THE WEB COLLECTION: MACROMEDIA® FLASH™ MX, DREAMWEAVER® MX, AND FIREWORKS® MX DESIGN PROFESSIONAL

By Sherry Bishop, Jim Shuman, and Barbara Waxer

THOMSON

COURSE TECHNOLOGY

The Web Collection: Macromedia® Flash™ MX, Dreamweaver® MX, and Fireworks® MX

by Sherry Bishop, Jim Shuman, and Barbara Waxer

Managing Editor:
Nicole Jones Pinard

Senior Product Manager:
Rebecca Berardy

Associate Product Manager:
Christina Kling Garrett

Editorial Assistant:
Elizabeth Harris

Production Editors:
Christine Spillett, Melissa Panagos

Developmental Editors:
Ann Fisher, Marjorie Hunt,
Barbara Waxer

Composition House:
GEX Publishing Services

QA Manuscript Reviewers:
Harris Bierhoff, Chris Carvalho,
Shawn Day, Christian Kunciw, Jeff
Schwartz, Ashlee Welz

Text Designer:
Ann Small

Illustrator:
Philip Brooker

Cover Design:
Philip Brooker

Design Professional Series Vision

The Design Professional Series is your guide to today's hottest multimedia applications. These comprehensive books teach the skills behind the application, showing you how to apply smart design principles to multimedia products, such as dynamic graphics, animation, Web sites, and video.

A team of design professionals including multimedia instructors, students, authors, and editors worked together to create this series. We recognized the unique learning environment of the digital media or multimedia classroom and have created a series that:

- Gives you comprehensive step-by-step instructions
- Offers in-depth explanation of the "why" behind a skill
- Includes creative projects for additional practice
- Explains concepts clearly using full-color visuals

It was our goal to create a book that speaks directly to the multimedia and design community—one of the most rapidly growing computer fields today.

This series was designed to appeal to the creative spirit. We would like to thank Philip Brooker for developing the inspirational artwork found on each unit opener and book cover. We would also like to give special thanks to Ann Small of A Small Design Studio for developing a sophisticated and instructive book design.
—The Design Professional Series

Author's Vision

What a joy it has been to be a part of such a creative and energetic team. The new Design Professional Series is a great format for teaching and learning Macromedia Flash, Dreamweaver, and Fireworks MX. Rebecca Berardy was the creator of this new series and the Design Professional Series team took the ball and ran with it. We would like to thank Nicole Pinard who provided the vision for the project and to thank everyone at Course Technology for their professional guidance.

Macromedia provided us with exceptional feedback in their review of the units, and we are grateful to Julie Hallstrom (Dreamweaver units), Jason Wylie (Flash units), and Mark Haynes (Fireworks units). A special thanks to Ann Fisher, Marjorie Hunt, and Barbara Waxer for their editorial expertise and encouragement. Our sincere appreciation goes out to Anita Quintana for her help with some of the graphic images used in the book. We would like to thank the reviewers— Tyler Feikema, the University of Health Sciences; Brenda Jacobsen, Idaho State University; James Kelley, Wor-Wic Community College; Piyush Patel, Northern Oklahoma College; Anita Philip, Oklahoma City Community College; Deborah Stockbridge, Quincy College—for their critiques and extremely helpful suggestions.
—The authors

I would like to give special thanks to my family and friends for their constant encouragement. My husband, Don, has been supportive in so many ways. Thank you is so inadequate.
—Sherry Bishop

I would like to thank my co-authors, Barbara and Sherry. I also want to give a heartfelt thanks to my wife, Barbara, for her patience and support. —Jim Shuman

Huge thanks to my partner, Lindy, and a to a house full of animals who deserve the utmost acknowledgement for their spontaneous contributions that never once bordered on combustion. —Barbara Waxer

Introduction to Macromedia Flash MX, Dreamweaver MX, and Fireworks MX

Welcome to *The Web Collection: Macromedia® Flash™ MX, Dreamweaver® MX, and Fireworks® MX —Design Professional.* This book offers creative projects, concise instructions, and complete coverage of basic to intermediate Flash, Dreamweaver, and Fireworks skills, helping you to create dynamic Web sites! Use this book both in the classroom and as your own reference guide.

This text is organized into 14 units. In these units, you will learn many skills including how to develop a Dreamweaver Web site, add Flash and Fireworks interactivity and animation, and integrate the tools of each application.

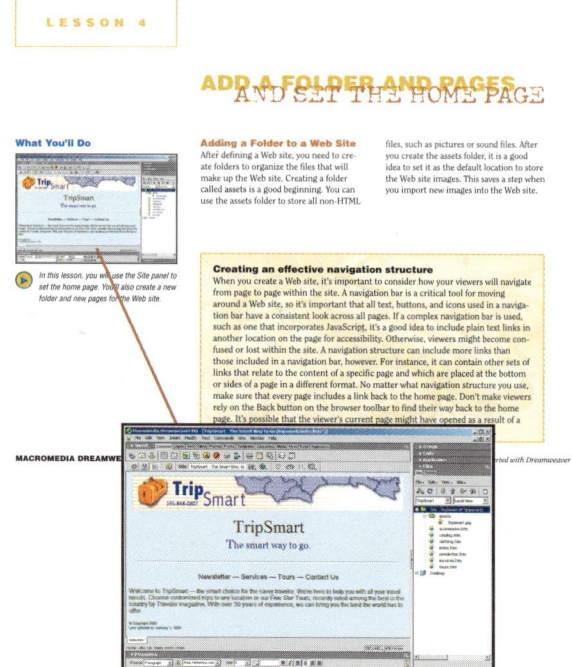

LESSON 4

ADD A FOLDER AND PAGES
AND SET THE HOME PAGE

What You'll Do

In this lesson, you will use the Site panel to set the home page. You'll also create a new folder and new pages for the Web site.

Adding a Folder to a Web Site
After defining a Web site, you need to create folders to organize the files that will make up the Web site. Creating a folder called assets is a good beginning. You can use the assets folder to store all non-HTML files, such as pictures or sound files. After you create the assets folder, it is a good idea to set it as the default location to store the Web site images. This saves a step when you import new images into the Web site.

Creating an effective navigation structure
When you create a Web site, it's important to consider how your viewers will navigate from page to page within the site. A navigation bar is a critical tool for moving around a Web site, so it's important that all text, buttons, and icons used in a navigation bar have a consistent look across all pages. If a complex navigation bar is used, such as one that incorporates JavaScript, it's a good idea to include plain text links in another location on the page for accessibility. Otherwise, viewers might become confused or lost within the site. A navigation structure can include more links than those included in a navigation bar, however. For instance, it can contain other sets of links that relate to the content of a specific page and which are placed at the bottom or sides of a page in a different format. No matter what navigation structure you use, make sure that every page includes a link back to the home page. Don't make viewers rely on the Back button on the browser toolbar to find their way back to the home page. It's possible that the viewer's current page might have opened as a result of a

MACROMEDIA DREAMWE...

Plus, there is an additional online unit covering the basics of HTML located on the Instructor's page for this book page at *www.course.com.*

What You'll Do

A What You'll Do figure begins every lesson. This figure gives you an at-a-glance look at the skills covered in the unit and shows you the completed data file of the lesson. Before you start the lesson, you will know—both on a technical and artistic level what you will be creating.

Comprehensive Conceptual Lessons

Before jumping into instructions, in-depth conceptual information tells you "why" skills are applied. This book provides the "how" and "why" through the use of professional examples. Also included in the text are helpful tips and sidebars to help you work more efficiently and creatively.

Step-by-Step instructions

This book combines in-depth conceptual information with concise steps to help you learn Dreamweaver, Fireworks, and Flash. Each set of steps guides you through a lesson where you will apply either Flash, Dreamweaver, or Fireworks tasks to a dynamic and professional data file. Step references to large colorful images and quick step summaries round out the lessons.

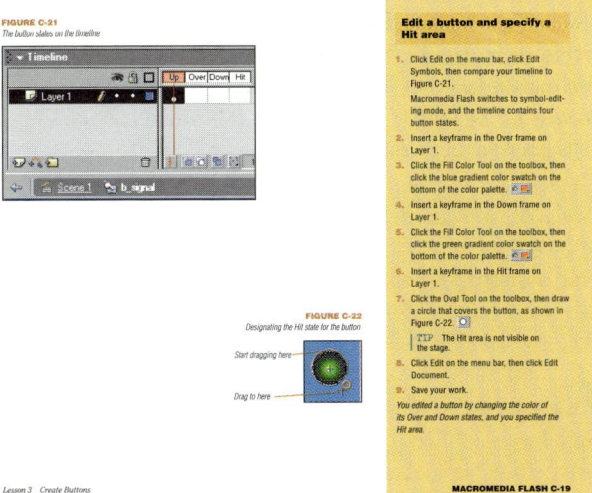

Projects

This book contains a variety of end-of-unit material for additional practice and reinforcement. The *Skills Review* contains hands-on practice exercises that mirror the progressive nature of the lesson material. The unit concludes with four projects: two Project Builders, one Design Project, and one Group Project. The Project Builder cases require you to apply the skills you've learned in the unit to create movies, Web sites, and animations. Design Projects examine Web site design and send students to the Web to research these issues. Group Projects encourage teamwork to create a project.

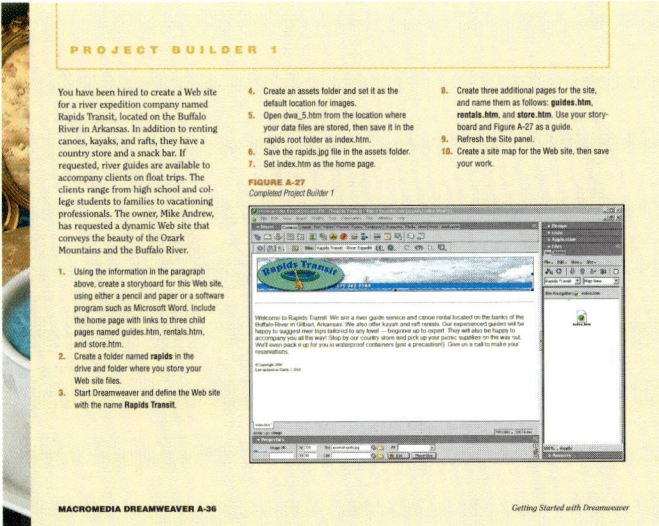

What instructor resources are available with this book?

The Instructor's Resource CD-ROM is Course Technology's way of putting the resources and information needed to teach and learn effectively into your hands. All the resources are available for both Macintosh and Windows operating systems, and many of the resources can be downloaded from *www.course.com*.

Instructor's Manual

Available as an electronic file, the Instructor's Manual is quality-assurance tested and includes unit overviews, detailed lecture topics for each unit with teaching tips, and comprehensive sample solutions to all lessons and end-of-unit material. The Instructor's Manual is available on the Instructor's Resource CD-ROM, or you can download it from *www.course.com*.

Syllabus

Prepare and customize your course easily using this sample course outline (available on the Instructor's Resources CD-ROM).

PowerPoint Presentations

Each unit has a corresponding PowerPoint presentation that you can use in lecture, distribute to your students, or customize to suit your course.

Figure Files

Figure Files contain all the figures from the book in bitmap format. Use the figure files to create transparency masters or in a PowerPoint presentation.

Solution to Exercises

Solution files are data files completed with comprehensive sample answers. Use these files to evaluate your students' work. Or, you can distribute them electronically or in hard copy so students can verify their work.

ExamView Test Bank and Test Engine

ExamView is a powerful testing software package that allows instructors to create and administer printed, computer (LAN-based), and Internet exams. ExamView includes hundreds of questions that correspond to the topics covered in this text, enabling students to generate detailed study guides that include page references for further review. The computer-based and Internet testing components allow students to take exams at their computers, and also save the instructor time by grading each exam automatically.

Data Files for Students

To complete most of the units in this book, your students will need data files. Put them on a file server for students to copy. The data files are available on the Instructor's Resource CD-ROM, the Review Pack, and can also be downloaded from *www.course.com*. Instruct students to use the Data Files List at the end of the book. This list gives instructions on copying and organizing files.

Online Appendix

If your students want to learn more about HTML, this book has a helpful online appendix. Instructor's can access this appendix at *www.course.com*. Navigate to the page for this book, click the link to Download Instructor's Files and Teaching Tools, and then click the link for HTML Basics.

Dreamweaver

UNIT A   GETTING STARTED WITH DREAMWEAVER

UNIT D — WORKING WITH LINKS

UNIT E WORKING WITH TABLES

UNIT A	GETTING STARTED WITH MACROMEDIA FLASH

CONTENTS

CONTENTS

Fireworks

UNIT B   WORKING WITH OBJECTS

CONTENTS

UNIT A	INTEGRATING MACROMEDIA MX PRODUCTS

CONTENTS

Intended Audience

This text is designed for the beginner or intermediate student who wants to learn how to use Macromedia Flash MX, Macromedia Dreamweaver MX, and Macromedia Fireworks MX. The book is designed to provide basic and in-depth material that not only educates, but encourages the student to explore the nuances of these exciting programs.

Approach

The text allows you to work at your own pace through step-by-step tutorials. A concept is presented and the process is explained, followed by the actual steps. To learn the most from the use of the text, you should adopt the following habits.

- Proceed slowly: Accuracy and comprehension is more important than speed.
- Understand what is happening with each step before you continue to the next step.
- After finishing a process, ask yourself: Can I do the process on my own? If the answer is no, review the steps.

Icons, buttons, and pointers

Symbols for icons, buttons, and pointers are shown each time they are used.

Fonts

Data and solution files contain a variety of commonly used fonts, but there is no guarantee that these fonts will be available on your computer. Each font is identified in cases where fonts beyond Times New Roman or Arial are used. If any of the fonts in use are not available on your computer, you can make a substitution realizing that the results may vary from those in the book.

Grading tips

Many students have Web-ready accounts to which they can post their completed assignments. The instructor can access the student accounts using a browser and view the site online.

There are some tasks that you will want to evaluate that are not apparent by simply viewing the pages of a Web site in a browser. For example, the settings for a Cascading Style Sheet file or the possibility of non-Web-safe colors in a Web site. In some of these instances, it is helpful to ask the students to print some of the reports available in Dreamweaver. Other times, a screen shot of a dialog box is helpful. To capture screens, ask the students to use the Print Screen key on the keyboard to capture the screen and then paste it into Microsoft Word or another word processing program

for printing. To keep from being overwhelmed with paperwork, you may develop a rubric to check key tasks in the assignments.

Creating a portfolio

One method for students to submit and keep a copy of all of their work is to create a portfolio of their projects that they link to a simple Web page and that can be saved on a CD-ROM.

Windows and Macintosh

Macromedia Flash, Dreamweaver, and Fireworks work virtually the same on Windows and Macintosh operating systems. In those cases where there is a difference the abbreviations (Win) and (Mac) are used.

Dreamweaver MX Workspace

If you are running Dreamweaver with a Windows operating system, you have the choice of using two different workspaces. One is based on the Dreamweaver 4 Workspace that uses floating windows. The document window and the site window do not display at the same time on the screen and the various documents, panels, and inspectors can float on the screen. You can easily reposition, open, or close, them to tailor your workspace.

The second layout option is the Dreamweaver MX Workspace, which is an integrated workspace. You can display the document window and the site window simultaneously, along with the panels and inspectors. The figures used in this text are captured using the integrated workspace layout. It is easy to change the workspace layout by using theGeneral dialog box option from the Preferences command on the Edit menu.

Macintosh users do not have the option of changing the workspace layout. Macintosh users must use the floating workspace layout.

Dreamweaver MX Units A–E

Building Web sites

The Dreamweaver units in this text use Web sites that students build from unit to unit. The lessons create and build the TripSmart Web site. The exercises at the end of each unit build three additional Web sites. To complete all of the work, it is recommended that you work consecutively through the book. However, if you do not; or if you have made mistakes and would like to start one of the Web sites with fresh files, contact you instructor for assistance.

Creating Dreamweaver Web sites that have not been built through previous consecutive units (Windows)

If you begin an assignment that requires a Web site that you did not create or maintain before a unit, you will need to perform the following steps:

1. Copy the solution files folder from the preceding unit for the Web site you wish to create onto the hard drive, Zip drive, or a high-density floppy disk. For example, if you are working on Unit E, you will need the solution files folder from Unit D. Your instructor will furnish this folder to you.

2. Start Dreamweaver.

3. Click Site on either menu bar, then click Edit Sites.

4. Click New to display the Site Definition for Unnamed Site 1 dialog box.

5. Type the name you want to use for your Web site in the Site Name text box. Spaces and upper-case letters are allowed in the Site name.

6. Click the Browse for File icon (folder) next to the Local Root Folder text box.

7. Click the drive and folder where your solution files folder is placed to locate the local root folder. The local root folder contains the name of the Web site you are working on. For example,

the local root folder for the TripSmart Web site is called tripsmart.

8. Double-click the local root folder, click Select, then click OK to close the Site Definition for Unnamed Site 1 dialog box.

9. A dialog box appears stating that the "Initial site cache will now be created. This scans the files in your site and starts tracking links as you change them." Click OK to accept this message.

10. Click Done to close the Edit Sites dialog box.

11. Click index.htm in the Local View list of the Site window to select it.

12. Click Site on the menu bar, then click Set as Home Page.

Creating Dreamweaver Web sites that have not been built through previous consecutive units (Macintosh)

If you begin an assignment that requires a Web site that you did not create or maintain before this unit, you will need to perform the following steps:

1. Copy the solution files folder from the preceding unit for the Web site you wish to create onto the hard drive, Zip drive, or a high-density floppy disk. For example, if you are working on Unit E, you will need the solution files folder

from Unit D. Your instructor will furnish this folder to you.

2. Start Dreamweaver and show the Site window by clicking Window on the menu bar and choosing Site.

3. Click Site on the menu bar, then click New Sites.

4. Type the name you want to use for your Web site in the Site Name text box. Spaces and upper case letters are allowed in the Site name.

5. Click the Browse for File icon (folder) next to the Local Root Folder text box.

6. Click the drive and folder where your solution files folder is stored to locate the local root folder. The local root folder contains the name of the Web site you are working on. For example, the local root folder for the TripSmart Web site is called tripsmart.

7. Click the local root folder, click Choose, then click OK to close the Site Definition for Unnamed Site 1 dialog box.

8. A dialog box appears stating that the "Initial site cache will now be created. This scans the files in your site and starts tracking links as you change them." Click OK to accept this message.

9. Click Done to close the Edit Sites dialog box.

10. Click index.htm in the Local Folder list of the Site window to select it.

11. Click Site on the menu bar, point to Site Map View, then click Set as Home Page.

Data Files

To complete the lessons and end-of-unit material in this book, you need to obtain the necessary data files. Please refer to the directions on the inside back cover for various methods to obtain these files. Once obtained, select where to store the files, such as the hard drive, a network server, or a Zip drive. The instructions in the lessons will refer to "the drive and folder where your data files are stored" when referring to the data files for the book.

In the Dreamweaver MX units, when opening a file from the Data Files folder to import into a Web site, it is necessary to check all internal links, including those to graphic images, and remove all absolute path references. For example: if a page with the TripSmart banner is opened and saved in the TripSmart Web site:

1. Click the image on the page to select it.

2. Use the Property Inspector to check the Src text box.

3. The Src text box should read assets/tripsmart.jpg.

4. If the Src text box has a longer path the extra characters should be removed.

   Example:
   file:/d:/data_files/unit_h/assets/tripsmart.jpg should be changed to assets/tripsmart.jpg

5. Save the file with the same name, overwriting the original file.

UNIT A

GETTING STARTED WITH DREAMWEAVER

1. Explore the Macromedia Dreamweaver workspace.

2. View a Web page and use Help.

3. Plan and define a Web site.

4. Add a folder and pages to a Web site and set the home page.

5. Create and view a site map.

GETTING STARTED WITH DREAMWEAVER

Introduction

Macromedia Dreamweaver MX is **Web design software** that lets you create dynamic, interactive Web pages containing text, images, hyperlinks, animation, sounds, video, and other elements. You can use Dreamweaver to create an individual Web page or a complex Web site consisting of many Web pages. A **Web site** is a group of related Web pages that are linked together and share a common interface and design. You can use Dreamweaver to create some Web page elements such as text, tables, and interactive buttons, or you can import elements from other software programs. You can save Dreamweaver files in many different file formats including HTML, JavaScript, or XML to name a few. **HTML** is the acronym for Hypertext Markup Language, the language used to create Web pages.

QUICKTIP

You use a browser to view your Web pages on the Internet. A **browser** is a program, such as Microsoft Internet Explorer or Netscape Communicator, that lets you display HTML-developed Web pages.

Using Dreamweaver Tools

Creating a good Web site is a complex task. Fortunately, Dreamweaver has an impressive number of tools that can help. Using Dreamweaver design tools, you can create dynamic and interactive Web pages without writing a word of HTML code. However, if you prefer to write code, Dreamweaver makes it easy to enter and edit the code directly and see the visual results of the code instantly. Dreamweaver also contains organizational tools that help you work with a team of people to create a Web site. You can also use Dreamweaver management tools to help you manage a Web site. For instance, you can use the **Site panel** to create folders to organize and store the various files for your Web site. You also use the Site panel to add pages to your Web site, and to set the **home page** in Dreamweaver, the first page that viewers will see when they visit the site. You can also use the **site map**, a graphical representation of how the pages within a Web site relate to each other, to view and edit the navigation structure of your Web site. The **navigation structure** is the way viewers navigate from page to page in your Web site.

Tools You'll Use

Property inspector —

Browse for
File icon

Refresh button

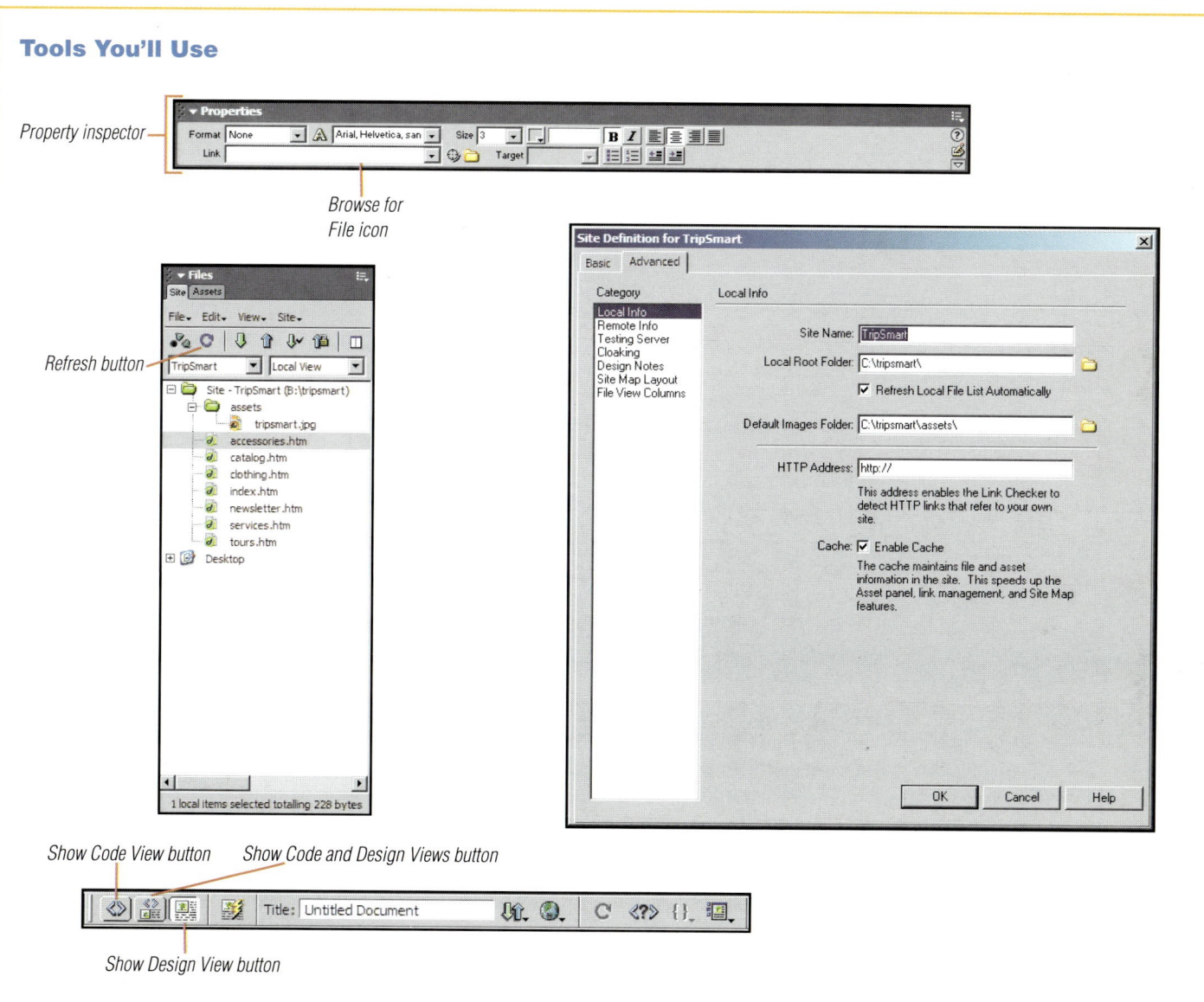

Show Code View button   Show Code and Design Views button

Show Design View button

EXPLORE THE DREAMWEAVER WORKSPACE

What You'll Do

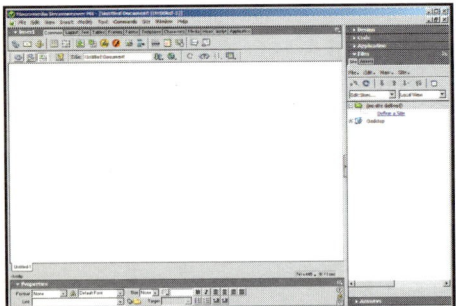

 In this lesson, you will start Dreamweaver, examine the components that make up the Dreamweaver workspace, and change views.

Examining the Dreamweaver Workspace

The **Dreamweaver workspace** is designed to provide you with easy access to all the tools you need to create Web pages. Refer to Figure A-1 as you locate the components described below.

The **document window** is the large white area in the Dreamweaver program window where you create and edit Web pages. The **menu bar**, located at the top of the document window, includes menu names, each of which contains Dreamweaver commands. To choose a menu command, click the menu name to open the menu, then click the menu command. The **Insert bar** contains buttons you can click to insert objects, such as images, tables, and horizontal rules.

The **Document toolbar** contains buttons you can use to change the current work mode, preview Web pages, debug Web pages, and view file-management options. The **Standard toolbar** contains buttons you can use to execute frequently used

commands also available on the File and Edit menus. The Standard toolbar is not part of the default workspace setup and might not be showing on your screen.

QUICKTIP

To hide or display the Standard or Document toolbars, click View on the menu bar, point to Toolbars, then click Document or Standard.

The **Property inspector**, located at the bottom of the Dreamweaver window, lets you view and change the properties of a selected object. The **Status bar** is located below the document window. The left end of the status bar displays the **tag selector**, which shows the HTML tags used at the insertion point location. The right side displays the window size and estimated download time for the current page.

A **panel** is a window that displays information on a particular topic or contains related commands. **Panel groups** are sets of related panels that are grouped together. To view the contents of a panel in a panel group, click the panel tab you want. Panel groups can be collapsed and docked on the right side of the screen, or undocked by dragging the gripper ⦙ on the left side of the panel group title bar. To collapse or expand a panel group, click the **expander arrow** ▽ on the left side of the panel group title bar, as shown in Figure A-2. When you use Dreamweaver for the first time, the Design, Code, Application, Files, and Answers panel groups are open by default.

Working with Dreamweaver Views

You view a Web page in the document window using one of three different views. A *view* is a particular way of displaying page content. **Design view** shows the page as it would appear in a browser, and is primarily used for designing and creating a Web page. **Code view** shows the underlying HTML code for the page; use this view to read or edit the underlying code. **Code and Design view** is a combination of Code view and Design view. Code and Design view is the best view for **debugging** or correcting errors because you can see immediately how code modifications will change the appearance of the page. The view buttons are located on the Document toolbar.

Title bar
Menu bar
Insert bar
Document toolbar
Standard toolbar

Document window

Tag selector
Status bar
Property inspector

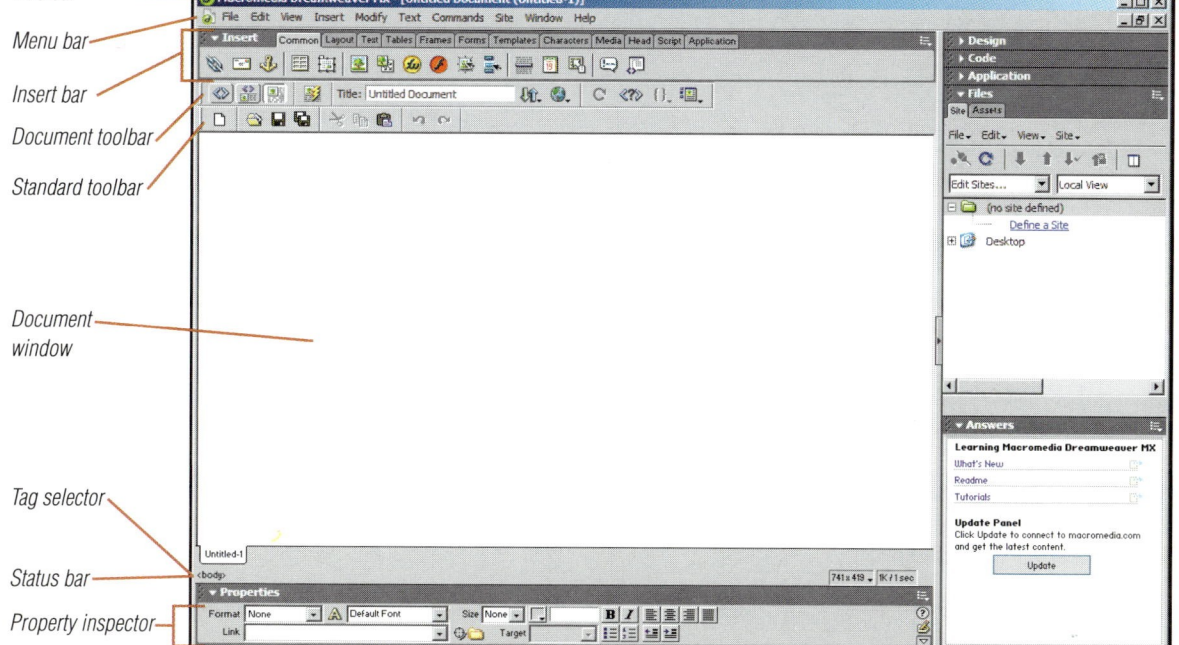

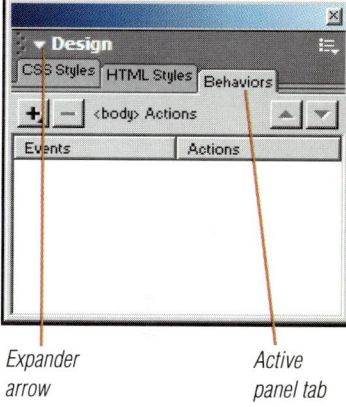

Expander arrow

Active panel tab

Start Dreamweaver (Windows)

1. Click the Start button on the taskbar.

   Start

2. Point to Programs or All Programs, point to Macromedia, then click Macromedia Dreamweaver MX, as shown in Figure A-3.

You started Dreamweaver MX for Windows.

Starting Dreamweaver MX (Windows)

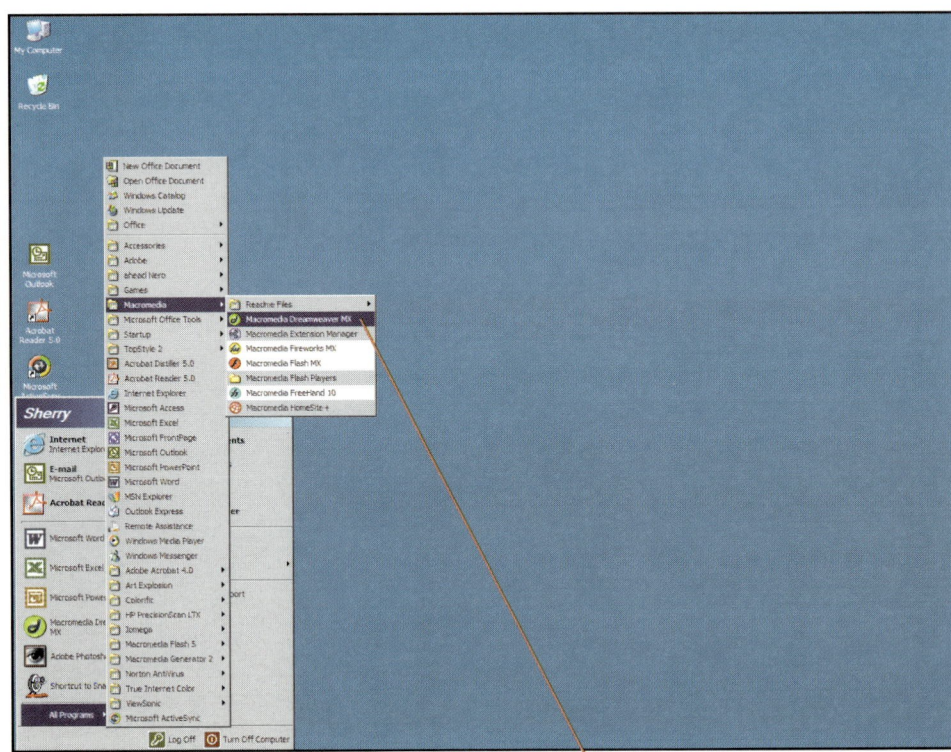

Click Macromedia Dreamweaver MX

Choosing a workspace layout (Windows)

If you are starting Dreamweaver MX for Windows for the first time after installing it, you will see the Workspace Setup dialog box, which asks you to choose between the Dreamweaver MX workspace layout and the Dreamweaver 4 workspace layout. The Dreamweaver MX workspace layout is an integrated workspace where the Dreamweaver windows and tools are positioned within one large application Window. The Dreamweaver 4 workspace is based on the Dreamweaver 4 interface and is composed of separate floating windows. Macintosh users must use the floating workspace. Most figures in this book show the Dreamweaver MX workspace. Ask your instructor which workspace layout option you should choose.

Getting Started with Dreamweaver

FIGURE A-4

Starting Dreamweaver MX (Macintosh)

Double-click the
hard drive icon

Start Dreamweaver (Macintosh)

1. Double-click the hard drive icon, as shown in Figure A-4.

The hard drive icon is usually in the upper-right corner of the desktop.

2. Double-click the Macromedia Dreamweaver MX folder.

> **TIP** Your Macromedia Dreamweaver folder might be in another folder called Applications. See your instructor or technical support person if you have trouble locating Dreamweaver.

3. Double-click the Macromedia Dreamweaver MX program icon.

You started Dreamweaver MX for Macintosh.

Change views and view panels

1. Click the Show Code View button on the Document toolbar as shown in Figure A-5.

   The HTML code for an untitled, blank document appears in the document window.

2. Click the Show Code and Design Views button on the Document toolbar.

3. Click the Show Design View button on the Document toolbar.

   (continued)

FIGURE A-5

Code view for blank document

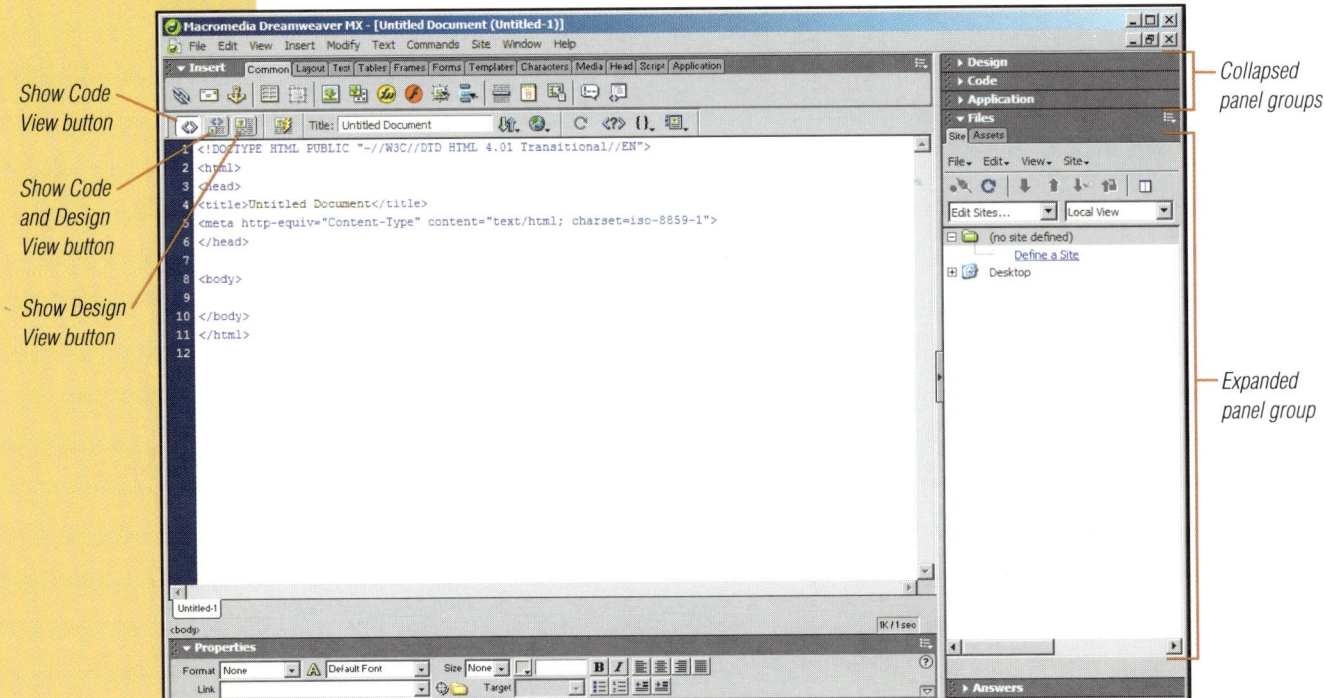

Show Code View button

Show Code and Design View button

Show Design View button

Collapsed panel groups

Expanded panel group

Getting Started with Dreamweaver

Displaying a panel group

Expander arrow

Drag to undock or "float" panel group

Code panel group

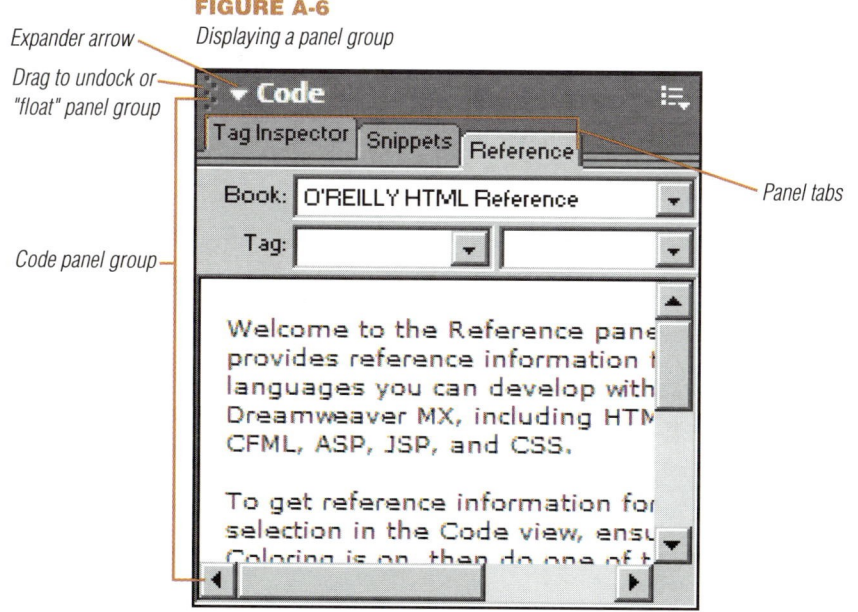

Panel tabs

4. Click the expander arrow on the Code panel group title bar, then compare your screen to Figure A-6. ▷

   TIP If the Code Panel group is not displayed, click Window on the menu bar, then click Snippets.

5. Click each panel tab to display the contents of each panel.

6. Click the expander arrow on the Code panel group title bar to collapse the Code panel group. ▽

7. Repeat Steps 4 through 6 to expand the Design, Application, Files, and Answers panel groups and view the contents of each panel.

   TIP If you are a Mac user, you first need to open the panel groups. To open each panel group, click Window on the menu bar, then click Snippets (for the Code panel group), or Bindings (for the Application group) or Assets (for the Files panel group).

You viewed a blank Web page using three views, opened each panel group and displayed the contents of each panel, and closed each panel group.

VIEW A WEB PAGE AND USE HELP

What You'll Do

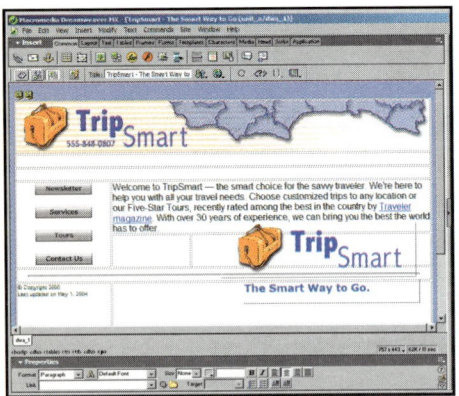

 In this lesson, you will open a Web page, view several page elements, and access the Help system.

Opening a Web page

After starting Dreamweaver, you can create a new Web site, create a new Web page, or open an existing Web site or Web page. The first Web page that appears when viewers go to a Web site is called the **home page**. The home page sets the look and feel of the Web site and directs viewers to the rest of the pages in the Web site.

Viewing basic Web page elements

There are many elements that make up Web pages. Web pages can be very simple, and designed primarily with text, or they can be media-rich with text, graphics, sound, and movies. Figure A-7 is an example of a Web page with several different page elements that work together to create a simple and attractive page.

Most information on a Web page is presented in the form of **text**. You can type text directly onto a Web page in Dreamweaver or import text created in other programs. You can then use the Property inspector to format text so that it is attractive and easy

to read. Text should be short and to the point to prevent viewers from losing interest and leaving your site.

Hyperlinks, also known as **links**, are graphic or text elements on a Web page that users click to display another location on the page, another Web page on the same Web site, or a Web page on a different Web site.

Graphics add visual interest to a Web page. The saying that "less is more" is certainly true with graphics, though. Too many graphics will cause the page to load too slowly and discourage viewers from waiting for the page to download. Many pages today have **banners**, which are graphics displayed across the top of the screen that can incorporate a company's logo, contact information, and links to the other pages in the site.

Navigation bars are bars that contain multiple links that are usually organized in rows or columns. Sometimes, navigation bars are used with an image map. An **image map** is a graphic that has been divided into sections, each of which contains a link.

Flash button objects are objects created in Macromedia Flash that can serve as links to other files or Web pages. You can insert them onto a Web page without requiring the Macromedia Flash program to be installed. They add "pizzazz" to a Web page.

Getting Help

Dreamweaver has an excellent Help feature that is both comprehensive and easy to use. When questions or problems arise, you can use the commands on the Help menu to find the answers you need. Clicking the Using Dreamweaver command on a Windows computer opens the Using Dreamweaver MX window that contains four tabs you can use to search for answers in different ways. The Contents tab lists Dreamweaver Help topics by category. The Index tab lets you view topics in alphabetical order, and the Search tab lets you enter a keyword to search for a specific topic. You can use the Favorites tab to bookmark topics that you might want to view later. On a Macintosh you can choose between Index or Table of Contents view and the Search field is always present at the top of the window. You can also use the Tutorials command on the Help menu to get step-by-step instructions on how to complete various tasks, and the What's New command to learn about the new features of Dreamweaver MX.

FIGURE A-7

Common Web page elements

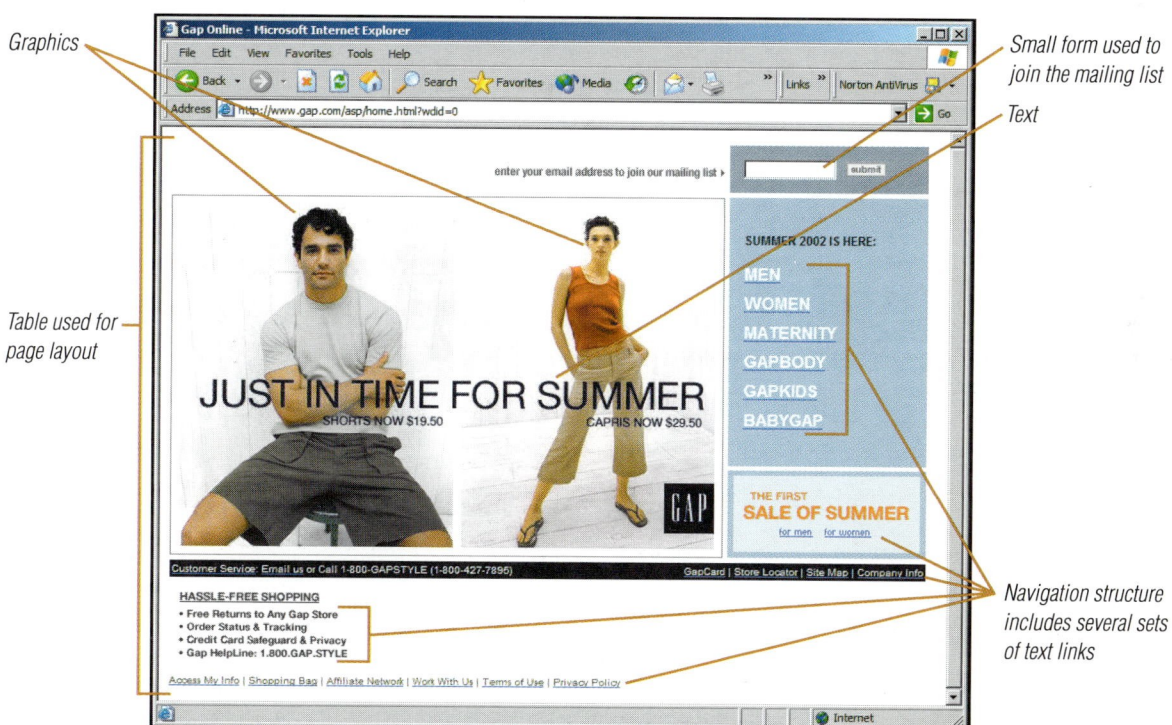

Open a Web page and view basic page elements

1. Click File on the menu bar, then click Open.

2. Click the Look in list arrow (Win), or From list arrow (Mac), locate the drive and folder where your data files are stored, then double-click the unit_a folder (Win), or click the Unit_a folder (Mac).

3. Click dwa_1.htm, then click Open.

4. Locate each of the Web page elements shown in Figure A-8.

5. Click the Show Code View button to view the code for the page. ⟨⟩

6. Scroll down to view all the code, then click the Show Design View button to return to Design view.

   TIP To view the code for a particular page element, select the page element in Design view, then click the Show Code View button.

7. Click File, then click Close to close the page without saving it.

You opened a Web page, located several page elements, viewed the code for the page, then closed the Web page without saving it.

FIGURE A-8

TripSmart Web page elements

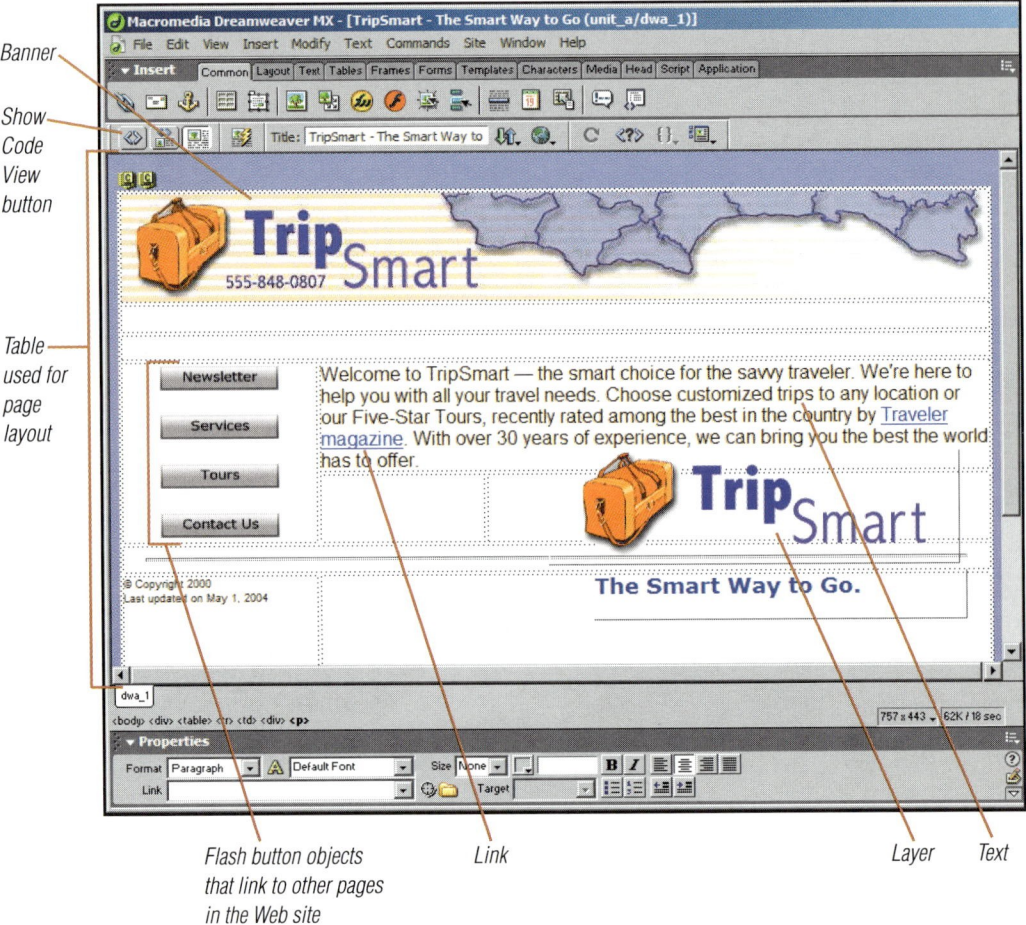

Banner

Show Code View button

Table used for page layout

Flash button objects that link to other pages in the Web site

Link

Layer   Text

FIGURE A-9
Using Dreamweaver Help

Click to see topics

Keywords

Topics found with keywords

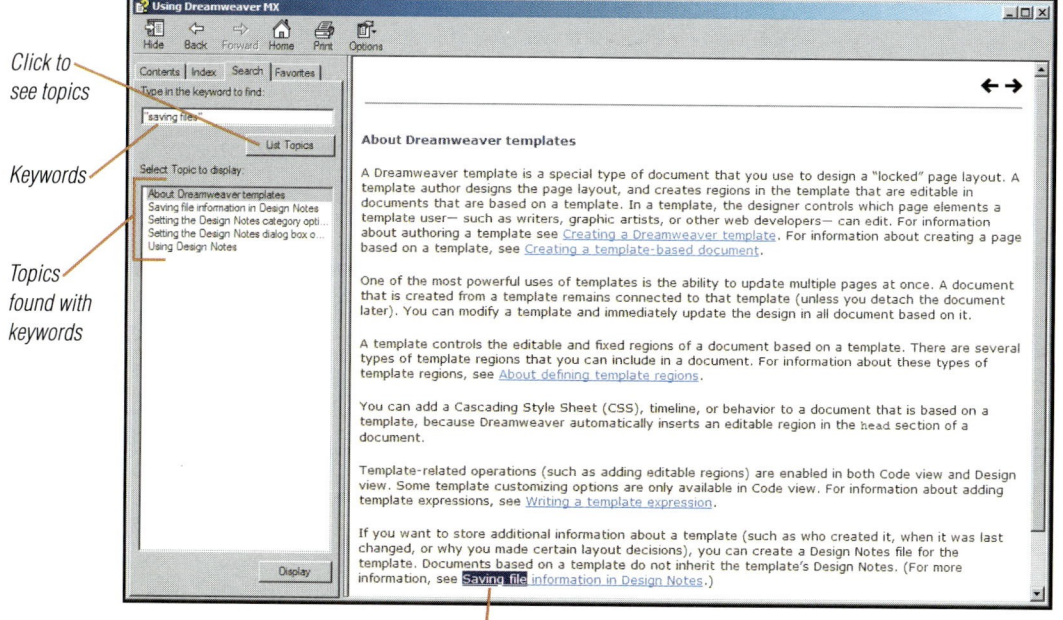

Keywords are highlighted in the text

1. Click Help on the menu bar, then click Using Dreamweaver.

2. Click the Search tab (Win).

3. Type **saving** in the Type in the keyword to find text box (Win) or type **saving** in the text box at the top of the Help window (Mac).

4. Click List Topics (Win), or Ask (Mac), then scroll down to view the topics.

5. Select saving in the keyword to find text box, type **"saving files"**, (be sure to type the quotation marks), then press [Enter] (Win) or [return] (Mac).

   Because you placed the keywords in quotation marks, Dreamweaver shows only the topics that contain the exact phrase "saving files." Topics that contain the individual words "saving" or "files" are not listed.

6. Double-click About Dreamweaver templates in the topic list.

   Information on Dreamweaver templates appears in the right frame, as shown in Figure A-9.

   > TIP   If you don't see the topic About Dreamweaver templates, double-click a different topic (Mac).

7. Scroll down and scan the text.

   The search words you used are highlighted in the Help text. Help will find both the exact words you enter and the derivatives of the words you enter.

8. Click Close (Win) or Quit (Mac).

You used the Dreamweaver Help files to read information about Dreamweaver templates.

MACROMEDIA DREAMWEAVER A-13

PLAN AND DEFINE A WEB SITE

What You'll Do

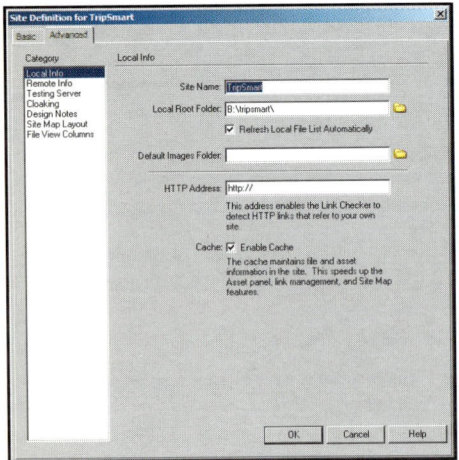

In this lesson, you will review a Web site plan for TripSmart, a full-service travel outfitter. You will also create a root folder for the TripSmart Web site, and then define the Web site.

Understanding the Web Site Creation Process

Creating a Web site is a complex process. It can often involve a large team of people working in various roles to ensure that the Web site contains accurate information, looks good, and works smoothly. Figure A-10 illustrates the steps involved in creating a Web site.

Planning a Web Site

Planning is probably the most important part of any successful project. Planning is an *essential* part of creating a Web site, and is a continuous process that overlaps the subsequent phases. To start planning your Web site, you need to create a checklist of questions and answers about the site. For example, what are your goals for

Understanding IP addresses and domain names

To be accessible over the Internet, a Web site must be published to a Web server with a permanent IP address. An **IP address** is an assigned series of numbers, separated by periods, that designate an address on the Internet. To access a Web page, you can enter either an IP address or a domain name in the address text box of your browser window. A **domain name** is a Web address that is expressed in letters instead of numbers, and usually reflects the name of the business represented by the Web site. For example, the domain name of the Macromedia Web site is *www.macromedia.com*, but the IP address would read something like 123.456.789.123. Because domain names use descriptive text instead of numbers, they are much easier to remember. Compare an IP address to your Social Security number and a domain name to your name. Both your Social Security number and your name are used to refer to you as a person, but your name is much easier for your friends and family to use than your Social Security number. You can type the IP address or the domain name in the address text box of the browser window to access a Web site.

the Web site? Who is the audience you want to target? Teenagers? Senior Citizens? How can you design the site to appeal to the target audience? The more questions you can answer about the site, the more prepared you will be when you begin the developmental phase. Because of the public demand for "instant" information, your plan should include not just how to get the site up and running, but how to keep it current. Table A-1 lists some of the basic questions you need to answer during the planning phase for almost any type of Web site. In addition to a checklist, you should also create a timeline and a budget for the Web site.

Setting up the Basic Structure

Once you complete the planning phase, you need to set up the structure of the site by creating a storyboard. A storyboard is a small sketch that represents every page in a Web site. Like a flowchart, a storyboard shows the relationship of each page in the Web site to all the other pages. Storyboards

Steps in creating a Web site

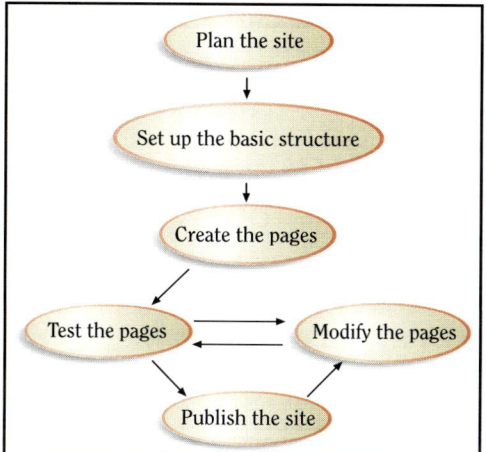

TABLE A-1: Web Site Planning Checklist

question	examples
1. Who is the target audience?	Seniors, teens, children
2. How can I tailor the Web site to reach that audience?	Specify an appropriate reading level, decide the optimal amount of multimedia content, use formal or casual language
3. What are the goals for the site?	Sell a product, provide information
4. How will I gather the information?	Recruit other company employees, write it myself, use content from in-house documents
5. What are my sources for multimedia content?	Internal production department, outside production company, my own photographs
6. What is my budget?	Very limited, well financed
7. How long do I have to complete the project?	Two weeks, 1 month, 6 months
8. Who is on my project team?	Just me, a complete staff of designers
9. How often should the site be updated?	Every 10 minutes, once a month
10. Who is responsible for updating the site?	Me, other team members

are very helpful when planning a Web site, because they allow you to visualize how each page in the site is linked to others. You can sketch a storyboard using a pencil and paper or using a graphics program on a computer. The storyboard shown in Figure A-11 shows all the pages that will be contained in the TripSmart Web site that you will create in this book. Notice that the home page appears at the top of the storyboard, and has four pages linked to it. The home page is called the **parent page**, because it is at a higher level in the Web hierarchy and has pages

linked to it. The pages linked to it below are called **child pages**. The Catalog page, which is a child page to the home page, is also a parent page to the Accessories and Clothing pages. You can refer to this storyboard as you create the actual links in Dreamweaver.

QUICK TIP

You can create a storyboard on a computer using a software program such as Word, Paint, Paintshop Pro, or Macromedia Freehand. You might find it easier to make changes to a computer-generated storyboard than to one created on paper.

In addition to creating a storyboard for your site, you should also create a folder hierarchy for all of the files that will be used in the Web site. Start by creating a folder for the Web site with a descriptive name, such as the name of the company. This folder, known as the **root folder**, will store all the Web pages or HTML files for the site. Then create a subfolder called **assets** in which you store all of the files that are not Web pages, such as images and video clips. You should avoid using spaces, special characters, or uppercase characters in your folder names.

FIGURE A-11

TripSmart Web site storyboard

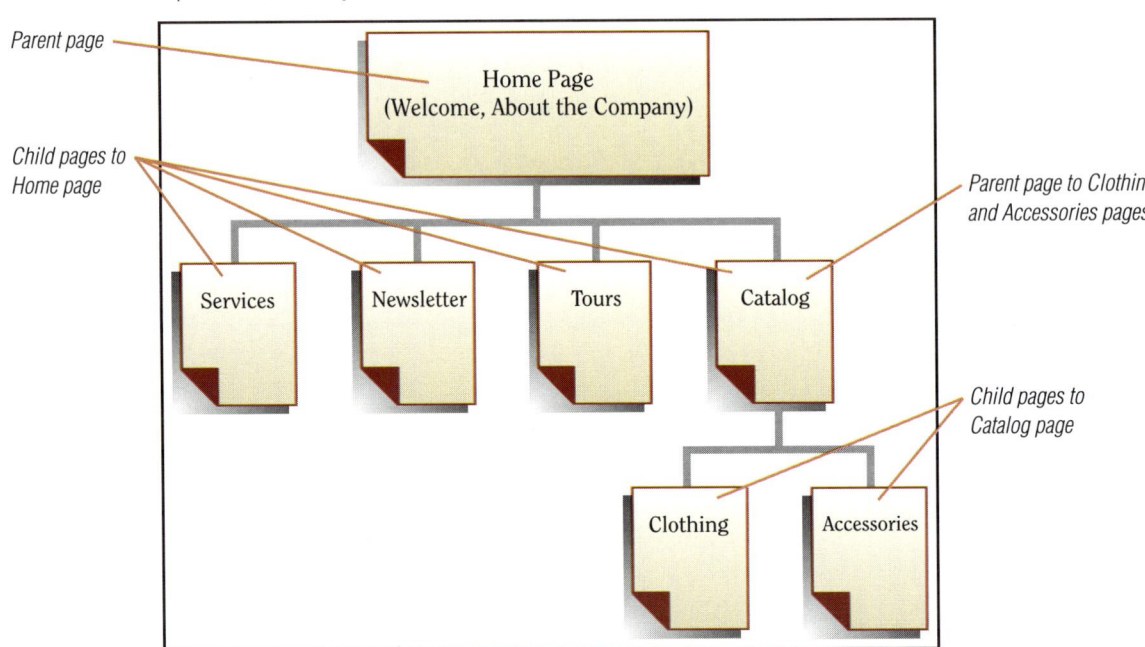

After you create the root folder, you need to define your Web site. When you **define** a Web site, the root folder and any folders and files it contains appears in the **Site panel**, the panel you use to manage your Web site's files and folders. Using the Site panel to manage your files ensures that the site links work correctly when the Web site is published. You also use the Site panel to add or delete pages.

Creating the Web Pages and Collecting the Page Content

This is the fun part! After you create your storyboard, you need to gather the files that will be used to create the pages, including text, graphics, buttons, video, and animation. Some of these files will come from other software programs, and some will be created in Dreamweaver. For example, you can create text in a word-processing program and insert it into Dreamweaver or you can create and format text in Dreamweaver. Graphics, tables, colors, and horizontal rules all contribute to making a page attractive and interesting. In choosing your elements, however, you should always carefully consider the file size of each page. A page with too many graphical elements might take a long time to load, which could cause visitors to leave your Web site. Before you actually add content to each

page, however, you need to use the Site panel to add all the pages to the site according to the structure you specified in your storyboard. Once all the blank pages are in place, you can add the content you collected.

Testing the Pages

Once all your pages are completed, you need to test the site to make sure all the links work and that everything looks good. It is important to test your Web pages using different browser software. The two most common browsers are Microsoft Internet Explorer and Netscape Navigator. You should also test your Web site using different versions of each browser. Older versions of Internet Explorer and Netscape Navigator do not support the latest Web technology. You should also test your Web site using a variety of screen sizes. Some viewers may have small monitors, while others may have large, high-resolution monitors. You should also consider modem speed. Although more people use cable modems or DSL (Digital Subscriber Line) these days, some still use slower dial-up modems. Testing is a continuous process, for which you should allocate plenty of time.

Modifying the Pages

After you create a Web site, you'll probably find that you need to keep making changes

to it, especially when informa site needs to be updated. Each make a change, such as adding ton or graphic to a page, you sh the site again. Modifying and testing pages in a Web site is an ongoing process.

Publishing the Site

Publishing a Web site means that you transfer all the files for the site to a **Web server**, a computer that is connected to the Internet with an IP (Internet Protocol) address, so that it is available for viewing on the Internet. A Web site must be published or users of the World Wide Web cannot view it. There are several options for publishing a Web site. For instance, many Internet Service Providers (ISPs) provide space on their servers for customers to publish Web sites and some commercial Web sites provide limited free space for their viewers. Although publishing happens at the end of the process, it's a good idea to set up Web server access in the planning phase. You use the Site panel to transfer your files using the FTP (**File Transfer Protocol**) capability. **FTP** is the process of uploading and downloading files to and from a remote site.

Create a root folder (Windows)

1. Click the Start button on the taskbar, point to Programs, point to Accessories, then click Windows Explorer. **Start**

2. Navigate to the drive and folder where you will create a folder to store your files for the TripSmart Web site.

3. Click File on the menu bar, point to New, then click Folder.

4. Type **tripsmart** to rename the folder, then press [Enter] as shown in Figure A-12.

   TIP   Your desktop will look different than Figure A-12 if you are not using Windows XP.

5. Close Windows Explorer.

You created a new folder to serve as the root folder for the TripSmart Web site.

Creating a root folder using Windows Explorer

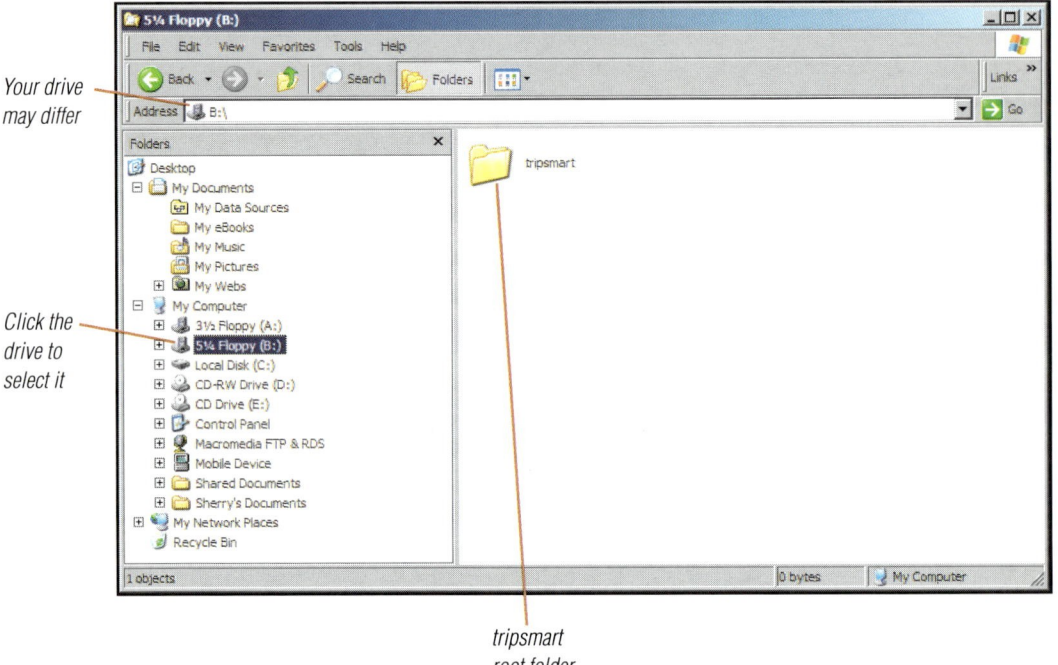

Your drive may differ

Click the drive to select it

tripsmart root folder

FIGURE A-13

Creating a root folder using a Macintosh

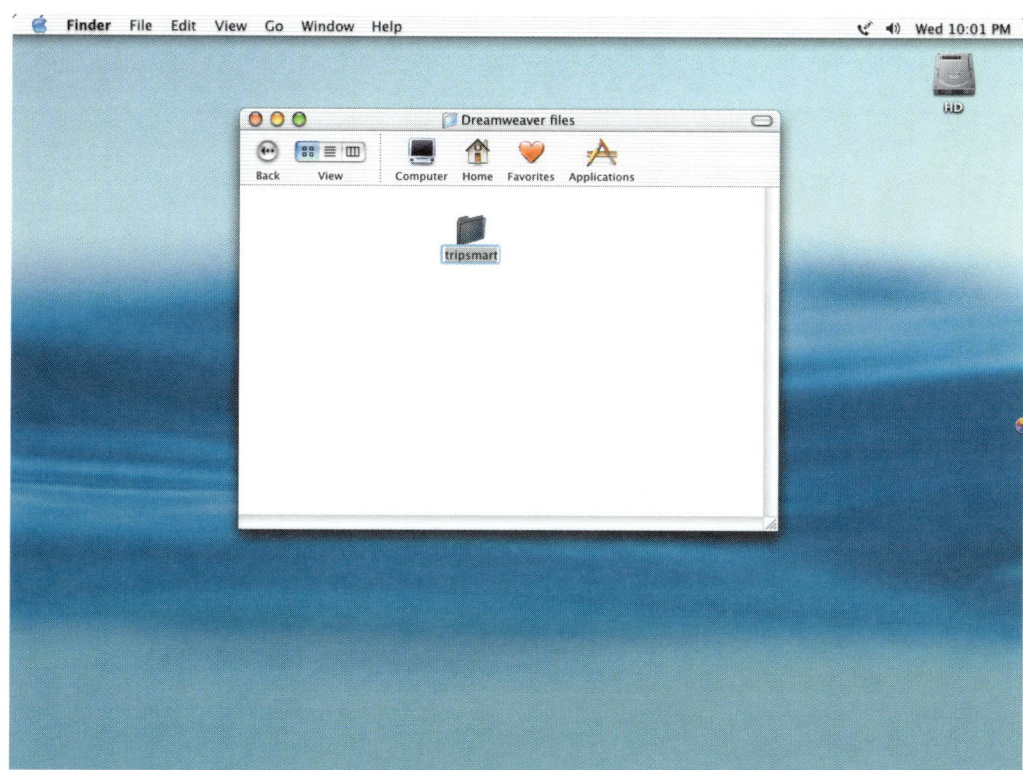

1. Double-click the Macintosh hard drive, then double-click the folder where you will create a folder to store your data files to open it.

2. Click File on the menu bar, then click New Folder.

3. Type **tripsmart** to rename the folder, as shown in Figure A-13.

   TIP If you cannot type a new folder name, click the current folder name once to highlight it, then type a new folder name.

You created a new folder to serve as the root folder for the TripSmart Web site.

...amweaver, click Site on the
...en click New Site.

...dvanced tab if necessary, then
ty... ...mart in the Site Name text box.

> TIP It is acceptable to use uppercase letters in the site name because it is not the name of a folder or a file.

3. Click the Browse for File icon next to the Local Root Folder text box, click the Select list arrow (Win) or click the From list arrow (Mac) in the Choose Local Folder dialog box, click the drive and folder where your data files are stored, then click the tripsmart folder.

4. Click Open (Win) or Choose (Mac), then click Select.

5. Verify that the Refresh Local File List Automatically and the Enable Cache check boxes are both checked, as shown in Figure A-14, then click OK.

   Clicking Enable Cache tells Dreamweaver to use your computer's temporary memory, or **cache**, while you work. The Refresh Local File List Automatically tells Dreamweaver to automatically display changes you make in your file lists, which eliminates the need to use the Refresh command.

You created a Web site and defined it with the name TripSmart. You verified that both the Refresh Local Files List Automatically and the Enable Cache options were enabled in the Site Definition dialog box.

FIGURE A-14

Site Definition dialog box

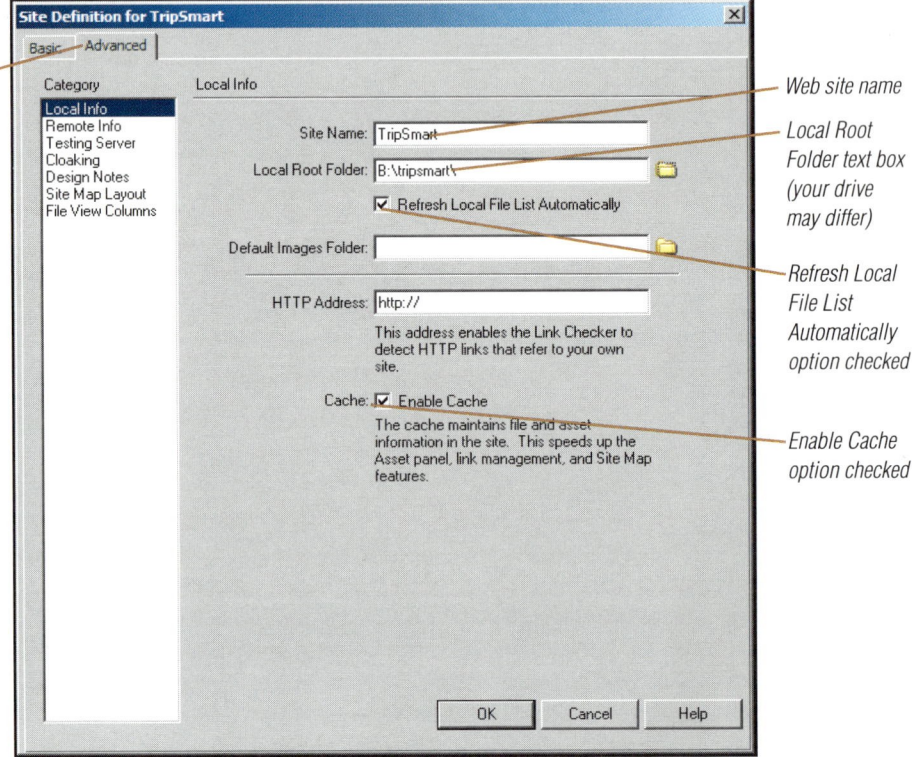

Advanced tab · · · · · · ·

Web site name

Local Root Folder text box (your drive may differ)

Refresh Local File List Automatically option checked

Enable Cache option checked

FIGURE A-15

Setting up remote access for the TripSmart Web site

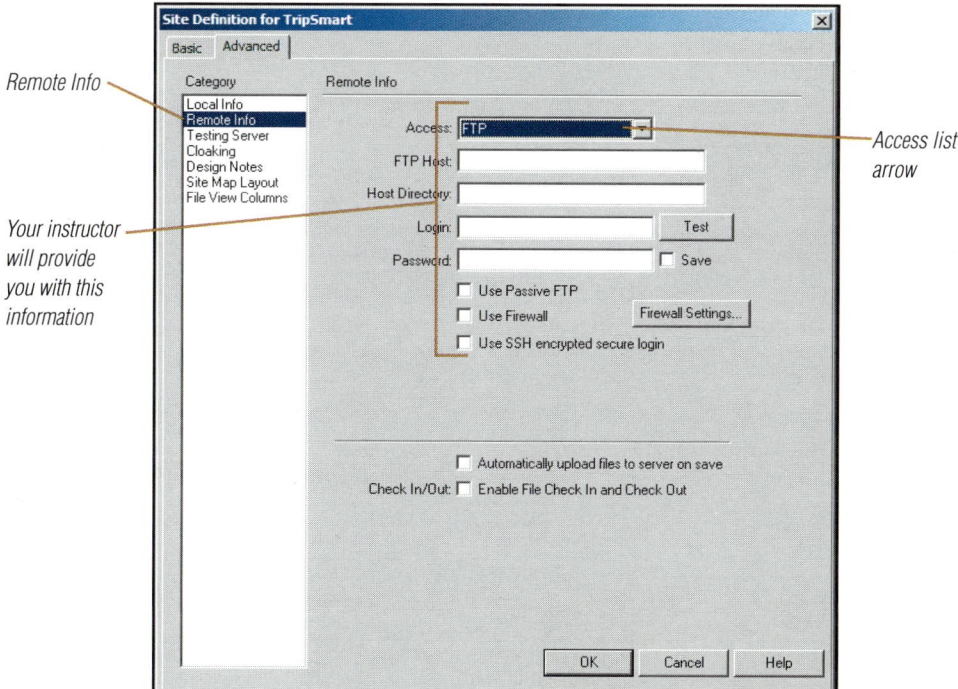

Remote Info

Your instructor will provide you with this information

Access list arrow

Set up Web server access

1. Click Site on the menu bar, then click Edit Sites.

2. Click TripSmart in the Edit Sites dialog box (if necessary), then click Edit.

3. Click the Advanced tab (if necessary), click Remote Info in the Category list, click the Access list arrow, then choose the method you will use to publish your Web site.

   TIP   Your instructor will provide you with this information. If you do not have the information to publish your Web site, choose None in the Site Definition dialog box. You can specify this information later.

4. Enter the necessary information in the Site Definition dialog box shown in Figure A-15, filling in the blanks with information from your instructor, click OK, then click Done.

You set up the remote access information to prepare you for publishing your Web site.

Understanding the process of publishing a Web site

Before publishing a Web site so that viewers of the Web can access it, you should first create a local root folder, called the **local site**, to house all the files for your Web site. Next, you need to gain access to a remote server. A **remote server** is a Web server that hosts Web sites and is not directly connected to the computer housing the local site. Many Internet Services Providers, or ISPs, provide space for publishing Web pages on their servers. Once you have access to a remote server, you can then use the Site Definition Remote Info dialog box to enter information such as the FTP host, host directory, login, and password. After entering this information, you can then use the Put File(s) icon in the Site panel to transfer the files to the designated remote server. Once the site is published to a remote server, it is called a **remote site**.

ADD A FOLDER AND PAGES
AND SET THE HOME PAGE

What You'll Do

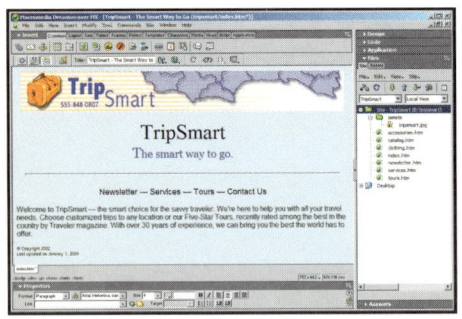

In this lesson, you will use the Site panel to set the home page. You'll also create a new folder and new pages for the Web site.

Adding a Folder to a Web Site

After defining a Web site, you need to create folders to organize the files that will make up the Web site. Creating a folder called **assets** is a good beginning. You can use the assets folder to store all non-HTML files, such as pictures or sound files. After you create the assets folder, it is a good idea to set it as the default location to store the Web site images. This saves a step when you import new images into the Web site.

Creating an effective navigation structure

When you create a Web site, it's important to consider how your viewers will navigate from page to page within the site. A navigation bar is a critical tool for moving around a Web site, so it's important that all text, buttons, and icons used in a navigation bar have a consistent look across all pages. If a complex navigation bar is used, such as one that incorporates JavaScript, it's a good idea to include plain text links in another location on the page for accessibility. Otherwise, viewers might become confused or lost within the site. A navigation structure can include more links than those included in a navigation bar, however. For instance, it can contain other sets of links that relate to the content of a specific page and which are placed at the bottom or sides of a page in a different format. No matter what navigation structure you use, make sure that every page includes a link back to the home page. Don't make viewers rely on the Back button on the browser toolbar to find their way back to the home page. It's possible that the viewer's current page might have opened as a result of a search and clicking the Back button will take the viewer out of the Web site.

Setting the Home Page

The home page of a Web site is the first page that viewers see when they visit your Web site. Most Web sites contain many other pages that all connect back to the home page. Dreamweaver uses the home page that you have designated as a starting point for creating a site map, a graphical representation of the Web pages in a Web site. When you set the home page, you tell Dreamweaver which page you have designated to be your home page. You set the home page in the Define Sites dialog box. The home page filename usually has the name index.htm.

Adding Pages to a Web Site

Web sites might be as simple as one page or might contain hundreds of pages. When you create a Web site, you need to add all the pages and specify where they should be placed in the Web site folder structure in the root folder. Once you add and name all the pages in the Web site, you can then add the content, such as text and graphics, to each page. It is better to add as many "empty" pages as you think you will need in the beginning, rather than adding them one at a time with all the content in place. This will enable you to set up the navigation structure of the Web site at the beginning of the development process, and view how each page is linked to others. When you are satisfied with the overall structure, you can then add the content to each page.

Using the Site panel for file management

You can use the Site panel to add, delete, move, or rename files and folders in a Web site. It is very important that you perform these file maintenance tasks in the Site panel rather than in Windows Explorer (Windows) or in the Finder (Mac). Dreamweaver will not recognize any changes you make to the Web site folder structure outside the Site panel. You use Windows Explorer (Win) or the Finder (Mac) only to create the root folder or to move or copy the root folder of a Web site to another location. If you move or copy the root folder to a new location, you will have to define the Web site again in the Site panel, as you did in Lesson 3 of this unit.

Add a folder to a Web site (Windows)

1. Click File on the Site panel menu bar, then click New Folder.

2. Type **assets** in the folder text box, then press [Enter].

3. Compare your screen with Figure A-16.

You used the Site panel to create a new folder in the TripSmart folder, and named it assets.

Add a folder to a Web site (Macintosh)

1. Click Window on the menu bar, click Site to open the Site panel (if necessary), press and hold [Ctrl], click the tripsmart folder, and then click New Folder.

2. Click the triangle to the left of the TripSmart folder to open it (if necessary), then click untitled on the new folder, type **assets** as the folder name, then press [return].

   > **TIP** You will not see the new folder until you expand the tripsmart folder by clicking the triangle to the left of the tripsmart folder (Mac).

3. Compare your screen with Figure A-17.

You used the Site panel, to create a new folder under the TripSmart folder, and named it assets.

FIGURE A-16

TripSmart site in Site panel with assets folder created (Windows)

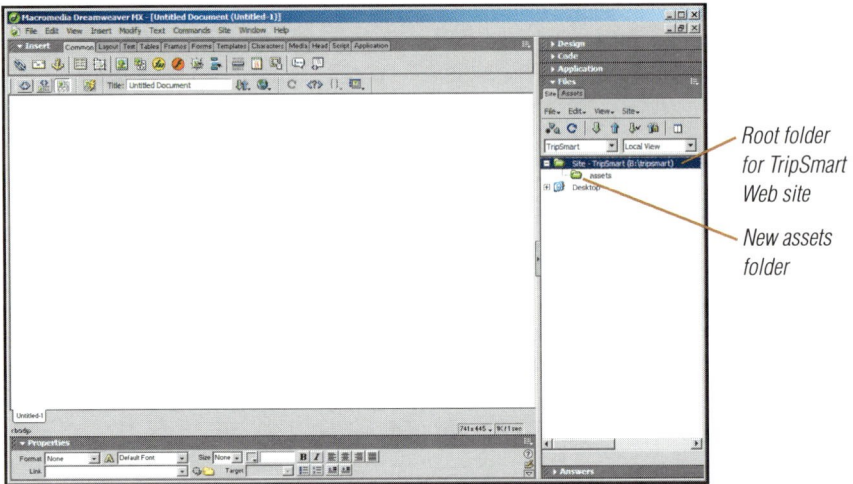

Root folder for TripSmart Web site

New assets folder

FIGURE A-17

TripSmart site in Site panel with assets folder created (Macintosh)

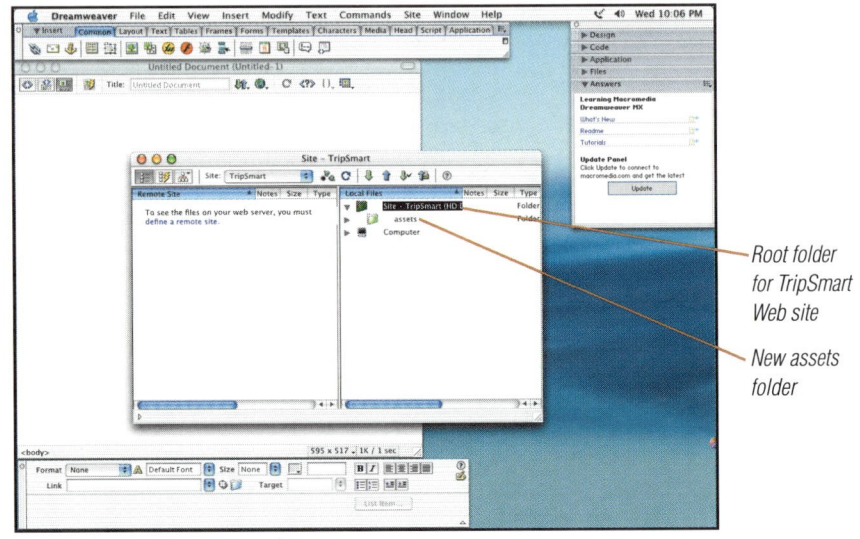

Root folder for TripSmart Web site

New assets folder

FIGURE A-18

Site Definition for TripSmart with assets folder set as the default images folder

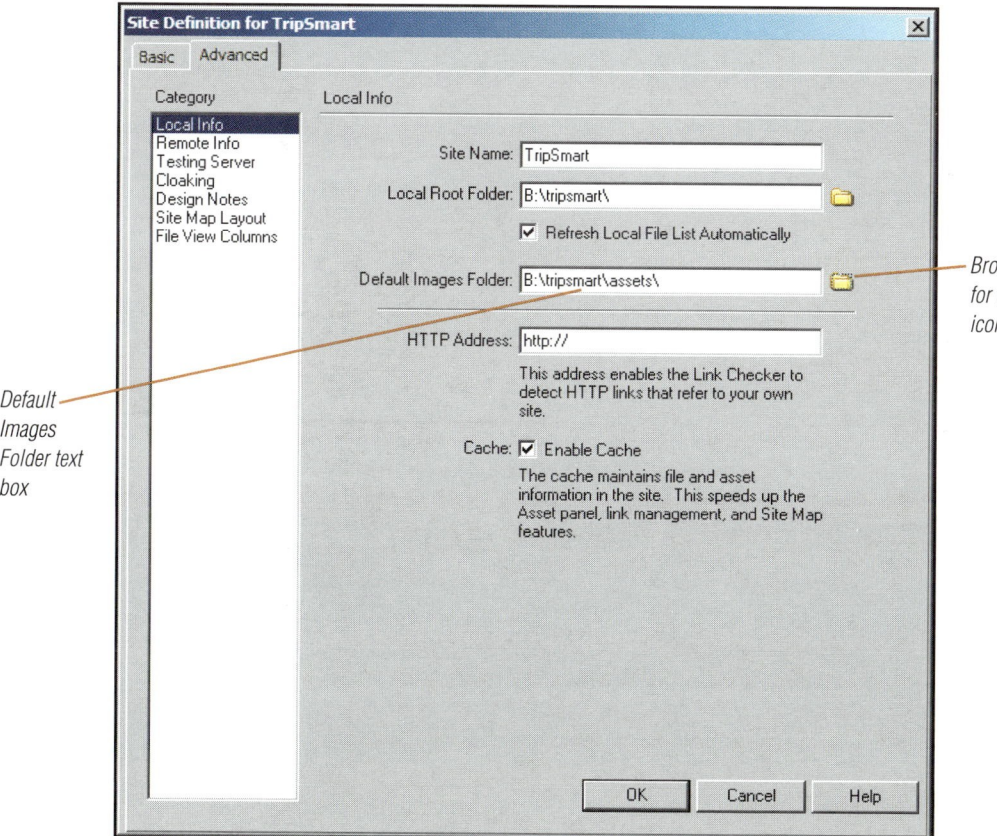

Default Images Folder text box

Browse for file icon

1. Click Site on the menu bar, click Edit Sites, select TripSmart if necessary, then click Edit.

2. Click the Browse for File icon next to the Default Images Folder text box.

3. Navigate to the folder where your Web site files are stored, double-click the tripsmart folder (Win), or click the tripsmart folder (Mac), double-click the assets folder (Win), or click the assets folder (Mac), then click Select (Win) or Choose (Mac).

   Compare your screen to Figure A-18.

4. Click OK, then click Done.

You set the assets folder as the default images folder so that imported images will be automatically saved in it.

Set the home page

1. Open the file dwa_2.htm from the Unit_a folder where your data files are stored.

2. Click File on the menu bar, click Save As, click the Save in list arrow (Win) or the Where list arrow (Mac), navigate to the tripsmart folder, type **index.htm** in the File name text box (Win), or Save As text box (Mac), then click Save.

   See Figure A-19. The title bar now displays the page title, TripSmart - The Smart Way to Go, followed by the root folder (tripsmart) and the name of the page (index.htm) in parentheses. The information within the parentheses is called the **path**, or location of the open file in relation to other folders in the Web site.

3. Click index.htm in the Site panel to select it, click Site on the Site panel menu bar, then click Set as Home Page (Win), or click Site on the menu bar, point to Site Map View, then click Set as Home Page (Mac).

   > **TIP** If you want your screen to match the figures in this book, make sure the document window is maximized.

You opened a file, saved it with the filename index.htm, and set it as the home page.

FIGURE A-19

index.htm placed in the tripsmart root folder

Page title and path for file

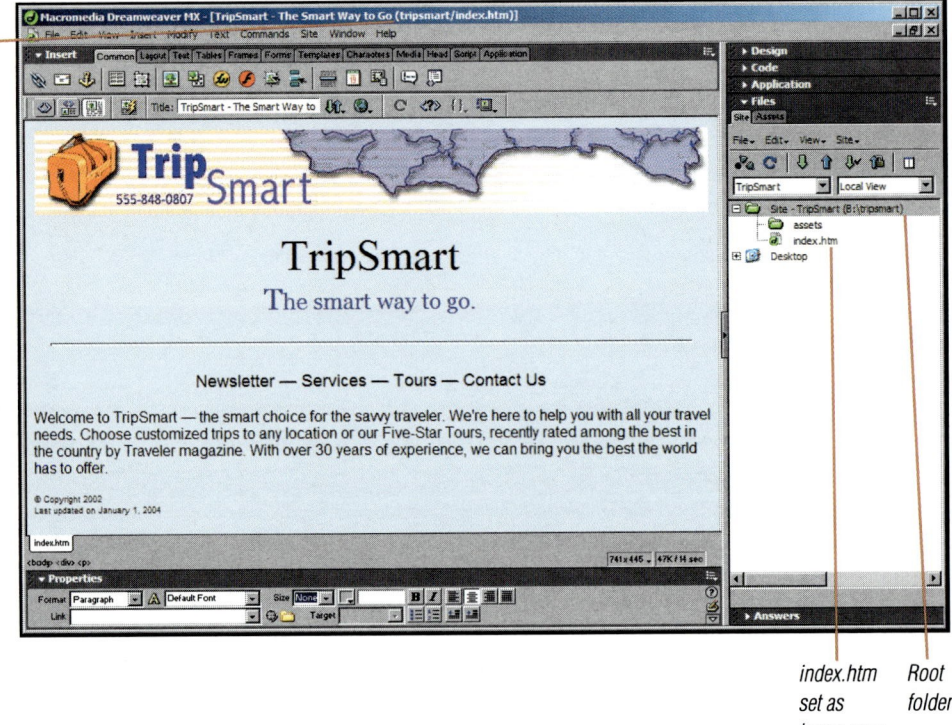

index.htm set as home page

Root folder

FIGURE A-20
Property inspector showing properties of the TripSmart banner

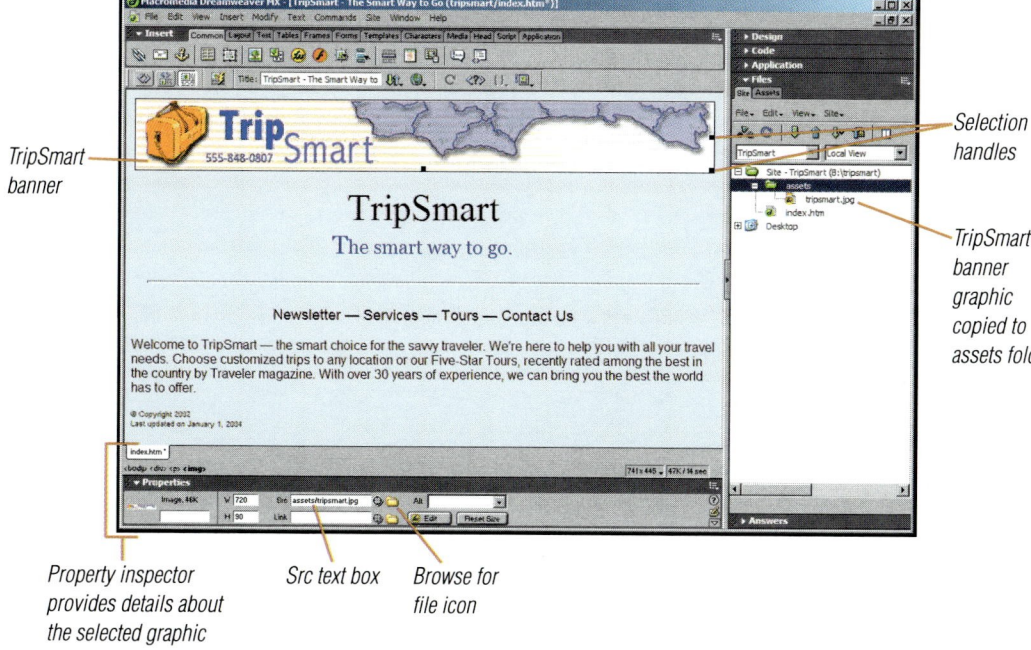

TripSmart banner

Selection handles

TripSmart banner graphic copied to assets folder

Property inspector provides details about the selected graphic

Src text box

Browse for file icon

Copy a graphic in an imported file and paste it to the assets folder

1. Click the TripSmart banner to select it.

   The Src text box in the Property inspector displays the current location of the selected banner.

2. Click the Browse for File icon next to the Src text box in the Property inspector, click the Look in list arrow (Win) or From list arrow (Mac), navigate to the unit_a assets folder, click tripsmart.jpg, then click OK (Win), or Choose (Mac).

   The TripSmart banner is automatically copied to the assets folder of the TripSmart Web site, the folder that you designated as the default images folder. The Src text box now shows the path of the banner to the assets folder in the Web site.

3. Compare your screen to Figure A-20.

   > **TIP** If you see a small gold icon next to the banner, click View on the menu bar, point to Visual Aids, then click Invisible Elements.

   Until you copy a graphic from an outside folder to your Web site, the graphic is not part of the Web site and the image will appear as a broken link on the page when the Web site is copied to a remote site.

   You copied the TripSmart banner to the assets folder.

Add pages to a Web site (Windows)

1. Click the plus sign to the left of the assets folder (if necessary) to open the folder and view its contents, tripsmart.jpg.

   TIP If you do not see any contents in the assets folder, click View on the Site panel menu bar, then click Refresh.

2. Click the tripsmart root folder to select it, click File on the Site panel menu bar, click New File, type **catalog.htm** to replace untitled.htm, then press [Enter].

   TIP If you create a new file in the Site panel, you must type the filename extension (.htm or .html) manually.

3. Repeat Step 2 to add five more blank pages to the TripSmart Web site, and name the new files services.htm, tours.htm, newsletter.htm, clothing.htm, and accessories.htm.

   TIP Make sure to add the new files to the root folder, not the assets folder. If you accidentally add them to the assets folder, just drag them to the root folder.

4. Click the Refresh button on the Site panel, then compare your screen to Figure A-21.

You added the following six pages to the TripSmart Web site: catalog, services, tours, newsletter, clothing, and accessories.

FIGURE A-21
New pages added to the TripSmart Web site (Windows)

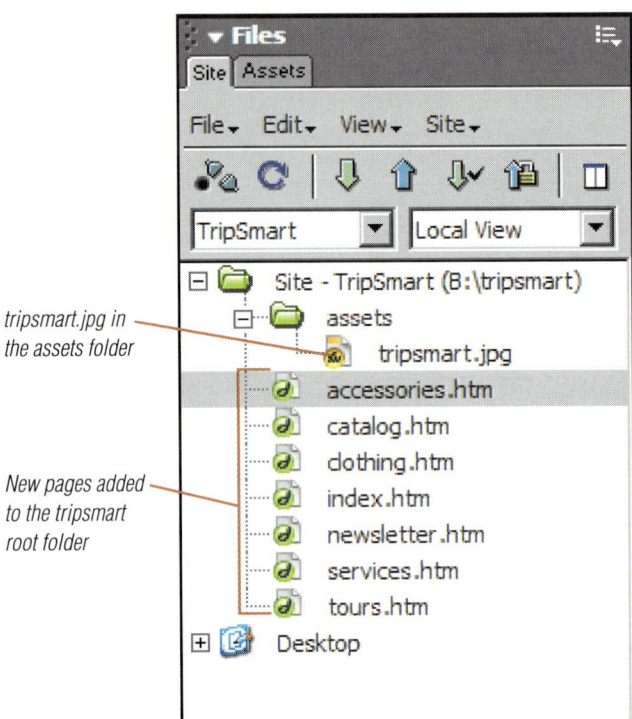

tripsmart.jpg in the assets folder

New pages added to the tripsmart root folder

FIGURE A-22

New pages added to the TripSmart Web site

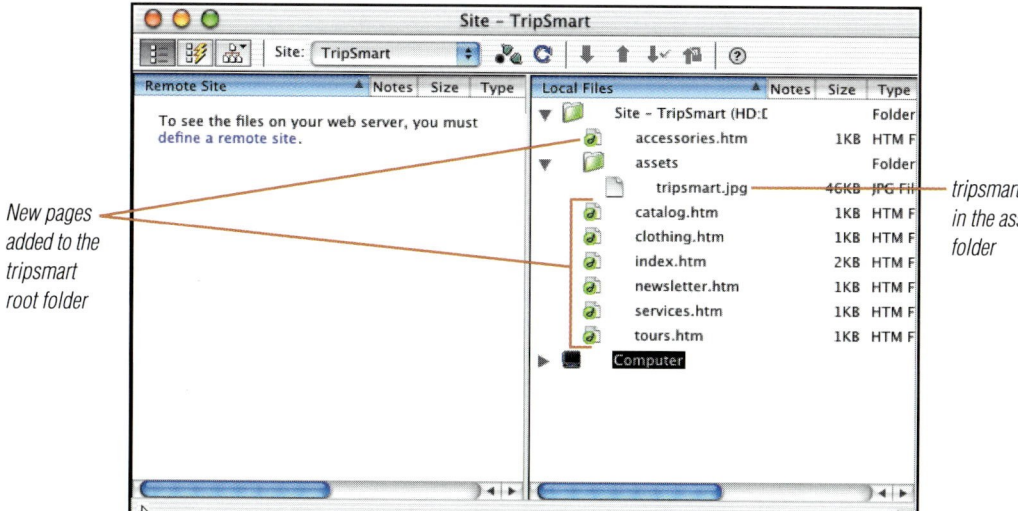

New pages added to the tripsmart root folder

tripsmart.jpg in the asssets folder

1. Click Site on the menu bar, then click Open Site to open the site panel.

2. Click the triangle to the left of the assets folder to open the folder and view its contents.

   TIP If you do not see any contents in the assets folder, click Site on the menu bar, then click Refresh.

3. Click the tripsmart root folder to select it.

4. Click Site on the menu bar, point to Site Files View, click New File, type **catalog.htm** to replace untitled.html, then press [return].

   TIP If you create a new file in the Site panel, you must type the filename extension (.htm or .html) manually.

5. Repeat Step 4 to add five more blank pages to the TripSmart Web site, and name the new files **services.htm**, **tours.htm**, **newsletter.htm**, **clothing.htm**, and **accessories.htm**.

6. Click Site on the menu bar, click Refresh to list the files alphabetically, then compare your screen to Figure A-22.

You added six pages to the TripSmart Web site: catalog, services, tours, newsletter, clothing, and accessories.

CREATE AND VIEW A SITE MAP

What You'll Do

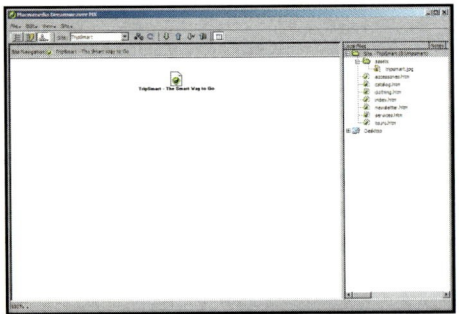

In this lesson, you will create and view a site map for the TripSmart Web site.

Creating a Site Map

As you add new Web pages to a Web site, it is easy to lose track of how they all link together. You can use the site map feature to help you keep track of the relationships between pages in a Web site. A **site map** is a graphical representation of the pages in the Web site and shows the folder structure for the Web site. You can find out details about each page by viewing the visual clues in the site map. For example, the site map uses icons to indicate pages with broken links, e-mail links, and links to external Web sites. It also indicates which pages are currently **checked out**, or being used by other team members.

Viewing a Site Map

You can view a site map using the Site Map command, or the Map View command. You can expand the Site panel to display both the site map and the Web site file list. You can specify that the site map show a filename or a page title for each page. You can also edit page titles in the site map. Figure A-23 shows the site map and file list for the TripSmart Web site. Only the home page and pages that are linked to the home page will display in the site map. As more child pages are added, the site map will display them using a

Verifying page titles

When you view a Web page in a browser, its page title is displayed in the browser window title bar. The page title should reflect the page content and set the tone for the page. It is especially important to use words in your page title that are likely to match keywords viewers may enter when using a search engine. Search engines compare the text in page titles to the keywords typed into the search engine. When a title bar displays "Untitled Document," the designer has neglected to give the page a title. This is like giving up free "billboard space," and looks very unprofessional.

tree structure, or a diagram that visually represents the way the pages are linked to each other.

Using Site Map Images in Web Pages

It is very helpful to include a graphic of the site map in a Web site to help viewers understand the navigation structure of the site. Using Dreamweaver, you have the options of saving a site map for printing purposes or for displaying a site map on a page in a Web site. Windows users can save site maps as either a BMP (bitmapped) file or as a PNG (Portable Network Graphics) file. The BMP format is the best format to use for printing the site map or inserting it into a page layout program or slide show. The PNG format is best for inserting the site map on a Web page. Macintosh users can save site maps as PICT or JPEG file. The PICT format is the best format for printing the site map and inserting it into a page layout program or a slide show. The JPEG format is best for inserting the site map on a Web page. Though gaining in popularity, PNG files are not available on the Macintosh platform and are not supported by older versions of browsers. However, they are capable of showing millions of colors, are small in size, and compress well without losing image quality.

FIGURE A-23
The TripSmart site map

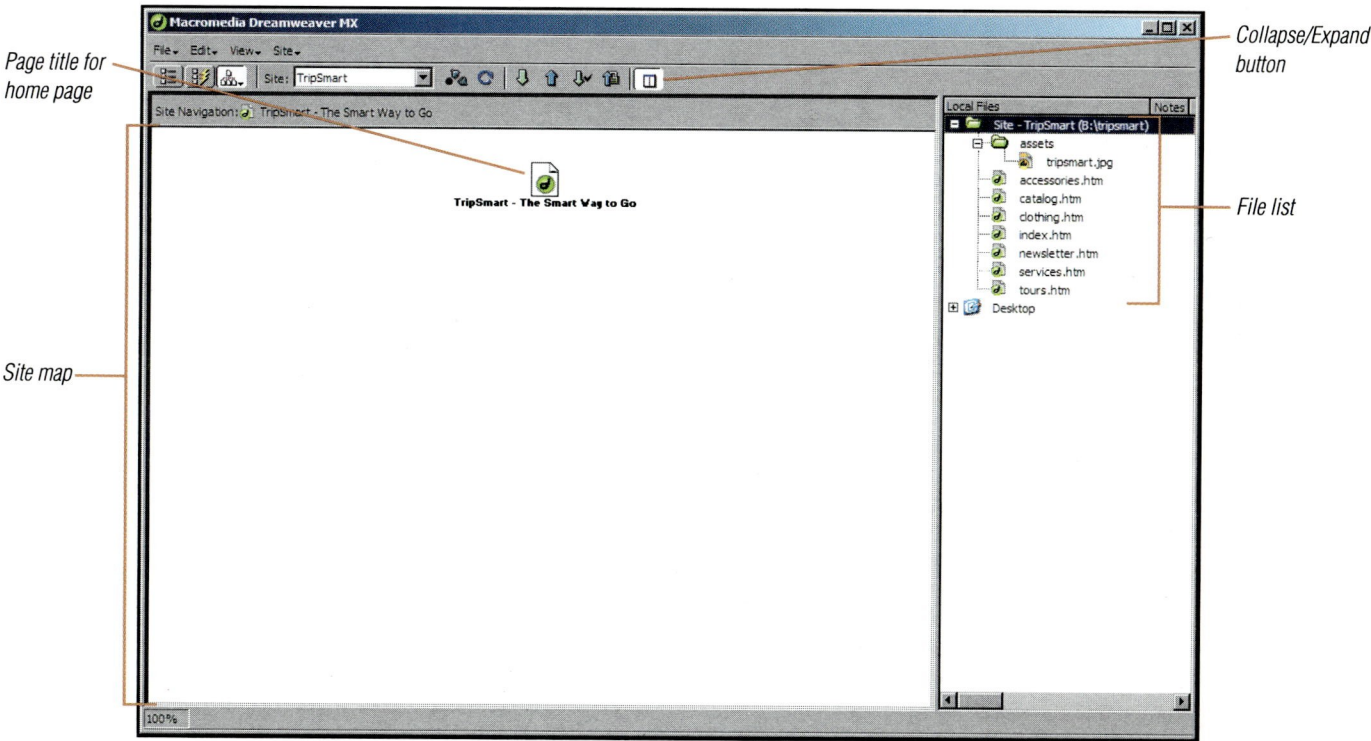

Page title for home page

Collapse/Expand button

File list

Site map

Select site map options

1. Click the Site list arrow in the Site panel, click Edit Sites, click TripSmart (if necessary), then click Edit to open the Site Definition dialog box.

2. Click Site Map Layout in the Category list.

3. Verify that index.htm is specified as the home page in the Home Page text box, as shown in Figure A-24.

   TIP If the index.htm file is not specified as your home page, click the Browse for File icon next to the Home Page text box, then locate and double-click index.htm.

4. Click the Page Titles option button to select it (if necessary).

5. Click OK, then click Done.

You designated index.htm as the home page for the TripSmart Web site to create the site map. You also specified that page titles instead of filenames display in the site map.

FIGURE A-24

Options for the site map layout

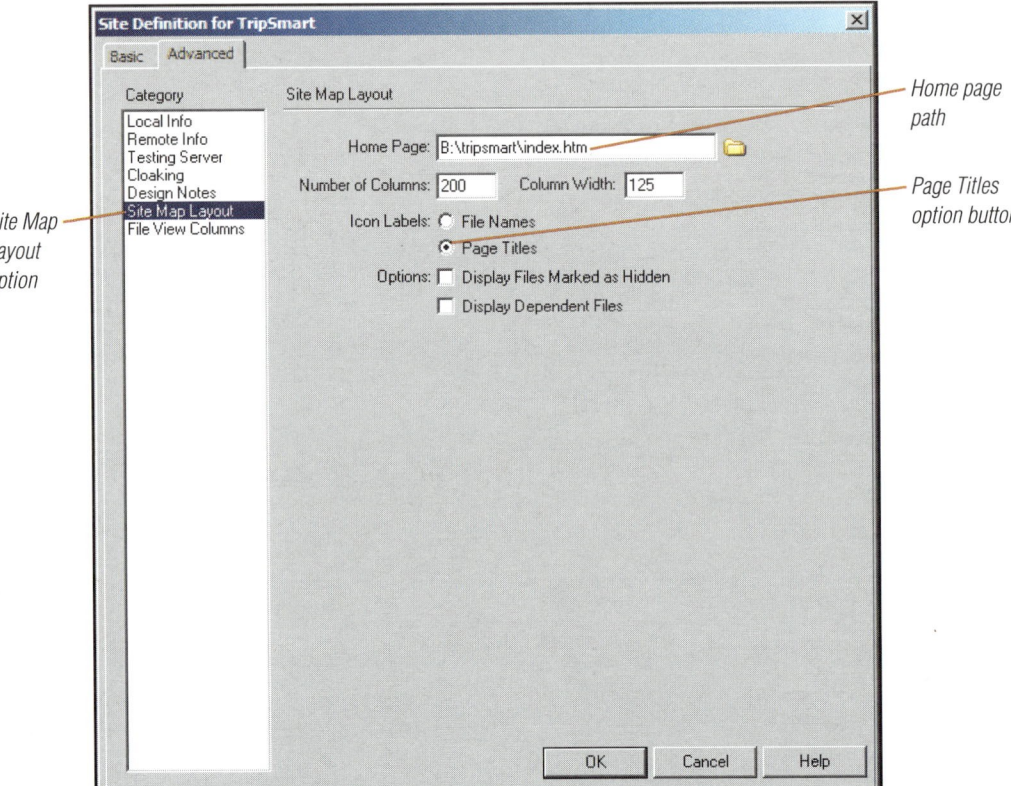

FIGURE A-25

Expanding the site map

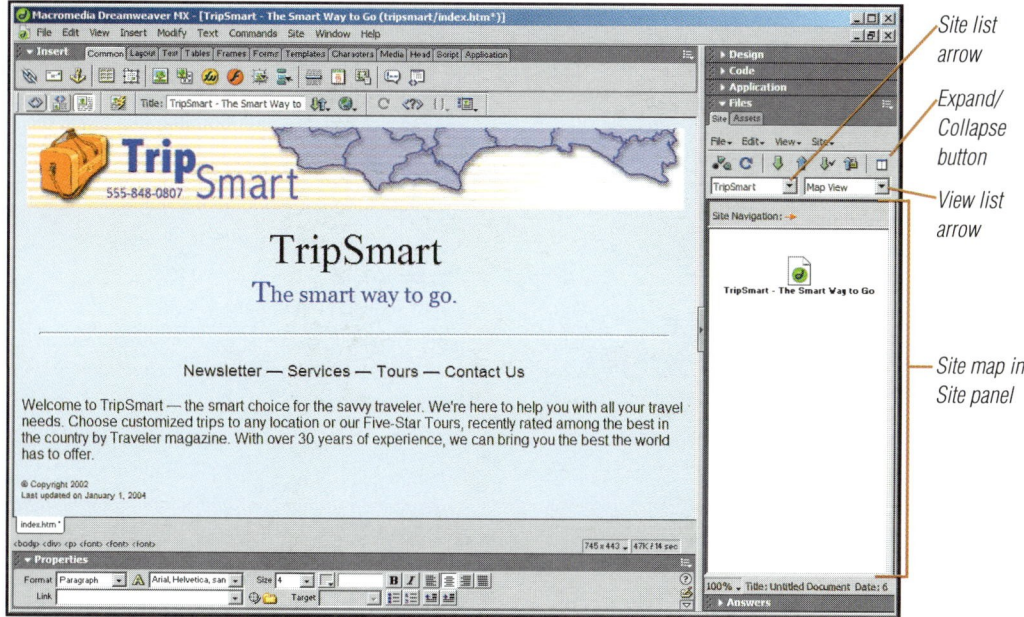

Site list arrow

Expand/ Collapse button

View list arrow

Site map in Site panel

1. Click the View list arrow on the Site panel, then click Map View (Win), or click the Site Map button (Mac).

2. Click the Expand/Collapse button on the Site panel toolbar, as shown in Figure A-25, to display the site map in the document window (Win).

   The site map shows the home page and pages that are linked to it. Because there are no pages linked to the home page, the site map shows only the home page.

   > TIP   You can drag the border between the two panes on the screen to resize them.

3. Click the Expand/Collapse button on the toolbar to collapse the site map.

4. Click the View list arrow, then click Local View (Win).

   The file list appears again in the Site panel.

You opened and closed the TripSmart site map in the Site panel.

Explore the Dreamweaver workspace.

1. Start Dreamweaver.
2. Change the view to Code view.
3. Change the view to Code and Design view.
4. Change the view to Design view.
5. Expand the Code panel group.
6. View each panel in the Code panel group.
7. Collapse the Code panel group.

View a Web page and use Help.

1. Open the file dwa_3.htm from the folder where your data files are stored.
2. Locate the following page elements: a table, a banner, a graphic, and some formatted text.
3. Change the view to Code view.
4. Change the view to Design view.
5. Use the Dreamweaver Help feature to search for information on panel groups.
6. Display and read one of the topics you find.
7. Close the Help window.
8. Close the page without saving it.

Plan and define a Web site.

1. Select the drive and folder where you will store your Web site files using Windows Explorer or Macintosh Finder.
2. Create a new root folder called **blooms**.
3. Close Explorer or Finder and activate the Dreamweaver window.
4. Create a new site called Blooms & Bulbs.
5. Specify the blooms folder as the Local Root folder.
6. Verify that the Refresh Local File List Automatically option and the Enable Cache option are both selected.
7. Use the Remote Info category in the Site Definition dialog box to set up Web server access by entering the information supplied to you by your instructor. (Specify None if you do not have the necessary information to set up Web server access.)
8. Close the Site Definition dialog box.

Add a folder and pages to a Web site and set the home page.

1. Create a new folder in the blooms root folder called **assets**.
2. Edit the site to set the assets folder as the default location for the Web site graphics.
3. Open the file dwa_4.htm from the folder where your data files are stored, then save this file in the blooms root folder as **index.htm**.
4. Set index.htm as the home page.
5. Select the banner on the page.
6. Use the Property inspector to browse for the file blooms.gif, and then save it in the assets folder of the Blooms & Bulbs Web site.
7. Create three new pages in the Site panel and name them: plants.htm, workshops.htm, and tips.htm.
8. Refresh the view to list the new files alphabetically.

Create and view a site map.

1. Use the Site Map Layout dialog box to verify that the index.htm file is shown as the home page.
2. Show the page titles.
3. View the expanded site map for the Web site and compare your screen to Figure A-26.
4. Save your work.

FIGURE A-26

Completed Skills Review

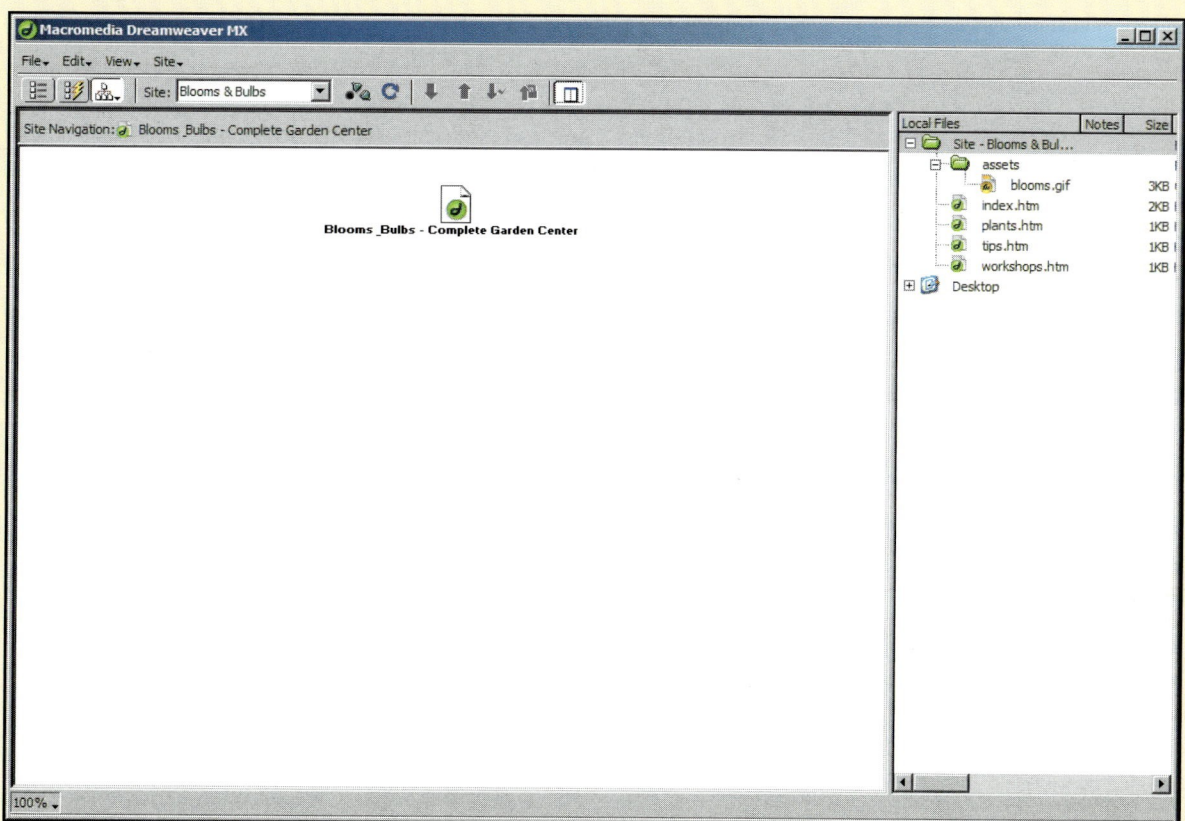

You have been hired to create a Web site for a river expedition company named Rapids Transit, located on the Buffalo River in Arkansas. In addition to renting canoes, kayaks, and rafts, they have a country store and a snack bar. If requested, river guides are available to accompany clients on float trips. The clients range from high school and college students to families to vacationing professionals. The owner, Mike Andrew, has requested a dynamic Web site that conveys the beauty of the Ozark Mountains and the Buffalo River.

1. Using the information in the paragraph above, create a storyboard for this Web site, using either a pencil and paper or a software program such as Microsoft Word. Include the home page with links to three child pages named guides.htm, rentals.htm, and store.htm.
2. Create a folder named **rapids** in the drive and folder where you store your Web site files.
3. Start Dreamweaver and define the Web site with the name **Rapids Transit**.

4. Create an assets folder and set it as the default location for images.
5. Open dwa_5.htm from the location where your data files are stored, then save it in the rapids root folder as index.htm.
6. Save the rapids.jpg file in the assets folder.
7. Set index.htm as the home page.

8. Create three additional pages for the site, and name them as follows: **guides.htm**, **rentals.htm**, and **store.htm**. Use your storyboard and Figure A-27 as a guide.
9. Refresh the Site panel.
10. Create a site map for the Web site, then save your work.

FIGURE A-27

Completed Project Builder 1

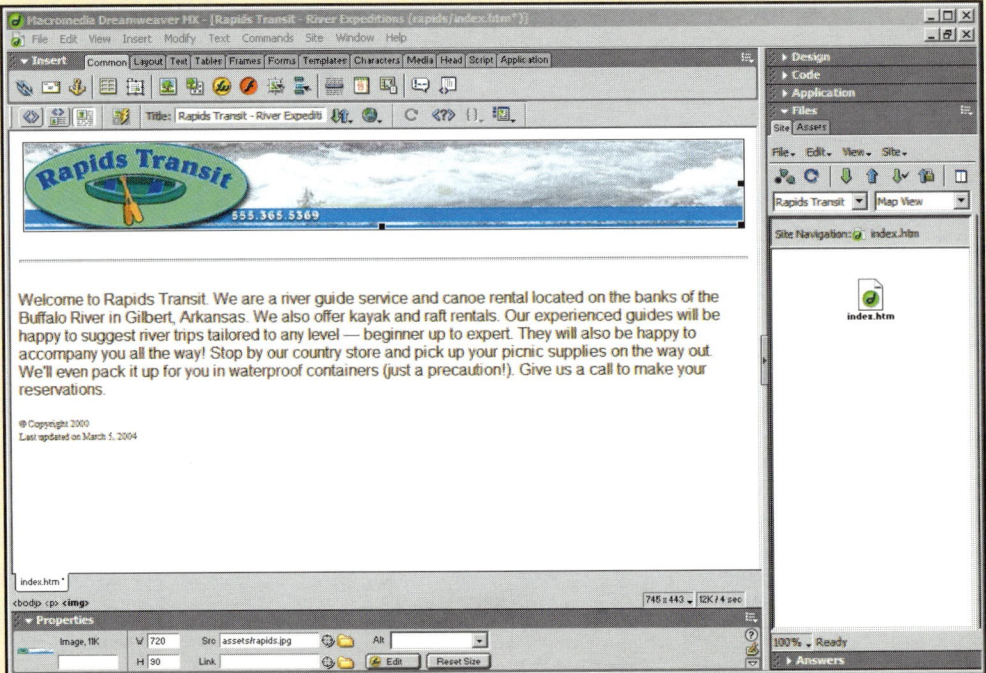

Your company has been selected to design a Web site for Jacob's, a new upscale restaurant in London that caters to business executives and theatre patrons. Jacob's has an extensive menu featuring French cuisine that includes set dinners and pre- and post-theatre dinner specials. They also like to feature some of their more popular recipes on their Web site. The chef, Jacob Richard, is famous in London for his creative cuisine and innovative culinary events.

1. Create a storyboard for this Web site that includes a home page and child pages called directions.htm, menus.htm, and recipes.htm.
2. Create a folder for the Web site in the drive and folder where you save your Web site files and name it **jacobs**.
3. Define the Web site with the name **Jacob's**.
4. Create an assets folder for the Web site and set the assets folder as the default location for images.
5. Open the file dwa_6.htm from the folder where your data files are stored, then save it as **index.htm** in the jacobs folder.
6. Save the jacobs.jpg file in the assets folder.
7. Set index.htm as the home page.
8. Using Figure A-28 and your storyboard as guides, create the additional pages shown for the Web site.
9. Create a site map that displays page titles, then save your work.

FIGURE A-28

Completed Project Builder 2

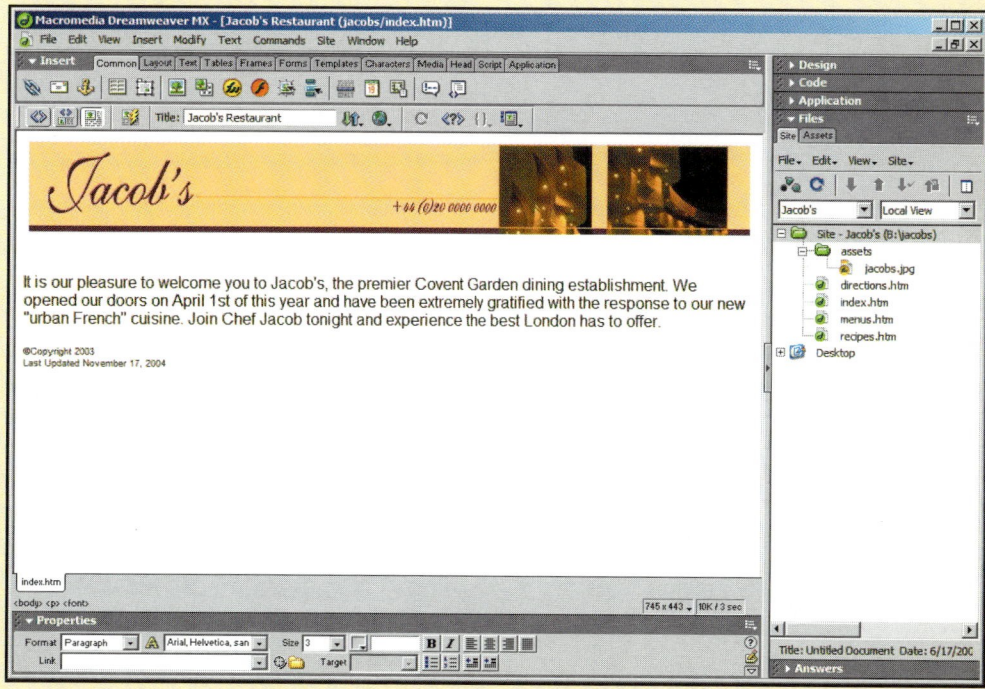

Figure A-29 shows the Audi Web site, a past selection for the Macromedia Site of the Day. To visit the current Audi Web site connect to the Internet, go to *www.course.com*, navigate to the page for this book, click the Student Online Companion link, then click the link for this unit. The current page might differ from the figure since dynamic Web sites are updated frequently to reflect current information. If you are viewing the Web page on a screen whose resolution is set to 800×600, you will see that the design fits very well. The main navigation structure is accessed through the images along the right side of the page. You can also click images in the center of the page to open new pages. You'll notice that as you place the pointer over an image, a tooltip appears with a description of the page that will open if the image is clicked. The page title is Audi World Site.

Go to the Macromedia Web site at *www.macromedia.com*, click the Visit Showcase link, then click the current Site of the Day. Explore the site and answer the following questions:

1. Do you see page titles for each page you visit?

2. Do the page titles accurately reflect the page content?

3. View the pages using more than one screen resolution, if possible. For which resolution does the site appear to be designed?

4. Is the navigation structure clear?

5. How is the navigation structure organized?

6. Why do you think this site was chosen as a Site of the Day?

FIGURE A-29
Design Project

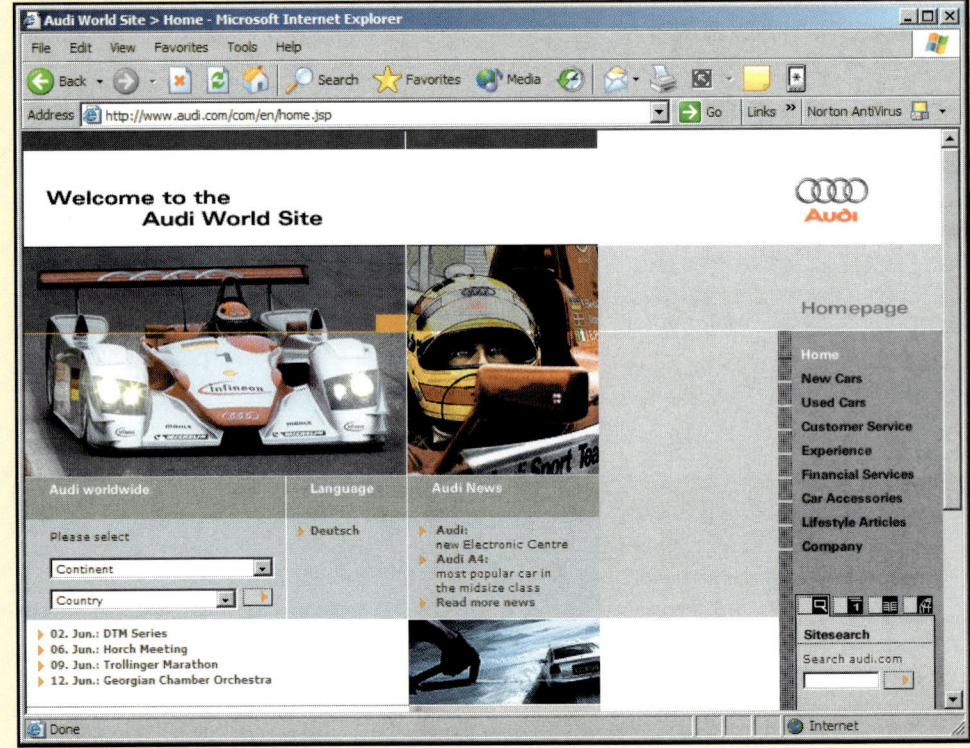

Work with a group to come up with a plan for a Web site that the group will create entirely on its own, without any data files. The focus of the Web site can be on any topic, organization, sports team, club, or company that you would like. Depending on the size of your group, you can assign individual elements of the project to group members, or work collectively to create the finished product. You will build on this Web site from unit to unit, so you must do each Group Project assignment in each unit to complete your Web site.

1. Decide among your members what type of Web site you would like to create. It can be a personal Web site about your class or school, a business Web site that promotes a fictitious or real company, or an informational Web site that provides information about a topic, cause, or organization. Your instructor may direct your choices for this assignment.

2. With the whole group participating and using Table A-2 as a guide, write a list of questions and answers about the Web site you have decided to create. Assign team members questions and have them report back to the group with answers.

3. Brainstorm as a group to construct a storyboard for your Web site to include at least four pages. The storyboard should include the home page with at least three child pages under it. Assign a team member the task of creating the storyboard.

4. Assign a team member the task of creating a root folder and an assets folder to house the Web site assets and set it as the default location for images.

5. Create a blank page named index.htm as a placeholder for the home page and set it as the home page.

6. Assign team members to collect content, such as pictures or text to use in your Web site. You can use a digital camera to take photos, scan pictures, or create your own graphics using a program such as Macromedia Fireworks. Gather the content in a central location that is accessible to the team as you develop your site.

UNIT B

DEVELOPING A WEB PAGE

1. Create head content and set page properties.

2. Create, import, and format text.

3. Add links to Web pages.

4. Use the History panel and Code Inspector.

5. Modify and test Web pages.

UNIT B
DEVELOPING A WEB PAGE

Introduction

The process of developing a Web page requires several steps. If the page is a home page, you need to decide on the head content. The head content contains information used by search engines to help viewers find your Web site. You also need to choose the colors for the page background as well as the links. You then need to add the page content and format it attractively, and add links to other pages in the Web site or to other Web sites. To ensure that all links work correctly and are current, you need to test them regularly.

Understanding Page Layout

Before you add content to a page, consider the following guidelines for laying out pages:

Use White Space Effectively. A living room crammed with too much furniture makes it difficult to appreciate the individual pieces. The same is true of a Web page. Too many text blocks, links, and images can be distracting. Consider leaving some white space on each page. White space, which is not necessarily white, is the area on a Web page that contains no text or graphics.

Limit Multimedia Elements. Too many multimedia elements, such as graphics, video clips, or sounds, may result in a page that takes too much time to load. Viewers may leave your Web site before the entire page finishes loading. Use multimedia elements only if you have a good reason.

Keep it Simple. Often the simplest Web sites are the most appealing and are also the easiest to create and maintain. A simple Web site that works well is far superior to a complex one that contains errors.

Use an Intuitive Navigation Structure. Make sure the navigation structure is easy to use. Viewers should always know where they are in the site and be able to find their way back to the home page. If viewers get lost, they may leave the site rather than struggle to find their way around.

Apply a Consistent Theme. To help give pages in your Web site a consistent appearance, consider designing your pages using elements that relate to a common theme.

Tools You'll Use

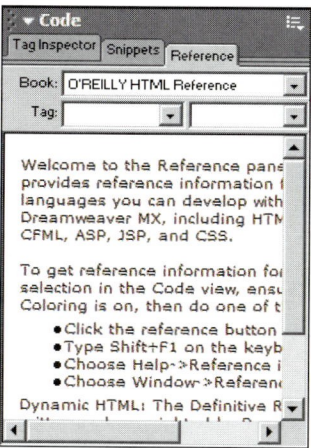

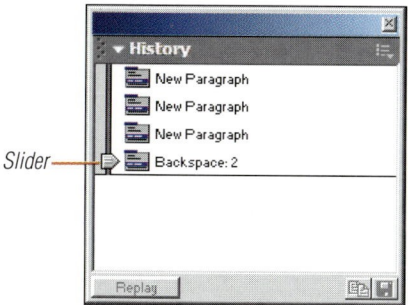

Slider

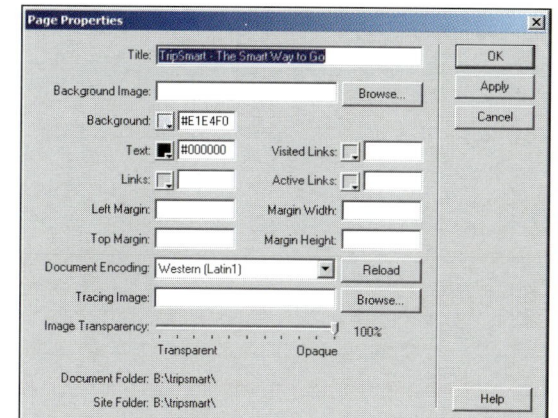

CREATE HEAD CONTENT AND SET PAGE PROPERTIES

What You'll Do

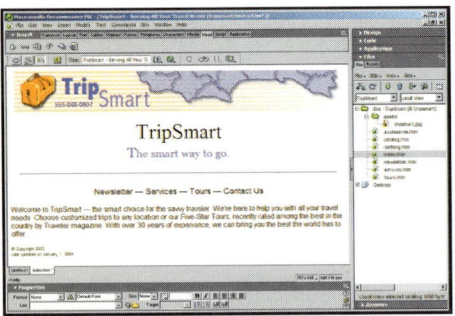

 In this lesson, you will learn how to enter titles, keywords, and descriptions in the head content section of a Web page. You will also change the background color for a Web page.

Creating the Head Content

A Web page is composed of two distinct sections: the head content and the body. The **head content** includes the page title that is displayed in the title bar of the browser and some important page elements, called meta tags, that are not visible in the browser. **Meta tags** are HTML codes that include information about the page, such as keywords and descriptions.

Keywords are words that relate to the content of the Web site. A **description** is a short paragraph that describes the content and features of the Web site. For instance, "travel" and "tours" would be appropriate keywords for the TripSmart Web site. It is important to include concise, useful information in the head content, because search engines find Web pages by matching the title, description, and keywords in

Using Web-Safe Colors

Before 1994, colors appeared differently on different types of computers. For instance, if a designer chose a particular shade of red in a document created on a Windows computer, he or she could not be certain that the same shade of red would appear on a Macintosh computer. In 1994, Netscape developed the first **Web-safe color palette**, a set of colors that appears consistently in all browsers and on Macintosh, Windows, and Unix platforms. If you want your Web pages to be viewed across a wide variety of computer platforms, make sure you choose Web-safe colors for all your page elements. Dreamweaver has two Web-safe color palettes, Color Cubes and Continuous Tones, each of which contains 216 Web-safe colors. Color Cubes is the default color palette. To choose a different color palette, click Modify on the menu bar, click Page Properties, click the Background, Text, or Links color box to open the color picker, click the Color Palette list arrow, then click the color palette you want.

the head content of Web pages with keywords that viewers enter in search engine text boxes. The **body** is the part of the page that appears in a browser window. It contains all the page content that is visible to viewers, such as text, graphics, and links.

Setting Web Page Properties

When you create a Web page, one of the first design decisions that you should make is choosing the **background color**, or the color that fills the entire Web page. The background color should complement the colors used for text, links, and graphics that are placed on the page. A strong contrast between the text color and the background color makes it easier for viewers to read the text on your Web page. You can choose a light background color and a dark text color, or a dark background color and a light text color. A white background with dark text, though not terribly exciting, provides good contrast and is the easiest to read for most viewers. The next important design decision you need to make is to choose the **default font** and **default link colors**, which are the colors used by the browser to display text, links, and visited links. The default color for **unvisited links**, or links that the viewer has not clicked yet, is blue. In Dreamweaver, unvisited links are simply called **links.** The default color for **visited links**, or links that have been previously clicked, is purple. You change the background color, text, and link colors using the color picker in the Page Properties dialog box. You can choose colors from one of the five Dreamweaver color palettes, as shown in Figure B-1.

QUICKTIP

Not all browsers recognize link color settings.

FIGURE B-1

Color picker showing color palettes

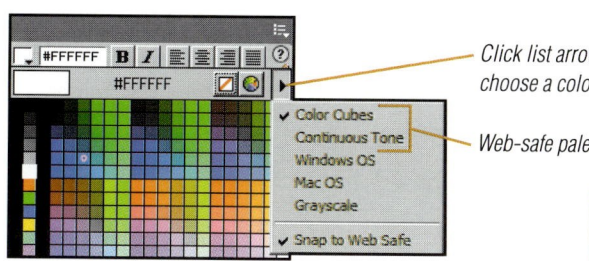

Click list arrow to choose a color palette

Web-safe palettes

Making pages accessible to viewers of all abilities

Never assume that all your viewers have perfect vision and hearing or full use of both hands. There are several techniques you can use to ensure that your Web site is accessible to individuals with disabilities. These techniques include using alternate text with graphic images, avoiding certain colors on Web pages, and supplying text as an alternate source for information that is presented in an audio file. You can test your Web site for accessibility before publishing it by submitting it to be tested by **Bobby**, a free service provided by **CAST**, the Center for Applied Special Technology. The Web site address for information about Bobby is *www.cast.org/bobby/.* Macromedia also provides a vehicle for testing Web site compliance with Section 508 accessibility guidelines. For more information, visit the Macromedia Web site at http://*www.macromedia.com/macromedia/accessibility/.*

Edit a page title

1. Click the Site pop-up menu on the Site panel, then click TripSmart (if necessary).

   If you do not have the completed TripSmart site from Unit A, contact your instructor.

2. Double-click index.htm in the Site panel to open the TripSmart home page, click View on the menu bar, then click Head Content.

   The Title icon and Meta icon are now visible in the head content section, as shown in Figure B-2.

3. Click the Title icon in the head content section.

   The page title TripSmart - The Smart Way To Go appears in the Title text box in the Property inspector.

4. Select TripSmart - The Smart Way To Go in the Title text box in the Property inspector, type **TripSmart - Serving All Your Travel Needs**, then press [Enter] (Win) or [return] (Mac).

   Compare your screen with Figure B-3. The new title is better, because it incorporates the word "travel," a word that potential customers might use as a keyword when using a search engine.

   > TIP You can also change the page title using the Title text box on the Document toolbar.

5. Click File on the menu bar, then click Save to save your work.

You opened the TripSmart Web site, opened the home page in Design view, opened the head content section, changed the page title, and saved your work.

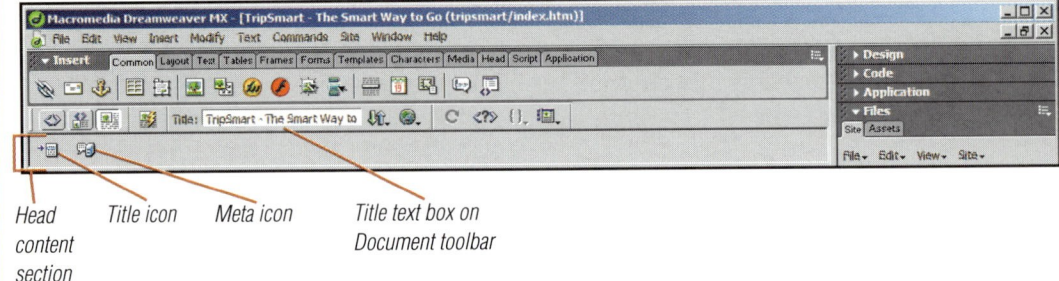

Head content section Title icon Meta icon Title text box on Document toolbar

FIGURE B-3
Property inspector displaying new page title

Planning the page layout

When you begin developing the content for your Web site, you need to decide what content to include and how to arrange each element on each page. You must design the content with the audience in mind. What is the age group of your audience? What reading level is appropriate? Should you use a formal or informal tone? Should the pages be simple, containing mostly text, or rich with images and multimedia files? Usually the first page that your audience will see when they visit your Web site is the home page. The home page should be designed so that viewers will feel "at home," and comfortable finding their way around the pages in your site. To ensure that viewers do not get lost in your Web site, make sure you design all the pages with a consistent look and feel. You can use templates to maintain a common look for each page. **Templates** are Web pages that contain the basic layout for each page in the site, including the location of a company logo or a menu of buttons.

Head
category
buttons

Keywords
button

Description
button

Head tab

Enter keywords

1. Click the Head tab on the Insert bar, then click the Keywords button on the Insert bar as shown in Figure B-4.

2. Type **travel**, **traveling**, **supplies**, **trips**, **vacations** in the Keywords text box, as shown in Figure B-5, then click OK.

3. Save your work.

You added keywords relating to travel to the head content of the TripSmart home page.

FIGURE B-5

Keywords dialog box

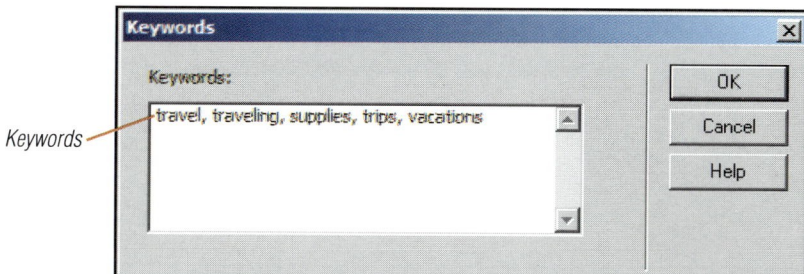

Keywords

Entering keywords and descriptions

Search engines use keywords, descriptions, and titles to find pages after a user enters search terms. Therefore, it is very important to anticipate the search terms your potential customers would use and include these words in the keywords, description, or title. Many search engines display page titles and descriptions in their search results. Some search engines limit the number of keywords that they will index, so make sure you list the most important keywords first. Keep your keywords and description concise to ensure that all search engines will include your site.

Enter a description

1. Click the Description button on the Insert bar.
2. Type **TripSmart is a comprehensive travel store. We can help you plan trips, make travel arrangements, and supply you with travel gear.**

   Compare your screen with Figure B-6.
3. Click OK.
4. Click the Show Code View button on the Document toolbar.

   Notice the title, keywords, and description appear in the HTML code in the document window, as shown in Figure B-7.
5. Click the Show Design View button to return to Design view.
6. Click View on the menu bar, then click Head Content to close the Head Content section.
7. Save your work.

You added a description of the TripSmart company to the head content of the home page. You then viewed the home page in Code view and examined the HTML code for the head content.

FIGURE B-6

Description dialog box

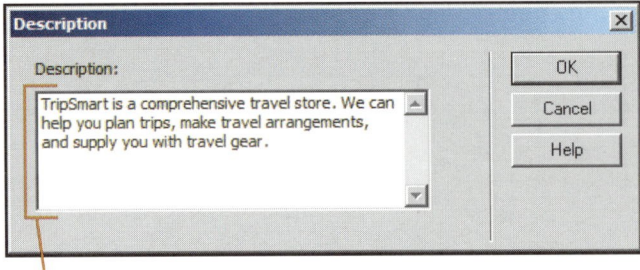

Description

FIGURE B-7

Head Content displayed in Code view

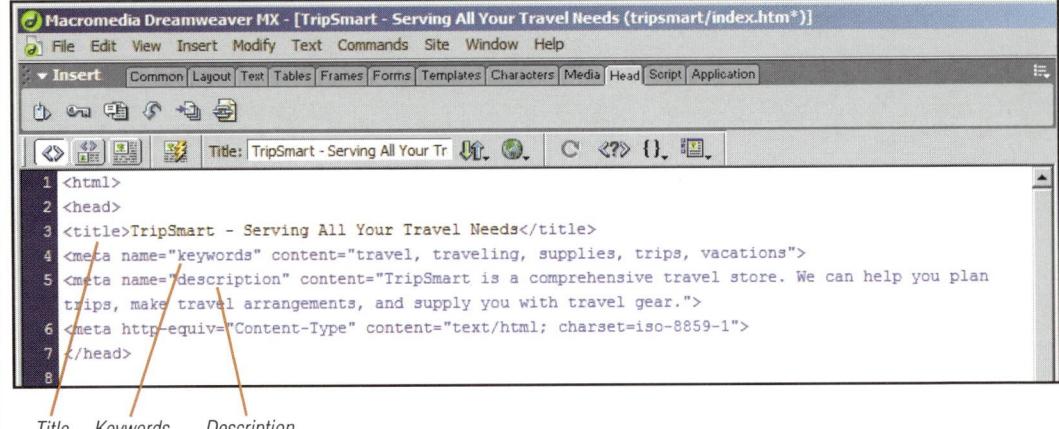

Title   Keywords   Description

FIGURE B-8

Page Properties dialog box

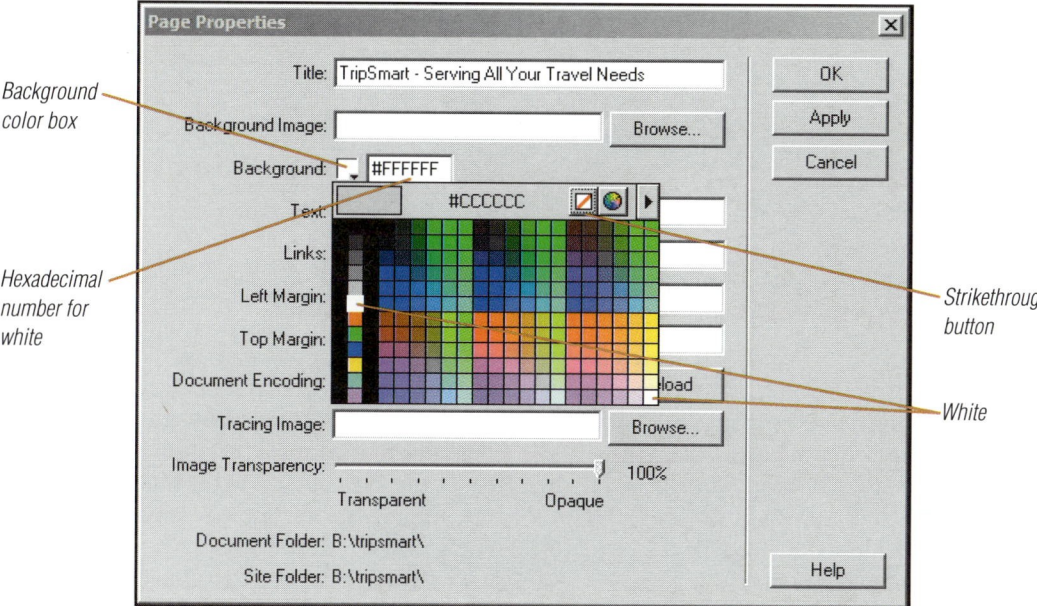

Background color box

Hexadecimal number for white

Strikethrough button

White

1. Click Modify on the menu bar, then click Page Properties to open the Page Properties dialog box.

2. Click the Background color box to open the color picker, as shown in Figure B-8.

3. Click the last color in the bottom row (white).

4. Click Apply, then click OK.

   Clicking Apply lets you see the changes you made to the Web page without closing the Page Properties dialog box. Clicking OK makes the changes you specified, then closes the dialog box.

   > **TIP** If you don't like the color you chose, click the Strikethrough button in the Page to switch back to the default color.

5. Save your work.

   The background color of the Web page is now white. The black text against the white background provides a nice contrast and makes the text easy to read.

   You used the Page Properties dialog box to change the background color to white.

Understanding hexadecimal values

Each color is assigned a **hexadecimal value**, a value that represents the amount of red, green, and blue present in the color. For example, white, which is made of equal parts of red, green, and blue, has a hexadecimal value of FFFFFF. Each pair of characters in the hexadecimal value represents the red, green, and blue values. The hexadecimal number system is based on 16, rather than 10 in the decimal number system. Since the hexadecimal number system includes only numbers up to 9, values after 9 use the letters of the alphabet. A represents the number 10 in the hexadecimal number system. F represents the number 15.

CREATE, IMPORT AND FORMAT TEXT

What You'll Do

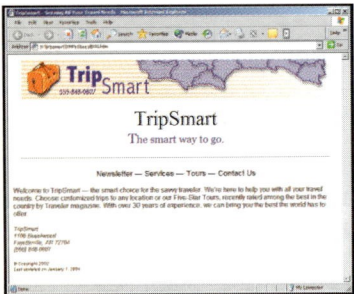

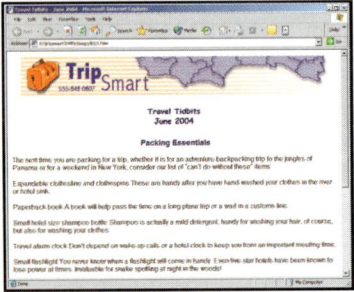

 In this lesson, you will apply heading styles and text styles to text on the TripSmart home page. You will also create a new page and import an HTML file created in Microsoft Word into it. Last, you will set text properties for the text on the new page.

Creating and Importing Text

Most information in Web pages is presented in the form of text. You can create text directly in Dreamweaver or copy and paste it from another software program. To import text from a Microsoft Word file, you use the Import Word HTML command, which deletes all extraneous HTML tags from a file and then shows the results of the cleanup in the Clean Up Word HTML Results window. You can then copy and paste the text from this window to another Dreamweaver page. When you import text, it is important to keep in mind that visitors to your site must have the same fonts installed on their computers as the fonts applied to the imported text. Otherwise, the text may appear incorrectly. Some software programs, such as Adobe Photoshop and Adobe Illustrator

Using keyboard shortcuts

When working with text, the standard Windows keyboard shortcuts for the Cut, Copy, and Paste commands are very useful. These are [Control] [X] for Cut, [Control] [C] for Copy, and [Control] [V] for Paste. You can view all Dreamweaver keyboard shortcuts using the Keyboard Shortcuts dialog box, which lets you view existing shortcuts for menu commands, tools, or miscellaneous functions, such as copying HTML or inserting an image. You can also create your own shortcuts or assign shortcuts from other applications, such as FreeHand or Adobe Illustrator and Photoshop. To view or modify keyboard shortcuts, click the Keyboard Shortcuts command on the Edit menu, then select the shortcut key set you want. The Keyboard Shortcuts feature is also available in Macromedia Fireworks and Flash. A printable version of all Dreamweaver keyboard shortcuts can be downloaded from the Dreamweaver Support Center at *http://www.macromedia.com/support/dreamweaver/documentation/dwmx_shortcuts/.*

can convert text into graphics so that the text retains the same appearance no matter what fonts are installed. However, text converted into graphics is no longer editable.

Formatting Text Using the Property Inspector

Because text is more difficult and tiring to read on a computer screen than on a printed page, you should make the text in your Web site attractive and easy to read. You can format text in Dreamweaver by changing its font, size, and color, just as you would in other software programs. To apply formatting to text, you first select the text you want to enhance, and then use the Property inspector to apply formatting attributes, such as font type, size, color, alignment, and indents.

Changing Fonts

You can format your text with different fonts by choosing a font combination from the Font list in the Property inspector. A **font combination** is a set of three fonts that specify which fonts a browser should use to display the text of your Web page. Font combinations are used so that if one font is not available, the browser will use the next one specified in the font combination. For example, if text is formatted with the font combination Arial, Helvetica, sans serif, the browser will first look on the viewer's system for Arial. If Arial is not available then it will look for Helvetica. If Helvetica is not available, then it will look for a sans-serif font to apply to the text. Using fonts within the default settings is wise, as fonts set outside the default settings may not be available on all viewers' computers.

Changing Font Sizes

There are two ways to change the size of text using the Property inspector. You can select a font size between 1 and 7, (where 1 is the smallest and 7 is the largest), or you can change the font size relative to the default base font. The **default base font** is size 3. For example, choosing +1 in the Size list increases the font size from 3 to 4.

Choosing −1 decreases the font size from 3 to 2. Font sizes on Windows and Macintosh computers may differ slightly, so it's important to view your page on both platforms, if possible.

Formatting Paragraphs

You can format blocks of text as paragraphs or as different sized headings. To format a paragraph as a heading, click anywhere in the paragraph, then select the heading size you want from the Format list in the Property inspector. The Format list contains six different heading styles. Heading 1 is the largest size, and Heading 6 is the smallest size. Browsers display text formatted as headings in bold, setting them off from paragraphs of text.

QUICKTIP

Avoid mixing too many different fonts and formatting attributes on a Web page. This can result in pages that are visually confusing and that may be difficult to read.

1. Position the insertion point directly after the text the "best the world has to offer" at the end of the paragraph, press [Enter] (Win) or [return] (Mac), then type **TripSmart**.

   Pressing [Enter] (Win) or [return] (Mac) creates a new paragraph that is two lines down from the previous paragraph.

2. Press and hold [Shift], press [Enter] (Win) or [return] (Mac), then type **1106 Beechwood**.

   Pressing and holding [Shift] while you press [Enter] (Win) or [return] (Mac) is called adding a soft return. A **line break** places a new line of text on the next line down without creating a new paragraph. Line breaks are useful when you want to add a new line of text directly below the current line of text.

3. Add the following text below the 1106 Beechwood text, using soft returns after each line:

   Fayetteville, AR 72704

   (555) 848-0807

4. Compare your screen with Figure B-9, then save your work.

You entered text for the address and telephone number on the home page.

Entering the address and telephone number on the TripSmart home page

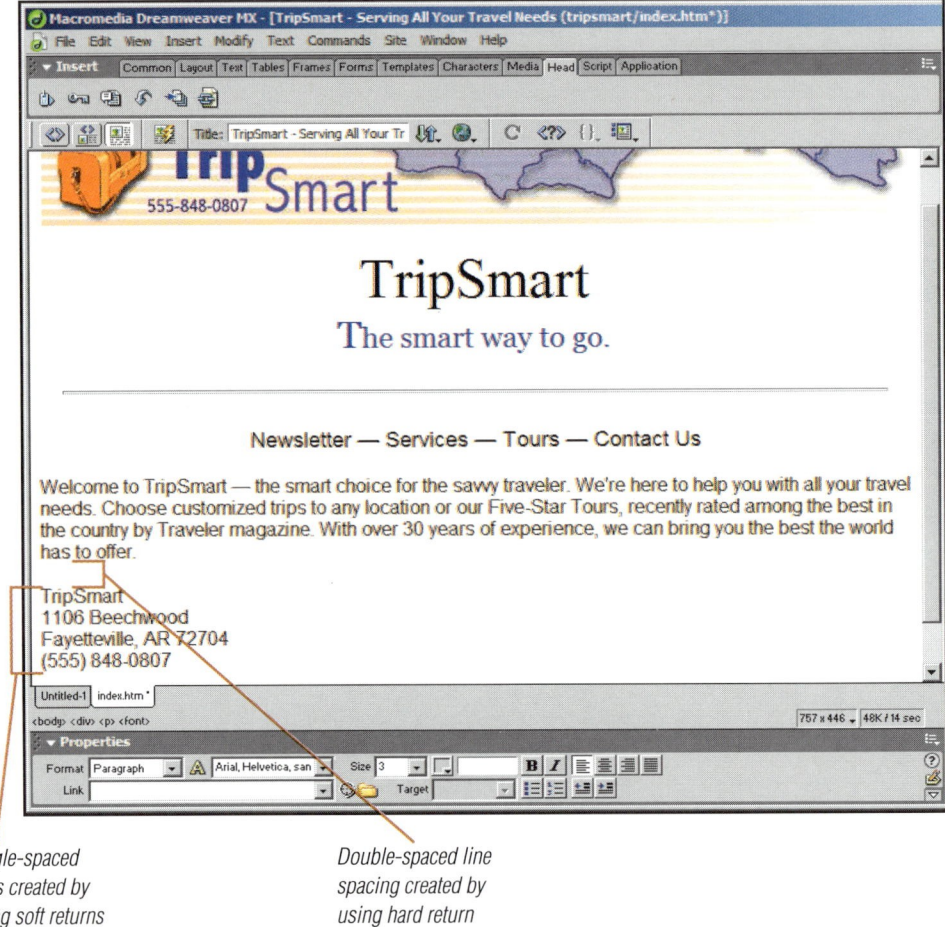

Single-spaced lines created by using soft returns

Double-spaced line spacing created by using hard return

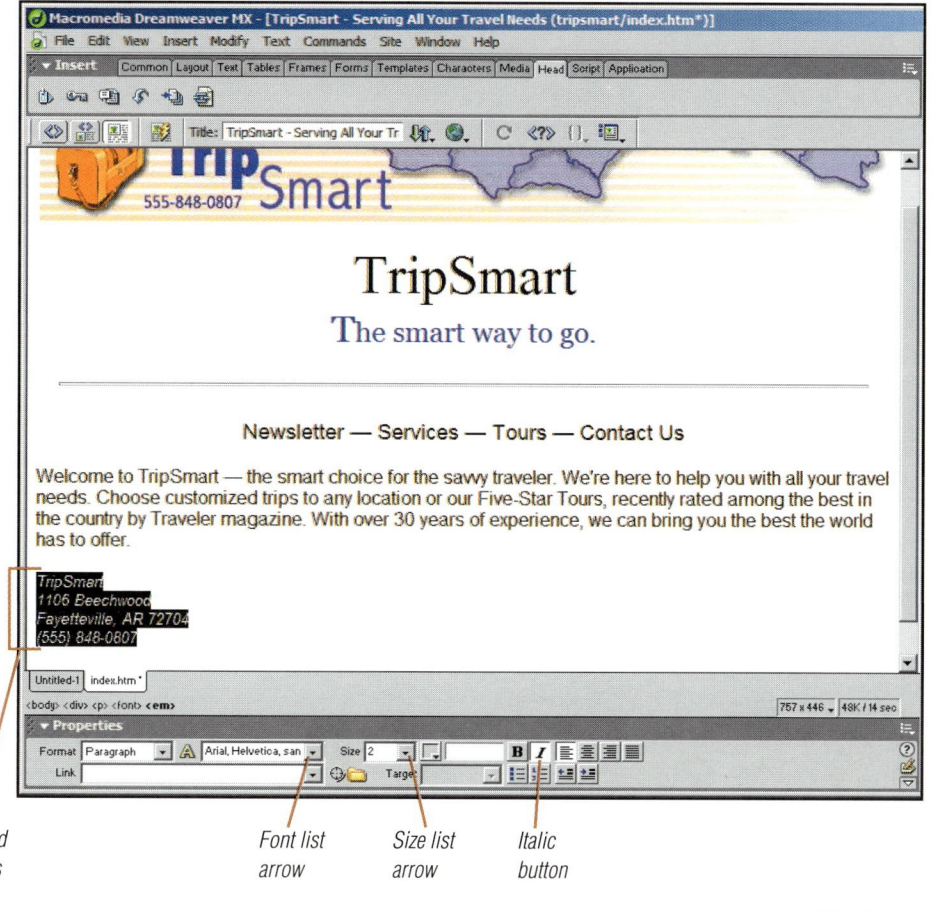

*Selected
address
text*

*Font list
arrow*

*Size list
arrow*

*Italic
button*

Format text

1. Select the address lines and telephone number, then click the Italic button in the Property inspector to italicize the text. *I*

2. With the text still selected, click the Size list arrow, click 2, then compare your screen to Figure B-10.

3. Save your work and close the file.

You formatted the address and phone number for TripSmart by changing the font style to italic and changing the size to 2.

Preventing data loss

When you are ready to stop working with a file in Dreamweaver, it is a good idea to save your changes, close the page or pages on which you are working, and exit Dreamweaver. Doing this will prevent the loss of data if power is interrupted. In some cases, loss of power can corrupt an open file and render it unusable.

Save graphics in the assets folder

1. Open dwb_1.htm from the unit_b data files folder, then save it as newsletter.htm in the tripsmart folder, overwriting the existing file.

2. Select the TripSmart banner.

   The Src box in the Property inspector shows the path as the unit_b assets folder. You need to change the path to the tripsmart.jpg file in the TripSmart assets folder.

3. Click the Browse for File icon next to the Src text box in the Property inspector, navigate to the tripsmart root folder, double-click the assets folder, click tripsmart.jpg, then click OK.

4. Click Travel Tidbits to select it, click the Browse for File icon next to the Src text box in the Property inspector, navigate to the unit_b assets folder, click tidbits.jpg, then click OK (Win) or Choose (Mac).

   Using the Browse for File icon to select the source of the original graphic file causes the file to be copied automatically to the assets folder of the Web site.

5. Click the Refresh button on the Site panel toolbar, then click the plus sign (Win) or expander arrow (Mac) next to the assets folder in the Site panel, if necessary.

   A copy of the tidbits.jpg file is now in the assets folder, as shown in Figure B-11.

6. Save your work.

   You opened a new file and saved it as the new newsletter page. You changed the path of the two graphics to the TripSmart assets folder.

Graphic file added to TripSmart assets folder

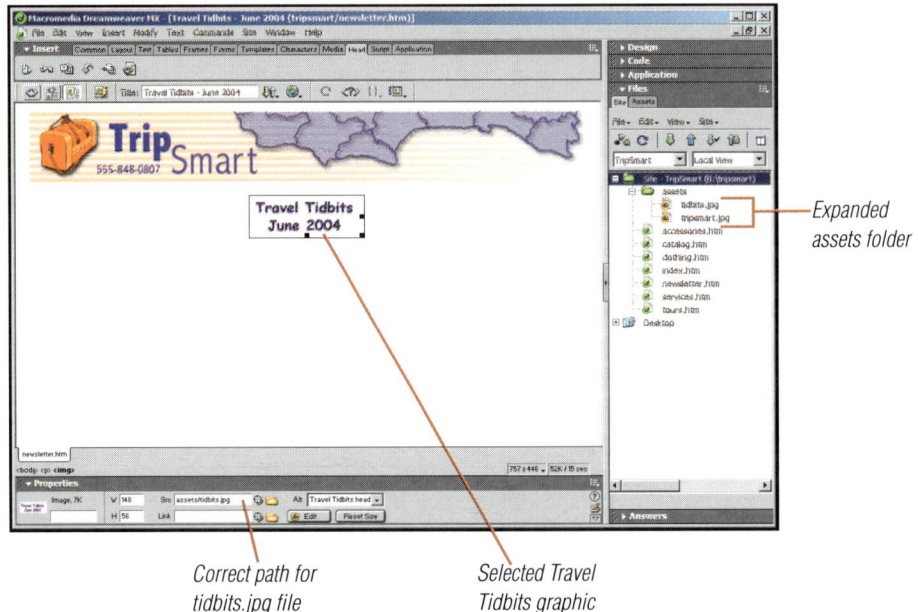

Expanded assets folder

Correct path for tidbits.jpg file

Selected Travel Tidbits graphic

Choosing filenames for Web pages

When you choose a name for a Web page, you should use a descriptive name that reflects the contents of the page. For example, if the page is about your company's products, you could name it products.htm. You should also follow some general rules for naming Web pages. For example, you should name the home page **index.htm**. Most file servers look for the file named index.htm to use as the initial page for a Web site. Do not use spaces, special characters, or punctuation in Web page filenames or the names of any graphics that will be inserted in your Web site. Spaces in filenames can cause errors when a browser attempts to read a file, and may cause your graphics to load incorrectly. You should also never use a number for the first character of a filename. To ensure that everything will load properly on all platforms, including UNIX, assume the filenames are case-sensitive and use lowercase characters. Files are saved with the .htm or .html file extension. While either file extension is appropriate, the default file extension is .htm for Windows platforms, and .html for Mac/UNIX platforms.

FIGURE B-12

Clean Up Word HTML dialog box

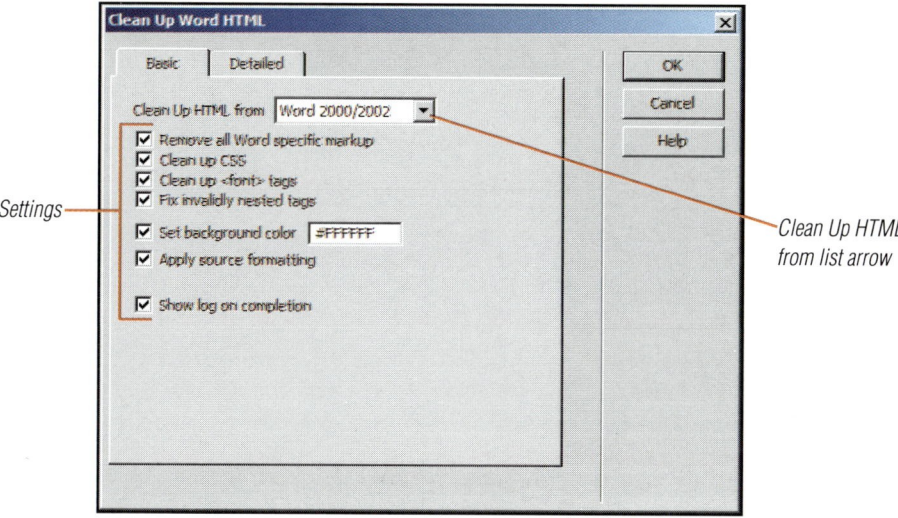

Settings

Clean Up HTML
from list arrow

Import text

1. Click File on the menu bar, point to Import, click Word HTML, navigate to the drive and folder where your data files are stored, double-click the unit_b folder (Win) or click the unit_b folder (Mac), then double-click packing_essentials.htm.

   TIP To specify a different version of Microsoft Word for the clean up, you can click the Clean Up HTML from list arrow, then click the appropriate version of Microsoft Word.

2. Make sure each check box in the Clean Up Word HTML dialog box is checked, as shown in Figure B-12, click OK, then click OK again to close the Clean Up Word HTML Results window.

3. Click Edit on the menu bar, click Select All, click Edit on the menu bar, click Copy, then close the file without saving changes.

4. Click to the right of the Travel Tidbits graphic on the newsletter.htm page, click Edit on the menu bar, then click Paste.

   TIP If the newsletter.htm page is not currently showing in the document window, click the newsletter.htm tab on the status bar.

5. Save your work.

You imported a Word HTML file and copied the text onto the newsletter page.

Saving a Word file as HTML

When you create text in Microsoft Word that you know will eventually be used on a Web page, you should not format the text. You should format the text after you import it into Dreamweaver. Formatting the text in Microsoft Word will create unnecessary HTML code that will be automatically removed when the file is imported into Dreamweaver. This practice will save time and avoid unnecessary frustration.

Set text properties

1. Click the Common tab on the Insert bar, then place the insertion point anywhere within the words Packing Essentials.

2. Click the Format list arrow in the Property inspector, then click Heading 3.

   The Heading 3 style is applied to the entire line of text. When you apply a heading, the entire paragraph in which the insertion point is placed becomes a heading and the appearance of the entire paragraph changes.

3. Click the Align Center button in the Property inspector to center the heading.

4. Select the words Packing Essentials, click the Font list arrow, then click Arial, Helvetica, sans-serif.

   Because setting a font is a character command, you must select all the characters you want to format before applying a font.

   TIP You can modify the font combinations in the Font list by clicking Text on the menu bar, pointing to Font, then clicking Edit Font List.

5. With the heading still selected, click the Text Color button in the Property inspector to open the color picker, then click the dark blue color in the third row of the first column (#000066).

   TIP You can also type #000066 in the color text box in the Property inspector to select the color in Step 5.

   (continued)

FIGURE B-13

Properties of Packing Essentials text

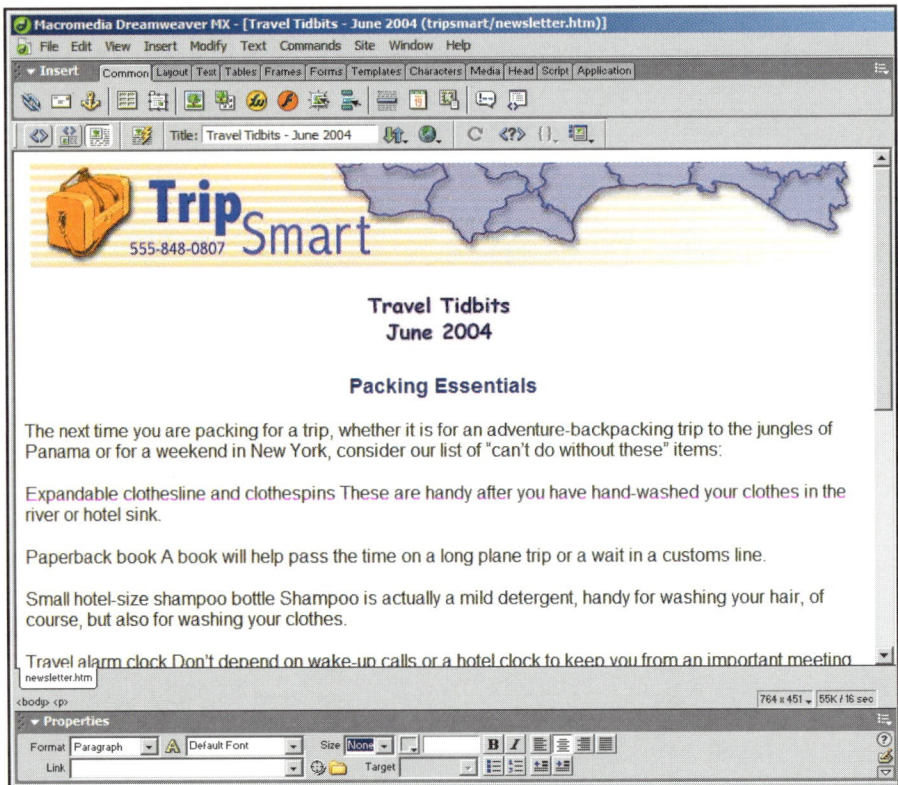

6. Click to the left of the T in The next time you are packing, press and hold [Shift], scroll to the end of the text, click to place the insertion point after the end of the last sentence, then release [Shift].

7. Click the Font list arrow in the Property inspector, click Arial, Helvetica, sans-serif, click the Size list arrow in the Property inspector, then click 3.

> TIP To change the size of selected text, use either the Format list arrow or the Size list arrow, but not both.

8. Click anywhere on the page to deselect the text, save your work, then compare your screen to Figure B-13.

You formatted the Packing Essentials text using the Heading 3 style and the Arial, Helvetica, sans-serif font combination. Next, you centered the heading on the page and changed the text color to a dark blue. You then selected the rest of the text on the page and changed it to the Arial, Helvetica, sans-serif font combination with a text size of 3.

Choosing fonts

There are two classifications of fonts: sans serif and serif. **Sans-serif fonts** are block-style characters that are often used for headings and subheadings. The headings in this book use a sans-serif font. Examples of sans-serif fonts include Arial, Verdana, and Helvetica. **Serif fonts** are more ornate, and contain small extra strokes at the beginning and end of the characters. Some people consider serif fonts easier to read in printed material, because the extra strokes lead your eye from one character to the next. This paragraph you are reading uses a serif font. Examples of serif fonts include Times New Roman, Times, and Georgia. Many designers feel that a sans-serif font is preferable when the content of a Web site is primarily intended to be read on the screen, but that a serif font is preferable if the content will be printed. When you choose fonts, you need to keep in mind the amount of text each page will contain and whether most viewers will read the text on-screen or print it out. A good rule of thumb is to limit each Web site to no more than three font variations. Using more than three may make your Web site look unprofessional and suggest the "ransom note effect." The phrase **ransom note effect** implies that fonts have been randomly used in a document without regard to style, similar to a ransom note made up of words cut from various sources and pasted onto a page.

ADD LINKS TO WEB PAGES

What You'll Do

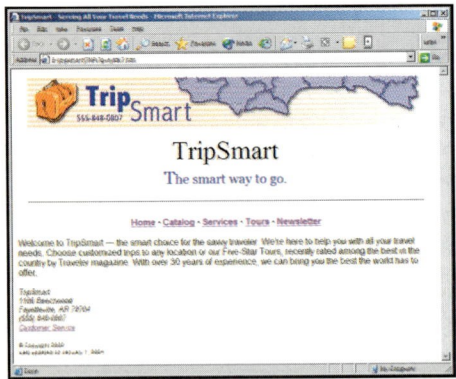

 In this lesson, you will open the home page and add links to the navigation bar that link to the Catalog, Services, Tours, and Newsletter pages. You will then insert an e-mail link at the bottom of the page and create page titles for the untitled pages in the site map.

Adding Links to Web Pages

Links provide the real strength for Web pages. Links make it possible for viewers to navigate through all the pages in a Web site and to connect to other pages you choose anywhere on the Web. Viewers are more likely to return to Web sites that have a user-friendly navigation structure. Viewers also enjoy Web sites that have interesting links to other Web pages or other Web sites.

To add links to a Web page, you first select the text or graphic that you want to serve as a link, then you specify a path to the page to which you want to link in the Link text box in the Property inspector. After you add all your links, you can open the site map to see a diagram of how the linked pages relate to each other.

When you create links on a Web page, it is important to avoid **broken links,** or links that cannot find their intended destinations. You can accidentally cause a broken link by typing the incorrect address for the link in the Link text box. Broken links are often caused by companies merging, going out of business, or simply moving their Web site addresses.

In addition to adding links to your pages, you should also provide a **point of contact,** or a place on a Web page that provides viewers with a means of contacting the company. A common point of contact is a **mailto: link,** which is an e-mail address that viewers with questions or problems can use to contact someone at the company's headquarters.

Using Navigation Bars

A navigation bar is an area on a Web page that contains links to the main pages of a Web site. Navigation bars are usually located at the top or side of the main pages of a Web site and can be created with text, graphics, or a combination of the two. To make navigating through a Web site as easy as possible, you should place navigation bars in the same position on each Web page. Navigation bars are the backbone of a Web site's navigation structure, which includes all navigation aids for moving around a Web site. You can, however, include additional links to the main pages of the Web site elsewhere on the page. The Web page in Figure B-14 shows an example of a navigation bar that contains both text and graphic links within a Flash movie. Notice that when the mouse is placed on the Features item at the top of the navigation bar, a menu appears.

Navigation bars can also be simple and contain only text-based links to the pages in the site. You can create a simple navigation bar by typing the names of your Web site's pages at the top of your Web page, formatting the text, and then adding links to each page name.

FIGURE B-14

Coca-Cola Web site

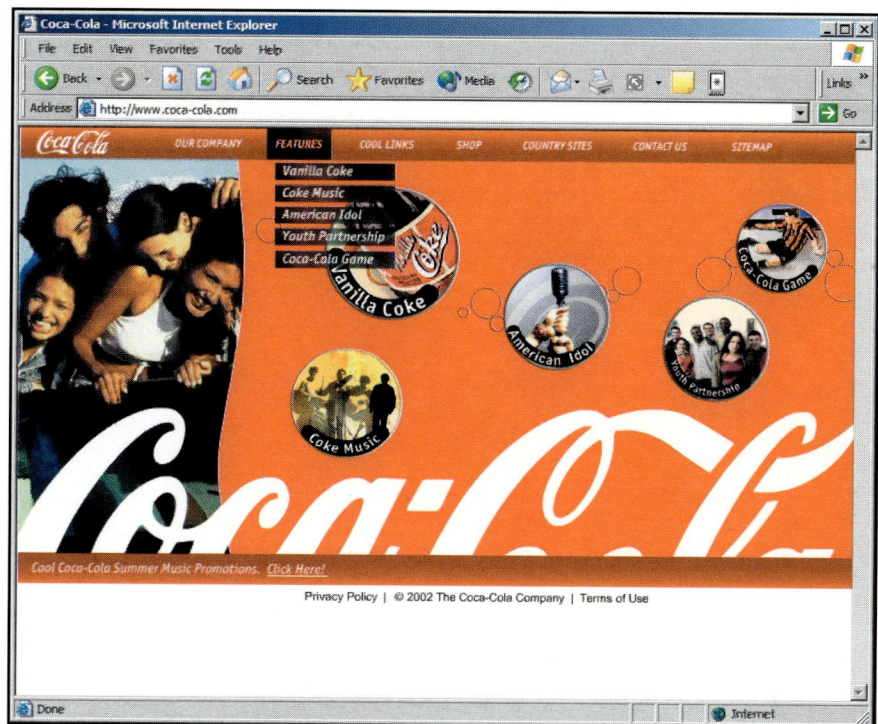

Create a navigation bar

1. Close the newsletter page, then open the home page.

2. Position the insertion point to the left of N in Newsletter, then drag to select Newsletter — Services — Tours — Contact Us, as shown in in Figure B-15.

3. Type **Home - Catalog - Services - Tours - Newsletter**.

   These five text labels will serve as a navigation bar. You will add the links later.

4. Save your work.

You created a new navigation bar using text, replacing the original navigation bar.

Format a navigation bar

1. Select Home - Catalog - Services - Tours - Newsletter, click the Size list arrow in the Property inspector, then click None.

   None is equal to size 3, the default text size. The None setting also eliminates any prior size formatting that was applied to the text.

   > **TIP** If your Property inspector is not displayed, click Window on the Document menu bar, then click Properties to open it.

2. Click the Format list arrow in the Property inspector, then click Heading 4.

3. Click the Font list arrow in the Property inspector, click Arial, Helvetica, sans-serif (if necessary), then compare your screen to Figure B-16.

4. Save your work.

You formatted the new navigation bar, using a heading and a font combination.

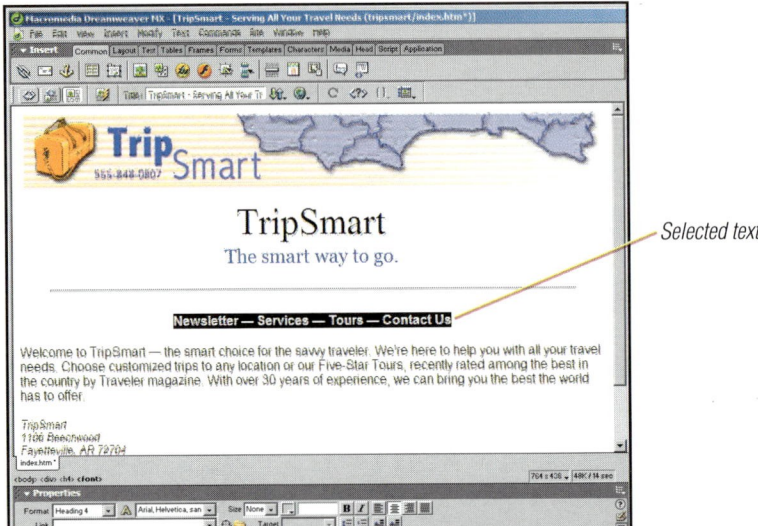

Selected text

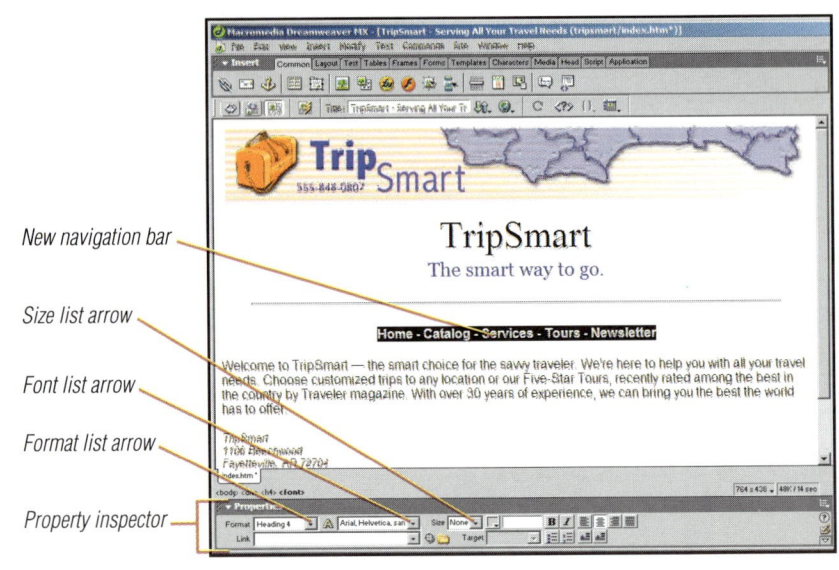

New navigation bar

Size list arrow

Font list arrow

Format list arrow

Property inspector

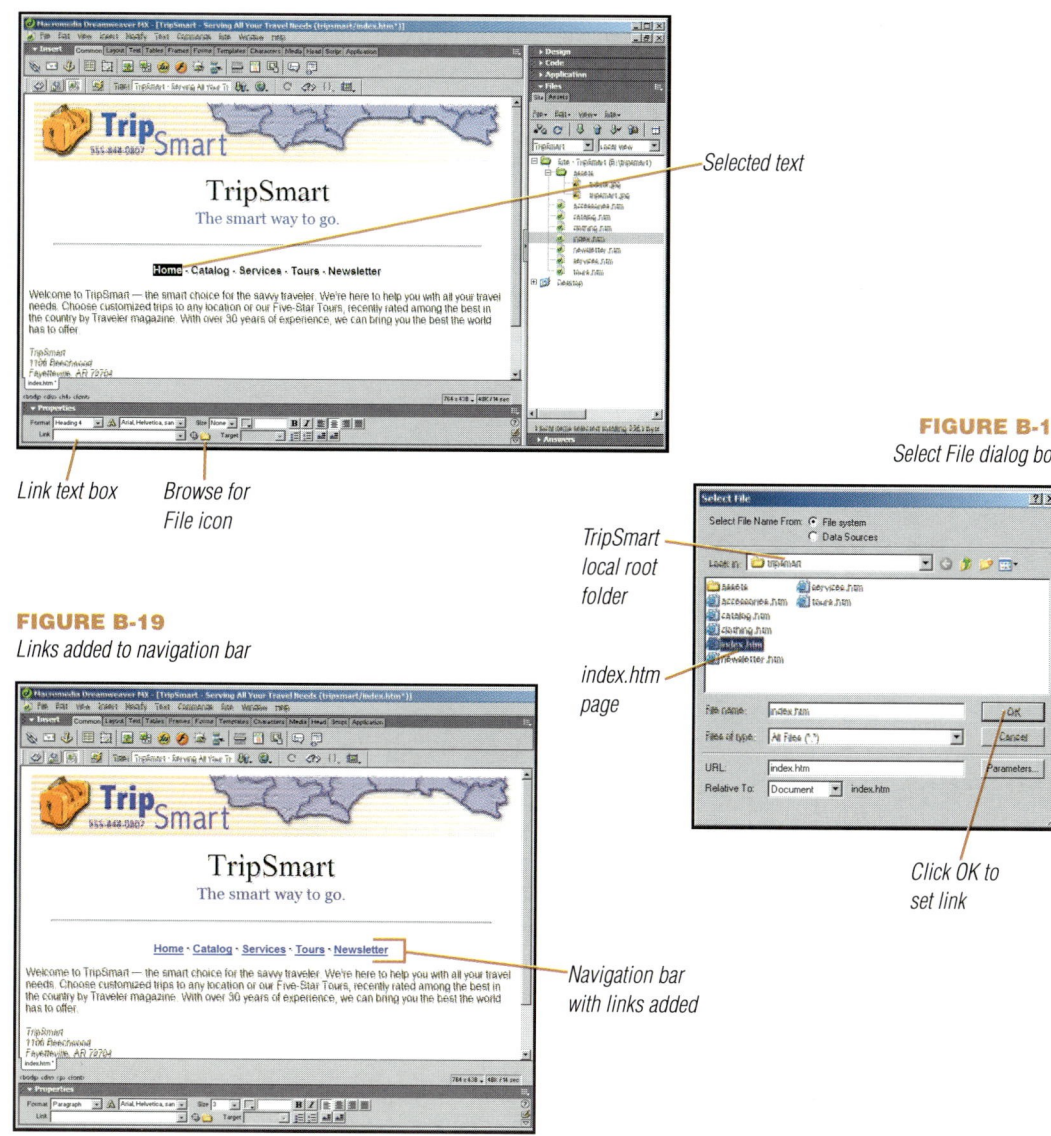

Selected text

Link text box   Browse for
File icon

TripSmart
local root
folder

index.htm
page

Click OK to
set link

Navigation bar
with links added

Add links to Web pages

1. Double-click Home to select it, as shown in Figure B-17.

2. Click the Browse for File icon next to the Link text box in the Property inspector, then navigate to the tripsmart root folder (if necessary).

3. Click index.htm as shown in Figure B-18, click OK (Win) or Choose (Mac), then click anywhere on the page to deselect Home.

    Home now appears in blue with an underline, indicating it is a link. In fact, clicking Home will not open a new page because the link is to the home page. It might seem odd to create a link to the same page on which the link appears, but this will be helpful when you copy the navigation bar to other pages in the site.

4. Repeat Steps 1–4 to create links for Catalog, Services, Tours, and Newsletter to their corresponding pages in the tripsmart root folder.

    When you finish adding the links to the other four pages, compare your screen to Figure B-19.

5. Save your work.

You created a link for each of the five navigation bar elements to their respective Web pages in the TripSmart Web site.

Create an e-mail link

1. Place the insertion point after the last digit in the telephone number, then insert a soft return.

2. Click the Common tab on the Insert bar (if necessary), then click the Email Link button on the Insert bar to insert an e-mail link.

3. Type **Customer Service** in the Text text box, and **mailbox@tripsmart.com** in the E-Mail text box, as shown in Figure B-20, then click OK to close the Email Link dialog box.

   TIP   You must enter the correct e-mail address in the E-Mail text box for the link to work. However, you can enter any descriptive name, such as customer service or Bob Smith in the Text text box.

4. Save your work.

   TIP   An asterisk after the filename in the title bar indicates that you have altered the page since you last saved it. After you save your work, the asterisk will disappear.

You inserted a mailto: link to serve as a point of contact for TripSmart.

Email Link dialog box

Text for e-mail link on the page (this could also be a person's name or position)

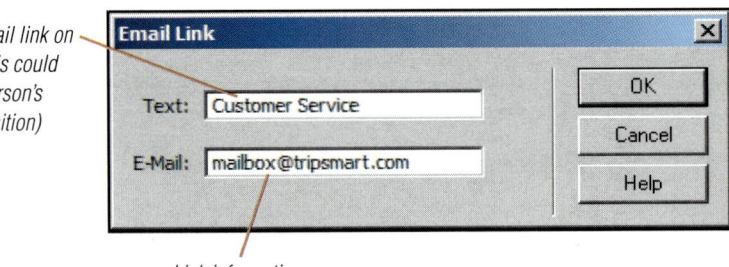

Link information

FIGURE B-21

TripSmart site map

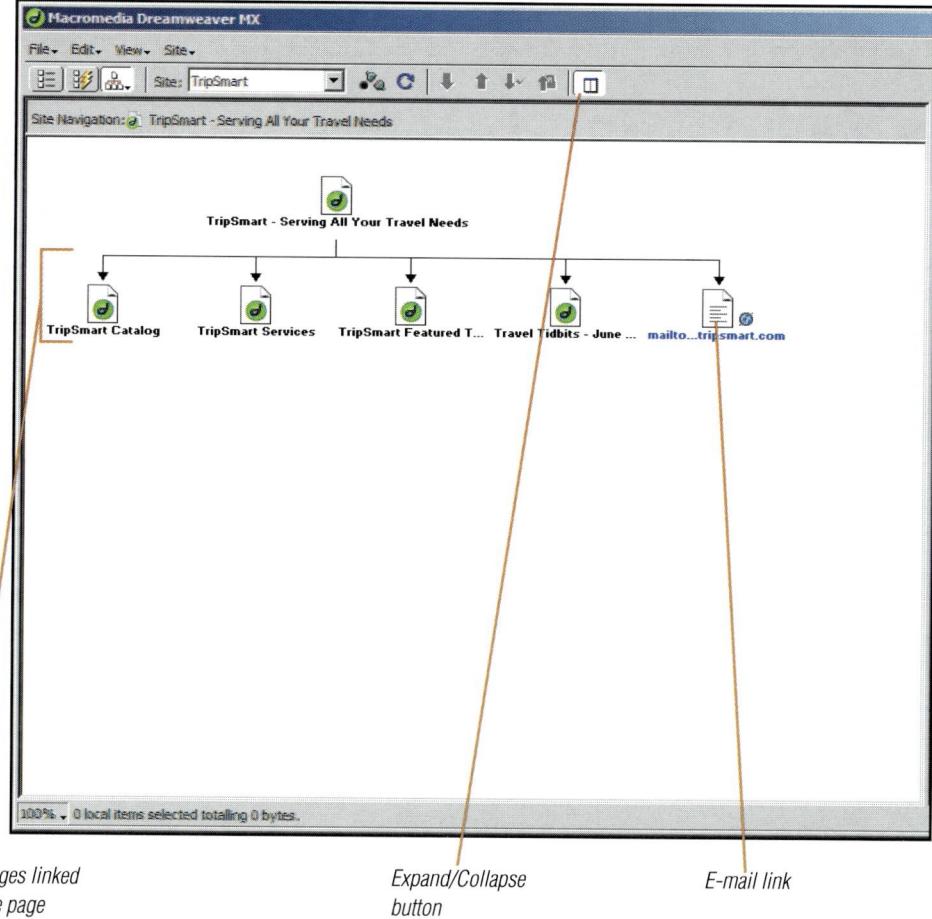

Four pages linked
to home page

Expand/Collapse
button

E-mail link

1. Click the View list arrow on the Site panel, then click Map View to view the site map **(Win)** or click Site on the menu bar, click Open Site, click TripSmart to open the Site panel, click the Site Map button to change to Map view, then click Map only (Mac).

2. Click the Expand/Collapse button on the Site panel to expand the site map (Win). ▣

   The site map shows the home page, the four pages that are linked to it, and the e-mail link on the home page.

3. Click View on the Site panel menu bar, then click Show Page Titles (Win), or click Site on the menu bar, point to Site Map View, then click Show Page Titles (Mac) to select it (if necessary.)

4. Select the first Untitled Document page in the site map, click the words Untitled Document, click again, type **TripSmart Catalog**, then press [Enter] (Win) or [return] (Mac).

5. Repeat Step 4 for the other two Untitled Document pages, naming them **TripSmart Services** and **TripSmart Featured Tours**, as shown in Figure B-21.

6. Click the Expand/Collapse button on the toolbar to collapse the site map (Win) or click the Site Files button on the Site panel to change to Local view (Mac). ▣

7. Click the View list arrow on the Site panel, then click Local View (Win).

You viewed the site map and added page titles to the untitled pages.

USE THE HISTORY PANEL AND USE THE CODE INSPECTOR

What You'll Do

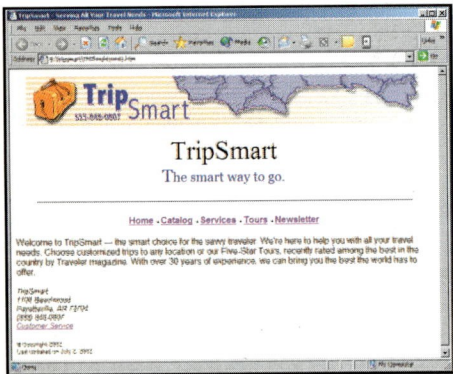

 In this lesson, you will use the History panel to undo formatting changes you make to a horizontal rule. You will then use the Code Inspector to view the HTML code for the horizontal rule. You will also insert a date object and then view its code in the Code Inspector.

Using the History Panel

Throughout the process of creating a Web page, it's likely that you will make mistakes along the way. Fortunately, you can use the History panel to undo your mistakes. The **History panel** records each editing and formatting task you perform and displays each one in a list in the order in which you completed them. Each task listed in the History panel is called a **step**. You can drag the **slider** on the left side of the History panel to undo or redo steps, as shown in Figure B-22. By default, the History panel records 50 steps. You can increase the number of steps the History panel records by adjusting the settings in the General category of the Preferences dialog box. However, keep in mind that setting this number too high might require additional memory and could hinder the way Dreamweaver operates.

Understanding other History panel features

Dragging the slider up and down in the History panel is a quick way to undo or redo steps. However, the History panel offers much more. It has the capability to "memorize" certain tasks and consolidate them into one command. This is a useful feature for steps that are executed repetitively on Web pages. Some Dreamweaver features, such as drag and drop, cannot be recorded in the History panel and have a red x placed next to them. The History panel also does not show steps performed in the Site panel.

Viewing HTML Code in the Code Inspector

If you enjoy writing code, you occasionally might want to make changes to Web pages by entering HTML code rather than using the panels and tools in Design view. You can view HTML code in Dreamweaver using Code view, Code and Design views, or the Code inspector. The **Code inspector,** shown in Figure B-23, is a separate floating window that displays the current page in Code view. The advantage of using the Code

inspector is that you can see a full-screen view of your page in Design view while viewing the underlying code in a floating window that you can resize and position wherever you want.

You can add advanced features, such as JavaScript functions, to Web pages by copying and pasting code from one page to another in the Code inspector. A **JavaScript** function is a block of code that adds dynamic content such as rollovers or interactive forms to a Web page. A **rollover** is a

special effect that changes the appearance of an object when the mouse "rolls over" it.

QUICK**TIP**

If you are new to HTML, you can use the Reference panel to find answers to your HTML questions. The Reference panel is part of the Code panel group and contains many resources besides HTML help, such as JavaScript help.

FIGURE B-22

History panel with Options menu open

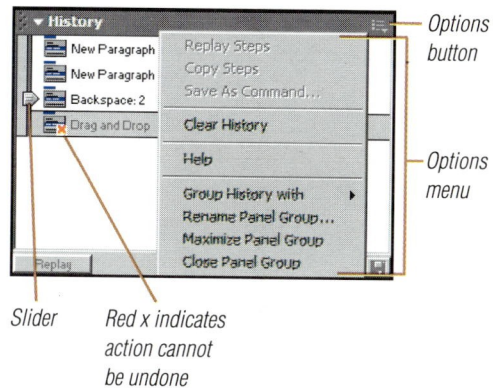

Options button

Options menu

Slider

Red x indicates action cannot be undone

FIGURE B-23

Code inspector

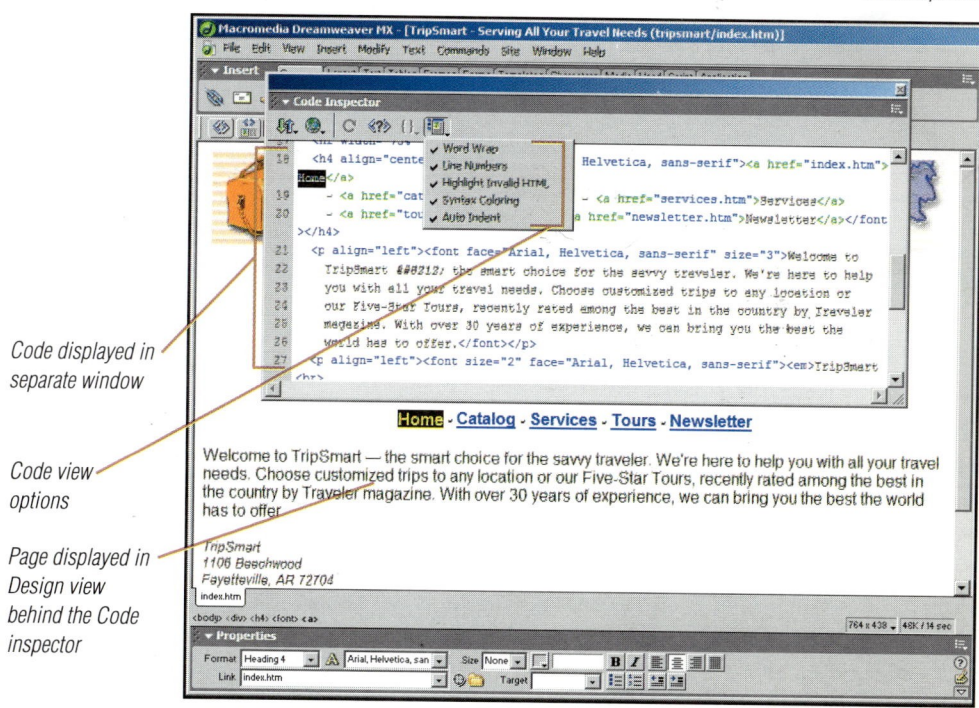

Code displayed in separate window

Code view options

Page displayed in Design view behind the Code inspector

Use the History panel

1. Click Window on the menu bar, point to Others, then click History.

   The History panel opens and displays steps you have recently performed.

2. Click the Options button on the History panel group title bar to open the Options menu, click Clear History, as shown in Figure B-24, then click Yes to close the warning box (if necessary).

3. Select the Horizontal Rule on the home page.

   A **horizontal rule** is a line used to separate page elements or to organize information on a page.

4. Select the number in the W text box, type **90**, click the list arrow next to the W text box, click %, press [Tab], then compare your screen to Figure B-25.

5. Using the Property inspector, change the width of the horizontal rule to 80%, then set the Align text box to Left.

6. Drag the slider on the History panel up to Set Width: 90%, as shown in Figure B-26.

   The bottom two steps in the History panel appear gray, indicating that these steps have been undone.

7. Save your work, click the Options button on the History panel group menu bar, then click Close panel group to close the History panel.

You formatted the horizontal rule, made changes to it, then used the History panel to undo the changes.

FIGURE B-24
Clearing the History panel

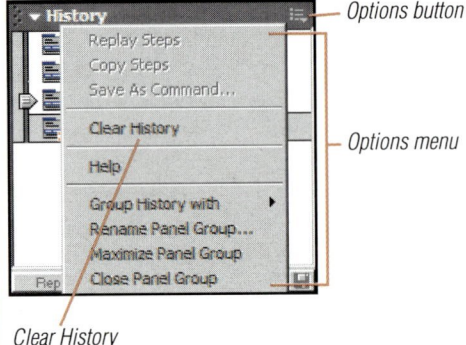

Options button

Options menu

Clear History

FIGURE B-25
Property inspector settings for horizontal rule

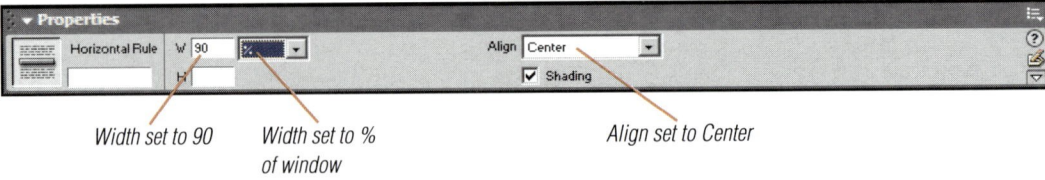

Width set to 90

Width set to % of window

Align set to Center

FIGURE B-26
Undoing steps using the History panel

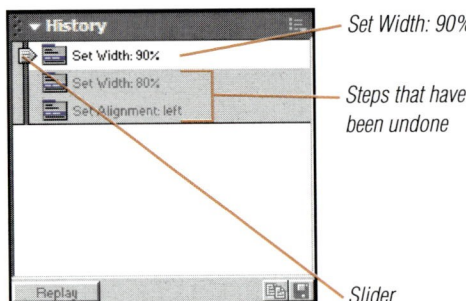

Set Width: 90%

Steps that have been undone

Slider

1. Click the horizontal rule to select it (if necessary), then click Window on the menu bar, point to Others, then click Code Inspector.

   The Code Inspector highlights the code for the horizontal rule.

   | TIP You can also press [F10] to open the Code Inspector.

2. Click the View Options button on the Code Inspector toolbar to open the View Options menu, then click Word Wrap (if necessary), to activate Word Wrap.

   Word Wrap forces the text to stay within the window, allowing you to read without scrolling sideways.

3. Click the View Options button to open the View Options menu, then verify that Highlight Invalid HTML and Syntax Coloring are checked, as shown in Figure B-27.

You viewed the underlying HTML code for the horizontal rule using the Code Inspector.

FIGURE B-27

Code Inspector View Options menu

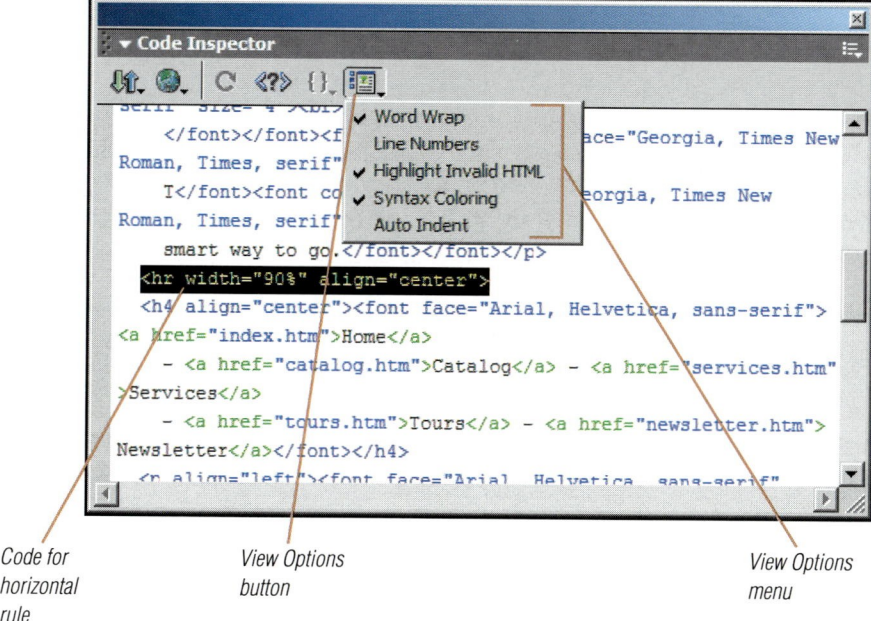

Code for horizontal rule

View Options button

View Options menu

Use the Reference panel

1. Click the Reference button on the Code Inspector toolbar, as shown in Figure B-28, to open the Code panel group with the Reference panel displayed. <?>

2. Read the information about horizontal rules in the Reference panel, as shown in Figure B-29, then click the expander arrow on the Code panel group title bar to collapse the Code panel group.

3. Click the Code Inspector Close button to close the Code Inspector.

You viewed the underlying HTML code for the horizontal rule using the Code Inspector and read information about horizontal rule settings in the Reference panel.

FIGURE B-28
Reference button on the Code Inspector toolbar

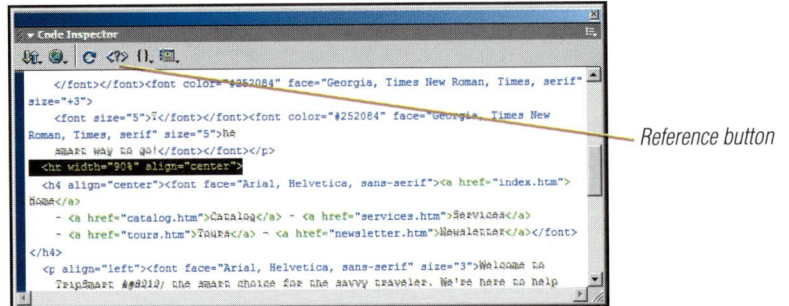

Reference button

FIGURE B-29
Viewing the Reference panel

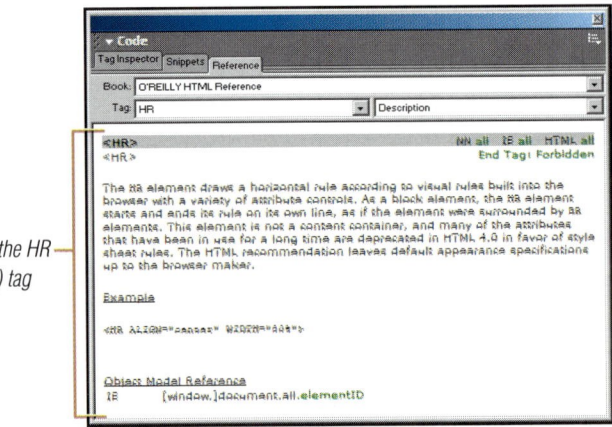

Information on the HR (horizontal rule) tag

Inserting comments

A handy Dreamweaver feature is the ability to insert comments into HTML code. Comments can provide helpful information describing portions of the code, such as a JavaScript function. You can create comments in any Dreamweaver view, but you must turn on Invisible Elements to see them in Design view. To create a comment, click the Common tab on the Insert bar, click the Comment button 🗭, type a comment in the Comment dialog box, then click OK. Comments are not visible in browser windows.

Developing a Web Page

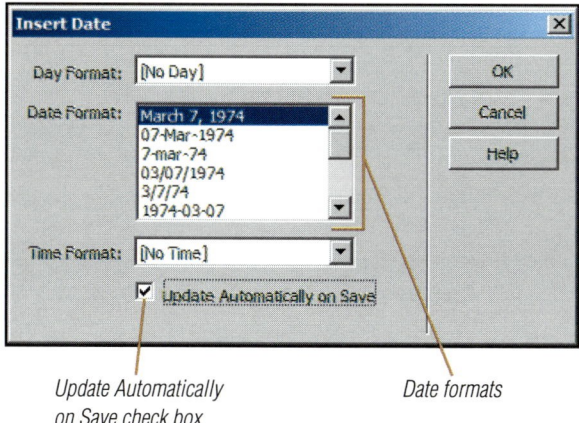

Update Automatically
on Save check box

Date formats

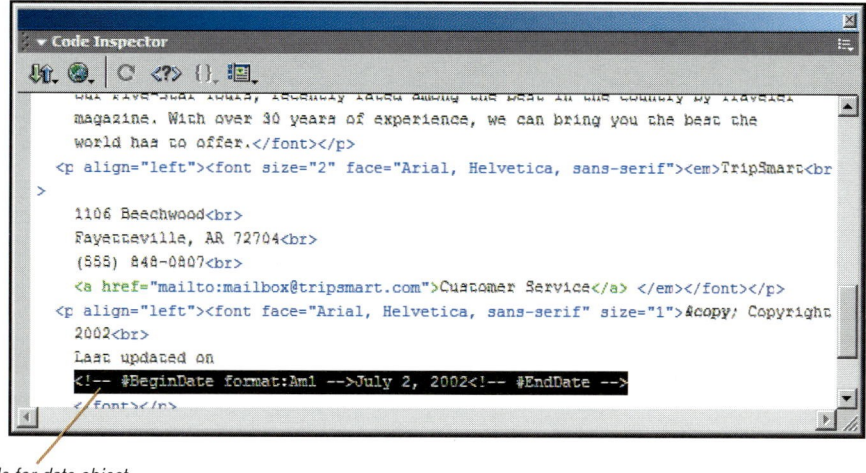

Code for date object

Insert a date object

1. Select January 1, 2004, then press [Delete] (Win) or [delete] (Mac) on your keyboard.

2. Click the Date button on the Insert bar, then click March 7, 1974 in the Date Format text box. 🗓

3. Click the Update Automatically on Save check box, as shown in Figure B-30, then click OK.

4. Open the Code Inspector.

   Notice that the code in the Code Inspector has changed to reflect the date object, as shown in Figure B-31.

5. Close the Code Inspector.

6. Save your work.

You inserted a date object that will be updated automatically when you open and save the home page.

MODIFY AND TEST WEB PAGES

What You'll Do

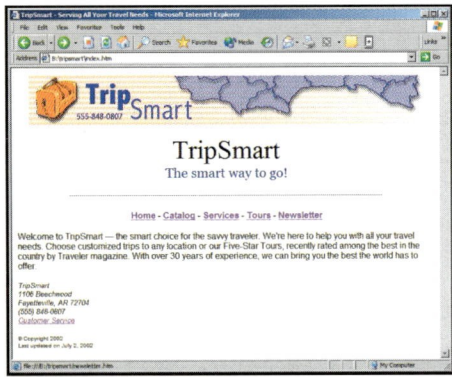

In this lesson, you will preview the home page in the browser to check for typographical errors, grammatical errors, broken links, and overall appearance. After previewing, you will make slight formatting adjustments to the page to improve its appearance.

Testing and Modifying Web Pages

Testing Web pages is a continuous process. You never really finish a Web site, as there are always additions and corrections to make. As you add and modify pages, you must test each page as part of the development process. The best way to test a Web page is to preview it in a browser window to make sure that all text and graphic elements appear the way you expect them to. You should also test your links to make sure they work properly. You also need to proofread your text to make sure it contains all the necessary information for the page and no typographical or grammatical errors. Designers typically view a page in a browser, return to Design view to make necessary changes, then view the page in a browser again. This process may be repeated many times before the page is ready for publishing. In fact, it is sometimes difficult to stop making improvements to a page and move on to another project. You need to strike a balance between quality, creativity, and productivity.

Using "Under Construction" pages

Many people are tempted to insert an unfinished page as a placeholder for a page that will be finished later. Rather than have real content, these pages usually contain text or a graphic that indicates the page is not finished, or "under construction". You should not publish a Web page that has a link to an unfinished page. It is frustrating to click a link for a page you want to open only to find an "under construction" note or graphic displayed. You want to make the best possible impression on your viewing audience. If you cannot complete a page before publishing it, at least provide enough information on it to make it "worth the trip."

Testing a Web Page Using Different Browsers

Because users access the Internet using a wide variety of computer systems, it is important to design your pages so that all browsers and screen sizes can display them well. You should test your pages using different browsers and a wide variety of screen sizes and resolutions to ensure the best view of your page by all types of computer equipment. Although the most common screen size that designers use today is 800×600, many viewers view at 1024×768. A page that is designed for a screen resolution of 800×600 will look much better at that setting than at a higher one. Many designers place a statement such as "this Web site is best viewed at 800×600" on the home page. To view your page using different screen sizes, click the Window Size pop-up menu in the middle of the status bar (Win) or at the bottom of the document window (Mac), then choose the setting you want to use. Table B-1 lists the default Dreamweaver window screen sizes.

TABLE B-1: Dreamweaver Default Window Screen Sizes

window size (inside dimensions of the browser window without borders)	monitor size
592W	
536×196	640×480, default
600×300	640×480, maximized
760×420	800×600, maximized
795×470	832×624, maximized
955×600	1024×768, maximized
544×378	Web TV

Modify a Web page

1. Click the Restore down button on the index.htm title bar to decrease the size of the home page window.

2. Click the Window Size list arrow on the status bar, as shown in Figure B-32, click 600 × 300 (640 × 480, Maximized).

   A viewer using this setting will be forced to use the horizontal scroll bar to view the entire page. This should be avoided, but very few people view at this resolution anymore.

   > **TIP** You cannot use the Window Size options if your document window is maximized.

3. Click the Window Size list arrow, click 760 × 420 (800 × 600, Maximized).

4. Replace the period after The smart way to go with an exclamation point.

5. Shorten the horizontal rule to 75%.

6. Select the text "The Smart way to go!" then change the text size to 5.

7. Click the Maximize button on the index.htm title bar to maximize the home page window.

8. Save your work.

You viewed the home page using two different window sizes and you made simple formatting changes to the page.

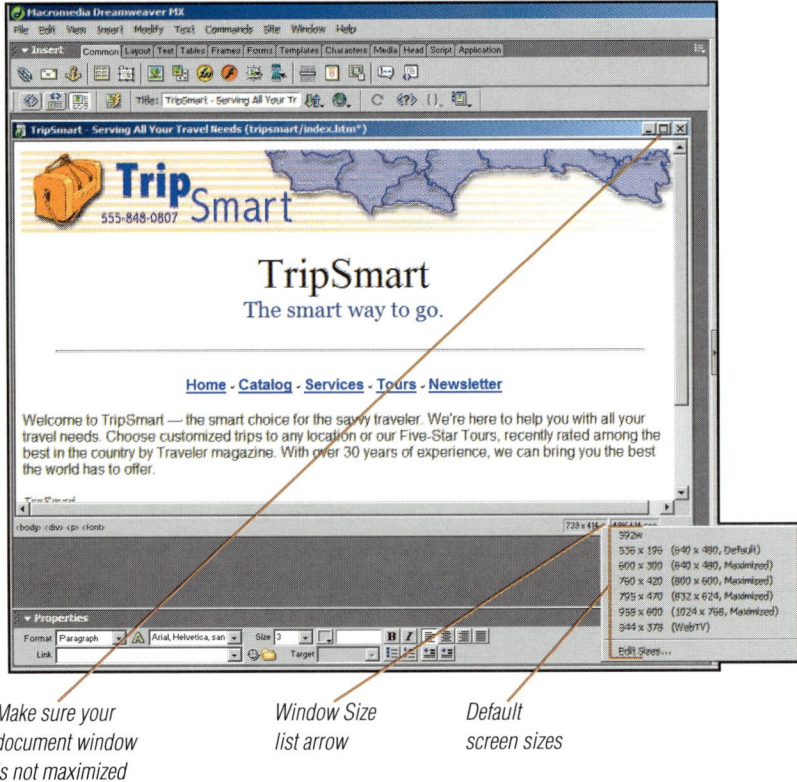

Make sure your document window is not maximized

Window Size list arrow

Default screen sizes

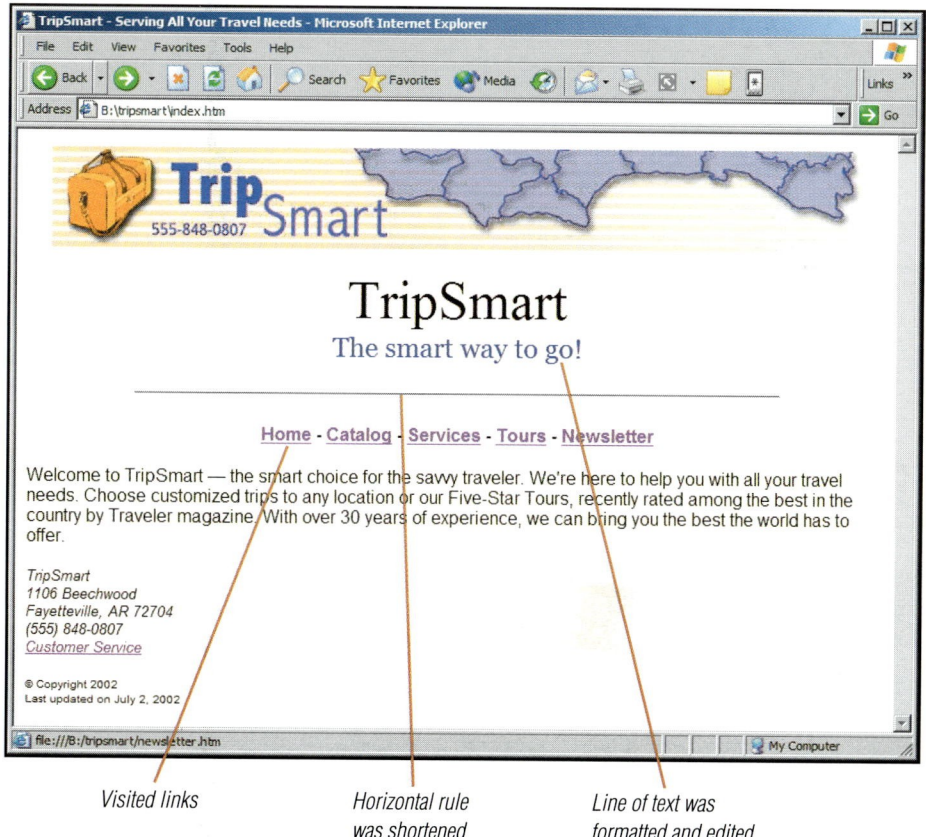

Visited links   *Horizontal rule
was shortened*   *Line of text was
formatted and edited*

1. Click the Preview/Debug in Browser button on the Document toolbar, then choose your browser from the menu that opens. 🌐

   The TripSmart home page opens in your default browser.

   > **TIP** If you do not see a browser listed after clicking Preview/Debug in Browser, contact your instructor for assistance.

2. Click all the links on the navigation bar, then use the Back button on the browser toolbar to return to the home page.

   Pages with no content at this point will appear as blank pages. Compare your screen to Figure B-33.

3. Close your browser window.

You viewed the TripSmart home page in your browser and tested each link on the navigation bar.

Choosing a window size

The 640 × 480 window size is not used by many viewers today, but you should still keep this size in mind when designing your Web pages. The 800 × 600 window setting is used on 15-inch monitors and some 17-inch monitors. Most consumers have at least a 15-inch monitor at their homes or offices, making this window size a good choice for a Web page.

Create head content and set Web page properties.

1. Open the Blooms & Bulbs Web site. (If you did not create this Web site in Unit A, contact your instructor for assistance.)
2. Open the home page and view the head content.
3. Change the page title to **Blooms & Bulbs - Your Complete Garden Center**.
4. Insert the following keywords: **garden, plants, water, nursery, flowers, supplies, landscape, annuals, perennials**, and **greenhouse**.
5. Insert the following description: **Blooms & Bulbs is a premier supplier of garden plants for both professional and home gardeners.**
6. Switch to Code view to view the HTML code for the head content, then switch back to Design view.
7. Open the Page Properties dialog box and view the current page properties.
8. Change the background color to a color of your choice.
9. Change the background color to white again, then save your work.

Create, import, and format text.

1. Select the current navigation bar and replace it with **Home, Featured Plants, Gardening Tips**, and **Workshops**. Use the [Spacebar] key and a hyphen to separate the items.
2. Using the Property inspector, apply the Heading 4 style to the navigation bar.

3. Create a hard return after the paragraph of text and type the following text, inserting a soft return after each line.
   Blooms & Bulbs
   Highway 7 North
   Alvin, TX 77511
   (555) 248-0806
4. Italicize the address and phone number lines and change them to a size 2.
5. Change the copyright and last updated statements to a size 2.
6. Save your work and close the home page.
7. Open dwb_2.htm and save it as **tips.htm** in the Blooms and Bulbs Web site, overwriting the existing file.
8. Set the banner path to the assets folder of the Blooms & Bulbs Web site and save the planting_tips.jpg in the assets folder of the Blooms & Bulbs Web site.
9. Import the gardening_tips.htm file from the drive and folder where your unit_b data files are stored, using the Import Word HTML command.
10. Copy the imported text and close the gardening_tips.htm file without saving the file.
11. Paste the text onto the tips.htm page below the navigation bar and left align the imported text (if necessary).
12. Format all the text on the page with the Arial, Helvetica, sans-serif font combination.
13. Select the Seasonal gardening checklist heading and use the Property inspector to center the text.

14. Use the Property inspector to format the selected text with a Heading 3 style, then save your work.
15. Apply the color #006633 (the third color in the second row) to the text.
16. Select the rest of the text on the page except for the Seasonal gardening checklist heading, then set the font to size 3.
17. Select the Basic Gardening Tips heading, then format this text in bold, with the color #006633 and a size of 3.
18. Save your work and close the tips page.

Add links to Web pages.

1. Open the home page (if necessary) and use the Property inspector to link Home on the navigation bar to the index.htm page.
2. Link Featured Plants on the navigation bar to the plants.htm page.
3. Link Gardening Tips on the navigation bar to the tips.htm page.
4. Link Workshops on the navigation bar to the workshops.htm page.
5. Using the Insert bar, create a mailto: link under the telephone number.
6. Type **Customer Service** in the Text text box and **mailbox@blooms.com** in the E-Mail text boxes.
7. Title the plants.htm page **Our Featured Plants**.
8. Title the workshops.htm page **Scheduled workshops**, then save your work.

Use the History Panel and Code Inspector.

1. Open the home page.
2. Open the History panel, then clear its contents.
3. Delete the current date in the Last updated statement and replace it with a date that will update automatically when the file is saved.
4. Change the font for the last updated statement.
5. Change the last updated statement to boldface.

6. Use the History panel to go back to the original font and style settings for the last updated statement.
7. Close the History panel.
8. Using the Code Inspector, examine the code for the last updated statement.
9. Close the Code Inspector.
10. Save your work.

Modify and test Web pages.

1. Using the Window Size pop-up menu, view the home page at 640 × 480 and at 800 × 600, then maximize the document window.

2. View the page in your browser.
3. Verify that all links work correctly.
4. Change the text Stop by and see us soon! to **We ship anywhere!**
5. Save your work, then view the pages in your browser, comparing your screens to Figure B-34 and Figure B-35.
6. Close your browser.
7. Adjust the spacing (if necessary), then save your work and preview the home page in the browser again.
8. Close the browser, save your work, then close all open pages.

FIGURE B-34

Completed Skills Review home page

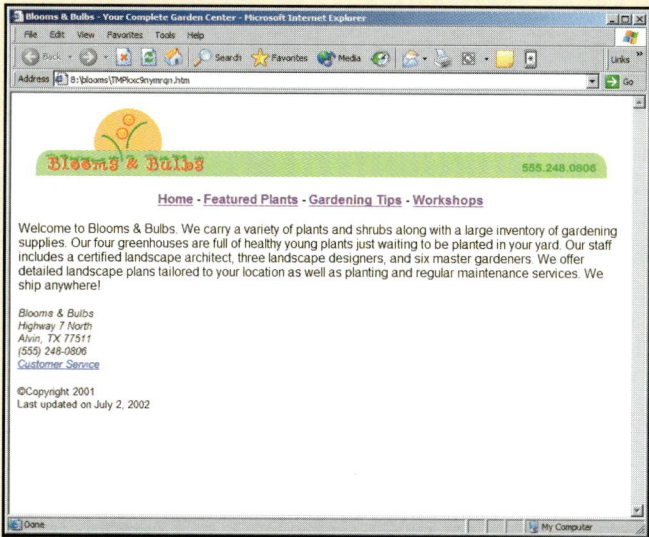

You have been hired to create a Web site for a river expedition company named Rapids Transit, located on the Buffalo River in Arkansas. You have created the basic framework for the Web site and are now ready to format and edit the home page to improve the content and appearance.

1. Open the Rapids Transit Web site, then open the home page. If you did not create this Web site in Unit A, contact your instructor.

2. Enter the following keywords: **river**, **rafting**, **Buffalo**, **Arkansas**, **Gilbert, kayak, canoe**, and **float**.

3. Enter the following description: **Rapids Transit is a river expedition company located on the Buffalo River in Gilbert, Arkansas.**

4. Change the page title to **Rapids Transit - Buffalo River Expeditions**.

5. Create a centered navigation bar below the Rapids Transit logo with the following text links: **Home**, **Our Guides**, **Equipment Rentals**, and **Country Store**. Place hyphens between each text link.

6. Apply the Heading 4 style to the text links and apply the Arial, Helvetica, sans-serif font combination.

7. Type the following address two lines below the paragraph about the company, using soft returns after each line:
Rapids Transit
Hwy 65
Gilbert, AR
(555) 365-5369

8. Insert an e-mail link in the line below the telephone number, using **Mike Andrew** for the Text text box and **mailbox@rapidstransit.com** for the E-mail text box in the Email Link dialog box.

9. Italicize the address, phone number, and e-mail link and format it to size 2, Arial, Helvetica, sans-serif.

10. Link the navigation bar entries to index.htm, guides.htm, rentals.htm, and store.htm.

11. Delete the horizontal rule.

12. View the HTML code for the page.

13. View the page using two different window sizes, then test the links in your browser window.

14. View the site map.

15. Create the following page titles:
guides.htm = **Meet Our Guides**
rentals.htm = **Equipment Rentals**
store.htm = **Shop At Our Country Store**

16. Verify that all the page titles are entered correctly.

17. Preview the page in your browser and test all the links.

18. Compare your page to Figure B-36, close the browser, save your work, then close all open pages.

FIGURE B-36
Completed Project Builder 1

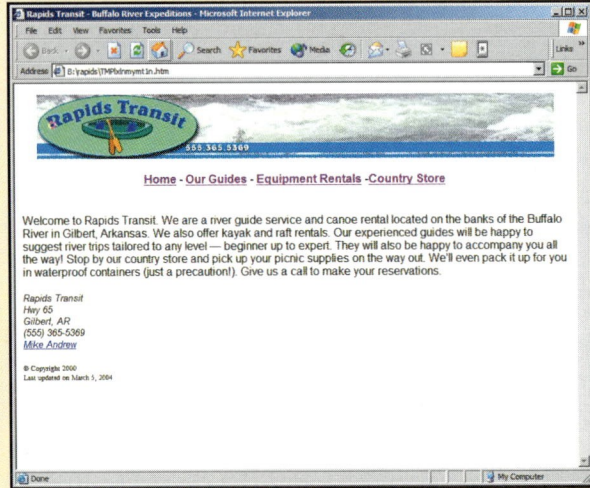

Your company has been selected to design a Web site for Jacob's, a new upscale restaurant in London catering to business executives and theatre patrons. You are now ready to add content to the home page and apply formatting options to improve the page appearance, using Figure B-37 as a guide.

1. Open the Jacob's Web site, then open the home page. If you did not create this Web site in Unit A, contact your instructor.
2. Add the following sentence to the end of the paragraph: **Dinner is served from 5:00 p.m. until 11:00 p.m. with our signature desserts and bar service until 2:00 a.m. Tuesday through Saturday.**
3. Add a navigation bar under the banner and above the paragraph that contains the following entries: **Home - Menus - Favorite Recipes - Directions and Hours**.
4. Center the navigation bar and apply a Heading 5 style.
5. Add the following 3 lines of text below the paragraph about the restaurant, using soft returns after each line:
   For reservations: please call
   +44 (0)20 0000 0000
   or e-mail reservations.
6. Delete the word reservations, then use the Email Link dialog box to insert an e-mail link using mailbox@jacobs.com for the e-mail address and reservations as the text.

7. Right-align the three lines of text that contain the reservation information.
8. Apply the Arial, Helvetica, sans-serif font to all text on the page.
9. Format the reservation information to size 2.
10. Create links from each navigation bar element to its corresponding Web page.
11. Replace the date that follows the text Last updated with a date object, then save your work.

FIGURE B-37
Completed Project Builder 2

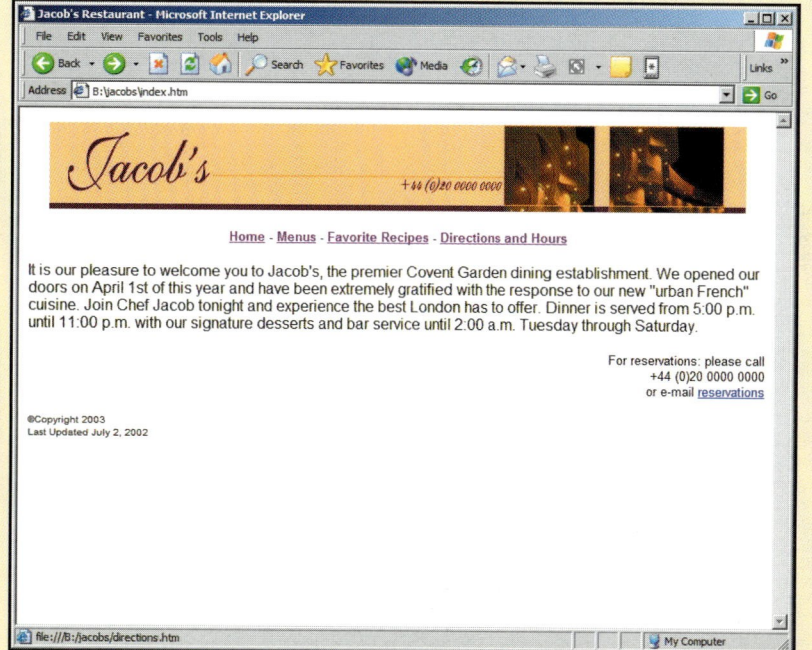

12. View the completed page in your default browser and test each link.
13. Close your browser.
14. View the site map and rename any untitled pages with appropriate titles.
15. Save your work and close all pages.

Angela Lou is a freelance photographer. She is searching the Internet looking for a particular type of paper to use in processing her prints. She knows that Web sites use keywords and descriptions in order to receive "hits" with search engines. She is curious about how they work. Follow the steps below and write your answers to the questions.

1. Connect to the Internet, go to *www.course.com*, navigate to the page for this book, click the Student Online Companion link, then click the link for this unit to see the Kodak Web site's home page. See Figure B-38.

2. View the page source by clicking View on the menu bar, then clicking Source (Internet Explorer) or Page Source (Netscape Navigator or Communicator).

3. Can you locate a description and keywords? If so, what are they?

4. How many keywords do you find?

5. Is the description appropriate for the Web site? Why or why not?

6. Look at the numbers of keywords and words in the description. Is there an appropriate number? Or are there too many or not enough?

7. Use a search engine such as Google at *www.google.com* and search for "photography" and "paper" in the Search text box.

8. Click the first link in the list of results and view the source code for that page. Do you see keywords and a description? Do any of them match the words you used in the search?

FIGURE B-38
Source for Design Project

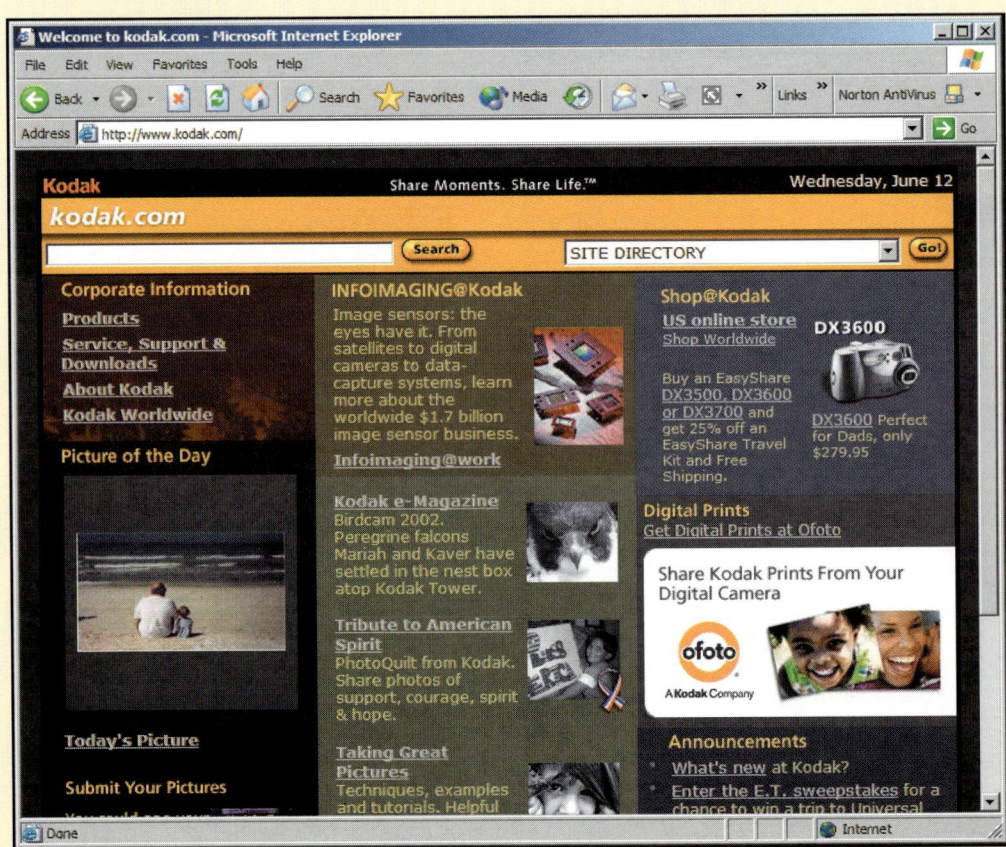

Depending on the size of your group, you can assign individual elements of the project to group members, or work collectively to create the finished product.

In this assignment, you will continue to work on the Web site your group defined in Unit A. In Unit A, you created a storyboard for your Web site with at least four pages. You also created a local root folder for your Web site and an assets folder to store the Web site asset files. You set the assets folder as the default storage location for your images. You began to collect information and resources for your Web site and started working on the home page.

1. Brainstorm as a group and come up with a title and several appropriate keywords for your site. Work together to write a description for the site.
2. Add the title, keywords, and description to the head content for the home page.
3. Assign a team member the task of creating the main page content for the home page and formatting it attractively.
4. Assign a team member the task of adding the address and other contact information to the home page, including an e-mail address.
5. Consult your storyboard and assign a team member the task of designing the navigation bar and linking it to the appropriate pages.
6. Add a last updated statement to the home page with a date that will automatically update when the page is saved.
7. Edit and format the page content until the group is satisfied with the results.
8. Verify that each page has a page title by viewing the site map.
9. Verify that all links, including the e-mail link, work correctly.
10. When you are satisfied with the home page, review the check list questions shown in Figure B-39, then make any necessary changes.
11. Save your work.

FIGURE B-39
Group Project check list

Web Site Check List

1. Do all pages have a page title?
2. Does the home page have a description and keywords?
3. Does the home page contain contact information, including an e-mail address?
4. Do all completed pages in the Web site have consistent navigation links?
5. Does the home page have a last updated statement that will automatically update when the page is saved?
6. Do all pages have attractively formatted text?
7. Do all paths for links and images work correctly?
8. Does the home page view well using at least two different screen resolutions?

UNIT C

WORKING WITH TEXT AND GRAPHICS

1. Create unordered and ordered lists.

2. Create, apply, and edit Cascading Style Sheets.

3. Insert and align graphics.

4. Enhance an image and use alternate text.

5. Insert a background image and perform site maintenance.

UNIT C

WORKING WITH TEXT AND GRAPHICS

Introduction

Most Web pages contain a combination of text and graphics. Dreamweaver provides many tools for working with text and graphics that you can use to make your Web pages attractive and easy to use. Dreamweaver also has tools that help you format text quickly and ensure a consistent appearance of text elements across all your Web pages.

Formatting Text as Lists

If a Web page contains a large amount of text, it can be difficult for viewers to digest it all. You can break up the monotony of large blocks of text by creating lists. You can create three types of lists in Dreamweaver: unordered lists, ordered lists, and definition lists.

Using Cascading Style Sheets

You can save time and ensure that all your page elements have a consistent appearance by using Cascading Style Sheets (CSS). You can use Cascading Style Sheets to define formatting attributes for page elements such as text and tables. You can then apply the formatting attributes you define to any element in a single document or to all of the pages in a Web site.

Using Graphics to Enhance Web Pages

Graphics make Web pages visually stimulating and more exciting than pages that contain only text. However, you should use graphics sparingly. If you think of text as the meat and potatoes of a Web site, the graphics would be the seasoning. You should add graphics to a page just as you would add seasoning to food. A little seasoning enhances the flavor and brings out the quality of the dish. Too much seasoning overwhelms the dish and masks the flavor of the main ingredients. Too little seasoning results in a bland dish. There are many ways to work with graphics so that they complement the content of pages in a Web site. There are specific file formats that should be used to save graphics for Web sites to ensure maximum quality with minimum file size. You should store graphics in a Web site's assets folder in an organized fashion.

Tools You'll Use

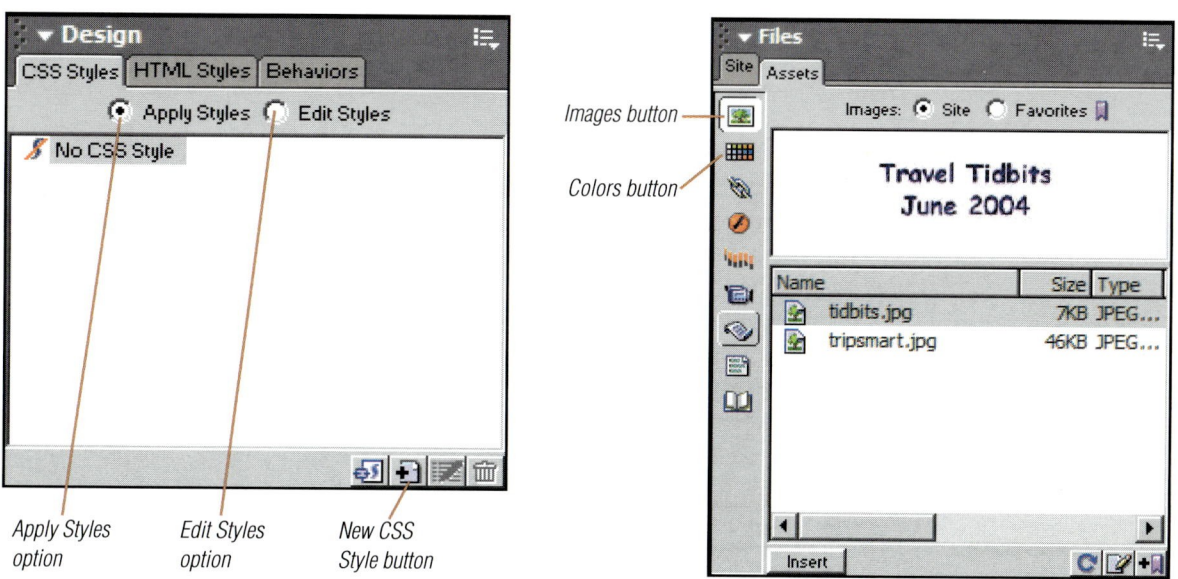

Apply Styles option

Edit Styles option

New CSS Style button

Images button

Colors button

Travel Tidbits
June 2004

Name	Size	Type
tidbits.jpg	7KB	JPEG...
tripsmart.jpg	46KB	JPEG...

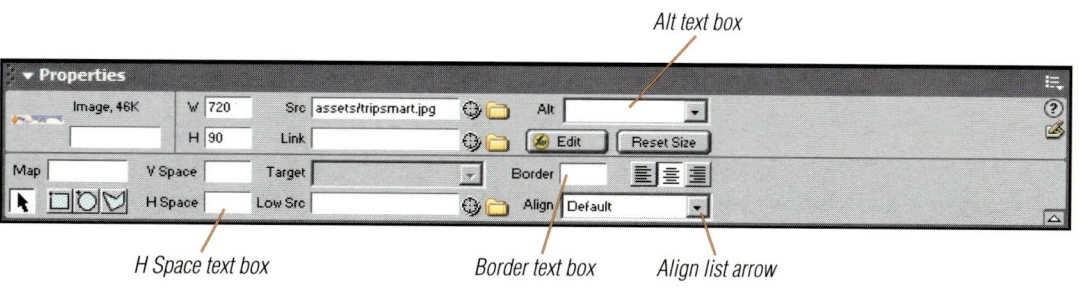

Alt text box

H Space text box

Border text box

Align list arrow

CREATE UNORDERED AND ORDERED LISTS

What You'll Do

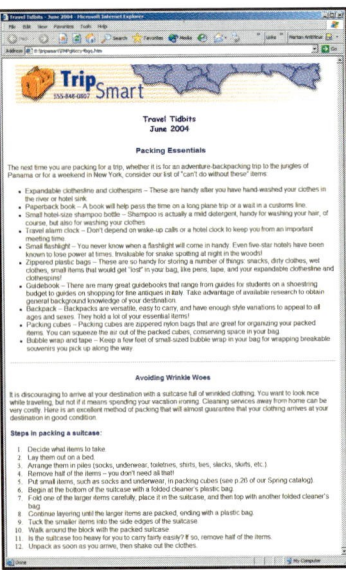

 In this lesson, you will create an unordered list of essential items to pack on the TripSmart newsletter page. You will also import text describing the steps for packing a suitcase, place a copy of the imported text on the newsletter page, and format it as an ordered list.

Creating Unordered Lists

Unordered lists are lists of items that do not need to be placed in a specific order. A grocery list that lists items in a random order is a good example of an unordered list. Items in unordered lists are usually preceded by a **bullet**, or a small raised dot or similar icon. Unordered lists that contain bullets are sometimes called **bulleted lists**. Though you can use paragraph indentations to create an unordered list, bullets can often make lists easier to read. To create an unordered list, you first select the text you want to format as an unordered list, then you use the Unordered List button in the Property inspector to insert bullets at the beginning of each paragraph of the selected text.

Formatting Unordered Lists

In Dreamweaver, the default bullet style is a round dot. To change the bullet style to square, you need to expand the Property inspector to its full size as shown in Figure C-1, click List Item in the Property inspector to open the List Properties dialog box, then set the style for bulleted lists to square. Be aware, however, that not all browsers display square bullets correctly, in which case the bullets will appear as round dots.

Creating Ordered Lists

Ordered lists, which are sometimes called **numbered lists**, are lists of items that are presented in a specific order and that are preceded by numbers or letters in sequence.

An order list is appropriate for a list in which each item must be executed according to its specified order. A list that provides numbered directions for driving from Point A to Point B or a list that provides instructions for assembling a bicycle are both examples of ordered lists.

Formatting Ordered Lists

You can format an ordered list to show different styles of numbers or letters using the List Properties dialog box, as shown in Figure C-2. You can apply numbers, Roman numerals, lowercase letters, or capital letters to an ordered list.

Creating Definition Lists

You can also use Dreamweaver to create definition lists. A **definition list** consists of a list of terms, where each term is followed by an indented paragraph. Definitions in a dictionary or topics in a book index are both examples of definition lists.

FIGURE C-1

Expanded Property inspector

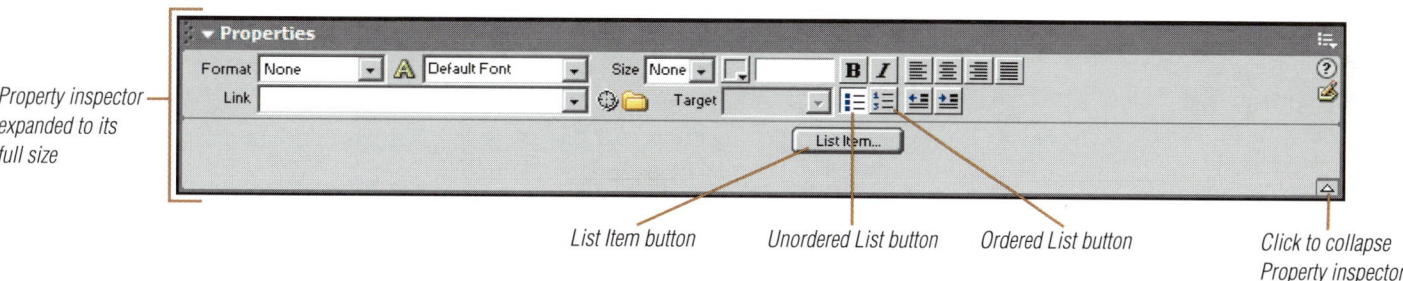

Property inspector expanded to its full size

List Item button   *Unordered List button*   *Ordered List button*   *Click to collapse Property inspector*

FIGURE C-2

Choosing a numbered list style in the List Properties dialog box

List Type list arrow

Numbered List styles

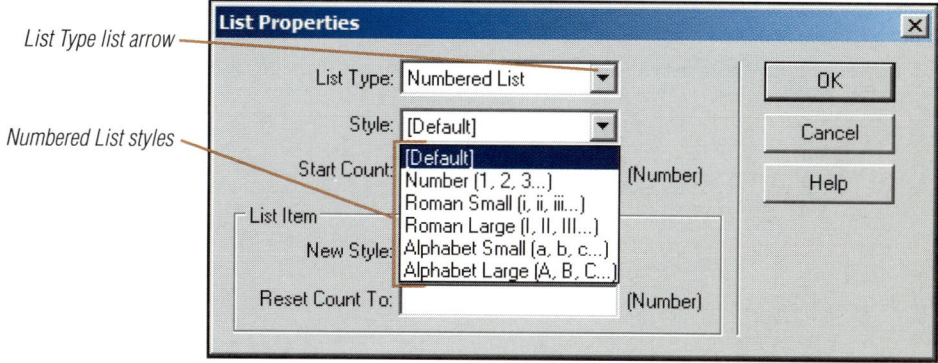

Create an unordered list

1. Open the newsletter page in the TripSmart Web site. (If you do not have the completed TripSmart Web site from Unit B, contact your instructor for assistance.)

2. Position the insertion point to the left of Expandable clothesline and clothespin in the second paragraph, scroll to the end of the page, press and hold [Shift], click to the right of the last sentence on the page, then release [Shift].

3. Click the Unordered List button in the Property inspector to format the selected text as an unordered list, click anywhere to deselect the text, then compare your screen to Figure C-3.

4. Click the insertion point after the last sentence on the page, then press [Enter] (Win) or [return] (Mac) twice to end the unordered list.

   TIP Pressing [Enter] (Win) or [return] (Mac) once at the end of an unordered list creates another bulleted item. To end an unordered list, press [Enter] (Win) or [return] (Mac) twice.

5. Save your work.

You opened the newsletter page in Design view and formatted the list of essential items to pack as an unordered list.

FIGURE C-3

Creating an unordered list

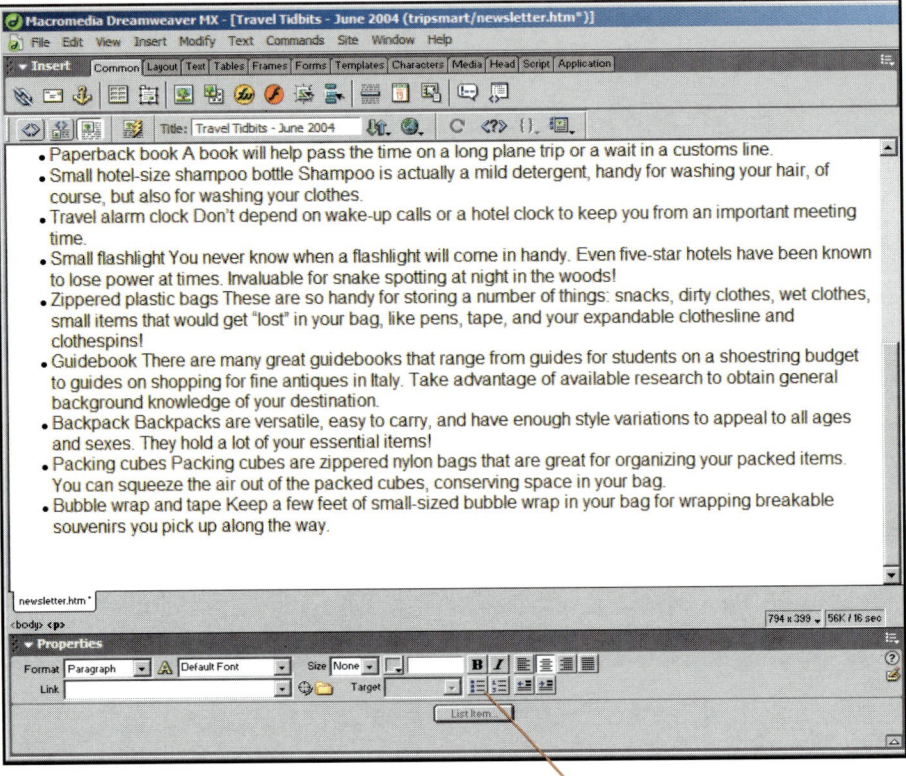

Unordered List button

FIGURE C-4
List Properties dialog box

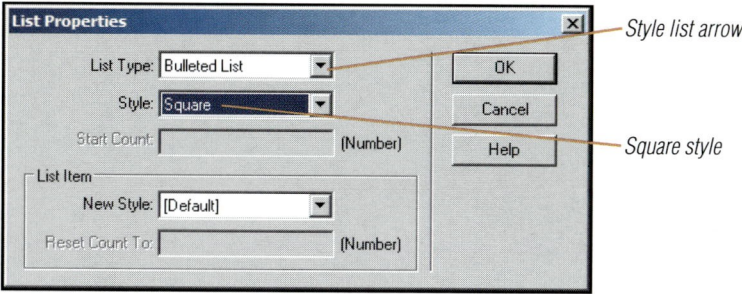

Style list arrow

Square style

Format an unordered list

1. Click any of the items in the unordered list to place the insertion point in the list.

2. Expand the Property inspector (if necessary), click the List Item button in the Property inspector to open the List Properties dialog box, click the Style list arrow, click Square, as shown in Figure C-4, then click OK. [List Item...]

   The bullets in the unordered list now have a square shape.

3. Position the insertion point to the left of the first item in the unordered list, then click the Show Code View button on the toolbar to view the code for the unordered list, as shown in Figure C-5. 〈◇〉

   Notice that there is a pair of HTML codes, or tags, surrounding each type of element on the page. The first tag in each pair begins the code for a particular element, and the last tag ends the code for the element. For instance, the tags <ul></ul> surround the unordered list. The tags <li> and </li> surround each item in the list.

4. Click the Show Design View button on the toolbar, then save your work. ▦

You used the List Properties dialog box to apply the square bullet style to the unordered list. You then viewed the HTML code for the unordered list in Code view.

FIGURE C-5
HTML tags in Code view for unordered list

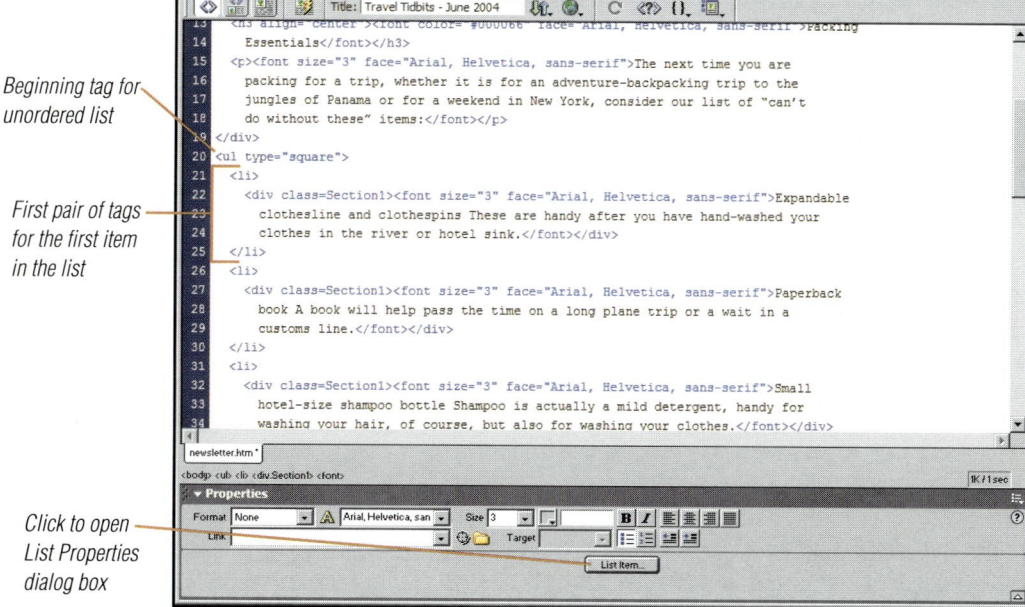

Beginning tag for unordered list

First pair of tags for the first item in the list

Click to open List Properties dialog box

Create an ordered list

1. Use the Import Word HTML command to import the data file how_to_pack.htm from the unit_c folder where your data files are stored, copy all the text in the how_to_pack.htm file, then close the file without saving it.

2. Paste the copied text just below the last unordered list item on the newsletter page.

3. Place the insertion point to the left of Avoiding Wrinkle Woes, then click the Horizontal Rule button on the Insert bar.

   A horizontal rule appears and helps to separate the unordered list from the text you just pasted.

4. Select the text beginning with Decide what items to take and ending with the last sentence on the page.

5. Click the Ordered List button in the Property inspector to format the selected text as an ordered list.

6. Deselect the text, compare your screen to Figure C-6, then save your work.

You imported text, copied it, and then pasted it on the newsletter page. You also added a horizontal rule to help organize the page. Finally, you formatted selected text as an ordered list.

FIGURE C-6

Creating an ordered list

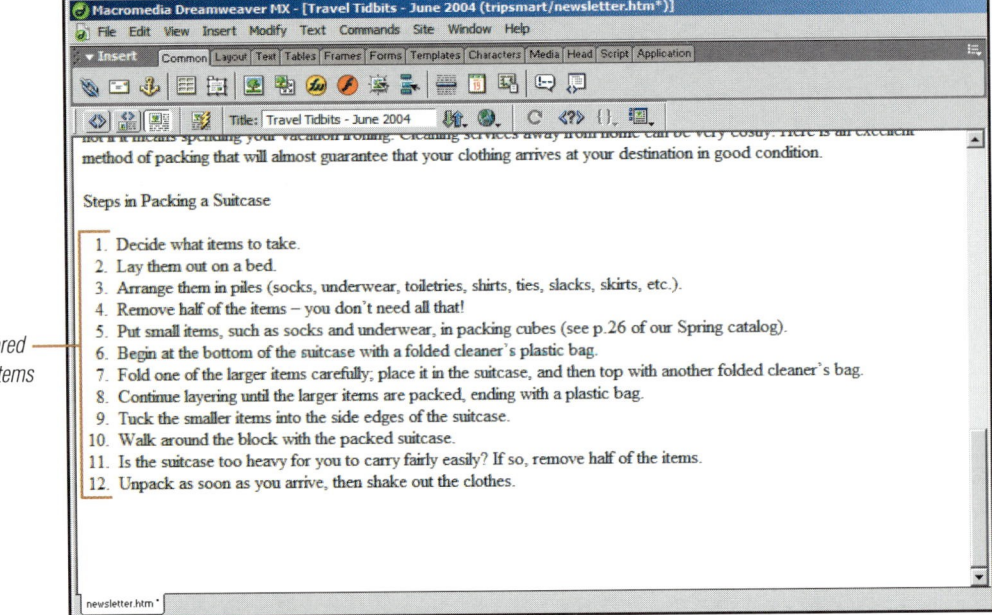

Ordered list items

FIGURE C-7
Newsletter page with ordered list

Formatted headings

Formatted body text

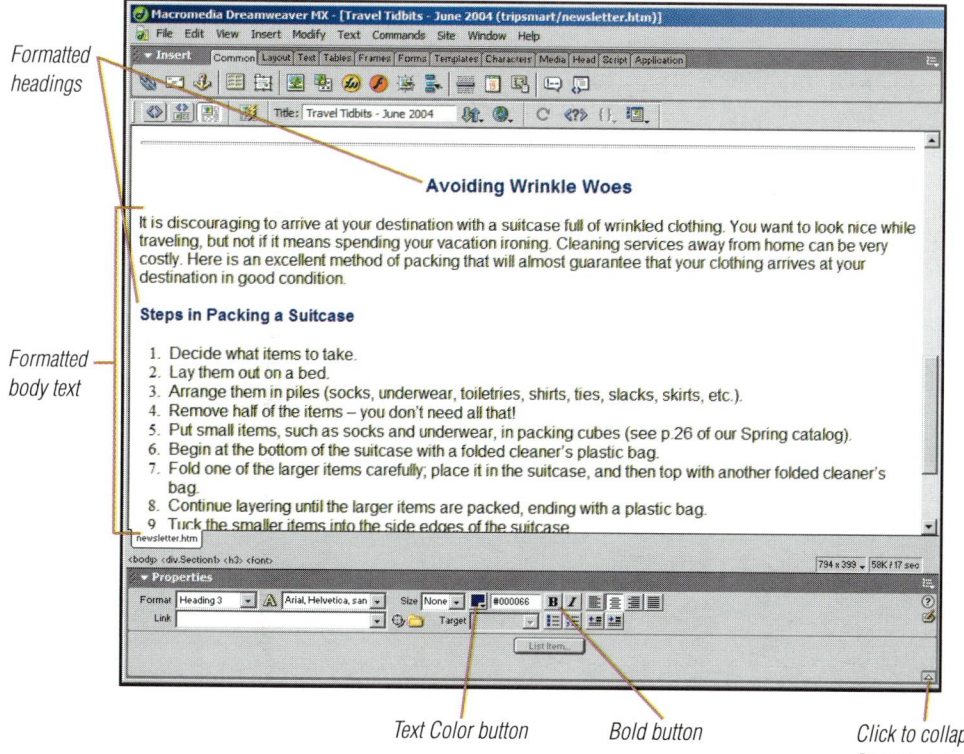

Text Color button   Bold button   Click to collapse Property inspector

1. Select all the text below the horizontal rule, then change the font to Arial, Helvetica, sans-serif, size 3.

2. Select the heading Steps in Packing a Suitcase, then click the Bold button in the Property inspector. **B**

3. Click the Text Color button in the Property inspector to open the color picker, then click the first square in the third row, color #000066.

4. Format the Avoiding Wrinkle Woes heading to match the Packing Essentials heading.

5. Compare your screen to Figure C-7, then save your work.

   TIP If you want to see more of your Web page in the document window, you can collapse the Property inspector.

You applied a new font and font size to the ordered list. You also formatted the Avoiding Wrinkle Woes heading to match the Packing Essentials heading.

CREATE, APPLY AND EDIT CASCADING STYLE SHEETS

What You'll Do

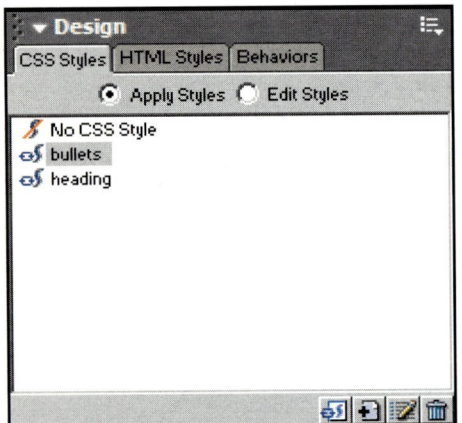

In this lesson, you will create a Cascading Style Sheet file for the TripSmart Web site. You also will create styles called bullets and heading and apply them to the newsletter page.

Using Cascading Style Sheets

When you want to apply the same formatting attributes to page elements such as text, objects, and tables, you can save a significant amount of time by using Cascading Style Sheets. A **Cascading Style Sheet** (CSS) is a made up of sets of formatting attributes that are either saved with a descriptive name or that redefine the appearance of an HTML tag. CSS style sheets are saved as individual files with the .css extension and stored in the directory structure of a Web site, as shown in Figure C-8. CSS style sheets contain styles, which are formatting attributes that can be applied to page elements.

You use the buttons on the CSS Styles panel to create, edit, and apply styles. To add a style, you use the New CSS Style dialog box to name the style and specify whether to add it to a new or existing style sheet. You then use the CSS Style Definition dialog box to set the formatting attributes for the style. Once you add a new style to a style sheet, it appears in a list in the CSS Styles panel. To apply a

style, you select the text to which you want to apply the style, then you click the style name in the CSS Styles panel. You can apply CSS styles to any element on a Web page or to all of the pages in a Web site. When you make a change to a style, all page elements formatted with that style are automatically updated. Once you create a CSS style sheet you can attach it to other pages in your Web site.

You can use CSS Styles to save an enormous amount of time. Being able to define a style and then apply it to page elements on all the pages of your Web site means that you can make hundreds of formatting changes in a few minutes. Be aware, however, that not all browsers can read CSS Styles. Versions of Internet Explorer that are 4.0 or lower do not support CSS styles. Only Netscape Navigator version 6.0 or higher supports CSS styles.

QUICKTIP

You can also use CSS styles to format other page content such as backgrounds, borders, lists, and boxes.

Understanding CSS Style Sheet Settings

If you open a style sheet file, you will see the coding for the CSS styles. A CSS style consists of two parts: the selector and the declaration. The **selector** is the name or the tag to which the style declarations have been assigned. The **declaration** consists of the property and the value. For example, Figure C-9 shows the code for the tripsmart.css style sheet. In this example, the first property listed for the bullets style is font-family. The value for this property is Arial, Helvetica, sans-serif.

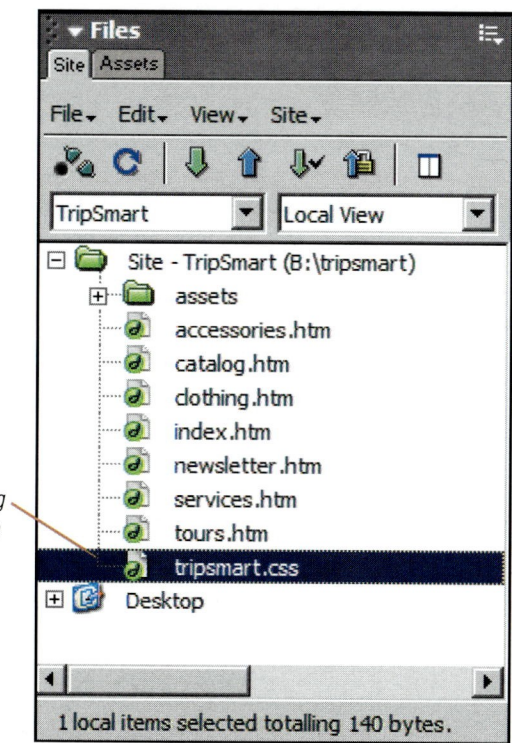

New Cascading Style Sheet file

```
1   .bullets {
2       font-family: Arial, Helvetica, sans-serif;
3       font-size: 16px;
4       font-style: normal;
5       font-weight: bold;
6       color: #000066;
7   }
8   .heading {
9       font-family: Arial, Helvetica, sans-serif;
10      font-size: 16px;
11      font-style: normal;
12      font-weight: bold;
13      color: #000066;
14      text-align: center;
15  }
16
```

Create a Cascading Style Sheet and a style

1. Click Window on the menu bar, then click CSS Styles to open the CSS Styles panel (if necessary).

2. Click the New CSS Style button at the bottom of the CSS Styles panel to open the New CSS Style dialog box, verify that the Make Custom Style (class) option button is selected, then type **bullets** in the Name text box.

   > TIP Class names are preceded by a period. If you don't enter a period when you type the name, Dreamweaver will add the period for you.

3. Click the Define in list arrow, click New Style Sheet File, compare your screen with Figure C-10, then click OK.

   The Save Style Sheet File As dialog box opens.

4. Type **tripsmart** in the File name text box (Win) or the Save As text box (Mac), then click Save to open the CSS Style Definition for .bullets in tripsmart.css dialog box.

   The bullets style will be stored within the tripsmart.css file.

5. Verify that Type is selected in the Category list, set the Font to Arial, Helvetica, sans-serif, set the Size at 12 pixels, set the Weight to bold, set the Color to #000066, set the Style to normal, compare your screen to Figure C-11, then click OK.

   The CSS style named bullets appears in the CSS Styles panel, as shown in Figure C-12.

6. Save your work.

You created a Cascading Style Sheet file named tripsmart.css and a style called .bullets.

FIGURE C-10

New CSS Style dialog box

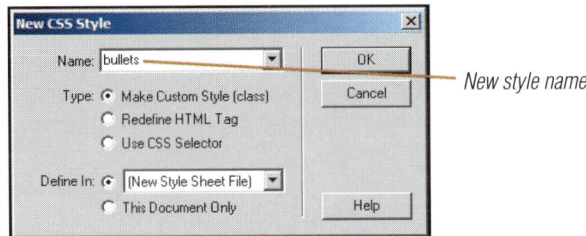

New style name

FIGURE C-11

CSS Style Definition for .bullets in tripsmart.css dialog box

Type category selected

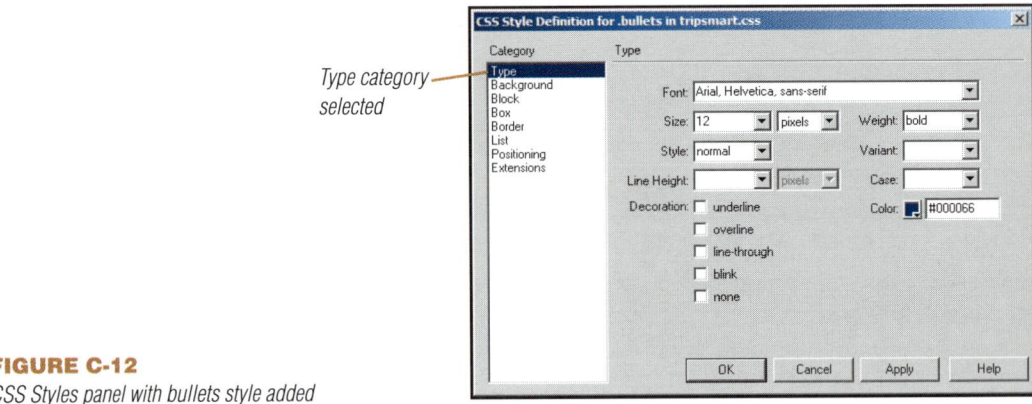

FIGURE C-12

CSS Styles panel with bullets style added

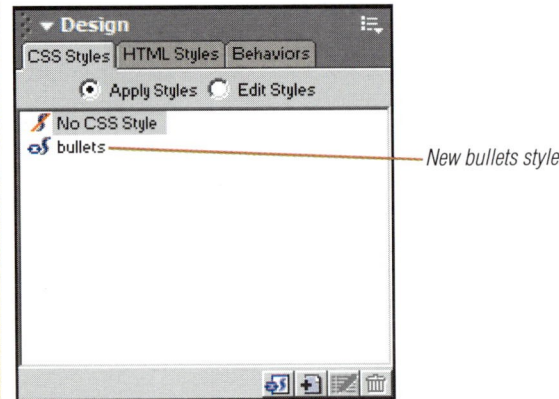

New bullets style

FIGURE C-13

Applying a CSS style to selected text

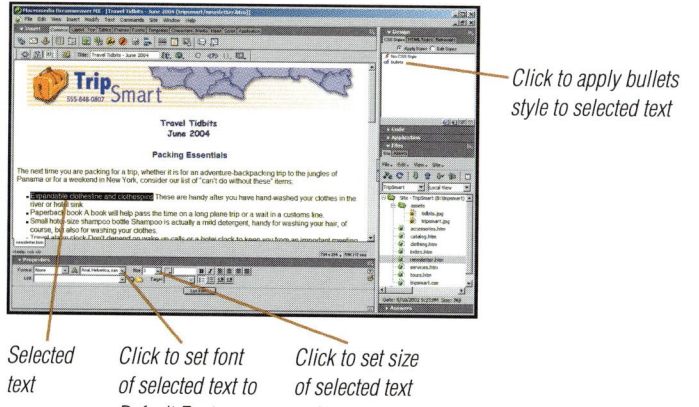

Click to apply bullets style to selected text

Selected text

Click to set font of selected text to Default Font

Click to set size of selected text to None

FIGURE C-14

Unordered list with bullets style applied

bullets style applied to each item in list

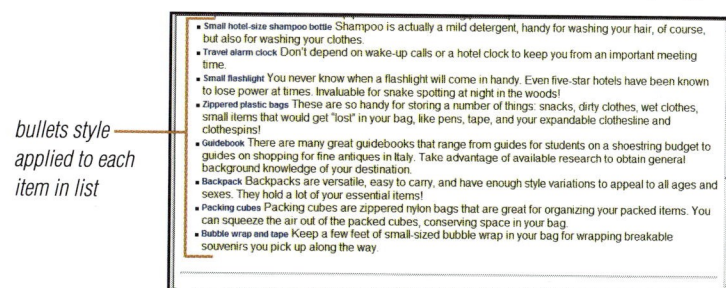

Apply a Cascading Style Sheet

1. Verify that the Apply Styles option is selected in the CSS Styles panel, select the text Expandable clothesline and clothespins, as shown in Figure C-13, then use the Property inspector to set the Format to Default Font and the Size to none.

   TIP Before you apply a style to selected text you need to remove all formatting attributes such as font and color from it, or the style will not be applied correctly.

2. Click bullets in the CSS Styles panel to apply the bullets style to the selected text.

3. Repeat Steps 1 and 2 to apply the bullets style to each of the nine remaining items in the unordered list.

4. Compare your screen to Figure C-14, then save your work.

You applied the bullets style to each item in the Packing Essentials list.

Attaching a style sheet file to another document

When you have several pages in a Web site, you will probably want to use the same CSS style sheet for each page to ensure that all your elements have a consistent appearance. To attach a style sheet to another document, click the Attach Style Sheet button 🔗 on the CSS Styles panel to open the Link External Style Sheet dialog box, make sure the Add as Link option is selected, browse to locate the file you want to attach, then click OK. The styles contained in the attached style sheet will appear in the CSS Styles panel in the Edit Styles mode, and you can use them to apply styles to any text on the page.

Edit a Cascading Style Sheet

1. Click the Edit Styles option at the top of the CSS Styles panel, click bullets in the CSS Styles panel, then click the Edit Style Sheet button at the bottom of the CSS Styles panel to open the CSS Style Definition for .bullets in tripsmart.css dialog box.

   > **TIP** You can also double-click a style in the CSS Styles panel to open the CSS Style Definition dialog box.

2. Click the Size list arrow, click 16, compare your screen to Figure C-15, click OK, then compare your screen to Figure C-16.

   The bullet text is now much bigger than before, reflecting the changes you made to the bullets style.

   > **TIP** If you position the insertion point in text that has a CSS style applied to it, that style is highlighted in the CSS Styles panel.

3. Save your work.

You edited the bullet style to change the font size to 16 pixels. You then viewed the results of the edited style in the unordered list.

FIGURE C-15

Editing a CSS Style

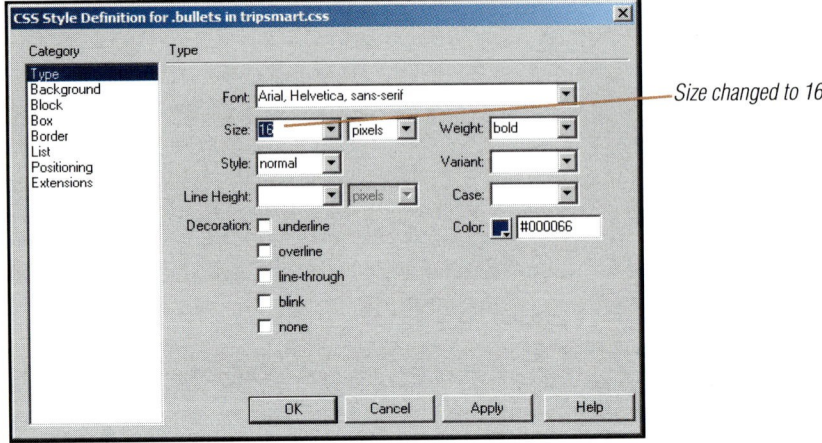

Size changed to 16

FIGURE C-16

Unordered list with edited bullets style applied

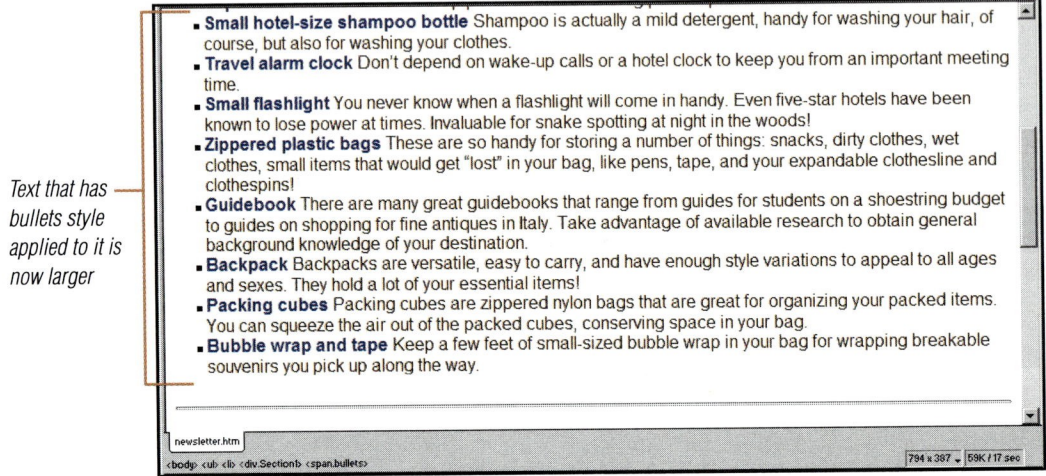

Text that has bullets style applied to it is now larger

Working with Text and Graphics

FIGURE C-17

Adding a style to a CSS style sheet

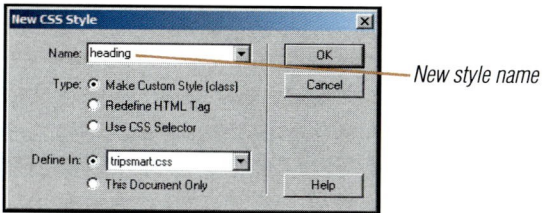

New style name

FIGURE C-18

Formatting options for heading style

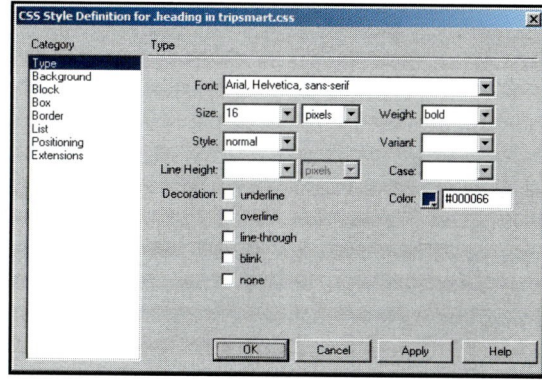

FIGURE C-19

Setting text alignment for headings style

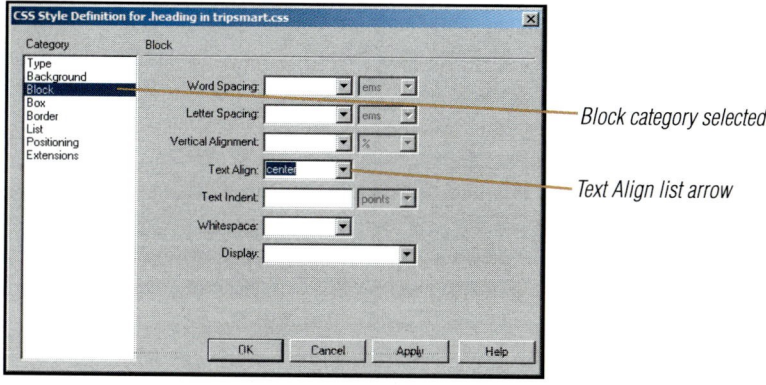

Block category selected

Text Align list arrow

Lesson 2   Create, Apply, and Edit Cascading Style Sheets

Add a style to a Cascading Style Sheet

1. Click the New CSS Style button at the bottom of the CSS Styles Panel.

2. Type **heading** in the Name Text box, as shown in Figure C-17, then click OK.

3. Set the Font to Arial, Helvetica, sans-serif, set the Size to 16, set the Style to normal, set the Weight to bold, set the Color to #000066, then compare your screen to Figure C-18.

4. Click the Block category in the New CSS Style Definition for .heading in tripsmart.css dialog box, click the Text Align list arrow, click center, as shown in Figure C-19, then click OK.

5. Select the heading Packing Essentials, use the Property inspector to set the Format to Paragraph and the Font to Default Font then click the Align Center button to remove the alignment setting.

6. With the heading still selected, click the Text Color button to open the color picker, then click the Strikethrough button.

7. Click the heading style in the CSS Styles panel to apply the heading style to the Packing Essentials heading.

8. Repeat Steps 5 through 7 to apply the heading style to the text Avoiding Wrinkle Woes, collapse the Design panel group, then save your work.

> TIP   Be careful not to click a style name with the insertion point in text unless you intend to apply that style to that text.

You added a new style called heading to the tripsmart .CSS file. You then applied the heading style to selected text.

MACROMEDIA DREAMWEAVER C-15

INSERT AND ALIGN GRAPHICS

What You'll Do

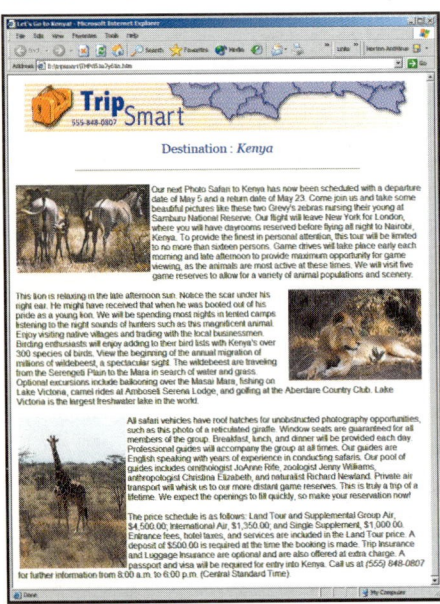

 In this lesson, you will insert three graphics on the tours page in the TripSmart Web site. You will then stagger the alignment of the images on the page to make the page more visually appealing.

Understanding Graphic File Formats

When you add graphics to a Web page, it's important to choose the appropriate graphic file format. The three primary graphic file formats used in Web pages are GIF (Graphics Interchange Format), JPEG (Joint Photographic Experts Group), and PNG (Portable Network Graphics). GIF files download very quickly, making them ideal to use on Web pages. Though limited in the number of colors they can represent, GIF files have the ability to show transparent areas. JPEG files can display many colors. Because they often contain many shades of the same color, photographs are often saved in JPEG format. Files saved with the PNG format share advantages of both GIFs and JPEGs, but are not universally recognized by older browsers.

QUICKTIP

The status bar displays the download time for the page. Each time you add a new graphic to the page, you can see how much additional time is added to the total download time.

Understanding the Assets Panel

When you add a graphic to a Web site, it is added automatically to the Assets panel. The **Assets panel,** located in the Files panel group, displays all the assets in a Web site. The Assets panel contains nine category buttons that you use to view your assets by category. These include Images, Colors, URLs, Flash, Shockwave, Movies, Scripts, Templates, and Library. To view a particular type of asset, click the appropriate category button. The Assets panel is split into two panes. When you click the Images button, as shown in Figure C-20, the lower pane displays a list of all the images in your site and contains four columns. The top pane displays a thumbnail of the selected image in the list. You can view assets in each category in two ways. You can use the Site option button to view all the assets in a Web site, or you can use the Favorites option button to view those assets that you have designated as **favorites,** or assets that you expect to use repeatedly while you work on the site.

Aligning Images

When you insert an image on a Web page, you need to position it in relation to other elements on the page. Positioning an image is referred to as **aligning** an image. By default, when you insert an image in a paragraph, its bottom edge aligns with the baseline of the first line of text or any other element in the same paragraph. When you select an image, the Align text box in the Property inspector displays the alignment setting for the image. You can change the alignment setting using the options on the Align list in the Property inspector.

FIGURE C-20
Assets panel

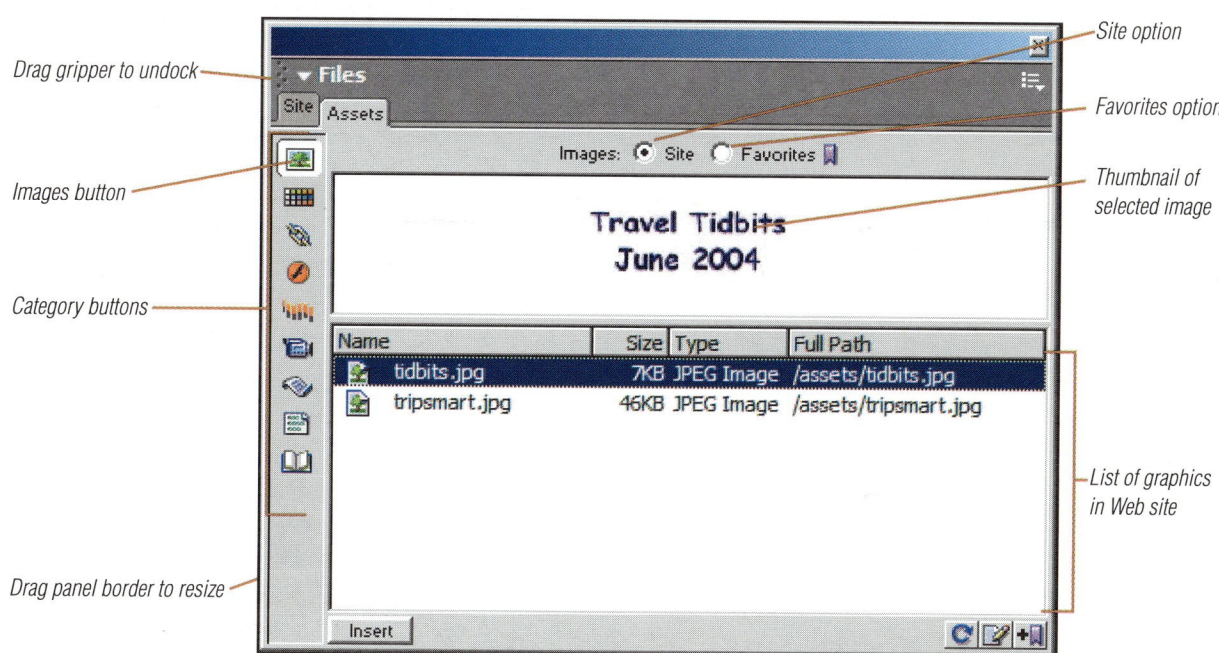

Drag gripper to undock

Images button

Category buttons

Drag panel border to resize

Site option

Favorites option

Thumbnail of selected image

List of graphics in Web site

Insert a graphic

1. Open dwc_1.htm from the unit_c folder where your data files are stored, then save it as **tours.htm** in the tripsmart root folder, overwriting the existing tours.htm file.

2. Set the path for the TripSmart banner as assets/tripsmart.jpg.

3. Position the insertion point in front of Our in the first paragraph, click the Image button on the Insert bar to open the Select Image Source dialog box, navigate to the unit_c assets folder, double-click zebra_mothers.jpg to insert this image on the page, then verify that the file was copied to your assets folder in the tripsmart root folder.

   Compare your screen to Figure C-21.

4. Click the Assets panel tab in the Files panel group (Win), or click the expander arrow next to the Files panel group (Mac), click the Images button on the Assets panel (if necessary), then click the Refresh Site List button at the bottom of the Assets panel to update the list of images in the TripSmart Web site.

   The Assets panel displays a list of all the images in the TripSmart Web site, as shown in Figure C-22. A thumbnail of the zebra image appears above the list.

   (continued)

MACROMEDIA DREAMWEAVER C-18

FIGURE C-21

TripSmart tours page with inserted image

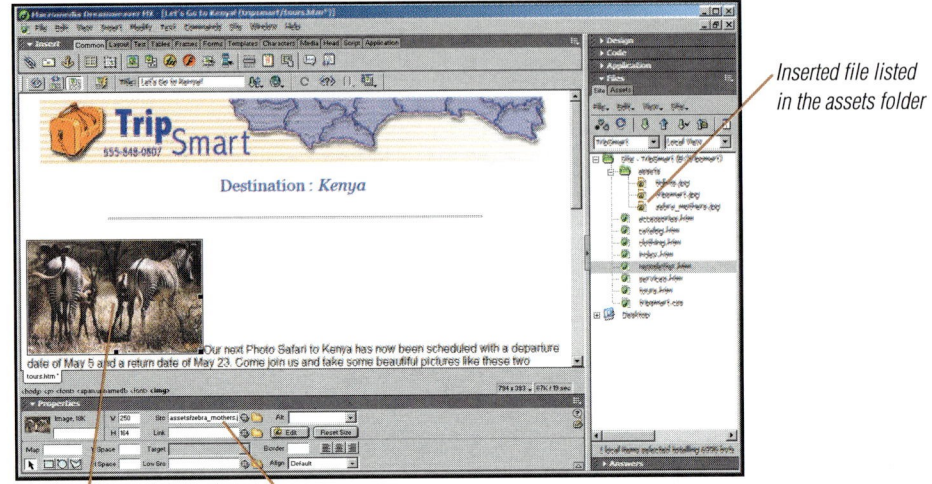

Inserted file listed in the assets folder

zebra_mothers.jpg file inserted

Path should begin with the word "assets"

FIGURE C-22

Image files for TripSmart Web site listed in Assets panel

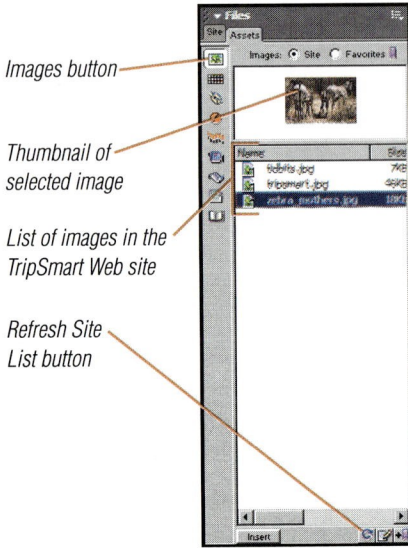

Images button

Thumbnail of selected image

List of images in the TripSmart Web site

Refresh Site List button

Working with Text and Graphics

FIGURE C-23
Assets panel with five images

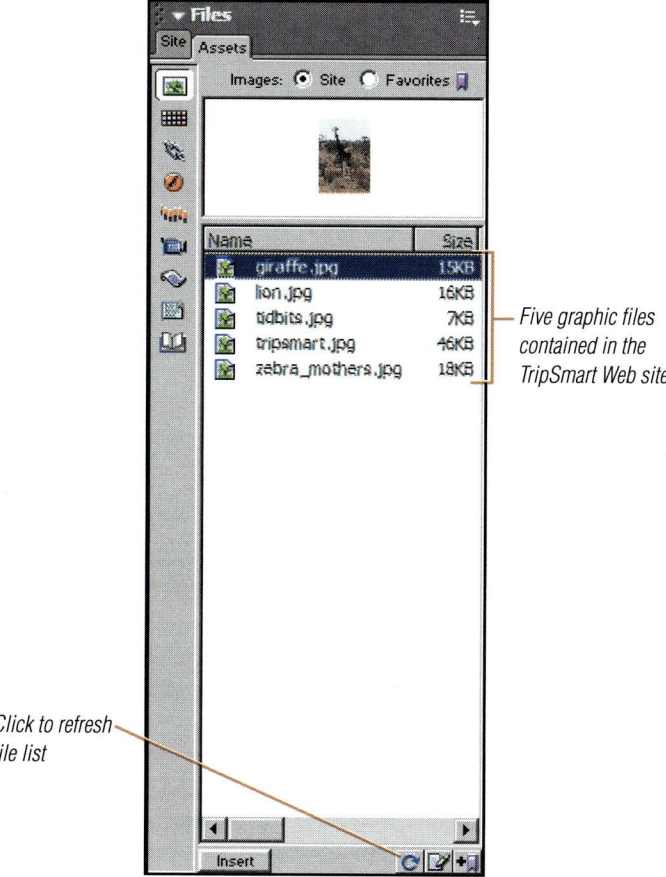

Five graphic files contained in the TripSmart Web site

Click to refresh file list

5. Insert the data file lion.jpg to the left of This at the beginning of the second paragraph, then refresh the Assets panel to verify that the lion.jpg file was copied to the assets folder of the TripSmart Web site.

> TIP The file lion.jpg is located in the assets folder in the unit_c folder where your data files are stored.

6. Insert the data file giraffe.jpg to the left of All safari vehicles at the beginning of the third paragraph, refresh the Assets panel to verify that the file was copied to the Web site, then save your work.

Your Assets panel should resemble Figure C-23.

You inserted the data file three images on the tours page and copied each image to the assets folder of the TripSmart Web site.

Align a graphic

1. Scroll to the top of the page, click the zebra image to select it, then expand the Property inspector (if necessary).

   Because an image is selected, the Property inspector displays tools you can use to set the properties of an image.

2. Click the Align list arrow in the Property inspector, then click Left.

   The zebra photo is now left-aligned and the paragraph text flows around its right edge as shown in Figure C-24. You might see a blue or yellow alignment icon next to the zebra image indicating that the image has been aligned.

   > **TIP** To show or hide alignment icons click View on the menu bar, point to Visual Aids, then click Invisible Elements.

   (continued)

FIGURE C-24
Left-aligned zebra image

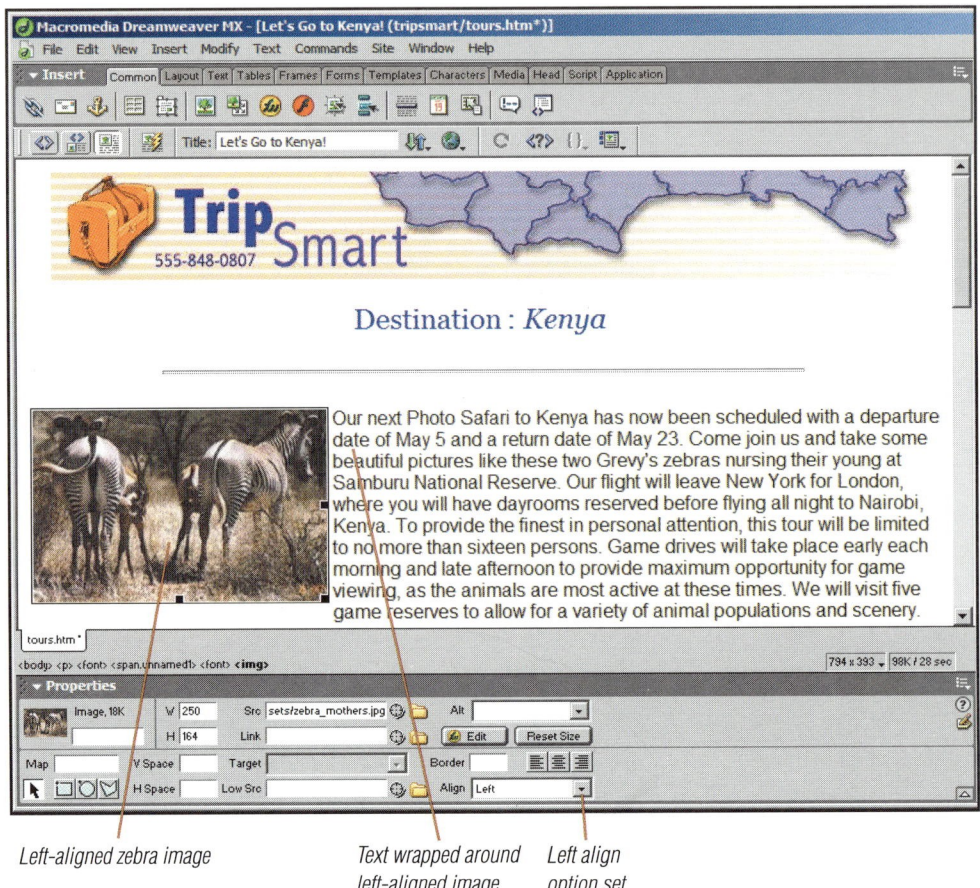

Left-aligned zebra image   Text wrapped around   Left align
                             left-aligned image   option set

Working with Text and Graphics

FIGURE C-25

Aligned images on the tours page

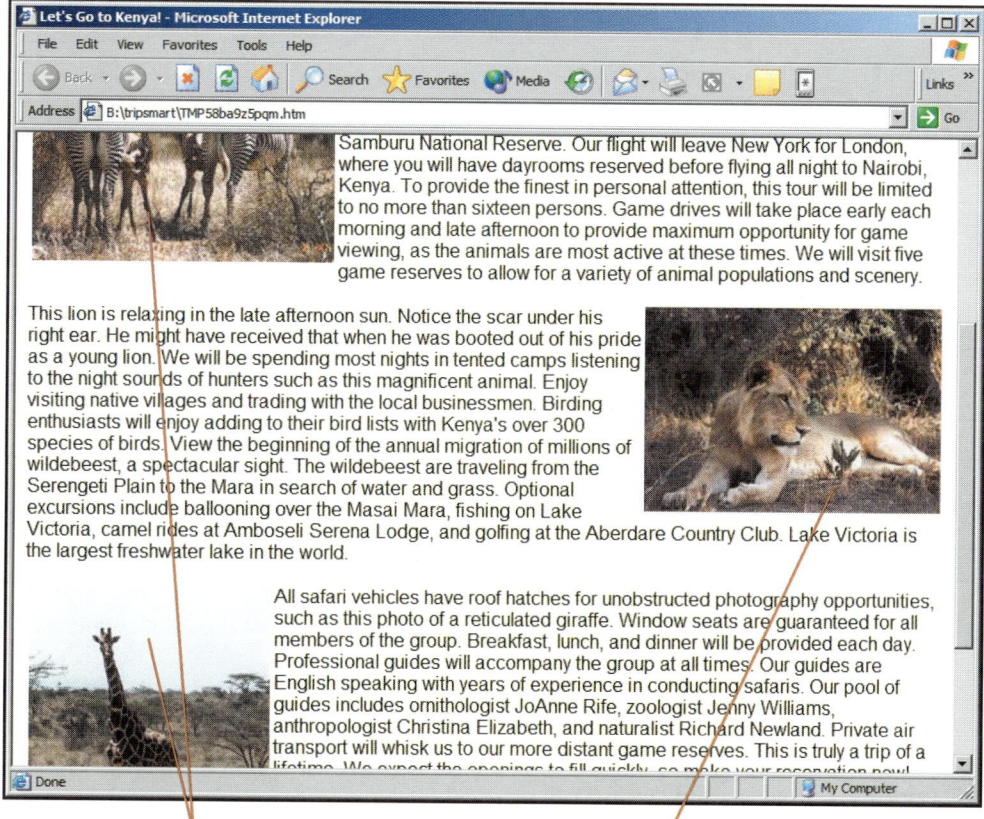

Left-aligned images   Right-aligned image

3. Select the the lion image, click the Align list arrow in the Property inspector, then click Right.

4. Align the giraffe image, using the Left Align option.

5. Save your work.

6. Preview the Web page in your browser, compare your screen to Figure C-25, then close your browser.

You used the Property inspector to set the alignment for the zebra, giraffe, and lion images. You then previewed the page in your browser.

ENHANCE AN IMAGE AND USE ALTERNATE TEXT

What You'll Do

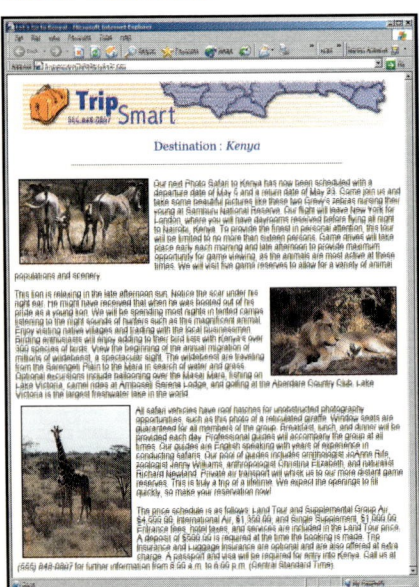

 In this lesson, you will add borders around the images on the tours page, adjust the horizontal space around the images to set them apart from the text, and then add alternate text to describe each image on the page.

Enhancing an Image

After you place an image on a Web page, you have several options for **enhancing** it, or improving its appearance. To make changes to the image itself, such as removing scratches from it, or making it lighter or darker, you need to use an image editor such as Macromedia Fireworks or Adobe Photoshop. However, you can use Dreamweaver to enhance certain aspects of how images appear on a page. For example, you can add borders around an image or add horizontal and vertical space. **Borders** are frames that surround an image. Horizontal and vertical space is blank space above, below, and on the sides of an image that separates the image from text or other elements on the page. Adding horizontal or vertical space, which is the same as adding white space, helps images

Resizing graphics using an external editor

Each image on a Web page takes a specific number of seconds to download, depending on the size of the file. Larger files (in kilobytes, not width and height) take longer to download than smaller files. It's important to figure out the smallest acceptable size for an image on your Web page. Then, if you need to resize an image to reduce the file size, use an external image editor to do so, *instead* of resizing it in Dreamweaver. Although you can adjust the width and height settings of an image in the Property inspector to change the size of the image as it appears on your screen, these settings do not affect the file size. Decreasing the size of an image using the H Size (height) and W Size (width) settings in the Property inspector does *not* reduce the time it will take the file to download. Ideally you should use graphics that have the smallest file size and the highest quality possible, so that each page downloads in eight seconds or less.

stand out on a page. In the Web page shown in Figure C-26, the horizontal and vertical space around the small images in the center column helps make these images more prominent. Adding horizontal or vertical space does not affect the width or height of the image.

QUICKTIP

Because some linked images are displayed with borders, viewers might mistake an image that contains a border with a hyperlink. For this reason, you should use borders sparingly.

Using Alternate Text

One of the easiest ways to make your Web page viewer-friendly and handicapped-accessible is to use alternate text. **Alternate text** is descriptive text that appears in place of an image while the image is downloading or when the mouse pointer is placed over it. You can program some browsers to display only alternate text and to download images manually. Alternate text can be "read" by a **screen reader**, a device used by the visually impaired to convert written text on a computer monitor to spoken words. Screen readers and alternate text make it possible for visually impaired viewers to have an image described to them in detail. You can also set up Dreamweaver to prompt you to enter alternate text whenever you insert an image on a page.

FIGURE C-26

Museum of Fine Arts Web site

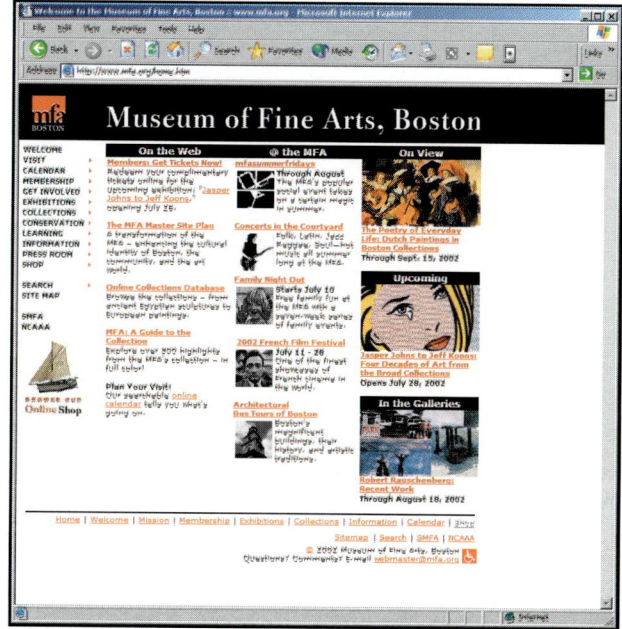

Add a border

1. Select the zebra image, then expand the Property inspector (if necessary).

2. Type **2** in the Border text box, as shown in Figure C-27, then press [Tab] to apply the border to the zebra image.

3. Repeat Step 2 to add borders to the lion and giraffe images.

4. Save your work.

You added a 2-pixel border to each image on the tours page.

Add horizontal space

1. Select the zebra image, type **10** in the H Space text box in the Property inspector, press [Tab], then compare your screen to Figure C-28.

   The text is more evenly wrapped around the image and is easier to read, since it is not so close to the edge of the image.

2. Repeat Step 4 to set the H Space to 10 for the lion and giraffe images.

   The spacing under each picture differs because of the difference in the lengths of the paragraphs.

3. Save your work.

You added horizontal spacing around each image on the tours page.

FIGURE C-27

Using the Property inspector to add a border

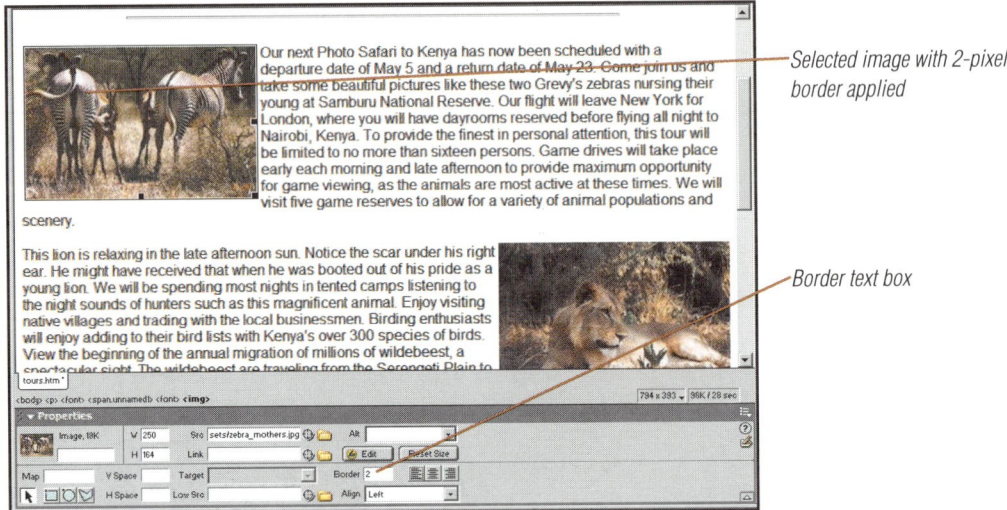

Selected image with 2-pixel border applied

Border text box

FIGURE C-28

Using the Property inspector to add horizontal space

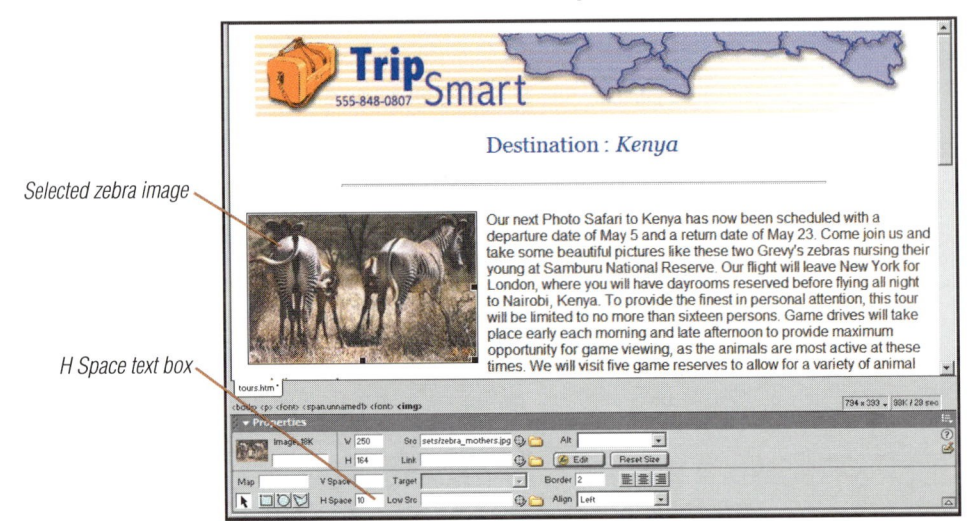

Selected zebra image

H Space text box

FIGURE C-29
Property inspector showing altered width and height settings of giraffe image

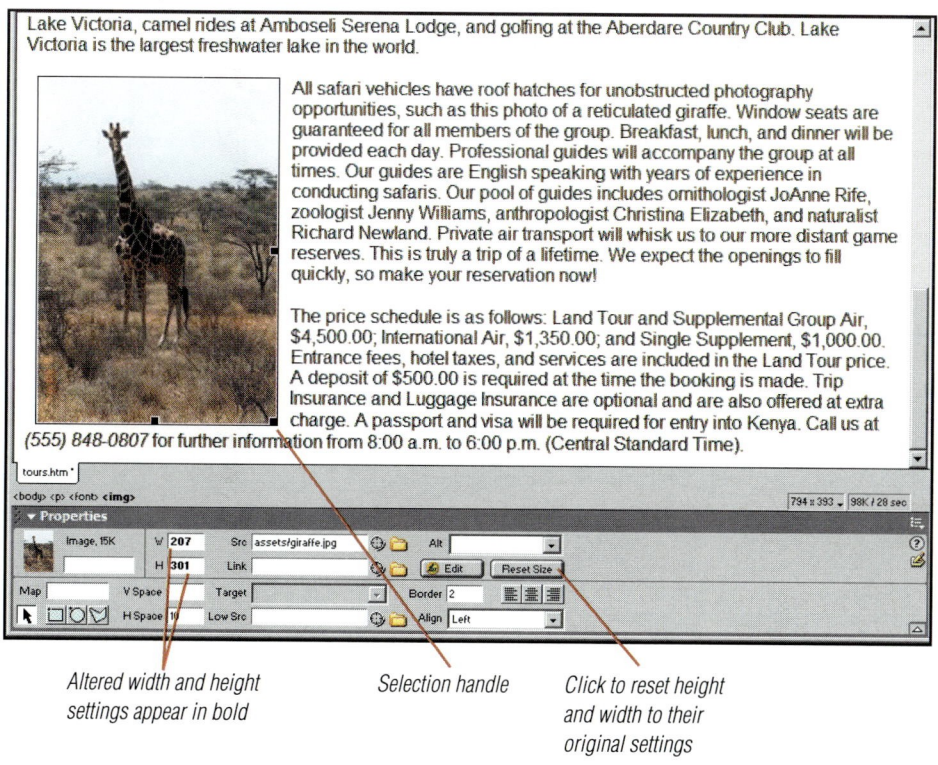

Altered width and height
settings appear in bold

Selection handle

Click to reset height
and width to their
original settings

1. Select the giraffe image, press and hold [Shift], then slowly drag the bottom-right corner selection handle of the giraffe image down and to the right about an eighth of an inch to increase the image size slightly, as shown in Figure C-29.

   Holding [Shift] while you drag a corner selection handle keeps the image in proportion.

   TIP To increase or decrease an image size significantly, resize the graphic using an image editor.

2. Resize the lion and giraffe images (if necessary).

   TIP To return a resized graphic to its original size, click the Reset Size button in the Property inspector.

3. Save your work.

You adjusted the size of the giraffe image to improve the appearance of text around it.

Use alternate text

1. Select the zebra image, type **Two zebra mothers with their babies** in the Alt text box in the Property inspector, as shown in Figure C-30, then press [Enter] (Win) or [return] (Mac).

2. Preview the page in your browser, then point to the zebra image until the alternate text appears, as shown in Figure C-31.

3. Close your browser.

4. Select the lion image, type **Lion relaxing in the Kenyan sun** in the Alt text box in the Property inspector, then press [Enter] (Win) or [return] (Mac).

5. Select the giraffe image, type **Reticulated giraffe posed among acacia trees and brush** in the Alt text box in the Property inspector, then press [Enter] (Win) or [return] (Mac).

6. Save your work.

7. Preview the page in your browser, view the alternate text for each image, then close your browser.

You added alternate text to each of the four images on the page, then you viewed the alternate text in your browser.

FIGURE C-30
Alternate text setting in the Property inspector

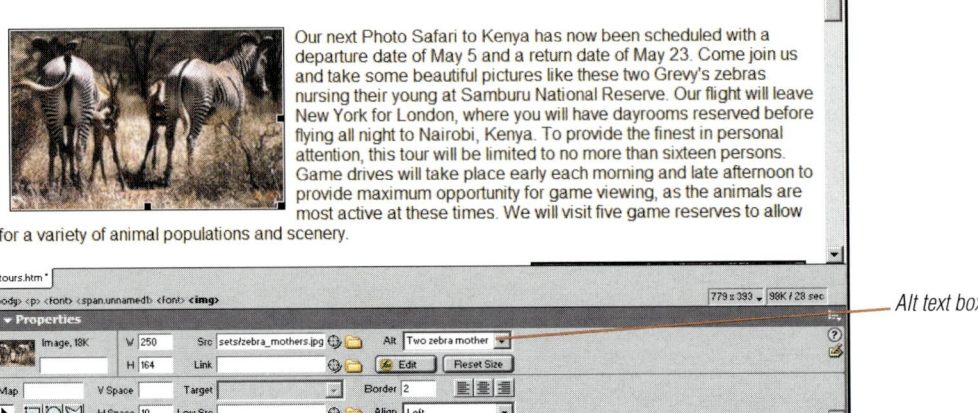

Alt text box

FIGURE C-31
Alternate text displayed in browser

Alternate text displayed on top of image

Working with Text and Graphics

FIGURE C-32

Preferences dialog box with Accessibility category selected

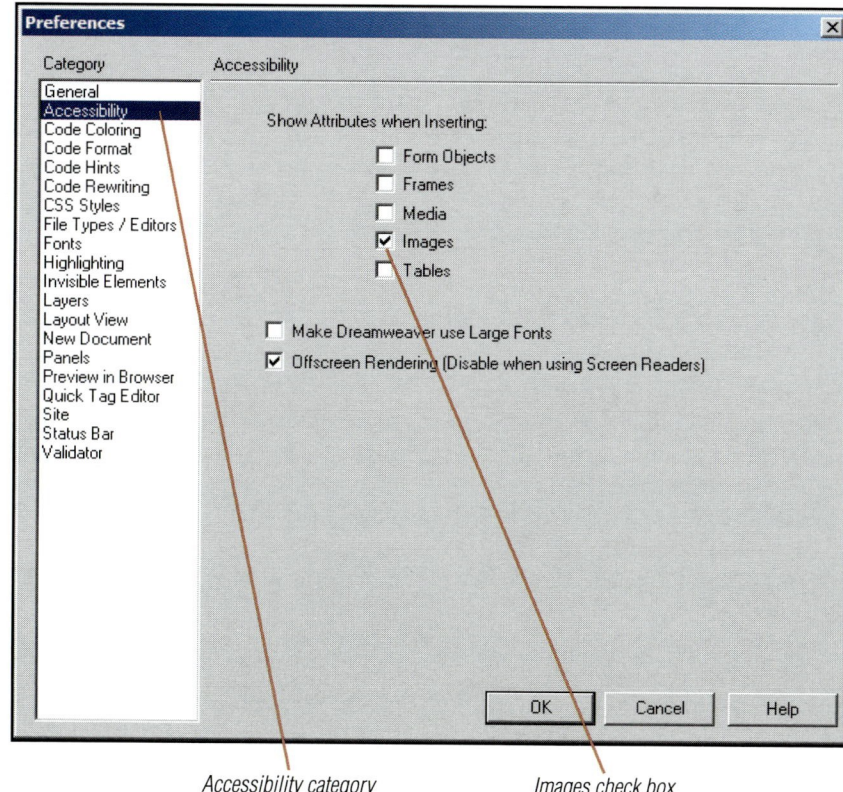

Accessibility category

Images check box

1. Click Edit on the menu bar, click Preferences to open the Preferences dialog box, then click the Accessibility category.

2. Click the Images check box as shown in Figure C-32, then click OK.

   TIP Once you set the Accessibility preferences, they will be in effect for all Web sites that you develop, not just the one that's open when you set them.

You set the Accessibility preferences to prompt you to enter alternate text each time you insert a graphic on a Web page.

INSERT A BACKGROUND IMAGE AND PERFORM SITE MAINTENANCE

What You'll Do

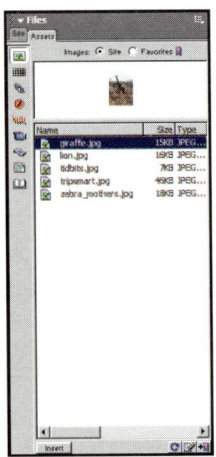 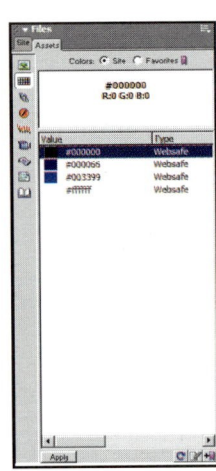

 In this lesson, you will insert a tiled image and then a seamless image. You will then use the Assets panel to delete them both from the Web site. You will also check for non-Web-safe colors in the Assets panel and delete one that you locate on the home page.

Inserting a Background Image

You can insert a background image on a Web page to provide depth and visual interest to the page, or to communicate a message or mood. **Background images** are graphic files used in place of background colors. Although you can use background images to create a dramatic effect, you should avoid inserting them on Web pages that have lots of text and other elements. Even though they might seem too plain, standard white backgrounds are usually the best choice for Web pages. If you choose to use a background image on a Web page, it should be small in file size, and preferably in GIF format. You can insert either a tiled image or a seamless image as a background. A **tiled image** is a small graphic that repeats across and down a Web page, appearing as individual squares or rectangles. A **seamless image** is a tiled image that is blurred at the edges so it appears to be one image. When you create a Web page, you should use either a background color or a background image, but not both, unless you have a need for the background color to be displayed while the background image finishes downloading. The background in the Web page shown in Figure C-33 contains several images arranged in a table format.

Managing Graphics

As you work on a Web site, you might find that you accumulate files in your assets folder that are not used in the site. To avoid accumulating unnecessary files, it's a good idea to look at a graphic on a page first, before you copy it to the assets folder. If you inadvertently copy an unwanted file to the assets folder, you should delete it or move it to another location. This is a good Web-site management practice that will prevent the assets folder from filling up with unwanted graphics.

Removing a graphic from a Web page does not remove it from the assets folder in the local root folder of the Web site. To remove an asset from a Web site, you can first locate the file you want to remove in the Assets panel. You then use the Locate in

Site command to open the Site panel with the unwanted file selected. You then use the Delete command to remove the file from the site.

QUICKTIP

You cannot use the Assets panel to delete a file. You must use the Site panel to delete files and perform all file-management tasks.

Removing Colors from a Web Site

You can use the Assets panel to remove non-Web-safe colors from a Web site. **Non-Web-safe** colors are colors that may not be displayed uniformly across platforms. After you remove colors from a Web site, you should use the Refresh Site List button on the Assets panel to verify that these colors have been removed. Sometimes it's necessary to press [Ctrl] (Win) or [Command] (Mac) while you click the Refresh Site List button. If refreshing the Assets panel does not work, try re-creating the site cache, then refreshing the Assets panel again

QUICKTIP

To re-create the site cache, open the Site panel, click Site on the Site panel menu bar, then click Recreate Site Cache (Win), or choose Site from the Document menu, then choose Recreate Site Cache (Mac).

FIGURE C-33

Mansion on Turtle Creek

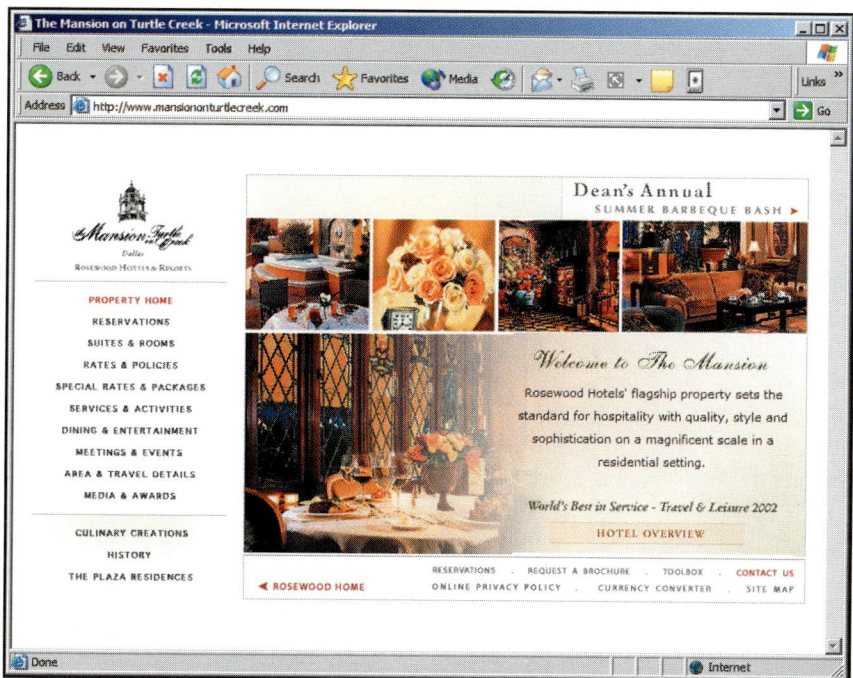

Insert a background image

1. Click Modify on the menu bar, then click Page Properties to open the Page Properties dialog box.

2. Click the Browse button next to the Background Image text box, navigate to the unit_c assets folder, then double-click tile_bak.gif.

   The tile_bak.gif file is automatically copied to the TripSmart assets folder.

3. Click OK to close the Page Properties dialog box, then click the Refresh button to refresh the file list in the Assets panel.

   A blue tiled background made up of individual squares replaces the white background. See Figure C-34.

4. Repeat Steps 1 and 2 to replace the tile_bak.gif background image with the data file seamless_bak.gif, located in the unit_c assets folder.

   See Figure C-35. The seamless background makes it hard to tell where one square stops and the other begins.

5. Save your work.

You applied a tiled background for the tours page. Then you replaced the tiled background with a seamless background.

FIGURE C-34

Tours page with a tiled background

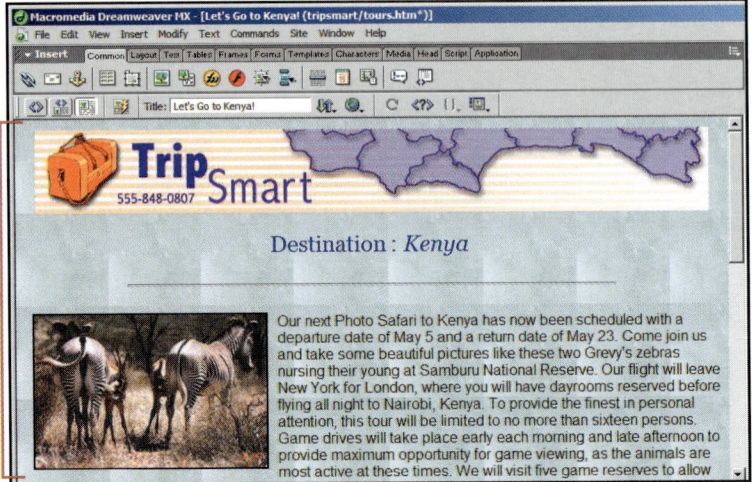

Blue tiled background

FIGURE C-35

Tours page with a seamless background

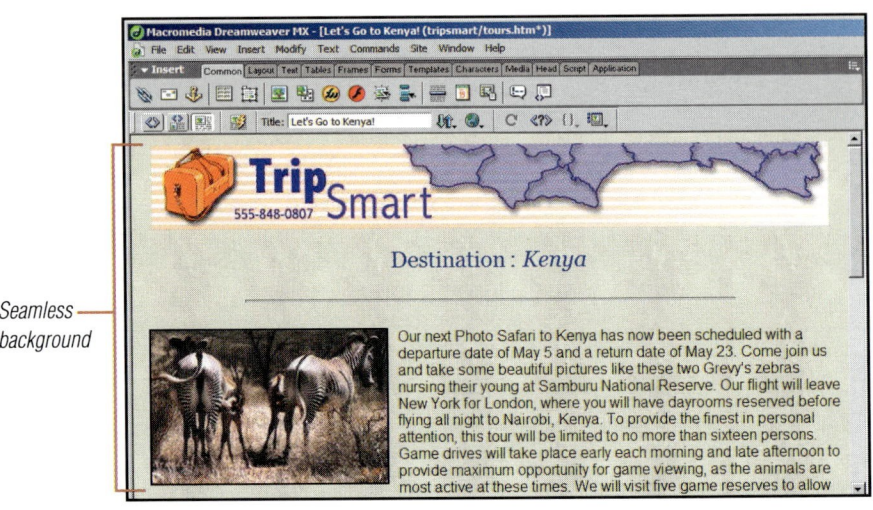

Seamless background

FIGURE C-36

Removing a background image

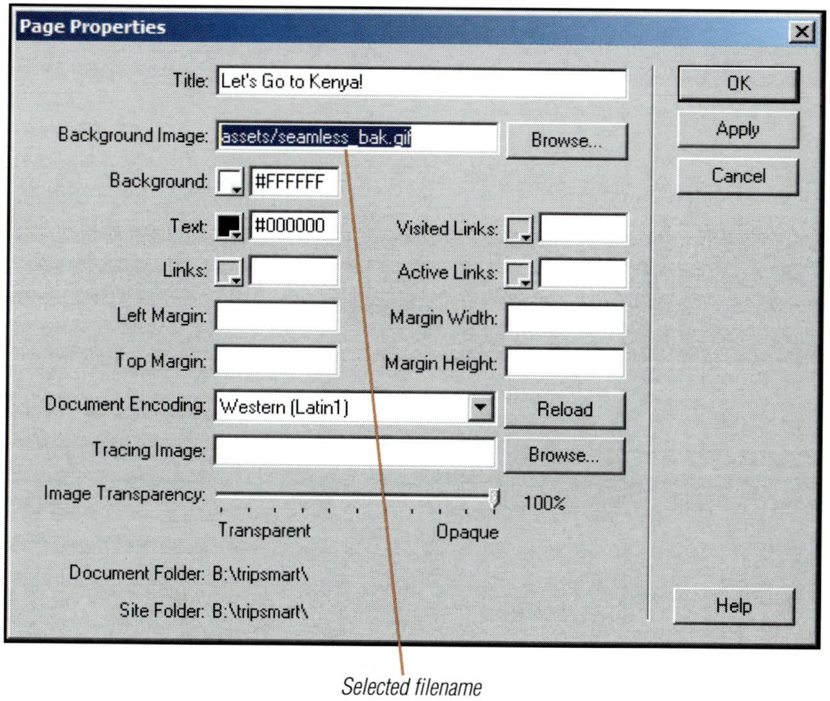
Page Properties
Title: Let's Go to Kenya!
Background Image: assets/seamless_bak.gif
Browse...
Background: #FFFFFF
Text: #000000
Links:
Visited Links:
Active Links:
Left Margin:
Top Margin:
Margin Width:
Margin Height:
Document Encoding: Western (Latin1)
Reload
Tracing Image:
Browse...
Image Transparency:
100%
Transparent
Opaque
Document Folder: B:\tripsmart\
Site Folder: B:\tripsmart\
OK
Apply
Cancel
Help
Selected filename

Remove a background image from a page

1. Click Modify on the menu bar, then click Page Properties.
2. Select the text in the Background Image text box as shown in Figure C-36, press [Delete], then click OK.

   The background of the tours page is white again.
3. Save your work.

You deleted the link to the background image file to change the tours page background back to white.

Delete files from a Web site

1. Click the Assets panel tab (Win), or expand the Files panel group (Mac) (if necessary).

2. Right-click (Win) or [control] click (Mac) seamless_bak.gif in the Assets panel, click Locate in Site to open the Site panel, select seamless_bak.gif in the Site panel (if necessary), press [Delete], then click OK in the dialog box that appears.

3. Repeat Step 2 to remove tile_bak.gif from the Web site, open the Assets panel, then refresh the Assets panel.

   Your Assets panel should resemble Figure C-37.

You removed two image files from the TripSmart Web site, then refreshed the Assets panel.

FIGURE C-37
Images listed in Assets panel

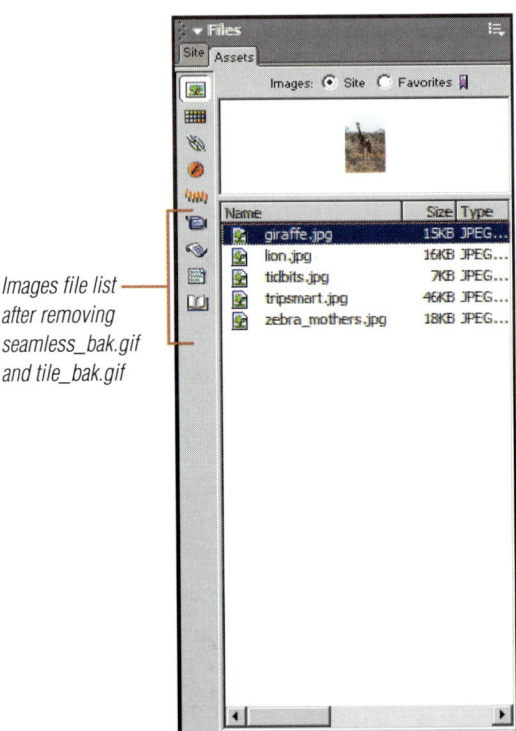

Images file list after removing seamless_bak.gif and tile_bak.gif

Managing graphic files

It is a good idea to store copies of your original Web site graphic files in a separate folder, outside the assets folder of your Web site. If you edit the original files, save them again using different names. Doing this ensures that you will be able to find a file in its original, unaltered state. You might have no need for certain files now, but you might need them later. Storing currently unused files also helps to keep your assets folder free of clutter. Storing copies of original Web site graphic files in a separate location also ensures that you have back-up copies in the event that you accidentally delete a file from the Web site that you need later.

FIGURE C-38
Colors listed in Assets panel

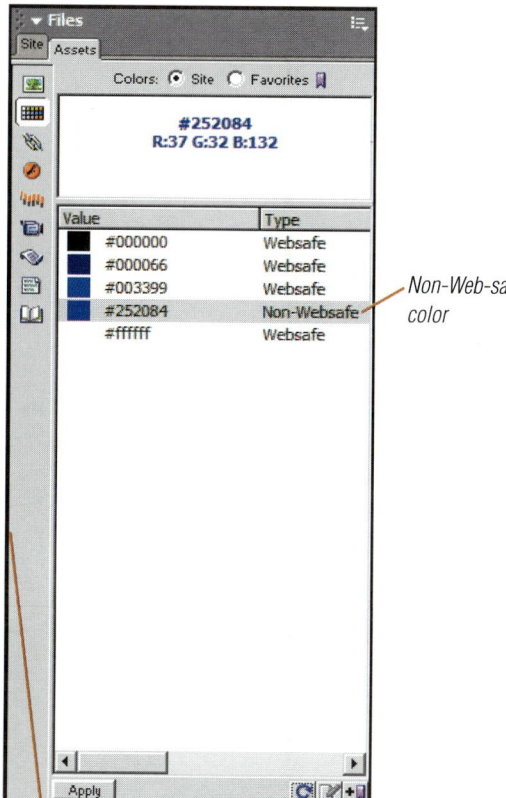

Non-Web-safe color

Drag this border to the left to expand panel width

FIGURE C-39
Non-Web-safe color removed from Assets panel

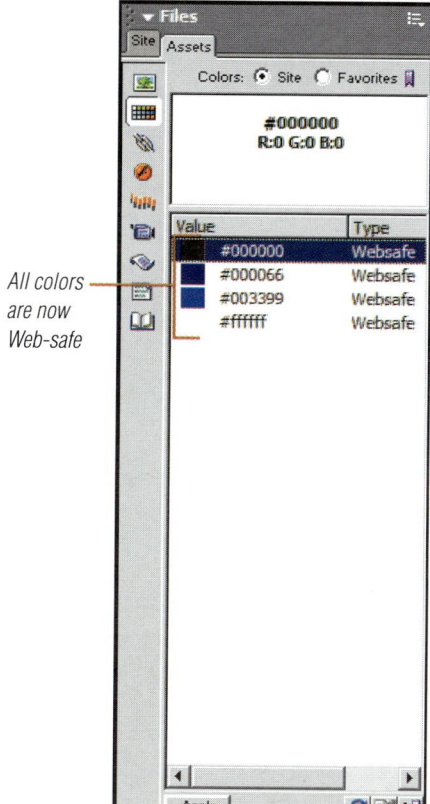

All colors are now Web-safe

1. Click the Colors button in the Assets panel to display the colors used in the Web site, then drag the left border of the Assets panel (if necessary) to expand it to the second column.

   The Assets panel shows that color 252084 is non-Web-safe, as shown in Figure C-38. This color appears in a heading on the home page.

2. Click the Site panel tab (Win), or click Site on the menu bar, place your pointer on Open Site, then click TripSmart (Mac).

3. Double-click index.htm to open the home page.

4. Select The smart way to go!, click the Text Color button in the Property inspector to open the color picker, click the Strikethough button, type #003399 in the Color text box, press [Tab] to apply the new color, then click anywhere to deselect the text.

   The heading text is now a different shade of blue with the Web-safe color #003399 applied.

5. Click the Assets panel tab, press and hold [Ctrl] (Win) or [Command] (Mac), click the Refresh Site List button then compare your screen to Figure C-39.

6. Save your work, preview the page in your browser, close your browser, then close all open files.

You removed one non-Web-safe color from the Web site, then refreshed the Assets panel.

Create unordered and ordered lists.

1. Open the Blooms & Bulbs Web site. (If you did not create this Web site in Units A and B, contact your instructor for assistance.)
2. Open the file dwc_2.htm from the unit_c data files folder, then save the file as **tips.htm** in the Blooms & Bulbs Web site, overwriting the existing tips.htm file.
3. Reset the path for the planting_tips.jpg graphic to the assets folder of the Blooms & Bulbs Web site.
4. Reset the path for the Blooms banner to the assets folder of the Blooms & Bulbs Web site.
5. Import the gardening_tips.htm file from the unit_c data files folder using the Import Word HTML command.
6. Copy the imported text, then close the gardening_tips.htm file without saving it.
7. Paste the copied text onto the tips page below the planting tips text graphic, then format the imported text as Arial, Helvetica, sans-serif, size 3.
8. Select the four lines of text below the Seasonal Gardening Checklist heading and format them as an unordered list.
9. Select the lines of text below the Basic Gardening tips heading and format them as an ordered list.
10. Save your work.

Create, apply, and edit Cascading Style Sheets.

1. Create a new CSS Style named **.seasons**, making sure the Make Custom Style (class) and the New Style Sheet File option buttons are both selected in the New CSS Style dialog box.
2. Name the style sheet file **blooms** in the Save Style Sheet File As dialog box.
3. Choose the following settings for the seasons style: Font = Arial, Helvetica, sans-serif, Size = 12 pixels, Style = normal, Weight = bold, and Color = #006633.
4. Change the Font setting to Default Font and the Size setting to None for the following text in the Seasonal Gardening Checklist: Fall:, Winter:, Spring:, and Summer:. (Be sure to include the colons.) Then, apply the seasons style to Fall:, Winter:, Spring:, and Summer:.
5. Edit the seasons style by changing the font size to 16 pixels.
6. Add an additional style called **headings** and define this style choosing the following type settings: Font = Arial, Helvetica, sans-serif, Size = 18 pixels, Style = normal, Weight = bold, and Color = #006633.
7. Apply the heading style to the two subheadings on the page: Seasonal Gardening Checklist and Basic Gardening Tips. (Make sure you remove any manual formatting before applying the style.)

8. Save your work and view the page in the browser.
9. Close the browser and the tips page.

Insert and align graphics.

1. Open the file dwc_3.htm from the unit_c data files folder, then save it as **plants.htm** in the Blooms & Bulbs Web site, overwriting the existing plants.htm file.
2. Verify that the path of the Blooms & Bulbs banner is set correctly to the assets folder in the blooms root folder.
3. Insert the iris.jpg file from the assets folder located in the unit_c data files folder to the left of the words Beautiful spring iris and add **Purple iris** as alternate text if prompted to do so.
4. Insert the tulips.jpg file from the unit_c assets folder file in front of the words Dramatic masses and add **Red and yellow tulips** as alternate text if prompted to do so.
5. Insert the pansies.jpg file from the unit_c assets folder in front of the words Pretty pansies and add **Deep violet pansies** as alternate text if prompted to do so.
6. Refresh the Site panel to verify that all three images were copied to the assets folder.
7. Left-align the iris image.
8. Left-align the tulips image.
9. Left-align the pansies image.
10. Save your work.

Working with Text and Graphics

Enhance an image and use alternate text.

1. Apply a 2-pixel border and horizontal spacing of 5 pixels around the iris image.
2. Apply a 2-pixel border and horizontal spacing of 5 pixels around the tulips image.
3. Apply a 2-pixel border and horizontal spacing of 5 pixels around the pansies image.
4. Add the text **Purple iris** as alternate text for the iris image (if necessary).
5. Add the text **Red and yellow tulips** as alternate text for the tulips image (if necessary).
6. Add the text **Deep violet pansies** as alternate text for the pansies image (if necessary).
7. Add the text **Blooms & Bulbs banner** as alternate text for the banner.
8. Edit the Accessibility Preferences to prompt you for alternate text when inserting images (if necessary).
9. Add appropriate alternate text to the banner on the index and tips pages.
10. Save your work and close the index and tips pages.

Insert a background image and manage graphics.

1. Make sure the plants page is open, then insert the daisies.gif file from the unit_c assets folder as a background image.
2. Save your work.
3. Preview the Web page in your browser, then close your browser.
4. Remove the daisies.gif file from the background.

5. Open the Assets panel, then refresh the Site list.
6. Use the Site panel to delete the daisies.gif file from the list of images.

7. Refresh the Assets panel and verify that the daisies.gif file has been removed from the Web site.
8. View the colors used in the site in the Assets panel and verify that all are Websafe.
9. Save your work, then close the tips.htm page.

FIGURES C-40 AND C-41
Completed Skills Review

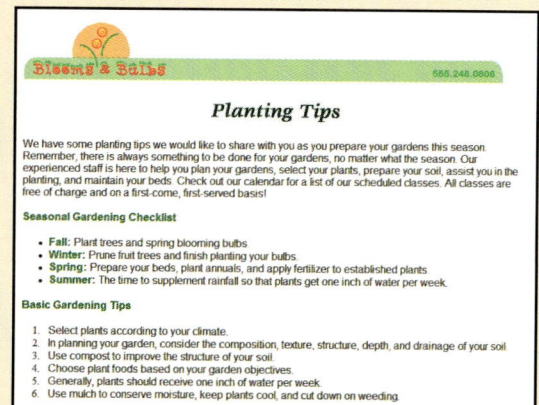

Use Figure C-42 as a guide to continue your work on the Rapids Transit Web site that you began in Project Builder 1 in Unit A. You are now ready to begin work on the guides page that explains the role of the guides in accompanying clients on float trips. You want to include a picture of one of the guides on the river and attractively format the text on the page. If you did not create this Web site in Unit A, contact your instructor for assistance.

1. Open the Rapids Transit Web site.
2. Open the file dwc_4.htm from the unit_c data files folder and save it in the rapids root folder as **guides.htm**, overwriting the existing guides.htm file.
3. Verify that the path for the banner is correctly set to the assets folder of the Rapids Transit Web site.
4. Insert the file buster_tricks.jpg from the assets folder located in the unit_c data files folder in an appropriate place on the page and copy the file to the assets folder.
5. Create alternate text for the buster_tricks image, add a border to the image, then choose an alignment setting for the image.
6. Add horizontal spacing of 5 to the buster_tricks image.

7. Create a new CSS Style called **.bodytext**, making sure that the Make Custom Style (class) and New Style Sheet File option buttons are checked in the New Style dialog box.
8. Save the style sheet file as **rapids** in the Rapids Transit Web site root folder.
9. Choose a font, size, style, color, and weight of your choice for the bodytext style.
10. Apply the bodytext style to the body text on the guides page.

11. Verify that the Accessibility Preference option is turned on, then add alternate text for any images in the Web site that do not yet have alternate text.
12. Save your work, then preview the page in your browser.
13. Close your browser, then close all open pages.

FIGURE C-42

Completed Project Builder 1

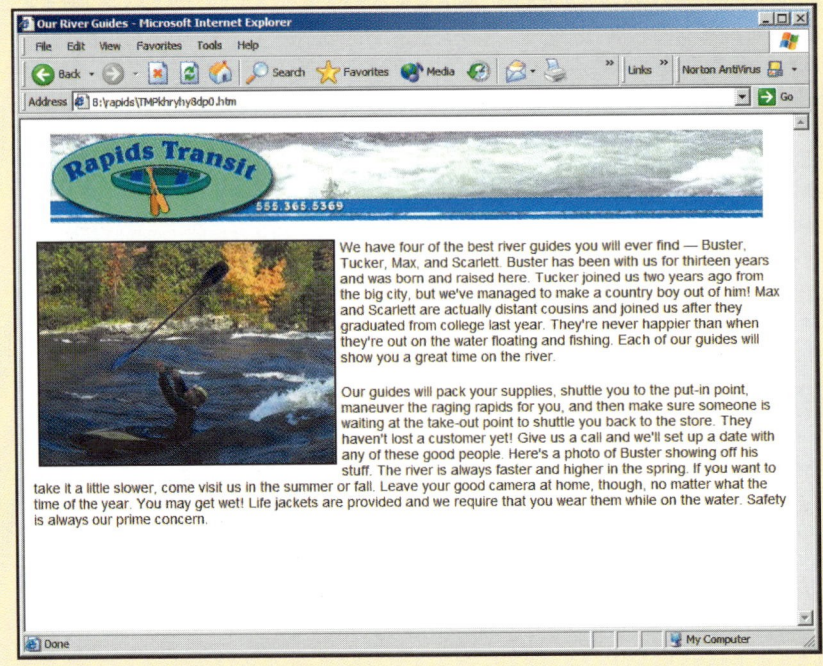

Working with Text and Graphics

In this exercise you continue your work on the Jacob's Web site that you started in Project Builder 2 in Unit A. You are now ready to add two new pages to the Web site. One page will display one of the restaurant's most popular recipes and another page will show three pictures of Jacob's special desserts. Figures C-43 and C-44 show possible solutions for this exercise. Your finished pages will look different if you choose different formatting options.

1. Open the Jacob's Web site (If you did not create this Web site in Units A and B, contact your instructor for assistance).

2. Open the file rolls.htm in the unit_c data files folder and save it to the jacobs root folder as **recipes.htm**, overwriting the existing recipes.htm file.

3. Format the list of ingredients as an unordered list.

4. Create a CSS style named **.ingredients** and save the style sheet file as **jacobs** in the Jacob's Web site root folder, using any formatting options that you like.

5. Apply the ingredients style to the ingredients in the unordered list.

6. Add a style called .bodytext to the jacobs style sheet file using any formatting options that you like, and apply it to the body text on the recipes page.

7. Create a style called **.subheadings** using appropriate formatting options and apply it to the words ingredients and directions.

8. Create a style called **.headings** using appropriate formatting options and apply it to the words Grandmother's Rolls, then save your work.

9. Open the file dwc_5.htm from the unit_c data files folder and save it in the Jacob's Web site as **after_theatre.htm**.

10. Set the path for the Jacob's banner to the assets folder of the Jacob's Web site.

11. Edit the accessibility preferences to prompt you for alternate text when inserting images (if necessary).

12. Add the poached_pear.jpg, oranges.jpg, and cheesecake.jpg images from the assets folder in the unit_c data files folder, adding appropriate alternate text to each image.

13. Add alternate text to the Jacob's banner.

14. Format the images with borders, spacing, and alignment that make the page look attractive.

15. Attach the jacobs style sheet to the after_theatre page, then apply the bodytext style to the body text on the page. (To attach the style sheet, click the Attach Style Sheet button at the bottom of the CSS Styles panel, click Browse to open the Link External Style Sheet dialog box, double-click the jacobs.css file, then click OK.)

16. Save your work, then preview both pages in your browser.

17. Close your browser, then close both pages.

FIGURE C-43
Completed Project Builder 2

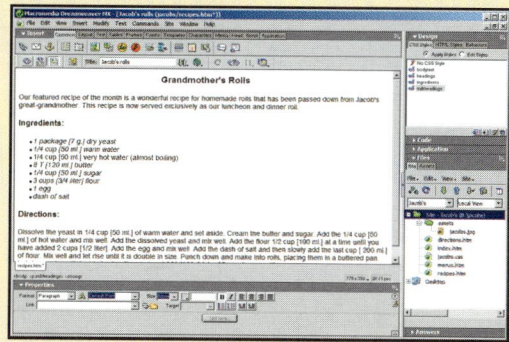

FIGURE C-44
Completed Project Builder 2

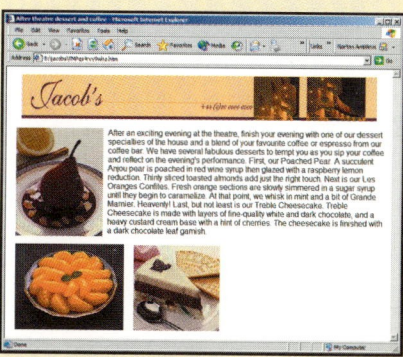

DESIGN PROJECT

Dr. Chappell is a government historian who is conducting research on the separation of church and state. He has gone to the Library of Congress Web site to look for information he can use.

1. Open your browser, connect to the Internet, go to *www.course.com*, navigate to the page for this book, click the Student Online Companion link, then click Link 1 for this unit. The Library of Congress Web site is shown in Figure C-45.

2. Which fonts are used for the main content on the home page? Are the same fonts used consistently on the other pages in the Web site?

3. Do you see ordered or unordered lists on any pages in the Web site? If so, how were they used?

4. Use the Source command on the View menu to view the source code to see if a set of fonts was used. If so, which one?

5. Do you see the use of Cascading Style Sheets noted in the source code?

6. Go to the Google Web site at *www.google.com* or the Alta Vista Web site at *www.altavista.com* to find another informational Web site of interest. Compare the use of text on that site with the use of text on the Library of Congress Web site.

FIGURE C-45
Design Project

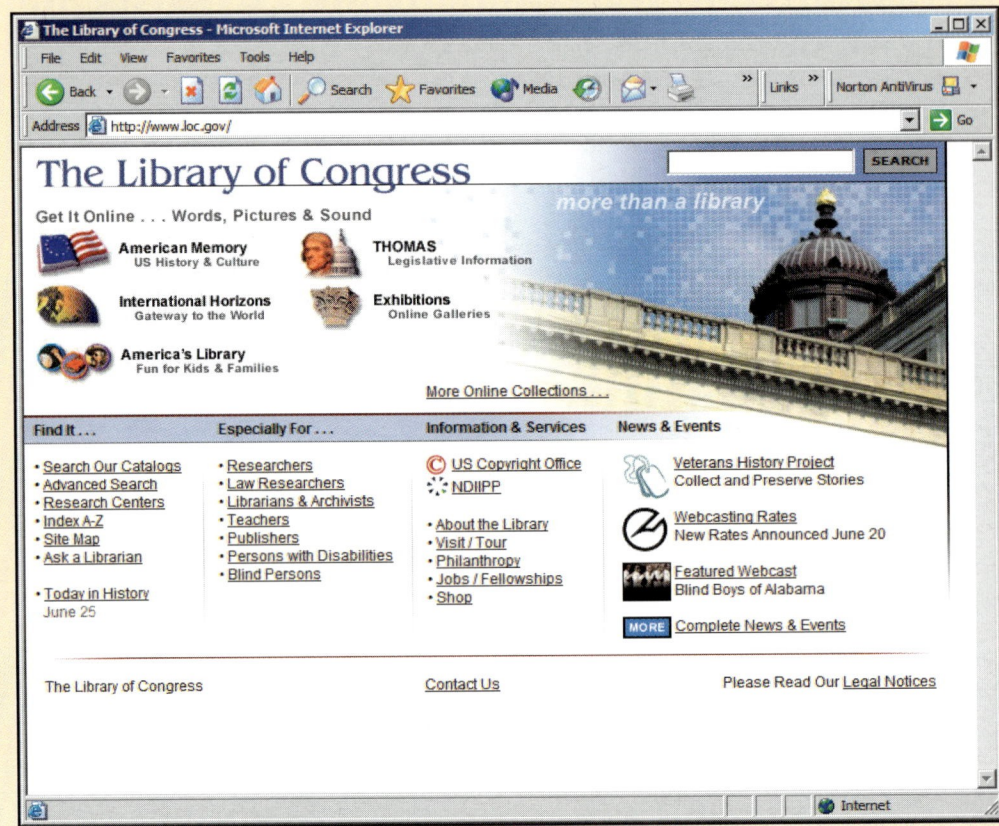

In this assignment, you continue to work on the group Web site that you started in Unit A. Depending on the size of your group, you can assign individual elements of the project to group members, or work collectively to create the finished product. There will be no data files supplied. You are building this Web site from unit to unit, so you must do each Group Project assignment in each unit to complete your Web site.

You will continue building your Web site by designing and completing a page that contains a list, headings, body text, graphics, and a background. During this process, you will develop a style sheet and add several styles to it. You will insert appropriate graphics on your page and enhance them for maximum effect. You will also check for non-Web-safe colors and remove any that you find.

1. Consult your storyboard and brainstorm as a group to decide which page to create and develop for this unit.
2. As a team, plan the page content for the page and make a sketch of the layout. You might want to create your sketch on a large piece of paper taped to the wall. Your sketch should include at least one ordered or unordered list, appropriate headings, body text, several graphics, and a background. Your sketch should also show where the body text and headings should be placed on the page and what styles should be used for each type of text. You should plan on creating at least two styles.
3. Assign a team member the task of creating this page and adding the text content to it.
4. Assign a team member the task of creating a Cascading Style Sheet for the Web site and adding to it the styles you decided to use. Assign the same team member the task of applying the styles to the appropriate content.
5. Access the graphics you gathered in Unit A and assign a team member the task of placing the graphics on the page so that the page matches the sketch you created in Step 2. This team member should also add a background image and appropriate alternate text for each graphic.
6. Assign a team member the task of checking for and removing any non-Web-safe colors.
7. Assign a team member the task of identifying any files in the Assets panel that are currently not used in the Web site. Decide as a group which of these assets should be removed, then assign a team member to delete these files.
8. As a team, preview the new page in a browser, then check for page layout problems and broken links. Make any necessary fixes in Dreamweaver, then preview the page again in a browser. Repeat this process until the group is satisfied with the way the page looks in the browser.
9. Use Figure C-46 to check all the pages of your site.
10. Close the browser, save your changes to the page, then close the page.

FIGURE C-46
Group Project check list

```
                    Web Site Check List

1.    Does each page have a page title?
2.    Does the home page have a description and keywords?
3.    Does the home page contain contact information?
4.    Does every page in the Web site have consistent navigation links?
5.    Does the home page have a last updated statement that will
6.    automatically update when the page is saved?
7.    Do all paths for links and images work correctly?
8.    Do all images have alternate text?
9.    Are all colors Web-safe?
10.   Are there any unnecessary files you can delete from the assets folder?
11.   Is there a style sheet with at least two styles?
12.   Did you apply the styles to page content?
13.   Do all pages view well using at least two different browser settings?
```

WORKING WITH LINKS

1. Create external and internal links.

2. Create internal links to named anchors.

3. Insert Flash text.

4. Create, modify, and copy a navigation bar.

5. Manage Web site links.

UNIT D
WORKING WITH LINKS

Introduction

What makes Web sites so powerful are the links that connect one page to another within a Web site or to any page on the Web. Though you can add graphics, animations, movies, and other enhancements to a Web site to make it visually attractive, the links you include are often the most essential components of a Web site. Links that connect the pages within a Web site are always very important because they help viewers navigate between the pages of the site. However, if one of your goals is to keep viewers from leaving your Web site, you might want to avoid including links to other Web sites. For example, most e-commerce sites include only links to other pages in the site to discourage shoppers from leaving the site. In this unit you will create links to other pages in the TripSmart Web site and to other sites on the Web. You will also insert a navigation bar that contains graphics instead of text, and check the links in the TripSmart Web site to make sure they all work.

Understanding Internal and External Links

Web pages contain two types of links: internal links and external links. **Internal links** are links to Web pages in the same Web site, and **external links** are links to Web pages in other Web sites or to e-mail addresses. Both internal and external links have two important parts that work together. The first part of a link is the element that viewers see and click on a Web page, for example, text, a graphic, or a button. The second part of a link is the **path**, or the name and location of the Web page or file that will open when the element is clicked. Setting and maintaining the correct paths for all your links is essential to avoid having broken links in your site.

Tools You'll Use

Named Anchor button

Flash text button

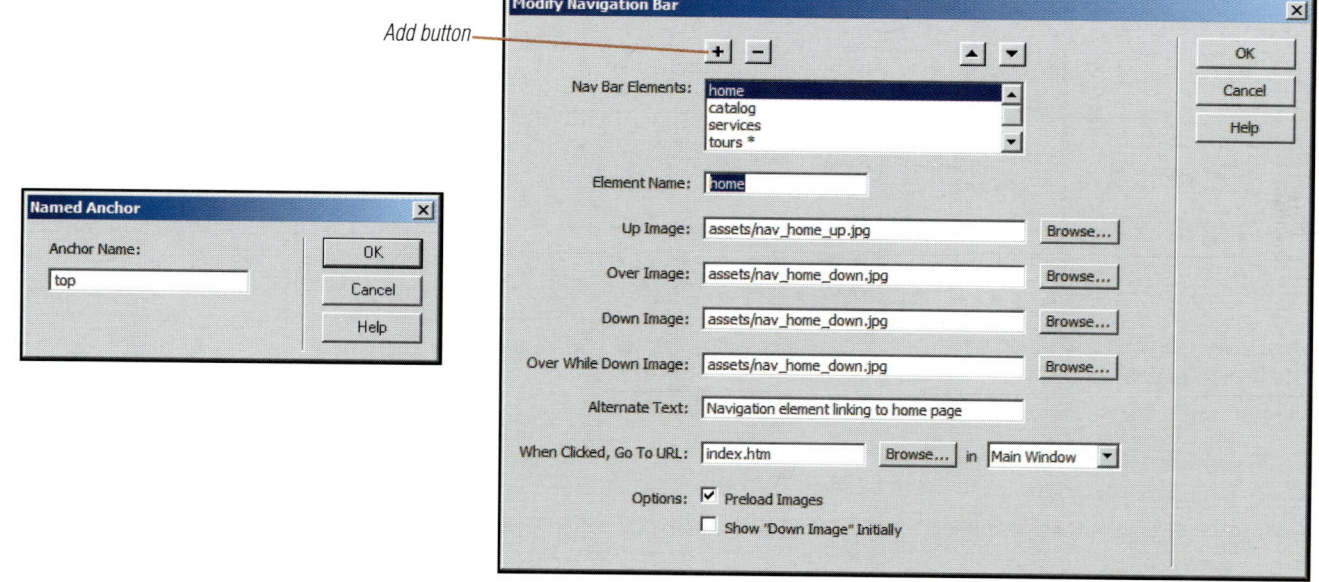

Add button

CREATE EXTERNAL AND INTERNAL LINKS

What You'll Do

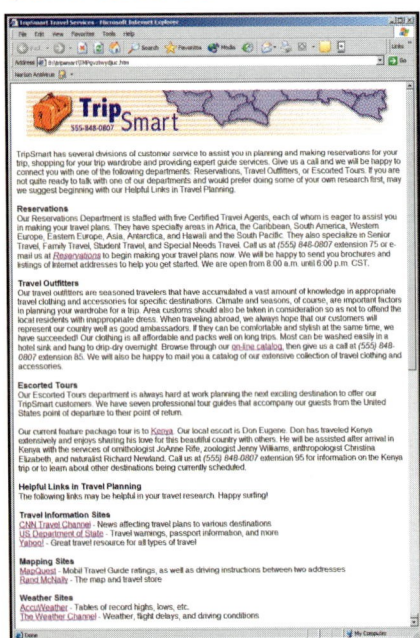

 In this lesson, you will create external links on the TripSmart services page that link to several Web sites related to travel. You will also create internal links to other pages within the TripSmart Web site.

Creating External Links

A good Web page usually includes a variety of external links to other related Web sites so that viewers can get more information on a particular topic. To create an external link, you first select the text or object that you want to serve as a link, then you type the absolute path to the destination Web page in the Links text box in the Property inspector. An **absolute path** is a path used for external links that includes the complete address for the destination page, including the protocol (such as http://) and the complete URL (Uniform Resource Locator), or address, of the destination page. When necessary, the Web page filename and folder hierarchy are also part of an absolute path. Figure D-1 shows an example of an absolute path showing the protocol, URL, and filename. After you enter external links on a Web page, you can view them in the site map.

FIGURE D-1

An example of an absolute path

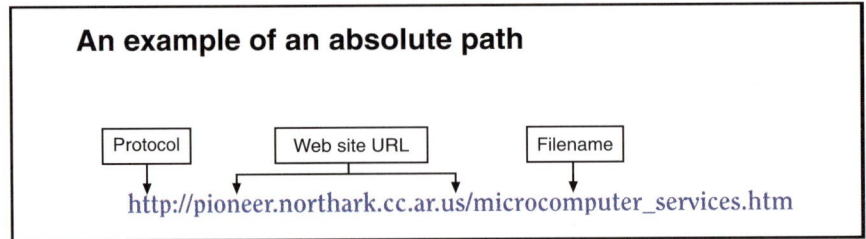

An example of an absolute path

| Protocol | Web site URL | Filename |

http://pioneer.northark.cc.ar.us/microcomputer_services.htm

Creating Internal Links

Each page in a Web site usually focuses on an individual category or topic. You should make sure that the home page provides links to each page in the site, and that all pages in the site contain numerous internal links so that viewers can move easily from page to page. To create an internal link, you first select the text element or graphic object that you want to make a link, then you use the Browse for File icon next to the Link text box in the Property inspector to specify the relative path to the destination page. A **relative path** is a type of path used to reference Web pages and graphic files within the same Web site. Relative paths include the filename and folder location of a file. Figure D-2 shows an example of a relative path. Table D-1 describes absolute paths and relative paths. Relative paths can either be site root relative or document relative.

You should take great care in managing your internal links to make sure they work correctly and are timely and relevant to the page content. You should design the navigation structure of your Web site so that viewers are never more than three or four clicks away from the page they are seeking.

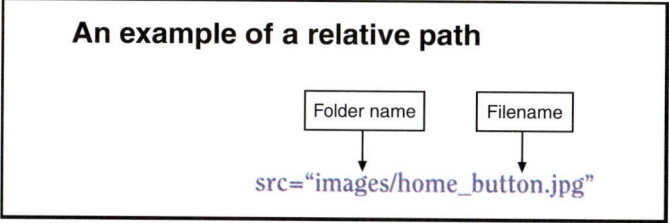

TABLE D-1: Description of absolute and relative paths

type of path	description	examples
Absolute path	Used for external links and specifies protocol, URL, and filename of destination page	http://www.yahoo.com/recreation
Relative path	Used for internal links and specifies location of file relative to the current page	services.htm or assets/tripsmart.gif
Root-relative path	Used for internal links when publishing to a server that contains many Web sites or where the Web site is so large it requires more than one server	/tripsmart/services.htm
Document-relative path	Used in most cases for internal links and specifies the location of file relative to current page	services.htm or assets/tripsmart.gif

Create an external link

1. Open the TripSmart Web site that you completed in Unit C, open dwd_1.htm from the unit_d folder where your data files are stored, then save it as **services.htm** to the tripsmart root folder, overwriting the existing services page.

2. Set the path for the TripSmart banner to the assets folder of the Web site.

3. Scroll down, then select CNN Travel Channel under the heading Travel Information Sites.

4. Click in the Link text box in the Property inspector, type **http://www.cnn.com/travel**, press [Enter] (Win) or [return] (Mac), then compare your screen to Figure D-3.

5. Repeat Steps 3 and 4 to create links for the following Web sites listed on the services page:

   US Department of State:
   http://travel.state.gov

   Yahoo!: **http://www.yahoo.com/Recreation/Travel**

   MapQuest: **http://www.mapquest.com**

   Rand McNally: **http://www.randmcnally.com**

   AccuWeather: **http://www.accuweather.com**

   The Weather Channel:
   http://www.weather.com

6. Save your work, preview the page in your browser, test all the links to make sure they work, then close your browser.

   > TIP You must have an active Internet connection to test the links. If clicking a link does not open a page, make sure you typed the URL correctly in the Link text box.

You opened the TripSmart Web site, replaced the existing services page, then added seven external links to other travel Web sites on the page. You also tested each link in your browser.

FIGURE D-3

Creating an external link to the CNN Travel Channel Web site

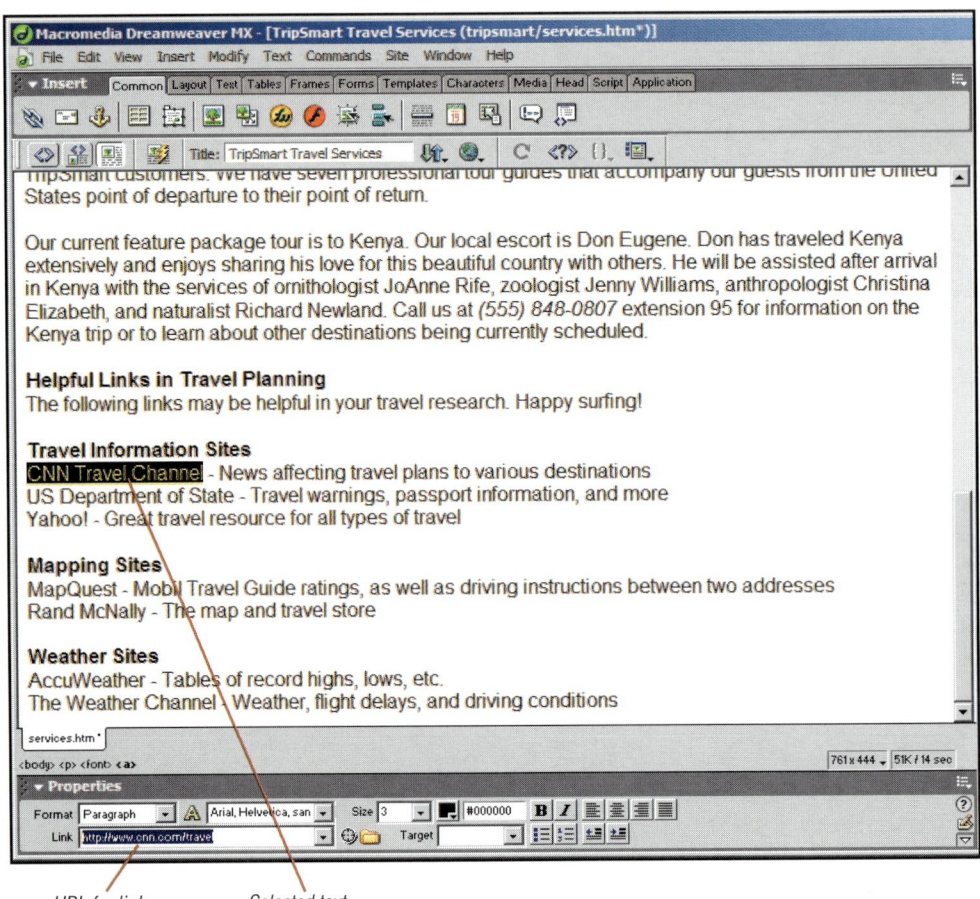

URL for link   Selected text

FIGURE D-4

Site map displaying external links on the services page

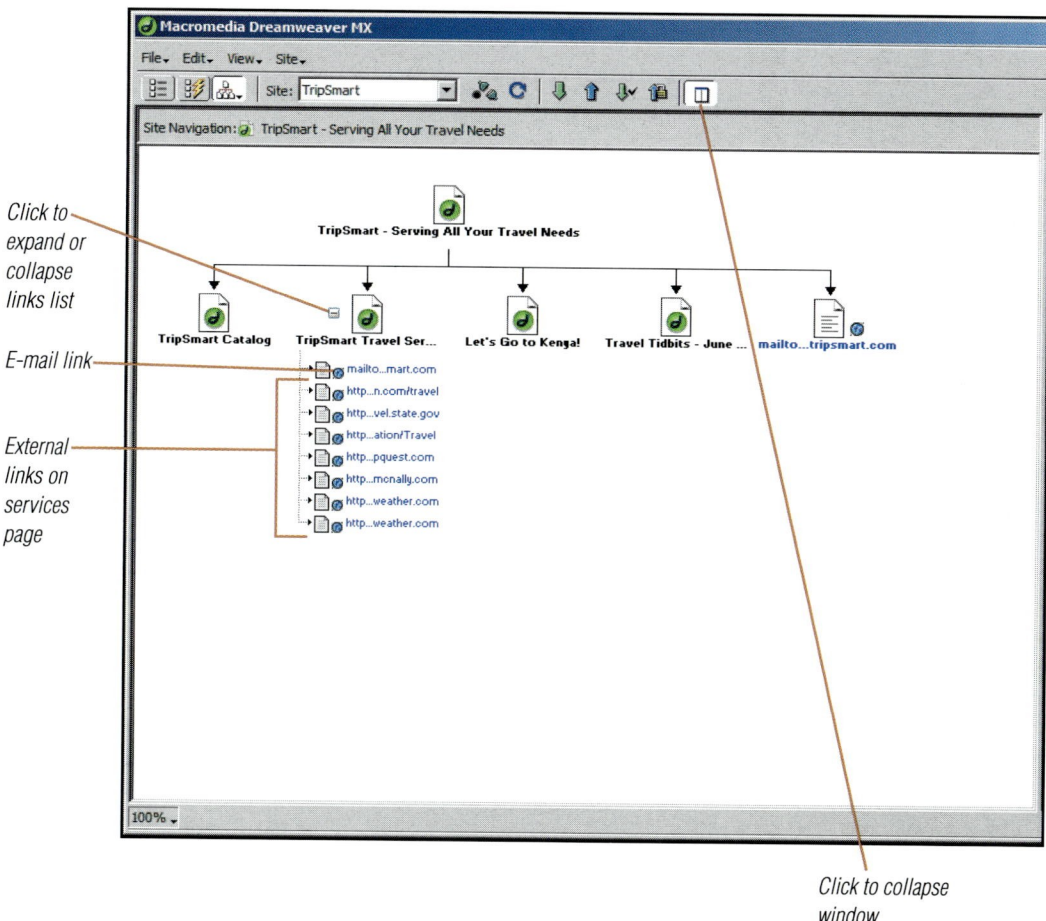

Click to expand or collapse links list

E-mail link

External links on services page

Click to collapse window

1. Mac users only: Click Site on the menu bar, point to Open Site, then click TripSmart to open the Site panel.

2. Click the View list arrow on the Site panel, click Map View (Win) or click the Site Map button (Mac), then click the Expand/Collapse button on the Site panel toolbar (Win).

   > **TIP** If you want to view or hide page titles in the site map, click View on the menu bar, then click Show Page Titles (Win) or click Site on the menu bar, point to Site Map View, then click Show Page Titles (Mac).

3. Click the plus sign to the left of the services page icon in the site map (if necessary) to view a list of the seven external links you created, as shown in Figure D-4.

   The TripSmart e-mail link also appears in the list.

4. Click the minus sign to the left of the services page icon in the site map to collapse the list of links.

5. Click the Expand/Collapse button on the toolbar, click the View list arrow on the Site panel, then click Local View (Win), or click the Site Files button on the Site panel to change to Local View (Mac).

You viewed the TripSmart site map and expanded the view of the services page to display the seven external links you added.

Create an internal link

1. Select on-line catalog in the paragraph under the Travel Outfitters heading.

2. Click the Browse for File icon in the Property inspector, then double-click catalog.htm in the Select File dialog box to set the relative path to the catalog page. 📁

   Notice that catalog.htm appears in the Link text box in the Property inspector, as shown in Figure D-5.

   > TIP Using the Browse for File icon to set the relative path for an internal link is easier than typing the filename in the Link text box.

3. Scroll down as necessary, then select Kenya in the second paragraph under the Escorted Tours heading.

4. Click the Browse for File icon next to the Links text box in the Property inspector, then double-click tours.htm in the Select File dialog box to specify the relative path to the tours page. 📁

   The word Kenya is now a link to the tours page.

5. Save your work, preview the page in your browser to verify that the internal links work correctly, then close your browser.

You created two internal links on the services page, and then tested the links in your browser.

FIGURE D-5

Creating an internal link on the services page

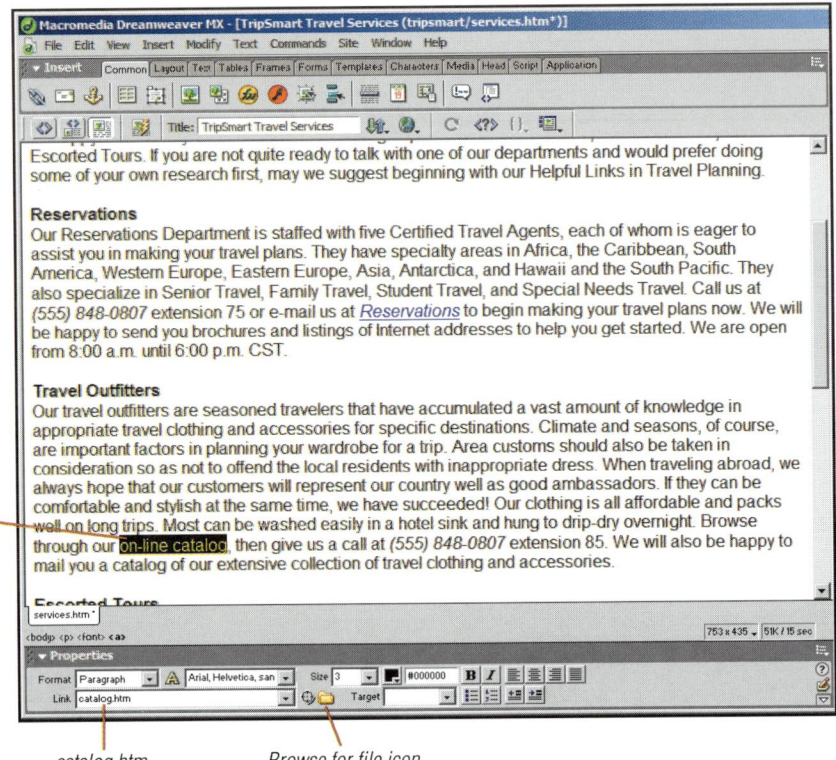

Selected text to be used for link

catalog.htm   Browse for file icon

Typing URLs

Typing URLs in the Link text box in the Property inspector can be very tedious. When you need to type a long and complex URL, it is easy to make mistakes and create a broken link. You can avoid such mistakes by copying and pasting the URL from the Address text box (Internet Explorer) or Location text box (Netscape Navigator and Communicator) to the Link text box in the Property inspector. Copying and pasting a URL ensures that the URL is entered correctly.

FIGURE D-6

Site map displaying external and internal links on the services page

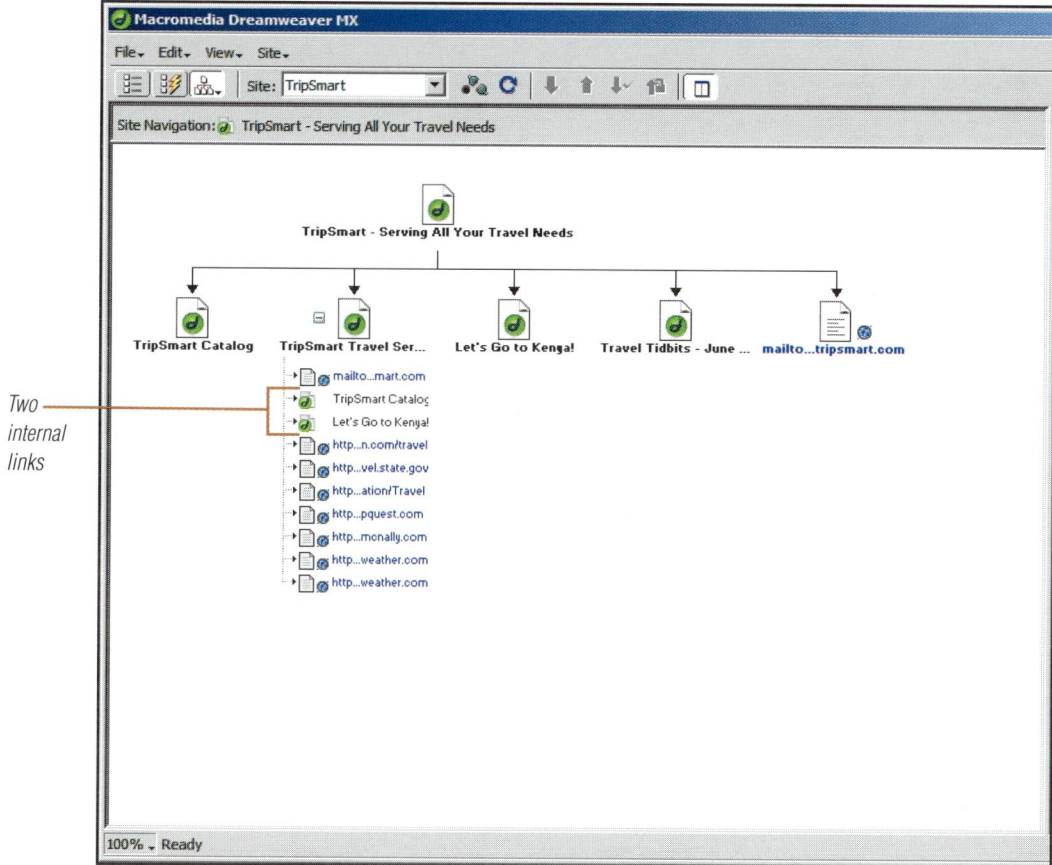

Two internal links

1. Click the View list arrow on the Site panel, click Map View, then click the Expand/Collapse button (Win) or click Site on the menu bar, point to Open Site, click TripSmart to open the Site panel, then click the Site Map button (Mac). ▣

2. Click the plus sign to the left of the services page icon.

   A list of 10 links appears below the services page icon as shown in Figure D-6. One is an e-mail link, seven are external links, and two are internal links.

   > TIP If your links do not display correctly, re-create the site cache. To re-create the site cache, click Site on the Site panel menu bar, then click Recreate Site Cache.

3. Click the Expand/Collapse button, click the View list arrow on the Site panel, then click Local View (Win), or click the Site Files button on the Site panel to change to Local view. ▣

You viewed the links on the services page in the site map.

CREATE INTERNAL LINKS
TO NAMED ANCHORS

What You'll Do

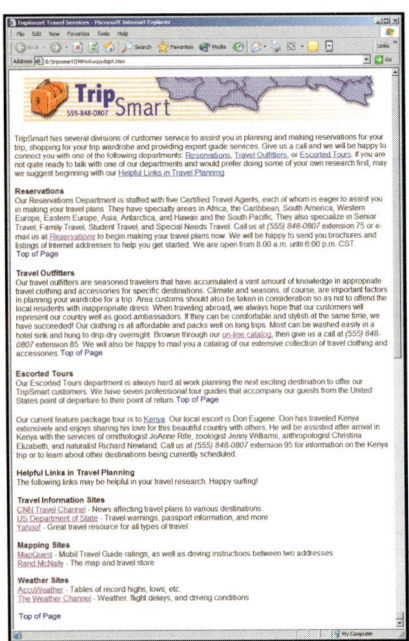

In this lesson, you will insert five named anchors on the services page: one for the top of the page and four for each heading. You will then create internal links to each named anchor.

Inserting Named Anchors

Some Web pages have so much content that viewers must scroll repeatedly to get to the bottom of the page and then back up to the top of the page. To make it easier for viewers to navigate to specific areas of a page without scrolling, you can use a combination of internal links and named anchors. A **named anchor** is a specific location on a Web page that has a descriptive name. Named anchors act as targets for internal links and make it easy for viewers to jump to a particular place on the same page quickly. A **target** is the location on a Web page that a browser displays when an internal link is clicked. For example, you can insert a named anchor called "top" at the top of a Web page, then create a link to

it at the bottom of the page. You can also insert named anchors in strategic places on a Web page, such as at the beginning of paragraph headings.

You insert a named anchor using the Insert Named Anchor button on the Common tab of the Insert bar, as shown in Figure D-7. You then enter the name of the Anchor in the Insert Named Anchor dialog box. You should choose short names that describe the named anchor location on the page. Named anchors are represented by yellow anchor icons on a Web page. You can show or hide named anchor icons by clicking View on the menu bar, pointing to Visual Aids, then clicking Invisible Elements.

Creating Internal Links to Named Anchors

Once you create a named anchor, you can create an internal link to it using one of two methods. You can select the text or graphic on the page that you want to make a link, then drag the Point to File icon from the Property inspector to the named anchor icon on the page. Or, you can select the text or graphic to which you want to make a link, then type the character # followed by the named anchor name (such as #top) in the Link text box in the Property inspector.

QUICKTIP

To avoid possible errors, you should create a named anchor before you create a link to it.

FIGURE D-7

Named Anchor button on the Insert bar

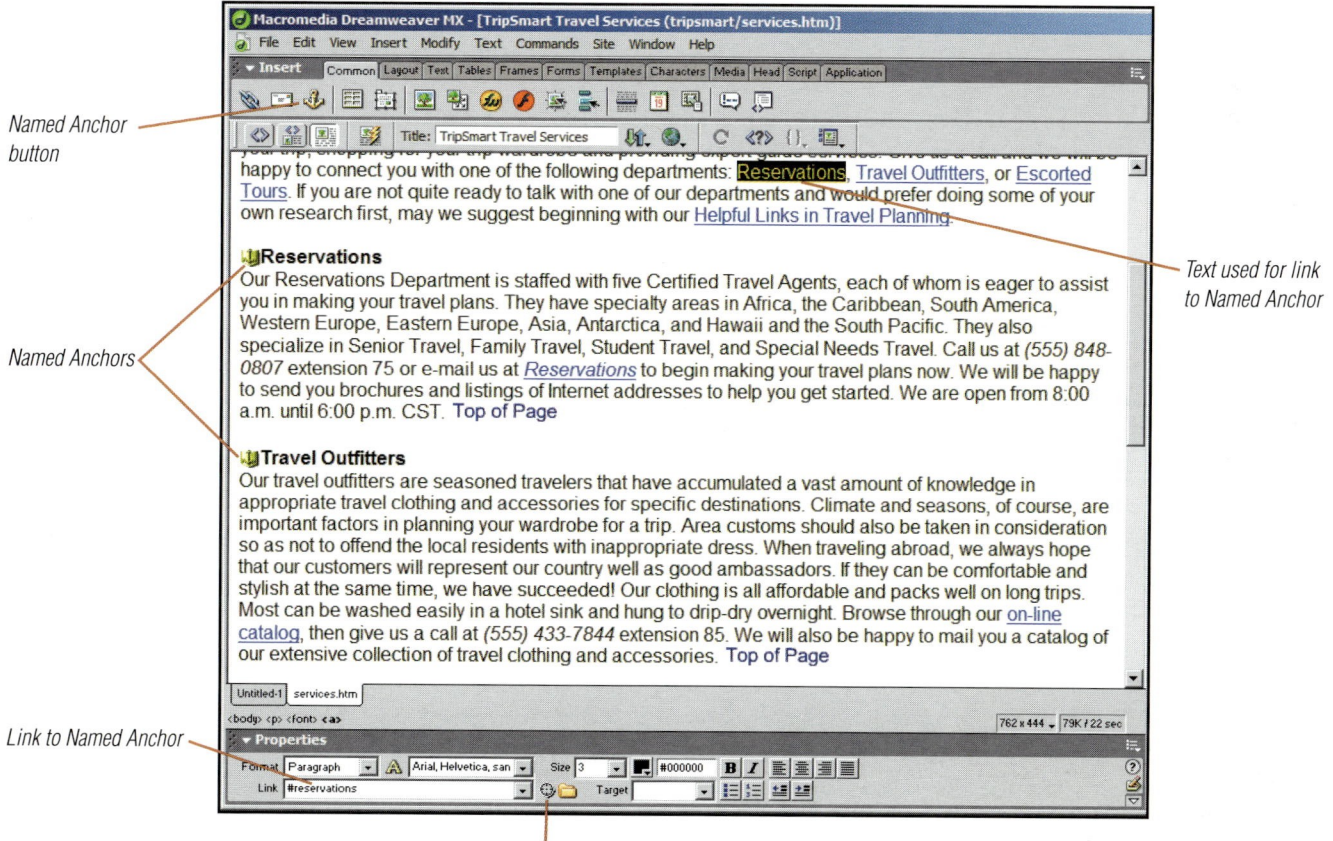

Named Anchor button

Named Anchors

Link to Named Anchor

Text used for link to Named Anchor

Point to File icon

Insert a named anchor

1. Click the TripSmart banner to select it, then press the Left Arrow key [←] to place the insertion point to the left of the banner.

2. Click View on the menu bar, point to Visual Aids, then verify that Invisible Elements is checked.

   TIP If there is no check mark next to Invisible Elements, then this feature is turned off. Click Invisible Elements to turn this feature on.

3. Click the Common tab on the Insert bar (if necessary).

4. Click the Named Anchor button on the Insert bar to open the Named Anchor dialog box, type **top** in the Anchor Name text box, compare your screen with Figure D-8, then click OK. ⚓

   An anchor icon now appears before the TripSmart banner.

   TIP Use lowercase letters, no spaces, and no special characters in named anchor names. You should also avoid using a number as the first character in a named anchor name.

   (continued)

FIGURE D-8
Named Anchor dialog box

Name of new anchor

Working with Links

FIGURE D-9

Named anchors on services page

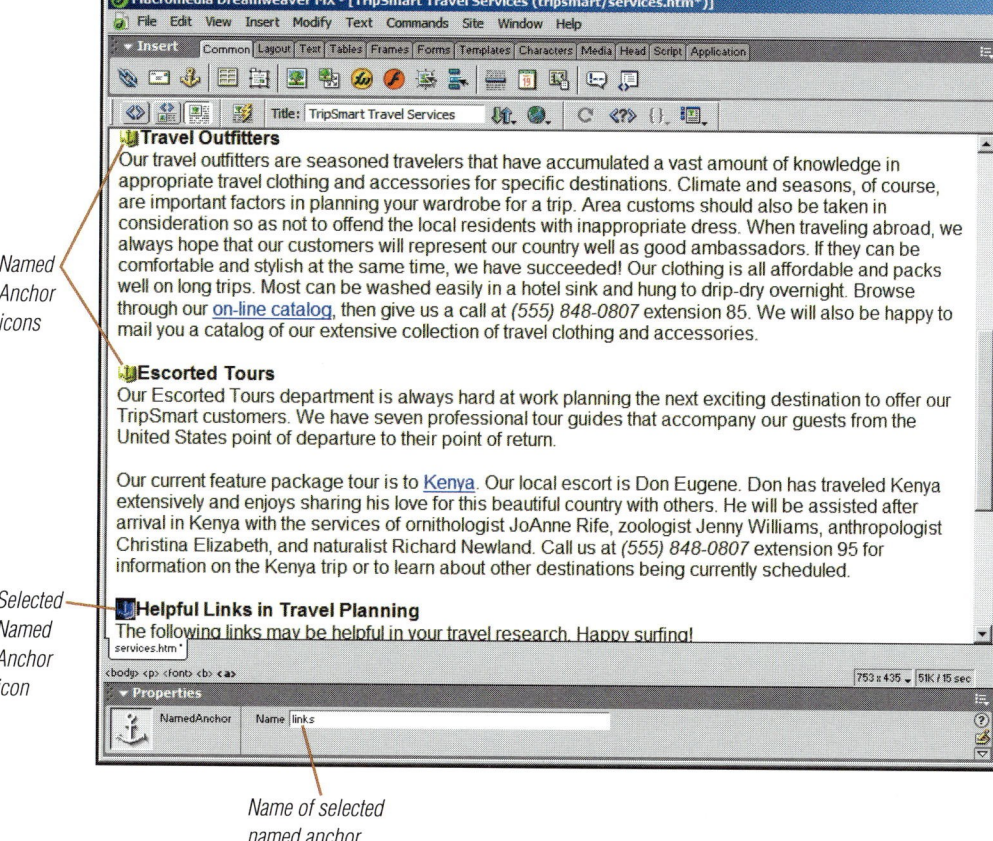

Named Anchor icons

Selected Named Anchor icon

Name of selected named anchor

5. Click to the left of the Reservations heading, then insert a named anchor called **reservations**.

6. Insert named anchors to the left of the Travel Outfitters, Escorted Tours, and Helpful Links in Travel Planning headings using the following names: **outfitters**, **tours**, and **links**.

   Your screen should resemble Figure D-9.

7. Save your work.

You created five named anchors on the services page; one at top of the page, and four that will help viewers quickly access the department headings on the page.

Create an internal link to a named anchor

1. Select the word Reservations in the second sentence of the first paragraph, then drag the Point to File icon from the Property inspector to the reservations named anchor as shown in Figure D-10. ☺

   The word Reservations is now linked to the reservations named anchor. When viewers click the word Reservations, the browser will display the Reservations paragraph at the top of the browser window.

   > TIP The name of a named anchor is always preceded by a pound (#) sign in the Link text box in the Property inspector.

2. Create internal links for Travel Outfitters, Escorted Tours, and Helpful Links in Travel Planning in the first paragraph by first selecting each of these phrases, then dragging the Point to File icon to the appropriate named anchor icon. ☺

   The phrases Travel Outfitters, Escorted Tours, and Helpful Links in Travel Planning are now links that connect to the Travel Outfitters, Escorted Tours, and Helpful Links in Travel Planning headings.

   > TIP Once you select the text you want to link, you might need to scroll down to view the named anchor on the screen. Once you see the named anchor on your screen, you can drag the Point to File icon on top of it.

   (continued)

FIGURE D-10

Dragging the Point to File icon to a named anchor

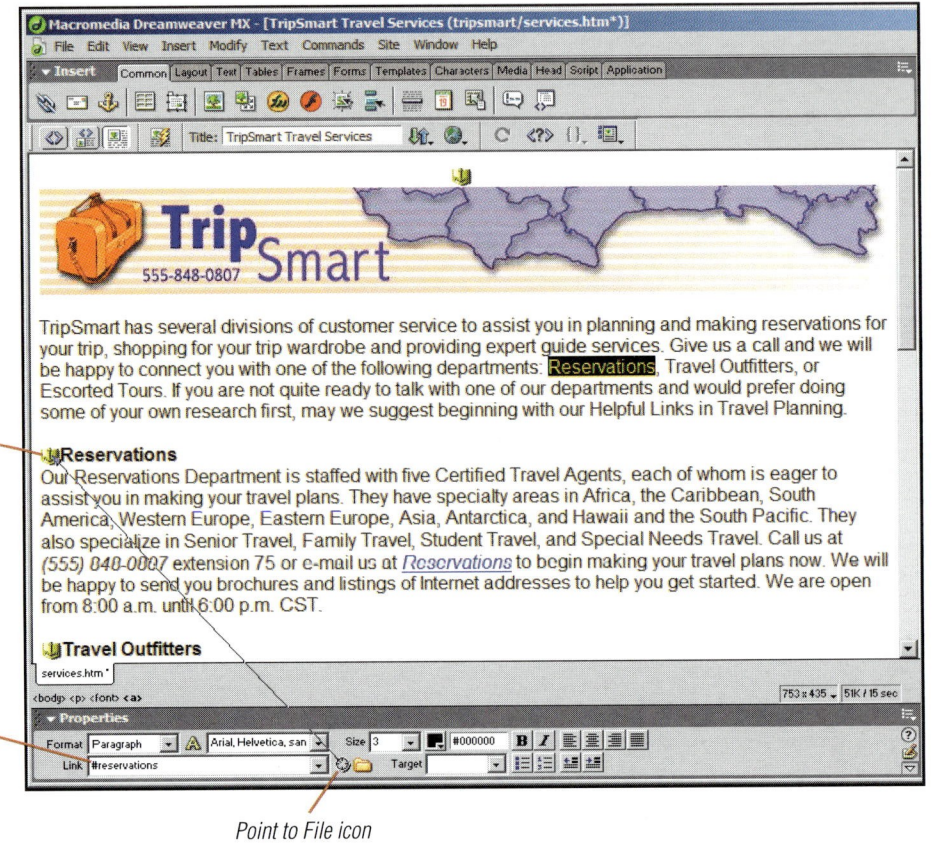

Point to File icon dragged to named anchor

Named anchor name preceded by #

Point to File icon

FIGURE D-11

Services page in Internet Explorer with three internal links to named anchors

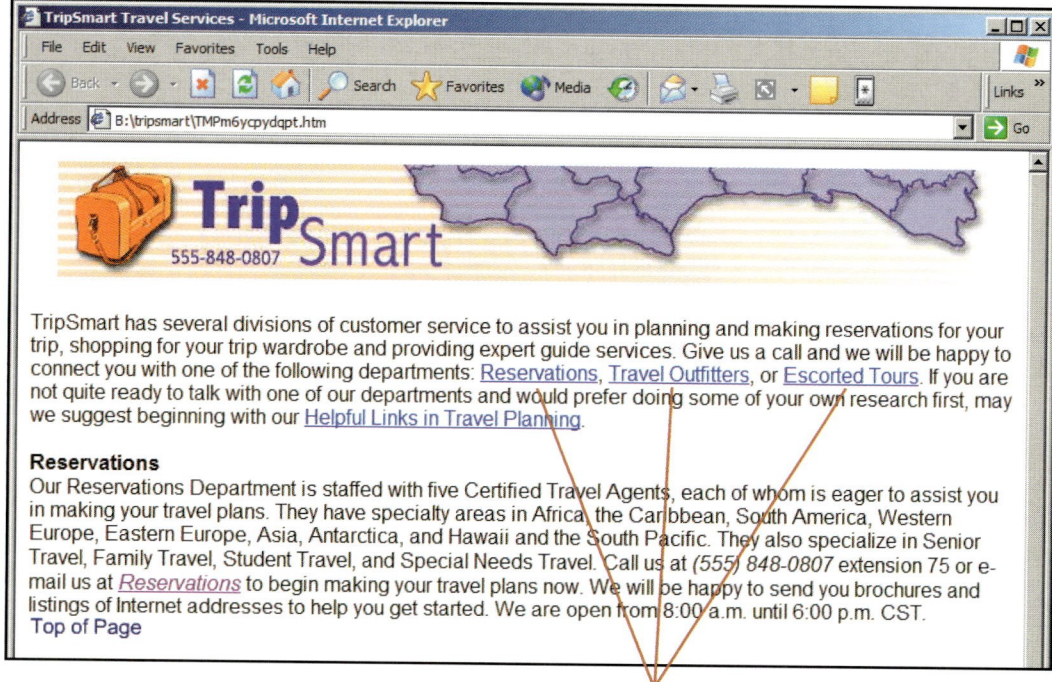

Internal links to named anchors

3. Save your work, preview the page in your browser as shown in Figure D-11, then test the links to each named anchor.

Notice that when you click the Escorted Tours and Helpful Links in Travel Planning in the browser, their associated named anchors appear in the middle of the page instead of at the top. This happens because the services page is not long enough to position these named anchors at the top of the page.

4. Close your browser.

You created internal links to the named anchors next to the department headings on the services page. You then previewed the page in your browser and tested each link.

INSERT FLASH TEXT

What You'll Do

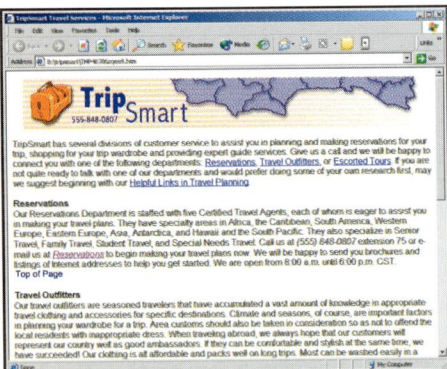

 In this lesson, you will use the Insert Flash Text dialog box to create a button that links to the top named anchor on the services page. You will copy this button to several locations on the services page, and then change the alignment of each button.

Understanding Flash Text

Flash is a Macromedia software program that you can use to create vector-based graphics and animations. **Vector-based graphics** are graphics that are based on mathematical formulas, as opposed to other types of graphic files such as JPG and BMP, which are based on pixels. Vector-based graphics have a smoother look and are smaller in file size than pixel-based graphics. Because they download quickly, vector-based graphics are ideal for Web sites. **Flash text** is a vector-based graphic file that contains text. You can insert Flash text to add visual interest to an otherwise dull Web page or to help deliver or reinforce a message. You can use Flash text to create internal or external links. Flash text files are saved with the .swf filename extension.

QUICKTIP

In order to view Flash animations, you must have the Flash player installed on your computer. The Flash player is free software that lets you view movies created with Macromedia software.

Inserting Flash Text on a Web Page

You can create Flash text in Dreamweaver without opening the Flash program. To insert Flash text on a Web page, you use the Flash Text button on the Media tab of the Insert bar, as shown in Figure D-12. Clicking this button opens the Insert Flash Text dialog box, which you use to specify the settings for the Flash text. You first need to specify the text you want to create as Flash text by typing it in the Text text box. You can then specify the font, size, and color of the Flash text, apply bold or italic styles to it, and align it using left, center, or right alignment options. You can also specify a **rollover color**, or the color in which the text will appear when the mouse pointer is placed on it. You also need to enter the path for the destination link in the Link text box. The destination link can be an internal link to another page in the site or to a named anchor on the same page, or an external link to a page on another Web site.

You then use the Target list in the Property inspector to specify how to open the destination page. The four options on the Target list arrow are described in Table D-2.

QUICKTIP

Notice that the _parent option in the table specifies to display the page in the parent frameset. A **frameset** is a group of Web pages displayed using more than one **frame** or window.

Before you close the Insert Flash Text dialog box, you need to type a descriptive name for your Flash text file in the Save As text box. Flash text files must be saved in the same folder as the page that contains the Flash text. For this reason, you should save your Flash text files to the root folder of the Web site.

FIGURE D-12
Insert bar Media tab

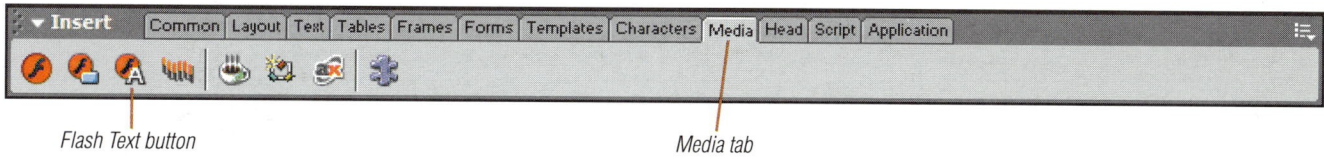

Flash Text button   *Media tab*

TABLE D-2: Options on the Target List

target	result
_blank	Displays the destination page in a separate browser window
_parent	Displays the destination page in the parent frameset (replaces the frameset)
_self	Displays the destination page in the same frame or window
_top	Displays the destination page in the whole browser window

Create Flash text

1. Click after the last word on the services page, then insert a hard return.

2. Click the Media tab on the Insert bar, then click the Flash Text button to open the Insert Flash Text dialog box, as shown in Figure D-13.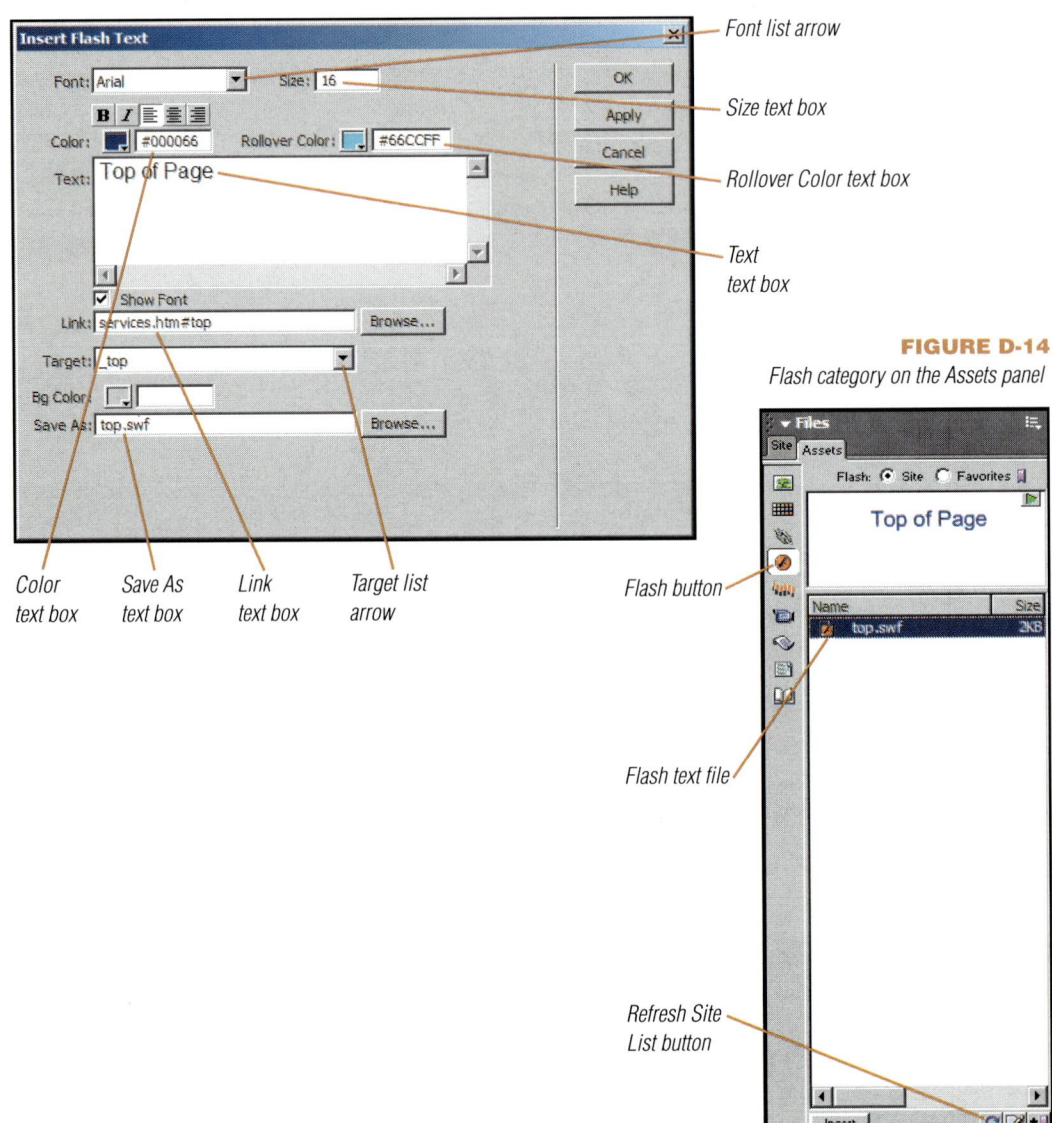

3. Type **Top of Page** in the Text text box, set the Font to Arial, set the Size to 16, set the Color to #000066, set the Rollover Color to #66CCFF, type services.htm#top in the Link text box, use the Target list arrow to set the Target at _top, type **top.swf** in the Save As text box, then click OK.

   The Top of Page Flash text now appears as a button at the bottom of the page. When a viewer clicks this button, the browser will display the top of the page.

4. Click the Assets tab in the Files panel group to open the Assets panel (Win), click the Flash button on the Assets panel (Win), or on Files panel group (Mac), as shown in Figure D-14, then click the Refresh Site List button.

5. Drag top.swf from the Assets panel to the end of the Reservations, Travel Outfitters, and Escorted Tours paragraphs to insert three more links to the top of the page.

6. Click the Site panel tab to open the Site panel (Win), then save your work.

(continued)

FIGURE D-13
Insert Flash Text dialog box

Font list arrow
Size text box
Rollover Color text box
Text text box

Color text box · Save As text box · Link text box · Target list arrow

FIGURE D-14
Flash category on the Assets panel

Flash button
Flash text file
Refresh Site List button

Working with Links

Flash text aligned to top

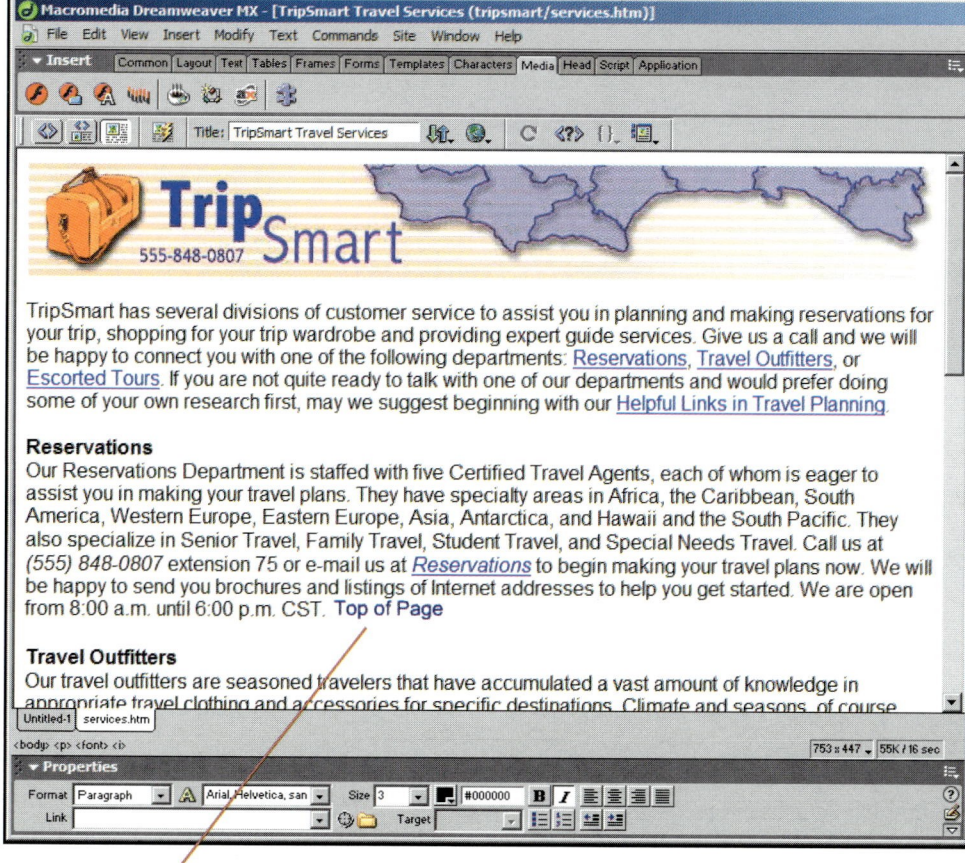

Flash text aligned with top of
paragraph text line

7. Preview the services page in your browser, test each Top of Page link, then close your browser.

> TIP If the top of the page is already displayed, the window will not move when you click the Flash text.

You used the Insert Flash Text dialog box to create a Top of Page button that links to the top named anchor on the services page. You also inserted the Top of Page button at the end of each department paragraph, so viewers will be able to go quickly to the top of the page without scrolling.

Change the alignment of Flash text

1. Click the Top of Page button at the end of the Reservations paragraph, expand the Property inspector, click the Align list arrow in the Property inspector, then click Top.

   The Top of Page button is now aligned with the top of the line of text, as shown in Figure D-15.

2. Apply the Top alignment setting to the Top of Page button located at the end of the Travel Outfitters and Escorted Tours paragraphs.

3. Collapse the Property inspector, turn off Invisible Elements, then save your work.

4. Preview the services page in your browser, test each Top of Page button, then close your browser.

You aligned the Flash text to improve its appearance on the page.

CREATE AND MODIFY A NAVIGATION BAR

What You'll Do

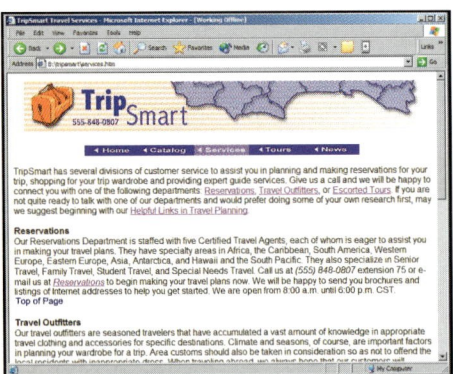

 In this lesson, you will create a navigation bar that can be used to link to each major page in the Web site. The navigation bar will have five elements: home, catalog, services, tours, and newsletter. You will also copy the new navigation bar to the index, newsletter, and tours pages. On each page you will modify the appropriate element state to reflect the current page.

Creating a Navigation Bar Using Images

To make your Web site more visually appealing, you can create a navigation bar with graphics rather than text. Any graphics you use in a navigation bar must be created in a graphics software program, such as Macromedia Fireworks or Adobe Illustrator. In order for a browser to display a navigation bar correctly, all graphic links in the navigation bar must be exactly the same size. You insert a navigation bar using the Navigation Bar button on the Insert bar or the Navigation Bar command on the Insert menu to open the Insert Navigation Bar dialog box. You use this dialog box to specify the appearance of each graphic link, called an **element**, in each of four possible states. A **state** is the condition of the element in relation to the mouse pointer. The four states are as follows: **Up Image** (the state when the mouse pointer is not on top of the element), **Over Image** (the state when the mouse pointer is positioned on top of

the element), **Down Image** (the state when you click the element), and **Over While Down Image** (the state when you click the element and continue pressing and holding the left mouse button). You can create a rollover effect by using different colors or images to represent each element state. You can add many special effects to navigation bars or to links on a Web page. For instance, the Web site shown in Figure D-16 contains a navigation bar that uses rollovers and also contains images that link to featured items in the Web site.

QUICKTIP

You can place only one navigation bar on a Web page using the Insert Navigation Bar dialog box.

Copying and Modifying a Navigation Bar

After you create a navigation bar, you can copy and paste it to the other main pages in your site to save time. Make sure you place the navigation bar in the same position on each page. This practice ensures that the navigation bar will look the same on each page, making it much easier for viewers to navigate to all the pages in a Web site.

You can then use the Modify Navigation Bar dialog box to customize the appearance of the copied navigation bar on each page. For example, you can change the appearance of the services navigation bar element on the services page so that it appears in a different color. Highlighting the navigation element for the current page provides a visual reminder so that viewers can quickly tell which page they are viewing. This process ensures that the navigation bar will look consistent across all pages, but will be customized for each page.

FIGURE D-16
Universal Studios Web site

Navigation bar with rollovers

Images serving as links

Create a navigation bar using images

1. Position the insertion point to the right of the TripSmart banner on the services page, then press [Enter] (Win) or [return] (Mac).

   The insertion point is now positioned between the TripSmart banner and the first paragraph of text.

2. Click the Common tab on the Insert bar, then click the Navigation Bar button on the Insert bar to open the Insert Navigation Bar dialog box.

3. Type **home** in the Element Name text box, click the Insert list arrow at the bottom of the dialog box, then click Horizontally (if necessary), to specify that the navigation bar be placed horizontally on the page.

4. Click the Browse button next to the Up Image text box, navigate to the drive and folder where your data files are stored, double-click the unit_d folder, double-click the assets folder, then double-click nav_home_up.jpg.

   The path to the file nav_home_up.jpg appears in the Up Image text box, as shown in Figure D-17.

5. Use the Browse button next to the Over Image text box to specify a path to the file nav_home_down.jpg located in the unit_d assets folder.

(continued)

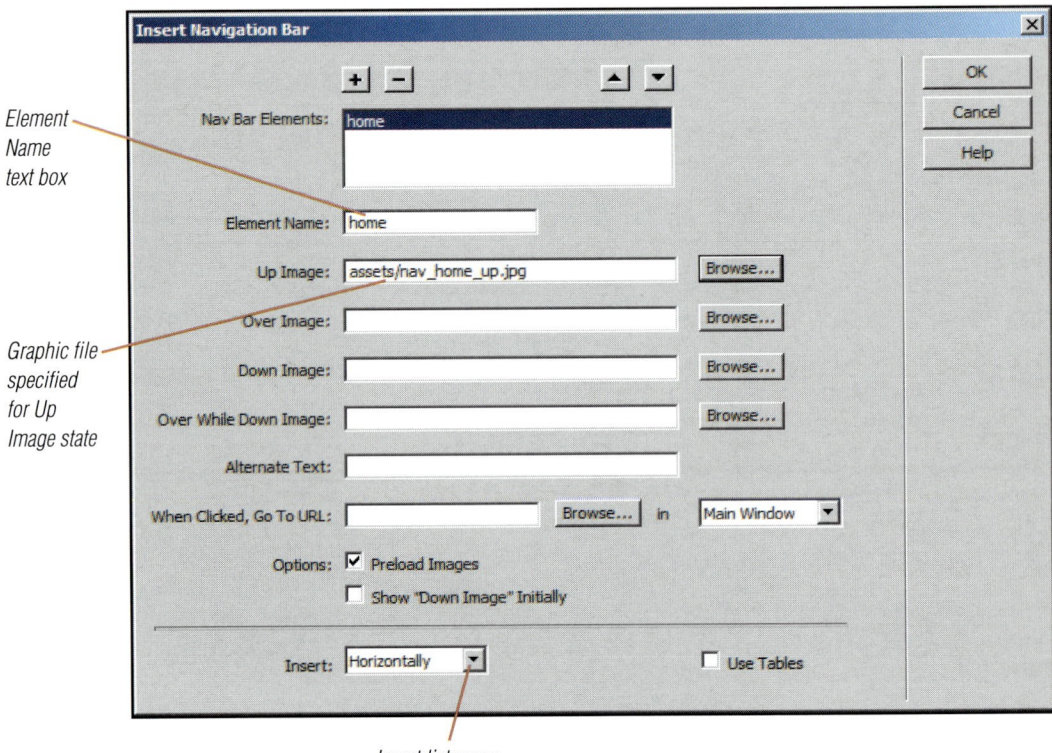

Element Name text box

Graphic file specified for Up Image state

Insert list arrow

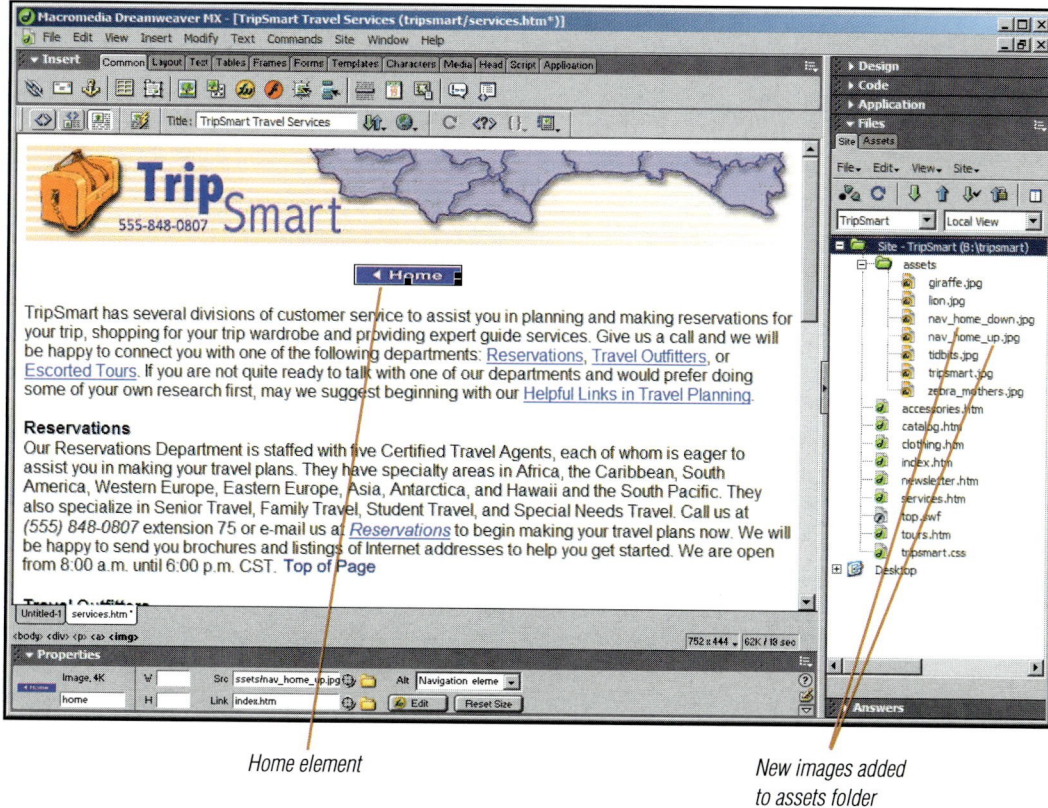

Home element

New images added
to assets folder

6. Use the Browse button next to the Down Image text box to specify a path to the file nav_home_down.jpg located in the unit_d assets folder, overwriting the existing file.

> TIP Instead of using the Browse button in Steps 6 and 7, you could copy the path of the nav_home_down.jpg file in the Over Image text box and paste it to the Down Image and Over While Down Image text boxes. You could also reference the nav_home_down.jpg file in the TripSmart assets folder once it is copied there in Step 5.

7. Use the Browse button next to the Over While Down Image text box to specify a path to the file nav_home_down.jpg located in the unit_d assets folder, overwriting the existing file.

   By specifying one graphic for the Up Image state, and another graphic for the Over Image, Down Image, and Over While Down Image states, you will create a rollover effect.

8. Type **Navigation bar element linking to home page** in the Alternate text box, click the Browse button next to the When Clicked, Go To URL text box, then double-click index.htm in the tripsmart root folder.

9. Click OK, refresh the Site panel to view the new images you added to the TripSmart assets folder, compare your screen to Figure D-18, then save your work.

You used the Insert Navigation Bar dialog box to create a navigation bar for the services page and added the home element to it. You used two images for each state, one for the up image state and one for the other three states.

Add elements to a navigation bar

1. Click Modify on the menu bar, then click Navigation Bar.

2. Click the Add button at the top of the Modify Navigation Bar dialog box, type **catalog** in the Element Name text box, then compare your screen with Figure D-19. ➕

   > TIP You use the Add button to add a new navigation element to the navigation bar, and the Delete button to delete a navigation element from the navigation bar. ➕ ➖

3. Click the Browse button next to the Up Image text box, navigate to the unit_d assets folder, click nav_catalog_up.jpg, then click OK (Win) or Choose (Mac).

   > TIP If a dialog box appears asking if you would like to copy the file to the root folder, click Yes, then click Save (Mac).

4. Use the Browse button next to the Over Image text box to specify a path to the file nav_catalog_down.jpg located in the unit_d assets folder.

5. Use the Browse button next to the Down Image text box to specify a path to the file nav_catalog_down.jpg located in the unit_d assets folder, overwriting the existing file.

6. Use the Browse button next to the Over While Down Image text box to specify a path to the file nav_catalog_down.jpg located in the unit_d assets folder, overwriting the existing file.

(continued)

FIGURE D-19

Adding navigation bar elements

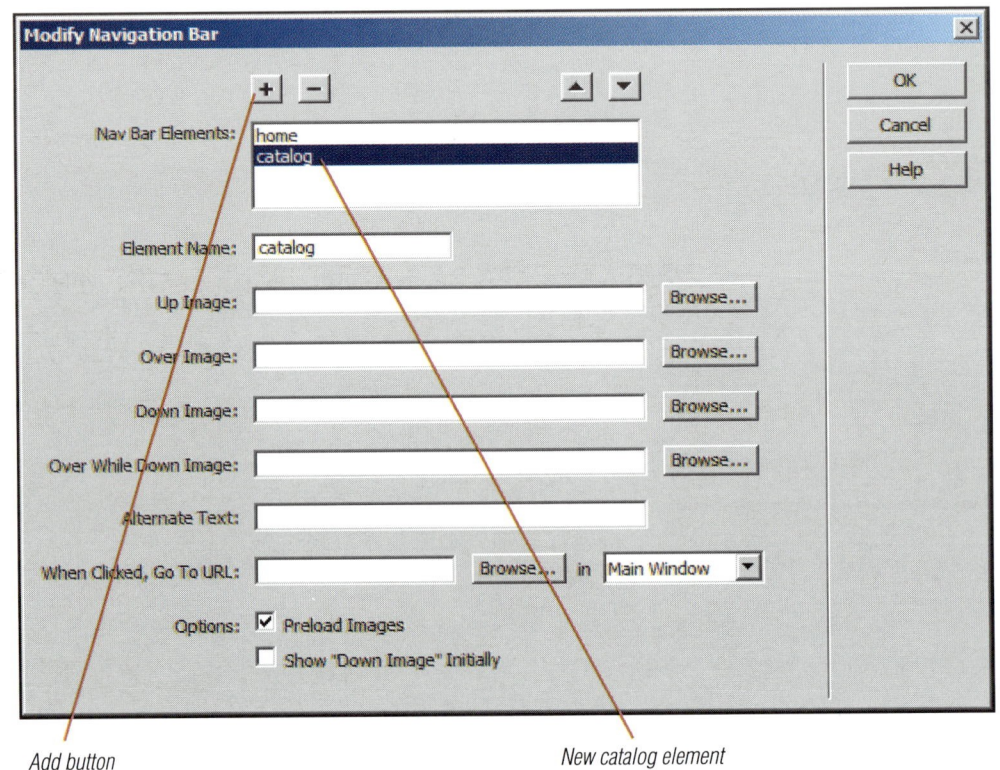

Add button   New catalog element

FIGURE D-20

The navigation bar with all elements added

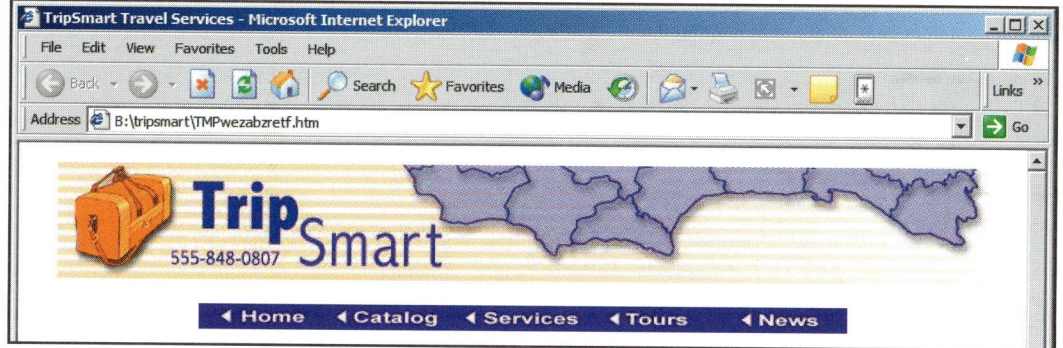

TABLE D-3: Settings to use in the Modify Navigation Bar dialog box for each new element

dialog box item	services element	tours element	newsletter element
Up Image file	nav_services_up.jpg	nav_tours_up.jpg	nav_news_up.jpg
Over Image file	nav_services_down.jpg	nav_tours_down.jpg	nav_news_down.jpg
Down Image file	nav_services_down.jpg	nav_tours_down.jpg	nav_news_down.jpg
Over While Down Image file	nav_services_down.jpg	nav_tours_down.jpg	nav_news_down.jpg
Alternate text	Navigation bar element linking to services page	Navigation bar element linking to tours page	Navigation bar element linking to newsletter page
When Clicked Go To URL	services.htm	tours.htm	newsletter.htm

7. Type **Navigation bar element linking to catalog page** in the Alternate text box, click the Browse button next to the When Clicked, Go To URL text box, then double-click catalog.htm.

8. Using the information provided in Table D-3, add three more navigation bar elements in the Modify Navigation Bar dialog box called **services**, **tours**, and **newsletter.**

   > TIP All files listed in the table are located in the assets folder of the unit_d folder where your data files are stored.

9. Click OK to close the Modify Navigation Bar dialog box, then compare your screen to Figure D-20.

10. Save your work, preview the page in your browser, check each link to verify that each element works correctly, then close your browser.

You completed the TripSmart navigation bar by adding four more elements to it, each of which contain links to the other four pages in the site. All images added to the navigation bar are now stored in the assets folder of the TripSmart Web site.

Copy and paste a navigation bar

1. Place the insertion point to the left of the navigation bar, hold down the [Shift] key, then click to the right of the navigation bar.

2. Click Edit on the menu bar, then click Copy.

3. Double-click newsletter.htm in the Site panel to open the newsletter page.

4. Click to the right of the TripSmart banner, then press [Enter] (Win) or [Return] (Mac).

5. Click Edit on the menu bar, click Paste, then compare your screen to Figure D-21.

6. Save your work.

You copied the navigation bar from the services page and pasted it on the newsletter page.

Customize a navigation bar

1. Click Modify on the menu bar, then click Navigation Bar to open the Modify Navigation Bar dialog box.

2. Click newsletter in the Nav Bar Elements text box, then click the Show "Down Image" Initially check box, as shown in Figure D-22.

   An asterisk appears next to newsletter in the Nav Bar Elements text box, indicating that this element will be displayed in the Down Image state initially. The light blue newsletter navigation element normally used for the Down Image state of the newsletter navigation bar element will remind viewers that they are on the tours page.

   (continued)

The navigation bar copied to the newsletter page.

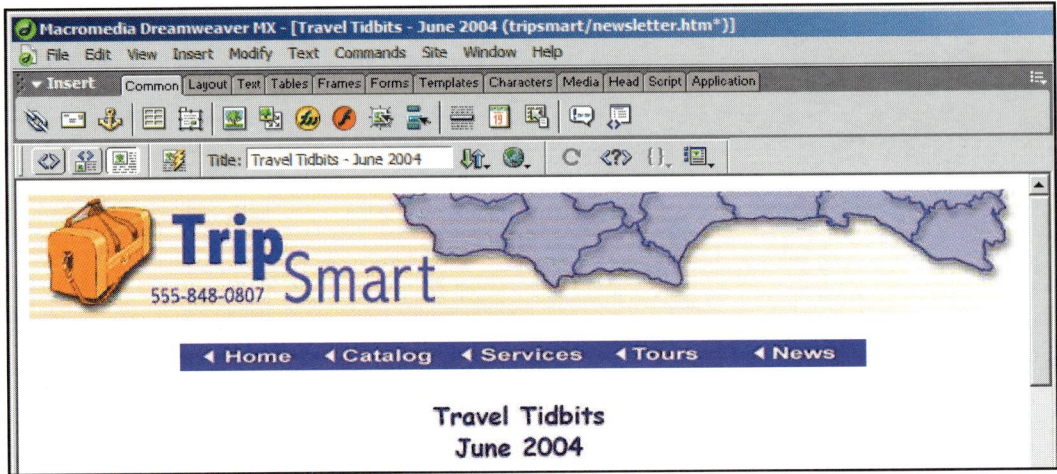

FIGURE D-22
Changing settings for the newsletter element

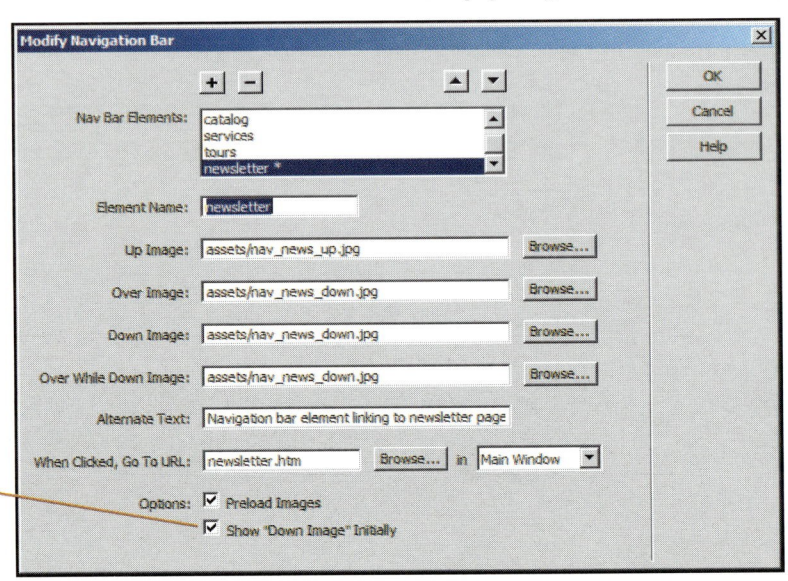

Show "Down Image" Initially Is selected

The Tours page with the modified navigation bar

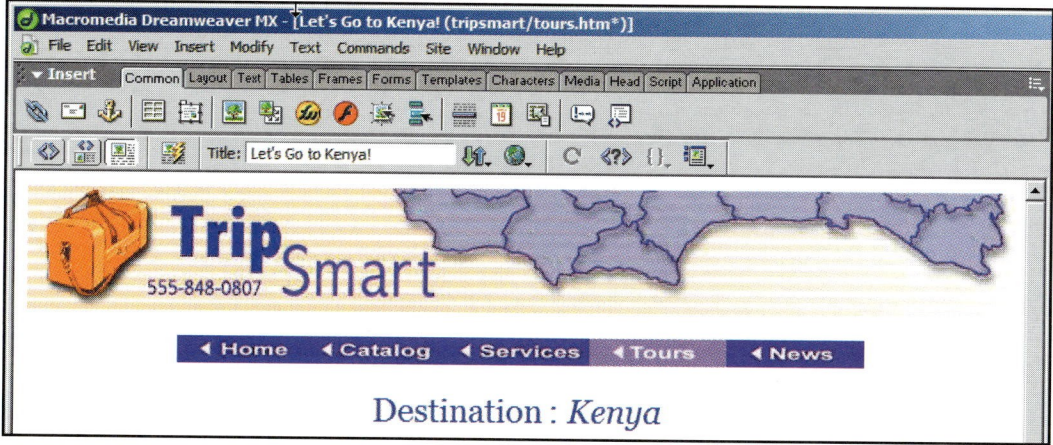

Creating an image map

Another way to create navigation links for Web pages is to create an image map. An **image map** is a graphic that has one or more hotspots placed on top of it. A **hotspot** is an area on a graphic that, when clicked, links to a different location on the page or to another Web page. For example, a map of the United States could have a hotspot placed on each state so that viewers could click a state to link to information about that state. To create a hotspot on an image, select the image on which you want to place the hotspot, then create the hotspot using one of the hotspot tools in the Property inspector.

3. Click OK to save the new settings and close the Modify Navigation Bar dialog box, then save and close the newsletter page.

4. Repeat Steps 1 through 3 to modify the navigation bar on the services page to show the Down Image initially for the services element, then save and close the services page.

5. Open the home page, paste the navigation bar under the TripSmart banner, then modify the navigation bar to show the Down Image Initially for the home element.

6. Delete the original navigation bar and the horizontal line on the home page, then save and close the home page.

7. Open the Tours page, paste the navigation bar under the TripSmart banner, then use the Modify Navigation Bar dialog box to specify that the Down Image be displayed initially for the tours element.

8. Delete the horizontal line on the page, then compare your screen to Figure D-23.

9. Save your work, preview the current page in your browser, test the navigation bar on the home, newsletter, services, and tours pages, then close your browser.

> TIP If you see some yellow HTML code on your page in Design View when you attempt to save your file, select both the beginning and ending tags, then press [Delete] to correct the error.

You modified the navigation bar on the newsletter page to show the newsletter element in the Down state initially. You then copied the navigation bar to two additional pages in the TripSmart Web site, modifying the navigation bar elements each time to show the down image state initially.

MANAGE WEB SITE LINKS

What You'll Do

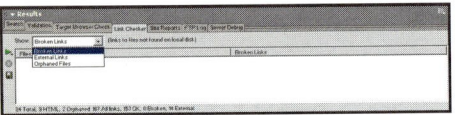

 In this lesson, you will use some of Dreamweaver's reporting features to check the TripSmart Web site for broken links and orphaned files.

Managing Web Site Links

Because the World Wide Web changes constantly, Web sites may be up one day and down the next. To avoid having broken links on your Web site, you need to check external links frequently. If a Web site changes server locations or goes down due to technical difficulties or a power failure, the links to it become broken. An external link can also become broken when an Internet connection fails to work properly. Broken links, like misspelled words on a Web page, indicate that a Web site is not being maintained diligently.

Checking links to make sure they work is an ongoing and crucial task you need to perform on a regular basis. You must check external links manually by reviewing your Web site in a browser and clicking each link to make sure it works correctly. The Check Links Sitewide feature is a helpful tool for managing your internal links. You can use it to check your entire Web site for the total number of links and the number of links that are OK, external, or broken, and then view the results of the link check in the Link Checker panel. The Link Checker panel also provides a list of all of the files used in a Web site, including those that are **orphaned files**, or files that are not linked to any pages in the Web site.

Considering navigation design issues

As you work on the navigation structure for a Web site, you should try to limit the number of links on each page to no more than is necessary. Too many links may confuse visitors to your Web site. You should also design links so that viewers can reach the information they want within three or four clicks. If finding information takes more than three or four clicks, the viewer may become discouraged or lost in the site. It's a good idea to provide visual clues on each page to let viewers know where they are, much like a "You are here" marker on a store directory at the mall.

FIGURE D-24

Link Checker panel displaying external links

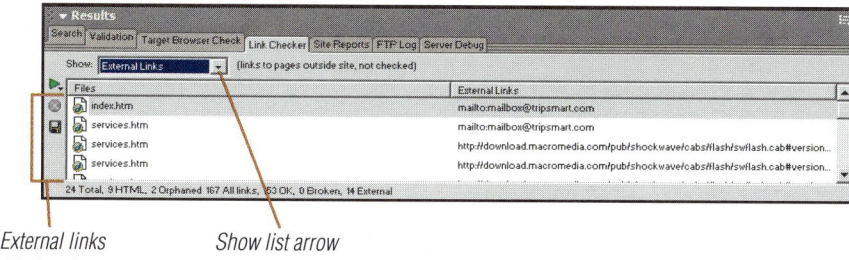

External links displayed

Show list arrow

Show list arrow

Orphaned files

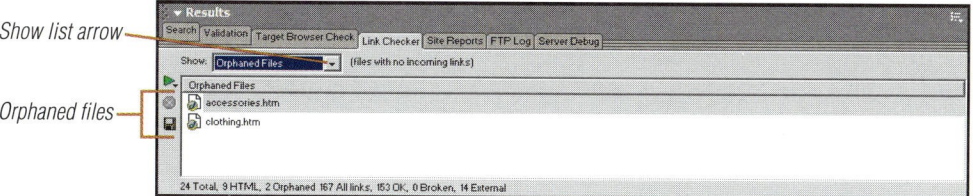

FIGURE D-26

Assets panel displaying links

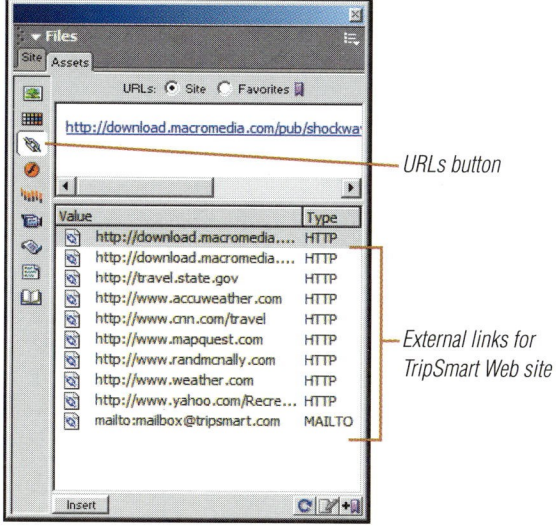

URLs button

External links for TripSmart Web site

---

1. Click Site on the Site panel menu bar, then click Check Links Sitewide (Win), or click Site on the menu bar, then click Check Links Sitewide (Mac).

   The Results panel group opens with the Link Checker panel displayed. By default the Link Checker panel initially displays any broken internal links found in the Web site. The TripSmart Web site has no broken links.

2. Click the Show list arrow in the Link Checker panel, click External Links, then compare your screen to Figure D-24.

   Some external links are listed more than once because the Link Checker displays each instance of an external link.

3. Click the Show list arrow, then click Orphaned Files to view the orphaned files in the Link Checker panel, as shown in Figure D-25.

4. Click the Options button in the Results panel group title bar, then click Close Panel Group.

5. Open the Assets panel (if necessary), then click the URLs button in the Assets panel to display the list of links in the Web site.

   The Assets panel displays the external links used in the Web site. See Figure D-26.

6. Save your work, then close all open pages.

You used the Link Checker panel to check for broken links, external links, and orphaned files in the TripSmart Web site.

Create external and internal links.

1. Open the Blooms & Bulbs Web site. (If you did not create this Web site in Units A through C, contact your instructor for assistance.)
2. Open dwd_2.htm from the unit_d data files folder, then save it as **master_gardener.htm** in the Blooms & Bulbs Web site.
3. Verify that the banner path is set correctly to the assets folder in the Web site, and correct it if it is not.
4. Scroll to the bottom of the page, then link the National Gardening Association text to *http://www.garden.org.*
5. Link the Better Homes and Gardens Gardening Home Page text to *http://bhg.com/gardening.*
6. Link the Southern Living text to *http://www.southernliving.com.*
7. Save the file, then preview the page in your browser, verifying that each link works correctly.
8. Close your browser, then return to the master_gardener page in Dreamweaver.
9. Scroll to the paragraph about gardening issues, select the gardening tips text in the last sentence, then link the selected text to the tips.htm file in the blooms root folder.
10. Save the file, test the links in your browser, then close your browser.

Create internal links to named anchors.

1. Show Invisible Elements (if necessary).
2. Click the Common tab on the Insert bar (if necessary).
3. Insert a named anchor in front of the Grass heading named **grass**.
4. Insert a named anchor in front of the Trees heading named **trees**.
5. Insert a named anchor in front of the Plants heading named **plants**.
6. Insert a named anchor at the top of the page named **top**.
7. Use the Point to File icon in the Property Inspector to create a link from the word grass in the Gardening Issues paragraph to the grass named anchor.
8. Create a link from the word trees in the Gardening Issues paragraph to the trees named anchor.
9. Create a link from the word plants in the Gardening Issues paragraph to the plants named anchor.
10. Save your work, view the page in your browser, test all the links to make sure they work, then close your browser.

Insert Flash text.

1. Insert Flash text at the bottom of the page that will take you to the top of the page. Use the following settings: Type: Arial, Size: 16, Color: #006600, Rollover Color: #009933, Link: master_gardener.htm#top, Target: _top.
2. Save the Flash text file as **top.swf**.
3. Save the file, view the page in your browser, test the Flash text link, then close your browser.

Create, modify, and copy a navigation bar.

1. Using the Common tab of the Insert bar, insert a horizontal navigation bar at the top of the master_gardener page below the banner.
2. Type **home** as the first element name, then use the blooms_home_up.gif file for the Up Image state. This file is in the assets folder of the unit_d data files folder.
3. Specify the file blooms_home_down.gif file for the three remaining states. This file is in the assets folder of the unit_d data files folder.
4. Enter **Navigation element linking to the home page** as the alternate text, then set the index.htm file as the link for the home element.
5. Create a new element named **plants**, and use the blooms_plants_up.gif file for the Up Image state and the blooms_plants_down.gif file for the remaining three states. These files are located in the assets folder of the unit_d data files folder.
6. Enter **Navigation element linking to the plants page** as the alternate text, then set the plants.htm file as the link for the plants element.
7. Create a new element named **workshops**, and use the blooms_workshops_up.gif file for the Up Image state and the blooms_workshops_down.gif file for the remaining three states. These files are located in the assets folder of the unit_d data files folder.

8. Enter **Navigation element linking to the workshops page** as the alternate text, then set the workshops.htm file as the link for the workshops element.

9. Create a new element named **tips**, and use the blooms_tips_up.gif file for the Up Image state and the blooms_tips_down.gif file for the remaining three states. These files are in the assets folder of the unit_d data files folder.

10. Enter **Navigation element linking to the tips page** as the alternate text, then set the tips.htm file as the link for the tips element.

11. Create a new element named **ask**, then use the blooms_ask_up.gif file for the Up Image state and the blooms_ask_down.gif file for the remaining three states. These files are in the assets folder of the unit_d data files folder.

12. Enter the alternate text **Navigation element linking to the master gardener page**, then set the master_gardener.htm file as the link for the ask element.

13. Center the navigation bar (if necessary), then save the page and test the links in your browser.

14. Select and copy the navigation bar, then open the home page.

15. Delete the current navigation bar on the home page, then paste the new navigation bar in its place.

16. Modify the home element on the navigation bar to show the Down Image state initially.

17. Save the page, test the links in your browser, then close the browser and the page.

18. Modify the navigation bar on the master_gardener page so the Down Image is shown initially for the ask element, then save and close the master_gardener page.

19. Paste the navigation bar to the plants.htm page and the tips.htm page, making the necessary modifications so that the Down Image is shown initially for each element.

20. Save your work, preview all the pages in your browser, test all the links, then close your browser.

FIGURE D-27
Completed Skills Review

Manage Web site links.

1. Use the Link Checker panel to view broken links, external links, and orphaned files in the Blooms & Bulbs Web site.

2. If you see broken links or orphaned files, refresh the Site list in the Site panel to remove them. If this does not remove the broken links, re-create the site cache. If you still see broken links, check for typing errors in the Link text box for any broken links to correct them.

3. View the external links in the Assets panel.

4. Save your work, then close all open pages.

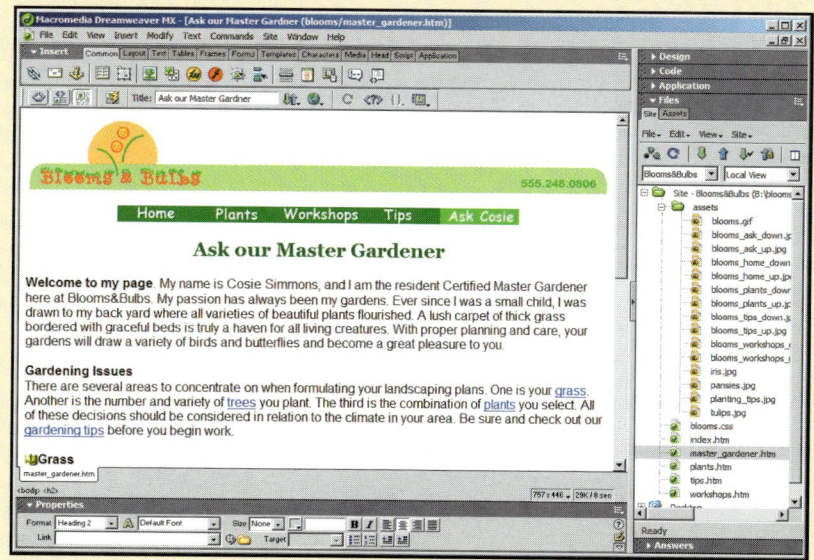

Use Figure D-28 as a guide to continue your work on the Rapids Transit Web site that you began in Project Builder 1 in Unit A. If you did not create this Web site in Unit A, contact your instructor for assistance. Mike Andrew, the owner, has asked you to create a new page for the Web site that lists helpful links for his customers. Also, because he no longer wants Equipment Rentals as an element in the navigation bar, he asked you to replace the existing navigation bar with a new one that contains the following elements: Home, Before You Go, Our Guides, and Country Store.

1. Open the Rapids Transit Web site. (If you did not create this Web site in Units A through C, contact your instructor for assistance.)
2. Open dwd_3.htm from the unit_d data files folder, then save it as **before.htm** in the Rapids Transit Web site root folder.
3. Save the buffalo_fall.gif file on the page in the assets folder of the Rapids Transit Web site, then set the path for the banner to the assets folder.
4. Create the following links:
   Buffalo National River in the Arkansas Ozarks: **http://www.ozarkmtns.com/buffalo**
   Map of the Buffalo National River: **http://www.ozarkmtns.com/buffalo/ buffmap.html**

Arkansas, the Natural State: **http://www.arkansas.com**
Buffalo River Floater's Guide: **http://www.ozarkmtns.com/buffalo/bfg.html**
5. Design a navigation bar using either text or graphics, then place it on each page of the Web site. If you decide to use graphics for the navigation bar, you will have to create your own graphic files using a graphics program. There are no data files for you to use. (*Hint*: if you create your own graphic files, be sure to create two graphic files for each element: one for the Up Image state and one for the Down Image state.) To design a navigation bar using text, you simply type the

text for each navigation bar element, format the text appropriately, and insert links to each text element as you did in Unit B. The navigation bar should contain the following elements: Home, Before You Go, Our Guides, and Country Store.

6. Save each page, then check for broken links and orphaned files. You should see one orphaned file, rentals.htm, which has no links to other pages yet. You will link this page to the country store page later.

7. Test all links in your browser, close your browser, then close all open pages.

FIGURE D-28

Completed Project Builder 1

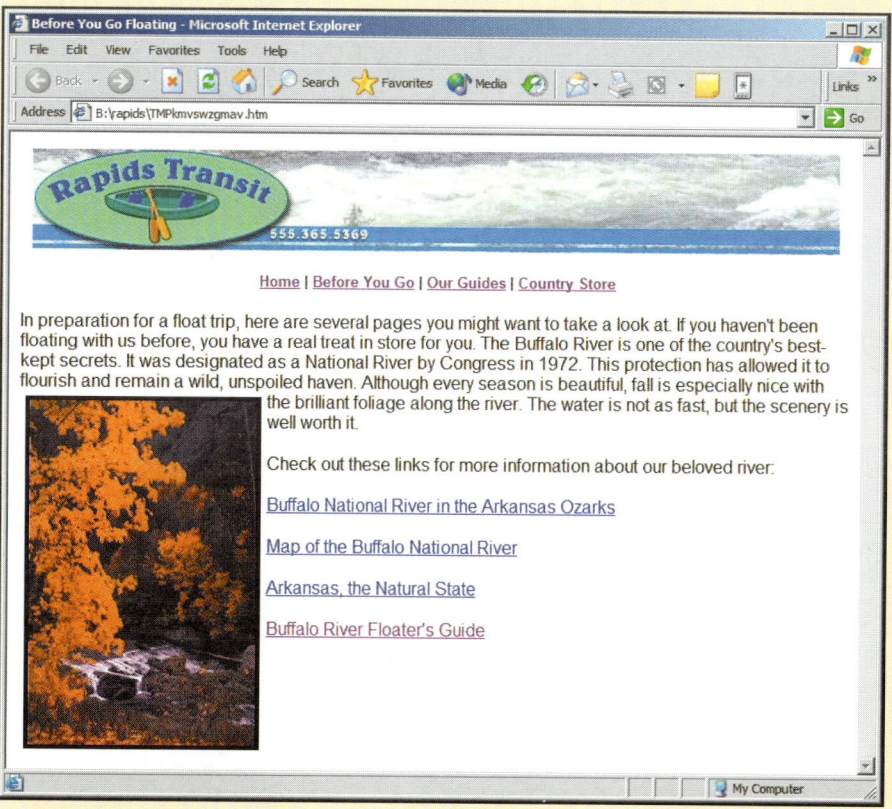

Use Figure D-29 as a guide to continue your work on the Jacob's Web site that you started in Project Builder 2 in Unit A. Chef Jacob has sent you a copy of this month's featured pre-theatre dinner menu to place on the Web site. He has also included some links to London theatre reviews. He has asked you to add this information to the Web site. He has also asked you to insert a new navigation bar on each page of the Web site to help viewers navigate through the site easily.

1. Open the Jacob's Web site. (If you did not create this Web site in Units A through C, contact your instructor for assistance.)

2. Open dwd_4.htm from the unit_d folder, then save it as **menus.htm** in the root folder of the Jacob's Web site, overwriting the existing file.

3. Change the path of the Jacob's banner so that it is set to the jacobs.jpg file in the assets folder of the Web site.

4. Select the text post-theatre dessert specials in the first paragraph, then link it to the after_theatre.htm page.

5. Select The London Theatre Guide - Online text, and link it to **http://www.londontheatre.co.uk/**.

6. Select the London Theatre Guide from the Society of London Theatre text, and link it to **http://www.officiallondontheatre.co.uk/**.

7. Select the London Theatre Tickets text, and link it to **http://www.londontheatrebookings.com/**.

8. Design a new navigation bar using either text or graphics, then place it at the top of the menus page. The navigation bar should contain the following elements: Home, Menus, Recipes, and Directions and Hours.

9. Copy the navigation bar, then paste it to the after_theatre.htm, index.htm, and directions.htm pages of the site. Delete the old navigation bar on any of the pages where it appears.

10. Insert a named anchor at the top of the menus page, then create Flash text at the bottom of the page to link to it.

11. Save all the pages, then check for broken links and orphaned files.

12. Preview all the pages in your browser, check to make sure the links work correctly, close your browser, then close all open pages.

FIGURE D-29
Completed Project Builder 2

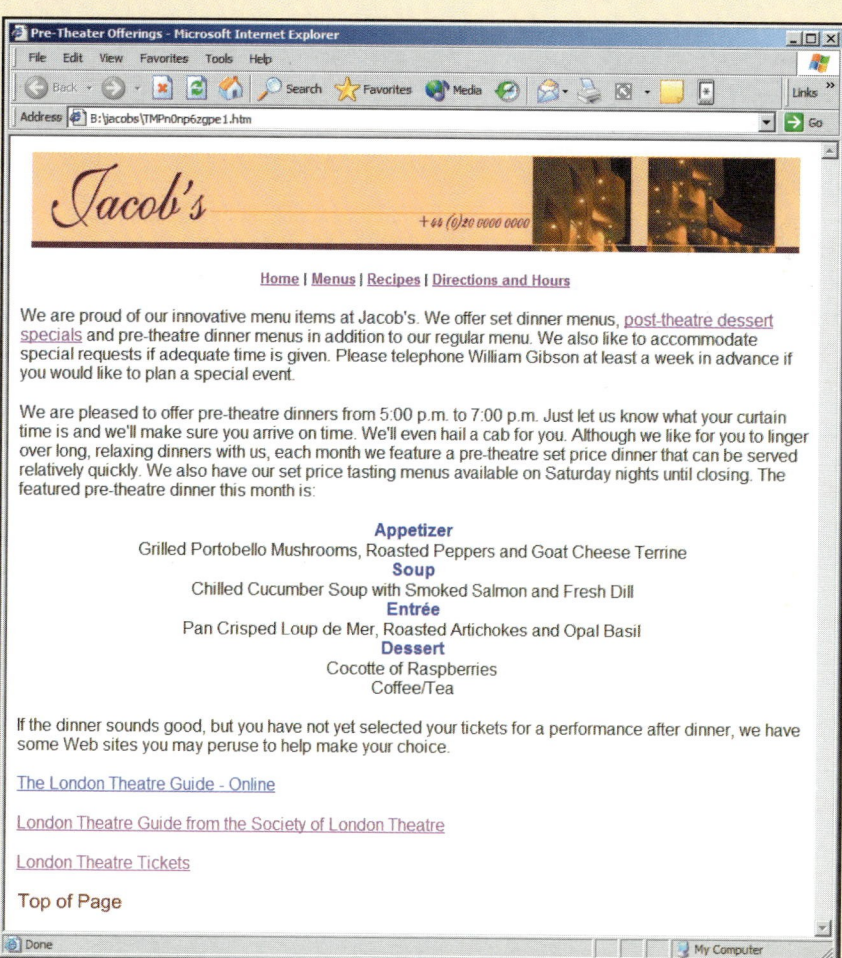

DESIGN PROJECT

Grace Keiko is a talented young water-color artist who specializes in botanical works. She wants to develop a Web site to advertise her work, but isn't sure what she would like to include in a Web site, or how to tie the pages together. She decides to spend several hours looking at other artists' Web sites to help her get started.

1. Connect to the Internet, go to www.google.com or your favorite search engine, then type in keywords that will help you locate artist Web sites, such as the one shown in Figure D-30.

2. Spend some time looking at several of the artist Web sites that you find to familiarize yourself with the types of content that each contains.

3. What categories of page content would you include on your Web site if you were Grace?

4. What external links would you consider including?

5. Describe how you would place external links on the pages, and list examples of ones you would use.

6. Would you use text or graphics for your navigation bar?

7. Would you include rollover effects on the navigation bar elements? If so, describe how they might look.

8. How could you incorporate named anchors on any of the pages?

9. Sketch a Web site plan for Grace, including the pages that you would use as links from the home page.

10. Refer to your Web site sketch, then create a home page for Grace that includes a navigation bar, a short introductory paragraph about her art, and a few external links.

FIGURE D-30
Source for Design Project

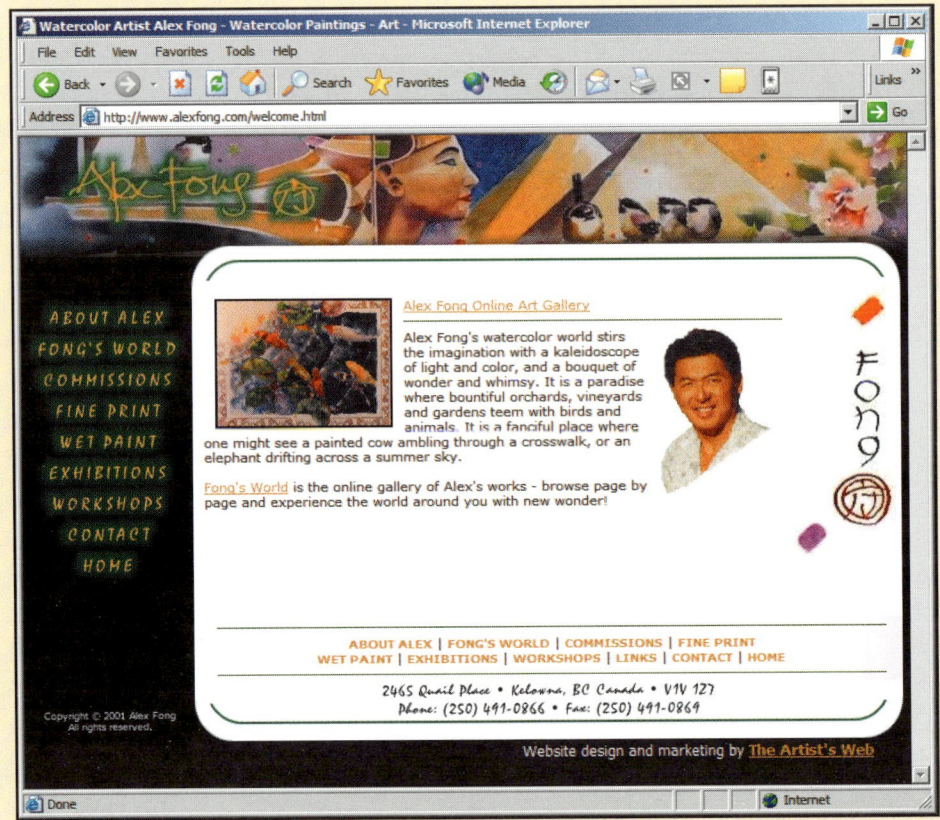

In this assignment, you will continue to work on the group Web site that you started in Unit A and developed in Units B and C. Depending on the size of your group, you can assign individual elements of the project to group members, or work collectively to create the finished product.

You will continue building your Web site by designing and completing a page with a navigation bar. After creating the navigation bar, you will copy it to each completed page in the Web site. In addition to the navigation bar, you will add several external links and several internal links to other pages as well as to named anchors. You will also link Flash text to a named anchor. After you complete this work, you will check for broken links and orphaned files.

1. Consult your storyboard and brainstorm as a team to decide which page or pages you would like to develop in this unit. Decide how to design and where to place the navigation bar, named anchors, Flash text, and any additional page elements you decide to use. Decide which reports should be run on the Web site to check for accuracy.

2. Assign everyone on the team the task of researching Web sites that could be included on one or more of your pages as external links of interest to your viewers.

Reconvene as a group to discuss your findings, then create a list of the external links you want to use. Using your storyboard as a guide, decide as a group where each external link should be placed in the site.

3. Assign a team member the task of adding external links to existing pages or creating any additional pages that contain external links.

4. Assign a team member the task of creating named anchors for key locations on the page, such as the top of the page, then linking appropriate text on the page to them.

5. Insert at least one Flash text object that links to either a named anchor or an internal link.

6. Brainstorm as a team to decide on a design for a navigation bar that will be used on all pages of the Web site.

7. Assign a team member the task of creating the navigation bar and copying it to all finished pages on the Web site. If you decided to use graphics for the navigation bar, assign a team member the task of creating the graphics that will be used.

8. Assign a team member the task of using the Link Checker panel to check for broken links and orphaned files.

9. Use the check list in Figure D-31 to make sure your Web site is complete, save your work, then close all open pages.

FIGURE D-31

Check list for Group Project

Web Site Check List
1. Do all pages have a page title?
2. Does the home page have a description and keywords?
3. Does the home page contain contact information?
4. Does every page in the Web site have consistent navigation links?
5. Does the home page have a last updated statement that will automatically update when the page is saved?
6. Do all paths for links and images work correctly?
7. Do all images have alternate text?
8. Do all pages have page titles?
9. Are all colors Web-safe?
10. Are there any unnecessary files that you can delete from the assets folder?
11. Is there a style sheet with at least two styles?
12. Did you apply the style sheet to page content?
13. Does at least one page contain links to one or more named anchors?
14. Does at least one page contain Flash text that links to either a named anchor or an internal link?
15. Do all pages view well using at least two different browser settings?

UNIT E
WORKING WITH TABLES

1. Create a table.

2. Resize, split, and merge cells.

3. Insert and align graphics in table cells.

4. Insert text and format cell content.

5. Perform Web site maintenance.

WORKING WITH TABLES

Introduction

You have learned how to place and align elements on a page and enhance them using various formatting options. However, page layout options are fairly limited without the use of tables. Tables offer another solution for organizing text and graphics on a page. **Tables** are placeholders made up of small boxes called **cells**, into which you can insert text and graphics. Cells in a table are arranged horizontally in **rows**, and vertically in **columns**. Using tables on a Web page gives you total control over the placement of each object on the page. In this unit, you will learn how to create and format tables, work with table rows and columns, and format the contents of table cells. You will also learn how to select and format table cells using table tags on the tag selector. Clicking a table tag on the tag selector selects the table element associated with that tag.

Inserting Graphics and Text in Tables

Once you insert a table on a Web page, it becomes very easy to place text and graphics exactly where you want them on the page. You can use a table to control both the placement of elements in relation to each other and the amount of space between each page element. Before you insert a table, however, you should always plan how your table will look with all the text and graphics in it. Even a rough sketch before you begin will save you time as you add content to the page.

Maintaining a Web Site

You already know how to check for broken links and non-Web-safe colors in your Web site. Dreamweaver also provides many other management tools to help you identify other problems. For instance, you can run a report to check for pages that have no page titles, or to search for images that contain no alternate text. It's a good idea to set up a schedule to run these and other reports on a regular basis.

Tools You'll Use

Table properties

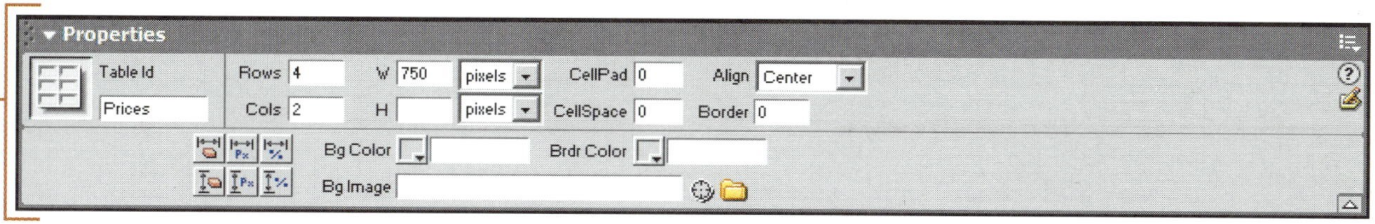

Row properties

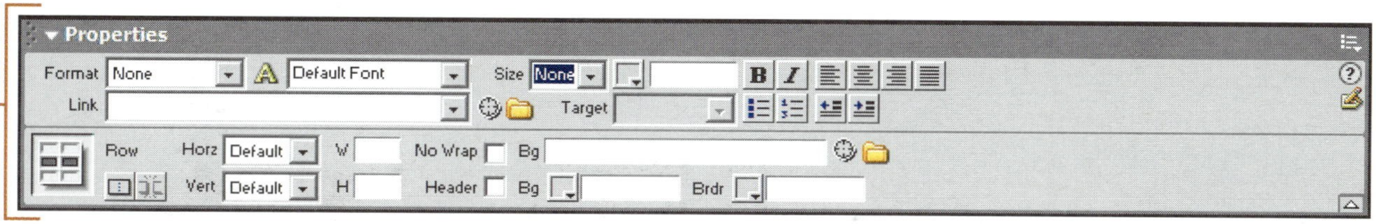

Cell properties

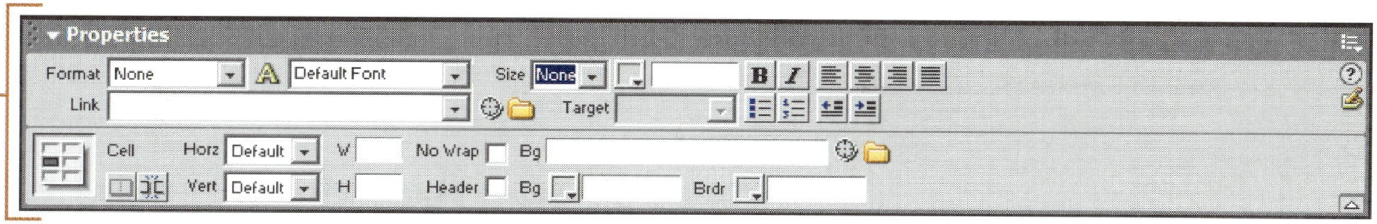

CREATE A TABLE

What You'll Do

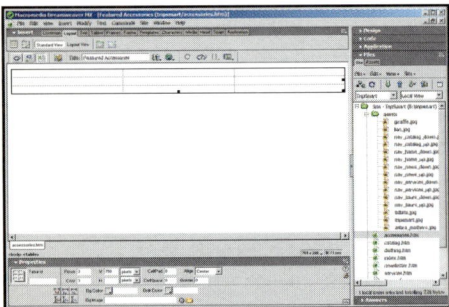

In this lesson, you will create a table for the accessories page in the TripSmart Web site to showcase several items in the TripSmart online catalog. This page, along with the clothing page, will be linked from the catalog page in the Web site.

Understanding Table Views

There are two ways to create a table in Dreamweaver. You can use the Insert Table button on the Common tab of the Insert bar, or you can draw a table using tools on the Layout tab of the Insert bar. Each method for creating a table requires a specific view. You use **Standard View** when you want to use the Insert Table button to insert a table. You use **Layout View** when you want to draw a table using the tools on the Insert bar. You can choose the view you want by clicking the Standard View button or the Layout View button on the Layout tab of the Insert bar.

Creating a Table in Standard View

Creating a table in Standard View is useful when you want to create a table with a specific number of columns and rows. To create a table in Standard View, you use the Insert Table button on the Common tab of the Insert bar to open the Insert Table dialog box, which you use to enter values for the number of rows and columns, the border size, table width, cell padding, and cell spacing. The **border** is the outline or frame around the table and the individual cells and is measured in pixels. The width, which can be specified in pixels or as a percentage, refers to the width of the table. When the table width is specified as a percentage, the table width will adjust to the width of the browser window. When the table width is specified in pixels, the table width stays the same, regardless of the size of the browser window. **Cell padding** is the distance between the cell content and the **cell walls**, the lines inside the cell borders. **Cell spacing** is the distance between cells.

Setting Table Accessibility Preferences for Tables

You can make a table more accessible to visually handicapped viewers by adding a table caption and a table summary that can be read by screen readers. The table caption appears on the screen. The table summary does not. You can use the Preferences dialog box to prompt you to enter a caption and summary every time you insert a table. These features are especially useful for tables that are used for tabular data.

Drawing a Table in Layout View

You use Layout view when you want to draw your own table. Drawing a table is a good idea for those situations where you want to place page elements on a Web page, and have no need for a specific number of rows and columns. You can use the Draw Layout Cell button or the Draw Layout Table button on the Layout tab of the Insert bar to draw a cell or a table. After you draw the first cell, Dreamweaver plots a table for you automatically.

Planning a Table

Before you create a table, you should sketch a plan for it that shows its location on the Web page and the placement of text and graphics in its cells. You should also decide whether to include borders around the tables and cells. Setting the border value to zero causes the table to appear invisible, so that viewers will never know you used a table for the page layout unless they looked at the code. Figure E-1 shows a sketch of the table you will create on the TripSmart accessories page to organize graphics and text.

FIGURE E-1

Sketch of table on the accessories page

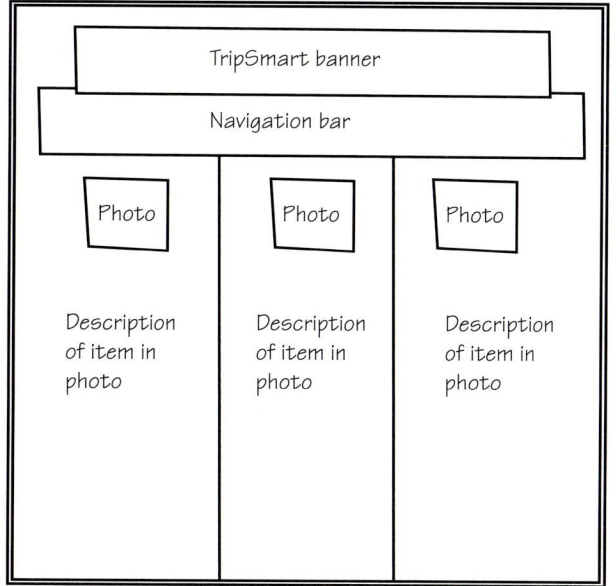

Set table accessibility preferences

1. Open the TripSmart Web site that you completed in Unit D, click Edit on the menu bar, then click Preferences to open the Preferences dialog box.
2. Click Accessibility in the Category list (if necessary).
3. Click the Show Attributes when Inserting Tables check box to place a checkmark in the option box, as shown in Figure E-2.
4. Click OK.

You set the Web site preferences to prompt you to enter accessibility properties when creating tables.

Create a table

1. Double-click accessories.htm in the Site panel to open the accessories page in Design view.

   The accessories page is a blank.

2. Select the text Untitled Document in the Title text box on the Document toolbar, type **Featured Accessories**, then press [Enter] (Win) or [return] (Mac) to enter a title for the table.
3. Click the Common tab on the Insert bar (if necessary), then click the Insert Table button.

(continued)

Setting accessibility preferences for tables

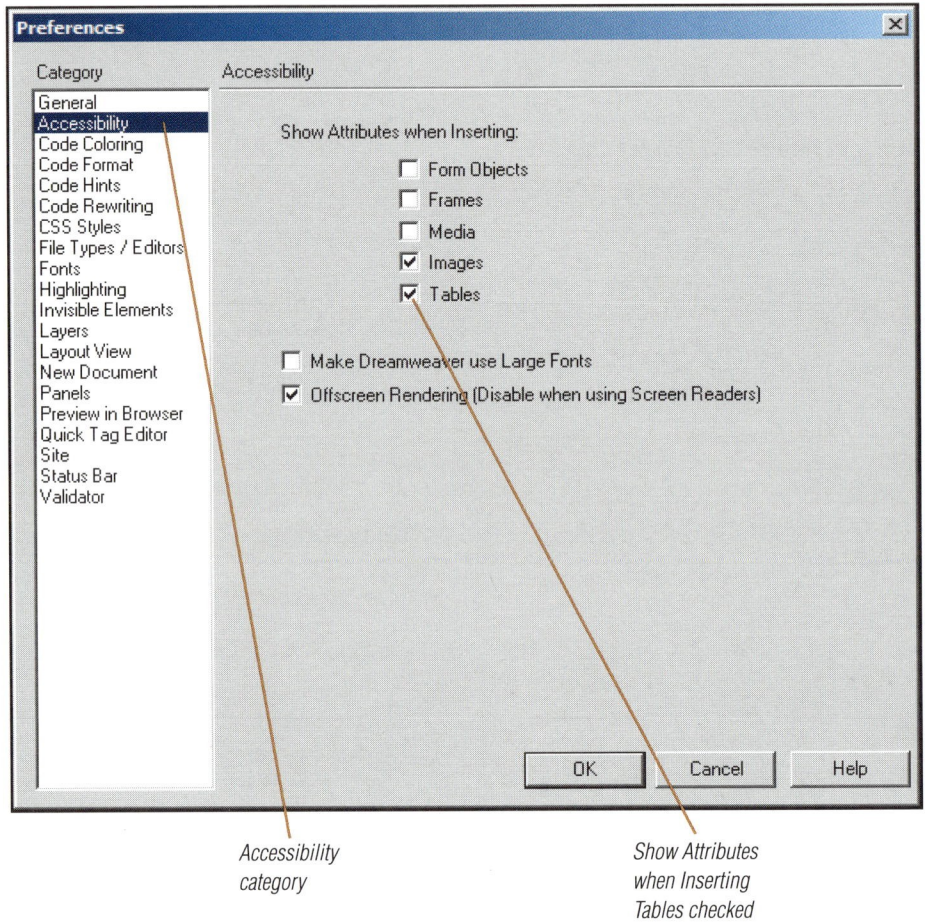

Accessibility category

Show Attributes when Inserting Tables checked

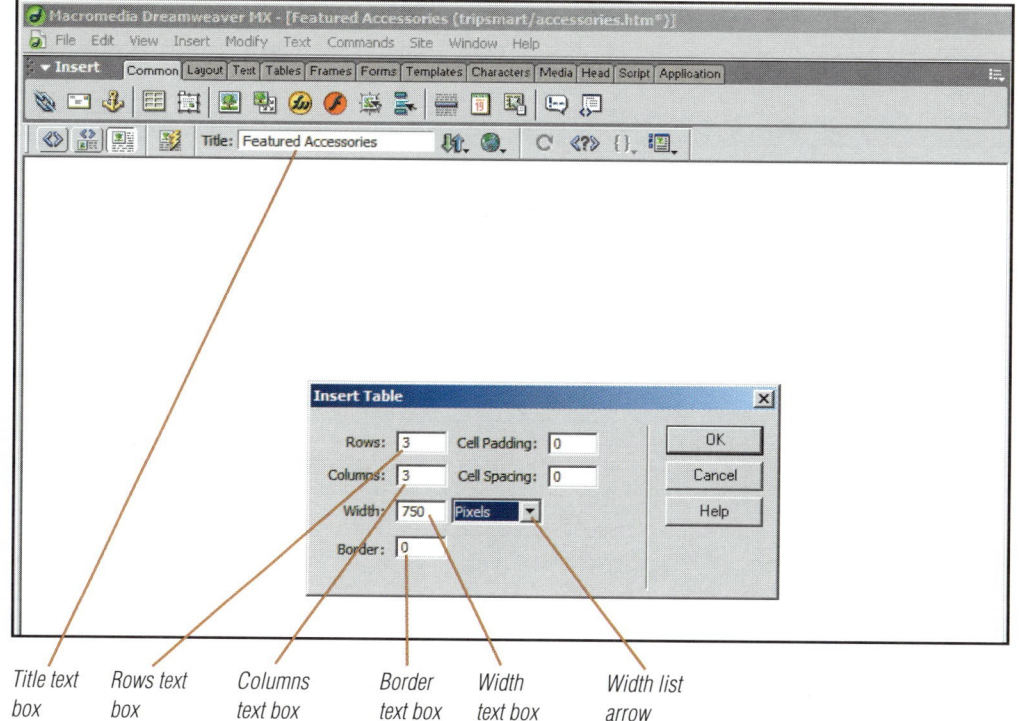

Title text box   Rows text box   Columns text box   Border text box   Width text box   Width list arrow

Table Summary

4. Type **3** in the Rows text box, type **3** in the Columns text box, type **750** in the Width text box, click the Width list arrow, click Pixels (if necessary), type **0** in the Border text box, as shown in Figure E-3, then click OK.

    The Accessibility Options for Tables dialog box opens.

5. Click in the Summary text box, type **This table was used for page layout.**, then compare your screen to Figure E-4.

6. Click OK to close the Accessibility Options for Tables dialog box.

    The table appears on the page, but the table summary is not visible. The summary will not appear in the browser, but will be read by screen readers.

    TIP   To edit accessibility preferences for a table, you must view the page in Code view or use the Code Inspector to edit the code directly.

7. Save your work.

You opened the accessories page in the TripSmart Web site and added a page title. You then created a table containing three rows and three columns and set the width at 750 pixels so it will appear in the same size regardless of the browser window size. Finally, you entered a table summary that will be read by screen readers.

Set table properties

1. Move the pointer slowly to the edge of the table until you see the pointer change to a four-sided arrow (Win), or 2-sided arrow (Mac), then click the table border to select the table, if necessary.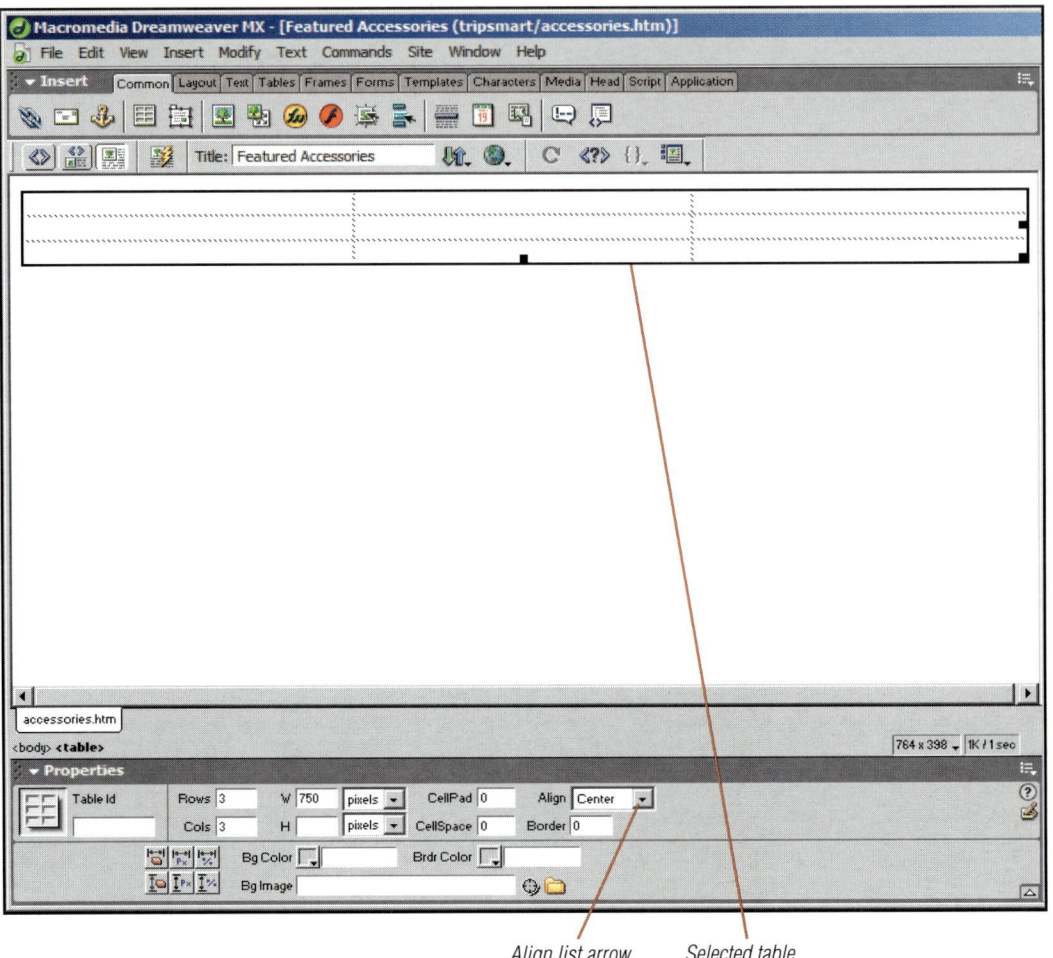

   TIP You can also select a table by (1) clicking the insertion point in the table, then clicking Modify, Table, Select Table; (2) selecting a cell in the table, then clicking Edit, Select All; or (3) clicking the table tag <table> on the tag selector.

2. Expand the Property inspector (if necessary) to display the current properties of the new table.

   TIP The Property inspector will only display information about the table if the table is selected.

3. Click the Align list arrow in the Property inspector, then click Center to center the table on the page, as shown in Figure E-5.

   The center alignment formatting ensures that the table will be centered in all browser windows, regardless of the screen size.

4. Save your work.

FIGURE E-5

Property inspector showing properties of selected table

Align list arrow   *Selected table*

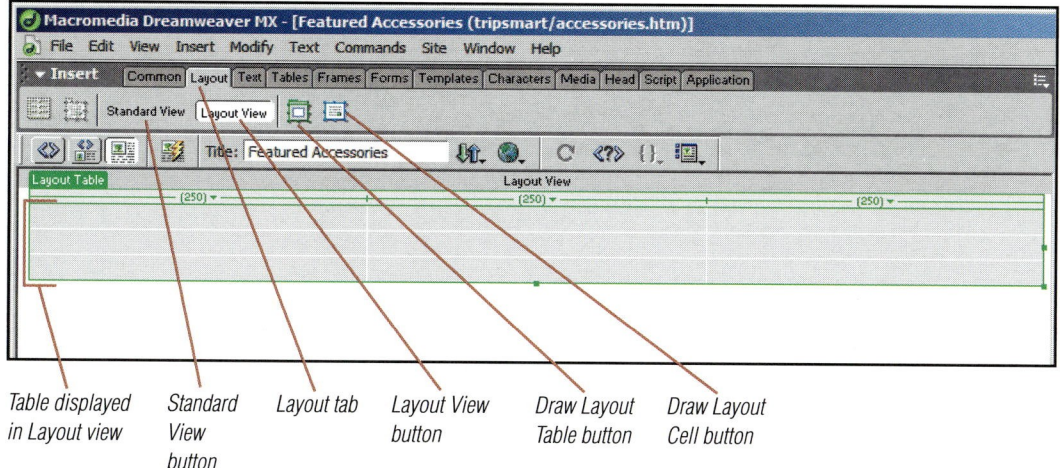

Table displayed
in Layout view

Standard
View
button

Layout tab

Layout View
button

Draw Layout
Table button

Draw Layout
Cell button

View the table in Layout View

1. Click the Layout tab on the Insert bar, then click the Layout View button. `Layout View`

   The Getting Started in Layout View window might open, providing instructions on creating and editing a table in Layout View.

2. Click OK (if necessary) to close the Getting Started in Layout View window.

   The table appears in Layout View, as shown in Figure E-6.

3. Click the Standard View button on the Insert bar to return to Standard view. `Standard View`

4. Click the Common tab on the Insert bar.

You viewed the table in Layout view, then switched back to Standard view.

Setting table and cell widths

If you use a table to place all the text and graphics contained on a Web page, it is wise to set the width of the table in pixels. This ensures that the table will not resize itself proportionately if the browser window size is changed. If you set the width of a table using pixels, the table will remain one size, regardless of the browser window size. For instance, if the width of a table is set to slightly less than 800, the table will stretch across the whole width of a browser window set at a resolution of 800×600. The same table would be the same size on a screen set at 1024×768 and therefore would not stretch across the entire screen. Most designers design to a resolution of 800×600. Be aware, however, that if you set the width of your table at 800 pixels, your table will be too wide to print the entire width of the page, and part of the right side of the page will be cut off. If you are designing a table layout for a page that is likely to be printed by the viewer, you should make your table narrower to fit on a printed page. If you set a table width as a percentage, however, the table would resize itself proportionately in any browser window, regardless of the resolution. You can also set each cell width as either a percentage of the table or as fixed pixels.

RESIZE, SPLIT, AND MERGE CELLS

What You'll Do

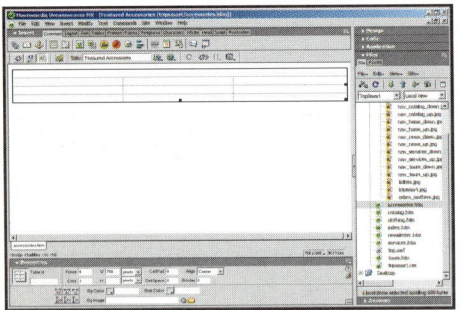

 In this lesson, you will set the width of the table cells to be split evenly across the table. You will then split each of the three cells and place images in those cells. You will also merge some cells to provide space for the banner.

Resizing Table Elements

You can resize the rows or columns of a table manually. To resize a table, row, or column, you must first select the table, then drag one of the table's three selection handles. To change all the columns in a table so that they are the same size, drag the middle-right selection handle. To resize the height of all rows simultaneously, drag the middle-bottom selection handle. To resize the entire table, drag the right-corner selection handle.

To resize a row or column individually, drag the interior cell borders up, down, to the left, or to the right. You can also resize selected columns, rows, or individual cells by entering specific measurements in the W and H text boxes in the Property inspector specified either in pixels or as a percentage. Cells whose width or height is specified as a percentage will maintain that percentage in relation to the width or height of the entire table if the table is resized.

Resetting table widths and heights

After resizing columns and rows in a table, you might want to change the sizes of the columns and rows back to their previous sizes. To reset columns and rows to their previous widths and heights, click Modify on the menu bar, point to Table, then click Clear Cell Heights or Clear Cell Widths. Using the Clear Cell Heights command also forces the cell border to snap to the bottom of any inserted graphics, so you can also use this command to tighten up extra white space in a cell.

Splitting and Merging Cells

Using the Insert Table command creates a new table with evenly spaced columns and rows. Sometimes you might want to adjust the cells in a table by splitting or merging them. To **split** a cell means to divide it into multiple rows or columns. To **merge** cells means to combine multiple cells into one cell. Using split and merged cells gives you more flexibility and control in placing page elements on a page and can help you create a more visually exciting layout. When you merge cells, the HTML tag used to describe the merged cell changes from a width size tag to a column span or row span tag. For example, <td colspan="2"> is the code for two cells that have been merged into one cell that spans two columns.

QUICKTIP

You can split merged cells and merge split cells.

Using nested tables

You can insert a nested table in a table. A nested table is a table inside a table. To create a nested table, you place the insertion point in the cell where you want to insert the nested table, then click the Insert Table button on the Insert bar. The nested table is a separate table that can be formatted differently from the table in which it is placed. Nested tables are useful when you want part of your table data to have visible borders and part to have invisible borders. For example, you can nest a table with red borders inside a table with invisible borders. You need to plan carefully when you insert nested tables. It is easy to get carried away and insert too many nested tables, which makes it more difficult to apply formatting and rearrange table elements. Before you insert a nested table, consider whether you could achieve the same result by adding rows and columns or by splitting cells.

Resize columns

1. Click inside the first cell in the bottom row, then click the cell tag on the tag selector, as shown in Figure E-7. **<td>**

   Clicking the cell tag (the HTML tag for that cell) selects the corresponding cell in the table. The cell now has a dark border surrounding it, indicating it is selected.

   > TIP To select the entire table, click the table tag on the tag selector.

2. Type **33%** in the W text box in the Property inspector to change the width of the cell to 33 percent of the table width.

   > TIP You need to type the % sign next to the number you type in the W text box. Otherwise, the width will be expressed in pixels.

3. Repeat Steps 1 and 2 for the next two cells in the last row, using **33%** for the middle cell and **34%** for the last cell.

   The combined widths of the three cells now add up to 100 percent. As you add content to the table, the first two columns will remain 33 percent of the width of the table, and the third column will remain 34%.

4. Save your changes.

   You set the width of each of the three cells in the bottom row to ensure that the width of all three cells is equal.

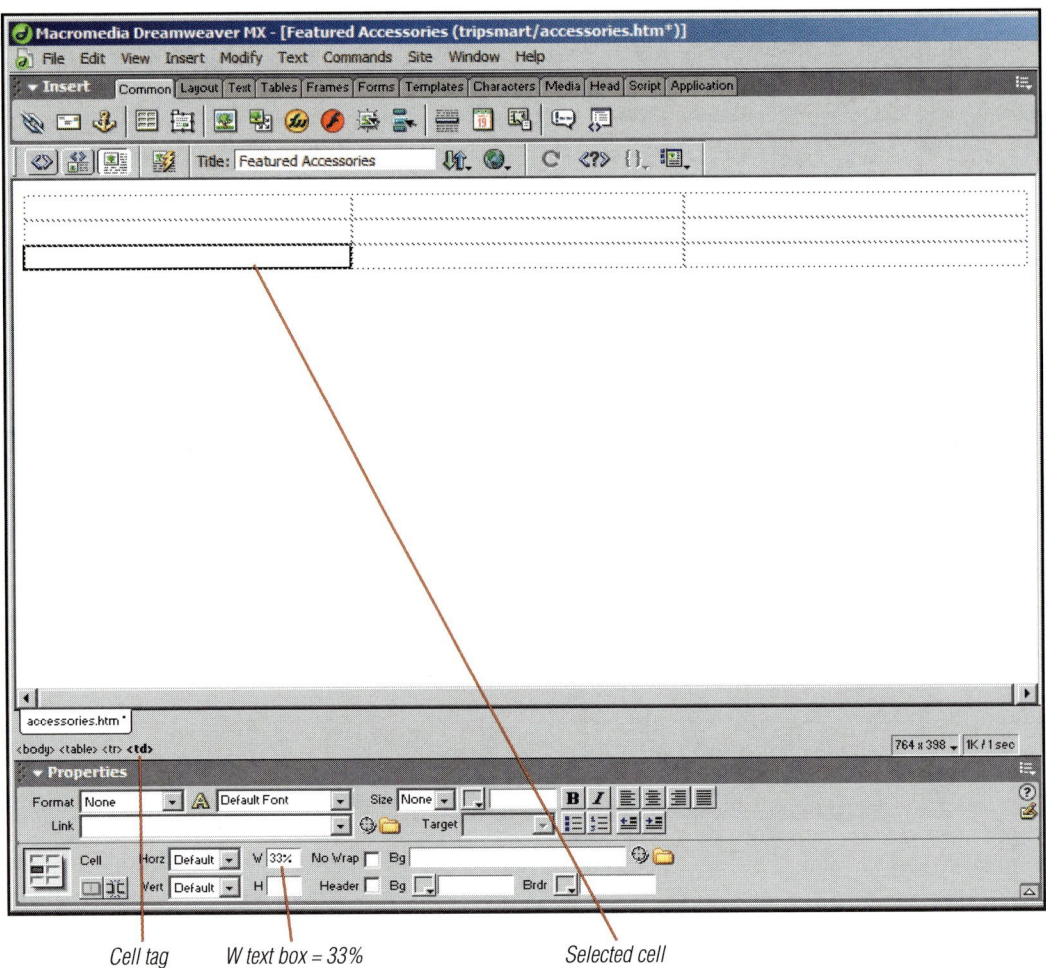

Cell tag   W text box = 33%   Selected cell

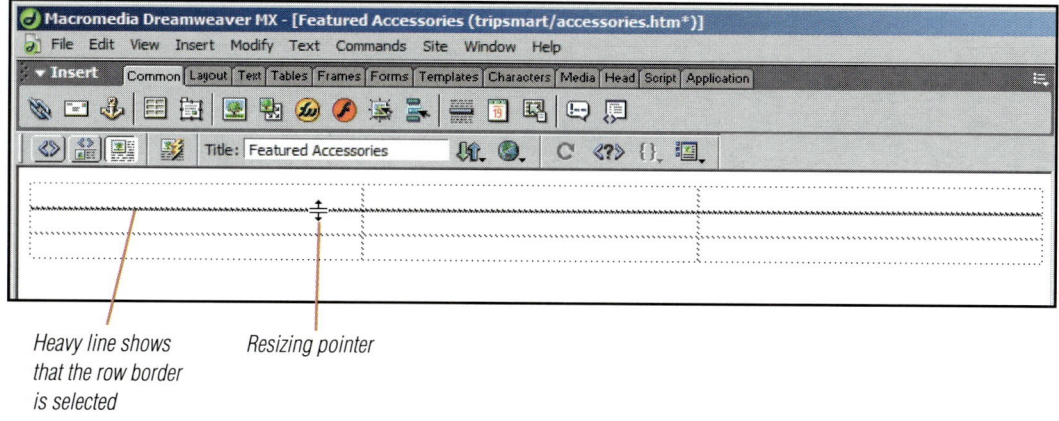

Heavy line shows
that the row border
is selected

Resizing pointer

Resize rows

1. Place the pointer over the bottom border of the first row until it changes to a two-sided arrow as shown in Figure E-8, then click and drag down about ¼ of an inch to increase the height of the row. ⬍

   The border turns darker when you select and drag it.

2. Click Window on the menu bar, point to Others, click History, then drag the slider in the History panel up one line to return the row to its original height.

3. Close the History panel group.

You changed the height of the top row, then used the History panel to change it back it to its original height.

HTML table tags

When formatting a table, it is important to understand the basic HTML table tags. The tags used for creating a table are <table> </table>. The tags used to create table rows are <tr></tr>. The tags used to create table cells are <td></td>. Dreamweaver places the   code into each empty table cell at the time it is created. The   code represents a **non-breaking space**, or a space that a browser will display on the page. Some browsers will collapse an empty cell, which can ruin the look of a table. The non-breaking space will hold the cell until content is placed in it, at which time it will be automatically removed.

Lesson 2   Resize, Split, and Merge Cells

Split cells

1. Click inside the first cell in the bottom row, then click the cell tag in the tag selector. **<td>**

2. Click the Splits Cells into Rows or Columns button in the Property inspector.

3. Click the Split Cells Into Rows option button (if necessary), type **2** in the Number of Rows text box (if necessary) as shown in Figure E-9, then click OK.

4. Repeat Steps 1 through 3 to split the other two cells in the bottom row to two rows each.

   TIP   To create a new row identical to the one above it, place the insertion point in the last cell of a table, then press [Tab].

5. Save your work.

You split the three cells in the bottom row into two rows, creating a new row of cells.

FIGURE E-9
Splitting a cell into two rows

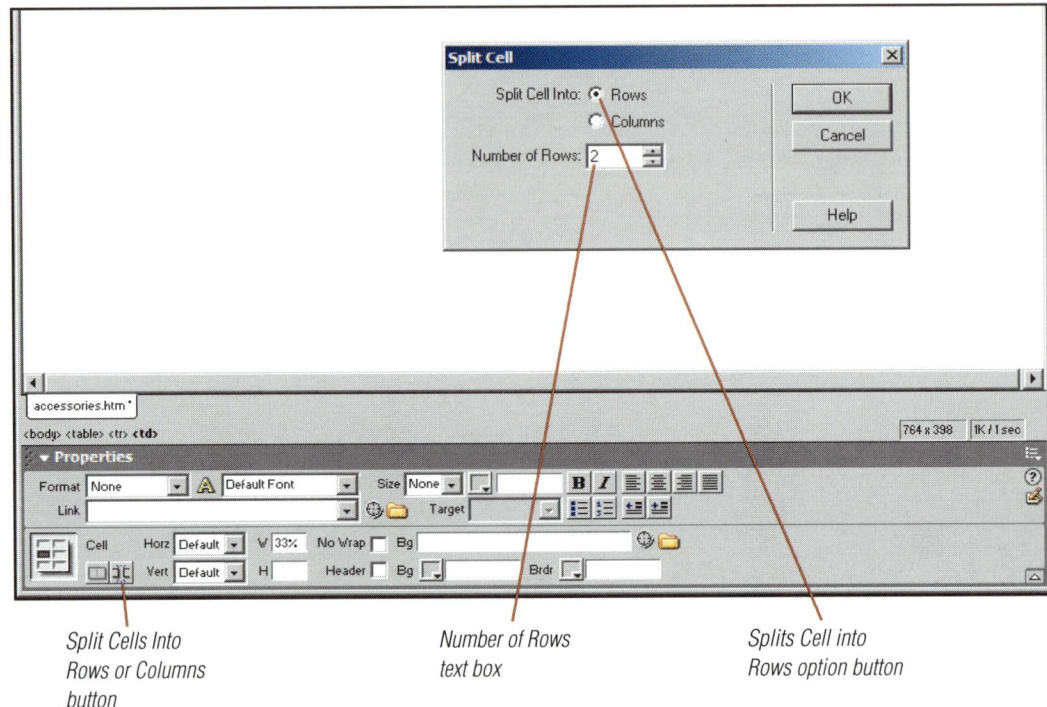

Split Cells Into Rows or Columns button

Number of Rows text box

Splits Cell into Rows option button

Adding or deleting a row

As you add new content to your table, you might find that you have too many or too few rows or columns. You can add or delete one row or column at a time or several at once. You use commands on the Modify menu to add and delete table rows and columns. When you add a new column or row, you must first select the existing column or row to which the new column or row will be adjacent. The Insert Row or Column dialog box lets you choose how many rows or columns you want to insert or delete, and where you want them placed in relationship to the selected row or column. The new column or row will have the same formatting and number of cells as the selected column or row.

Merging selected cells into one cell

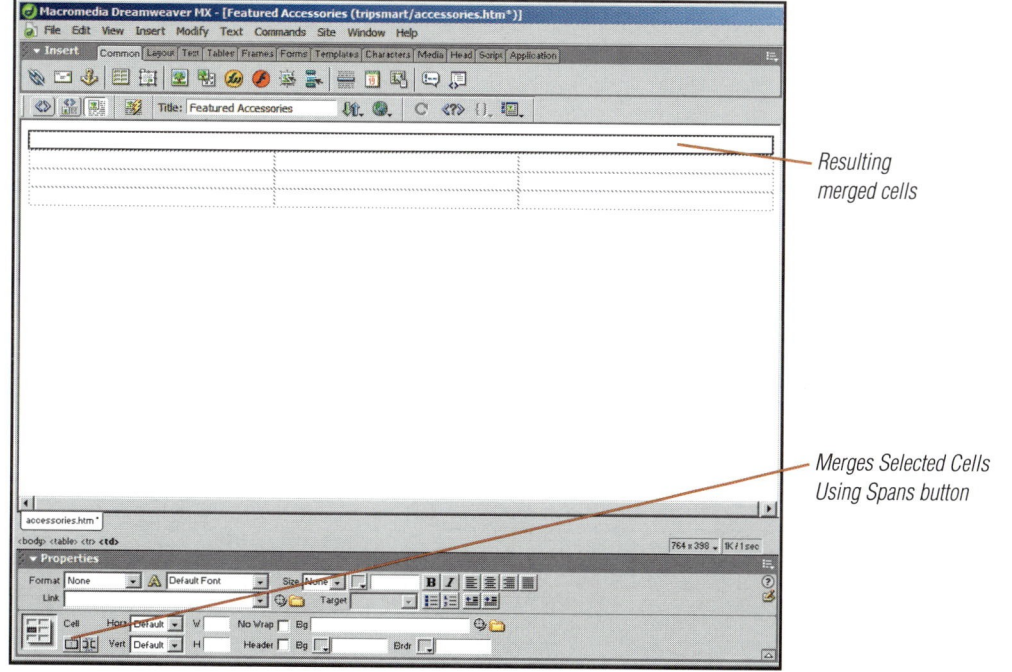

— Resulting merged cells

— Merges Selected Cells Using Spans button

accessories.htm

764 x 398 | 1K / 1 sec

Merge cells

1. Click in the first cell in the top row of the table to place the insertion point, then click and drag the pointer to the right to select the second and third cells in the top row.

2. Click the Merges Selected Cells Using Spans button in the Property inspector. 🔲

   The three cells are merged into one cell, as shown in Figure E-10. Merged cells are good placeholders for banners or page headings.

   > TIP   You can only merge cells that are adjacent to each other.

3. Click the Show Code View button, then view the code for the split and merged cells, as shown in Figure E-11. ◇

   Notice the table tags denoting the column span (td colspan="3") and the non-breaking spaces ( ) inserted in the empty cells.

4. Click the Show Design View button then save your work. ▦

You merged three cells in the first row to make room for the TripSmart banner.

FIGURE E-11
Code View for merged cells

```
7
8    <body>
9    <table width="750" border="0" align="center" cellpadding="0" cellspacing="0" summary="This table was
     used for page layout.">
10    <tr>
11      <td colspan="3"> </td>
12    </tr>
13    <tr>
14      <td> </td>
15      <td> </td>
16      <td> </td>
17    </tr>
18    <tr>
19      <td width="33%"> </td>
20      <td width="33%"> </td>
```

colspan tag

INSERT AND ALIGN GRAPHICS IN TABLE CELLS

What You'll Do

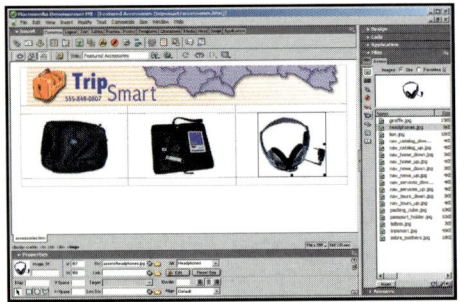

 In this lesson, you will insert the TripSmart banner in the top row of the table. You will then insert three graphics showing three TripSmart catalog items. After placing the three graphics, you will center them within their cells.

Inserting Graphics in Table Cells

You can insert graphics in the cells of a table using the Image button on the Insert bar or the Image command on the Insert menu. If you already have graphics saved in your Web site that you would like to insert in a table, you can drag them from the Assets panel into the table cells. When you add a large graphic to a cell, the cell expands to accommodate the inserted graphic. If you set the Preferences dialog box to prompt you for alternate text when inserting graphics, the Image Tag Accessibility Attributes dialog box will open after you insert a graphic, prompting you to enter alternate text. Figure E-12 shows the John Deere Web site, which uses a table for page layout and contains several images in its table cells. Notice that some images appear in cells by themselves, and some appear in cells containing text or other graphics.

Aligning Graphics in Table Cells

You can align graphics both horizontally and vertically within a cell. You can align a graphic horizontally using the Align Left, Align Right, and Align Center buttons or the Horz list arrow in the Property inspector. You can also align a graphic vertically by the top, middle, bottom, or baseline of a cell. To align a graphic vertically within a cell, use the Vert list arrow in the Property inspector, then choose an alignment option, as shown in Figure E-13.

FIGURE E-12

John Deere Web site

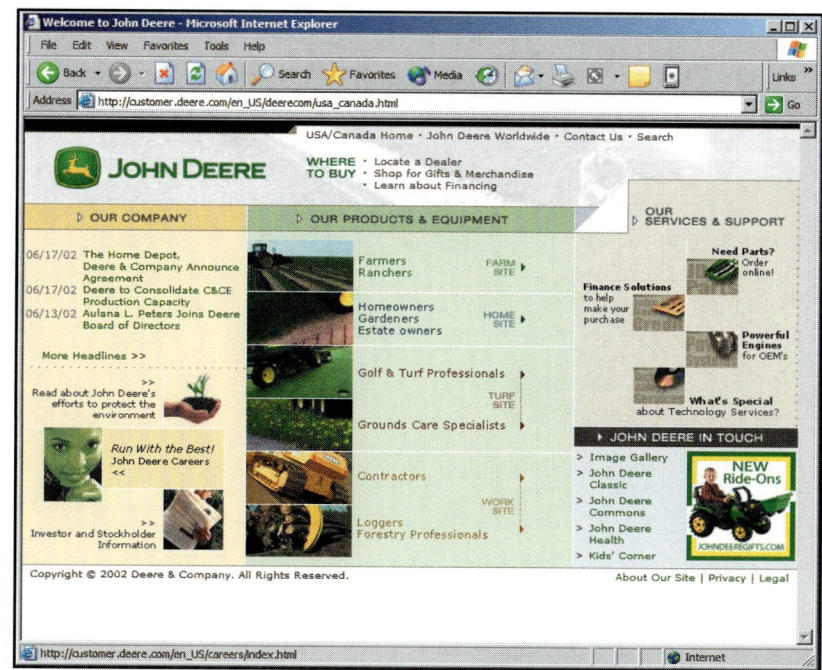

FIGURE E-13

Vertically aligning cell contents

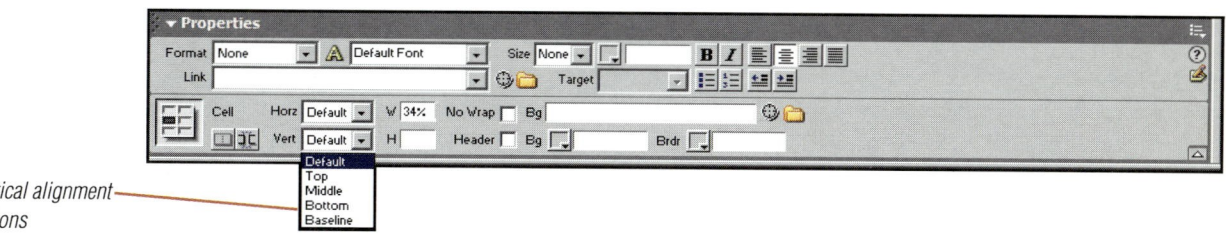

Vertical alignment options

Insert graphics in table cells

1. Open the Assets panel (if necessary), click the Images button on the Assets panel (if necessary), then drag the tripsmart.jpg graphic from the Assets panel to the top row of the table.

   The Image Tag Accessibility Attributes dialog box opens.

2. Type **TripSmart banner** in the Alternate Text text box, then click OK.

3. Click in the first cell in the third row to place the insertion point, insert packing_cube.jpg from the unit_e assets folder, then enter **Packing Cube** for the alternate text.

4. Repeat Step 3 to insert passport_holder.jpg and headphones.jpg in the next two cells, using **Passport Holder** and **Headphones** for the alternate text, then compare your screen to Figure E-14.

   TIP   Press [Tab] to move your insertion point to the next cell in a row. Press [Shift][Tab] to move your insertion point to the previous cell.

5. Refresh the Assets panel to verify that the three new graphics were copied to the TripSmart Web site assets folder.

6. Save your work.

7. Preview the page in your browser.

   Notice that the page would look better if each graphic were evenly distributed across the page.

8. Close your browser.

You inserted images into four cells of the table on the accessories page.

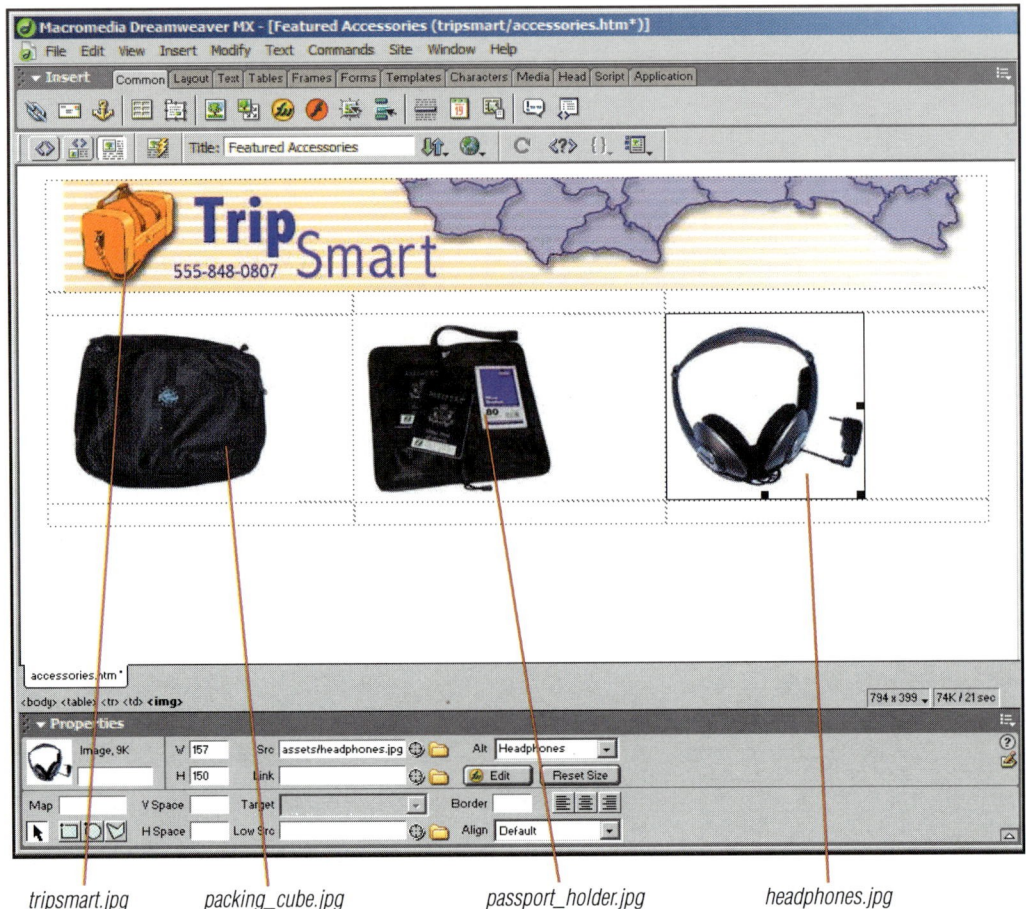

tripsmart.jpg   packing_cube.jpg   passport_holder.jpg   headphones.jpg

1. Click the TripSmart banner, then click the Align Center button in the Property inspector. ▤

2. Center-align the packing cube, passport holder, and headphones images, as shown in Figure E-15.

3. Save your work.

4. Preview the page in your browser, view the centered images, then close your browser.

You center-aligned the TripSmart banner and the three graphics within their respective cells.

FIGURE E-15
Centering images in cells

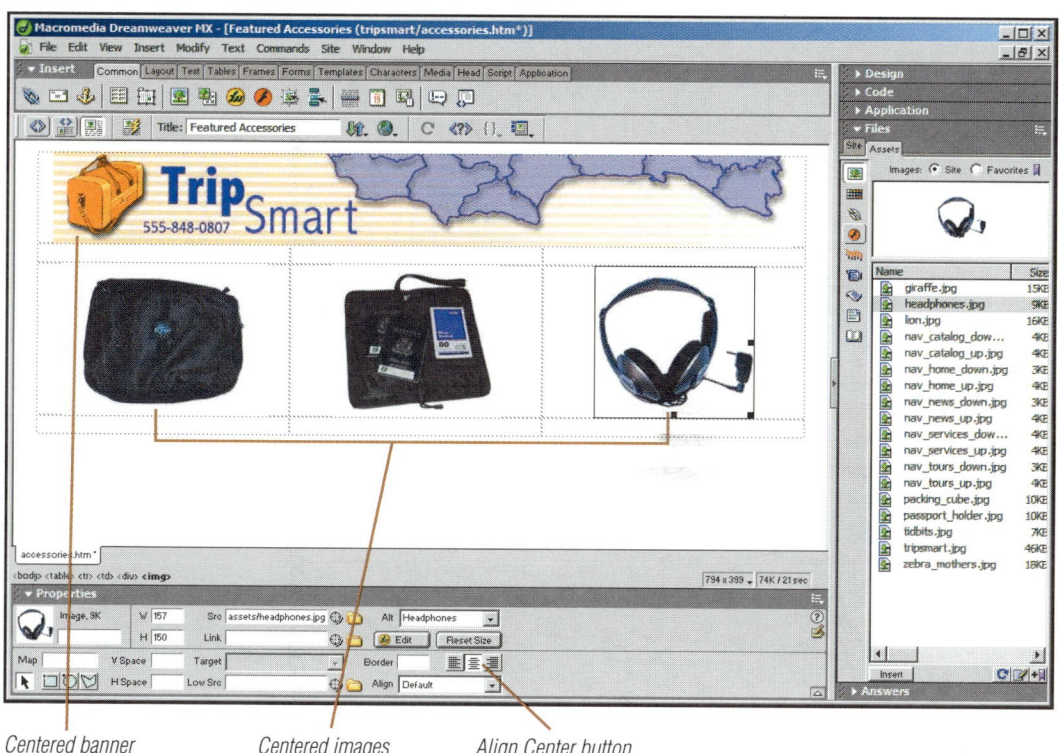

Centered banner   Centered images   Align Center button

INSERT TEXT AND FORMAT CELL CONTENT

What You'll Do

 In this lesson, you will type a heading for the accessories page and copy and paste descriptive text for each item on the page. You will then format the text to enhance its appearance on the page. Last, you will add descriptive names for each item and then format the text you added.

Inserting Text in a Table

You can enter text in a table either by typing it in a cell, copying it from another source and pasting it into a cell, or importing it from another program. Once you place text in a table cell, you can format it to make it more readable and more visually appealing on the page.

Formatting Cell Content

Making modifications and formatting changes to a table and its contents is easier to do in Standard view than in Layout view. To format the contents of a cell in Standard view, you select the contents in the cell, and then apply formatting to it. If a cell contains multiple objects of the same type, such as text, you can either format each item individually or select the entire cell and apply formatting that will be applied identically to all items. You can tell whether you have selected the cell contents or the cell by looking to see what options are showing in the Property inspector. Figure E-16 shows a selected graphic in a cell. Notice that the Property inspector displays options for formatting the object, rather than options for formatting the cell.

Formatting cells

Formatting cells is different than formatting cell contents. Formatting a cell can include setting properties that visually enhance the cell appearance, such as setting a cell width, assigning a background color, or setting global alignment properties for the cell content. To format a cell, you need to either select the cell or place the insertion point inside the cell you want to format, then choose the cell formatting options you want in the Property inspector. For example, to choose a fill color for a selected cell, you click the Background Color button in the Property inspector, then choose a color from the color picker.

In order to format a cell, you must expand the Property inspector to display the cell formatting options. In Figure E-17, notice that the insertion point is positioned in the passport holder cell, but the passport holder graphic is not selected. The Property inspector displays the formatting options for cells.

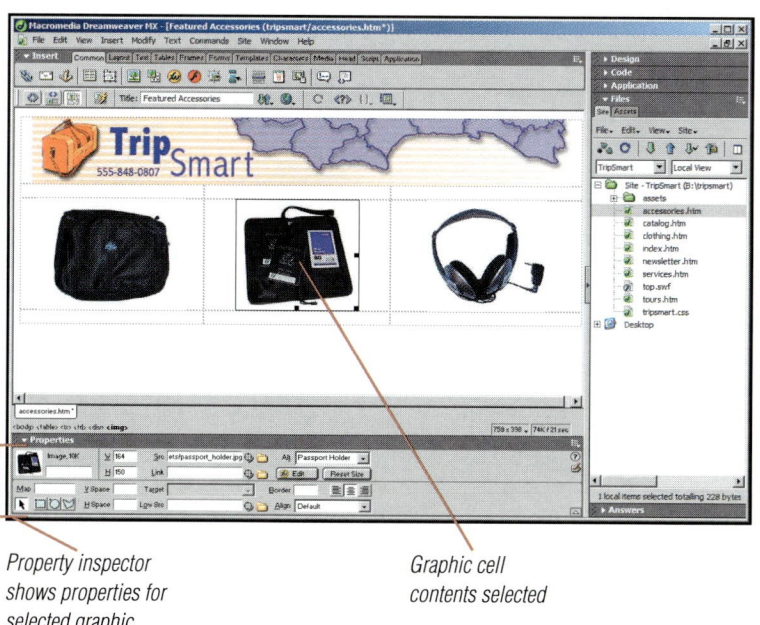

Property inspector shows properties for selected graphic

Graphic cell contents selected

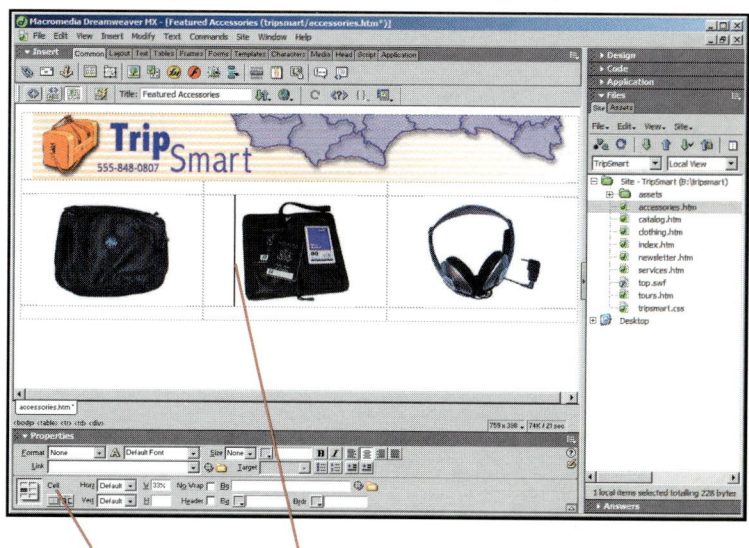

Property inspector shows cell properties

Insertion point in cell

Insert text

1. Click to the right of the TripSmart banner to place the insertion point, press [Enter] (Win) or [return] (Mac), then type **Featured Catalog Accessories**.

2. Open packing_cube.htm from the unit_e data files folder, click Edit on the menu bar, click Select All, click Edit on the menu bar, click Copy, then close packing_cube.htm.

3. Click in the cell under the packing cube image to place the insertion point, click Edit on the menu bar, then click Paste.

4. Repeat Steps 2 and 3 to paste all the text contained in the data files passport_holder.htm and headphones.htm in the cells below their respective images.

5. Click in the cell above the packing cube image to place the insertion point, type **Packing Cubes**, press [Tab], type **Passport Holder**, press [Tab], then type **Headphones**, as shown in Figure E-18.

6. Save your work.

You typed headings into four cells and copied and pasted descriptive text in the three cells under the three images.

Copying and pasting text into cells

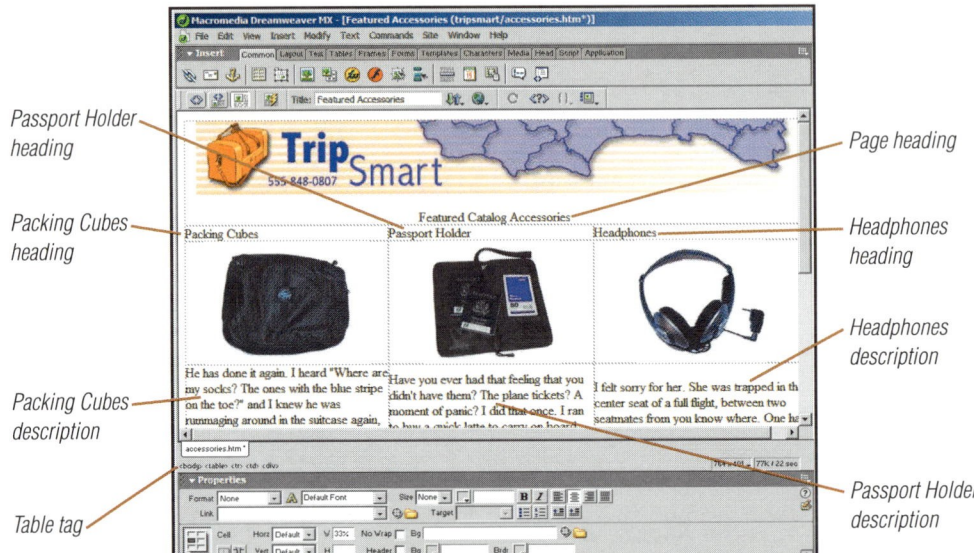

Passport Holder heading

Packing Cubes heading

Packing Cubes description

Table tag

Page heading

Headphones heading

Headphones description

Passport Holder description

Importing and exporting data from tables

You can import and export tabular data into and out of Dreamweaver. Tabular data is data that is arranged in columns and rows and separated by a **delimiter**: a comma, tab, colon, semicolon, or similar character. **Importing** means to bring data created in another software program into Dreamweaver, and **exporting** means to save data created in Dreamweaver in a special file format that can be inserted into other programs. Files that are imported into Dreamweaver must be saved as delimited files. **Delimited files** are database or spreadsheet files that have been saved as text files with delimiters such as tabs or commas separating the data. Programs such as Microsoft Access and Microsoft Excel offer many file formats for saving files. To import a delimited file, you click File on the menu bar, point to Import, then click Tabular Data. The Import Tabular Data dialog box opens, offering you formatting options for the imported table. To export a table that you created in Dreamweaver, you click File on the menu bar, point to Export, then click Table. The Export Table dialog box opens, letting you choose the type of delimiter you want for the delimited file.

Formatting text using the Property inspector and Assets panel

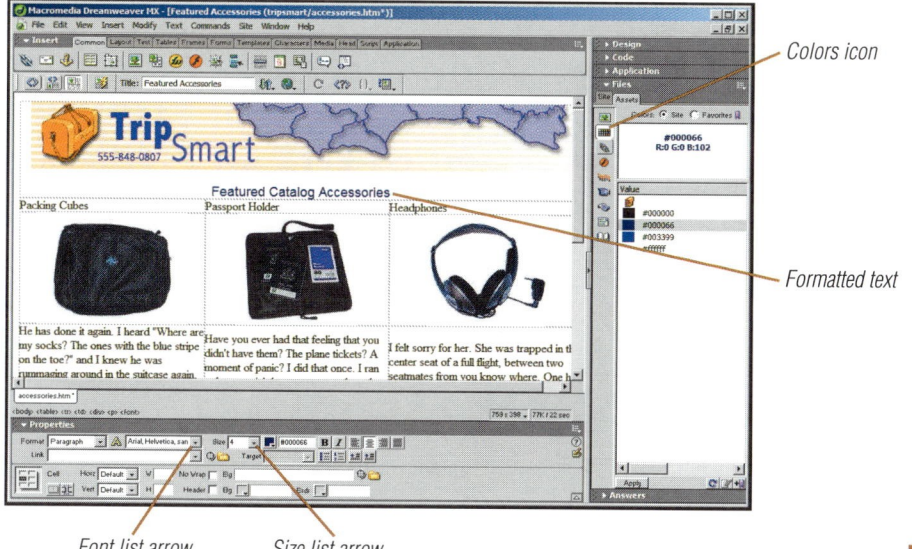

Colors icon

Formatted text

Font list arrow   Size list arrow

Format cell content

1. Select the Featured Catalog Accessories text, click the Font list arrow in the Property inspector, click Arial, Helvetica, sans-serif, click the Size list arrow, then click 4.

2. Make sure that Featured Catalog Accessories is still selected, click the Colors button on the Assets panel, click and drag one of the shades of blue from the list of colors onto the selected text, then deselect the text.

   Compare your screen to Figure E-19.

3. Click in the cell below the packing cube image, then use the Property inspector to set the horizontal alignment to Left and the vertical alignment to Top.

4. Make sure the description text is still selected, then change the font to Arial, Helvetica, sans serif, size 2.

5. Repeat Steps 3 and 4 to format the description text in the cells below the passport holder and headphones graphics, using the same formatting applied to the packing cubes description text.

   Your screen should resemble Figure E-20.

You formatted text in table cells.

FIGURE E-20

Formatting catalog item descriptions

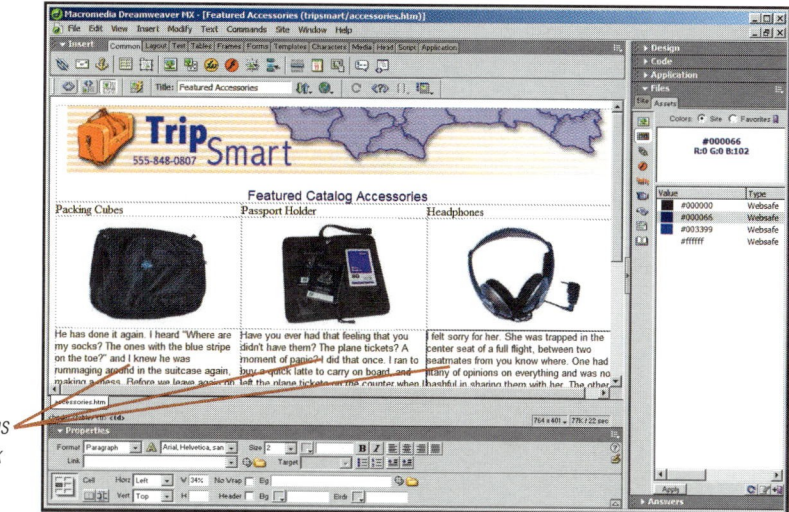

Three descriptions
with uniform look

Format cells

1. Click the table tag on the tag selector to select the entire table.

2. Type **12** in the CellSpace text box in the Property inspector, then press [Enter](Win) or [return](Mac) to add 12 pixels of space between the cells, as shown in Figure E-21.

   The descriptions are easier to read now because you inserted a little white space between the columns.

3. Click in the cell with the Packing Cubes heading to place the insertion point.

4. Click the Background Color button in the Property inspector, then click the second color in the fourth row (#003399).

5. Repeat Step 4 to apply the background color #003399 to the next two cells containing the text Passport Holder and Headphones, then compare your screen to Figure E-22.

   The headings are no longer visible against the blue background.

6. Save your work.

You formatted table cells by adding cell spacing. You set the background color for three cells to blue.

MACROMEDIA DREAMWEAVER E-24

FIGURE E-21

Changing the CellSpace amount

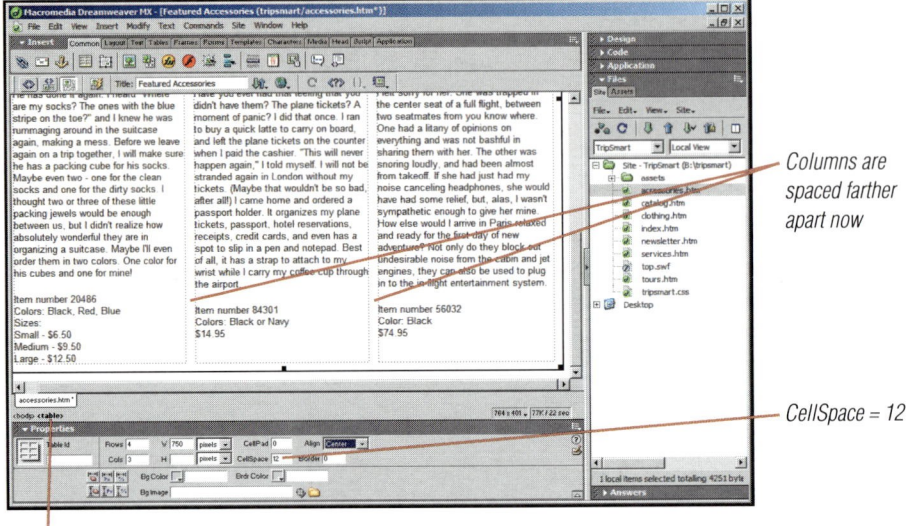

Columns are spaced farther apart now

CellSpace = 12

Table tag

FIGURE E-22

Formatted cell backgrounds

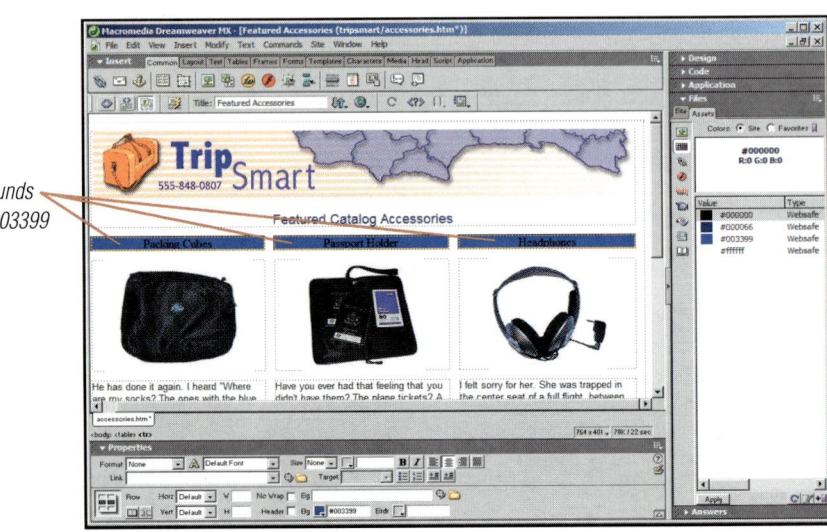

Cell backgrounds with color #003399 applied

Working with Tables

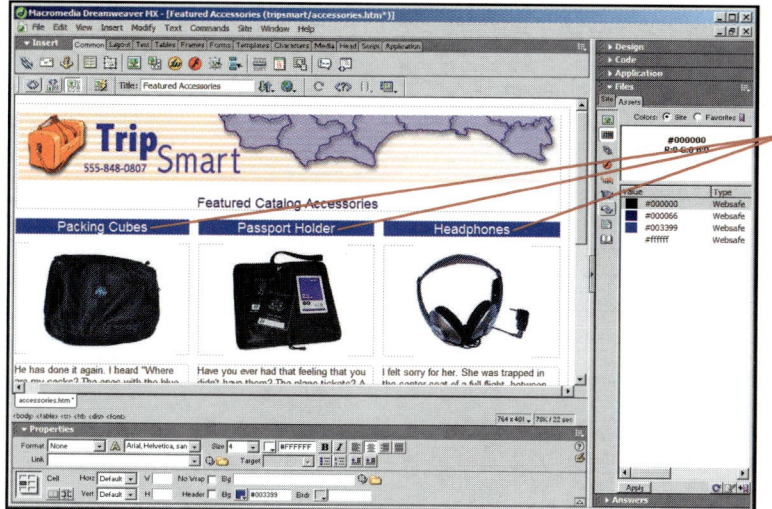

Formatted text labels

Item numbers with bold formatting applied

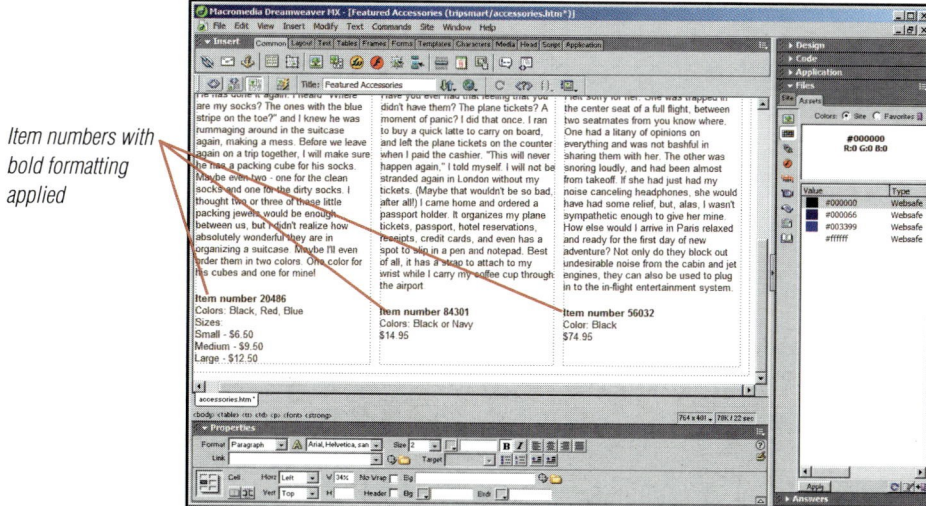

Modify cell content

1. Select the Packing Cubes text label in the cell above the packing cube image, use the Property inspector to format the text as Arial, Helvetica, sans-serif, Size 4, center-aligned, white (#FFFFFF) then deselect the text.

    Compare your screen with Figure E-23.

2. Repeat Step 1 to format the Passport Holder and Headphones text labels.

3. Scroll to the bottom of the page, select Item number 20486, then click the Bold button in the Property inspector. **B**

4. Apply bold formatting to the item numbers in the next two cells, as shown in Figure E-24.

5. Save your work, preview the accessories page in your browser, then close your browser.

6. Close the accessories page.

You formatted the text headings and the item numbers on the accessories page.

PERFORM WEB SITE MAINTENANCE

What You'll Do

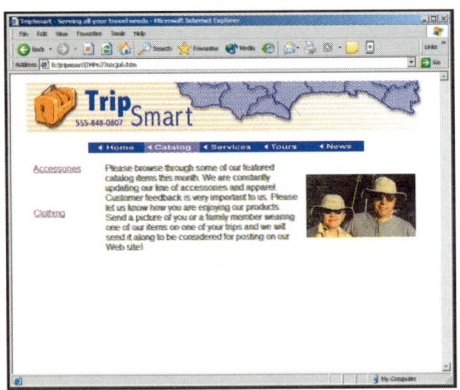

In this lesson, you will use some of Dreamweaver's site maintenance tools to check for broken links, orphaned files, and missing alternate text. You will also verify that all colors are Web-safe. You will then correct any problems that you find.

Maintaining a Web Site

As you add pages, links, and content to a Web site, it can quickly become difficult to manage. It's important to perform maintenance tasks frequently to make sure your Web site operates smoothly. To keep a Web site "clean," you should use Dreamweaver site maintenance tools frequently. You have already learned about some of the tools described in the paragraphs below. While it is important to use them as you create and modify your pages, it is also important to run them at periodic intervals after publishing your Web site to make sure your Web site is always error-free.

Checking Links Sitewide

Before and after you publish your Web site, you should use the Link Checker panel to make sure all internal links are working. If the Link Checker panel displays any broken links, you should repair them. If the Link Checker panel displays any orphaned files, you should evaluate whether to delete them or link them to existing pages.

Using the Assets Panel

You should also use the Assets panel to check the list of images and colors used in your Web site. If you see images listed that are not being used, you should move them to a storage folder outside the Web site until you need them. You should also check the Colors list to make sure that all colors in the site are Web-safe. If there are non-Web-safe colors in the list, locate the elements to which these colors are applied and apply Web-safe colors to them.

Using Site Reports

You can use the Reports command on the Site menu to generate six different reports that can help you maintain your Web site. You choose the type of report you want to run in the Reports dialog box, shown in Figure E-25. You can specify whether to generate the report for the entire current local site, selected files in the site, or a selected folder. You can also generate a Workflow report to see files that have been checked out by others or to view the Design Notes attached to files.

Using the Site Map

You can use the site map to check your navigation structure. Does the navigation structure shown in the site map reflect a logically organized flowchart? Is each page three or four clicks from the home page? If the answer is no to either of these questions, you can make adjustments to improve the navigation structure.

Testing Pages

Finally, you should test your Web site using many different types and versions of browsers, platforms, and screen resolutions. You should test all links to make sure they connect to valid, active Web sites. Pages that download slowly should be trimmed in size to improve performance. You should analyze all feedback on the Web site objectively, saving both positive and negative comments for future reference to help you make improvements to the site.

FIGURE E-25
Reports dialog box

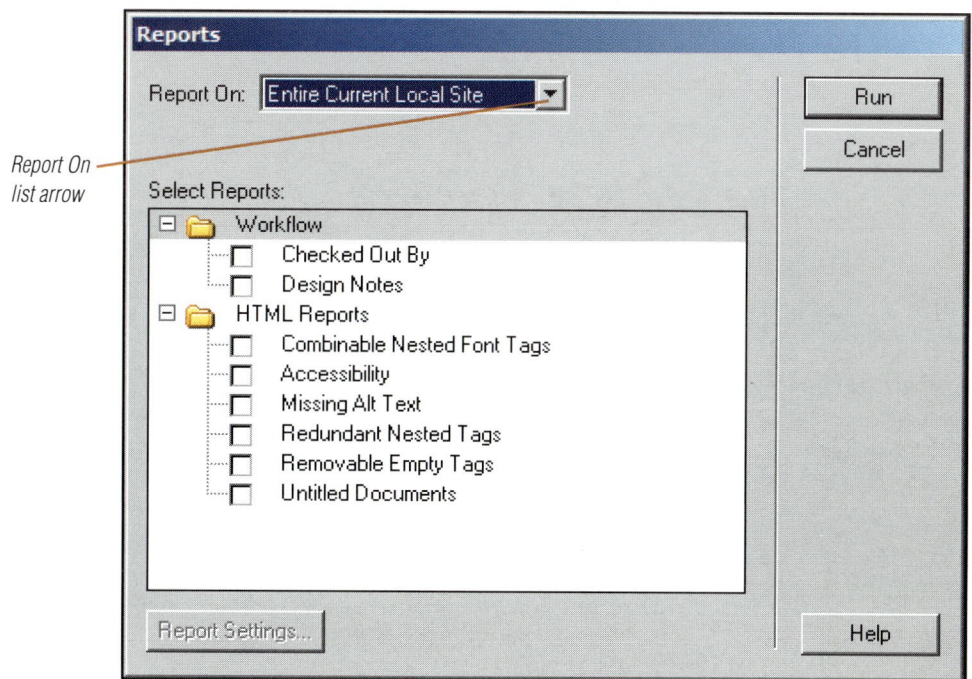

Report On list arrow

Check for broken links

1. Open the Site panel (if necessary).

2. Click Site on the Site panel menu bar, then click Recreate Site to Cache (Win) or click Site on the menu bar, then click Recreate Site Cache (Mac).

3. Click Site on the Site panel menu bar, point to Check Links Sitewide, click the Show list arrow in the Link Checker panel, then click Broken Links (if necessary).

   No broken links are listed in the Link Checker, as shown in Figure E-26.

You verified that there are no broken links in the Web site.

FIGURE E-26
Link Checker displaying no broken links

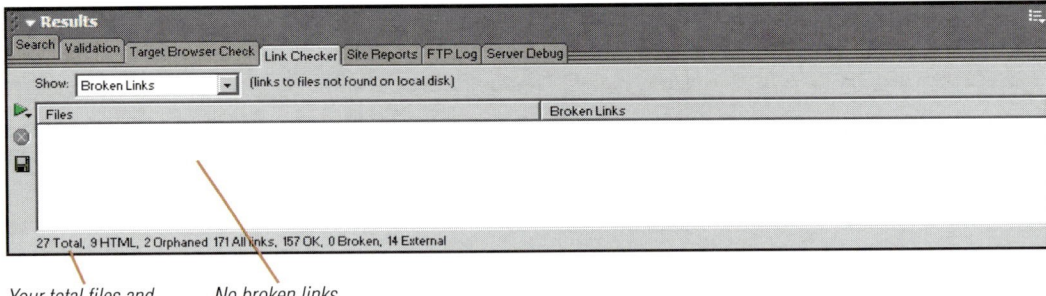

Your total files and total links may differ   *No broken links*

Check for orphaned files

1. Click the Show list arrow, then click Orphaned Files.

   As Figure E-27 shows, the accessories page and the clothing page appear as orphaned files. You will link the catalog page to these pages later.

   > TIP   If you have more than two orphaned files, click Site on the Site panel menu bar, click Recreate Site Cache, then check for orphaned files again.

2. Close the Results panel group.

You used the Link Checker to find two orphaned files in the Web site.

FIGURE E-27

Link Checker displaying orphaned files

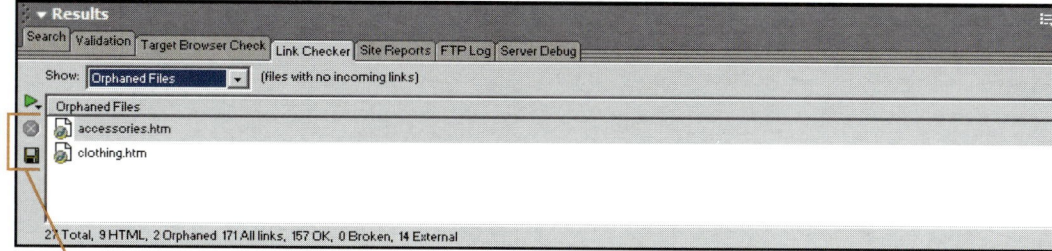

Two orphaned
files listed

Remove orphaned files

1. Open dwe_1.htm from the unit_e data files folder and save it in the Web site as **clothing.htm**, overwriting the existing file.

2. Copy the hat.jpg, vest.jpg, and pants.jpg files on the clothing page to the assets folder in the Web site.

3. Change the path of the TripSmart banner path to the tripsmart.jpg image in the assets folder in the TripSmart Web site, then save and close the clothing page.

4. Open dwe_2.htm from the unit_e data files folder, then save it in the TripSmart Web site as **catalog.htm**, overwriting the existing file.

5. Copy the hats_on_the_amazon.jpg file to the assets folder in the Web site.

6. Check all internal links and images to verify that all paths are set correctly, then save and close the catalog page.

   > TIP Use the Modify Navigation Bar dialog box to change the paths of the navigation bar images and links to appropriate files in the TripSmart Web site.

7. Open the accessories page.

8. Place the insertion point in the last cell in the table, press [Tab] to insert a new row, then type **Back to catalog page**.

9. Format the Back to Catalog page text as Arial, Helvetica, sans serif, size 3, then link the Back to Catalog page text to catalog.htm.

   Compare your screen to Figure E-28.

   (continued)

FIGURE E-28

Link to catalog page on accessories page

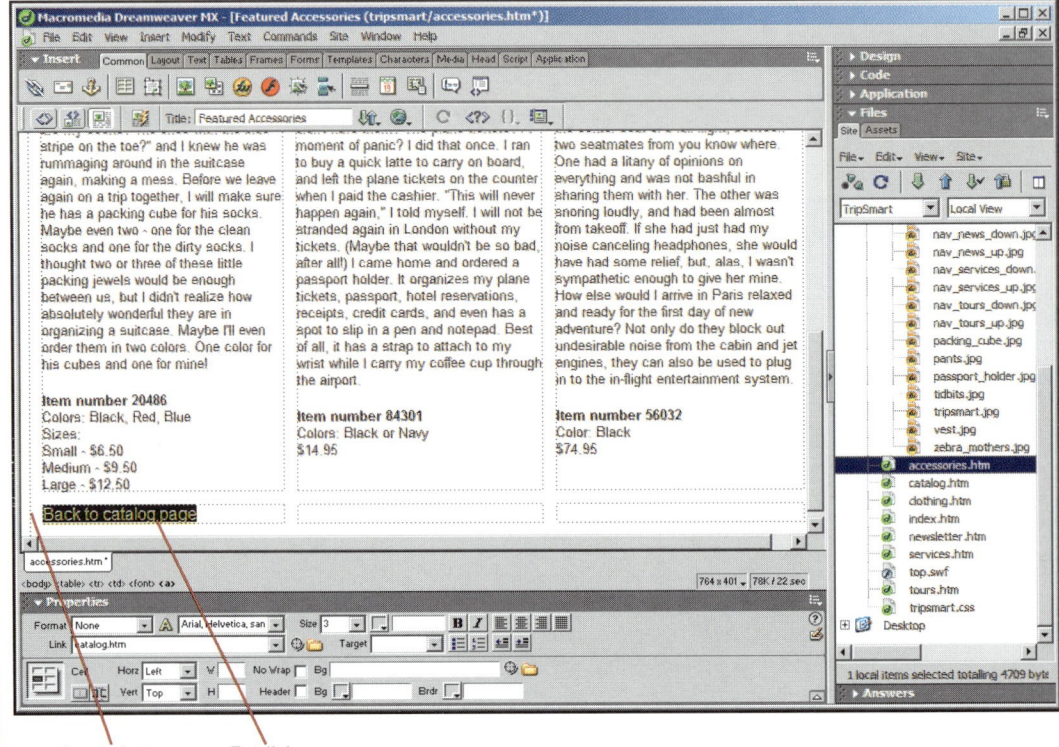

Inserted row   Text link

Working with Tables

Link to catalog page on clothing page

As we rounded the bend in the river, a gust of east wind whipped hats off heads and into the murky Amazon river that piranhas call home. Others peered sadly over the rail. I grinned like a caiman. My hat was tied securely and snug in place. Thank you, Safari Hat! My fellow explorers ended the day with red faces in more ways than one.

Item number 50501
Colors: Khaki, White
Sizes: Small, Medium, Large
$29.00

"Can you hold these for a few minutes, dear?" I've heard that before. She handed me her binoculars while she bartered with the natives. I slipped them into my pocket with my extra film and batteries. I was glad I had on my photographer's vest today. It held all our necessities: bottled water, guidebook, compass, and snacks; in addition to the camera, lenses, and flash attachment. What a worker!

Item number 52301
Colors: Khaki, Moss
Sizes: Small, Medium, Large
$54.95

Weather changes quickly in Kenya. As I sipped my English tea before we headed out to our early morning game viewing, I decided to wear my Kenya Convertible Pants. As the weather warmed, I unzipped the legs to cool off a bit. After the safari, we arrived for lunch at the Mount Kenya Safari Club. I zipped them back on and felt more presentable at such an elegant establishment. Propriety and comfort at one low price.

Item number 62495
Color: Khaki
Sizes: Small, Medium, Large, Extra-large
$39.50

Back to Catalog page

Link to catalog page

10. Save and close the accessories page, then open the clothing page.

11. Click the table tag to select it, then click Modify on the menu bar, point to Table, then click Clear Cell Heights to clear the cell heights for the new row.

12. Repeat Steps 8 and 9 to create a Back to Catalog page text link at the bottom of the clothing page, compare your screen with Figure E-29, then save and close the clothing page.

13. Re-create the Site Cache, click the Refresh button on the Site Panel, then run the Check Links Sitewide report again to verify that there are no orphaned files.

> TIP   If the Link Checker panel shows orphaned files, re-create the Site Cache. If orphaned files still appear in the report, locate them in the Web site, then correct the paths that contain errors.

You corrected the two orphaned files by linking the accessories and clothing pages from the catalog page.

Verify that all colors are Web-safe

1. Click the Colors button on the Assets panel to view the Web site colors, as shown in Figure E-30.

    The Assets panel shows that all colors used in the Web site are Web-safe.

You verified that the Web site contains all Web-safe colors.

Check for untitled documents

1. Click Site on the menu bar, then click Reports to open the Reports dialog box.

2. Click the Untitled Documents check box, click the Report On list arrow, click Entire Current Local Site, as shown in Figure E-31, then click Run.

    The Site Reports panel opens and shows no files, indicating that all documents in the Web site contain titles.

3. Close the Results panel group.

You verified that the Web site contains no untitled documents.

Assets panel displaying Web-safe colors

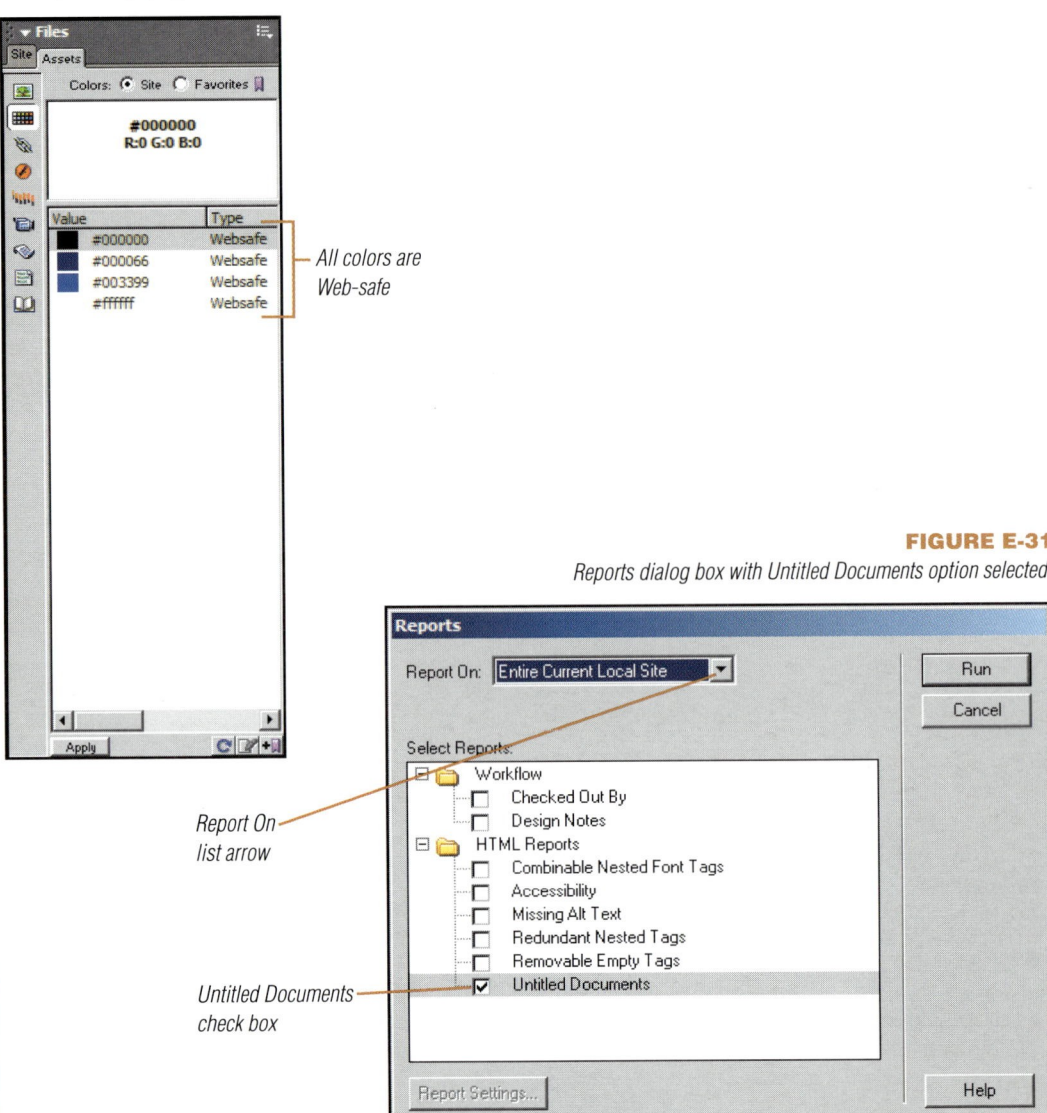

All colors are Web-safe

FIGURE E-31
Reports dialog box with Untitled Documents option selected

Report On list arrow

Untitled Documents check box

Working with Tables

FIGURE E-32

Reports dialog box with Missing Alt Text option selected

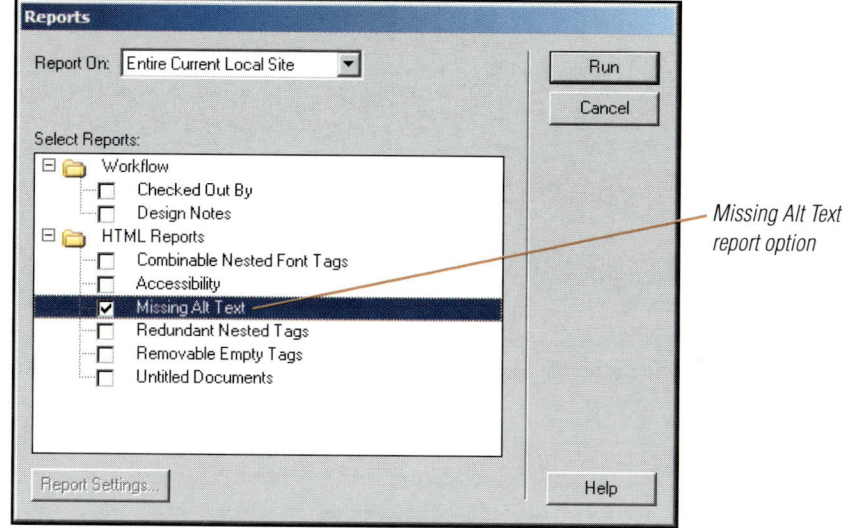

Missing Alt Text report option

1. Using Figure E-32 as a guide, run another report that checks the entire current local site for missing alternate text.

   Two pages contain images that are missing alternate text, as shown in Figure E-33.

2. Open the catalog page, then find the image that contains no alternate text.

3. Add appropriate alternate text to the image.

4. Repeat Steps 2 and 3 to locate the image on the home page that contains no alternate text, then add alternate text to it.

5. Save your work, then run the report again to check the entire site for missing alternate text.

   No files should appear in the Site Reports panel.

6. Close the Results panel group, then close all open pages.

You ran a report to check for missing alternate text in the entire site. You then added alternate text to two images.

FIGURE E-33

Missing Alt Text Results dialog box

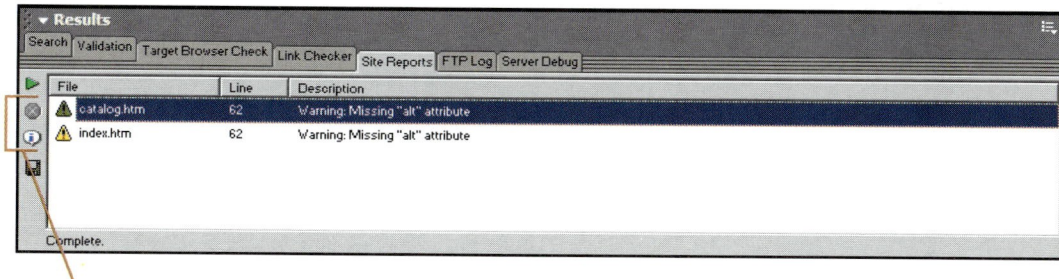

Two missing "alt" tags found

Create a table.

1. Open the Blooms & Bulbs Web site. (If you did not create this Web site in Units A through D, contact your instructor for assistance.)
2. Open workshops.htm from the Web site.
3. Insert a table on the page with the following settings: Rows: 5, Columns: 3, Width: 750 pixels, Border: 0.
4. Enter the text **This table was used for page layout.** in the Summary text box of the Accessibility Options for Table dialog box.
5. Center the table on the page, then use Figure E-34 as a guide for completing this exercise.
6. Save your work.

Resize, split, and merge cells.

1. Select the first cell in the first row, then set the cell width to **35%**.
2. Select the second cell in the first row, then set the cell width to **35%**.
3. Select the third cell in the first row, then set the cell width to **30%**.
4. Merge the third cell in the third row with the third cell in the fourth row.
5. Split the first cell in the third row into two rows.
6. Split the second cell in the third row into two rows.
7. Merge the three cells in the first row.
8. Merge the three cells in the second row.
9. Save your work.

Insert and align graphics in table cells.

1. Use the Assets panel to insert the Blooms & Bulbs banner in the first row and enter appropriate alternate text when prompted.
2. Center the banner.
3. Copy the navigation bar from the home page, paste it in the second row of the table, then center the navigation bar using the Horz list arrow in the Property inspector.
4. Modify the navigation bar to show the workshops element in the down image state and the home element in the up image state.
5. Use the Insert bar to insert the texas_rose.jpg file in the third cell of the third row (the merged cell) directly below the navigation bar. You can find the texas_rose.jpg file in the in the unit_e assets folder where your data files are stored. Add the alternate text **Texas Rose Festival logo** to the texas_rose.jpg when prompted, then center the image in the cell.
6. Use the tag selector to select the cell containing the texas_rose.jpg image, then set the vertical alignment to Top.
7. Use the Insert bar to insert the yellow_rose.jpg file from the unit_e assets folder in the second cell in the fifth row. Add the alternate text **Yellow roses** to the yellow_rose.jpg when prompted.
8. Use the Align list arrow to set the alignment of the yellow_rose.jpg to Left.

9. Select the cell containing the yellow_rose.jpg, then set the vertical alignment of the selected cell to Top.
10. Insert the tearoom.jpg file from the unit_e assets folder in the second cell of the last row, adding the alternate text **Rose arrangement in antique pitcher** when prompted.
11. Center the tearoom.jpg image.
12. Set the vertical alignment of the cell containing the tearoom.jpg image to Top.
13. Save your work.

Insert text and format cell content.

1. Type **Texas Rose Festival** in the second cell in the fourth row, insert a soft return, then type **Tyler, Texas**.
2. Type **Agenda** in the first cell in the fourth row.
3. Open the file agenda.htm from the unit_e data files folder, copy all the text in this file, close agenda.htm, then paste the text into the first cell in the fifth row.
4. Open the file nursery.htm from the unit_e data files folder, copy all the text from this file, paste it into the cell containing the yellow_rose.jpg image to the right of the image, then close the file.
5. Open the file tearoom.htm from the unit_e data files folder, copy all the text from this file, close the tearoom.htm file, then paste the text in the first cell in the last row.
6. Open the file exhibition.htm from the unit_e data files folder, copy all the text from this file, close the exhibition.htm file, then paste the text in the last cell in the last row.

7. Click to place the insertion point to the right of the texas_rose.jpg image, then insert a hard return.

8. Type **Price: $60**, create a soft return, type **includes:**, insert a soft return, type **Admissions, lunch,** insert a soft return, then type **snacks, and tea**. (*Hint*: if your table expands too much, select the table tag on the tag selector and it will revert back to its original size.)

9. Select the Texas Rose Festival text, then format it using the following settings: Font: Arial, Helvetica, sans-serif; Size: 5; Style: Bold; Alignment: Right; Color: #336633.

10. Select the Tyler, Texas text and format it using the following settings: Font: Arial, Helvetica, sans-serif; Size: 4; Color: #336633.

11. Select the cell containing Texas Rose Festival, Tyler, Texas, then set the vertical alignment to Top.

12. Select each of the paragraphs of text and format them using the following settings: Font: Arial, Helvetica, sans-serif; Size: 3; Vertical Alignment: Top.

13. Select the text under the texas_rose.jpg and format it using the following settings: Font: Arial, Helvetica, sans-serif; Size: 2; Style: Bold; Alignment: Center.

14. Select the cell with the word Agenda in it, then change the cell background color to #336633.

15. Format the word Agenda using the following settings: Font: Arial, Helvetica, sans-serif;

Size: 4; Style: Bold; Alignment: Center; Color: #FFFFFF.

16. Select the table, then change the cell spacing to 5.

17. Save your work, preview the page in your browser, then close your browser.

Perform Web site maintenance.

1. Use the Link Checker panel to check for broken links, then fix any broken links that appear.

2. Use the Link Checker panel to check for orphaned files. If any orphaned files appear in the report, take steps to link them to appropriate pages or remove them.

FIGURE E-34
Completed Skills Review

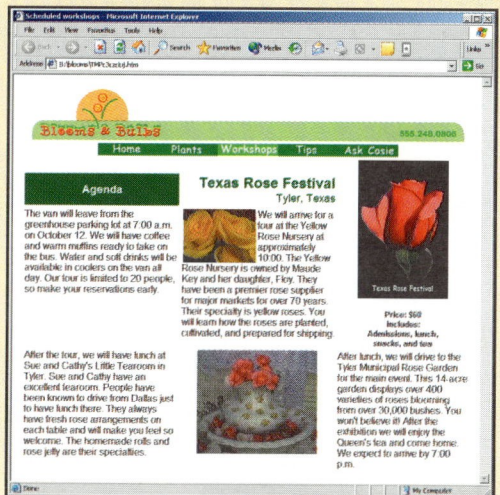

3. Use the Assets panel to check for non-Web-safe colors.

4. Run an Untitled Documents report for the entire local site. If the report lists any pages that have no titles, add page titles to the untitled pages. Run the report again to verify that all pages have page titles.

5. Run a report to look for missing alternate text. Add alternate text to any graphics that need it, then run the report again to verify that all images contain alternate text.

6. Save your work, then close all open pages.

In this exercise you will continue your work on the Rapids Transit Web site that you began in Project Builder 1 in Unit A and developed in Units B through D. Mike Andrew, the owner, has asked you to work on the page for his equipment rentals. He wants you to use a table for page layout.

1. Open the Rapids Transit Web site. If you did not create this Web site in Unit A, contact your instructor for assistance.

2. Open rentals.htm from the Web site.

3. Insert a table with the following settings: Rows: four, Columns: two, Width: 750 pixels, Border: 0. Enter an appropriate table summary when prompted. Center the table.

4. Merge the cells in the top row, then place the Rapids Transit banner into the resulting merged cell. Add the following alternate text to the image: **Rapids Transit banner,** then center the banner.

5. Merge the cells in the second row, copy the navigation bar from another page, then paste it into the merged cell.

6. Center the navigation bar.

7. Split the first cell in the third row into two rows, type **Equipment Rentals** in the first of these two rows, then format the Equipment Rentals text using the following settings: Font: Arial, Helvetica, sans serif; Color: #000099; Size: 4, Alignment: centered.

8. Format the E and R in Equipment Rentals one size larger than the rest of the text.

9. Place the kayak.jpg file from the unit_e assets folder in the first cell in the fourth row, add the following alternate text to the image, **Kayaking on the river**, then center the kayak.jpg image.

10. Use the tag selector to select the cell with the kayak.jpg image, then change the cell width to 30%.

11. Open the file rental_info.htm, paste the contents into the cell to the right of the image, then close the rental_info.htm file.

12. Format the paragraph as Arial, Helvetica, sans-serif, size 3, then set the vertical alignment to Top.

13. Merge the cells in the bottom row, then insert a new (nested) table with 3 rows, 4 columns, 100% width, and a border of 1. Set the cell padding and cell spacing for the nested table to 0. Enter **Rental prices** for the table summary.

14. Format the nested table border to color #000066, then set each cell width in any row to 25%.

15. Enter the equipment data below into your table then format the text as Arial, Helvetica, sans-serif, size 3.

Canoe	**$8.00**	**Life Jacket**	**$2.00**
Kayak	**$9.00**	**Helmet**	**$2.00**
Two-Man Rubber Raft	**$7.00**	**Dry Packs**	**$1.00**

16. Save your work, view the page in your browser, then compare your screen with Figure E-35.

17. Close the browser, open store.htm from the unit_e data files folder, then save it in the Web site, overwriting the existing store.htm file.

18. Save the fruit_basket.jpg file in the Web site assets folder, then set the banner path to the rapids.jpg file in the Rapids Transit Web site assets folder.

19. Run reports for broken links, orphaned files, missing alternate text, and untitled documents. Make corrections as necessary.

20. Save your work, then close all open pages.

FIGURE E-35

Completed Project Builder 1

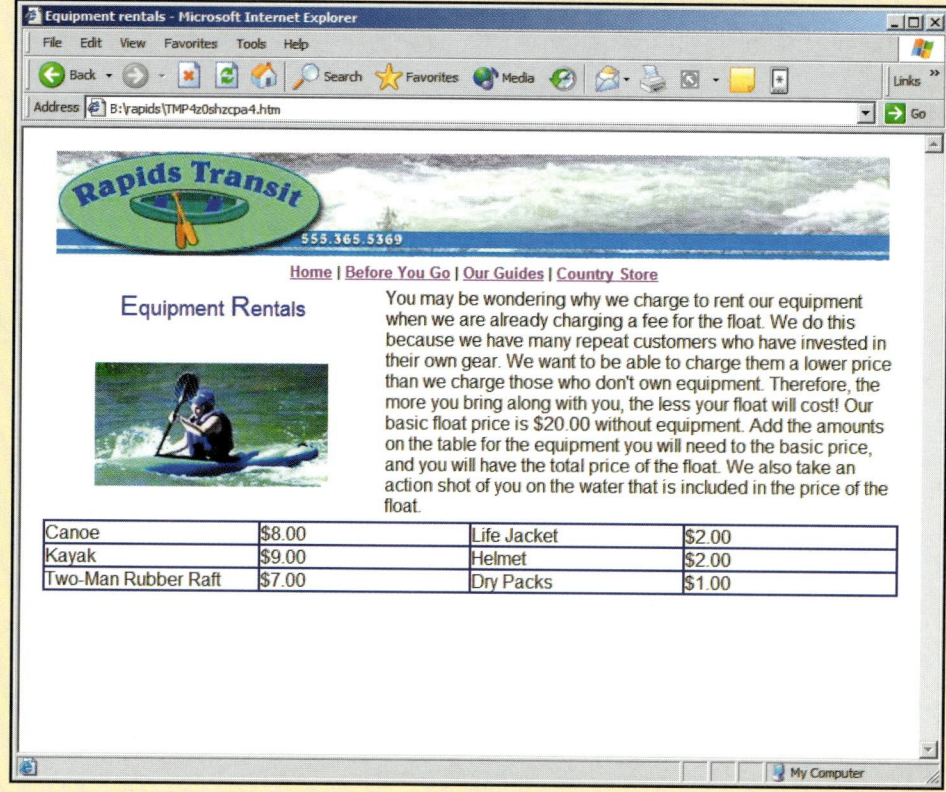

Use Figure E-36 as a guide to continue your work on the Jacob's Web site that you started in Project Builder 2 in Unit A and developed in Units B through D. Chef Jacob would like you to develop a short page listing his hours and directions to the restaurant. You decide to use a table to lay out the page.

1. If you did not create this Web site in Units A through D, contact your instructor for assistance.

2. Open the Jacob's Web site, then open directions.htm.

3. Type **Hours and Directions to Jacob's** for the page title, replacing the original title.

4. Create a table on the page with the following settings: Rows: seven, Columns: two, Width: 750 pixels, Border: 0, adding an appropriate table summary when prompted.

5. Center the table and set the two cells in the bottom row to 50% widths.

6. Merge the cells in the first row, then insert the Jacob's banner. Center-align the banner, then enter appropriate alternate text for it.

7. Merge the cells in the second row, copy the navigation bar from another page, then paste the navigation bar in the resulting merged cell. Center-align the navigation bar.

8. Merge the cells in the fourth row and enter **Our hours are:**, then format it as Arial, Helvetica, sans-serif, size 3, centered, and bold.

9. In the first cell in the fifth row, type **Sunday through Thursday**, enter a soft return, then type **11:00 a.m. to 10:00 p.m.** Format the text as Arial, Helvetica, sans-serif, size 2, centered.

10. In the second cell in the fifth row, type **Fridays and Saturdays**, enter a soft return, then type **11:00 a.m. to 12:00 a.m.** Format the text as Arial, Helvetica, sans-serif, size 2, centered.

11. Merge the cells in the sixth row, then type **We have three private rooms that are available for private parties with advance reservations.** Insert a soft return in front of the text. Format the text as Arial, Helvetica, sans-serif, size 3, centered.

12. Insert the file signature_dish.jpg from the unit_e assets folder in the first cell in the last row, enter appropriate alternate text when prompted, then center the image.

13. Open the file directions_paragraph.htm, copy and paste the text in the second cell in the last row then format the paragraph as Arial, Helvetica, sans-serif, size 3. Then set the vertical alignment to Middle.

14. Place the insertion point to the right of the signature_dish image, create a soft return, type **Set-price dinners**, create a soft return, then type **are served on Saturday evenings**.

15. Format the text as Arial, Helvetica, sans-serif, size 2, centered.

16. Save your work, then preview the page in your browser.

17. Run reports for broken links, orphaned files, missing alternate text, and untitled documents. Make corrections as necessary, then close all open pages.

FIGURE E-36
Completed Project Builder 2

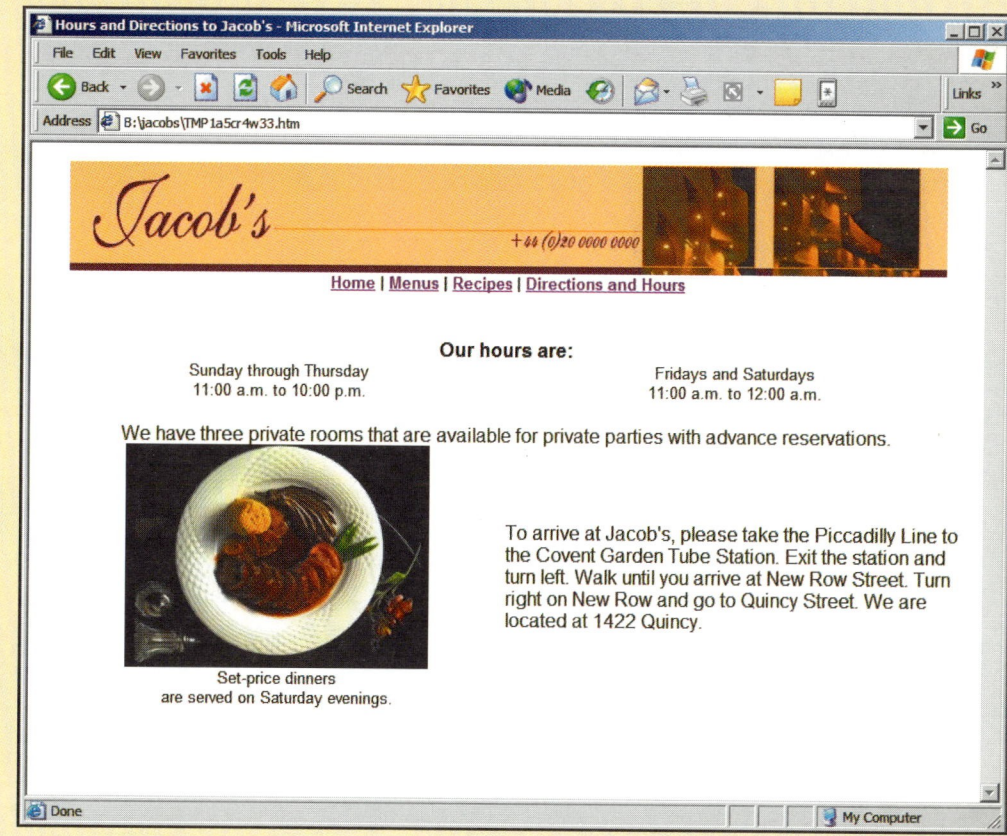

DESIGN PROJECT

Vesta Everitt has opened a new shop called Needles and Thread that carries needlepoint, cross-stitching, and smocking supplies. She is considering creating a Web site to promote her services and products and would like to gather some ideas before she hires a Web designer. She decides to visit the L.L. Bean and Neiman Marcus Web sites to look for design ideas, as shown in Figures E-37 and E-38.

1. Connect to the Internet, go to *www.course.com*, navigate to the page for this book, click the Student Online Companion link, then click the first link for this unit.
2. Click View on your browser's menu bar, then click Source Command to view the source code for the Neiman Marcus home page.
3. Search the code for table tags. Note the number that you find.
4. Go to *www.course.com*, navigate to the page for this book, click the Student Online Companion link, then click the second link for this unit.
5. Repeat Steps 2 and 3 for the L.L. Bean home page.
6. Using a word processor or scrap paper, list five design ideas that you like from either of these pages. Be sure to specify which page was the source of each idea.

FIGURE E-37
Source for Design Project

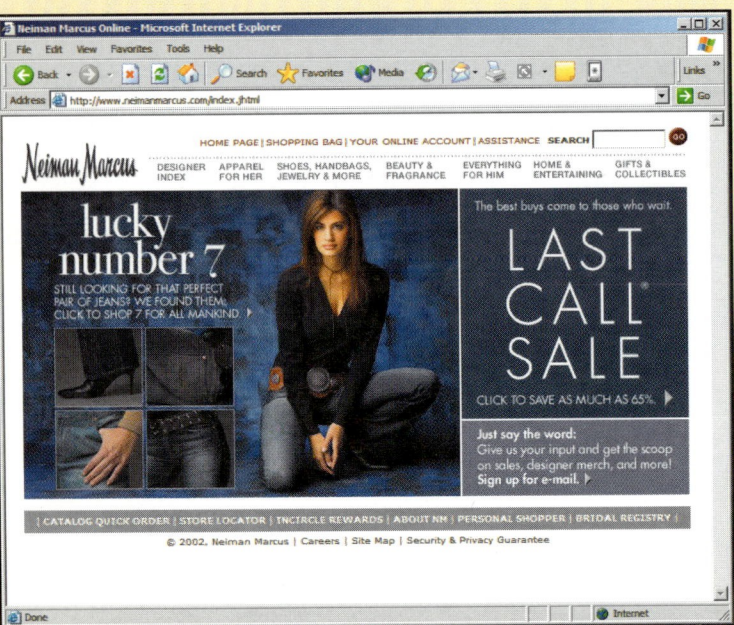

FIGURE E-38
Source for Design Project

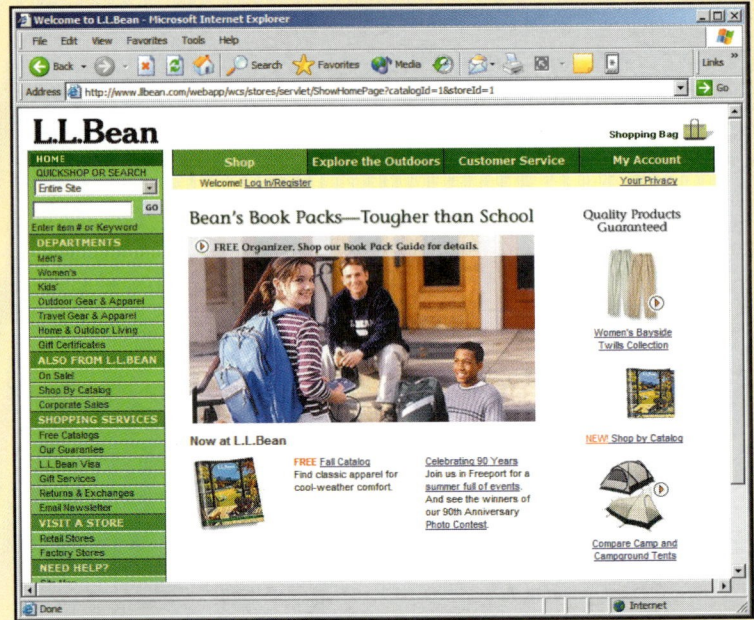

GROUP PROJECT

In this assignment, you will continue to work on the group Web site that you started in Unit A and developed in Units B through D. Depending on the size of your group, you can assign individual elements of the project to group members, or work collectively to create the finished product. There will be no data files supplied. You are building this Web site from unit to unit, so you must do each Group Project assignment in each unit to complete your Web site.

You will continue building your Web site by designing and completing a page that contains a table used for page layout. After completing your page, you will run several reports to test the Web site.

1. If you did not create this Web site in Units A through D, contact your instructor for assistance.
2. Meet as a group to review and evaluate your storyboard. Choose a page or pages to develop in which you will use a table for page layout.
3. Plan the content for the new page (or pages) by making a sketch of the table that shows where the content will be placed in the table cells. Split and merge cells and align each element as necessary to create a visually attractive layout.

4. Assign one or more team members the task of creating the table and placing the content in the cells using the sketch for guidance.
5. After you complete the pages, assign a team member to run a report that checks for broken links in the Web site. The team member should also correct any broken links that appear in the report.
6. Assign a team member the task of running a report on the Web site for orphaned files and correct any if found.
7. Assign a team member the task of running a report on pages that are missing alternate text. The team member should also add alternate text to elements that need it.

8. Assign a team member the task of running a report on any pages that do not have page titles and add titles to any pages, as needed.
9. Assign a team member the task of checking for any non-Web-safe colors in the Web site. If any are found, the team member should replace them with Web-safe colors.
10. As a group, preview all the pages in your browser and test all links. Evaluate the pages for both content and layout, then use the checklist in Figure E-39 to make sure your Web site is completed.
11. Assign team members the task of making any modifications necessary to improve the pages.

FIGURE E-39
Group Project check list

Web Site Checklist
1. Title any pages that have no page titles.
2. Check to see that all pages have consistent navigation links.
3. Check to see that all links work correctly.
4. Check to see that all images have alternate text.
5. Remove any non-Web-safe colors.
6. Delete any unnecessary files.
7. Remove any orphaned files.
8. Use tables for layout when possible.
9. View all pages using at least two different browser settings.
10. Verify that the home page has keywords, a description, and a point of contact.

GETTING STARTED WITH
MACROMEDIA FLASH

1. Understand the Macromedia Flash environment.

2. Open a document and play a movie.

3. Create and save a movie.

4. Work with layers and the timeline.

5. Plan a Web site.

6. Distribute a Macromedia Flash movie.

GETTING STARTED WITH MACROMEDIA FLASH

Introduction

Macromedia Flash is a program that allows you to create compelling interactive experiences, primarily by using animation. Yet, while it is known as a tool for creating complex animations for the Web, Macromedia Flash also has excellent drawing tools and tools for creating interactive controls, such as navigation buttons and menus. In addition, you can use its publishing capabilities to create Web sites and Web-based applications.

In only a few short years, Macromedia Flash has become the standard for both professional and casual Web developers. The reason that Macromedia Flash has become so popular is that the program is optimized for the Web. Web developers try to provide high-impact experiences for the user, to make sites come alive and turn them from static text and pictures to dynamic, interactive experiences. The problem has been that incorporating high-quality graphics and motion into a Web site can dramatically increase the download time and frustrate viewers as they wait for an image to appear or for an animation to play. Macromedia Flash directly addresses this problem by allowing developers to use vector images, which reduce the size of graphic files. Vector images appeal to developers for two reasons. First, they are scalable, which means they can be resized and reshaped without distortion. For example, you could easily have an object, such as an airplane, become smaller as it moves across the screen without having to create the plane in different sizes. Second, Macromedia Flash provides for streaming content over the Internet. Instead of waiting for the entire contents of a Web page to load, the viewer sees a continuous display of images. For example, if your Web site has a Macromedia Flash movie that is played when the viewer first visits your Web site, the viewer does not have to wait for the entire movie to be downloaded before it starts. Streaming allows the movie to start playing when the Web site is opened, and it continues as frames of the movie are delivered to the viewer's computer.

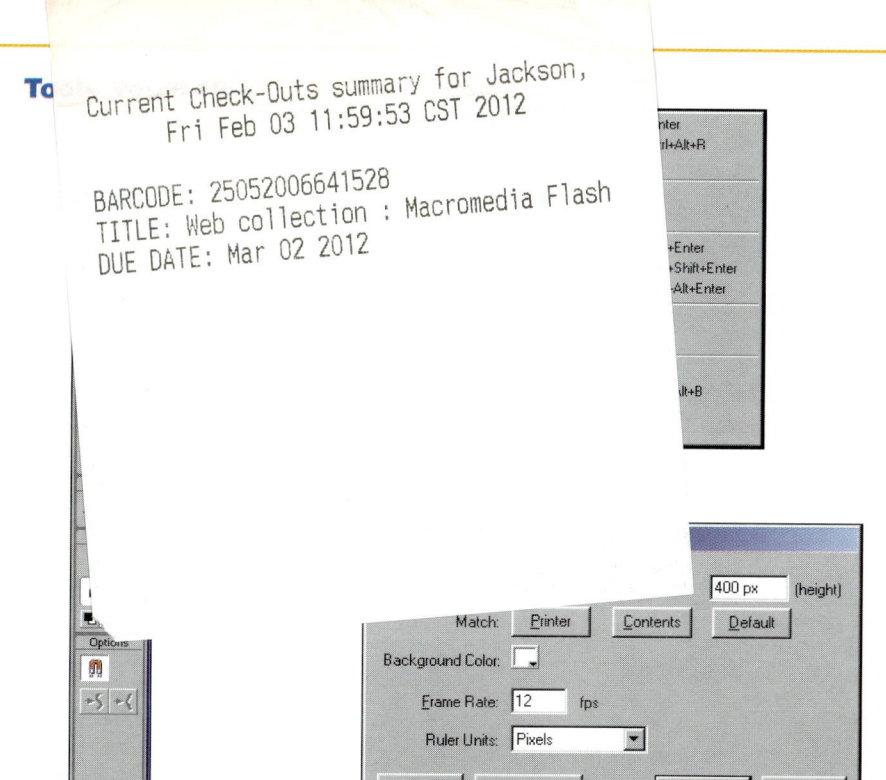

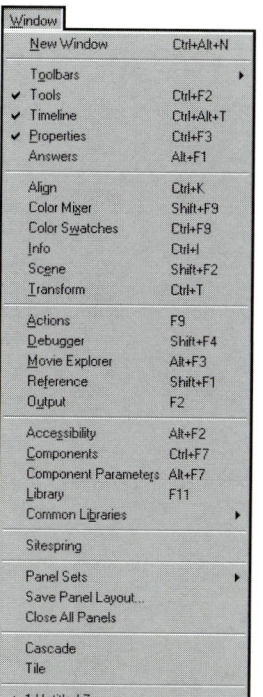

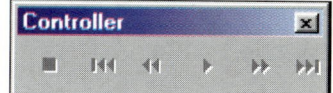

UNDERSTAND THE MACROMEDIA FLASH ENVIRONMENT

What You'll Do

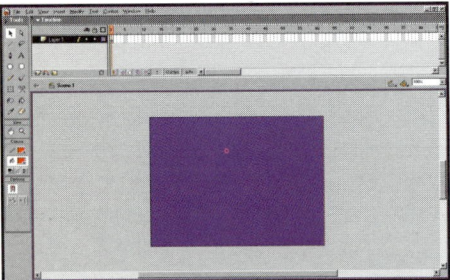

 In this lesson, you will learn about the development environment in Macromedia Flash and how to change Macromedia Flash settings to customize your workspace.

Organizing the Macromedia Flash Development Environment

As a developer, one of the most important things to do is to organize your workspace—that is, to decide what to have displayed on the screen and how to arrange the various tools and windows. Because **Macromedia Flash** is such a powerful program with many tools, your workspace may become cluttered. Fortunately, it is easy to customize the workspace to display only the tools needed at any particular time.

The development environment in Macromedia Flash operates according to a movie metaphor: you create scenes on a stage; these scenes run in frames on a timeline. As you work in Macromedia Flash, you create a movie by arranging objects (such as graphics and text) on the stage, and animate the objects using the

timeline. You can play the movie on the stage, as you are working on it, by using the movie controls (start, stop, rewind, and so on). In addition, you can test the movie in a browser. When the movie is ready for distribution, you can export it as a Macromedia Flash Player movie, which viewers can access using a Macromedia Flash Player. A **Macromedia Flash Player** is a program that is installed on the viewer's computer to allow Macromedia Flash movies to be played in Web browsers or as stand-alone applications. Millions of people have installed the Macromedia Flash Player (a free download from the Macromedia Web site), allowing them to view and interact with Macromedia Flash movies and Web applications. Macromedia Flash movies can also be saved as executable files, called projectors, which can be viewed without the need for the Macromedia Flash Player.

When you start Macromedia Flash, three basic parts of the development environment are displayed: the stage, the timeline, and the workspace. In addition, you can choose to have other parts of the program displayed. You use the toolbox to create and edit graphics, and you use panels to control the characteristics and change the attributes of selected objects. A description of the Macromedia Flash development environment follows.

Stage

The **stage** contains all of the objects that are part of the movie that will be seen by your viewers. It shows how the objects behave within the movie and how they interact with each other. You can resize the stage and change the background color applied to it. You can draw objects on or import objects to the stage, and then edit and animate them.

Timeline

The **timeline** is used to organize and control the movie's contents by specifying when each object appears on the stage. The timeline is critical to the creation of movies, because a movie is merely a series of still images that appear over time. The images are contained within **frames**, which are units of the timeline. Frames in a Macromedia Flash movie are similar to frames in a motion picture. When a Macromedia Flash movie is played, a playhead moves from frame to frame in the timeline, causing the contents of each frame to appear on the stage in a linear sequence.

The timeline indicates where you are at any time within the movie and allows you to insert, delete, select, and move frames. It shows the animation in your movie and the layers that contain objects. Layers help to organize the objects on the stage. You can draw and edit objects on one layer without affecting objects on other layers. Layers are a way to stack objects so they can overlap and give a 3-D appearance on the stage.

Toolbox

The **toolbox** contains a set of tools used to draw and edit graphics and text. It is divided into four sections.

Tools—Includes draw, paint, text, and selection tools, which are used to create lines, shapes, illustrations, and text. The selection tools are used to select objects so that they can be modified in a number of ways.

View—Includes the Zoom Tool and the Hand Tool, which are used to zoom in on and out of parts of the stage and to pan the stage window, respectively.

Colors—Includes tools and icons used to change the stroke (border of an object) and fill (area inside an object) colors.

Options—Includes options for selected tools, such as allowing you to choose the size of the brush when using the Brush Tool.

Panels are used to view, organize, and modify objects and features in a movie. For example, the Properties panel (also called the Property Inspector) is used to change the properties of an object, such as the fill color of a circle. The Properties panel is context sensitive so that if you are working with text it displays the appropriate options, such as font and font size.

Although several panels are available, you may choose to display them only when they are needed. This keeps your workspace from becoming too cluttered. The toolbox and panels are floating elements, meaning that you can move them around the work-space. This allows you to dock (link) panels together as a way of organizing them in the workspace. You can also make room in the workspace by collapsing panels so only their title bars are displayed.

Regardless of how you decide to customize your development environment, the stage and the menu bar are always displayed. Usually, you display the timeline, toolbox, and one or more panels. Figure A-1 shows the Macromedia Flash default development environment with the stage, timeline, tool-box, and panels displayed.

When you start a new Macromedia Flash document (movie), you can set the docu-ment properties, such as the size of the

window (stage) the movie will play in, the background color, and the speed of the movie in frames per second. You can change these settings using the Document command on the Modify menu. To increase the size of the stage so that the objects on the stage can be more easily edited, you can change the magnification setting using commands on the View menu.

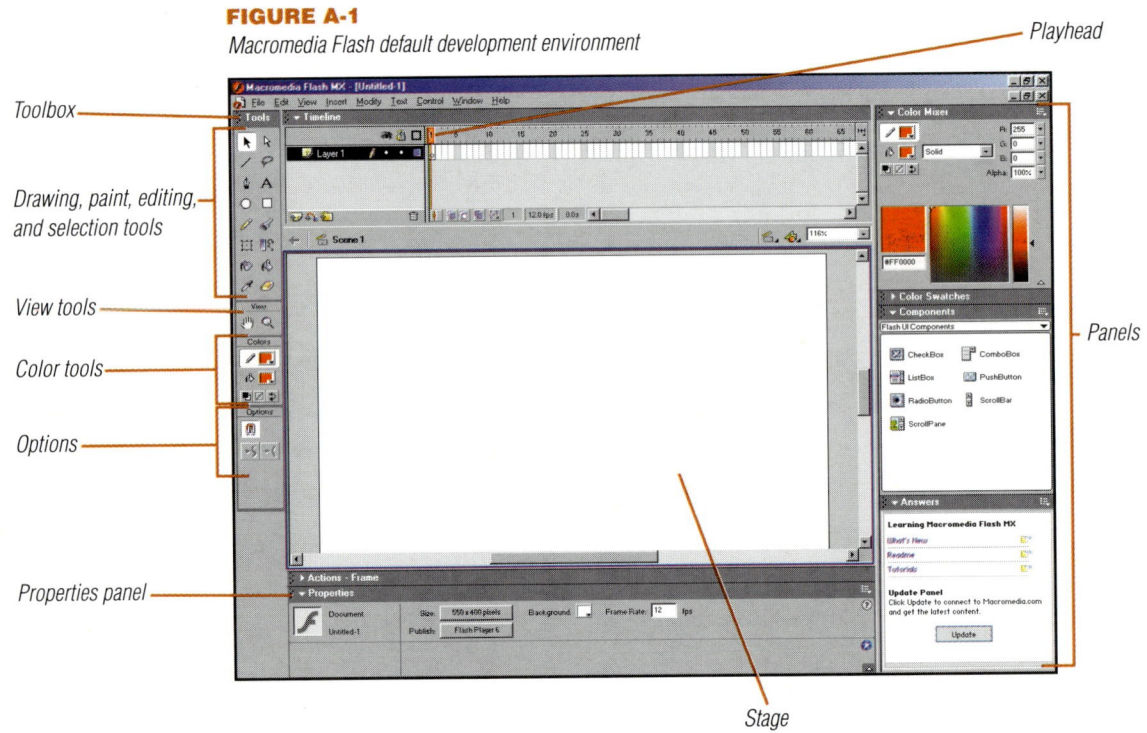

FIGURE A-1

Macromedia Flash default development environment

Playhead

Toolbox

Drawing, paint, editing, and selection tools

View tools

Color tools

Options

Properties panel

Panels

Stage

FIGURE A-2
Document Properties dialog box

Click Background color swatch to change background color

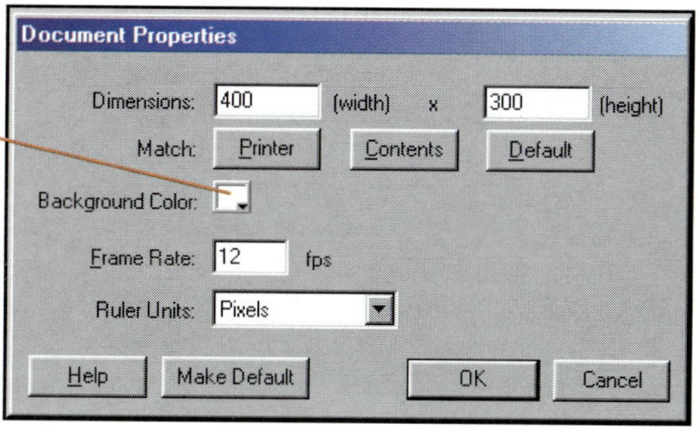

Document Properties

Dimensions:	400	(width)	x	300	(height)
Match:	Printer	Contents	Default	
Background Color:				
Frame Rate:	12	fps		
Ruler Units:	Pixels			

Help   Make Default   OK   Cancel

Start Macromedia Flash and set the movie properties and magnification

1. Click the Start button on the taskbar, point to All Programs, point to the Macromedia folder, then click the Macromedia Flash MX program icon (Win).

   TIP If you are starting Macromedia Flash on a Macintosh, double-click the hard drive icon, double-click the Applications folder, double-click the Macromedia Flash MX folder, and then double-click the Macromedia Flash MX program icon.

2. Click the Maximize button in the movie title bar, if necessary.

3. Click Window on the menu bar, then verify that Properties is checked.

4. Click the Document properties button in the Properties panel to display the Document Properties dialog box. 550 x 400 pixels

5. Double-click the width text box (if necessary), type **400**, double-click the height text box, then type **300**.

6. Click the Background Color swatch, shown in Figure A-2, then click the blue color swatch on the left column of the color palette.

   (continued)

7. Accept the remaining default values, then click OK to close the Document Properties dialog box.

8. Drag the scroll bars at the bottom and the right of the screen to center the stage.

9. Click View on the menu bar, point to Magnification, then click 100%.

10. Click 100% in the View magnification box at the top of the stage, as shown in Figure A-3, type **90**, and then press [Enter] (Win) or [return] (Mac).

11. Click File on the menu bar, click Save As, then save your file as **devenvironment.fla**.

You started the Macromedia Flash program, set the document properties and background color, then named the movie.

FIGURE A-3
View magnification box

View magnification box

FIGURE A-4

The Properties panel

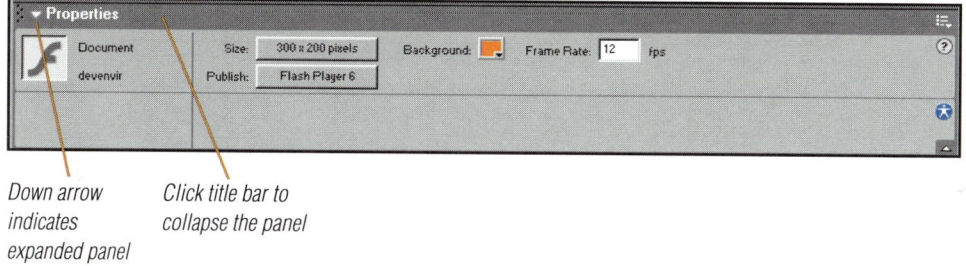

Down arrow indicates expanded panel

Click title bar to collapse the panel

Understanding your workspace

Organizing the Macromedia Flash development environment is like organizing your desktop. You may work more efficiently if you have many of the most commonly used items in view and ready to use. Alternately, you may work better if your workspace is relatively uncluttered, giving you more free "desk space." Fortunately, Macromedia Flash makes it easy for you to decide which items to display and how they are arranged while you work. You should become familiar with quickly opening and closing the various windows and panels in Macromedia Flash, and experimenting with different layouts and screen resolutions to find the environment that works best for you.

1. Click Window on the menu bar, point to Panel Sets, then click Default Layout.

2. Click the Properties panel title bar to collapse the panel, as shown in Figure A-4 (Win).

   Only the title bar displays.

3. Click the Properties panel title bar to expand the panel (Win).

4. Right-click (Win) the Properties panel title bar, then click Close Panel, or click the circled X in the upper-left corner (Mac) to close the panel and remove it from the workspace.

5. Click Window on the menu bar, then click Close All Panels.

   Instead of removing the panels from the workspace, the Close All Panels option collapses all panels so that only their title bars are displayed (Win), or the panels close (Mac).

6. Right-click (Win) the title bar of each panel, then click Close Panel to close each panel.

7. Click Window on the menu bar, then click Properties.

   The Properties panel displays fully.

8. Click File on the menu bar, then click Close.

You customized the development environment by displaying panels, using the default panel layout, and collapsing and closing panels.

OPEN A DOCUMENT AND PLAY A MOVIE

What You'll Do

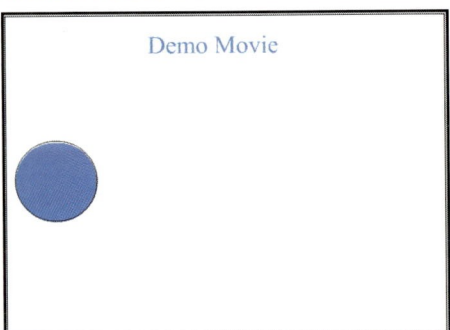

Demo Movie

 In this lesson, you will open a Macromedia Flash document (movie) and then preview, test, and save the movie.

Opening a Movie in Macromedia Flash

Macromedia Flash gives movies a .fla file extension. For example, if you have created a movie and saved it with the name mymovie, the file name will be mymovie.fla. Files with the .fla file extension can only be opened using Macromedia Flash. After they are opened, you can edit and resave them. Another file format for Macromedia Flash movies is the Macromedia Flash Player (.swf) format. These files are created from Macromedia Flash movies using the Publish command, which allows them to be played in a browser without the Macromedia Flash program. However, the viewer would need to have the Macromedia Flash Player installed on his or her computer. Because .swf files cannot be edited in the Macromedia Flash program, you should preview them on the stage and test them using Macromedia Flash Player before you publish them. Be sure to keep the original .fla file so that you can make changes at a later date.

Previewing a Movie

After opening a Macromedia Flash movie, you can preview it within the development environment in several ways. When you preview a movie, you play the frames by directing the playhead to move through the timeline, and you watch it on the stage.

Control menu commands (and keyboard shortcuts)

Figure A-5 shows the Control menu commands, which resemble common VCR-type options:

- Play ([Enter] (Win) or [return] (Mac)) begins playing the movie, frame by frame, from the location of the playhead and continuing until the end of the movie. For example, if the playhead is on Frame 5 and the last frame is Frame 40, choosing the Play command will play Frames 5–40 of the movie.

- Rewind ([Ctrl][Alt] R (Win)) or [alt] [command] [R] (Mac) moves the playhead to Frame 1.
- Step Forward (.) moves the playhead forward one frame at a time.
- Step Backward (,) moves the playhead backward one frame at a time.

You can turn on the Loop Playback setting to allow the movie to continue playing repeatedly. A check mark next to the Loop Playback command on the Control menu indicates that the feature is turned on. To turn off this feature, click the command.

Controller

You can also preview a movie using the Controller, shown in Figure A-6. To display the Controller, click the Controller option on the Toolbar command of the Window menu (Win), or click the Controller command on the Window menu (Mac).

Testing a Movie

When you preview a movie, some interactive functions, such as buttons, that are used to jump from one part of the movie to another, do not work unless the movie is played using a Macromedia Flash Player. You can use the Test Movie command on the Control menu to test the movie using the Macromedia Flash Player.

FIGURE A-5

Control menu commands

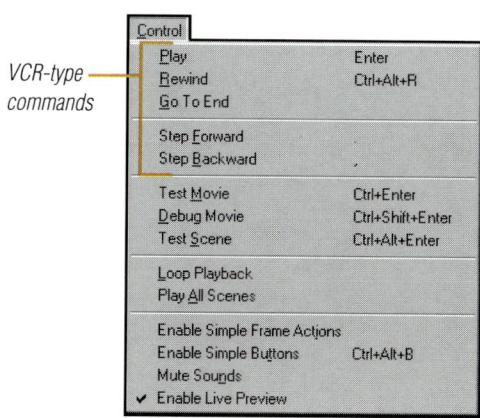

VCR-type commands

FIGURE A-6

Controller toolbar

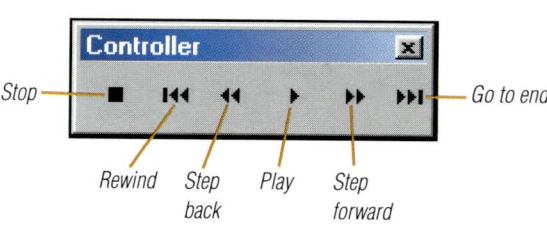

Stop — Go to end

Rewind Step back Play Step forward

Open and play a movie using the Control menu and the Controller

1. Open fla_1.fla from the drive and folder where your data files are stored for Unit A, then save it as **demomovie.fla**.

2. Click Control on the menu bar, click Play, then notice how the playhead moves across the timeline, as shown in Figure A-7.

3. Click Control on the menu bar, then click Rewind.

4. Press [Enter] (Win) or [return] (Mac) to play the movie, then press [Enter] (Win) or [return] (Mac) again to stop the movie before it ends.

5. Click Window on the menu bar, point to Toolbars (Win), then click Controller.

6. Use all of the Controller buttons to preview the movie, then close the Controller.

7. Click Control on the menu bar, click Loop Playback to turn it on, then play the movie.

   The movie plays continuously.

8. After viewing the movie looping, click Control on the menu bar, then click Loop Playback to turn it off.

9. Save your work.

You opened a Macromedia Flash movie and previewed it in the development environment, using various controls.

FIGURE A-7

Playhead moving across timeline

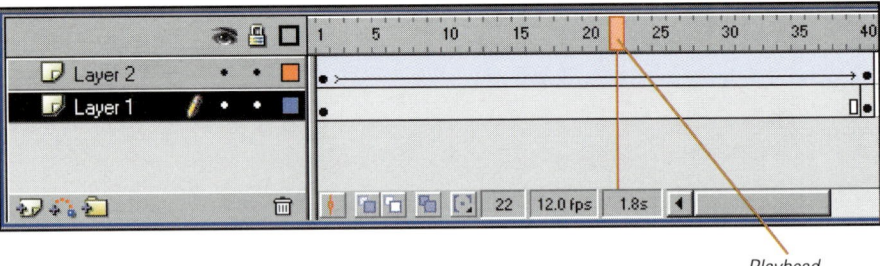

Playhead

Getting Started with Macromedia Flash

FIGURE A-8

Macromedia Flash Player window

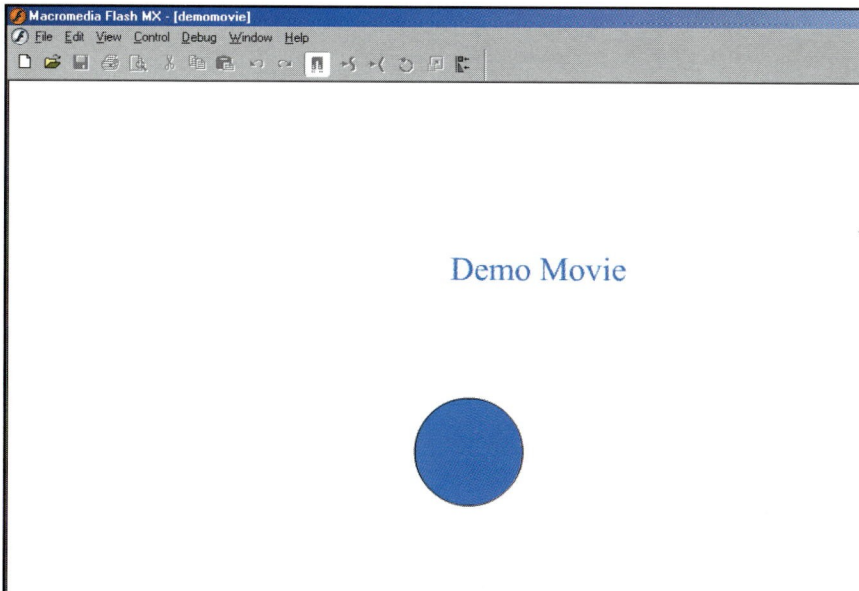

Demo Movie

1. Click Control on the menu bar, then click Test Movie to view the movie in the Macromedia Flash Player window, as shown in Figure A-8.

2. Click Control on the menu bar, noting the respective commands.

3. Click File on the menu bar, then click Close to close the Macromedia Flash Player window.

   TIP   When you test a movie, Macromedia Flash automatically runs the movie in Macromedia Flash Player, which creates a file that has a .swf extension in the folder where your movie is stored.

4. Close demomovie.fla.

You tested a movie in the Macromedia Flash Player window.

Using the Macromedia Flash Player

In order to view a Macromedia Flash movie on the Web, your computer needs to have the Macromedia Flash Player installed. An important feature of multimedia players, such as Macromedia Flash Player, is that they can decompress a file that has been compressed to give it a small file size that can be more quickly delivered over the Internet. In addition to Macromedia, companies such as Apple, Microsoft, and RealNetworks create players that allow applications, developed with their and other company's products, to be viewed on the Web. The multimedia players are distributed free and can be downloaded from the company's Web site. The Macromedia Flash Player is created by Macromedia and is available at *www.macromedia.com/downloads*.

CREATE AND SAVE A MOVIE

What You'll Do

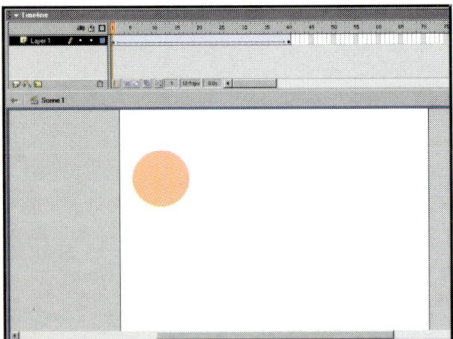

 In this lesson, you will create a Macromedia Flash movie that will include a simple animation, and then save the movie.

Creating a Macromedia Flash Movie

Macromedia Flash movies are created by placing objects (graphics, text, sounds, photos, and so on) on the stage, editing these objects (for example, changing their brightness), animating the objects, and adding interactivity with buttons and menus. You can create graphic objects in Macromedia Flash using the drawing tools, or you can develop them in another program, such as Macromedia Fireworks or Adobe Photoshop, and then import them into a Macromedia Flash movie. In addition, you can acquire clip art and stock photographs and import them into a movie. When objects are placed on the stage, they are automatically placed in a layer and in the currently selected frame of the timeline.

Figure A-9 shows a movie that has an oval object created in Macromedia Flash. Notice that the playhead is on Frame 1 of the movie. The objects placed on the stage appear in Frame 1 and appear on the stage when the playback head is on Frame 1. The dot in Frame 1 on the timeline indicates that this frame is a keyframe. A **keyframe** is always the first frame of every animation and is also a frame you can add that allows you to define a change in an animation.

The oval object in Figure A-9 was created using the Oval Tool. To create an oval or a rectangle, you select the desired tool and then drag the pointer over an area on the stage. If you want to draw a perfect circle or square, press and hold [Shift] when the tool is selected, and then drag the shape. If you make a mistake, you can click Edit on the menu bar, and then click Undo. In order to edit an object, you must first select it. You can use the Arrow Tool to select an entire object or group of objects. You drag the Arrow Tool pointer around the entire object to make a marquee selection. An object that has been selected displays a dot pattern.

Creating an Animation

Figure A-10 shows another movie that has 40 frames, as specified in the timeline. The arrow in the timeline indicates a motion animation. In this case, the object will move from left to right across the stage. The movement of the object is caused by having the object in different places on the stage in different frames of the movie. A basic motion animation requires two keyframes. The first keyframe sets the starting position of the object, and the second keyframe sets the ending position of the object. The number of frames between the two keyframes determines the length of the animation. For example, if the starting keyframe is Frame 1 and the ending keyframe is Frame 40, the object will be animated for 40 frames. Once the two keyframes are set, Macromedia Flash automatically fills in the frames between them, with a process called **motion tweening**.

Adding an Effect to an Object

In addition to animating the location of an object (or objects), you can also animate an object's appearance; for example, its shape, color, brightness, or transparency. The color of the circle on the left of the stage in Figure A-10 has been lightened using the Brightness effect on the Properties panel. When the movie is played, the color of the circle will start out light and then become darker as it moves to the right.

FIGURE A-9

Oval object in Frame 1

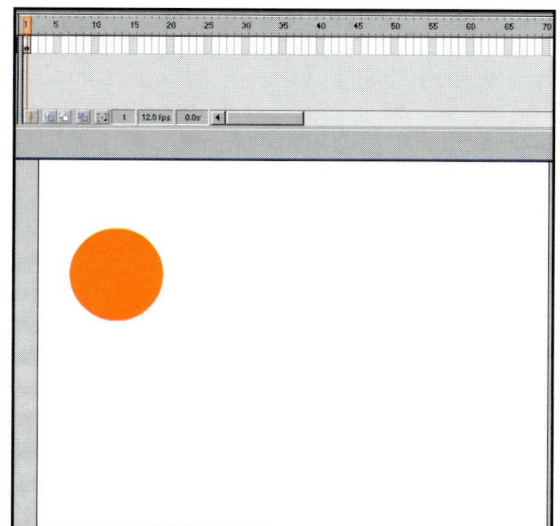

FIGURE A-10

Motion animation

Arrow indicates motion animation

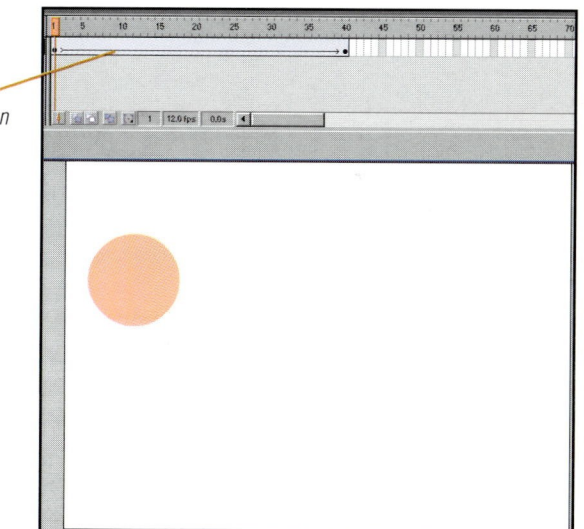

Create objects using drawing tools

1. Click File on the menu bar, click New, then save the movie as **tween.fla**.

2. Click the Oval Tool on the toolbox.

3. Click the Fill Color Tool on the toolbox, then, if necessary, click the red color swatch in the left column of the color palette.

4. Press and hold [Shift], then drag the Oval Tool on the stage to draw the circle shown in Figure A-11.

5. Click the Arrow Tool on the toolbox, then drag a marquee selection around the object to select it, as shown in Figure A-12.

   The object appears covered with a dot pattern.

6. Save your work.

You created an object using the Oval Tool and then selected the object using the Arrow Tool.

Create basic animation

1. Click Insert on the menu bar, then click Create Motion Tween.

   A blue border surrounds the object.

2. Click Frame 40 on Layer 1 of the timeline.

3. Click Insert on the menu bar, then click Keyframe.

   A second keyframe is defined in Frame 40, and Frames 1–40 appear shaded.

   (continued)

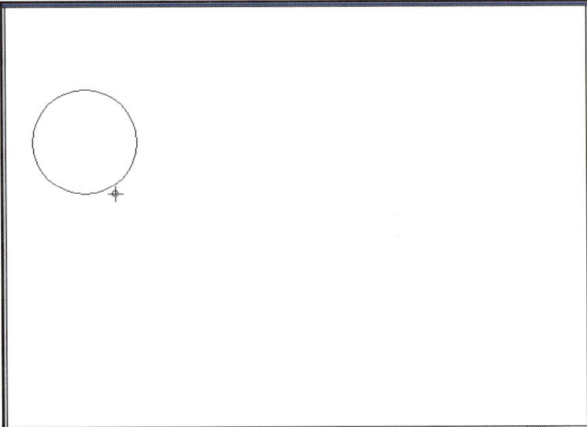

FIGURE A-12
Creating a marquee selection

The circle on the right side of the stage

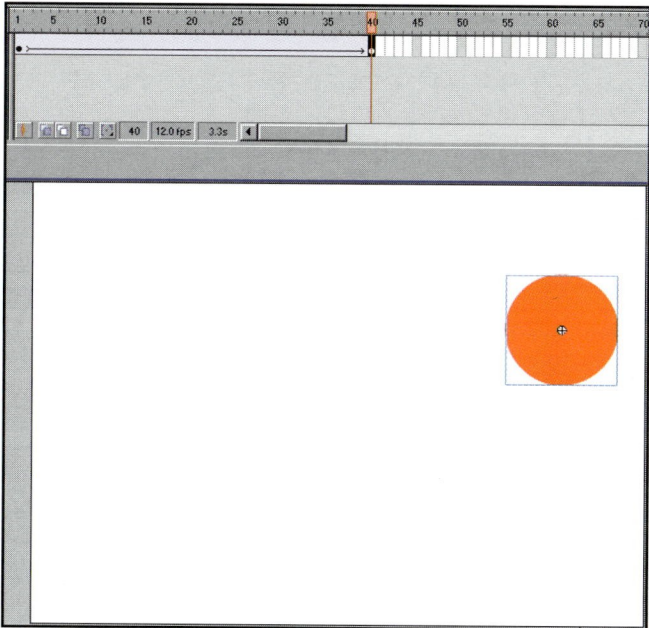

Using options and shortcuts

There is often more than one way to complete a particular function when using Macromedia Flash. For example, if you want to change the font for text you have typed, you can use Text menu options or the Properties panel. In addition, Macromedia Flash provides context menus that are relevant to the current selection. For example, if you point to a graphic and right-click (Win) or [control] click (Mac), a menu appears with graphic-related commands, such as rotate and skew. Shortcut keys are also available for many of the most common commands, such as [Ctrl] Z (Win) or [command] Z (Mac) for Undo.

4. Drag the circle to the right side of the stage, as shown in Figure A-13.

   The movement of the circle on the stage corresponds to the new location of the circle as defined in the keyframe in Frame 40.

5. Play the movie.

   The playhead moves through the timeline in Frames 1–40, and the circle moves across the stage.

6. Save your work.

You created a basic motion tween animation by inserting a keyframe and changing the location of an object.

Change the brightness of an object

1. Click Window on the menu bar, then verify that the Properties command is checked.

2. Click Frame 1 on Layer 1, then click the circle.

3. Click the Color Styles list arrow in the Properties panel, then click Brightness.

4. Click the Brightness Amount list arrow, then drag the slider to 70%.

   TIP You can also double-click the Brightness Amount box and type a percentage.

5. Click anywhere in the workspace to close the slider.

6. Play the movie, save your work.

   The circle becomes brighter as it moves across the stage.

You used the Properties panel to change the brightness of the object in one of the keyframes.

WORK WITH LAYERS AND THE TIMELINE

What You'll Do

In this lesson, you will add another layer, allowing you to create additional animation, and you will use the timeline to help organize your movie.

Understanding the Timeline

The timeline organizes and controls a movie's contents over time. By learning how to read the information provided in the timeline, you can determine and change what will be happening in a movie, frame by frame. You can determine which objects are animated, what types of animations are being used, when the various objects will appear in a movie, which objects will appear on top of others, and how fast the movie will play. Features of the timeline are shown in Figure A-14 and explained in this lesson.

Using Layers

Each new Macromedia Flash movie contains one layer, named Layer 1. **Layers** are like transparent sheets of acetate that are stacked on top of each other, as shown in Figure A-15. Each layer can contain one or more objects. You can add layers using the Layer command on the Insert menu or by clicking the Insert Layer icon on the timeline. When you add a new layer, Macromedia Flash stacks it on top of the other layer(s) in the timeline. The stacking order of the layers in the timeline is important because objects on the stage will appear in the same stacking order. For example, if you had two overlapping layers, and the top layer had a drawing of a tree and the bottom layer had a drawing of a house, the tree would appear as though it were in front of the house. You can change the stacking order of layers simply by dragging them up or down in the list of layers. You can name layers, hide them so their contents do not appear on the stage, and lock them so that they cannot be edited.

Using Frames

The timeline is made up of individual units called **frames**. The content of each layer is displayed in frames as the playhead moves over them while the movie plays. Frames are numbered in increments of five for easy reference, and colors and symbols are used to indicate the type of frame (for example, keyframe or motion animation). The upper-right corner of the timeline contains a pop-up menu. This menu provides different views of the timeline, showing more frames or showing thumbnails of the objects on a layer, for example. The status bar at the bottom of the timeline indicates the current frame (the frame that the playhead is currently on), the frame rate (frames per second), and the elapsed time from Frame 1 to the current frame.

Using the Playhead

The **playhead** indicates which frame is playing. You can manually move the playhead by dragging it left or right. This makes it easier to locate a frame that you may want to edit. Dragging the playhead also allows you to do a quick check of the movie without having to play it.

Understanding Scenes

When you create a new movie, Scene 1 also appears in the timeline. A **scene** is a section of the timeline designated for a specific part of the movie. For example, a movie created for a Web site could be divided into a number of scenes: an introduction, a home page, and content pages. Scenes are a way to organize long movies. Without them, scrolling through the timeline to work on different parts of the movie could become a very frustrating and inefficient way to work. You can insert new scenes by using the Insert menu. Scenes can be given descriptive names, which will help you find them easily if you need to edit a particular scene. You can click the Scene command on the Modify menu to change the play order of scenes in your movie. The number of scenes is limited only by the computer's memory.

FIGURE A-14
Elements of the timeline

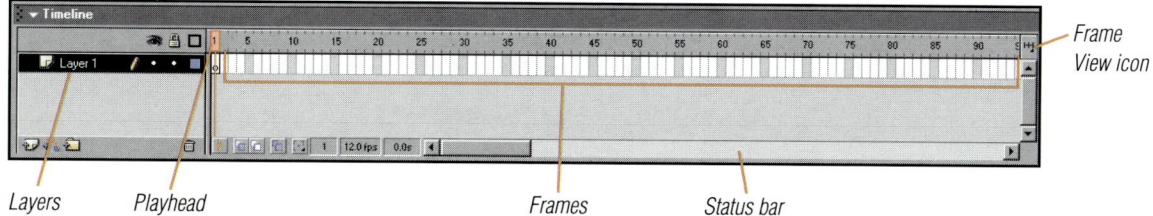

Frame
View icon

Layers Playhead Frames Status bar

FIGURE A-15
The concept of layers

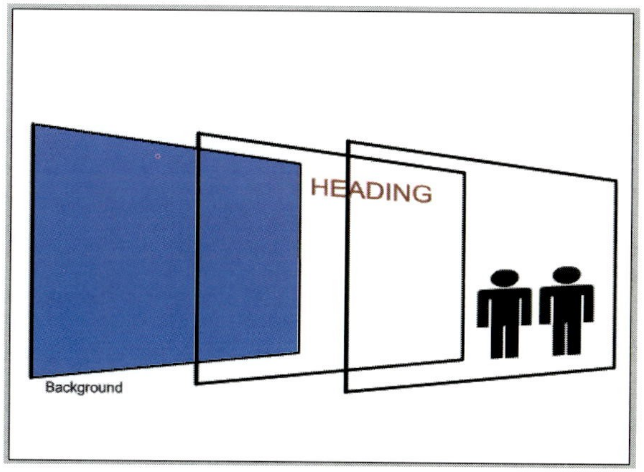

HEADING

Background

Working with the Timeline

Figure A-16 shows the timeline of a movie created in Lesson 2 with a second object, a square at the top of the stage. By studying the timeline, you can learn several things about this movie. First, the second object is placed on its own layer, Layer 2. Second, the layer has a motion animation (indicated by the arrow and blue background in the frames). Third, the animation runs from Frame 1 to Frame 40. Fourth, if the objects intersect, the square will be on top of the circle, because the layer it is placed on is above the layer that the circle is placed on. Fifth, the frame rate is set to 12, which means that the movie will play 12 frames per second. Sixth, the playhead is at Frame 1, which causes the contents for both layers of Frame 1 to be displayed on the stage.

QUICKTIP

You can adjust the size of the timeline by positioning the mouse over the bottom edge, and then dragging the border up or down.

FIGURE A-16

The timeline of a movie with a second object

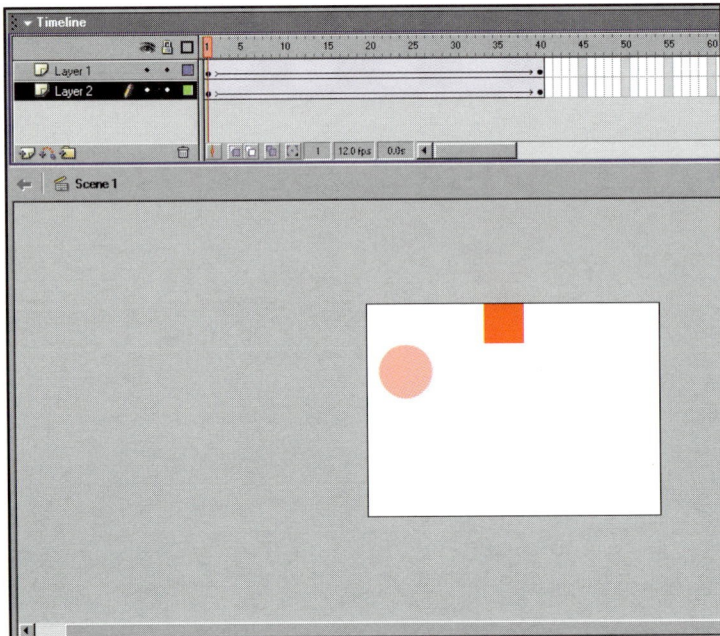

FIGURE A-17
Drawing a square

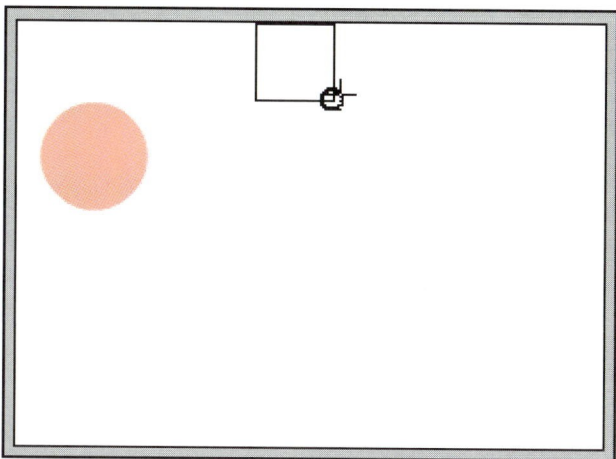

FIGURE A-18
Positioning the square at the bottom of the stage

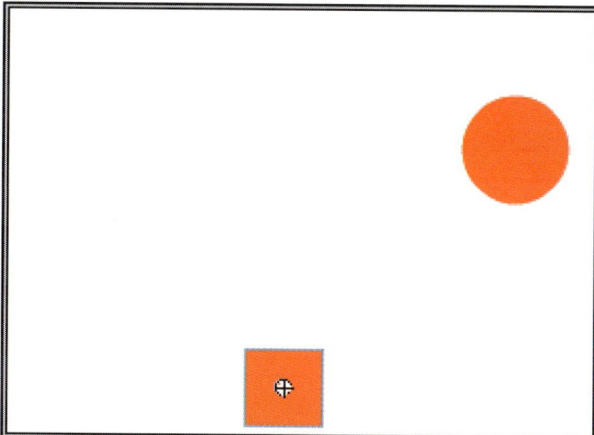

Add a layer

1. Save tween.fla as **layers.fla**.
2. Click Frame 1 on Layer 1.
3. Click View on the menu bar, point to Magnification, then click 50%.
4. Click Insert on the menu bar, then click Layer.

   A new layer—Layer 2—appears at the top of the timeline.
5. Save your work.

You added a layer to the timeline.

Create a second animation

1. Click the Rectangle Tool on the toolbox, press and hold [Shift], then draw a square resembling the dimensions shown in Figure A-17. ▢
2. Click the Arrow Tool on the toolbox, then drag a marquee around the square. ▸
3. Click Insert on the menu bar, then click Create Motion Tween.
4. Click Frame 40 on Layer 2, then insert a keyframe.
5. Drag the square to the bottom of the stage, as shown in Figure A-18, then play the movie.

   The square appears on top when the two objects intersect.
6. Save your work.

You drew an object and used it to create a second animation.

Work with layers and view features in the timeline

1. Click Layer 2 on the timeline, then drag it below Layer 1.

   Layer 2 is now the bottom layer.

2. Play the movie and notice how the square appears beneath the circle when they intersect.

3. Click the Frame View icon on the end of the timeline to display the menu shown in Figure A-19.

4. Click Tiny to display more frames.

5. Click the Frame View icon, click Preview, then note the object thumbnails that appear on the timeline.

6. Click the Frame View icon, then click Normal.

7. Save your work.

You changed the order of the layers and changed the display of frames on the timeline.

FIGURE A-19

Changing the view of the timeline

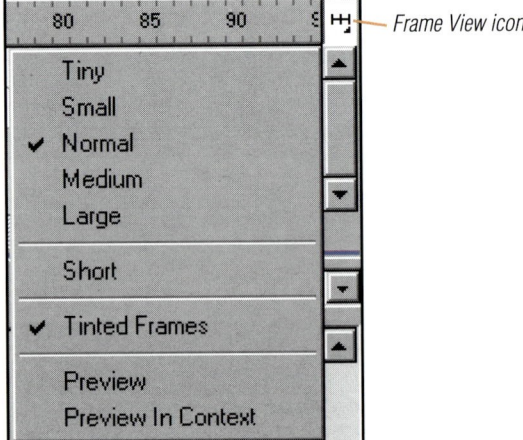

Frame View icon

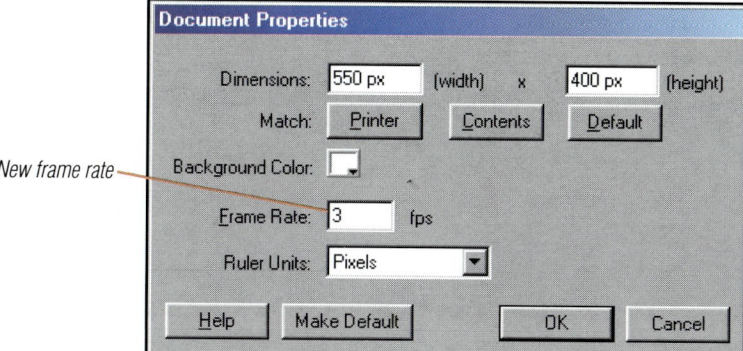

New frame rate

1. Double-click the Frame Rate box on the bottom of the timeline. `12.0 fps`

2. Double-click the Frame Rate text box, type **3**, click OK, then compare your Document Properties dialog box to Figure A-20. `12.0 fps`

3. Play the movie and notice how slowly the movie plays.

4. Repeat Steps 1 and 2, but change the frame rate to 18 and then to 12.

5. Click Frame 1 on the timeline.

6. Drag the playhead left and right to display specific frames.

7. Save your work, then close layers.fla.

You changed the frame rate of the movie.

Getting Help

Macromedia Flash provides a comprehensive Help feature that can be very useful when first learning the program. You can access Help by clicking commands on the Help menu. The Help feature includes the Macromedia Flash manual, which is organized by topic and can be accessed through the index or by using a keyword search. In addition, the Help menu contains samples and tutorials that cover basic Macromedia Flash features.

PLAN A WEB SITE

What You'll Do

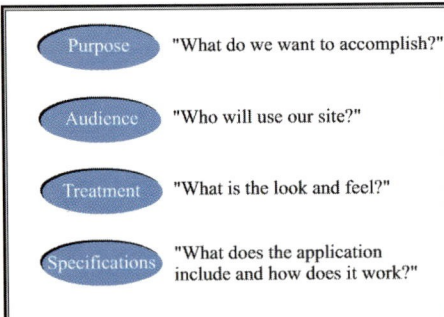

Purpose	"What do we want to accomplish?"
Audience	"Who will use our site?"
Treatment	"What is the look and feel?"
Specifications	"What does the application include and how does it work?"

In this lesson, you will learn how to plan a Macromedia Flash application. You will also learn about the guidelines for screen design and the interactive design of Web pages.

Planning an Application

Macromedia Flash can be used to develop animations (movies) that are part of a product, such as a game or educational tutorial, delivered on CD-ROM or DVD. You can use Macromedia Flash to create enhancements to Web pages, such as animated logos and interactive navigation buttons. You can also use Macromedia Flash to create entire Web sites. No matter what the application, the first step is planning. Often, the temptation is to jump right into the program and start developing movies. The problem is that this invariably results in a more time-consuming process at best; and wasted effort, resources, and money at worst. The larger in scope and the more complex the project is, the more critical the planning process. Planning an entire Web site should involve the following steps:

Step 1: Stating the Purpose (Goals). "What, specifically, do we want to accomplish?"

Determining the goals of a site is a critical step in planning, because goals guide the development process, keep the team members on track, and provide a way to evaluate the site both during and after its development.

Step 2: Identifying the Target Audience. "Who will use the Web site?"

Understanding the potential viewers helps in developing a site that can address their needs. For example, children respond to exploration and surprise, so having a dog wag its tail when the mouse pointer rolls over it might appeal to this audience.

Step 3: Determining the Treatment. "What is the look and feel?"

The treatment is how the Web site will be presented to the user, including the tone, approach, and emphasis.

Tone. Will the site be humorous, serious, light, heavy, formal, or informal? The tone of a site can often be used to make a statement projecting a progressive, high-tech, well-funded corporate image, for instance.

Approach. How much direction will be provided to the user? An interactive game site might focus on exploration, while an informational site might provide lots of direction, such as menus.

Emphasis. How much emphasis will be placed on the various multimedia elements? For example, a company may want to develop an informational site that shows the features of their new product line, including animated demonstrations of how each product works. The budget might not allow for the expense of creating the animations, so the emphasis would shift to still pictures with text descriptions.

Step 4: Developing the Specifications and Storyboard. "What precisely does the application include and how does it work?"

The specifications state what will be included in each screen, including the arrangement of each element and the functionality of each object (for example, what happens when you click the button

labeled Skip Intro). Specifications should include the following:

Playback System. The choice of what configuration to target for playback is critical, especially Internet connection speed, browser versions, screen resolution, and plug-ins.

Elements to Include. The specifications should include details about the various elements that are to be included in the site. What are the dimensions for the animations, and what is the frame rate? What are the sizes of the various objects such as photos, buttons, and so on? What fonts, font sizes, and type styles will be used?

Functionality. The specifications should include the way the program reacts to an action by the user, such as a mouse click. For example, clicking on a door (object) might cause the door to open (an animation), a doorbell to ring (sound), an "exit the program" message to appear (text), or an entirely new screen to be displayed.

User Interface. The user interface involves designing the appearance of objects (how each object is arranged on the screen) and the interactivity (how the user navigates through the site).

A storyboard is a representation of what each screen will look like and how the screens are linked. The purpose of the storyboard is to provide an overview of the project, provide a guide (road map) for the developer, illustrate the links among screens, and illustrate the functionality of the objects. Figure A-21 shows a storyboard. The exact content (such as a specific photo) does not have to be decided upon, but it is important to show where text, graphics, photos, buttons, and other elements, will be placed. Thus, the storyboard includes placeholders for the various elements. An important feature of the storyboard is the navigation scheme. The Web site designer decides how the various screens will be linked and represents this in the storyboard. In this way, problems with the navigation scheme can be identified before the development begins.

Using Screen Design Guidelines

The following screen design guidelines are used by Web developers. The implementation of these guidelines is affected by the goals of the site, the intended audience, and the content.

Balance—Balance in screen design refers to the distribution of optical weight in the layout. Optical weight is the ability of an object to attract the viewer's eye, as determined by the object's size, shape, color, and so on. In general, a balanced design is more appealing to a viewer.

FIGURE A-21
Sample storyboard

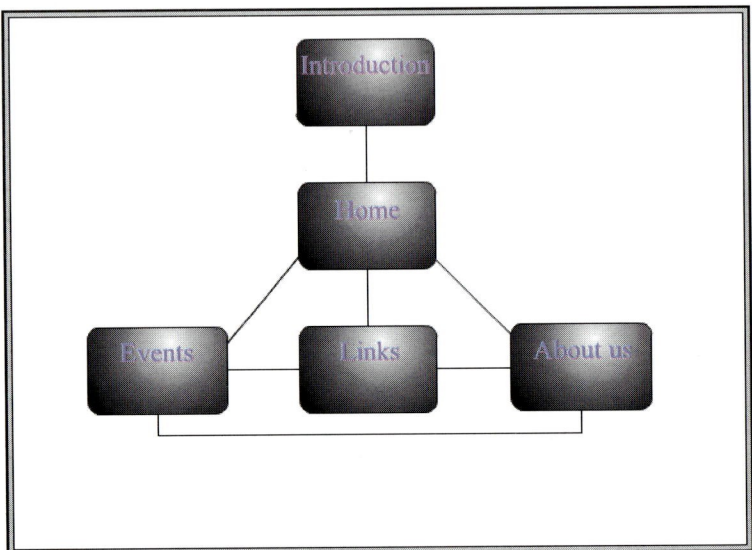

Unity—Intra-screen unity has to do with how the various screen objects relate and how they all fit in. Unity helps them reinforce each other. Inter-screen unity refers to the design that viewers encounter as they navigate from one screen to another, and it provides consistency throughout the site.

Movement—Movement refers to the way the viewer's eye moves through the objects on the screen. Techniques in an animation, such as movement, can be used to draw the viewer to a location on the screen.

Using Interactive Design Guidelines

In addition to screen design guidelines, interactive guidelines determine the interactivity of the site. The following guidelines are not absolute rules but are affected by the goals of the site, the intended audience, and the content:

- Make it simple, easy to understand, and easy to use. Make the site intuitive so that viewers do not have to spend time learning what the site is all about and what they need to do.
- Build in consistency in the navigation scheme. Help the users know where they are in the site and help them avoid getting lost.
- Provide feedback. Users need to know when an action, such as clicking a button, has been completed. Changing its color or shape, or adding a sound can indicate this.
- Give the user control. Allow the user to skip long introductions; provide controls for starting, stopping, and rewinding animations, video, and audio; and provide controls for adjusting audio.

DISTRIBUTE A MACROMEDIA FLASH MOVIE

What You'll Do

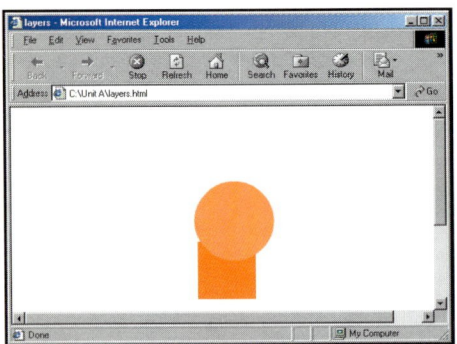

In this lesson you will prepare a movie for distribution in various formats.

Distributing Movies

When you develop Macromedia Flash movies, the application saves them in a file format (.fla) that only users who have the Macromedia Flash program installed on their computers can view. Usually, Macromedia Flash movies are viewed on the Web as part of a Web site or directly from a viewer's computer using the Macromedia Flash Player. In order to view your Macromedia Flash movies on the Web, you must change the movie to a Macromedia Shockwave (.swf) file format and generate the HTML code that references the Macromedia Shockwave file. You can accomplish both of these tasks by using the publish feature of Macromedia Flash.

The process for publishing a Macromedia Flash movie is to create and save a movie and then click the Publish command on the File menu. You can also specify various settings such as dimensions for the window that the movie plays within in the browser, before publishing the movie. Publishing a movie creates two files: an HTML file and a Macromedia Shockwave file. Both of these files retain the same name as the Flash movie file, but with different file extensions:

- .html—the HTML document
- .swf—the Macromedia Shockwave file

You can change these names as you would any files on your computer. The HTML document contains the code that the browser interprets to display the movie on the Web. The code also specifies the Macromedia Shockwave movie that the browser will play. Sample HTML code referencing a Macromedia Shockwave movie is shown in Figure A-22.

Macromedia Flash provides several other ways to distribute your movies that may or may not involve delivery on the Web. You can create a stand-alone movie called a **projector**. Projector files, such as Windows .exe files, maintain the movie's interactivity. Alternately, you can create self-running movies, such as Quicktime .mov files, that are not interactive.

You can play projector and non-interactive files directly from a computer, or you can incorporate them into an application, such as a game, that is delivered from a download on a CD or DVD.

FIGURE A-22

Sample HTML code

```
<HTML>
<HEAD>
<meta http-equiv=Content-Type content="text/html;  charset=ISO-8859-1">
<TITLE>layers</TITLE>
</HEAD>
<BODY bgcolor="#FFFFFF">
<!-- URL's used in the movie-->
<!-- text used in the movie-->
<OBJECT classid="clsid:D27CDB6E-AE6D-11cf-96B8-444553540000"
 codebase="http://download.macromedia.com/pub/shockwave/cabs/flash/swflash.cab#version=6,0,0,0"
WIDTH="550" HEIGHT="400" id="layers" ALIGN="">
 <PARAM NAME=movie VALUE="layers.swf"> <PARAM NAME=quality VALUE=high> <PARAM NAME=bgcolor
VALUE=#FFFFFF> <EMBED src="layers.swf" quality=high bgcolor=#FFFFFF  WIDTH="550" HEIGHT="400" NAME="layers"
ALIGN=""
 TYPE="application/x-shockwave-flash" PLUGINSPAGE="http://www.macromedia.com/go/getflashplayer"></EMBED>
</OBJECT>
</BODY>
</HTML>
```

Code specifying the Macromedia Shockwave movie that the browser will play

.swf extension indicates a Macromedia Shockwave file

Publish a movie for distribution on the Web

1. Open layers.fla.
2. Click File on the menu bar, then click Publish.
3. Open the file management tool that is on your operating system, then navigate to the drive and folder where you save your work for this unit.
4. Notice the three files that begin with "layers", as shown in Figure A-23.

   Layers.fla, the Flash movie; layers.swf, the Macromedia Shockwave file; and layers.htm, the HTML document, appear in the window.
5. Open your browser.
6. Open layers.htm, then notice that the movie plays in the browser.
7. Close the browser.

You used the Publish command to create an HTML document and a Macromedia Shockwave file, then displayed the HTML document in a Web browser.

The three layers files after publishing the movie

Name	Size	Type
layers.fla	18KB	Flash Document
layers.html	1KB	Mozilla Hypertext Markup Language Document
layers.swf	1KB	Flash Movie

Your browser icon may be different

FIGURE A-24

The Flash Player window playing the Macromedia Shockwave movie

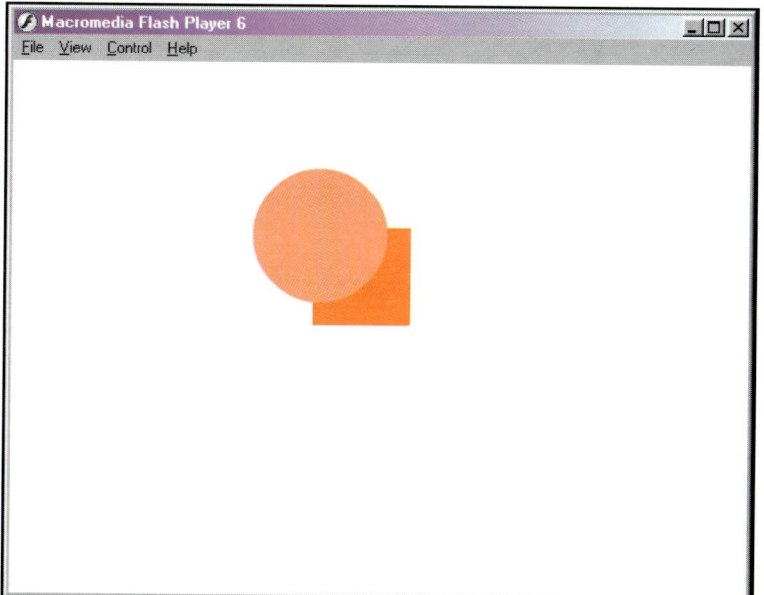

1. Click File on the menu bar, then click Publish Settings.

2. Click the Windows Projector (.exe) (Win) or Macintosh Projector (Mac) option, then deselect other file formats, if necessary.

3. Click Publish, then click OK.

4. Open the file management tool that is on your operating system, then navigate to the drive and folder where you save your work for this unit.

5. Double-click layers.exe (Win), or layers Projector (Mac), then notice that the application plays in the Macromedia Flash Player window, as shown in Figure A-24.

6. Close the Macromedia Flash Player window.

7. Close layers.fla in Macromedia Flash.

You created and displayed a stand-alone projector file.

Start Macromedia Flash, open a movie, and set the movie properties and magnification.

1. Start Macromedia Flash, open fla_2.fla, and then save it as **skillsdemoA.fla**.
2. Display the Document Properties dialog box.
3. Change the movie window dimensions to width: 550 px and height: 400 px.
4. Change the background color to yellow. (*Hint*: Select the yellow color swatch in the left column of the color palette.)
5. Close the Document Properties dialog box.
6. Change the magnification to 50% using the View menu.
7. Change the magnification to 75% using the View magnification box.
8. If necessary, use the scroll bars at the bottom and the right of the screen to center the stage in the workspace.

Display, close, and collapse panels.

1. Set panels to their default layout. (*Hint*: Use the Panel Sets command on the Window menu.)
2. Collapse all panels.
3. Close each panel to remove them from the screen.
4. Display the Properties panel.
5. Close and open the Toolbox.

Play and test a movie.

1. Use the controls in the Control menu to play and rewind the movie.
2. Use the Controller to rewind, play, stop, and start the movie.
3. Turn Loop Playback on, play the movie, and then stop it.
4. Test the movie in the Macromedia Flash Player window, and then close the window.

Create an object, create a basic animation, and apply an effect.

1. Rewind the movie, insert a layer, and then draw a red circle in the lower-right corner of the stage, approximately the same size as the green ball. (*Hint*: Use the scroll bar on the timeline to view the new layer, if necessary.)
2. Select the circle, and then add Create Motion Tween animation to it.
3. Animate the circle so that it moves across the screen from right to left beginning in Frame 1 and ending in Frame 65. (*Hint*: Add a keyframe in the ending frame.)
4. Use the Arrow Tool to select the circle, then change brightness from 0% to -100%.
5. Play the movie, then rewind it.

Add a layer, change the frame rate, and change the view of the timeline.

1. Add a layer, select Frame 1, and then create a second circle approximately the same size as the previously created circle in the lower-left corner of the stage.
2. Animate the circle so that it moves across the screen from left to right beginning in Frame 1 and ending in Frame 65.
3. Use the Arrow Tool to select the circle, then change brightness from 0% to 100%.
4. Play the movie.
5. Use the timeline to change the frame rate to 8 frames per second.

6. Change the view of the timeline to display more frames.
7. Change the view of the timeline to display a preview of the object thumbnails.
8. Change the view of the timeline to display the Normal view.
9. Use the playhead to display each frame.
10. Save the movie, and then compare your movie to Figure A-25.

Publish a movie.

1. Click File on the menu bar, then click Publish.
2. Open your browser, then open skillsdemoA.htm.
3. View the movie, then close your browser.

Create a projector.

1. Display the Publish Setting dialog box.
2. Select the appropriate projector setting for your operating systems and remove all of the other settings.
3. Publish the movie.
4. Open the file management tool that is on your operating system, navigate to the drive and folder where you save your work for this unit, then open skillsdemoA.fla.
5. View the movie, then close the Macromedia Flash Player window.
6. Close the movie in Macromedia Flash.

FIGURE A-25
Completed Skills Review

A friend cannot decide whether to sign up for a class in Macromedia Flash or Dreamweaver. You help her decide by showing her what you already know about Macromedia Flash. Since you think she'd love a class in Macromedia Flash, you decide to show her how easy it is to create a simple animation involving two objects that move diagonally across the screen.

1. Open a new movie, and then save it as **demonstration.fla**.
2. Create a simple shape or design, and place it in the upper-left corner of the stage.
3. Animate the object using the Create Motion Tween command.
4. Insert a keyframe in Frame 50.
5. Move the object to the lower-right corner of the stage.
6. Insert a new layer, and then select Frame 1.
7. Create another object in the upper-right corner of the stage.
8. Animate the object using the Create Motion Tween command.
9. Insert a keyframe in Frame 50.
10. Move the object to the lower-left corner of the stage.
11. Play the movie, and then click Frame 1.
12. Change the brightness for both objects to 80%.
13. Preview the movie and test it.
14. Save the movie, and then compare your movie to Figure A-26.

FIGURE A-26
Completed Project Builder 1

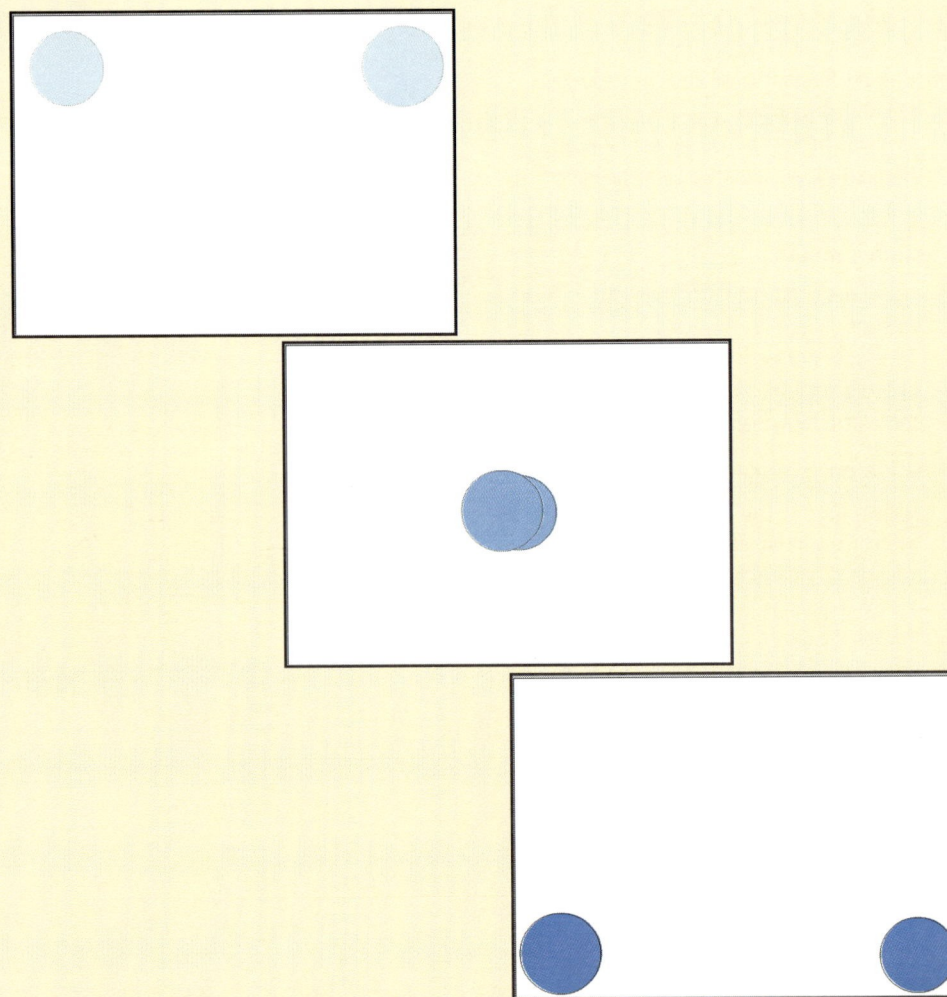

You've been asked to develop a simple movie about recycling for a day care center. For this project, you will add two animations to an existing movie. You will show three objects that appear on the screen at different times, and then move to a recycle bin at different times. You can use any objects you can draw easily.

1. Open fla_3.fla, then save it as **recycle.fla**.
2. Play the movie and study the timeline to familiarize yourself with the movie's current settings.
3. Insert a new layer, insert a keyframe in Frame 10 of the new layer, then draw a small object in the upper-left corner of the stage.
4. Create a motion animation that moves the object to the recycle bin.
5. Insert a new layer, insert a keyframe in Frame 20, draw a small object in the upper center of the stage, then create a motion animation that moves the object to the recycle bin.
6. Insert a new layer, insert a keyframe in Frame 30, draw a small object in the upper-right corner of the stage, then create a motion animation that moves the object to the recycle bin.
7. Play the movie.
8. Save the movie, then compare your movie to Figure A-27.

FIGURE A-27
Completed Project Builder 2

DESIGN PROJECT

Figure A-28 shows the home page of a Web site. Study the figure and answer the following questions. For each question, indicate how you determined your answer.

1. Connect to the Internet, and go to *www.course.com*. Navigate to the page for this book, click the Student Online Companion, then click the link for this unit.

2. Open a document in a word processor or open a new Macromedia Flash movie, save the file as **dpuUnitA**, then answer the following questions. (*Hint*: Use the Text Tool in Macromedia Flash.)

   - Whose Web site is this?
   - What is the goal(s) of the site?
   - Who is the target audience?
   - What treatment (look and feel) is used?
   - What are the design layout guidelines being used (balance, movement, etc.)?
   - How can animation enhance this page?
   - Do you think this is an effective design for the company, its products, and its target audience? Why, or why not?
   - What suggestions would you make to improve on the design, and why?

FIGURE A-28
Design Project

Your group can assign elements of the project to individual members, or work collectively to create the finished product.

There are numerous companies in the business of developing Web sites for others. Many of these companies use Macromedia Flash as one of their primary development tools. These companies promote themselves through their own Web sites and usually provide online portfolios with samples of their work. Use your favorite search engine (use keywords such as Macromedia Flash developers and Macromedia Flash animators) to locate three of these companies, and generate the following information for each one. A sample is shown in Figure A-29. Each member of your group will work independently on the following research project, and then you will meet to compare your results and choose the three companies that you feel are the best.

1. Company name:
2. Contact information (address, phone, and so on):
3. Web site URL:
4. Company mission:
5. Services provided:
6. Sample list of clients:

7. Describe three ways they seem to have used Macromedia Flash in their own sites. Were these effective? Why, or why not?
8. Describe three applications of Macromedia Flash that they include in their portfolios (or showcases or samples). Were these effective? Why, or why not?

9. Would you want to work for this company? Why, or why not?
10. Would you recommend this company to another company that was looking to enhance its Web site? Why, or why not?

FIGURE A-29
Group Project

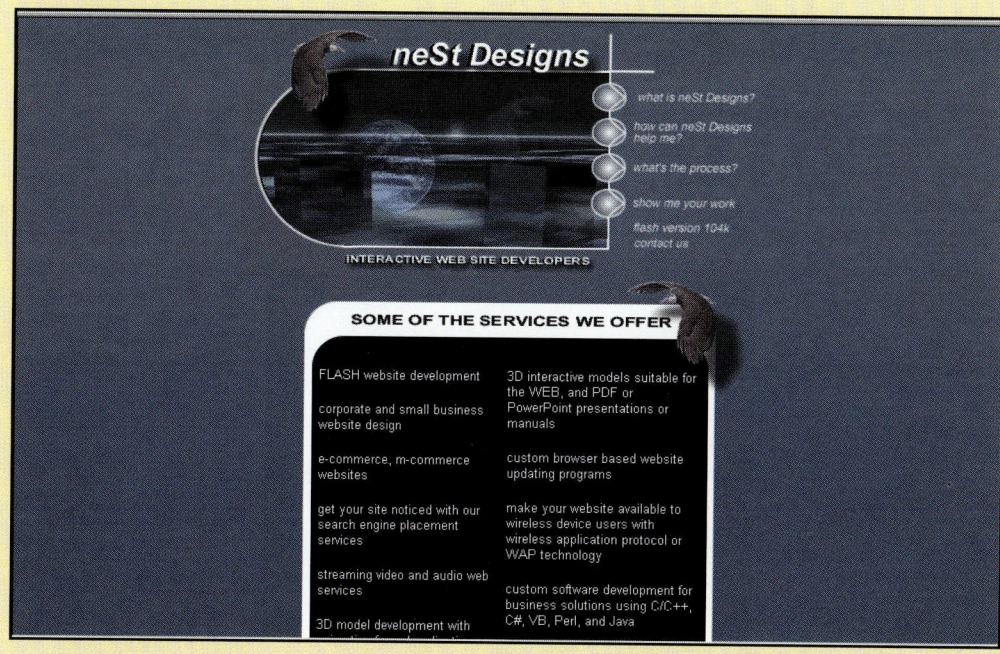

UNIT B

DRAWING IN MACROMEDIA FLASH

1. Use the Macromedia Flash drawing tools.

2. Edit drawings.

3. Work with objects.

4. Work with text.

5. Work with layers.

UNIT B

DRAWING IN MACROMEDIA FLASH

Introduction

One of the most compelling features of Macromedia Flash is its ability to create and manipulate vector graphics. Computers can display graphics in either a bitmap or a vector format. The difference between these formats is in how they describe an image. Bitmap graphics represent the image as an array of dots, called **pixels**, which are arranged within a grid. Each pixel in an image has an exact position on the screen and a precise color. To make a change in a bitmap, you modify the pixels. When you enlarge a bitmap graphic, the number of pixels remains the same, resulting in jagged edges that decrease the quality of the image. Vector graphics represent the image using lines and curves, which you can resize without losing image quality. Also, because vector images are generally smaller than bitmap images, they are particularly useful for a Web site. However, vector graphics are not as effective as bitmap graphic for representing photo-realistic images.

As you learned in Unit A, images created using Macromedia Flash drawing tools have a stroke, a fill, or both. In addition, the stroke of an object can be segmented into smaller lines. You can modify the size, shape, rotation, and color of each stroke, fill, and segment.

Tools You'll Use

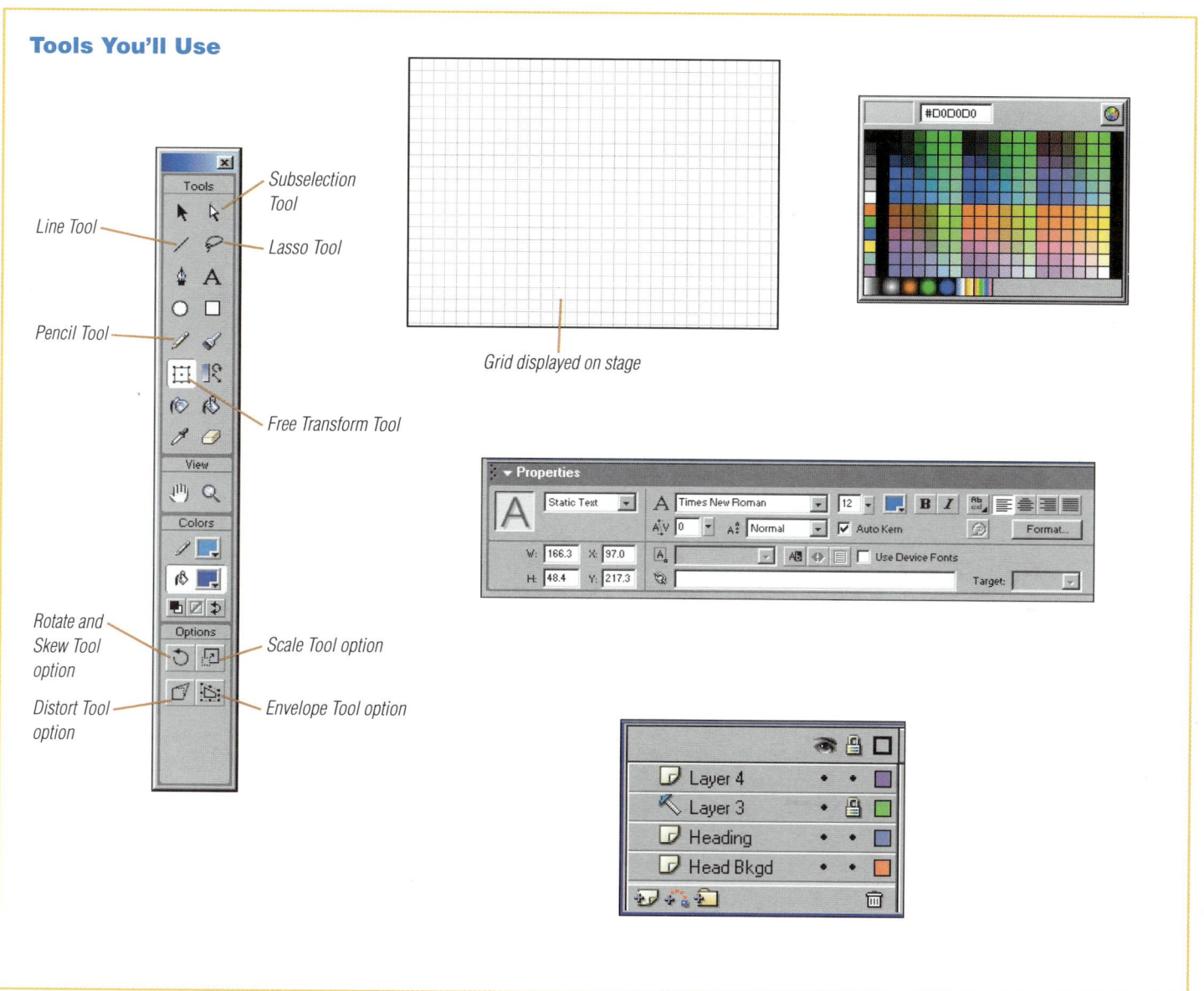

Subselection Tool

Line Tool

Lasso Tool

Pencil Tool

Free Transform Tool

Grid displayed on stage

Rotate and Skew Tool option

Scale Tool option

Distort Tool option

Envelope Tool option

USE THE MACROMEDIA FLASH DRAWING TOOLS

What You'll Do

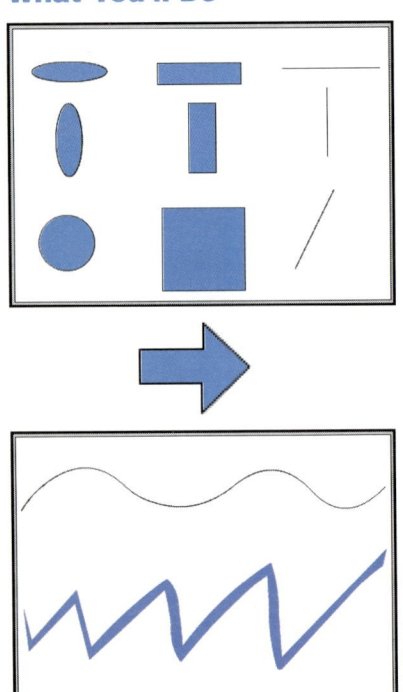

 In this lesson, you will use several drawing tools to create various vector graphics.

Using Macromedia Flash Drawing and Editing Tools

When you point to a tool on the toolbox, its name appears next to the tool and a description of its function is displayed on the Status bar at the bottom of the screen. Figure B-1 identifies the tools described below. Several of the tools have options that modify their use.

Arrow—Used to select an object or parts of an object, such as the stroke or fill; and to reshape objects. The options available for the Arrow Tool are Snap to Objects (aligns objects), Smooth (smoothes lines), and Straighten (straightens lines).

Subselection—Used to select, drag, and reshape an object. Vector graphics are composed of lines and curves (each of which is a segment) connected by **anchor points**. Selecting an object with this tool displays the anchor points and allows you to use them to edit the object.

Line—Used to draw straight lines. You can draw vertical, horizontal, and 45° diagonal lines by pressing and holding [Shift] while drawing the line.

Lasso—Used to select objects or parts of objects. The Polygon Mode Tool option allows you to draw straight lines when selecting an object.

Pen—Used to draw lines and curves by creating a series of dots, known as anchor points, that are automatically connected.

Text—Used to create and edit text.

Oval—Used to draw oval shapes. Press and hold [Shift] to draw a perfect circle.

Rectangle—Used to draw rectangular shapes. Press and hold [Shift] to draw a perfect square. The Round Rectangle Radius Tool option allows you to round the corners of a rectangle.

Drawing in Macromedia Flash

Pencil—Used to draw freehand lines and shapes. The options available for the Pencil Tool are Straighten (draws straight lines), Smooth (draws smooth curved lines), and Ink (draws freehand with no modification).

Brush—Used to draw (paint) with brush-like strokes. Options allow you to set the size and shape of the brush, and to determine the area to be painted, such as inside or behind an object.

Free Transform—Used to transform objects by rotating, scaling, skewing, and distorting them.

Fill Transform—Used to transform a gradient fill by adjusting the size, direction, or center of the fill.

Ink Bottle—Used to apply line colors and thickness to the stroke of an object.

Paint Bucket—Used to fill enclosed areas of a drawing with color. Options allow you to fill areas that have gaps and to make adjustments in a gradient fill.

Eyedropper—Used to copy stroke, fill, and text attributes from one object to another.

Eraser—Used to erase lines and fills. Options allow you to choose what part of the object to erase, as well as the size and shape of the eraser.

The Oval, Rectangle, Pencil, Brush, Line, and Pen Tools are used to create vector objects.

Displaying Gridlines and Rulers

Gridlines and rulers can be used to position objects on the stage. The Grid and Ruler commands, found on the View menu, are used to turn on and off these features. You can modify the grid size and color, and you can specify the units for the rulers.

FIGURE B-1

Macromedia Flash tools

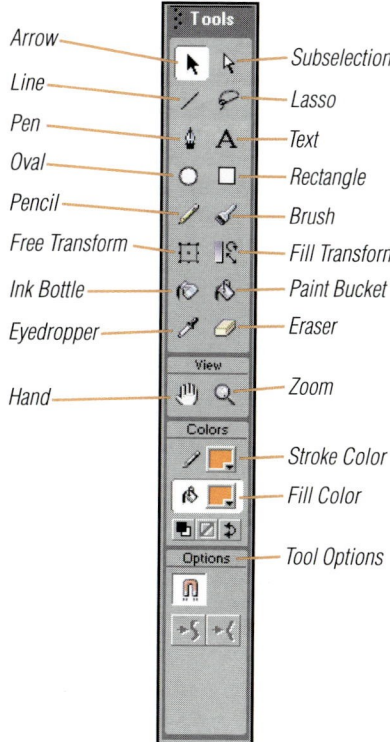

Show gridlines and check settings

1. Open a new movie, then save it as **tools.fla**.

2. Verify that the movie size is 550 × 400 pixels.

   > TIP In addition to clicking the Document properties button to access document properties, you can also click Modify on the menu bar and then click Document.

3. Click the Stroke Color Tool on the toolbox, then click the black color swatch in the left column of the color palette (if necessary).

4. Click the Fill Color Tool on the toolbox, then click the blue color swatch in the left column of the color palette (if necessary).

5. Click View on the menu bar, point to Grid, then click Show Grid to display the gridlines.

   A gray grid appears on the stage.

6. Click Window on the menu bar, point to Toolbars, then click Main and Status if they do not have check marks next to them (Win).

7. Point to several tools on the toolbar, then read about their functions on the Status bar (Win), as shown in Figure B-2.

8. Save your work.

You displayed the grid and viewed tool descriptions on the Status bar.

Tool description on the Status bar

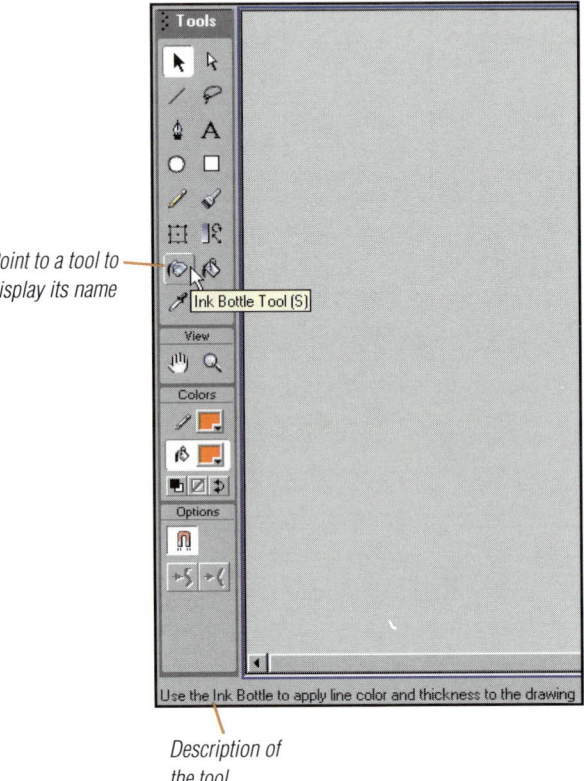

Point to a tool to display its name

Description of the tool

FIGURE B-3

Objects created with drawing tools

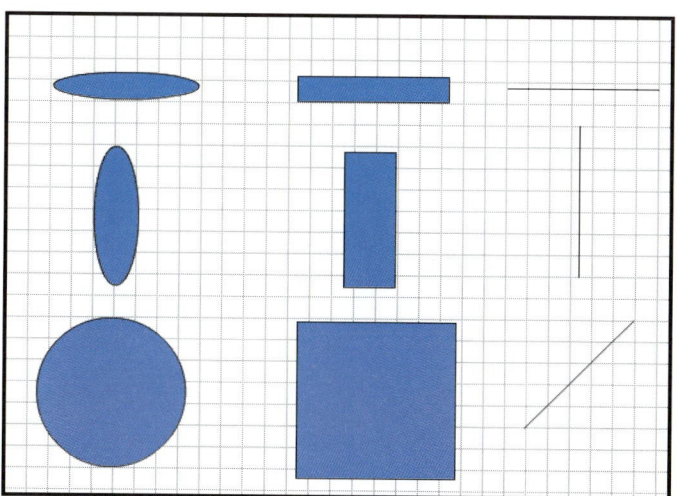

FIGURE B-4

Positioning the Pen Tool on the stage

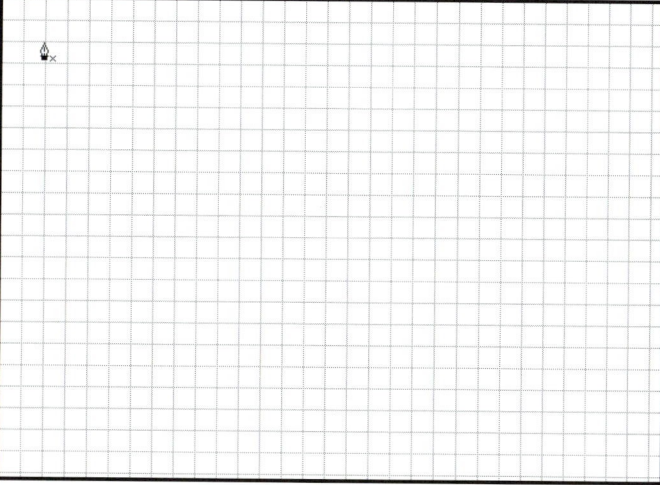

Use the Oval, Rectangle, and Line Tools

1. Click the Oval Tool on the toolbox, then using Figure B-3 as a guide, draw the three oval shapes. ⦿

   TIP   Use the grid to approximate shape sizes.

2. Repeat Step 1 using the Rectangle Tool. ▢

3. Repeat Step 1 using the Line Tool. ╱

   TIP   To undo an action, click the Undo command on the Edit menu.

4. Save your work.

You used the Oval, Rectangle, and Line Tools to draw objects on the stage.

Use the Pen Tool

1. Click Insert on the menu bar, then click Layer.

   A new layer—Layer 2—appears above Layer 1.

   TIP   Macromedia Flash numbers new layers sequentially, even if you delete previously created layers.

2. Insert a keyframe in Frame 5 on Layer 2.

   Since the objects were drawn in Frame 1, they are no longer visible when you insert a keyframe in Frame 5.

3. Click View on the menu bar, point to Magnification, click 200%, then center the upper-left corner of the stage in the workspace.

4. Click the Pen Tool on the toolbox, position it in the upper-left quadrant of the stage as shown in Figure B-4, then click to set an anchor point. ✍

(continued)

5. Using Figure B-5 as a guide, click the remaining anchor points to complete drawing an arrow.

   TIP   To close an object, be sure to re-click the first anchor point as your last action.

6. Save your work.

You added a layer, inserted a keyframe, and then used the Pen Tool to draw an arrow.

Use the Pencil and Brush Tools

1. Click View on the menu bar, point to Magnification, then click 100%.

2. Insert a new layer, Layer 3, then insert a keyframe in Frame 10.

3. Click the Pencil Tool on the toolbox.

4. Click the Pencil Mode Tool in the Options section of the toolbox, then click the Smooth Tool option, as shown in Figure B-6.

   TIP   A small arrow in the corner of an icon indicates that you can access additional icons.

   (continued)

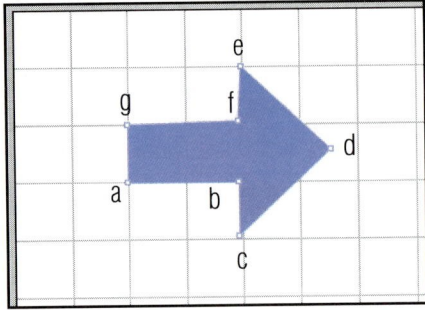

Click Pencil Mode Tool to display remaining options

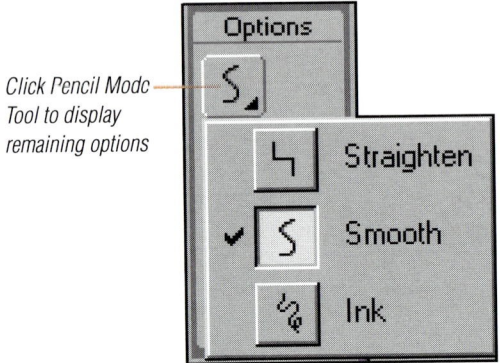

FIGURE B-7

Images drawn using drawing tools

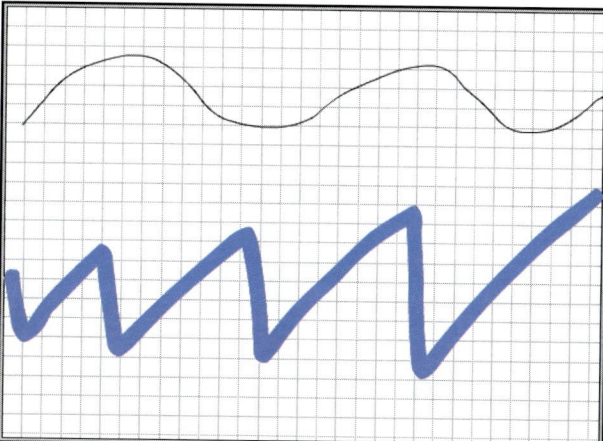

FIGURE B-8

Changing the brush size

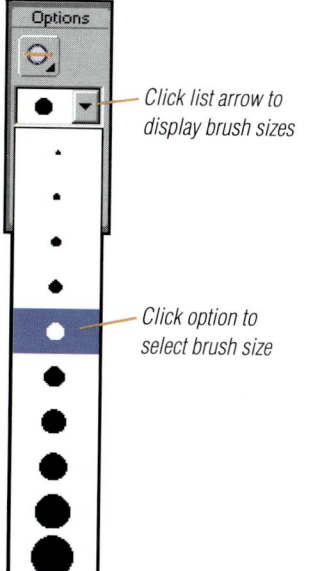

Click list arrow to
display brush sizes

Click option to
select brush size

5. Draw the top image shown in Figure B-7.

   TIP Collapse the Properties panel, if necessary.

6. Click the Brush Tool on the toolbox.

7. Click the Brush Size list arrow in the Options section of the toolbox, then click the 5th option from the top, as shown in Figure B-8.

8. Repeat Step 4, drawing the bottom image.

9. Save your work.

You selected the Smooth option for the Pencil Tool and drew an object; you selected a brush size for the Brush Tool and drew an object.

Modify an object using tool options

1. Click the Arrow Tool on the toolbox, then drag a marquee around the top object to select it.

   Options for the Arrow Tool appear in the Options section of the toolbox.

2. Click the Smooth Tool option in the Options section of the toolbox at least three times.

   The line becomes smoother.

3. Select the bottom object, then click the Straighten Tool option in the Options section of the toolbox at least three times.

   The segments of the line become straighter.

4. Save your work.

You smoothed and straightened objects.

Lesson 1   Use the Macromedia Flash Drawing Tools

EDIT DRAWINGS

What You'll Do

▶ *In this lesson, you will use several techniques to select objects, change the color of strokes and fills, and create a gradient fill.*

Selecting Objects

Before you can edit a drawing, you must first select the objects on which you want to work. Objects are made up of a stroke(s) and a fill. Strokes can have several segments. For example, a rectangle will have four stroke segments, one for each side of the object. These can be selected separately or as a whole. Macromedia Flash highlights objects that have been selected, as shown in Figure B-9. When the stroke of an object is selected, a colored line appears. When the fill of an object is selected, a dot pattern appears; and when objects are grouped, a bounding box appears.

Using the Arrow Tool

You can use the Arrow Tool to select part or all of an object, and to select multiple objects. To select only the fill, click just the fill; to select only the stroke, click just the stroke. To select both the fill and the stroke, double-click the object or draw a marquee around it. To select part of an object, drag a marquee that defines the area you wish to select, as shown in Figure B-10. To select multiple objects or combinations of strokes and fills, press and hold [Shift], then click each item. To deselect an item(s), click a blank area of the stage.

Using the Lasso Tool

The Lasso Tool provides more flexibility when selecting an area on the stage. You can use the tool in a freehand manner to select any size and shape of area. Alternately, you can use the Polygon Mode Tool option to draw straight lines and connect them.

Working With Colors

Macromedia Flash allows you to change the color of the stroke and fill of an object. Figure B-11 shows the Colors section of the toolbox. To change a color, you click the Stroke Color Tool or the Fill Color Tool, and then select a color swatch on the color palette.

You can set the desired colors before drawing an object, or you can change a color of a previously drawn object. You can use the Ink Bottle Tool to change the stroke color, and you can use the Paint Bucket Tool to change the fill color. You can also use the Properties panel to change the stroke and fill colors.

Working With Gradients

A gradient is a color fill that makes a gradual transition from one color to another. Gradients can be very useful for creating a 3-D effect, drawing attention to an object, and generally enhancing the appearance of an object. You can apply a gradient fill by using the Paint Bucket Tool. The position of the Paint Bucket Tool over the object is important because it determines the direction of the gradient fill.

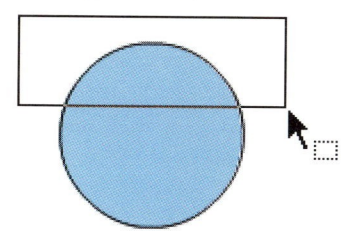

FIGURE B-10
Selecting part of an object

FIGURE B-9
Objects or parts of objects are highlighted when selected

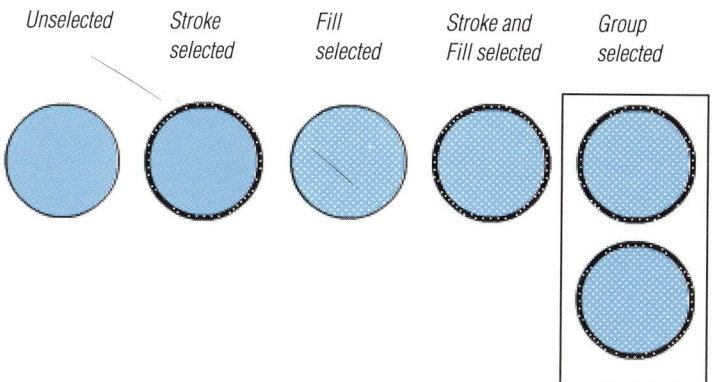

Unselected | Stroke selected | Fill selected | Stroke and Fill selected | Group selected

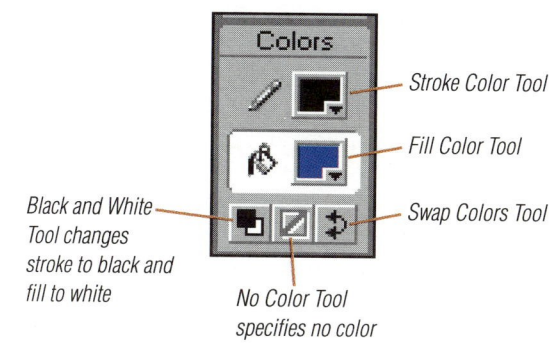

FIGURE B-11
The Colors section of the toolbox

Stroke Color Tool

Fill Color Tool

Swap Colors Tool

Black and White Tool changes stroke to black and fill to white

No Color Tool specifies no color

Select a drawing using the mouse and the Lasso Tool

1. Click Frame 1 on the timeline.

   TIP The actions you perform on the stage will produce very different results depending on whether you click a frame on the timeline or on a layer.

2. Click the Arrow Tool on the toolbox (if necessary), then drag the marquee around the perfect circle to select the entire object (both the stroke and the fill).

3. Click anywhere on the stage to deselect the object.

4. Click inside the circle to select the fill only, then click outside the circle to deselect it.

5. Click the stroke of the circle to select it, as shown in Figure B-12, then deselect it.

6. Double-click the circle to select it, press and hold [Shift], double-click the square to select both objects, then deselect both objects.

7. Click the right border of the square to select it, as shown in Figure B-13, then deselect it.

8. Click the Lasso Tool on the toolbox, then encircle the objects, as shown in Figure B-14.

   TIP The encircled objects are selected when you release the mouse.

9. Save your work.

You used the Arrow Tool to select the stroke and fill of an object, and you used the Lasso Tool to select a group of objects.

FIGURE B-12
Using the Arrow Tool to select the stroke of the circle

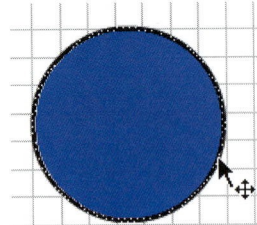

FIGURE B-13
Using the Arrow Tool to select a segment of the stroke of the square

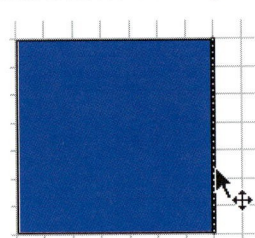

FIGURE B-14
Using the Lasso Tool to select several objects

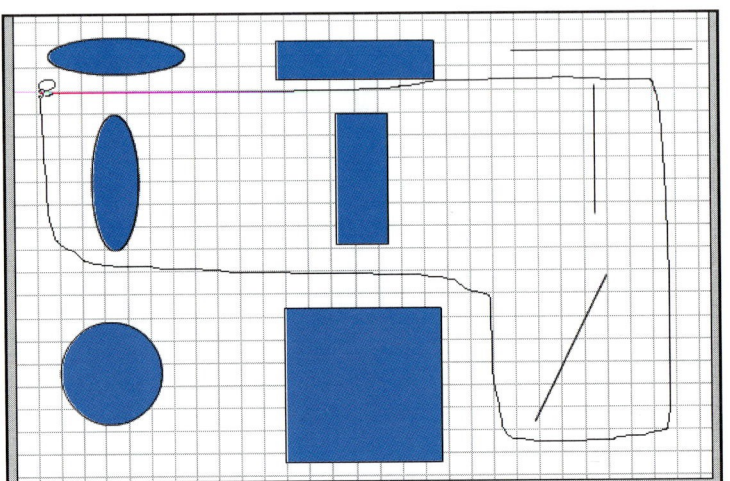

Drawing in Macromedia Flash

Circles drawn with the Oval Tool

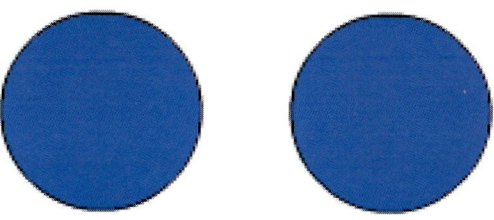

Changing the stroke color

Change fill and stroke colors

1. Click Layer 3, insert a new layer—Layer 4— then insert a keyframe in Frame 15.

2. Click View on the menu bar, point to Grid, then click Show Grid to remove the gridlines.

3. Click the Oval Tool on the toolbox, then draw circles similar to those shown in Figure B-15.

4. Click the Fill Color Tool on the toolbox, then click the yellow color swatch in the left column of the color palette.

5. Click the Paint Bucket Tool on the toolbox, then click the fill of the right circle.

6. Click the Stroke Color Tool on the toolbox, then click the yellow color swatch in the left column of the color palette.

7. Click the Ink Bottle Tool on the toolbox, then click the stroke of the left circle, as shown in Figure B-16.

8. Save your work.

You changed the fill and stroke colors of an object.

Create a gradient

1. Click the Fill Color Tool on the toolbox, then click the red gradient color swatch in the bottom row of the color palette, as shown in Figure B-17.

2. Click the Paint Bucket Tool on the toolbox, then click the yellow circle.

3. Continue to click different parts of the circle, then click the right side, as shown in Figure B-18.

4. Click the Fill Transform Tool, then click the gradient-filled circle.

(continued)

FIGURE B-17
Selecting the red gradient

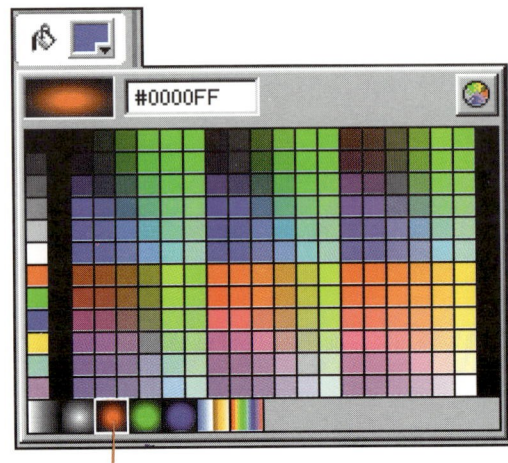

#0000FF

Click red gradient color swatch to select it

FIGURE B-18
Clicking the right side of the circle

Drawing in Macromedia Flash

5. Drag each of the four handles, shown in Figure B-19, to determine their effects on the gradient, then click the stage to deselect the circle.

6. Click the Fill Color Tool, then click the blue color swatch in the left column of the color palette.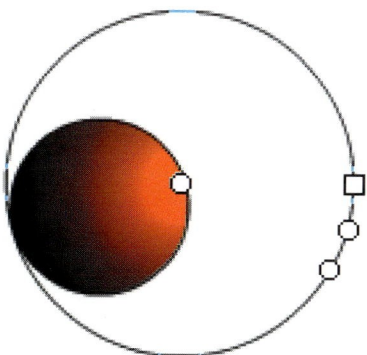

7. Save your work.

You applied a gradient fill and you used the Fill Transform Tool to alter the gradient.

FIGURE B-19

Fill Transform handles

WORK WITH OBJECTS

What You'll Do

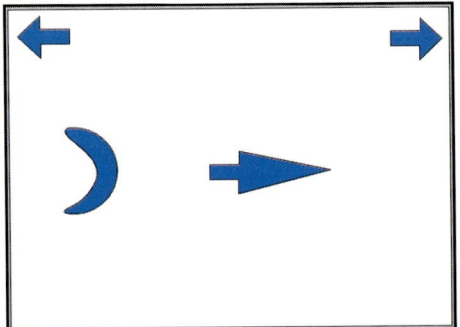

In this lesson, you will copy, move, and transform (resize, rotate, and reshape) objects.

Copying and Moving Objects

To copy one or more objects, select them, then click the Copy command on the Edit menu. Macromedia Flash places a copy of the object on the clipboard. To paste the object, click the Paste command on the Edit menu. You can copy an object to another layer by selecting the layer prior to pasting the object.

You can move an object by selecting it and dragging it to a new location. You can precisely position an object by selecting it and then pressing the arrow keys, which move the selection up, down, left, and right in small increments.

Transforming Objects

You can use the Free Transform Tool to resize, rotate, skew, and reshape objects. After selecting an object, you can click the Free Transform Tool to display eight square-shaped handles used to transform the object, and a circle-shaped transformation point located at the center of the object. The transformation point is the point around which the object can be rotated. You can also change its location. The Free Transform Tool has four options: Rotate and Skew, Scale, Distort, and Envelope. These tool options restrict the transformations that can be completed; you can select only one option at a time.

Resizing an Object

You can enlarge or reduce the size of an object using the Scale Tool option of the Free Transform Tool. The process is to select the object and click the Free Transform Tool, then click the Scale Tool option in the Options section of the tool-box. Eight handles appear around the selected object. You can drag the corner handles to resize the object without changing its proportions. That is, if the object starts out as a square, dragging a corner handle will change the size of the object, but it will still be a square. On the other hand, if you drag one of the middle handles, the object will be reshaped as taller, shorter, wider, or narrower.

Rotating and Skewing an Object

You can use the Rotate and Skew Tool option of the Free Transform Tool to rotate an object and to skew it. Select the object, click the Free Transform Tool, then click the Rotate and Skew Tool option in the Options section of the toolbox. Eight square-shaped handles appear around the object. You can drag the corner handles to rotate the object, or you can drag the middle handles to skew the object, as shown in Figure B-20. The Transform panel can be used to rotate and skew an object in a more precise way; select the object, display the Transform dialog box, enter the desired rotation of skew, then press [Enter] (Win) or [return] (Mac).

Distorting an Object

You can use the Distort and Envelope Tool options to reshape an object by dragging its handles. The Envelope Tool option provides more than eight handles to allow for more precise distortions.

Reshaping a Segment of an Object

You can use the Subselection Tool to reshape a segment of an object. Click an edge of the object to display handles that can be dragged to reshape the object.

You can use the Arrow Tool to reshape objects. When you point to the edge of an object, the pointer displays an arc symbol. Using the Arc pointer, you can drag the edge of the object you want to reshape, as

shown in Figure B-21. If the Arrow Tool points to a corner of an object, the pointer displays an L-shaped symbol—dragging the pointer reshapes the corner of the object.

Flipping an Object

You can use an option under the Transform command to flip an object either horizontally or vertically. Select the object, click the Transform command on the Modify menu, and then choose Flip Vertical or Flip Horizontal. Other Transform options allow you to rotate and scale the selected object, and the Remove Transform command allows you to restore an object to its original state.

Using handles to manipulate an object

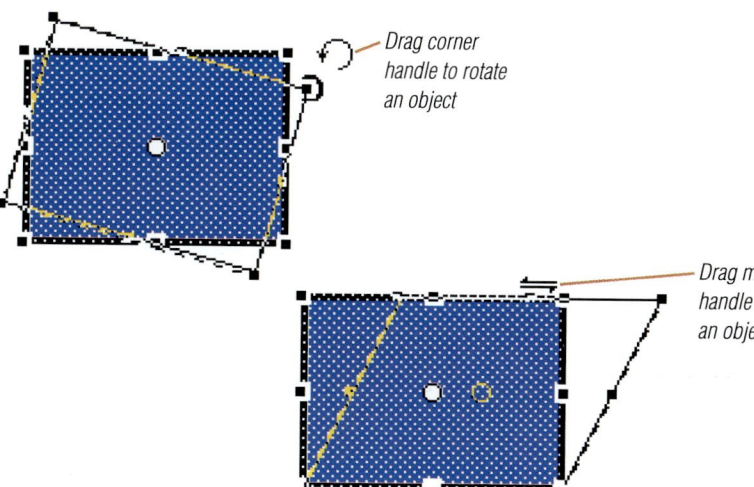

Drag corner handle to rotate an object

Drag middle handle to skew an object

FIGURE B-21

Using the Envelope Tool option to distort an object

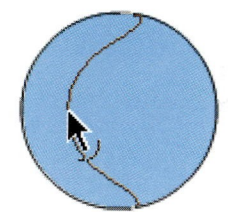

Copy and move an object

1. Click Frame 5 on the timeline.

2. Click the Arrow Tool on the toolbox, then double-click the arrow object to select it.

3. Click Edit on the menu bar, click Copy, click Edit on the menu bar, click Paste, then compare your image to Figure B-22.

   Macromedia Flash pastes a copy of the arrow on the stage.

4. Drag and align the newly copied arrow under the original arrow, as shown in Figure B-23.

5. Save your work.

You used the Arrow Tool to select an object, then you copied and moved the object.

A copy of the arrow on the stage

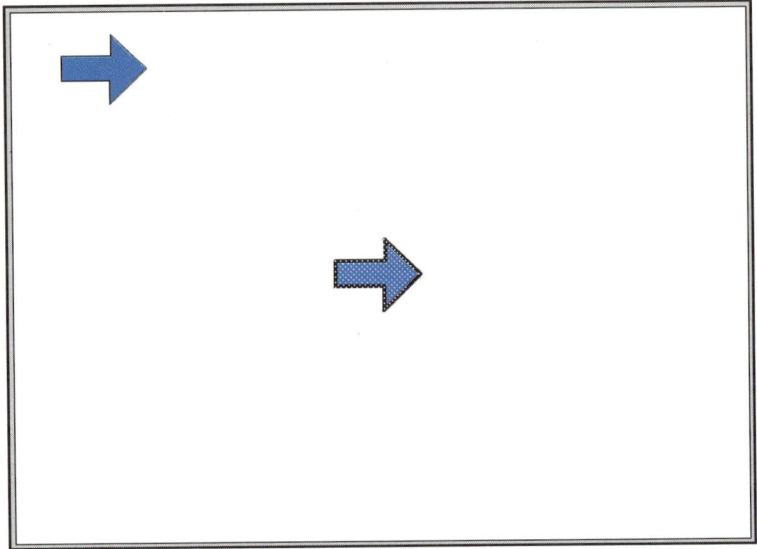

Aligning the arrows

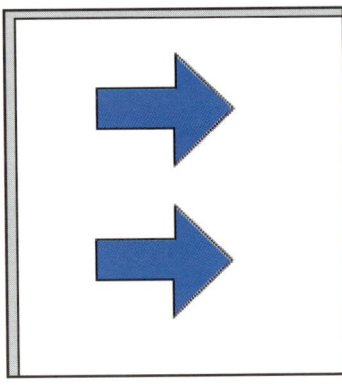

Drawing in Macromedia Flash

Resize and reshape an object

1. Verify that the arrow is selected, then click the Free Transform Tool on the toolbox.

2. Click the Scale Tool option in the Options section of the toolbox.

3. Drag each corner handle towards and then away from the center of the object, as shown in Figure B-24.

   As you drag the corner handles, the object's size is changed, but its proportions remain the same.

4. Drag each middle handle towards and then away from the center of the object.

   As you drag the middle handles, the object's size and proportions are changed.

5. Save your work.

You used the Free Transform Tool and the Scale Tool options to display an object's handles, and you used the handles to resize and reshape the object.

FIGURE B-24
Resizing an object using the corner handles

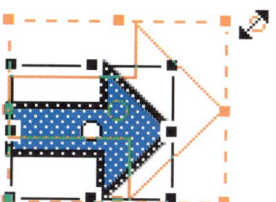

Rotate, skew, and flip an object

1. Verify that the arrow is selected, then click the Rotate and Skew Tool option in the Options section of the toolbox. ↻

2. Click the upper-right corner handle, then rotate the object clockwise as shown in Figure B-25.

3. Click the upper-middle handle, then drag it to the right.

    The arrow slants to the right.

4. Click Edit on the menu bar, click Undo, then repeat until the arrow is in its original shape.

5. Click the Arrow Tool on the toolbox, double-click the bottom arrow, click Window on the menu bar, then click Transform. ▶

6. Double-click the Rotate text box, type **45**, then press [Enter] (Win) or [return] (Mac).

7. Click Edit on the menu bar, then click Undo.

8. Close the Transform panel.

9. Verify that the arrow is selected, click Modify on the menu bar, point to Transform, then click Flip Horizontal.

10. Move the arrows to the positions shown in Figure B-26.

    TIP   Double-click each arrow or drag a marquee around them to select the fill and the stroke.

11. Save your work.

You used toolbox options, the Transform panel, and Modify menu commands to rotate, skew, and flip an object.

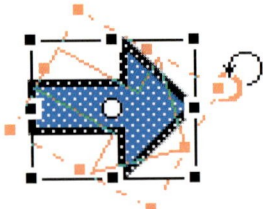

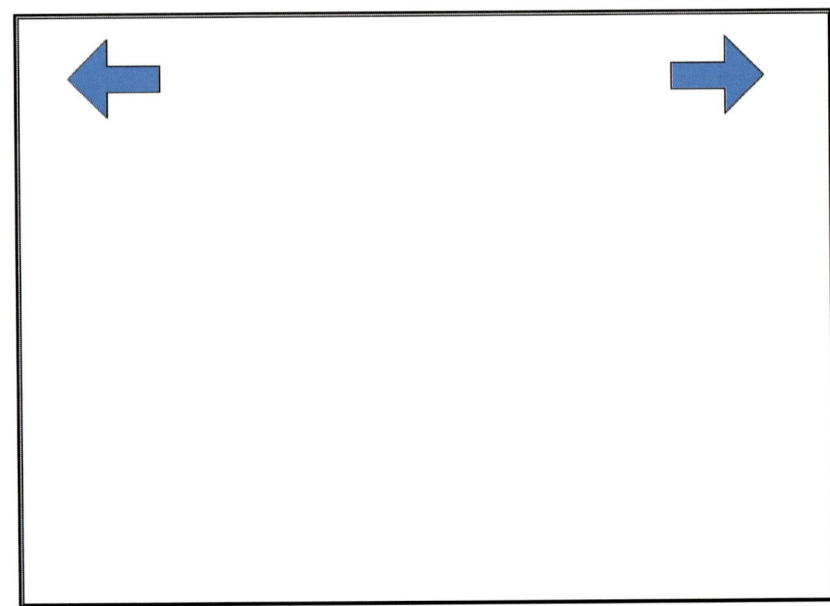

Drawing in Macromedia Flash

FIGURE B-27

Using the Subselection Tool to select an object

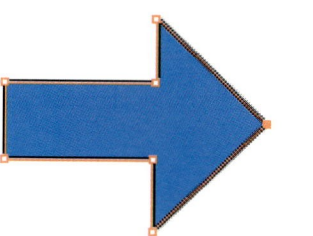

FIGURE B-28

Using the Subselection Tool to drag a handle to reshape the object

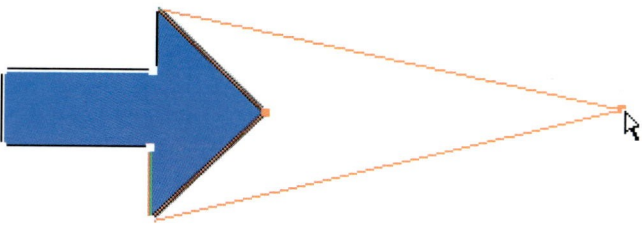

FIGURE B-29

Using the Arrow Tool to drag an edge to reshape the object

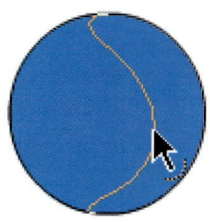 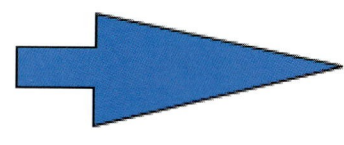

Change view and reshape an object using the Subselection Tool

1. Select the arrow in the upper-right corner of the stage, click Edit on the menu bar, click Copy, click Edit on the menu bar, then click Paste.

2. Click the Zoom Tool on the toolbox, then click the middle of the copied object to enlarge the view. 🔍

3. Click the Subselection Tool on the toolbox, then click the tip of the arrow to display the handles, as shown in Figure B-27. ▷

   | TIP   The handles allow you to change any segment of the object.

4. Click the handle at the tip of the arrow, then drag it as shown in Figure B-28.

5. Click the Zoom Tool on the toolbox, press and hold [Alt] (Win) or [option] (Mac), then click the middle of the arrow. 🔍

6. Click the Oval Tool on the toolbox, then draw a circle to the left of the middle arrow. ○

7. Click the Arrow Tool on the toolbox, then point to the left edge of the circle until the Arc pointer is displayed. ↖

8. Drag the pointer to the position shown in Figure B-29.

9. Save your work.

You used the Zoom Tool to change the view, and you used the Subselection and Arrow Tools to reshape objects.

WORK WITH TEXT

What You'll Do

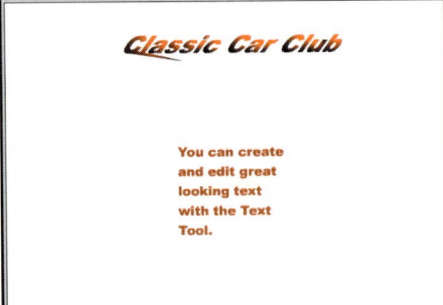

 In this lesson, you will enter text using text blocks. You will also resize text blocks, change text attributes, and transform text.

Learning About Text

Macromedia Flash provides a great deal of flexibility when using text. Among other settings, you can select the typeface (font), size, style (bold, italic), and color (including gradients) of text. You can transform the text by rotating, scaling, skewing, and flipping it. You can even break apart a letter and reshape its segments.

Entering Text and Changing the Text Block

It is important to understand that text is entered into a text block, as shown in Figure B-30. You use the Text Tool to place a text block on the stage and to enter and edit text. A text block expands as more text is entered and may even extend beyond the edge of the stage. You can adjust the size of the text block so that it is a fixed width by dragging the handle in the upper- right corner of the block. Figure B-31 shows the process of using the Text Tool to enter text and resize the text block. Once you select the tool, you click the pointer on the stage where you want the text to appear. An

insertion point indicates where in the text block the next character will appear when typed. You can reshape the text block by pressing [Enter] (Win) or [return] (Mac) or by dragging the circle handle. After reshaping the text block, the circle handle changes to a square, indicating that the text block now has a fixed horizontal width. Then, when you enter more text, it automatically wraps within the text block. You can resize or move the text block at any time by selecting it with the Arrow Tool and dragging the section.

Changing Text Attributes

You can use the Properties panel to change the font, size, and style of a single character or an entire text block. Figure B-32 shows the Properties panel when a text object is selected. You select text, display the Properties panel, and make the desired changes. You can use the Arrow Tool to select the entire text block by drawing a box around it. You can use the Text Tool to select a single character or string of characters by dragging the

I-beam pointer over them, as shown in Figure B-33.

Working with Paragraphs

When working on large bodies of text, such as paragraphs, Macromedia Flash provides many of the features found in a word processor. You can align paragraphs (left, right, center, justified) within a text block. You can use the Properties panel to set margins (space between the border of a text block and the paragraph text), indents for the first line of a paragraph, and line spacing (distance between paragraphs).

Transforming Text

It is important to understand that a text block is an object. Therefore, you can transform (reshape, rotate, skew, and so on) a text block as you would other objects. If you want to transform individual characters within a text block, you must first break it apart. Use the Arrow Tool to select the text block, and then click the Break Apart command on the Modify menu. Each character (or a group of characters) in the text block can now be selected and transformed.

FIGURE B-30

A text block

This is a text block used to enter text

FIGURE B-31

Using the Text Tool

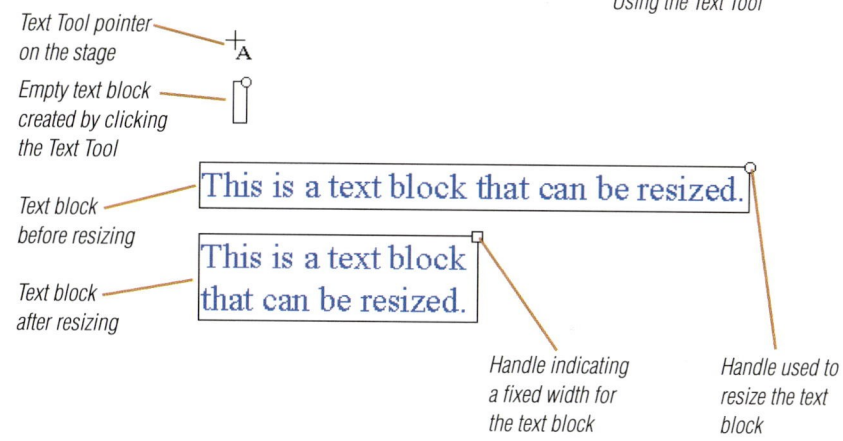

Text Tool pointer on the stage

Empty text block created by clicking the Text Tool

Text block before resizing

Text block after resizing

This is a text block that can be resized.

This is a text block that can be resized.

Handle indicating a fixed width for the text block

Handle used to resize the text block

FIGURE B-32

The Properties panel when a text object is selected

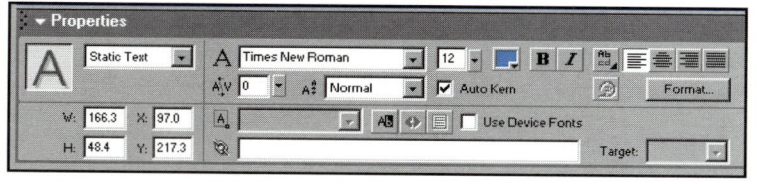

FIGURE B-33

Dragging the I-Beam pointer to select text

This is a text block that can be resized.

I-Beam pointer

Create text

1. Click Layer 4, click Insert on the menu bar, then click Layer to insert a new layer—Layer 5.

2. Insert a keyframe in Frame 20 on Layer 5.

3. Click the Text Tool on the toolbox, click the center of the stage, then type **You can create great looking text with the Text Tool**. A

4. Click the I-Beam pointer before the word "great," as shown in Figure B-34, then type and edit. I

5. Save your work.

You used the Text Tool to create text.

FIGURE B-34
Using the Text Tool to enter text

You can create great looking text with the Text Tool.

Drawing in Macromedia Flash

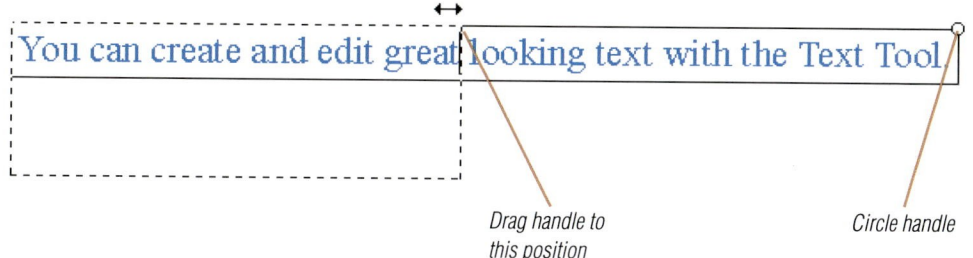

You can create and edit great looking text with the Text Tool

Drag handle to
this position

Circle handle

Change text attributes

1. Position the text pointer over the circle handle until the pointer changes to a double arrow, then drag the handle to the left, as shown in Figure B-35. $+_A$

2. Drag the I-Beam pointer across all lines of text to select all the text. $\mathbb{I}$

3. Click Window on the menu bar, then verify that Properties is checked.

4. Click the Font list arrow, click Arial Black, click the Font Size list arrow, then drag the slider to **16**.

5. Click the Text (fill) color swatch, click the Hex Edit text box, type **990000** as shown in Figure B-36, then press [Enter] (Win) or [return] (Mac).

6. Click a blank area of the stage, then save your work.

You resized the text block and changed the font and type size.

FIGURE B-36

Changing text color on the Properties panel

Type Hex color
number here

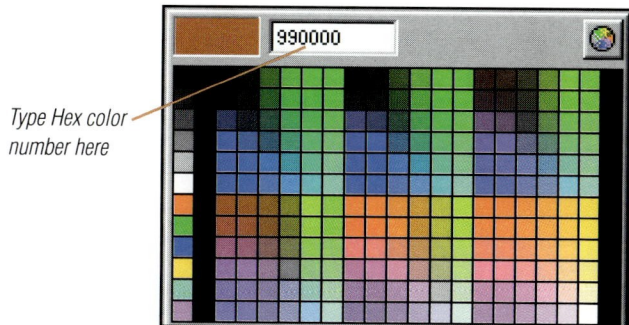

Skew text

1. Verify that the Text Tool is selected, click the pointer near the top of the stage, approximately even with Frame 20, then type **Classic Car Club**.

   The new text reflects the most recent settings changed in the Properties panel.

2. Drag the I-Beam pointer across all lines of text to select it, click the Font Size list arrow on the Property inspector, then drag the slider to **30**.

3. Click the Arrow Tool on the toolbox, click the Free Transform Tool, then click the Rotate and Skew Tool option in the Options section of the toolbox.

4. Drag the top middle handle to the right to skew the text, as shown in Figure B-37.

5. Save your work.

You skewed text using the Free Transform Tool.

FIGURE B-37
Skewing the text

Drawing in Macromedia Flash

Apply a gradient to text

1. Click the Arrow Tool on the toolbox, click the text block to select it, click Modify on the menu bar, then click Break Apart.

   The words are separated into individual text blocks.

2. Click Modify on the menu bar, then click Break Apart.

   The letters are filled with a dot pattern, indicating that they can now be edited.

3. Click the Zoom Tool on the toolbox, then click the "C" in Classic.

4. Click the Subselection Tool on the toolbox, then click the edge of the letter "C" to display the object's segment handles.

5. Drag a lower handle on the "C" in Classic, as shown in Figure B-38.

   A portion of the letter extends outward.

6. Click the Arrow Tool on the toolbox, click the Fill Color Tool on the toolbox, then click the red gradient color swatch in the bottom row of the color palette.

7. Click the Paint Bucket Tool on the toolbox, then click the top of each letter to change the fill to a red gradient as shown in Figure B-39.

   | TIP   Scroll across the stage as necessary.

8. Click the Zoom Tool on the toolbox, press and hold [Alt] (Win) or [option] (Mac), then click the letter "C" in Classic to zoom out.

9. Save your work, then close the movie.

You converted and reshaped text, and added a gradient to the text.

WORK WITH LAYERS

What You'll Do

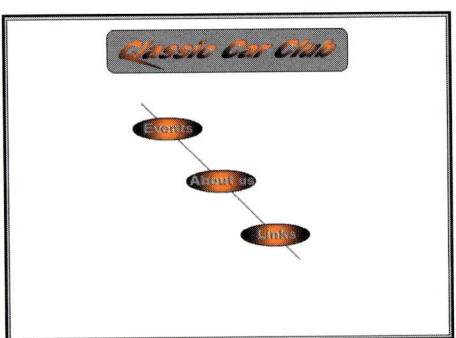

 In this lesson, you will create, rename, reorder, delete, hide, and lock layers. You will also display outline layers, use a Guide layer, distribute text to layers, and create a folder layer.

Learning About Layers

Macromedia Flash uses two types of spatial organization. First, there is the position of objects on the stage, and then there is the stacking order of objects that overlap. An example of overlapping objects is text placed on a banner. Layers are used on the timeline as a way to organize objects. Placing objects on their own layer makes them easier to work with, especially when reshaping them, repositioning them on the stage, or rearranging their order in relation to other objects. In addition, layers are useful for organizing other elements such as sounds, animations, and ActionScripts.

There are six types of layers:

Normal—The default layer type. All objects on these layers appear in the movie.

Guide (Standard and Motion)—Standard Guide layers serve as a reference point for positioning objects on the stage. Motion Guide layers are used to create a path for animated objects to follow.

Guided—A layer that contains an animated object, linked to a Motion Guide layer.

Mask—A layer that hides and reveals portions of another layer.

Masked—A layer that contains the objects that are hidden and revealed by a Mask layer.

Folder—A layer that can contain other layers.

Motion Guide and Mask layer types will be covered in a later unit.

Drawing in Macromedia Flash

Working with Layers

The Layer Properties dialog box allows you to specify the type of layer. It also allows you to name, show (and hide), and lock them. Naming a layer provides a clue to the objects on the layer. For example, naming a layer Logo might indicate that the object on the layer is the company's logo. Hiding a layer(s) may reduce the clutter on the stage and make it easier to work with selected objects from the layer(s) that are not hidden. Locking a layer(s) prevents the objects from being accidentally edited. Other options in the Layer Properties dialog box allow you to view layers as outlines and change the outline color. Outlines can be used to help you determine which objects are on a layer. When you turn on this feature, each layer has a colored box that corresponds with the color of the objects on its layer, as shown in Figure B-40. Icons on the Layers section of the timeline correspond to features in the Layer Properties dialog box, as shown in Figure B-41.

FIGURE B-40
Displaying outlines

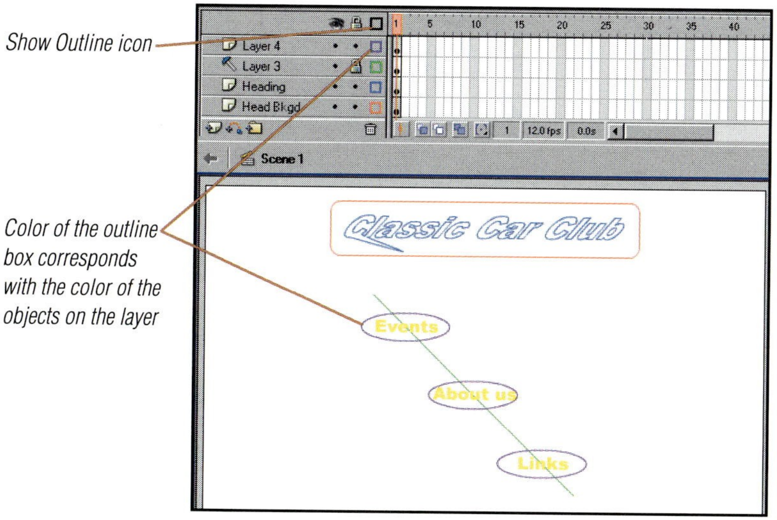

FIGURE B-41
The Layers section of the timeline

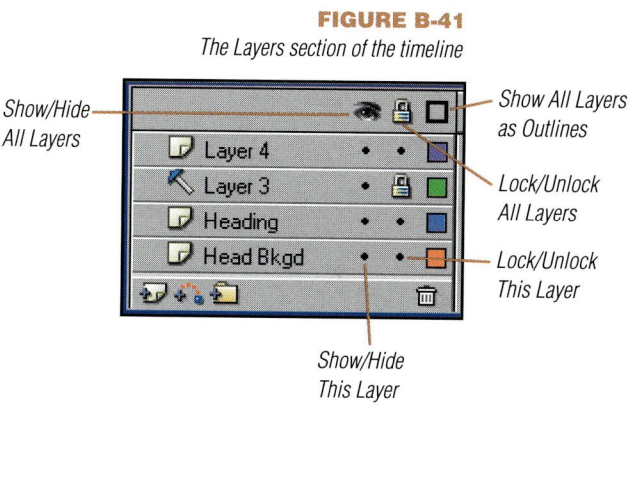

Show Outline icon

Color of the outline box corresponds with the color of the objects on the layer

Show/Hide All Layers

Show All Layers as Outlines

Lock/Unlock All Layers

Lock/Unlock This Layer

Show/Hide This Layer

Using a Guide Layer

Guide layers are useful in aligning objects on the stage. Figure B-42 shows a Guide layer that has been used to align three buttons along a diagonal path. The process is to insert a new layer, click the Layer command on the Modify menu to display the Layer Properties dialog box, select Guides as the layer type, and then draw a path that will be used as the guide to align objects. You then display the Guides options from the View menu, turn on Snap to Guides, and drag the desired objects to the Guide line. Objects have a registration point that is used to snap when snapping to a guide. By default, this point is at the center of the object. Figure B-43 shows the process.

FIGURE B-42

A Guide layer used to align objects on the stage

FIGURE B-43

The registration point of an object

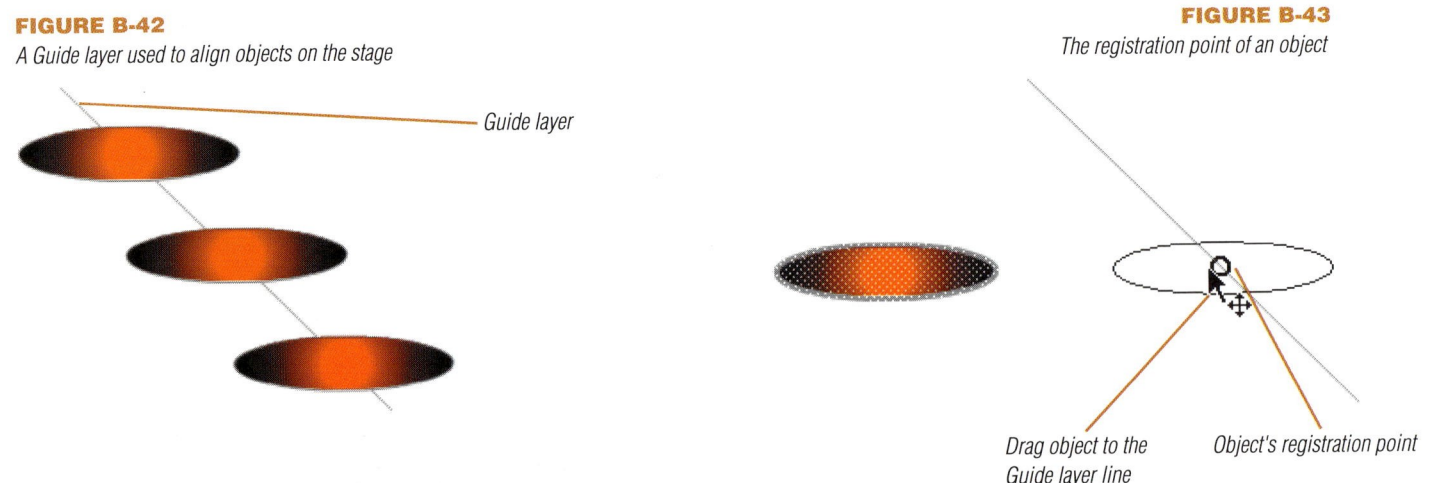

Guide layer

Drag object to the Guide layer line

Object's registration point

Distributing Text to Layers

Text blocks are made up of one or more characters. When you break apart a text block, each character becomes an object that can be edited independent of the other characters. You can use the Distribute to Layers command to cause each character to automatically be placed on its own layer. Figure B-44 shows the seven layers created after the text block containing 55 Chevy has been broken apart and distributed to layers.

Using Folder Layers

As movies become larger and more complex, the number of layers increases. Macromedia Flash allows you to organize layers by creating folders and grouping other layers in them. Figure B-45 shows a layers folder—Layer 6—with three layers in it. You can click the Folder layer triangle next to Layer 6 to open and close the folder.

FIGURE B-44
Distributing text to layers

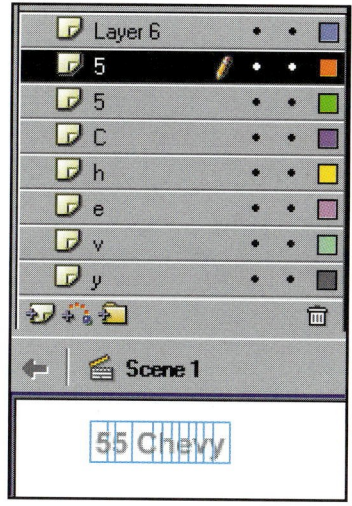

FIGURE B-45
A folder layer

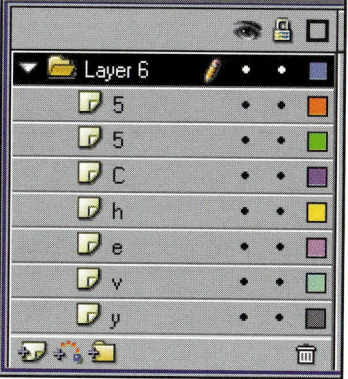

Create and reorder layers

1. Open flb_1.fla, then save it as **layersB.fla**.

2. Click the Insert Layer icon on the bottom of the timeline to insert a new layer, Layer 2.

3. Click the Rectangle Tool on the toolbox, then click the Round Rectangle Radius Tool option in the Options section of the toolbox.

4. Type **10**, then click OK.

5. Click the Fill Color Tool on the toolbox, click the Hex Edit text box, type **999999**, then press [Enter] (Win) or [return] (Mac).

6. Click the Stroke Color Tool on the toolbox, click the Hex Edit text box, type **000000**, then press [Enter] (Win) or [return] (Mac).

7. Draw the rectangle shown in Figure B-46 so that it covers the text heading.

8. Drag Layer 1 above Layer 2 on the timeline, as shown in Figure B-47.

9. Save your work.

You created a layer and reordered layers.

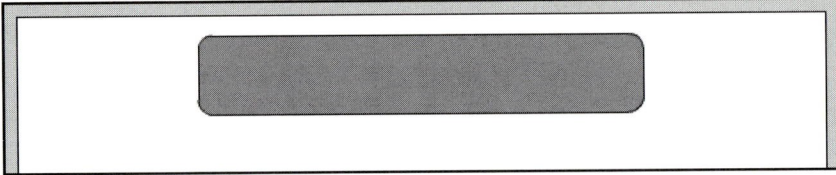

Drag Layer 1 above Layer 2

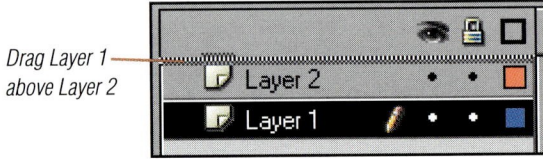

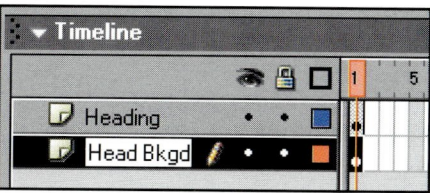

Rename and delete layers on the timeline

1. Double-click Layer 1 on the timeline, type **Heading** in the Layer Name text box, then press [Enter] (Win) or [return] (Mac).

2. Repeat Step 1 for Layer 2, but type **Head Bkgd**, then compare your timeline to Figure B-48.

3. Click the Heading layer, then click the Delete Layer icon on the bottom of the timeline to delete the layer. 🗑

4. Click Edit on the menu bar, then click Undo.

5. Save your work.

You renamed, deleted, and restored a layer.

FIGURE B-48

Renaming layers

Hide, lock, and display layer outlines

1. Click the Show/Hide All Layers icon to hide all layers, then compare your image to Figure B-49. 👁

2. Click the Show/Hide All Layers icon to show all the layers.

3. Click the Lock/Unlock All Layers icon to lock all layers. 🔒

4. With the layers locked, try to select and edit an object. ✚

5. Click the Lock/Unlock All Layers icon again to unlock the layers. 🔓

6. Click the Heading layer, then click the Show/Hide dot icon under the Show/Hide icon twice to hide and show the layer. ✚

7. Click the Show All Layers as Outlines icon twice to display and turn off the outlines of all objects. ▢

8. Save your work.

You hid and locked layers and displayed the outlines of objects in a layer.

FIGURE B-49
Hiding all the layers

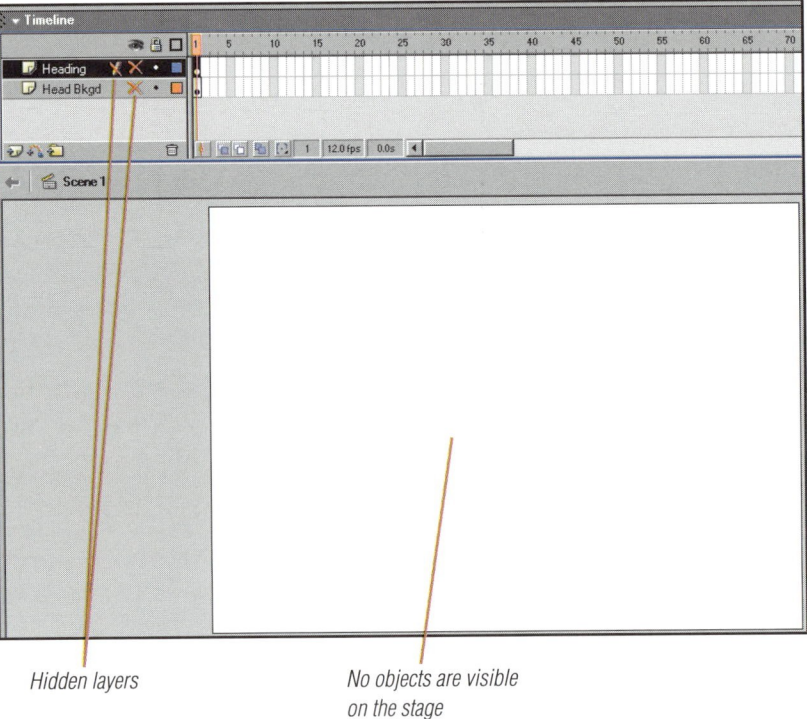

Hidden layers

No objects are visible on the stage

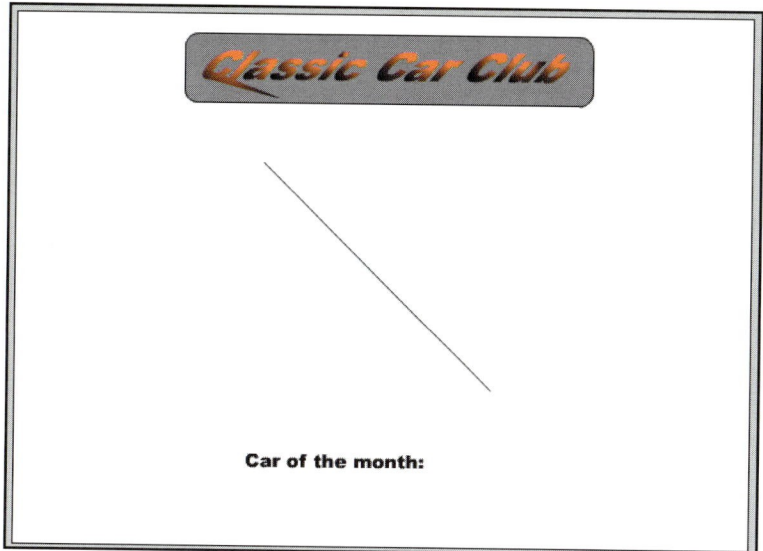

Car of the month:

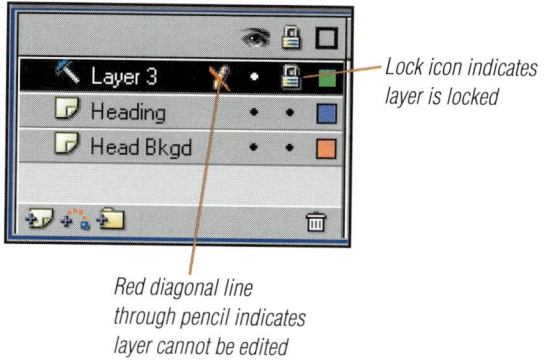

Lock icon indicates layer is locked

Red diagonal line through pencil indicates layer cannot be edited

Create a guide for a Guide layer

1. Click the Heading layer, then click the Insert Layer icon on the timeline to add a new layer, Layer 3.

2. Click Modify on the menu bar, click Layer to display the Layer Properties dialog box, click Guide, then click OK.

3. Click the Line Tool on the toolbox, press and hold [Shift], then draw the diagonal line shown in Figure B-50. /

4. Click the Lock/Unlock This Layer dot icon under the Lock/Unlock All Layers icon in Layer 3 to lock it, then compare your layers to Figure B-51. ✦

5. Save your work.

You created a guide for a Guide layer.

Add objects to a Guide layer

1. Click the Insert Layer icon on the timeline to add a new layer, Layer 4.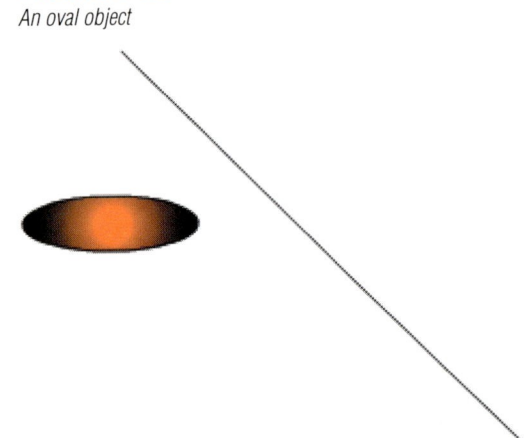

2. Click the Fill Color Tool on the toolbox, then click the red gradient color swatch in the bottom row of the color palette, if necessary.

3. Click the Oval Tool on the toolbox, then draw the oval shown in Figure B-52.

4. Click the Arrow Tool on the toolbox, then double-click the oval object to select it.

5. Point to the center of the oval, click, then slowly drag it to the Guide layer line, as shown in Figure B-53.

6. With the oval object selected, click Edit on the menu bar, then click Copy.

7. Click Edit on the menu bar, click Paste, then, if necessary, align the copied object to the Guide layer line beneath the first oval.

(continued)

FIGURE B-52
An oval object

FIGURE B-53
Dragging an object to the Guide layer line

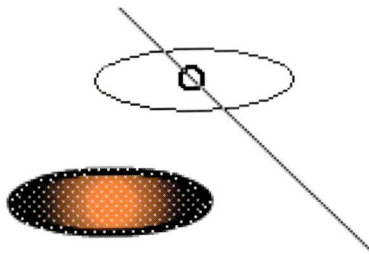

Drawing in Macromedia Flash

FIGURE B-54
Adding text to the oval objects

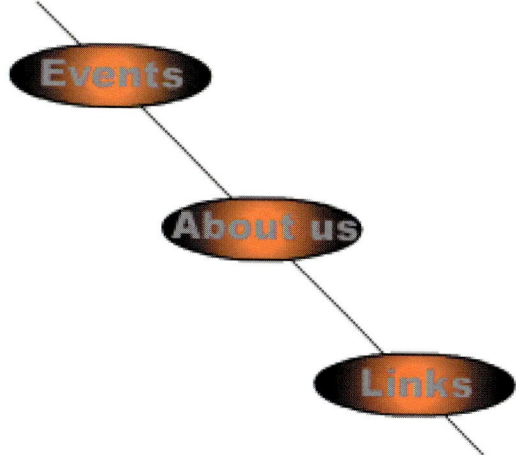

8. Click Edit on the menu bar, click Paste, then align the copied object to the bottom of the Guide layer line.

   TIP Objects are pasted in the center of the stage, and one object may cover up another object.

9. Click the Insert Layer icon on the timeline to insert a new layer, Layer 5.

10. Click the Text Tool on the toolbox, then, if necessary, click the Font list arrow on the Property inspector, click Arial Black, click the Font Size list arrow, then drag the slider to **14**. A

11. Click the Text (fill) color swatch in the Property inspector, click the Hex Edit text box, type **999999**, then press [Enter] (Win) or [return] (Mac).

12. Click on the top oval, then type **Events**.

13. Click the Arrow Tool on the toolbox, click the text box to select it, then drag the text box to center it on the oval, as shown in Figure B-54.

14. Repeat Steps 11 through 13, typing **About us** and **Links** text blocks.

15. Save your work.

You created a Guide layer and used it to align objects on the stage.

Distribute to layers and create a Folders layer

1. Insert a new layer—Layer 6—click the Text Tool on the toolbox, then type **55 Chevy** following the words "Car of the Month:".

2. Click the Arrow Tool on the toolbox, then select the 55 Chevy text block.

3. Click Modify on the menu bar, then click Break Apart.

4. Click Modify on the menu bar, then click Distribute to Layers.

   Layers are created for each letter.

5. Click Layer 6, click Modify in the menu bar, then click Layer.

   TIP You may need to use the scroll bar at the right side of the timeline to display Layer 6.

6. Click Folder in the Layer Properties dialog box, then click OK.

   Layer 6 becomes a Folder layer.

7. Click the y layer, then drag it to Layer 6, as shown in Figure B-55.

(continued)

Layer dragged to folder

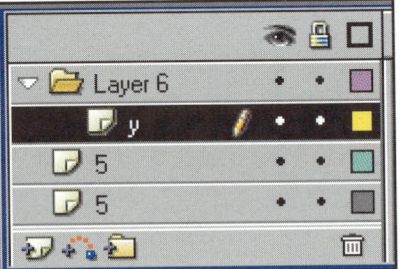

8. Repeat Step 8 for the v, e, h, C, 5, and 5 layers.

9. Click the Collapse triangle next to Layer 6 to collapse the folder, then compare your timeline to Figure B-56. ▽

10. Click the Expand triangle to expand the folder. ▷

11. Save and close the document.

You broke apart a text block and distributed the letters to a Folder layer.

FIGURE B-56

Collapsing Layer 6

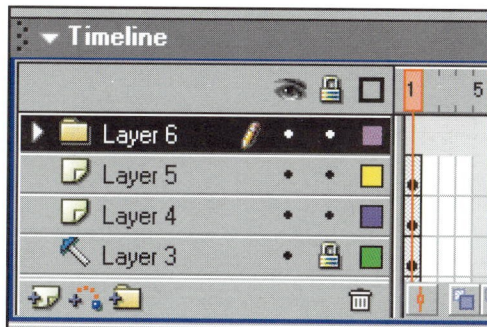

Draw objects with the drawing tools.

1. Open a new movie, then save it as **skillsdemoB.fla**.
2. Display the Grid.
3. Set the stroke color to black (hex: 000000) and the fill color to blue (hex: 0000FF).
4. Use the Oval Tool to draw an oval on the left side of the stage, then draw a circle beneath the oval.
5. Use the Rectangle Tool to draw a rectangle in the middle of the stage, then draw a square beneath the rectangle.
6. Use the Line Tool to draw a horizontal line on the right side of the stage, then draw a vertical line beneath the horizontal line and a diagonal line beneath the vertical line.
7. Use the Pen Tool to draw an arrow-shaped object above the rectangle.
8. Use the Pencil Tool to draw a freehand line above the oval, then use the Smooth Tool option to smooth out the line.
9. Save your work.

Select and edit objects.

1. Use the Arrow Tool to select the stroke of the circle, then deselect the stroke.
2. Use the Arrow Tool to select the fill of the circle, then deselect the fill.
3. Use the Lasso Tool to select several of the objects, then deselect them.
4. Use the Ink Bottle to change the stroke color of the circle to red (Hex FF0000).
5. Use the Paint Bucket to change the fill color of the square to red (Hex FF0000).
6. Change the fill color of the oval to a blue gradient.
7. Save your work.

Work with objects.

1. Copy the arrow object.
2. Move the copied arrow to another location on the stage.
3. Rescale both arrows to approximately half their original size.

4. Flip the copied arrow horizontally.
5. Rotate the rectangle to a 45° angle.
6. Skew the square to the right.
7. Copy one of the arrows and use the Subselection Tool to reshape it, then delete it.
8. Use the Arrow Tool to reshape the circle to a crescent shape.
9. Save your work.

Enter and edit text.

1. Enter the following text in a text block at the top of the stage: **Portal to the Pacific**.
2. Change the text to font: Tahoma, size: 24, color: red.
3. Use the gridlines to help align the text block to the top center of the stage.
4. Skew the text block to the right.
5. Save your work.

Work with layers.

1. Insert a layer into the movie.
2. Change the name on the new layer to **Heading Bkgnd**.
3. Draw a rounded corner rectangle that covers the words Portal to the Pacific.
4. Switch the order of the layers.
5. Lock all layers.
6. Unlock all layers.
7. Hide the Heading Bkgnd layer.
8. Show the Heading Bkgnd layer.
9. Show all layers as outlines.
10. Turn off the view of the outlines.
11. Create a Guide layer and move the arrows to it.
12. Add a layer and use the Text Tool to type **SEATTLE** below the heading.
13. Break the text block apart and distribute the text to layers.
14. Create a Folder layer and add each of the text layers to it.
15. Save your work, then compare your image to Figure B-57.

FIGURE B-57
Completed Skills Review

A local travel company, Ultimate Tours, has asked you to design several sample homepages for their new Web site. The goal of the Web site is to inform potential customers of their services. The company specializes in exotic treks, tours, and cruises. Thus, while their target audience spans a wide age range, they are all looking for something out of the ordinary.

1. Open a new movie and save it as **ultimatetoursB.fla**.
2. Set the movie properties, including the size and background color.
3. Create the following on separate layers and name the layers:
   - A text heading; select a font size and font color. Skew the heading, break it apart, then reshape one or more of the characters.
   - A subheading with a different font size and color.
   - A guide path.
   - At least three objects.
4. Snap the objects to the guide path.
5. On another layer, add text to the objects and place them on the guide path.
6. Compare your image to Figure B-58.
7. Save your work.

FIGURE B-58
Completed Project Builder 1

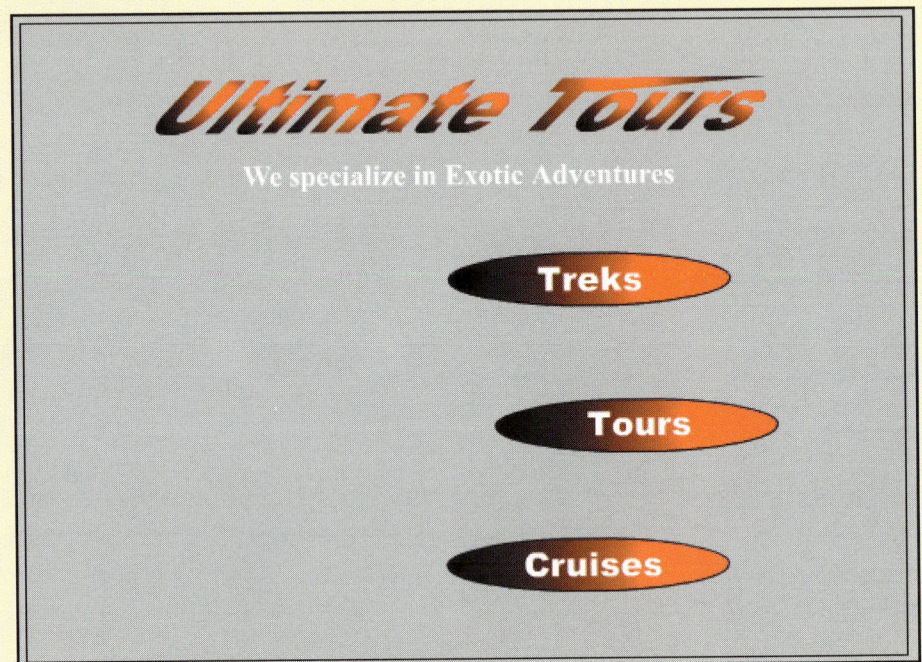

After weeks of unsuccessful job hunting, you have decided to create a personal portfolio of your work. The portfolio will be a Web site done completely in Macromedia Flash.

1. Research what should be included in a portfolio.
2. Plan the site by specifying the goal, target audience, treatment ("look and feel"), and elements you want to include (text, graphics, sound, and so on).
3. Sketch out a storyboard that shows the layout of the objects on the various screens and how they are linked together. Be creative in your design.
4. Design the homepage to include personal data, contact information, previous employment, education, and samples of your work.
5. Open a new movie and save it as **portfolioB.fla**.
6. Set the movie properties, including the size and background color, if desired.
7. Display the gridlines and rulers and use them to help align objects on the stage.

8. Create a heading with its own background, then create other text objects and drawings to be used as links to the categories of information provided on the Web site. (*Hint*: In this file, the Tahoma font is used. You can replace this font with Impact or any other appropriate font on your computer.)
9. Save your work, then compare your image to Figure B-59.

FIGURE B-59
Completed Project Builder 2

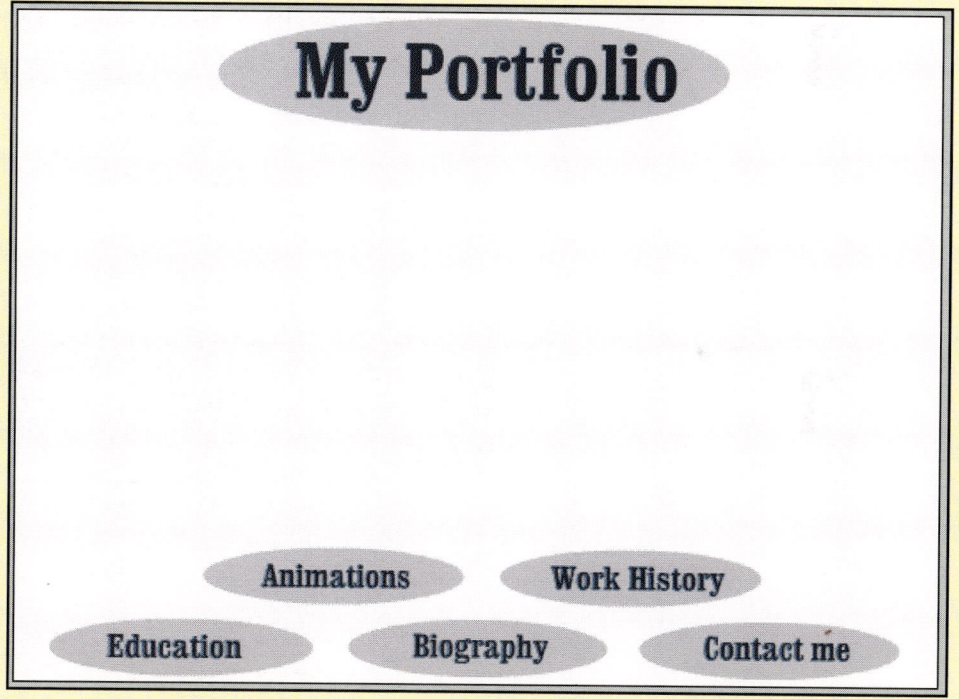

Drawing in Macromedia Flash

DESIGN PROJECT

Figure B-60 shows the homepage of the Billabong Web site. Study the figure and complete the following. For each question indicate how you determined your answer.

1. Connect to the Internet, and go to *www.course.com*. Navigate to the page for this book, click the Student Online Companion, then click the link for this unit.
2. Open a document in a word processor or open a new Macromedia Flash movie, save the file as **dpuUnitB**, then answer the following questions. (*Hint*: Use the Text Tool in Macromedia Flash.)
   - Whose Web site is this?
   - What is the goal(s) of the site?
   - Who is the target audience?
   - What is the treatment ("look and feel") that is used?
   - What are the design layout guidelines being used (balance, movement, and so on)?
   - What may be animated on this homepage?
   - Do you think this is an effective design for the company, its products, and its target audience? Why or why not?
   - What suggestions would you make to improve on the design and why?

FIGURE B-60
Design Project

Your group can assign elements of the project to individual members, or work collectively to create the finished product.

Your group has been asked to create several sample designs for the homepage of a new student organization called the Jazz Club. The club is being organized to bring together music enthusiasts for social events and charitable fund-raising activities. They plan to sponsor weekly jam sessions and a show once a month. Because the club is just getting started, the organizers are looking to you for help in developing a Web site.

1. Plan the site by specifying the goal, target audience, treatment ("look and feel"), and elements you want to include (text, graphics, sound, and so on).
2. Sketch out a storyboard that shows the layout of the objects on the various screens and how they are linked together. Be creative in your design.
3. Open a new movie and save it as **jazzclub.fla**.
4. Set the movie properties, including the size and background color, if desired.
5. Display the gridlines and rulers and use them to help align objects on the stage.

6. Create a heading with a background, text objects, and drawings to be used as links to the categories of information provided on the Web site.

7. Save your work, then compare your image to Figure B-61.

FIGURE B-61
Completed Group Project

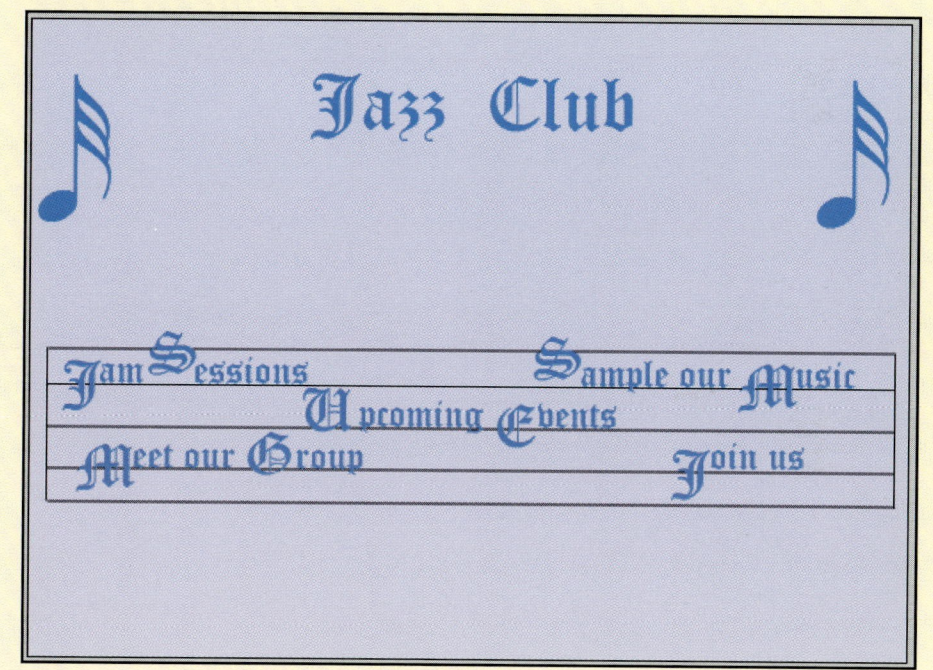

UNIT C

WORKING WITH SYMBOLS AND INTERACTIVITY

1. Work with symbols and instances.

2. Work with Libraries.

3. Create buttons.

4. Assign actions to buttons.

UNIT C

WORKING WITH SYMBOLS AND INTERACTIVITY

Introduction

An important feature of Macromedia Flash is its ability to create movies with small file sizes. This allows the movies to be delivered from the Web more quickly. One way to keep the file sizes small is to create reusable graphics, buttons, and movie clips. Macromedia Flash allows you to create a graphic (drawing) and then make unlimited copies, which you can use in other movies. Macromedia Flash calls the original drawing a **symbol** and the copied drawings **instances**. Using instances reduces the movie file size because Macromedia Flash needs to store only the symbol's information (size, shape, color). When you want to use a symbol in a movie, Macromedia Flash creates an instance (copy), but does not save the instance in the Macromedia Flash movie; this keeps down the movie's file size. What is especially valuable about this process is that you can change the attributes (such

as color and shape) for each instance. For example, if your Web site contains drawings of cars, you have to create just one drawing, insert as many instances of the car as you like, and then change the instances accordingly. Macromedia Flash stores symbols in the Library panel—each time you need a copy of the symbol, you can open the Library panel and drag the symbol to the stage, creating an instance of the symbol.

There are three categories of symbols (called behaviors): graphic, button, and movie clip. A graphic symbol is useful because you can reuse a single image and make changes in each instance of the image. A button symbol is useful because you can create buttons for interactivity, such as starting or stopping a movie. A movie clip symbol is useful because you can create a movie within a movie. Movie clips will be covered in a later unit.

Tools You'll Use

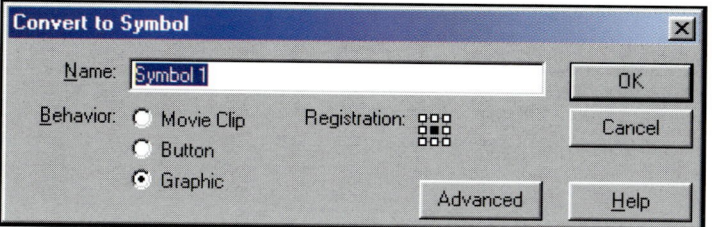

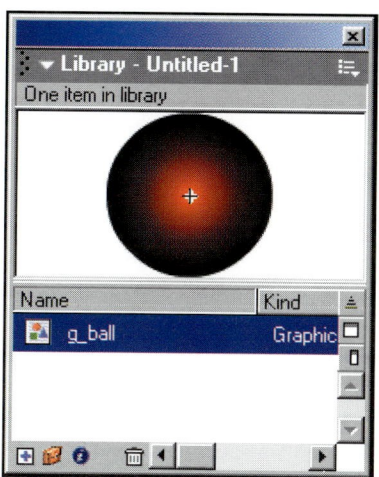

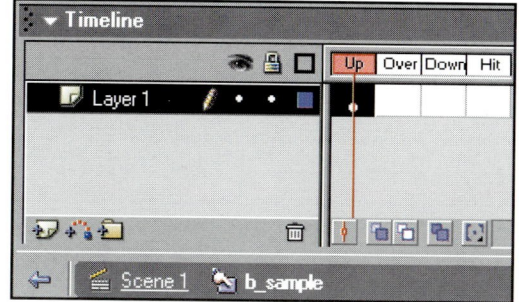

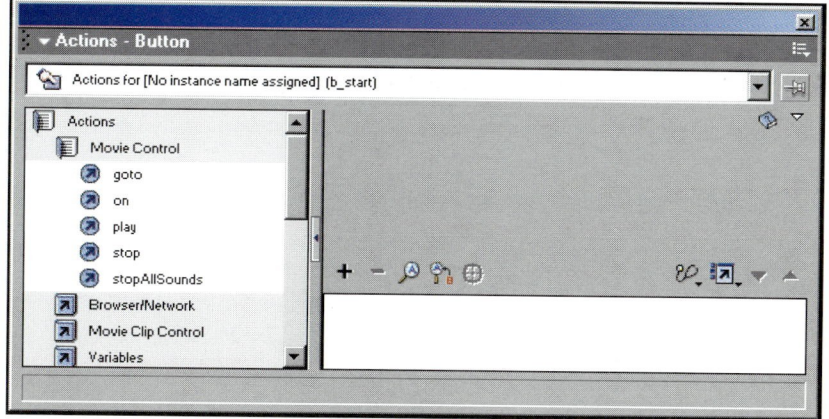

WORK WITH SYMBOLS AND INSTANCES

What You'll Do

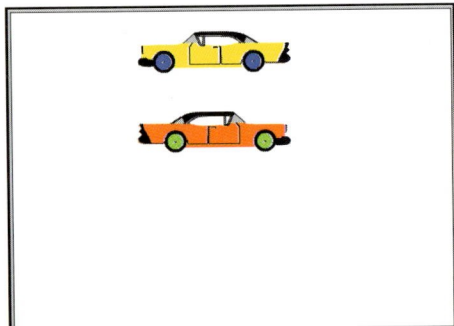

 In this lesson, you will create graphic symbols, turn them into instances, and then edit the instances.

Creating a Graphic Symbol

You can use the New Symbol command on the Insert menu to create and then draw a symbol. You can also draw an object and then use the Convert to Symbol command on the Insert menu to convert the object to a symbol. The Convert to Symbol dialog box, shown in Figure C-1, allows you to name the symbol and specify the type of symbol you want to create (Movie Clip, Button, or Graphic). When naming a symbol, it's a good idea to use a naming convention that allows you to quickly identify the type of symbol and to group like symbols together. For example, you could identify all graphic symbols by naming them g_*name*.

After you complete the Symbol Properties box, Macromedia Flash places the symbol in the Library panel, shown in Figure C-2. To create an instance of the symbol, you simply drag a symbol from the Library panel to the stage. To edit a symbol, you select it from the Library panel or use the Edit Symbol command on the Edit menu. When you edit a symbol, the changes are reflected in all instances of that symbol in your movie. For example, you can draw a car, convert this object to a symbol, and then create several instances of the car. You can uniformly change the size of all of the cars by selecting the car symbol from the Library panel and then rescaling it to the desired size.

Working with Instances

You can have as many instances as needed in your movie, and you can edit each one to make it somewhat different than the others. You can rotate, skew (slant), and resize graphic and button instances. In addition, you can change the color, brightness, and transparency. However, there are some limitations to the editing that you can perform. An instance is a single object with no segments or parts, such as a stroke and a fill—you cannot select a part of an instance. Therefore, any changes to the color of the instance are made to the entire object. Of course, you can use layers to stack other objects on top of an instance to change its appearance. In addition, you can use the Break Apart command on the Modify menu to break the link between an instance and a symbol. Once the link is broken, you can make any changes to the object, such as changing its stroke and fill color. However, because the link is broken, the object is no longer an instance, and any changes you make to the original symbol would not affect the object.

The process for creating an instance is to open the Library panel and drag the desired symbol to the stage. You select an instance by using the Arrow Tool to draw a box around it. A blue border indicates that the object has been selected. Then, you can use the Free Transform Tool options (such as Rotate and Skew, or Scale) to modify the entire image, or you can break apart the instance and edit individual lines and fills.

FIGURE C-1
Using the Convert to Symbol dialog box to convert a symbol

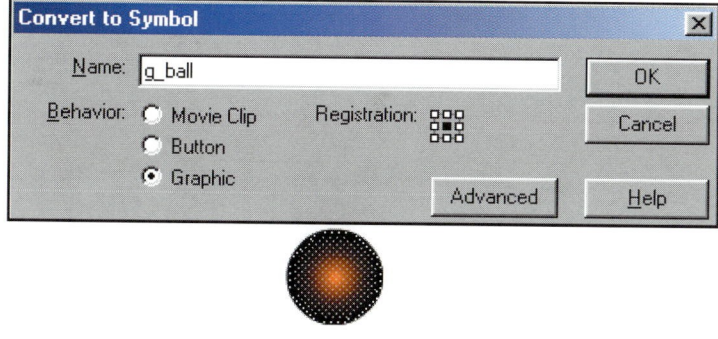

FIGURE C-2
A graphic symbol in the Library panel

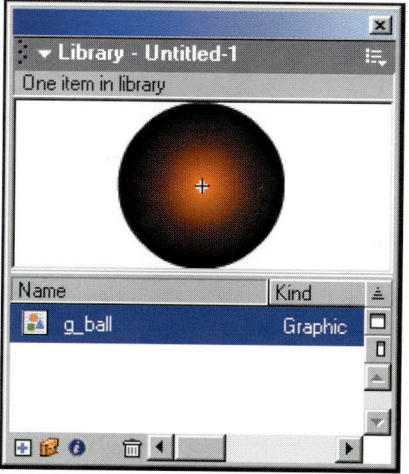

Create a symbol

1. Open flc_1, then save it as **coolcar.fla**.

2. Click the Arrow Tool on the toolbox, then drag the marquee around the car to select it. ▶

3. Click Insert on the menu bar, then click Convert to Symbol.

4. Type **g_car** in the Name text box.

5. Click the Graphic Behavior option, as shown in Figure C-3, then click OK.

6. Click Window on the menu bar, then click Library.

7. Click the g_car symbol in the Library panel to display the car, as shown in Figure C-4.

8. Point to the Library panel title bar, then drag the panel to the right side of the screen so it does not obscure your view of the stage.

9. Save your work.

You opened a file with an object, converted the object to a symbol, and displayed the symbol in the Library panel.

FIGURE C-3
Options in the Convert to Symbol dialog box

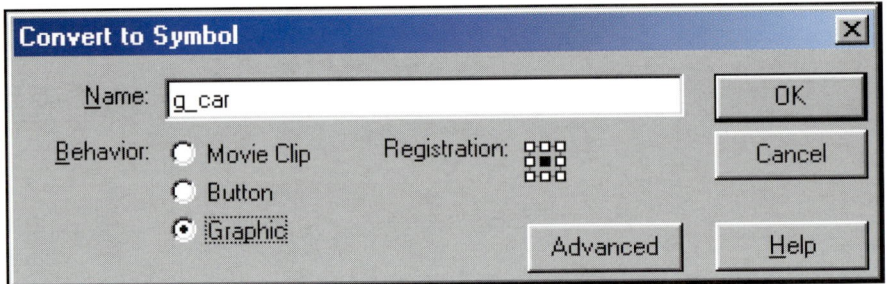

FIGURE C-4
Newly created symbol in the Library panel

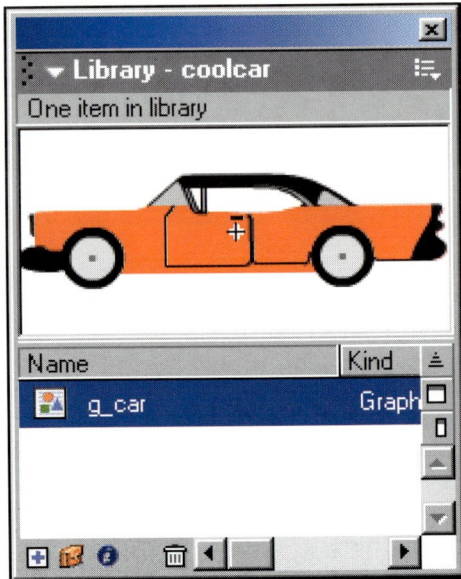

FIGURE C-5
Creating an instance

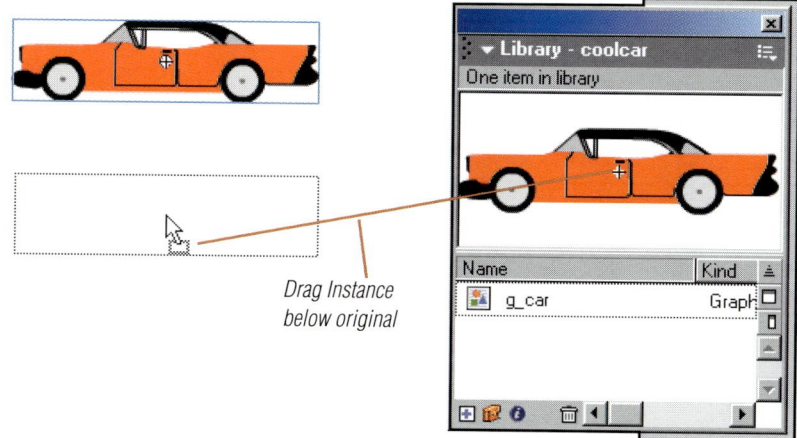

Drag Instance
below original

FIGURE C-6
The Advanced Effect dialog box

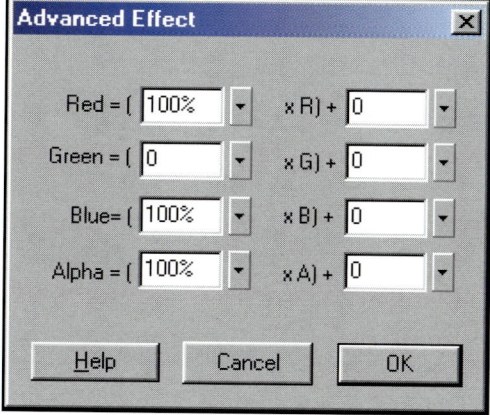

Create and edit an instance

1. Point to the car image in the Item Preview window, then drag the image to the stage beneath the first car, as shown in Figure C-5.

   You can also drag the name of the symbol from the Library panel to the stage.

2. Click the Arrow Tool on the toolbox, verify that the bottom car is selected, click Modify on the menu bar, point to Transform, then click Flip Horizontal.

3. Click Window on the menu bar; then, if necessary, display the Properties panel.

4. Click the Color list arrow, then click Advanced.

5. Click the Settings button, double-click the Green=(text box, type **0**, then compare your dialog box to Figure C-6. `Settings...`

6. Click OK, then click a blank area of the stage.

   The windshield and tires become purple.

7. Save your work.

You created an instance of a symbol and edited its instance on the stage.

Edit a symbol in symbol-editing mode

1. Double-click the g_car symbol icon in the Library panel to enter symbol-editing mode, then compare your screen to Figure C-7.

   The g_car symbol appears on the stage below the timeline, indicating that you are editing the g_car symbol.

   > **TIP** You can also edit a symbol by clicking Edit on the menu bar, then clicking Edit Symbols.

2. Click a blank area of the stage to deselect the car.

3. Click the Arrow Tool on the toolbox, then click the light gray hubcap inside the front wheel to select it.

4. Press and hold [Shift], then click the hubcap inside the back wheel to select the fills of both wheels.

5. Click the Fill Color Tool on the toolbox, click the blue color swatch in the left column of the color palette, then compare your image to Figure C-8.

   Changes you make to the symbol affect every instance of the symbol on the stage. The hubcap color becomes blue in the Library panel and on the stage.

6. Click Edit on the menu bar, then click Edit Document to return to movie-editing mode.

   The hubcap color of the instances on the stage reflects the color changes you made to the symbol.

7. Save your work.

You edited a symbol in symbol-editing mode.

FIGURE C-7

Symbol-editing mode

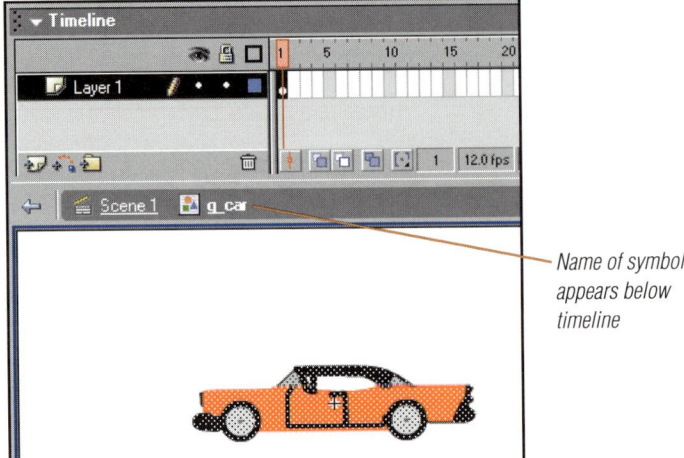

Name of symbol appears below timeline

FIGURE C-8

Edited symbol

Working with Symbols and Interactivity

FIGURE C-9
The car with the red body selected

FIGURE C-10
Changing the symbol affects only the one instance of the symbol

Instance of the symbol ————

Object that is no longer an ————
instance of the symbol

Break apart an instance

1. Click the Arrow Tool on the toolbox, then drag the marquee around the bottom car to select it.

2. Click Modify on the menu bar, then click Break Apart.

   The object is no longer linked to the symbol, and its parts (strokes and fills) can now be edited.

3. Click a blank area of the stage to deselect the object.

4. Click the Arrow Tool on the toolbox, click the front hubcap, press and hold [Shift], then click the back hubcap to select both wheels.

5. Click the Fill Color Tool, then click the green color swatch in the left column of the color palette.

6. Double-click the g_car symbol icon in the Library window to enter symbol-editing mode.

7. Click the red body of the car, as shown in Figure C-9.

8. Click the Fill Color Tool, then click the yellow color swatch in the left column of the color palette.

9. Click Edit on the menu bar, click Edit Document, then compare your image to Figure C-10.

   The original instance is a different color, but the one to which you applied the Break Apart command remains unchanged.

10. Save and close the movie.

You used the Break Apart command to break the link of the instance to its symbol, then you edited the object and the symbol.

WORK WITH LIBRARIES

What You'll Do

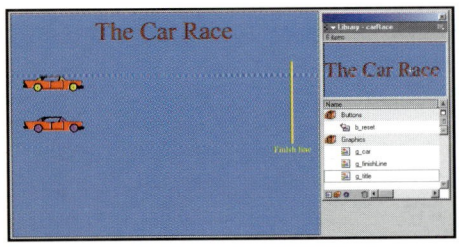

In this lesson, you will use the Library panel to organize the symbols in a movie.

Understanding the Library

The Library in a Macromedia Flash movie contains the movie symbols. The Library provides a way to view and organize the symbols, and allows you to change the symbol name, display symbol properties, and add and delete symbols. Figure C-11 shows the Library panel for a movie. Refer to this figure as you read the following description of the parts of the Library.

Title bar—Names the movie with which the Library is associated. This is important because if you have multiple movies open, you could be working on one movie, but have displayed the Library panel for a different movie. In addition to the movie

libraries, you can create permanent libraries that are available whenever you start Macromedia Flash. Macromedia Flash also has sample libraries that contain buttons, graphics, and movie clips. The permanent and sample libraries are accessed through the Common Libraries command in the Windows menu. All of the assets in all of the libraries are available for use in any movie.

Options menu—Shown in Figure C-12; provides access to several features used to edit symbols (such as renaming symbols) and organize symbols (such as creating a new folder).

Item preview—Displays the selected symbol. If the symbol is a movie clip, a control button appears allowing you to preview the animation.

Toggle Sorting Order icon—Allows you to reorder the list of folders and symbols within folders.

Wide Library View and Narrow Library View icons—Used to expand and collapse the Library window to display more or less of the symbol properties.

Name text box—Lists the folder and symbol names. Each symbol type has a different icon associated with it. Clicking a symbol name or icon displays the symbol in the Item Preview window.

New Symbol icon—Displays the Create New Symbol dialog box, allowing you to create a new symbol.

New Folder icon—Allows you to create a new folder.

Properties icon—Displays the Symbol Properties dialog box for the selected symbol.

Delete Item icon—Deletes the selected symbol or folder.

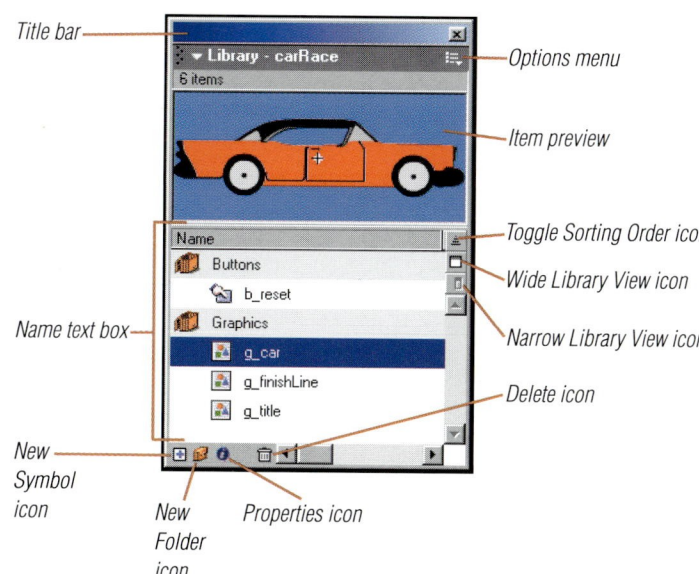

FIGURE C-11
The Library panel

Title bar
Options menu
Item preview
Toggle Sorting Order icon
Wide Library View icon
Narrow Library View icon
Name text box
Delete icon
New Symbol icon
New Folder icon
Properties icon

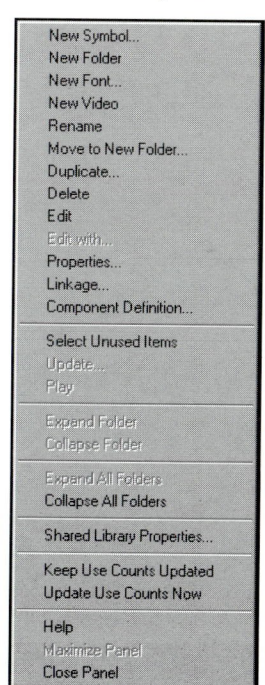

FIGURE C-12
The Options menu

Create folders in the Library panel

1. Open flc_2.fla, then save it as **carRace.fla**.

2. Click Window on the menu bar, then click Library.

3. Point to the bottom of the Library panel, then when the pointer changes to a double-headed arrow (Win), drag the bottom-right corner of the window to enlarge it to the size shown in Figure C-13.

4. Click the New Folder icon.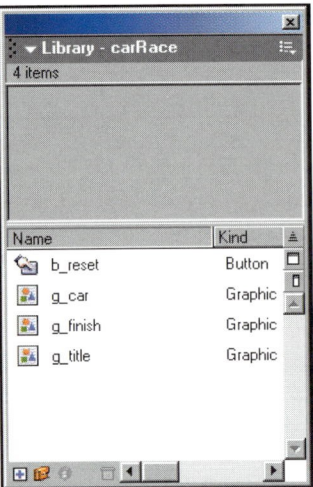

5. Type **Graphics** in the Name text box, then press [Enter] (Win) or [return] (Mac).

6. Drag the g_finish symbol to the Graphics folder, as shown in Figure C-14.

   TIP You can double-click the Folder icon to view the contents.

(continued)

FIGURE C-13

Enlarging the Library panel

FIGURE C-14

Moving a symbol to a folder

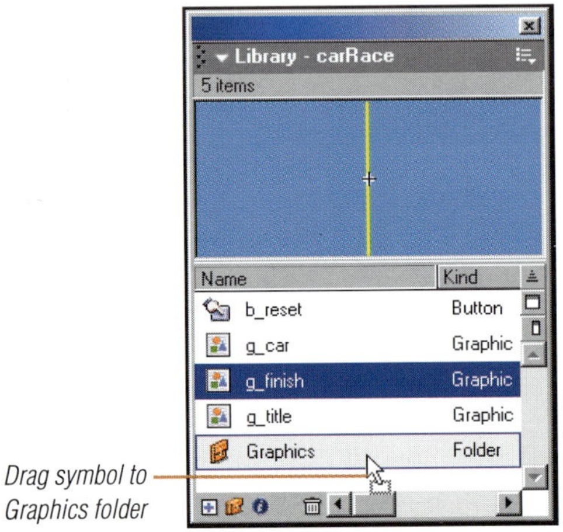

Drag symbol to — Graphics folder

Working with Symbols and Interactivity

7. Drag the g_title and g_car symbols to the Graphics folder.

8. Click the b_reset symbol, then click the New Folder icon.

9. Type **Buttons** in the Name text box, then press [Enter] (Win) or [return] (Mac).

10. Drag the b_reset symbol to the Buttons folder, then compare your panel to Figure C-15.

11. Save your work.

You opened a Macromedia Flash movie, displayed the Library panel, created folders, and organized the symbols within the folders.

FIGURE C-15

Folders added to the Library panel

Display the properties of a symbol and rename a symbol

1. Double-click the Graphics folder icon to display the symbols.

2. Click the g_finish symbol, then click the Properties icon to display the Symbol Properties dialog box. *(icon)*

3. Type **g_finishLine** in the Name text box, as shown in Figure C-16, then click OK.

4. Save your work.

You used the Library panel to display the properties of a symbol and rename a symbol.

FIGURE C-16

Renaming a symbol

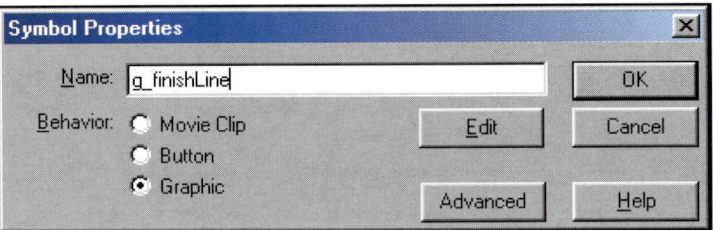

Working with Symbols and Interactivity

FIGURE C-17

The Library panel with the folders expanded

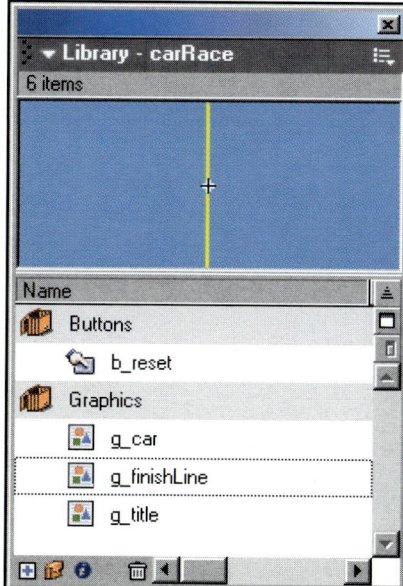

1. Click the Wide Library View icon to expand the window. ▯

2. If necessary, click the Arrow Tool on the toolbox, point to the Library panel title bar, then drag the panel to the center of the screen. ▸

3. Click the Narrow Library View icon to collapse the panel. ▯

4. Click the Graphics folder to highlight it.

5. Click the Toggle Sorting Order icon to move the Graphics folder above the Button folder. ▲

6. Click the Toggle Sorting Order icon again to move the Graphics folder below the Button folder.

7. Click the Options menu icon near the top right of the panel, then click Collapse All Folders. ☰

8. Click the Options menu icon, click Expand All Folders, then compare your Library window to Figure C-17.

9. Click the Arrow Tool on the toolbox, point to the Library panel title bar, then drag the panel to the right side of the screen. ▸

10. Save your work.

You expanded and collapsed the Library panel, and sorted folders.

CREATE BUTTONS

What You'll Do

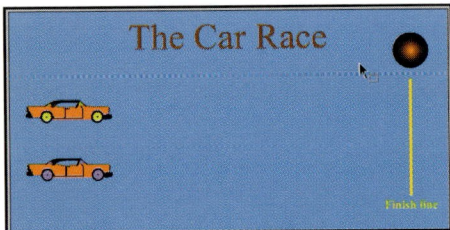

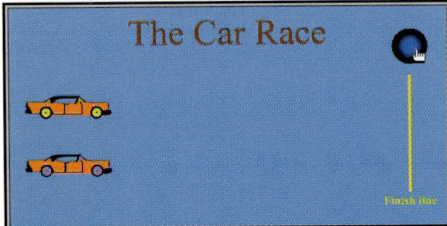

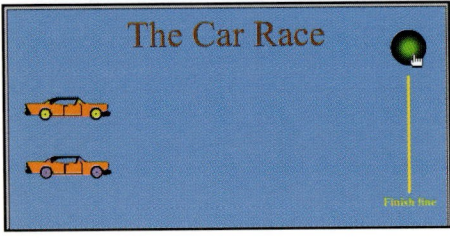

In this lesson, you will create buttons, edit the four button states, and test a button.

Understanding Buttons

Button symbols are used to provide interactivity. When you click a button, an action occurs, such as starting an animation or jumping to another frame on the timeline. Any object, including Macromedia Flash drawings, text blocks, and imported graphic images, can be made into buttons. Unlike graphic symbols, buttons have four states: Up, Over, Down, and Hit. These states correspond to the use of the mouse and recognize that the user requires feedback when the mouse is pointing to a button and when the button has been clicked. This is often shown by a change in the button (such as a different color or different shape). These four states are explained below and shown in Figure C-18.

Up—Represents how the button appears when the mouse pointer is not over it.

Over—Represents how the button appears when the mouse pointer is over it.

Down—Represents how the button appears after the user clicks the mouse.

Hit—Defines the area of the screen that will respond to the click. In most cases, you will want the Hit state to be the same or similar to the Up state in location and size.

When you create a button symbol, Macromedia Flash automatically creates a new timeline. The timeline has only four frames, one for each state. The timeline does not play; it merely reacts to the mouse pointer by displaying the appropriate button state and performing an action, such as jumping to a specific frame on the main timeline.

The process for creating and previewing buttons is as follows:

Create a button symbol—Draw an object or select an object that has already been created and placed on the stage. Use the Convert to Symbol command on the Insert menu to convert the object to a button symbol and to enter a name for the button.

Edit the button symbol—Select the button and choose the Edit Symbols command on the Edit menu. This displays the button timeline, shown in Figure C-19, which allows you to work with the four button states. The Up state is the original button symbol that Macromedia Flash automatically places in Frame 1. You need to determine how the original object will change for the other states. To change the button for the Over state, click Frame 2 and insert a keyframe. This automatically places a copy of the button in Frame 1 into Frame 2. Then, alter the button's appearance for the Over state. Use the same process for the Down state. For the Hit state, you insert a keyframe on Frame 4 and then specify the area on the screen that responds to the pointer.

Return to the main timeline—Once you've finished editing a button, choose the Edit Document command on the Edit menu to return to the main timeline.

Preview the button—By default, Macromedia Flash disables buttons so that you can manipulate them on the stage. You can preview a button by choosing the Enable Simple Buttons command on the Control menu. You can also click the Test Movie command on the Control menu to play the movie and test the buttons.

FIGURE C-18

The four button states

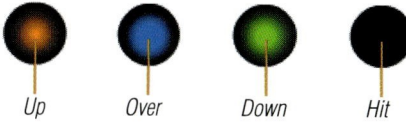

Up Over Down Hit

FIGURE C-19

The button timeline

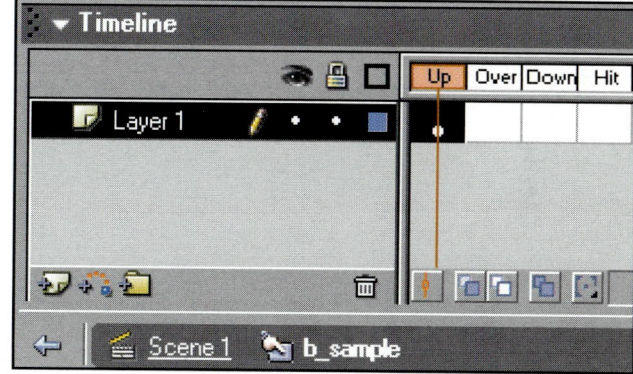

Create a button

1. Click the title layer on the timeline.

2. Click the Insert Layer icon on the timeline.

   | TIP The number of your newly created layer will vary.

3. Double-click the new layer, type **signal**, then press [Enter] (Win) or [return] (Mac).

4. Click the Oval Tool on the toolbox, click the Stroke Color Tool on the toolbox, then click the black color swatch in the left column of the color palette.

5. Click the Fill Color Tool on the toolbox, then click the red gradient color swatch in the bottom row of the color palette.

6. Draw the circle shown in Figure C-20.

7. Click the Arrow Tool on the toolbox, then drag the marquee around the circle to select it.

8. Click Insert on the menu bar, then click Convert to Symbol.

9. Type **b_signal** in the Name text box, click the Button option, then click OK.

10. Drag the b_signal symbol to the Buttons folder in the Library panel.

11. Save your work.

You created a button symbol on the stage and dragged it to the Buttons folder in the Library panel.

FIGURE C-20
The circle object

The Car Race

Finish line

FIGURE C-21

The button states on the timeline

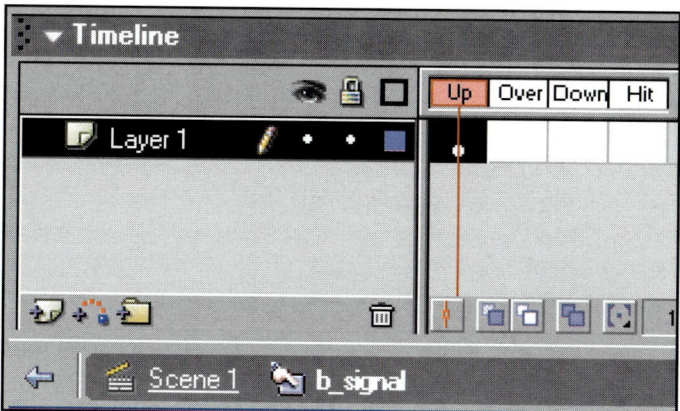

FIGURE C-22

Designating the Hit state for the button

Start dragging here

Drag to here

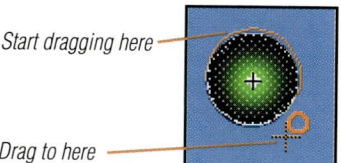

1. Click Edit on the menu bar, click Edit Symbols, then compare your timeline to Figure C-21.

   Macromedia Flash switches to symbol-editing mode, and the timeline contains four button states.

2. Insert a keyframe in the Over frame on Layer 1.

3. Click the Fill Color Tool on the toolbox, then click the blue gradient color swatch on the bottom of the color palette.

4. Insert a keyframe in the Down frame on Layer 1.

5. Click the Fill Color Tool on the toolbox, then click the green gradient color swatch on the bottom of the color palette.

6. Insert a keyframe in the Hit frame on Layer 1.

7. Click the Oval Tool on the toolbox, then draw a circle that covers the button, as shown in Figure C-22.

   TIP   The Hit area is not visible on the stage.

8. Click Edit on the menu bar, then click Edit Document.

9. Save your work.

You edited a button by changing the color of its Over and Down states, and you specified the Hit area.

Test a button

1. Click the Arrow Tool on the toolbox, then click a blank area of the stage.

2. Click Control on the menu bar, then click Enable Simple Buttons.

3. Point to the signal button on the stage; notice that the button changes to a blue gradient, the color you selected for the Over state, then compare your image to Figure C-23.

4. Press and hold the mouse, then notice that the button changes to a green gradient, the color you selected for the Down state, as shown in Figure C-24.

(continued)

FIGURE C-23
The button's Over state

FIGURE C-24
The button's Down state

FIGURE C-25

The button's Up state

5. Release the mouse and notice that the button changes to the Over state color.

6. Move the mouse away from the signal button, and notice that the button returns to a red gradient, the Up state color, as shown in Figure C-25.

7. Click Window on the menu bar, then click Library to close the Library panel.

You used the mouse to test a button and view the button states.

ASSIGN ACTIONS TO BUTTONS

What You'll Do

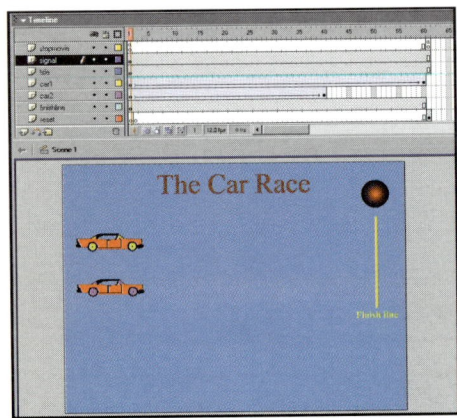

In this lesson, you will use ActionScripts to assign actions to frames and buttons.

Understanding Actions

In a basic movie, Macromedia Flash plays the frames sequentially, repeating the movie without stopping for user input. However, you may often want to provide users with the ability to interact with the movie by allowing them to perform actions such as starting and stopping the movie or jumping to a specific frame. One way to provide user interaction is to assign an action to the Down state of a button or preferably to the instance of a button. Then, whenever the user clicks on the button, the action occurs. Macromedia Flash provides a scripting language, called ActionScript, that allows you to add actions to buttons and frames within a movie. For example, you can place a stop action in a frame that pauses the movie and then assign a play action to a button that starts the movie when the user clicks the button.

Analyzing ActionScript

ActionScript is a powerful scripting language that allows those with programming expertise to create very sophisticated actions. For example, you can create order forms that capture user input, or volume controls that display when sounds are played. A basic ActionScript involves an event (such as a mouse click) that causes some action to occur by triggering the script. Following is an example of a basic ActionScript:

```
on (release) {gotoAndPlay
(10);}
```

In this example, the event is a mouse click (indicated by the word `release`) that causes the movie's playback head to go to Frame 10 and play the frame. This is a simple ActionScript and is easy to follow. Other ActionScripts can be quite complex and may require programming expertise to understand. Fortunately, Macromedia Flash provides an easy way to use ActionScripts without having to learn the scripting language. The Actions panel allows you to assign basic actions to frames and objects, such as buttons. Figure C-26 shows the Actions panel displaying an ActionScript indicating that when the user clicks on the selected object (a button), the movie plays.

The process for assigning actions to buttons, shown in Figure C-27, is as follows.

- Select the desired button on the stage.
- Display the Actions panel.
- Select the appropriate category. Macromedia Flash provides several Action categories. The Movie Control category allows you to create scripts for controlling movies and navigating within movies. You can use these actions to start and stop movies, jump to specific frames, and respond to user mouse movements and keystrokes.
- Select the desired action.

Button actions respond to one or more of the following mouse events:

Press—With the pointer inside the button Hit area, the user presses the mouse button.

Release—With the pointer inside the button Hit area, the user presses and releases (clicks) the mouse button.

Release Outside—With the pointer inside the button Hit area, the user presses and holds down the mouse button, moves the pointer outside the Hit area, and releases the mouse button.

Key Press—With the Macromedia Flash button displayed, the user presses a predetermined key on the keyboard.

Roll Over—The user moves the pointer into the button Hit area.

Roll Out—The user moves the pointer out of the button Hit area.

Drag Over—The user holds down the mouse button, moves the pointer out of the button Hit area and then back into the Hit area.

Drag Out—With the pointer inside the button Hit area, the user holds down the mouse button and moves the pointer outside the Hit area.

FIGURE C-26

The Actions panel displaying an ActionScript

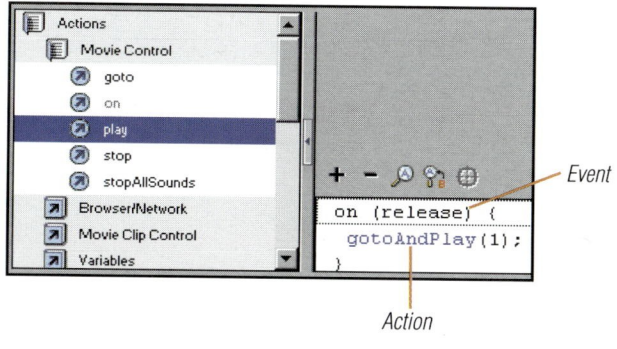

Event

Action

FIGURE C-27

The process for assigning actions to buttons

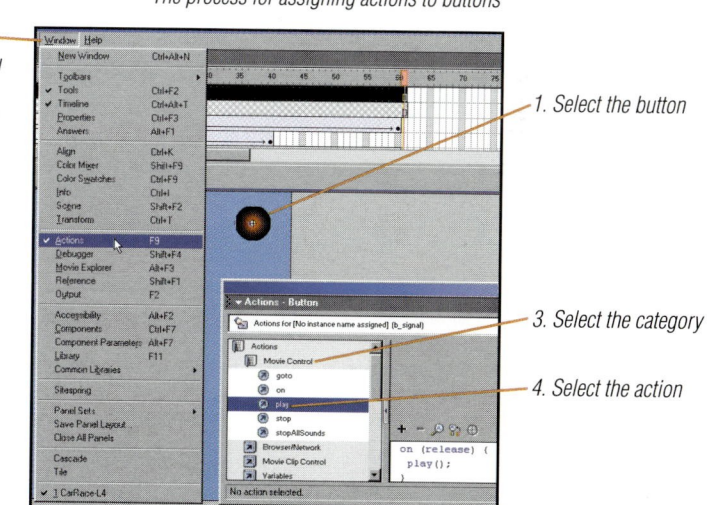

2. Use the Window menu to display the Actions panel

1. Select the button

3. Select the category

4. Select the action

Assign a stop action to frames

1. Click Control on the menu bar, then click Test Movie.

   The movie plays and continues to loop.

2. Click File on the menu bar, then click Close.

   > **TIP** You can also click the Close button on the Test Movie window to close the window, but be careful not to click the Close button for the Macromedia Flash window.

3. Click the Insert Layer icon on the timeline to insert a new layer.

4. Double-click the new layer's name, type **stopmovie**, then press [Enter] (Win) or [return] (Mac).

5. Click Frame 1 on the stopmovie layer.

6. Click Window on the menu bar, then click Actions to display the Actions panel, as shown in Figure C-28.

   > **TIP** Close or minimize the Properties panel if it is open and obscures your view of the stage.

(continued)

FIGURE C-28

The Actions panel

FIGURE C-29

Assigning an action to Frame 1 on the stopmovie layer

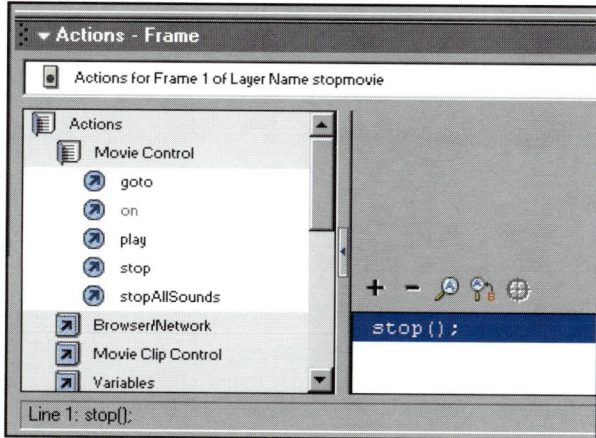

7. Click Actions (if necessary), click Movie Control, double-click stop, then compare your Actions panel to Figure C-29.

8. Insert a keyframe in Frame 61 on the stopmovie layer.

9. Double-click stop in the Actions panel.

10. Click Frame 1 on the timeline, click Control on the menu bar, then click Test Movie.

    The movie does not play because there is a stop action assigned to Frame 1.

11. Click File on the menu bar, then click Close to close the test movie window.

12. Save your work.

You inserted a layer and assigned a stop action to the first and last frames on the layer.

Assign a start action to a button

1. Click the Arrow Tool on the toolbox, then drag the pointer around the signal button on the stage to select it.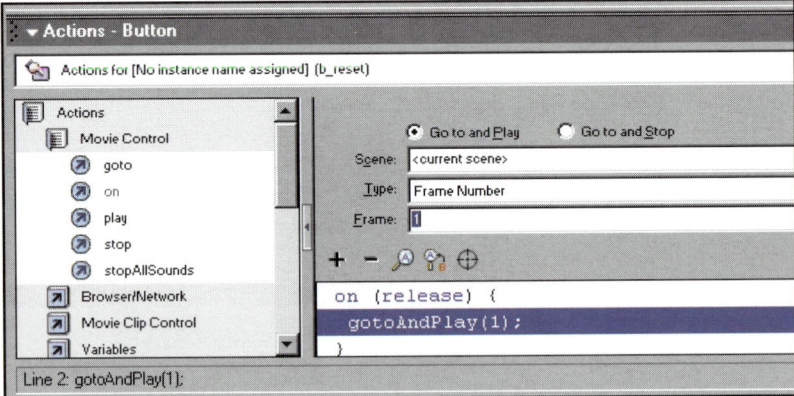

2. Double-click play in the Actions panel.

3. Click Control on the menu bar, then click Test Movie.

4. Click the signal button.

   The movie plays and stops. The reset button appears but it does not have an action assigned to it.

5. Close the test movie window and save your work.

You assigned a start action to a button.

Assign a goto frame action to a button

1. Click Frame 61 on the timeline to display the Reset button.

2. Click the Arrow Tool on the toolbox, then drag the marquee around Reset to select it.

3. Double-click goto in the Actions panel to display the goto settings shown in Figure C-30.

   TIP The default settings for the goto action are release (click the mouse button and release it) for the event, and Frame 1 for the frame to which the movie jumps. You can specify another frame, change the event, or add multiple events.

   (continued)

FIGURE C-30

The default settings for the goto *action*

Working with Symbols and Interactivity

FIGURE C-31

FIGURE C-31

Displaying the list of events

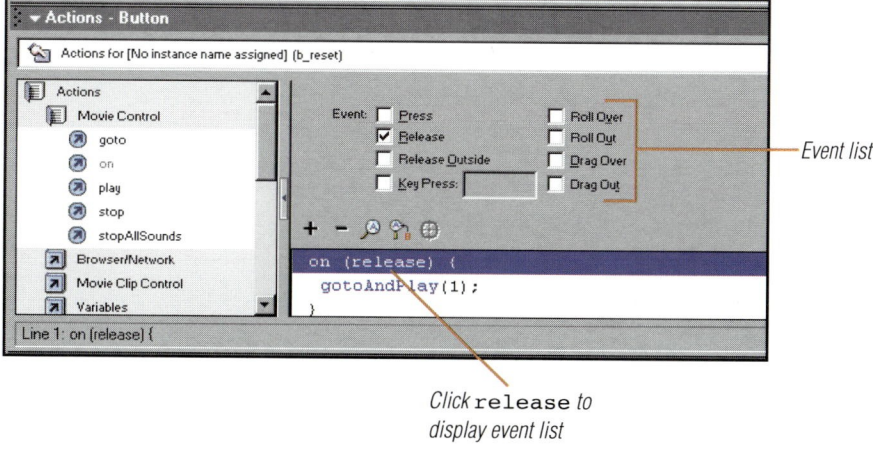

Click release *to display event list*

— Event list

4. Click release in the ActionScript to display the list of events, as shown in Figure C-31.

| TIP Expand the Actions panel, if necessary.

5. Click the Key Press check box, then type **r** in the text box.

| TIP The letter you specify for the key press is case-sensitive.

6. Click Control on the menu bar, then click Test Movie.

7. Click the signal button to start the movie, then when the movie stops, click Reset or press **r**.

8. Close the test window, then save and close the movie.

You assigned a start action to a button and a goto *frame action to another button. You also added an event that triggers the action.*

Create a symbol.

1. Open flc_3.fla and save it as **skillsdemoC.fla**.
2. Add a new layer above the ballspin layer and name it **title-bkgnd**.
3. Draw a black rectangle behind the title text Color Spin, using the Rounded Rectangle Radius Tool option, and set the corner radius points to 10.
4. Select the rectangle, convert it to a graphic symbol, then name it **g_bkgnd**.
5. Save your work.

Create and edit an instance.

1. Add a new layer above the titlebkgnd layer and name it **vballs-sm.**
2. Display the Library panel.
3. Drag the g_vball-sm symbol to the upper-left corner of the stage.
4. Drag the g_vball-sm symbol three more times to each of the other corners.
5. Double-click the g_vball-sm symbol icon in the Library panel to switch to symbol-editing mode.
6. Change the color of the ball to red.
7. Return to the document and notice how all instances have been changed to red.
8. Select the ball in the upper-right corner of the stage and break apart the object.

9. Change the color to blue.
10. Select, break apart, and change the bottom-left ball to green and the bottom-right ball to yellow.
11. Save your work.

Create a folder in the Library panel.

1. Use the Options menu in the Library panel to create a new folder.
2. Name the folder **Graphics**.
3. Move the three graphic symbols to the Graphics folder.
4. Expand the Graphic folder.
5. Save your work.

Work with the Library window.

1. Rename the g_bkgnd symbol to g_title-bkgnd in the Library panel.
2. Expand and narrow your view of the Library panel.
3. Collapse and expand the folder.
4. Save your work.

Create a button.

1. Add a new layer above the vballs-sm layer and name it **start**.
2. Drag the g_title-bkgnd symbol from the Library panel to the bottom center of the stage.

3. Create a white 30-pt Arial text block on top of the title-bkgnd object, then type **Start**. (*Hint*: Center the text block in the background object.)
4. Select the rectangle and the text. (*Hint*: Select the Arrow Tool, then press and hold [Shift].)
5. Convert the selected objects to a button symbol and name it **b_start**.
6. Create a new folder named **Buttons** in the Library panel and move the button symbol to the folder.
7. Display the button timeline.
8. Insert a keyframe in the Over frame.
9. Select the text and change the color to gray.
10. Insert a keyframe in the Down frame.
11. Select the text and change the color to blue.
12. Insert a keyframe in the Hit frame.
13. Draw a rectangular object that covers the area for the Hit state.
14. Return to movie-editing mode.
15. Save your work.

Test a button.

1. Turn on Enable Simple Buttons.
2. Point to the button and notice the color change.
3. Click the button and notice the other color change.

Stop a movie.

1. Insert a new layer and name it **stopmovie**.
2. Insert a keyframe in Frame 40 on the new layer.
3. With Frame 40 selected, display the Actions panel.
4. Assign a stop action to the frame.
5. Click Frame 1 on the new layer.
6. Assign a stop action to Frame 1.
7. Save your work.

Assign an action to a button.

1. Click Control on the menu bar, then click Enable Simple buttons to turn off this feature.
2. Use the Arrow Tool to select the button on the stage.
3. Use the Actions panel to assign a play action to the button.
4. Test the movie.
5. Save your work, then compare your image to Figure C-32.

FIGURE C-32
Completed Skills Review

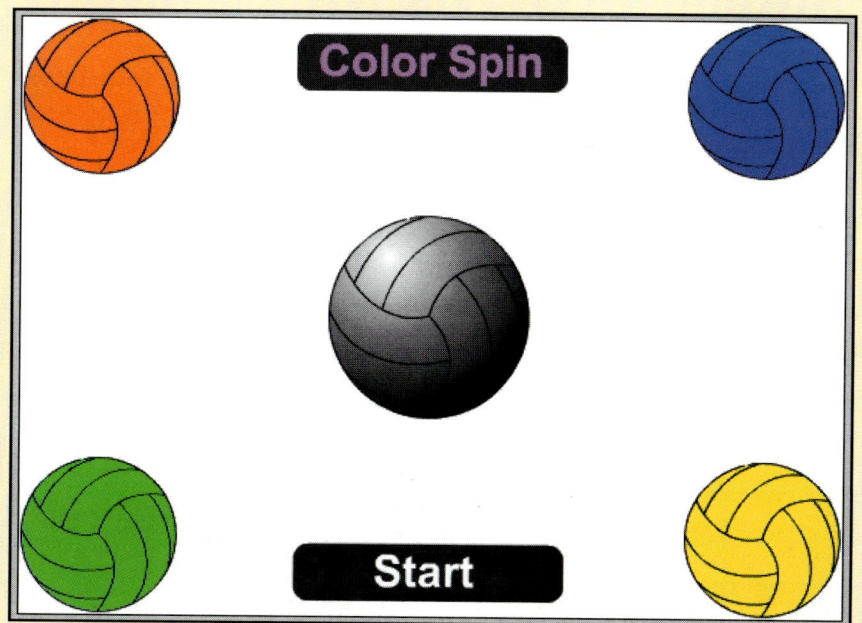

The Ultimate Tours travel company has asked you to design a sample navigation scheme for its Web site. The company wants to see how its homepage will link with one of its main categories (Treks). Figure C-33 shows a sample homepage and Treks screen. Using these or the homepage you created in Unit B as a guide, you will add a Treks screen and link it to the homepage. (*Hint*: Assume that all of the drawings on the homepage are on Frame 1, unless noted.)

1. Open ultimatetoursB.fla (the file you created in Unit B Project Builder 1) and save it as **utlimatetoursC.fla**. (*Hint*: If you did not create ultimatetoursB.fla in Unit B, see your instructor.)
2. Select the layer that the Ultimate Tours is on, and insert a keyframe on a frame at least five frames further along the timeline.
3. Add a new layer, add a keyframe on the last frame of the movie, then create the Treks screen, except for the home graphic, using layers for each of the elements on the screen.
4. Convert the Treks graphic on the homepage to a button symbol, and edit the symbol so that different colors appear for the different states.
5. Assign a `goto` action that jumps the playhead to the Treks screen when the button is clicked.

6. Add a new layer and name it **stopmovie**. Add stop actions that cause the movie to stop after displaying the homepage and after displaying the Treks page.
7. Insert a new layer and name it **homeButton**, insert a keyframe on the appropriate frame, and draw the home button image with the Home text.

FIGURE C-33
Completed Project Builder 1

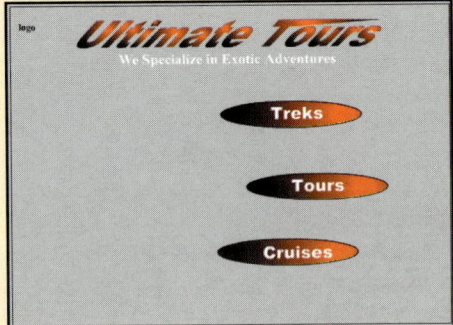

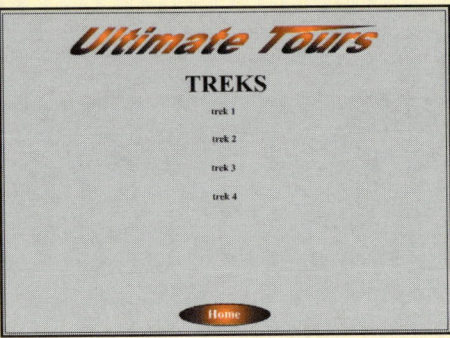

8. Convert the image to a button symbol, and edit the symbol so that different colors appear for the different states. Assign a `goto` action for the button that jumps the movie to Frame 1.
9. Test the movie.
10. Save your work, then compare your Web page to Figure C-33.

This is a continuation of Project Builder 2 in Unit B, which is the development of a personal portfolio. If you did not create portfolioB.fla in Unit B, see your instructor. The homepage has several categories, including the following:

- Personal data
- Contact information
- Previous employment
- Education
- Samples of your work

In this project, you will create a button that will be used to link the homepage of your portfolio to the animations page. Next, you will create another button to start the animation.

1. Open portfolioB.fla (the file you created in Project Builder 2, Unit B) and save it as **portfolioC.fla**. (*Hint*: In this file, the Tahoma font is used. You can replace this font with Impact or any other appropriate font on your computer.)
2. Add a new layer, insert a keyframe on Frame 3 (or one frame past the last frame of the movie), and create an animation using objects that you create.
3. Add a new layer, insert a keyframe on Frame 2 (or one frame before the animation frame), and create a Sample Animation screen.

4. Convert the title into a button symbol and edit the symbol so that different colors appear for the different states. Assign an action that jumps to the frame that plays an animation.
5. Change the Animations graphic on the homepage to a button, and edit the symbol so that different colors appear for the different states. Assign an action that jumps to the Sample Animation screen.

FIGURE C-34
Completed Project Builder 2

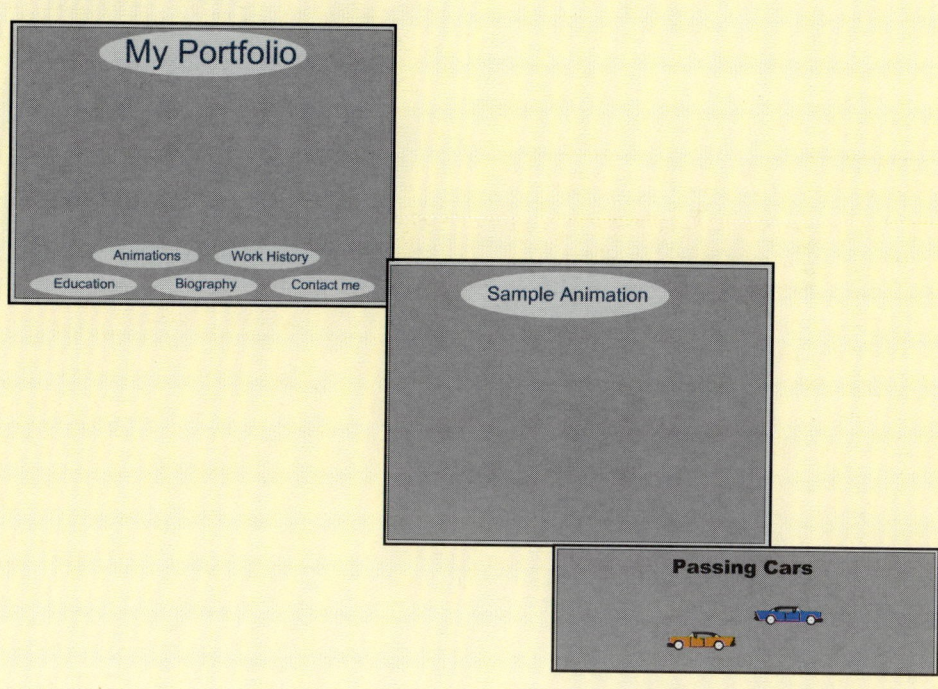

6. Add a new layer and name it **stopmovie**. Insert keyframes and assign stop actions to the appropriate frames.
7. Test the movie.
8. Save your work, then compare your movie to Figure C-34.

Figure C-35 shows the homepage of a Web site. Study the figure and complete the following questions. For each question, indicate how you determined your answer.

1. Connect to the Internet, and go to *www.course.com*. Navigate to the page for this book, click the Student Online Companion, then click the link for this unit.

2. Open a document in a word processor or open a new Macromedia Flash movie, save the file as **dpuUnitC**, then answer the following questions. (*Hint*: Use the Text Tool in Macromedia Flash.)

   ■ Whose Web site is this?
   ■ What is the goal(s) of the site?
   ■ Who is the target audience?
   ■ What is the treatment ("look and feel") that is used?
   ■ What are the design layout guidelines being used (balance, movement, and so on)?
   ■ What animations would you suggest to enhance this site?
   ■ Do you think this is an effective design for the company, its products, and its target audience? Why or why not?
   ■ What suggestions would you make to improve on the design, and why?

FIGURE C-35
Design Project

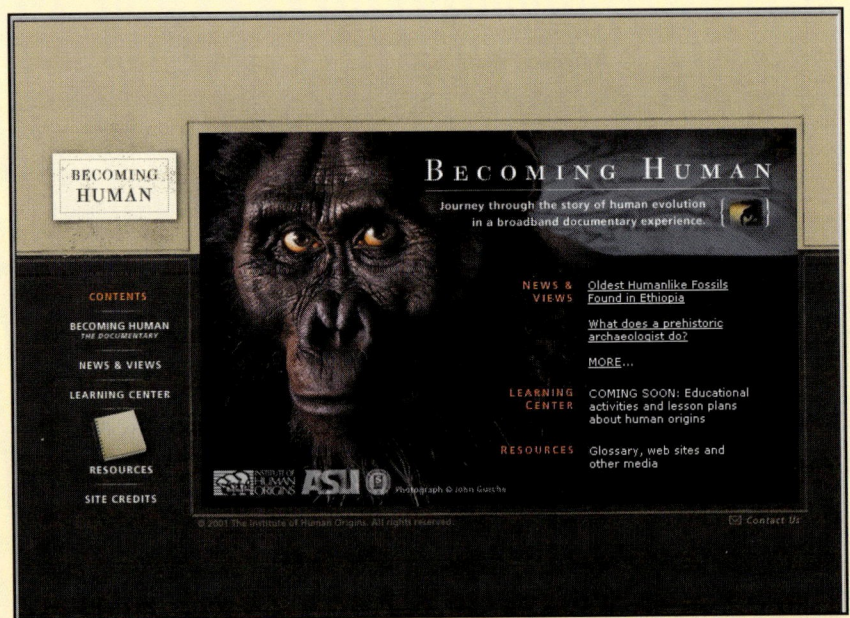

Working with Symbols and Interactivity

Your group can assign elements of the project to individual members, or you can work collectively to create the finished product.

Your group has been asked to assist your school's International Student Association (ISA). The association sponsors a series of monthly events, each focusing on a different culture from around the world. The events are led by a guest speaker who makes a presentation, followed by a discussion. The events are free and they are open to everyone. ISA would like you to design a Macromedia Flash movie that will be used with its Web site. The movie starts by providing information about the series, and then provides a link to the upcoming event.

1. Open a new movie and save it as **isa.fla**. (*Hint*: In this file, the CloisterBack BT font is used. You can replace this font with Georgia or any other appropriate font on your computer.)
2. Create an initial screen with Information about the association's series.
3. Assign an action that stops the movie.
4. Add a button on the Information screen that jumps the movie to a screen that presents information about the next event.

5. Add a button on the Information screen that jumps the movie to a screen that lists the series (all nine events for the school year- September through May).
6. On the next Event and Series screens, add a Return button that jumps the movie back to the Information screen.

FIGURE C-36
Completed Group Project

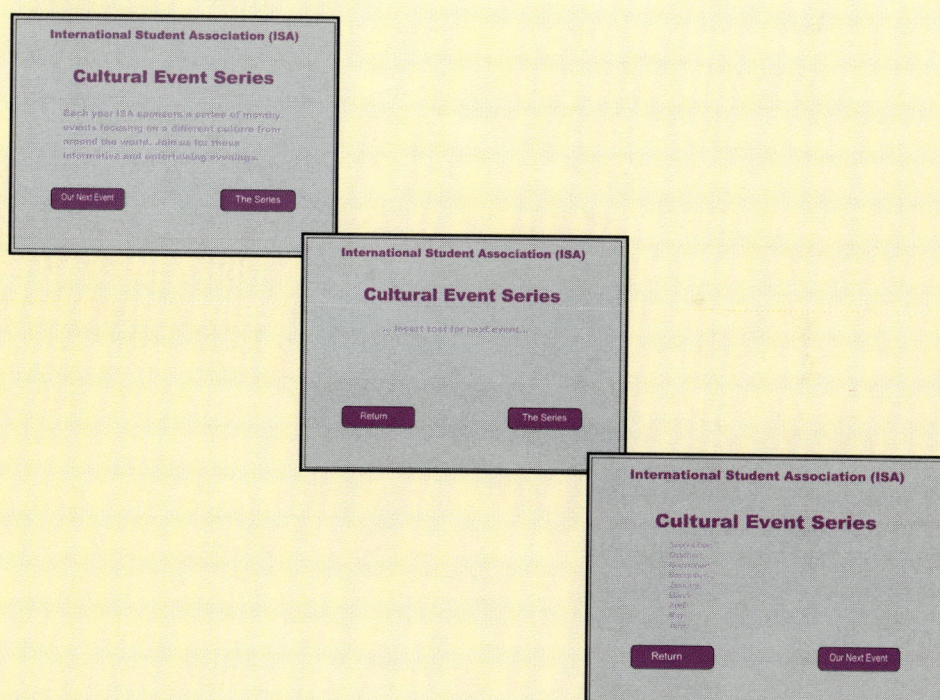

7. Specify different colors for each state of each button.
8. Test the movie.
9. Save your work, then compare your movie to Figure C-36.

UNIT D

CREATING ANIMATIONS

1. Create frame animations.

2. Create motion-tweened animation.

3. Work with motion guides.

4. Create motion animation effects.

5. Animate text.

CREATING ANIMATIONS

Introduction

Animation can be an important part of your Web site, whether the site focuses on e-commerce (attracts attention and provides product demonstrations), education (simulates complex processes such as DNA replication), or entertainment (provides interactive games).

How Does Animation Work?

The perception of motion in an animation is actually an illusion. Animation is like a motion picture in that it is made up of a series of still images. Research has found that our eye captures and holds an image for one-tenth of a second before processing another image. By retaining each impression for one-tenth of a second, we perceive a series of rapidly displayed still images as a single, moving image. This phenomenon is known as persistence of vision and provides the basis for the frame rate in animations. Frame rates of 10–12 frames-per-second (fps) generally provide an acceptably smooth computer-based animation. Lower frame rates result in a jerky image, while higher frame rates may result in a blurred image. Macromedia Flash uses a default frame rate of 12 fps.

Macromedia Flash Animation

Creating animation is one of the most powerful features of Macromedia Flash, yet developing basic animations is a simple process. Macromedia Flash allows you to create animations that can move and rotate an object around the stage, and change its size, shape, or color. You can also use the animation features in Macromedia Flash to create special effects, such as an object zooming or fading in and out. You can combine animation effects so that an object changes shape and color as it moves across the stage. Animations are created by changing the content of successive frames. Macromedia Flash provides two animation methods: frame-by-frame animation and tweened animation.

Tools You'll Use

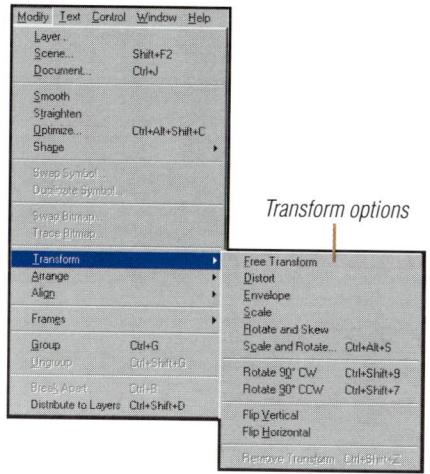

Transform options

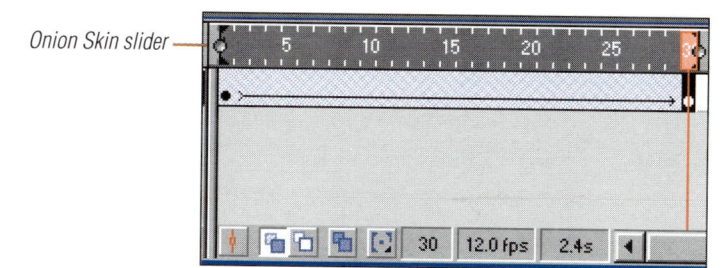

Onion Skin slider

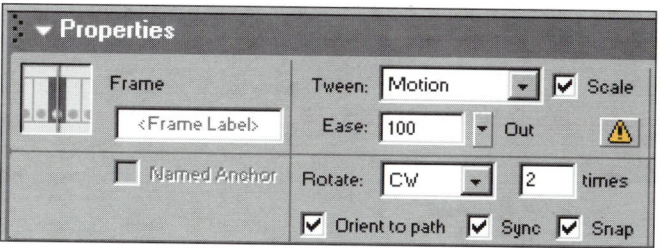

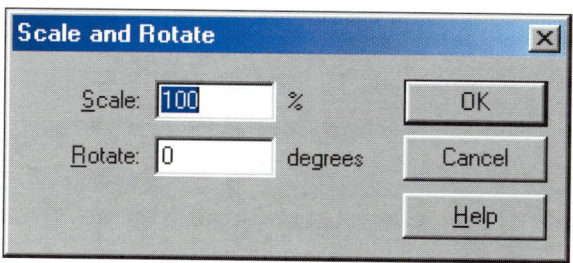

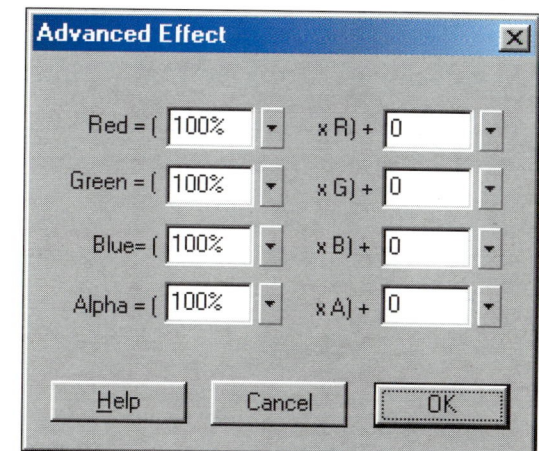

CREATE FRAME ANIMATIONS

What You'll Do

 In this lesson you will create frame animations.

Understanding Frame Animations

A frame animation (also called a frame-by-frame animation) is created by specifying the object that is to appear in each frame of a sequence of frames. Figure D-1 shows three images that are variations of a cartoon character. In this instance, the head and body remain the same, but the arms and legs change to represent a walking motion. If these individual images are placed into succeeding frames (with keyframes), an animation is created.

Frame-by-frame animations are useful when you want to change individual parts of an image. The images in Figure D-1 are simple—only three images are needed for the animation. However, depending on the complexity of the image and the desired movements, the time needed to display each change can be large. When creating a frame-by-frame animation, you need to consider the following points:

- The number of different images. The more images there are, the more time is needed to create them. However, the greater the number of images, the less change you need to make in each image. Therefore, the movement in the animation may seem more realistic.
- The number of frames in which each image will appear. If each image appears in only one frame, the animation may appear rather jerky, since the changes are made very rapidly. In some instances, you may want to give the impression of a rapid change in an object, such as rapidly blinking colors. The number of frames creates varied results.
- The movie frame rate. Frame rates below 10 may appear jerky, while those above 30 may appear blurred.

Keyframes are critical to the development of frame animations because they signify a change in the object. Because frame animations are created by changing the object, all frames in a frame animation may need to be keyframes. The exception is when you want an object displayed in several frames before it changes.

Creating a Frame Animation

To create a frame animation, select the frame on the layer where you want the animation to begin, insert a keyframe, and then place the object on the stage. Next, select the frame where you want the change to occur, insert a keyframe, and then change the object. You can also add a new object in place of the original one. Figure D-2 shows the first six frames of an animation in which the front end of a car raises up and down in place. The movement of the animation is visible because the Onion Skin feature is turned on; this feature will be discussed later in this unit. In this case, the car stays in place during the animation. A frame animation can also involve movement of the object around the stage.

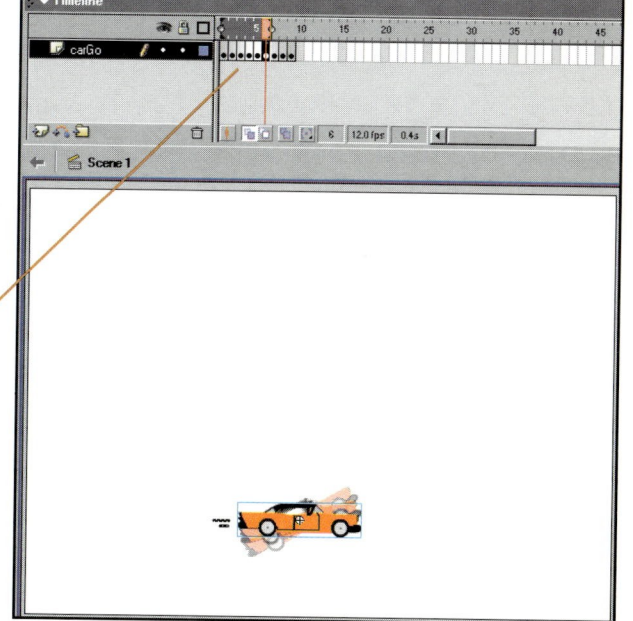

In each frame, the car is in a different position

Create an in-place frame animation

1. Open fld_1.fla, then save it as **frameAn.fla**.

2. Insert a keyframe in Frame 2 on the carGo layer.

3. Verify that the car is selected, click the Free Transform Tool on the toolbox, then click the Rotate and Skew Tool option in the Options section of the toolbox.

4. Drag the top-right handle up one position, as shown in Figure D-3.

5. Insert a keyframe in Frame 3 on the carGo layer.

6. Drag the top-right handle up one more position.

7. Insert a keyframe in Frame 4 on the carGo layer, then drag the top-right handle down one position.

8. Insert a keyframe in Frame 5 on the carGo layer, then drag the top-right handle down to position the car to its original horizontal position.

9. Insert a keyframe in Frame 6 on the carGo layer, then compare your timeline to Figure D-4.

10. Save your work.

You created an in-place frame animation.

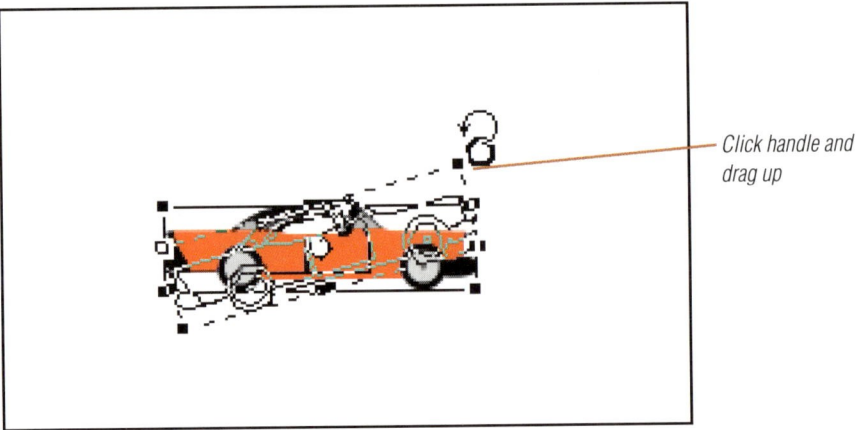

Click handle and drag up

Creating Animations

Add detail to the animation

1. Click the Pencil Tool on the toolbox, click the Stroke Color Tool on the toolbox, then select the black color swatch in the left column of the color palette. 🖊

   | TIP Adjust the Zoom percentage as needed.

2. Draw the two lines shown in Figure D-5.

3. Click Control on the menu bar, then click Play.

4. Save your work.

You added lines to the animation that indicate motion.

FIGURE D-5

Adding lines to the object

Create a moving frame animation

1. Insert a keyframe in Frame 7 on the carGo layer.

2. Click the Arrow Tool on the toolbox, drag a marquee around the car and the lines, then drag the car and the two lines to the right approximately half the distance to the right edge of the stage.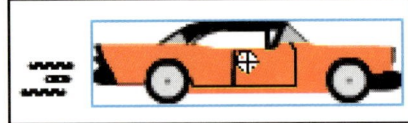

3. Insert a keyframe in Frame 8 on the carGo layer.

4. Click the Pencil Tool on the toolbox, then draw a third line as shown in Figure D-6.

5. Click the Arrow Tool on the toolbox, drag a marquee around the car and lines, then drag the car and the three lines to the right, as shown in Figure D-7.

(continued)

The car with a third line

FIGURE D-7
The car and three lines after dragging them to the right

FIGURE D-8

Positioning the car off the stage

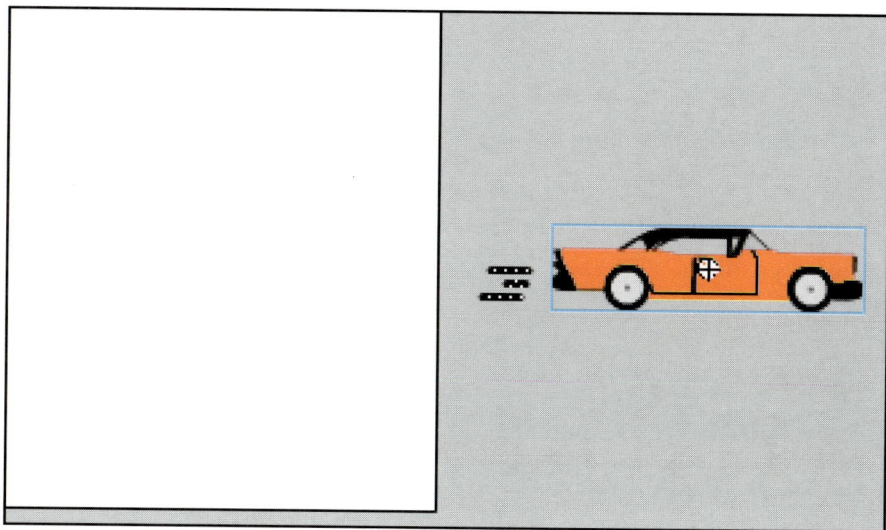

6. Insert a keyframe in Frame 9 on the carGo layer, then drag the car and the three lines completely off the right side of the stage, as shown in Figure D-8.

7. Play the movie, then save your work.

You created a moving frame animation.

Change the frame rate

1. Double-click the Frame Rate icon on the timeline, type **6** in the Frame Rate text box, click OK, then play the movie. 12.0 fps

2. Repeat Step 1, typing **18** and **12** in the Frame Rate text box, respectively.

3. Save your work, then close the movie.

You changed the frame rate for the movie.

CREATE MOTION-TWEENED ANIMATION

What You'll Do

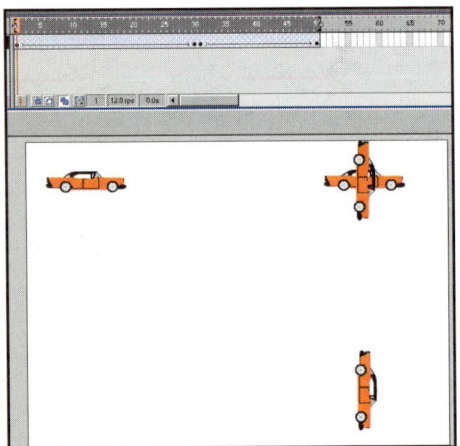

 *In this lesson, you will create motion-tweened animations.*

Understanding Motion Tweening

Frame-by-frame animation can be a tedious process, especially if you have to alter an object's position an infinitesimal amount in every frame. Fortunately, once you create start and end frames, Macromedia Flash can fill in the in-between frames, a process called tweening. In tweened animation, Macromedia Flash stores only the attributes that change from frame to frame. For example, if you have an object that moves across the stage, Macromedia Flash stores the location of the object in each frame, but not the other attributes of the object, such as its dimensions and color. In contrast, for frame animation, all of the attributes for the object need to be stored in each frame. Frame animations have larger file sizes than tweened animations.

There are two types of tweened animation: shape and motion. Shape animations are similar to the process of image morphing in which one object slowly turns into another—often unrelated—object, such as a robot that turns into a man. Shape-tweened animations will be covered in the next unit. You can use motion tweening to create animations in which objects move and in which they are resized, rotated, and recolored. Figure D-9 shows a motion-tweened animation of a car moving diagonally across the screen. There are only two keyframes needed for this animation: a keyframe in Frame 1 where the car starts, and a keyframe in Frame 30 where the car ends. Macromedia Flash automatically fills in the other frames.

To create a motion-tweened animation, select the starting frame and, if necessary, insert a keyframe. Position the object on the stage and verify that it is selected. Next, choose the Create Motion Tween command from the Insert menu, then insert a keyframe in the ending frame of the animation. Figure D-10 shows the timeline after creating a Motion Tween and specifying an ending keyframe. Motion tweening is represented by black dots displayed in the keyframes and a black arrow linking the keyframes against a light blue background. The final step is to move the object and/or make changes to the object, such as changing its size or rotating it. Keep in mind the following points as you create motion-tweened animations.

- If you change the position of the object, it will move in a direct line from the starting position to the ending position. To move the object on a predetermined path, you can create several motion-tweened animations in succeeding frames, or you can use a motion guide as explained in the next lesson.
- If you reshape an object in the ending keyframe, the object will slowly change from the starting to the ending keyframes. If this is not the effect you want, you can add a keyframe immediately after the tweened animation and reshape the object at that point.
- When you select an object and create a motion tween, Macromedia Flash automatically creates a symbol and names it Tween 1.

FIGURE D-9
Sample motion-tweened animation

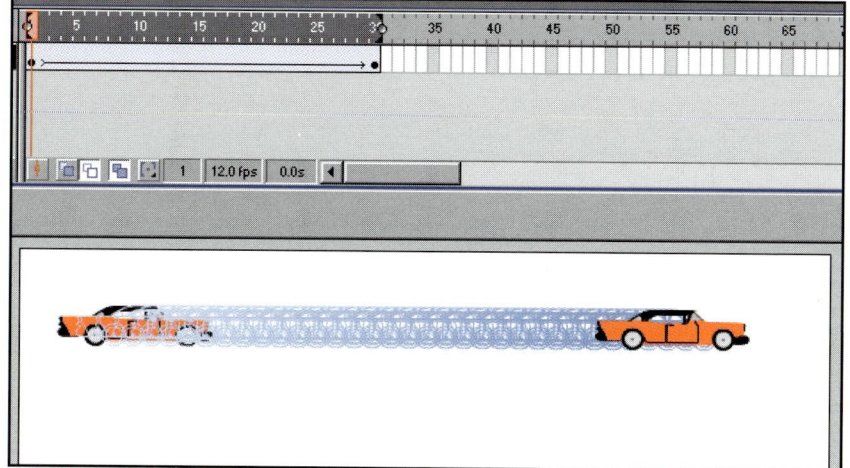

FIGURE D-10
Motion tweening as it appears on the timeline

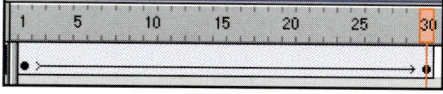

Create a motion-tweened animation

1. Open fld_2.fla, then save it as **carAn**.

2. Click Frame 1 on the carTurn layer, click Insert on the menu bar, then click Create Motion Tween.

3. Insert a keyframe in Frame 30 on the carTurn layer.

4. Click the Arrow Tool on the toolbox (if necessary), then drag the car to the position on the stage shown in Figure D-11.

5. Play the movie, then save your work.

You created a motion-tweened animation.

FIGURE D-11
Final position of the first motion tween

Creating Animations

FIGURE D-12

Final position of the combined motion tween

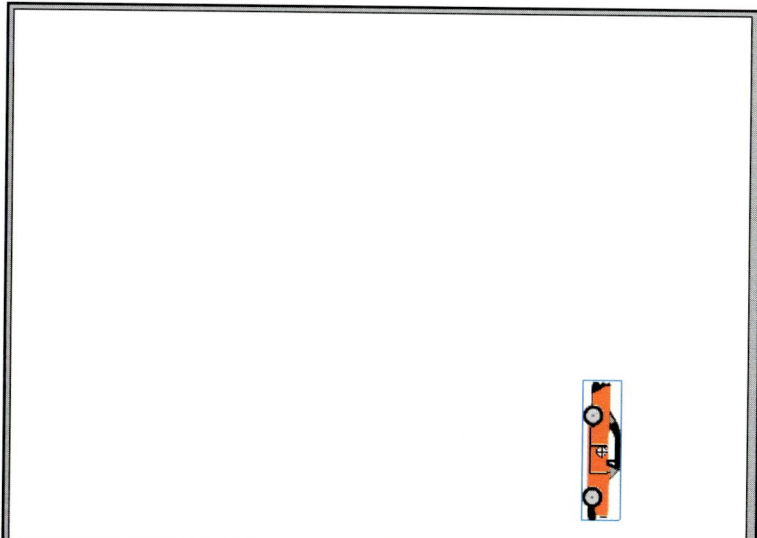

Combine motion-tweened animations

1. Insert a keyframe in Frame 31 on the carTurn layer.

2. Verify that the car is selected, click Modify on the menu bar, point to Transform, then click Rotate 90° CW.

3. Insert a keyframe in Frame 50 on the carTurn layer.

4. Click the Arrow Tool on the toolbox (if necessary), then drag the car to the location shown in Figure D-12.

5. Play the movie.

6. Save your work, then close the movie.

You combined two motion-tweened animations with a rotation between the animations.

WORK WITH MOTION GUIDES

What You'll Do

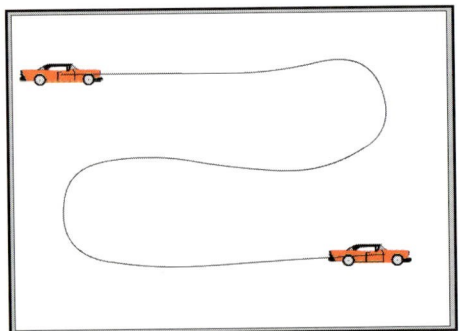

▶ *In this lesson, you will create a motion guide and attach an animation to it.*

Understanding Motion Guides

In the previous lesson, you combined two animations to cause an object to change directions. Macromedia Flash provides a way for you to create a path that will guide moving objects around the stage in any direction, as shown in Figure D-13. Motion guide layers allow you to draw a path and attach motion-tweened animations to the path. The animations are placed on their own layer beneath the motion guide layer. There are two ways to work with motion guides. First, you can create the guide layer and draw a path, then create an animation and attach the animated object to the path. Second, you can create an animation, create a motion guide layer and draw a path, then attach the animated object to the path. The process for using the second method is as follows:

- Create a motion-tweened animation.
- Select a layer and insert a motion guide layer. The selected layer is indented below the motion guide layer, as shown in Figure D-14. This indicates that the selected layer is associated with the motion guide layer.

- Draw a path using the Pen, Pencil, Line, Circle, Rectangle, or Brush Tools.
- Attach the object to the path by dragging the object by its registration point to the beginning of the path in the first frame, and to the end of the path in the last frame.

Depending on the type of object you are animating and the path, you may need to orient the object to the path. This means that the object will rotate in response to the direction of the path, as shown in Figure D-15. The Property inspector is used to specify that the object will be oriented to the path. The advantages of using a motion guide are that you can have an object move along any path, including a path that intersects itself, and you can easily change the shape of the path, allowing you to experiment with different motions. A disadvantage of using a motion guide is that, in some instances, orienting the object along the path may result in an unnatural-looking animation. You can fix this by stepping through the animation one frame at a time until you reach the frame where the object is positioned poorly. You can then insert a keyframe and adjust the object as desired.

Working with the Property Inspector When Creating Motion-Tweened Animations

Figure D-16 shows the Property inspector with the following options:

- Tween—specifies Motion, Shape, or None.

- Scale—tweens the size of an object. Select this option when you want an object to grow smaller or larger.
- Ease—specifies the rate of change between tweened frames. For example, you may want to have an object—such as a car—start out slowly and accelerate gradually. Ease values are between –100 (slow) to 100 (fast).

- Rotate—specifies the number of times an object rotates clockwise (CW) or counterclockwise (CCW).
- Orient to path—orients the baseline of the object to the path.
- Sync—ensures that the object loops properly.
- Snap—attaches the object to the path by its registration point, the point around which the object rotates and the point that snaps to a motion guide.

FIGURE D-13

Comparing orientations

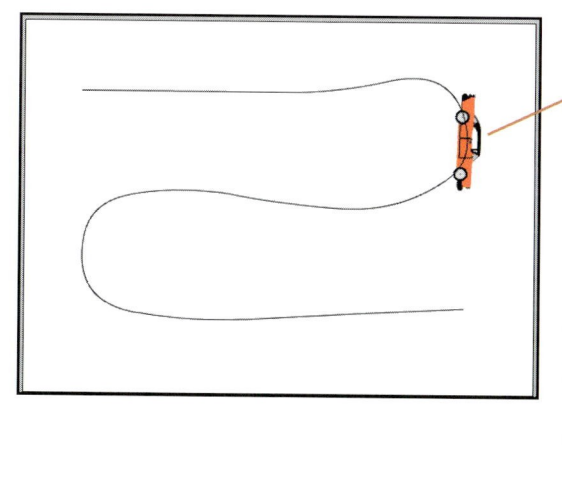

Object oriented to path

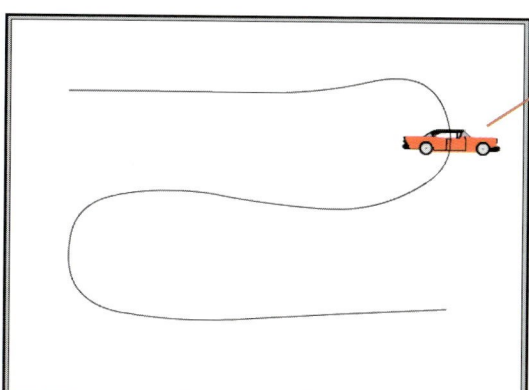

Object not oriented to path

FIGURE D-14

A motion guide layer

Create an animation without a motion guide

1. Open fld_3.fla, then save it as **carPath.fla**.

2. Make sure that the car is selected, click Insert on the menu bar, then click Create Motion Tween.

3. Insert a keyframe in Frame 40 on the carRoute layer.

4. Drag the car to the lower-right corner of the stage, as shown in Figure D-15.

5. Play the movie.

6. Click Frame 1 on the timeline, then save your work.

   The car moves diagonally down to the corner of the stage.

You created a motion animation without a motion guide.

FIGURE D-15

Positioning the car

FIGURE D-16
Motion path

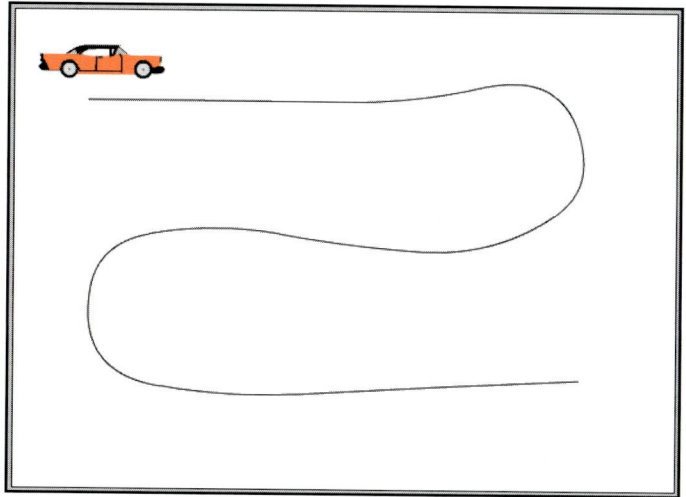

FIGURE D-17
Snapping an object to the path

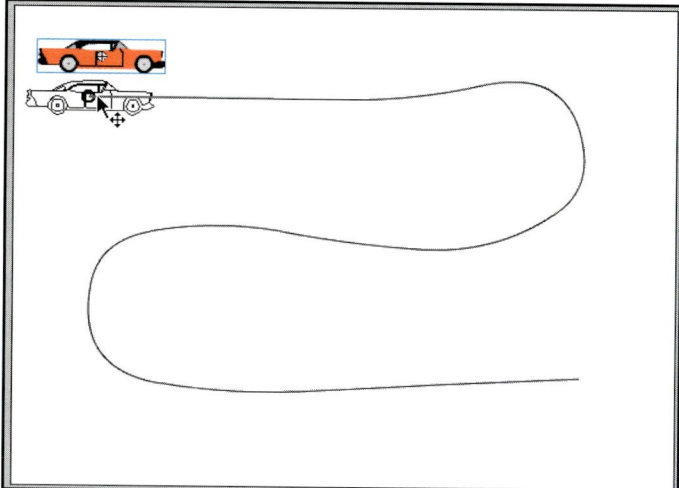

1. Click Frame 1 on the carRoute layer.

2. Click Insert on the menu bar, then click Motion Guide.

   The carRoute layer is indented beneath the guide layer on the timeline.

3. Click the Pencil Tool on the toolbox, click the Smooth Tool option in the Options section of the toolbox, then draw a path similar to the one shown in Figure D-16.

   > **TIP** You can smooth out a path by selecting it with the Arrow Tool, then clicking the Smooth Tool option several times.

4. Click the Arrow Tool on the toolbox.

5. If the car does not snap to the beginning of the path, click the car to select it, click the registration point of the car, then drag it to the beginning of the path, as shown in Figure D-17.

   > **TIP** An object is snapped to the beginning or end of a motion path when the start or end point of the motion path intersects the car's registration point.

6. Click Frame 40 on the carRoute layer.

7. If the car does not snap to the end of the path, click the Arrow Tool on the Tools panel, click the registration point of the car, then drag it to the end of the path.

8. Play the movie, then save your work.

You created a motion guide on a path and attached an animation to it.

Orient an object to the path

1. Play the movie again and notice how the car does not turn front-first in response to the turns in the path.

2. Make sure the Property inspector is displayed, then click Frame 1 on the carRoute layer.

3. Make sure the car is selected, click the Orient to path check box, then compare your Property inspector to Figure D-18 (Win).

4. Play the movie, then save your work.

   Notice the car is oriented front-first to the turns in the path and that CarRoute appears on the timeline to identify the animation.

You used the Property inspector to specify that the object is oriented to the path.

Orient to path option

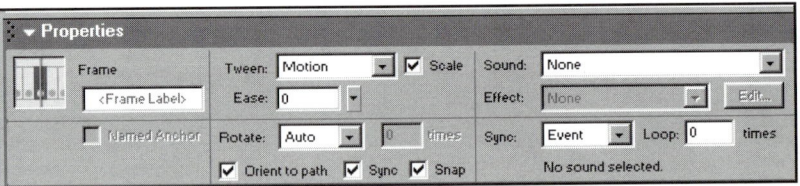

FIGURE D-19
Setting the Ease value

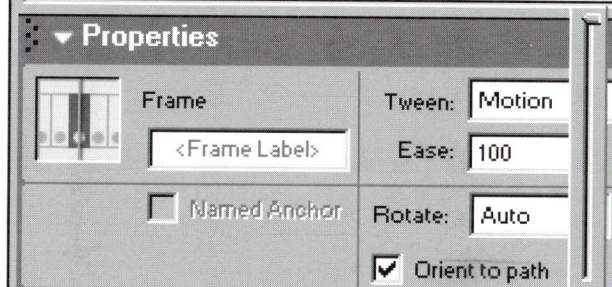

1. Play the movie and notice the speed of the car is constant.

2. Click Frame 1 on the carRoute layer.

3. Click the Ease list arrow in the Property inspector, then drag the slider up to 100, as shown in Figure D-19.

4. Click a blank area outside the stage.

5. Play the movie and notice how the car starts out fast and decelerates as it moves toward the end of the path.

6. Click Frame 1 on the carRoute layer.

7. Click the Ease list arrow in the Property inspector, drag the slider down to –100, then click a blank area outside the stage.

8. Play the movie and notice how the car starts out slow and accelerates as it moves toward the end of the path.

9. Save your work.

You set Ease values to alter the starting and ending speed of the car.

CREATE MOTION ANIMATION EFFECTS

What You'll Do

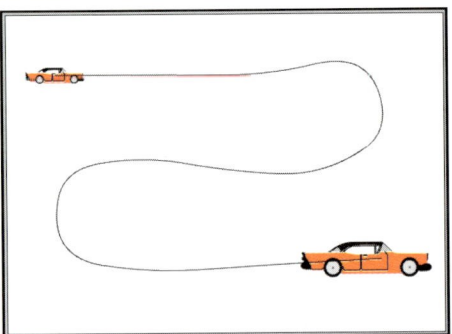

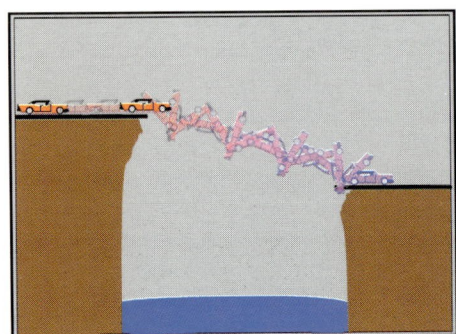

In this lesson, you will use motion tween- ing to resize, rotate, and change the color of animated objects.

Creating Motion Animation Effects

Up to this point, you have created motion-tweened animations that cause an object to move around the stage. There are sev- eral other effects that you can create using motion tweening, including resizing, rotating, and changing the color of an object as it is in motion.

Resizing an Object Using a Motion Tween

The simplest process for resizing an object during a motion tween is to select a frame as the starting frame, draw or place an object on the stage, and then create a motion tween. You can select an ending frame and resize the object using the resize handles that are displayed when you select the Free Transform Tool and the Scale Tool options on the toolbox. The results of this process are shown in Figure D-20. By moving and resizing an object, you can create the effect that it is moving away from you or towards you. If you have the object remain stationary while it is being resized, the effect is simi- lar to zooming in or out.

Rotating an Object Using a Motion Tween

You have several options when rotating an object using a motion tween. You can cause the object to rotate clockwise or counterclockwise any number of degrees and any number of times. You can also stipulate an Ease value to cause the rotation to accelerate or decelerate. These effects can be specified using the Rotate Tool option of the Free Transform Tool on the toolbox, adjusting settings in the Property inspector, or clicking a Transform option on the Modify menu. Notice that these options include Flip Vertical and Flip Horizontal. Choosing these options causes the object to slowly flip throughout the length of the anima- tion. You can combine effects so that they occur simultaneously during the anima- tion. For example, you can have a car rotate and get smaller as it moves across the stage. The Scale and Rotate dialog box allows you to specify a percentage for scaling and a number of degrees for rotating.

Changing an Object's Color Using a Motion Tween

Macromedia Flash provides several ways in which you can alter the color of objects using a motion tween. The most basic change involves starting with one color for the object and ending with another color. The tweening process slowly changes the color across the specified frames. When the movie is played, the colors are blended as the object moves across the stage. At the middle of the animation, the object's color is purple with equal portions of the blue and red colors mixed together. Figure D-21 displays the animation using the Onion Skin feature. Normally, Macromedia Flash displays one frame of an animation sequence at a time on the stage. Turning on the Onion Skin feature allows you to view an outline of the object(s) in any number of frames. This can help in positioning animated objects on the stage.

More sophisticated color changes can be made using the Property inspector. You can adjust the brightness; tint the colors; adjust the transparency (Alpha option); and change the red, green, and blue values of an object. One of the most popular animation effects is to cause an object to slowly fade in. You can accomplish this by motion tweening the object, setting the Alpha value to 0 (transparent) in the starting frame, and then setting it to 100 in the

ending frame. To make the object fade out, just reverse the values.

Combining Various Animation Effects

Macromedia Flash allows you to combine the various motion-tween effects so that you can rotate an object as it moves across the stage, changes color, and changes size. Macromedia Flash allows you to combine

motion-tweened animations to create various effects. For example, if you create an airplane object, you can apply the following aerial effects:

- enter from off stage and perform a loop;
- rotate the plane horizontally to create a barrel roll effect;
- grow smaller as it moves across the screen to simulate the effect of the plane speeding away;
- change colors on the fuselage to simulate the reflection of the sun.

FIGURE D-20

Resizing an object using a motion tween

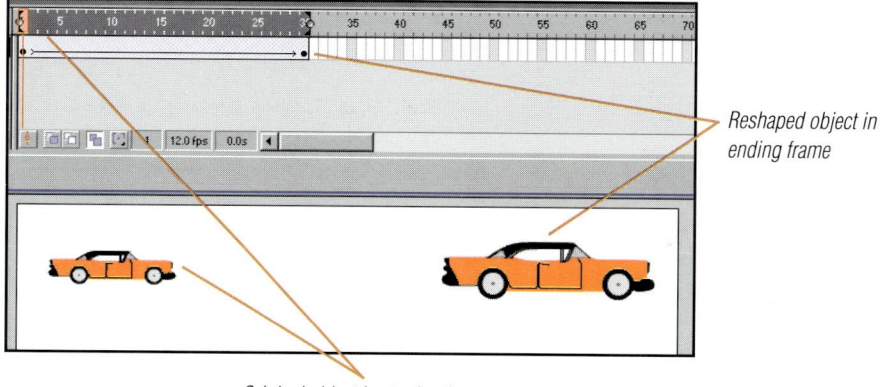

Reshaped object in ending frame

Original object in starting frame

FIGURE D-21

Onion Skin feature

Use motion tweening to resize an object

1. Make sure that the carPath.fla movie is open.

2. Click Frame 1 on the carRoute layer.

3. Make sure the car is selected, click the Free Transform Tool on the toolbox, then click the Scale Tool option in the Options section of the toolbox.

4. Drag the upper-left corner handle inward until the car is approximately half the original size, as shown in Figure D-22.

5. Click Frame 40 on the carRoute layer.

6. Make sure the car is selected, then click the Scale Tool option in the Options section of the toolbox.

7. Drag the upper-right corner handle outward until the car is approximately twice the original size, as shown in Figure D-23.

8. Play the movie and notice how the car is resized.

9. Save your work, then close the movie.

You used the Scale Tool option to resize an object in a motion animation.

Using the handles to reduce the size of the car

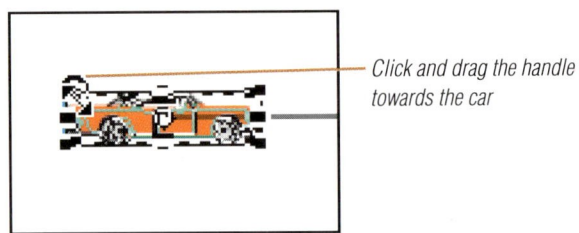

Click and drag the handle towards the car

Using the handles to increase the size of the car

Click and drag the handle away from the car

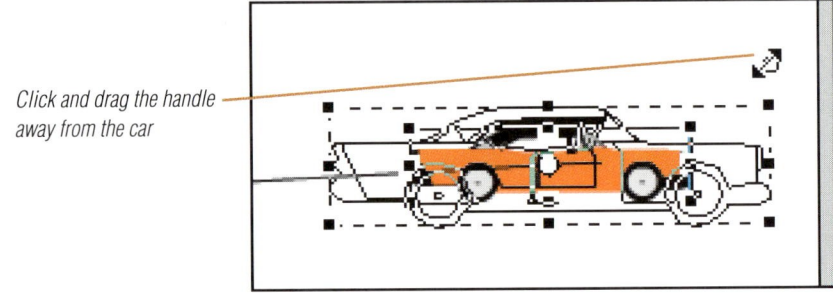

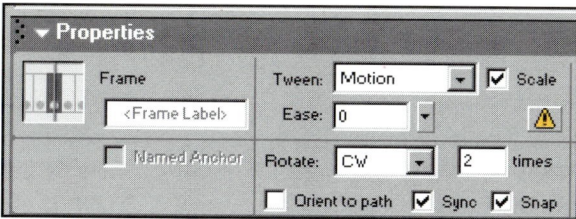

Use motion tweening to rotate an object

1. Open fld_4.fla, then save it as **carRotate**.

2. Click Frame 5 on the carJump layer.

3. Make sure the car is selected, click Insert on the menu bar, then click Create Motion Tween.

4. Click the Rotate list arrow in the Property inspector, click CW, double-click the times text box, then type **2**, as shown in Figure D-24.

5. Insert a keyframe in Frame 20 on the carJump layer.

6. Play the movie; notice the car moves forward, then rotates in place at the edge of the cliff.

7. Click Frame 20 on the carJump layer, then drag the car across the stage to the edge of the right cliff, as shown in Figure D-25.

8. Play the movie; notice that the car rotates as it moves to the new location, then save your work.

You created a motion animation and rotated the object.

Use motion tweening to change the color of an object

1. Click Frame 20 on the carJump layer.

2. Click the Arrow Tool on the toolbox (if necessary), then single-click the car to select it. ▶

3. Click the Color list arrow in the Property inspector, click Advanced, then click the Settings button. `Settings...`

4. Click the xB)+ list arrow, then drag the slider to **255**, as shown in Figure D-26.

5. Click OK.

6. Play the movie and notice how the color slowly changes from red to fuchsia.

   > TIP   Because motion tweening is per-formed on instances of symbols and text blocks, changing the color of a motion-tweened object affects the entire object. To make changes in individual areas of an object, you must first select the object and choose the Break Apart command from the Modify menu.

7. Save your work.

You used the Property inspector to change the color of an object as it was being animated.

MACROMEDIA FLASH D-24

FIGURE D-26

Changing the color settings

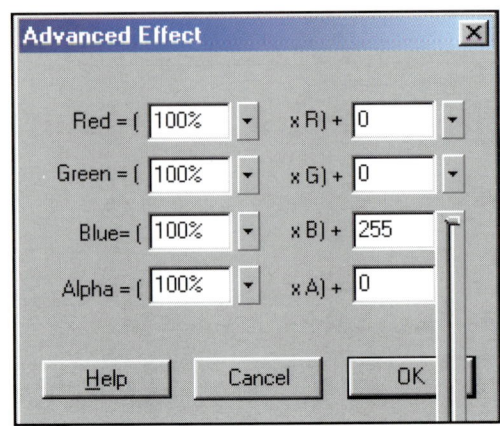

1. Click Frame 1 on the carJump layer, then click the Onion Skin icon on the timeline.

2. Click the Edit Multiple Frames icon on the timeline.

3. Drag the End Onion Skin slider to Frame 20, then compare your image to Figure D-27.

   Each frame of the animation is visible on the stage.

4. Click the Onion Skin icon and the Edit Multiple Frames icon on the timeline to turn off these features.

5. Save and close the movie.

You displayed the animation using the Onion Skin feature.

FIGURE D-27
Using the Onion Skin feature

Start Onion Skin slider

Drag End Onion Skin slider to Frame 20

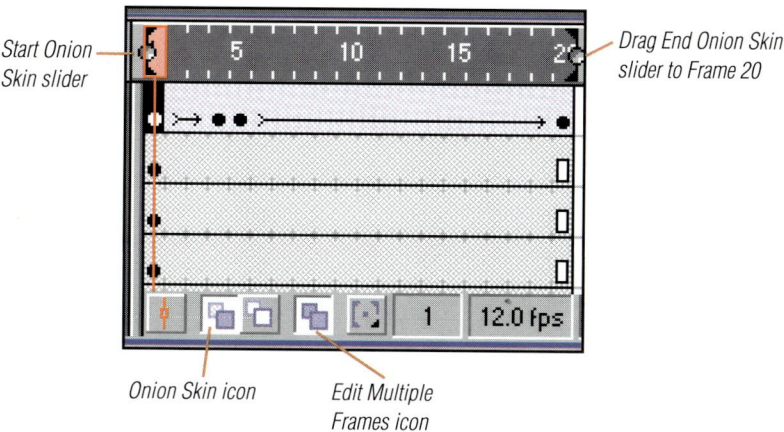

Onion Skin icon

Edit Multiple Frames icon

ANIMATE TEXT

What You'll Do

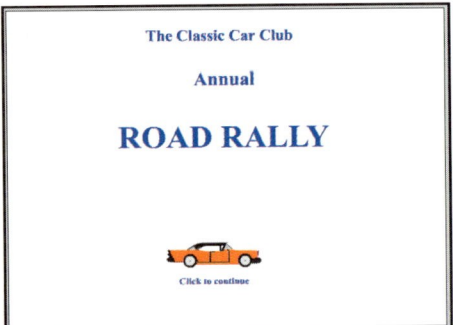

 In this lesson, you will animate text by scrolling, rotating, zooming, and resizing it.

Animating Text

You can motion tween text block objects just as you do graphic objects. You can resize, rotate, reposition, and change their colors. Figure D-28 shows three examples of animated text. When the movie starts, each of the following can occur one after the other:

- The Classic Car Club text block scrolls in from the left side to the top center of the stage. This is done by positioning the text block off the stage and creating a motion-tweened animation that moves it to the stage.
- The Annual text block appears and rotates five times. This occurs after you create the Annual text block, position it in the middle of the stage under the heading, and use the Property inspector to specify a clockwise rotation that repeats five times.

- The ROAD RALLY text block slowly zooms out and appears in the middle of the stage. This occurs after you create the text block and use the Free Transform Tool handles to resize it to a small block. You use the Property inspector to specify a transparent value. Finally, the text block is resized to a larger size at the end of the animation.

Once you create a motion animation using a text block, the text block becomes a symbol and you are unable to edit individual characters within the text block. You can, however, edit the symbol as a whole.

FIGURE D-28

Three examples of animated text

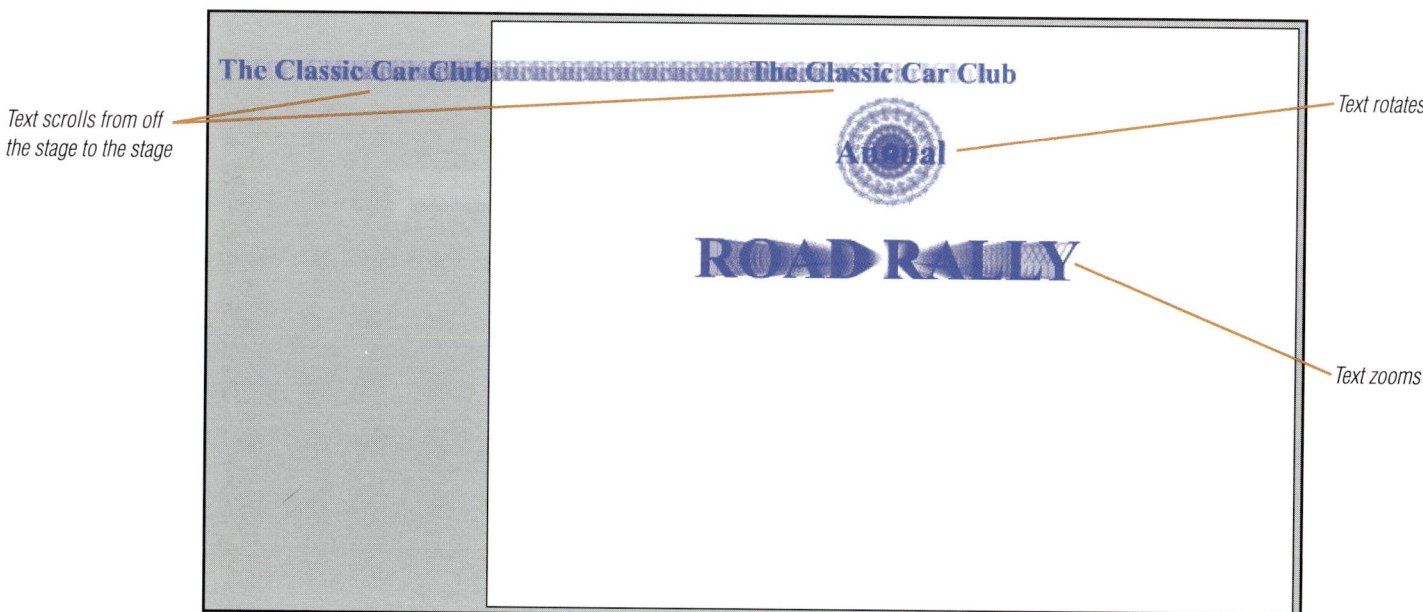

Text scrolls from off the stage to the stage

Text rotates

Text zooms

Select, copy, and paste frames

1. Open frameAn.fla.
2. Click Frame 10 on the carGo layer, then drag left to Frame 1 until you select all the frames, as shown in Figure D-29.
3. Click Edit on the menu bar, then click Cut Frames.
4. Click Frame 71 on the carGo layer.
5. Click Edit on the menu bar, then click Paste Frames.
6. Play the movie, then save your work.

You selected, copied, and pasted frames on the timeline.

FIGURE D-29
Selecting frames

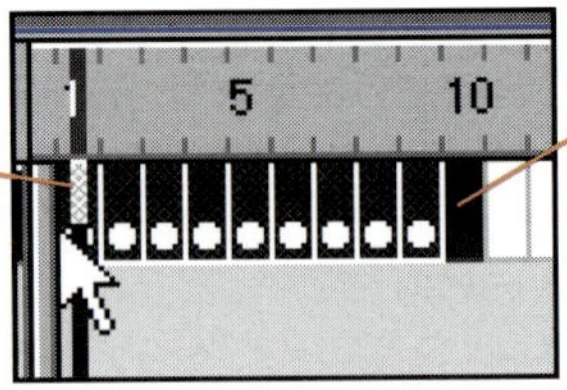

Drag to here

Start here

FIGURE D-30

Positioning the Text Tool pointer outside the stage

*Position Text Tool
pointer off the stage*

FIGURE D-31

Positioning the text block

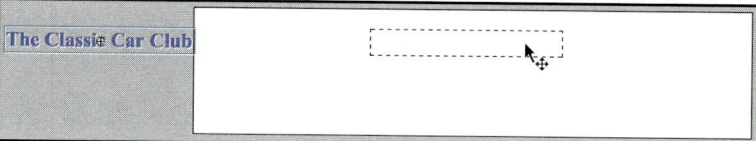

1. Insert a new layer, rename it **scrollText**, then press [Enter] (Win) or [return] (Mac).

2. Click Frame 1 on the scrollText layer, then verify that the Property inspector is displayed.

3. Click the Text Tool on the toolbox, click the Font list arrow in the Property inspector, then click Times New Roman. **A**

4. Click the Font Size list arrow in the Property inspector, then drag the slider to **20**.

5. Click the Text (fill) color swatch in the Property inspector, then click the blue color swatch on the left column of the color palette.

6. Click the Text Tool pointer outside the stage in the upper-left corner of the workspace, as shown in Figure D-30. $+_\mathrm{A}$

7. Type **The Classic Car Club**.

8. Click the Arrow Tool on the toolbox, click the text box, click Insert on the menu bar, then click Create Motion Tween.

9. Insert a keyframe in Frame 20 on the scrollText layer.

10. Drag the text block horizontally to the center of the stage, as shown in Figure D-31.

11. Insert a keyframe in Frame 80 on the scrollText layer.

12. Play the movie, then save your work.

    The text moves to center stage from offstage left.

You created a text block object and applied a motion tween animation to it.

Create rotating text

1. Insert a new layer, rename it **rotateText**, then press [Enter] (Win) or [return] (Mac).

2. Insert a keyframe in Frame 21 on the rotateText layer.

3. Click the Text Tool on the toolbox, click the font size list arrow in the Property inspector, drag the slider to **24**, position the pointer beneath the "a" in "Classic", type **Annual**, then compare your image to Figure D-32. **A**

4. Click the Arrow Tool on the toolbox, click Insert on the menu bar, then click Create Motion Tween. ▸

5. Click Frame 21 on the rotateText layer, click the Rotate list arrow in the Property inspector, click CW, drag the pointer to select 1 in the times text box, then type **2**.

6. Insert keyframes in Frames 40 and 80 on the rotateText layer.

7. Play the movie, then save your work.

   The text rotates clockwise two times.

You created a rotating text block.

Positioning the text for rotation

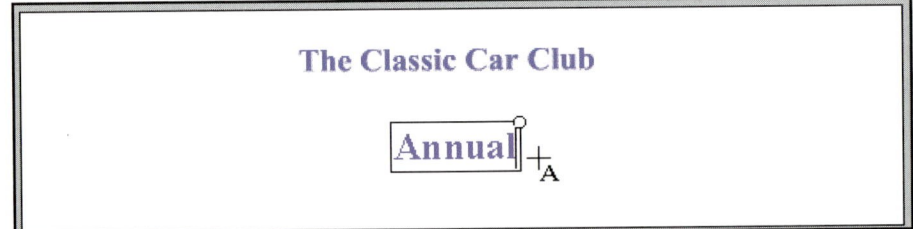

Using the Text Tool to type ROAD RALLY

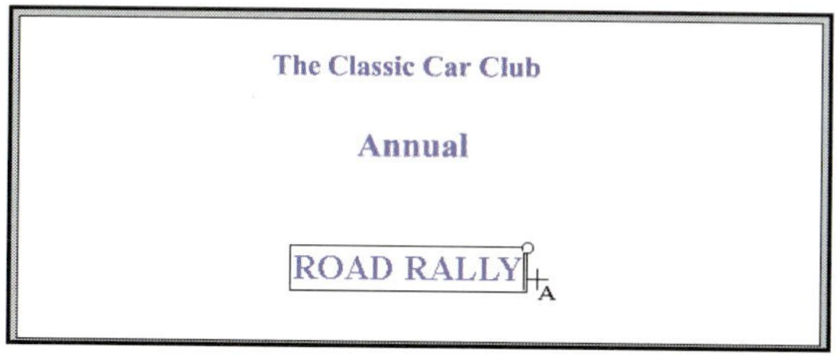

The Classic Car Club

Annual

ROAD RALLY

FIGURE D-34
Resizing and repositioning the text block

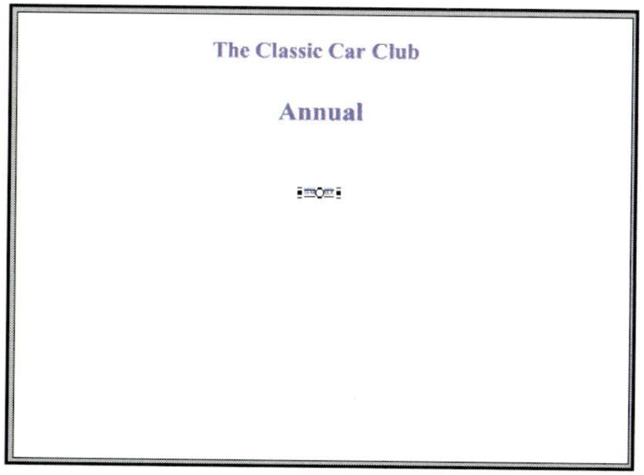

The Classic Car Club

Annual

FIGURE D-35
Resizing the text block

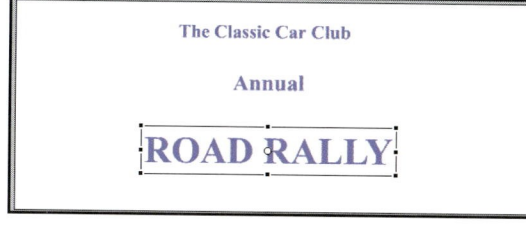

The Classic Car Club

Annual

ROAD RALLY

Resize and fade in text

1. Insert a new layer, rename it **fadeinText**, then press [Enter] (Win) or [return] (Mac).

2. Insert a keyframe in Frame 40 on the fadeinText layer.

3. Click the Text Tool on the toolbox, position the pointer beneath the Annual text block and even with the "T" in "The", type **ROAD RALLY**, then compare your image to Figure D-33. ◪A

4. Click the Free Transform Tool on the toolbox, then click the Scale Tool option in the Options section of the toolbox. ⊞

5. Drag the upper-left corner handle inward to resize the text block, then position the text block as shown in Figure D-34. ⊞

6. Click Insert on the menu bar, then click Create Motion Tween.

7. Click the Color list arrow in the Property inspector, click Alpha, click the Alpha Amount list arrow, drag the slider to **0**, then click a blank area outside the stage.

8. Insert a keyframe in Frame 60 on the fadeinText layer, then click the Arrow Tool on the toolbox (if necessary). ▶

9. Click the Alpha Amount list arrow in the Property inspector, then drag the slider to **100**.

10. Click the Free Transform Tool on the toolbox, click the Scale Tool option in the Options section of the toolbox, drag the upper-left corner handle outward to resize the text block, then position it as shown in Figure D-35. ▣

(continued)

11. Insert a keyframe in Frame 80 on the fadeinText layer.

12. Play the movie, then save your work.

You created a motion animation that caused a text block to fade in and zoom out.

Add a play button

1. Insert a new layer, rename it **continue**, then press [Enter] (Win) or [return] (Mac).

> TIP Scroll up the timeline to view the new layer.

2. Insert a keyframe in Frame 71 on the continue layer.

3. Click the Text Tool on the toolbox, click the Font Size list arrow in the Property inspector, drag the slider to **12**, then click the Arrow Tool. A

4. Make sure the bottom of the stage is visible, position the Text Tool pointer beneath the back wheel of the car, type **Click to continue**, then compare your image to Figure D-36. +A

5. Click the Arrow Tool on the toolbox to select the text block, click Insert on the menu bar, click Convert to Symbol, type **b_continue** in the Name text box, make sure the Button option is selected, then click OK.

6. Click the Arrow Tool on the toolbox (if necessary), then double-click the text block to edit the button.

(continued)

FIGURE D-36
Adding a button

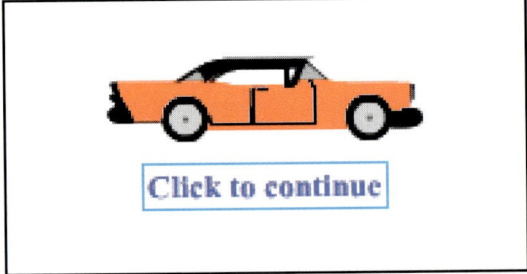

The rectangle that defines the hit area

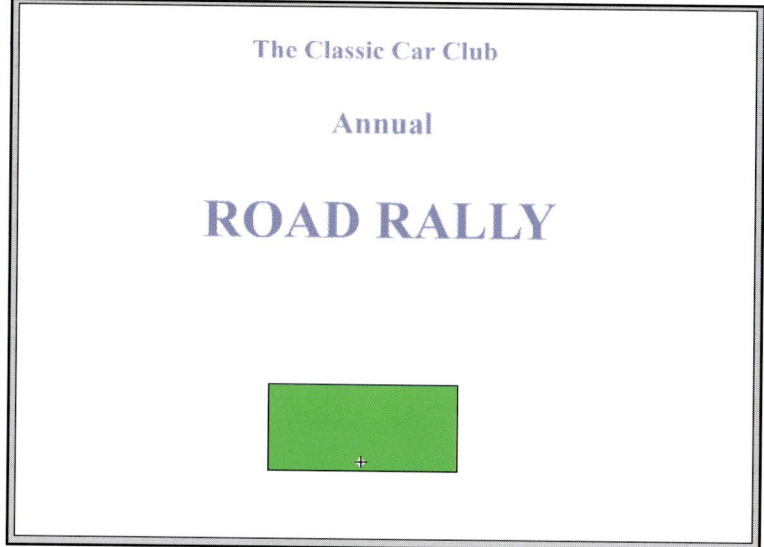

The Classic Car Club

Annual

ROAD RALLY

FIGURE D-38

Adding a stop action

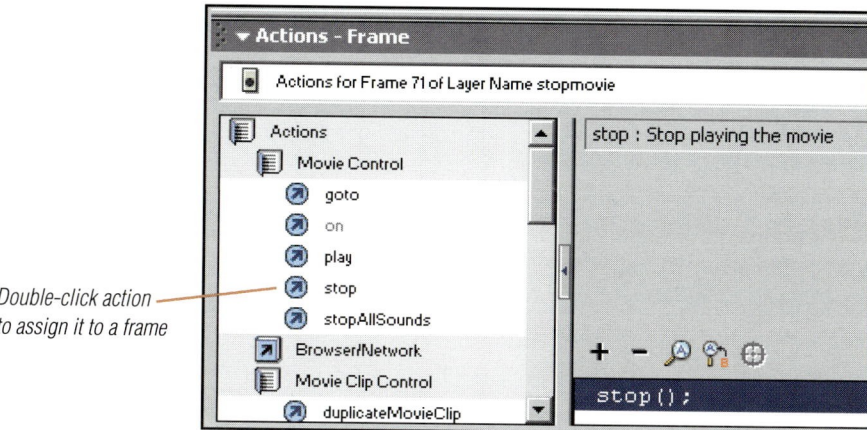

*Double-click action
to assign it to a frame*

7. Insert a keyframe in the Over frame, click the Fill Color Tool on the toolbox, then click the black color swatch in the left column of the color palette.

8. Insert a keyframe in the Down frame, click the Fill Color Tool on the toolbox, then click the bright green color swatch in the left column of the color palette.

9. Insert a keyframe in the Hit frame, click the Rectangle Tool on the toolbox, then draw a rectangle that covers the text block and the car, as shown in Figure D-37.

10. Click Edit on the menu bar, click Edit Document, then save your work.

You inserted a play button.

Add an action to the button

1. Click the Arrow Tool on the toolbox, click Window on the menu bar, then click Actions.

2. Double-click `play` in the Actions panel to assign a `play` action to the button.

3. Insert a new layer, rename the layer **stopmovie**, then insert a keyframe in Frame 71.

4. Double-click `stop` in the Actions panel to assign a `stop` action to Frame 71 on the stopmovie layer, as shown in Figure D-38.

5. Test the movie, then save and close the movie.

   The movie plays the animated text blocks, then plays the animated car when you click the ActionScript text.

You inserted a play button and added a `stop` action to it.

Create a frame animation.

1. Open fld_5.fla and save it as **skillsdemoD.fla**.
2. Insert a keyframe in Frame 22 on the v-ball layer.
3. Resize the object to approximately one-fourth its original size.
4. Insert a keyframe in Frame 23 on the v-ball layer.
5. Resize the object back to approximately its original size.
6. Insert a keyframe in Frame 24 on the v-ball layer, then drag the object to the upper-left corner of the stage.
7. Insert a keyframe in Frame 25 on the v-ball layer, then drag the object to the lower-left corner of the stage.
8. Insert a keyframe in Frame 26 on the v-ball layer, then drag the object to the upper-right corner of the stage.
9. Insert a keyframe in Frame 27 on the v-ball layer, then drag the object to the lower-right corner of the stage.
10. Change the movie frame rate to 3 frames per second, then play the movie.
11. Change the movie frame rate to 12 frames per second, play the movie, then save your work.

Create a motion-tweened animation.

1. Insert a new layer and name it **ballAn**.
2. Insert a keyframe in Frame 28 on the ballAn layer.
3. Display the Library panel, then drag the g_vball graphic symbol to the lower-left corner of the stage.
4. Make sure the object is selected, then create a Motion Tween.
5. Insert a keyframe in Frame 60 on the ballAn layer.
6. Drag the object to the lower-right corner of the stage.
7. Play the movie, then save your work.

Create a motion guide.

1. Click Frame 28 on the ballAn layer.
2. Insert a Motion Guide layer.
3. Use the Pencil Tool to draw a motion path in the shape of an arc, as shown in Figure D-39.
4. Attach the object to the left side of the path in Frame 28 on the ballAn layer.
5. Attach the object to the right side path in Frame 60 on the ballAn layer.
6. Use the Property inspector to orient the object to the path.
7. Play the movie, then save your work.

Accelerate the animated object.

1. Click Frame 28 on the ballAn layer.
2. Use the Property inspector to change the Ease value to −100.
3. Play the movie, then save your work.

Create motion animation effects.

1. Click Frame 60 on the ballAn layer, and use the Free Transform Tool and the Scale Tool option handles to resize the object to approximately one-fourth its original size.
2. Click Frame 28 on the ballAn layer, and use the Property inspector to specify a clockwise rotation that plays five times.
3. Play the movie.
4. Select Frame 60 on the ballAn layer, then select the ball.
5. Use the Advanced Color option in the Property inspector to change the color of the object to green.
6. Play the movie, then save your work.

Animate text.

1. Click the guide layer, then insert a new layer and name it **heading**.
2. Click Frame 1 on the heading layer.
3. Use the Text Tool to type **Having fun with a** in a location off the top-left of the stage.
4. Change the text to Arial, 20 point, red, and boldface.
5. Insert a motion tween.
6. Insert a keyframe in Frame 10 on the heading layer.
7. Drag the text to the top center of the stage.
8. Insert a keyframe in Frame 60 on the heading layer.
9. Play the movie and save your work.
10. Add a layer and name it **zoom**.
11. Insert a keyframe in Frame 11 on the zoom layer.
12. Use the Text Tool to type **Volleyball** below the heading, then center it as needed.

Creating Animations

13. Create a motion tween.

14. Insert a keyframe in Frame 20 on the zoom layer.

15. Click Frame 11 on the zoom layer and select the text block.

16. Use the Property inspector to set the Alpha color option to 0.

17. Resize the text block to approximately one-half inch in Frame 11 on the zoom layer.

18. Select Frame 20 on the zoom layer, and resize the text block to approximate the size shown in Figure D-39.

19. Insert a keyframe in Frame 60 of the zoom layer.

20. Test the movie, then save your work.

FIGURE D-39

Completed Skills Review

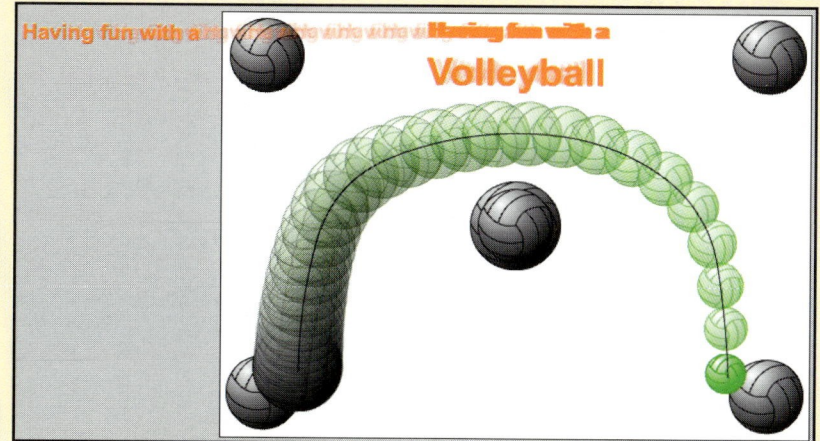

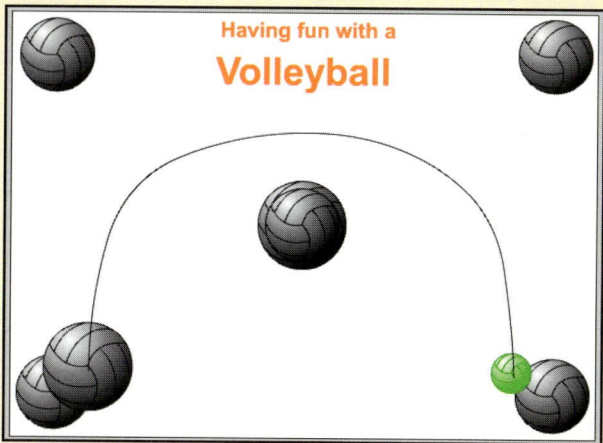

The Ultimate Tours travel company has asked you to design several sample animations for their Web site. Figure D-44 shows a sample homepage and the Cruises screen. Using these (or one of the homepages you created in Unit C) as a guide, complete the following:

For the Ultimate Tours homepage:

1. Open ultimatetoursC.fla (the file you created in Unit C Project Builder 1) and save it as ultimatetoursD.fla. (*Hint*: If you did not create ultimatetoursC.fla in Unit C, see your instructor.)

2. Have the heading **Ultimate Tours** zoom out from a transparent text block.

3. After the heading appears, make the subheading **We Specialize in Exotic Adventures** appear.

4. Make each of the buttons (Treks, Tours, Cruises) scroll from off the bottom of the stage to their positions on the stage. Stagger the buttons so that each one scrolls after the other.

5. Make the logo text appear.

6. Assign a stop action after the homepage appears.

7. Assign a go-to action to the Cruises button to jump to the frame that has the Cruises screen.

8. Add a Cruises screen, then display the heading, subheading, and logo.

9. Create a motion-tweened animation that moves a boat across the screen.

10. Add a motion path that has a dip in it.

11. Attach the boat to the motion path, and orient it to the path.

12. Add the three placeholders (Cruise 1, Cruise 2, Cruise 3).

13. Add the Home button.

14. Test the movie, then compare your movie to Figure D-40.

FIGURE D-40
Completed Project Builder 1

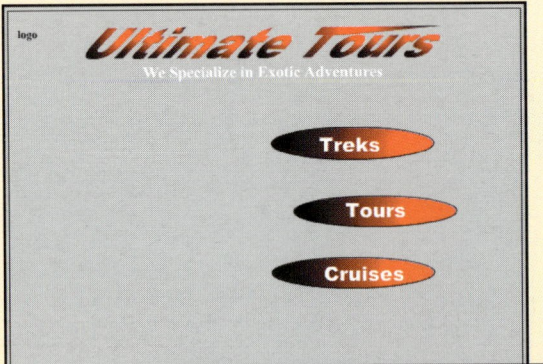

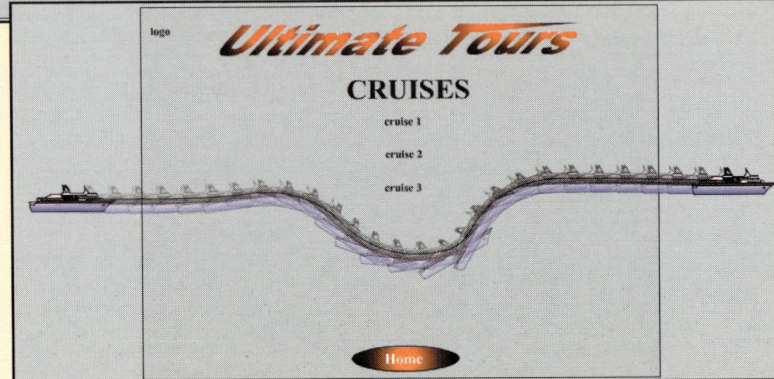

This is a continuation of Project Builder 2 in Unit C, which is the development of a personal portfolio. If you have not completed the previous project, see your instructor. The homepage has several categories, including the following:

- Personal data
- Contact information
- Previous employment
- Education
- Samples of your work

In this project, you will create several buttons for the sample animations screen and link them to the animations.

1. Open portfolioC.fla (the file you created in Project Builder 2, Unit C) and save it as **portfolioD.fla**. (*Hint*: In this file, the Tahoma font is used. You can replace this font with Impact or any other appropriate font on your computer.)
2. Display the Sample Animation screen and change the heading to Sample Animations.
3. Add layers and create buttons for the tweened animation, frame-by-frame animation, motion path animation, and animated text.
4. Create a tweened animation or use the passing cars animation from Unit C, and link it to the appropriate button on the Sample Animations screen.

5. Create a frame-by-frame animation, and link it to the appropriate button on the Sample Animations screen.
6. Create a motion path animation, and link it to the appropriate button on the Sample Animations screen.
7. Create several text animations, using scrolling, rotating, and zooming; link them to the appropriate button on the Sample Animations screen.

FIGURE D-41
Completed Project Builder 2

8. Add a layer and create a Home button that links the Sample Animation screen to the Home screen.
9. Create frame actions that cause the movie to return to the Sample Animations screen after each animation has been played.
10. Test the movie.
11. Save your work, then compare sample pages from your movie to Figure D-41.

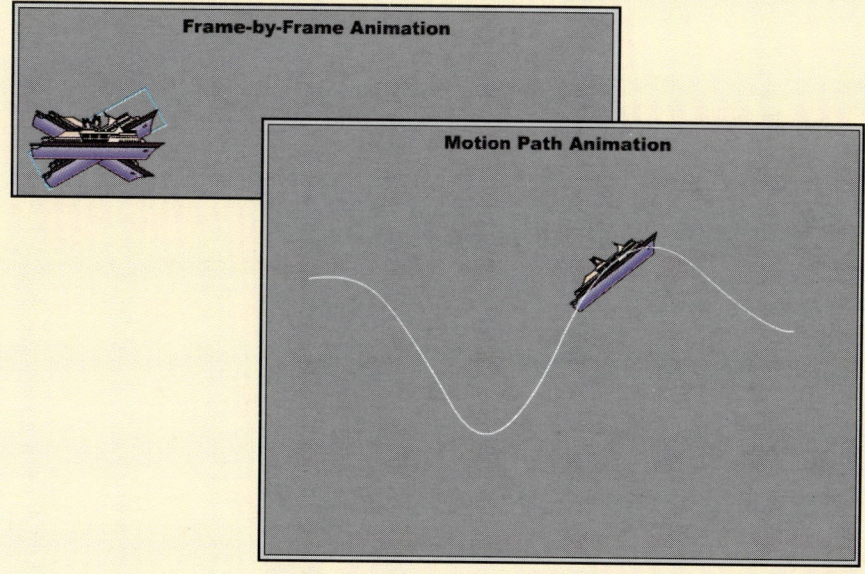

DESIGN PROJECT

Figure D-42 shows the homepage of a Web site. Study the figure and complete the following. For each question, indicate how you determined your answer.

1. Connect to the Internet and go to *www.course.com*. Navigate to the page for this book, click the Student Online Companion, then click the link for this unit.
2. Open a document in a word processor or open a new Macromedia Flash movie, save the file as **dpuUnitD**, then answer the following questions. (*Hint*: Use the Text Tool in Macromedia Flash.)
   - What seems to be the purpose of this site?
   - Who would be the target audience?
   - How might a frame animation be used in this site?
   - How might a motion-tweened animation be used?
   - How might a motion guide be used?
   - How might motion animation effects be used?
   - How might text be animated?

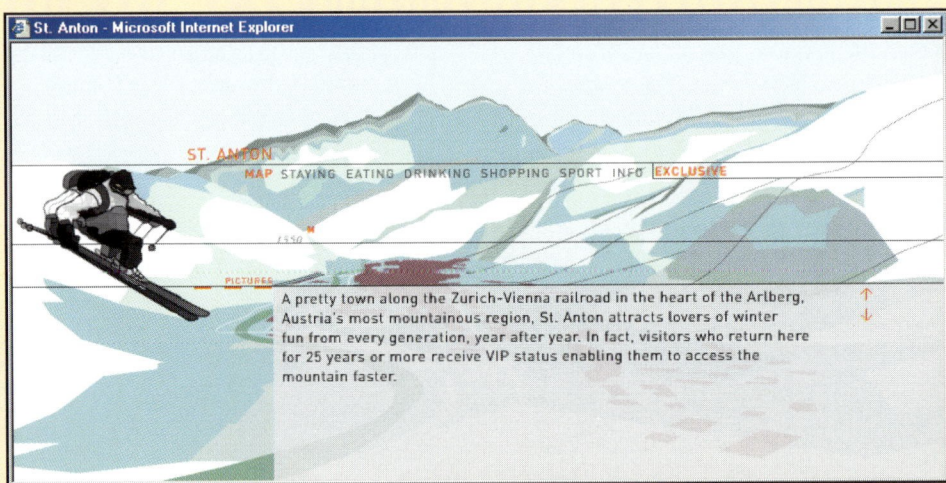

A pretty town along the Zurich-Vienna railroad in the heart of the Arlberg, Austria's most mountainous region, St. Anton attracts lovers of winter fun from every generation, year after year. In fact, visitors who return here for 25 years or more receive VIP status enabling them to access the mountain faster.

Your group can assign elements of the project to individual members, or work collectively to create the finished product.

Your group has been asked to develop a Web site for the school's summer basketball camp. The camp caters to kids from 6 to 12 years old. Participants are grouped by ability and given instruction on the fundamentals of basketball such as dribbling, passing, and shooting; the rules of the game; teamwork; and sportsmanship. A tournament is played at the end of the two-week camp.

Include the following in the Web site:

1. An initial screen with information about the camp (you provide the camp name, dates, and so on).
2. A black border around the stage.
3. A frame-by-frame animation.
4. A motion-tweened animation.
5. One or more animations that has an object(s) change location on the stage, rotate, change size, and change color.
6. One or more animations that has a text block(s) change location on the stage, rotate, change size, change color, zoom in or out, and fade in or out.
7. An animation that uses a motion guide.
8. An animation that changes the Ease setting.
9. Save the movie as **summerBB**, then compare your image to Figure D-43.

FIGURE D-43
Completed Group Project

Creating Animations

UNIT E

CREATING SPECIAL EFFECTS

1. Create shape-tweened animations.

2. Create a mask effect.

3. Add sound.

4. Add scenes.

5. Create a slide show presentation.

UNIT E

CREATING SPECIAL EFFECTS

Introduction

Now that you are familiar with the basics of Macromedia Flash, you can begin to apply some of the special features that can enhance a movie. Special effects can provide variety and add interest to a movie, as well as draw the viewer's attention to a location or event in the movie. One type of special effect is a morph. That is, making one shape appear to change into another shape over time, such as an airplane changing into a hot air balloon as it flies across the sky. Another special effect is a

spotlight that highlights an area(s) of the movie or reveals selected contents on the stage. You can use sound effects to enhance a movie by creating moods and dramatizing events.

In addition to working with special effects, you now also have experience in developing several movies around one theme, Classic Car Club, and are ready to incorporate these individual movies into a single movie with several scenes. Scenes provide a way to organize a large movie that has several parts, such as a Web site.

Tools You'll Use

Sound settings

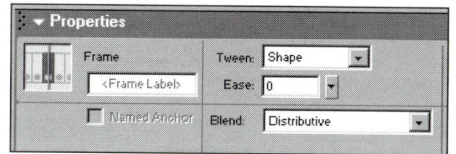

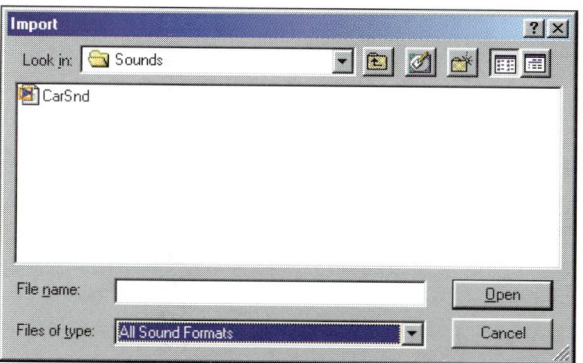

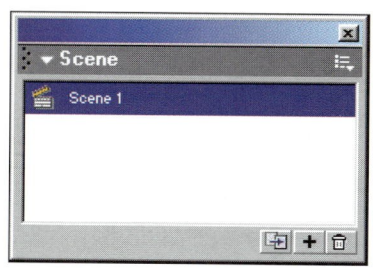

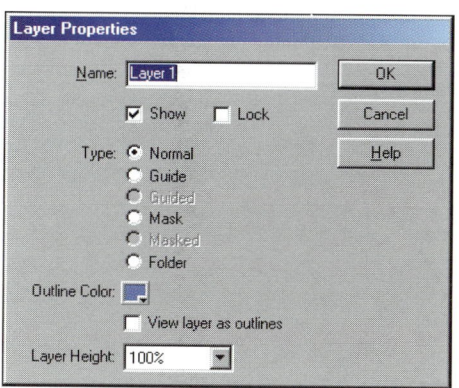

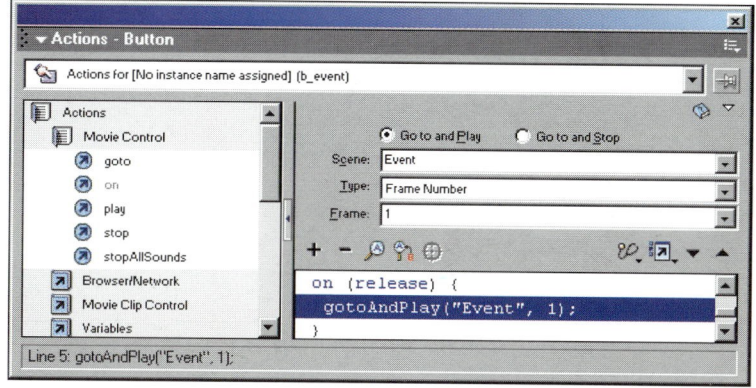

CREATE SHAPE TWEEN ANIMATIONS

What You'll Do

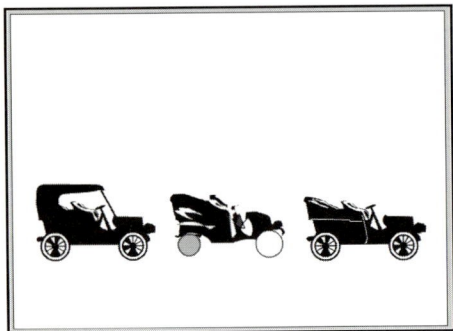

(▶) *In this lesson, you will create a shape-tweened animation and specify shape hints.*

Shape Tweening

In Unit D, you learned that you can use motion tweening to change the shape of an object. You accomplish this by selecting the Free Transform Tool and then dragging the handles. This process allows you to resize and skew the object. While this is easy and allows you to include motion along with the change in shape, there are two drawbacks. First, you are limited in the type of changes (resizing and skewing) that can be made to the shape of an object. Second, you must work with the same object throughout the animation. When you use shape tweening, however, you can have an animation change the shape of an object to any form you desire, and you can include two objects in the animation with two different shapes. As with motion tweening, you can use shape tweening to change other properties of an object, such as the color, location, and size.

Using Shape Tweening to Create a Morphing Effect

Morphing involves changing one object into another, sometimes unrelated, object. For example, you could turn a robot into a man, or turn a football into a basketball. The viewer sees the transformation as a series of incremental changes. In Macromedia Flash, the first object appears on the stage and changes into the second object as the movie plays. The number of frames included from the beginning to the end of this shape-tweened animation determines how quickly the morphing effect takes place. The first frame in the animation displays the first object and the last frame displays the second object. The in-between frames display the different shapes that are created as the first object changes into the second object.

When working with shape tweening you need to keep the following points in mind:

- Shape tweening can be applied only to editable graphics. To apply shape tweening to instances, groups, symbols, text blocks, or bitmaps, you can use the Break Apart command on the Modify menu to break apart an object and make it editable. When you break apart an instance of a symbol, it is no longer linked to the original symbol.

- You can shape tween more than one object at a time as long as all the objects are on the same layer. However, if the shapes are complex and/or if they involve movement in which the objects cross paths, the results may be unpredictable.
- You can use shape tweening to move an object in a straight line, but other options, such as rotating an object, are not available.
- You can use the settings in the Property inspector to set options (such as acceleration or deceleration) for a shape tween.
- Shape hints can be used to control more complex shape changes.

Properties Panel Options

Figure E-1 shows the Property inspector options for a shape tween. The options allow you to adjust several aspects of the animation, as described below.

- Adjust the rate of change between frames to create a more natural appearance during the transition by setting an ease value. Setting the value between -1 and -100 will begin the shape tween gradually and accelerate it toward the end of the animation. Setting the value between 1 and 100 will begin the shape tween rapidly and decelerate it toward the end of the animation. By default, the rate of change is set to 0, which causes a constant rate of change between frames.
- Choose a blend option. The Distributive option creates an animation in which the in-between shapes are smoother and more irregular. The Angular option preserves the corners and straight lines and works only with objects that have these features. If the objects do not have corners, Macromedia Flash will default to the Distributive option.

Shape Hints

You can use shape hints to control the shape's transition appearance during animation. Shape hints allow you to specify a location on the beginning object that corresponds to a location on the ending object. Figure E-2 shows two shape animations of the same objects, one using shape hints and the other not using shape hints. The figure also shows how the object being reshaped appears in one of the in-between frames. Notice that with the shape hints the object in the in-between frame is more recognizable.

FIGURE E-1

The Property inspector options for a shape tween

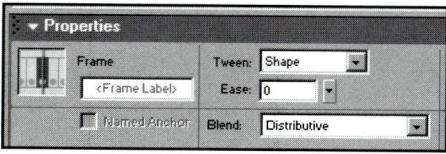

FIGURE E-2

Two shape animations: with and without shape hints

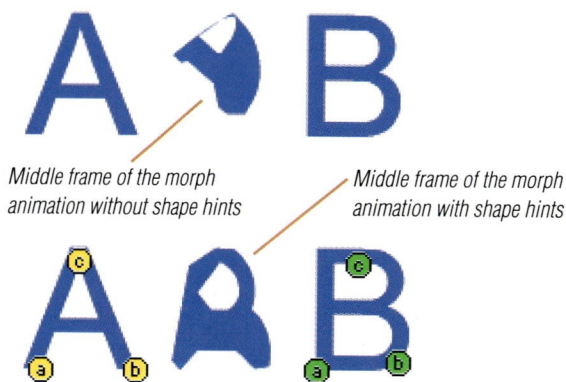

Middle frame of the morph animation without shape hints

Middle frame of the morph animation with shape hints

Create a shape tween animation

1. Open fle_1.fla, then save it as **antiqueCar.fla**.

2. Insert a keyframe in Frame 30 on the shape layer.

3. Click a blank area outside the stage, point to the left side of the top of the car, then drag the car top to the shape shown in Figure E-3.

4. Click anywhere on the shape layer between Frames 1 and 30.

5. Make sure the Property inspector is displayed, click the Tween list arrow, then click Shape.

6. Click Frame 1 on the shape layer, then play the movie.

7. Click Frame 30 on the shape layer.

8. If necessary, click the Arrow Tool on the toolbox, then drag a marquee around the car to select it.

9. Drag the car to the right side of the stage.

10. Play the movie, then save and close it.

You created a shape-tweened animation.

FIGURE E-3
The reshaped object

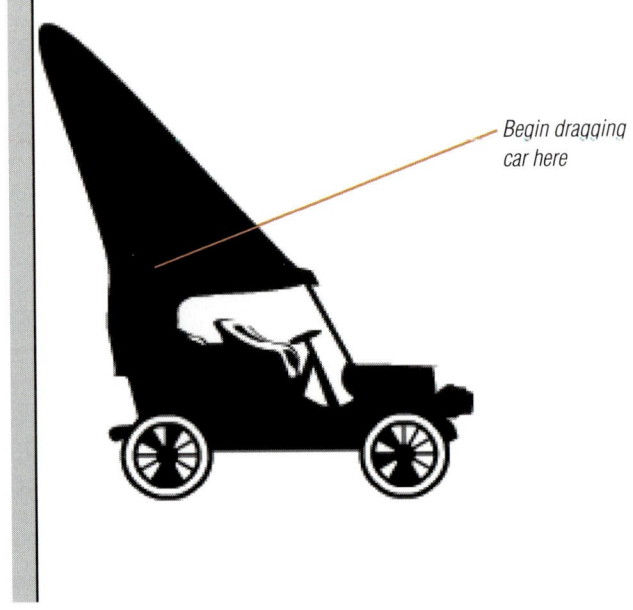

Begin dragging car here

FIGURE E-4

Positioning the car instance on the stage

Create a morphing effect

1. Open fle_2.fla, then save it as **morphCar.fla**.

2. Insert a blank keyframe in Frame 40 on the morph layer.

   TIP Inserting a blank keyframe prevents the object in the preceding keyframe from automatically being inserted into the blank frame.

3. Click the Edit Multiple Frames icon on the timeline.

   Turning on the Edit Multiple Frames will allow you to align the two objects to be morphed.

4. Make sure the Library panel is open.

5. Drag the g_antiqueCarTopDown graphic symbol from the Library panel directly on top of the car on the stage, as shown in Figure E-4.

   TIP Use the arrow keys to move the object in small increments.

6. Make sure that the antiqueCarTopDown object is selected, click Modify on the menu bar, then click Break Apart.

7. Click the Edit Multiple Frames icon on the timeline to turn off the feature.

8. Click anywhere between Frames 1 and 40 on the morph layer, click the Tween list arrow on the Property inspector, then click Shape.

9. Play the movie, then save your work.

   The first car morphs into the second car.

You created a morphing effect.

Adjust the rate of change in a shape-tweened animation

1. Click Frame 40 on the morph layer.

2. If necessary, click the Arrow Tool on the toolbox, then drag a marquee around the car to select it.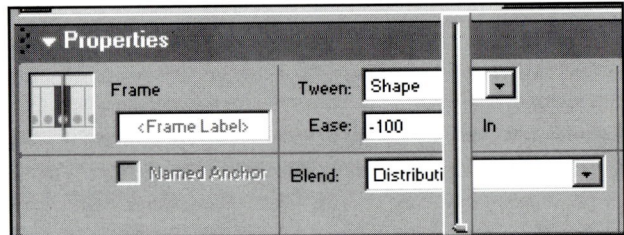

3. Drag the car to the right side of the stage.

4. Click Frame 1 on the morph layer.

5. Click the Ease list arrow in the Property inspector, then drag the slider down to **–100**, as shown in Figure E-5.

6. Click Frame 1 on the timeline, then play the movie.

7. Repeat Steps 4 and 5, but change the value to 100.

8. Click Frame 1 on the timeline, then play the movie.

   The car starts out fast and slows down as the morph process is completed.

9. Save your work, then close the movie.

You added motion to a shape-tweened animation and changed the Ease values.

Changing the Ease value for the morph

FIGURE E-6

Positioning a shape hint

FIGURE E-7

Adding shape hints

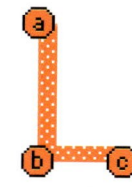

FIGURE E-8

Matching shape hints

Use shape hints

1. Open fle_3.fla, then save it as **shapeHints.fla**.

2. Play the movie and notice how the L morphs into a Z.

3. Click Frame 15 on the timeline, the midpoint of the animation, then notice the shape.

4. Click Frame 1 on the hints layer to display the first object.

5. Make sure the object is selected, click Modify in the menu bar, point to Shape, then click Add Shape Hint.

6. Drag the Shape Hint icon to the location shown in Figure E-6.

7. Repeat Steps 5 and 6 to set a second and third Shape Hint icon, as shown in Figure E-7.

8. Click Frame 30 on the hints layer, then drag the Shape Hint icons to match Figure E-8.

   TIP   The shape hints are stacked on top of each other.

9. Click Frame 15 on the hints layer, then notice how the object is more recognizable now that the shape hints have been added.

10. Play the movie.

11. Save your work, then close the movie.

You added shape hints to a morph animation.

CREATE A MASK EFFECT

What You'll Do

Cla

'ar

'lut

 In this lesson, you will apply a mask effect.

Understanding Mask Layers

A mask layer allows you to cover up the objects on another layer(s) and, at the same time, create a window through which you can view various objects on the other layer. You can determine the size and shape of the window and specify whether it moves around the stage. Moving the window around the stage can create effects such as a spotlight that highlights certain contents on the stage, drawing the viewer's attention to a specific location. Because the window can move around the stage, you can use a mask layer to reveal only the area of the stage and the objects you want the viewer to see.

You need at least two layers on the timeline when you are working with a mask layer. One layer, called the mask layer, contains the window object through which you view the objects on the second layer below. The second layer, called the masked layer, contains the object(s) that are viewed through the window. Figure E-9 shows how a mask layer works: The top part of the figure shows the mask

layer with the window in the shape of a circle. The next part of the figure shows the layer to be masked. The last part of the figure shows the results of applying the mask. Figure E-9 illustrates the simplest use of a mask layer. In most cases, you want to have other objects appear on the stage and have the mask layer affect only a certain portion of the stage.

Following is the process for using a mask layer:

- Select an original layer that will become the masked layer—it contains the objects that you want to display through the mask layer window.
- Insert a new layer above the masked layer that will become the mask layer. A mask layer always masks the layer(s) immediately below it.
- Draw a filled shape, such as a circle, or create an instance of a symbol that will become the window on the mask layer. Macromedia Flash will ignore bitmaps, gradients, transparency colors, and line styles on a mask layer. On a mask layer, filled areas become

Creating Special Effects

transparent and non-filled areas become opaque.

- Select the new layer and open the Layer Properties dialog box after selecting the Layer command on the Modify menu, then choose Mask. Macromedia Flash converts the layer to become the mask layer.

- Select the original layer and open the Layer Properties dialog box after selecting the Layer command on the Modify menu, then choose Masked. Macromedia Flash converts the layer to become the masked layer.
- Lock both the mask and masked layers.
- To mask additional layers: Drag an existing layer to beneath the mask

layer, or create a new layer beneath the mask layer and use the Layer Properties dialog box to convert it to a masked layer.

- To unlink a masked layer: Drag it above the mask layer, or select it and select Normal from the Layer Properties dialog box.

FIGURE E-9

A mask layer with a window

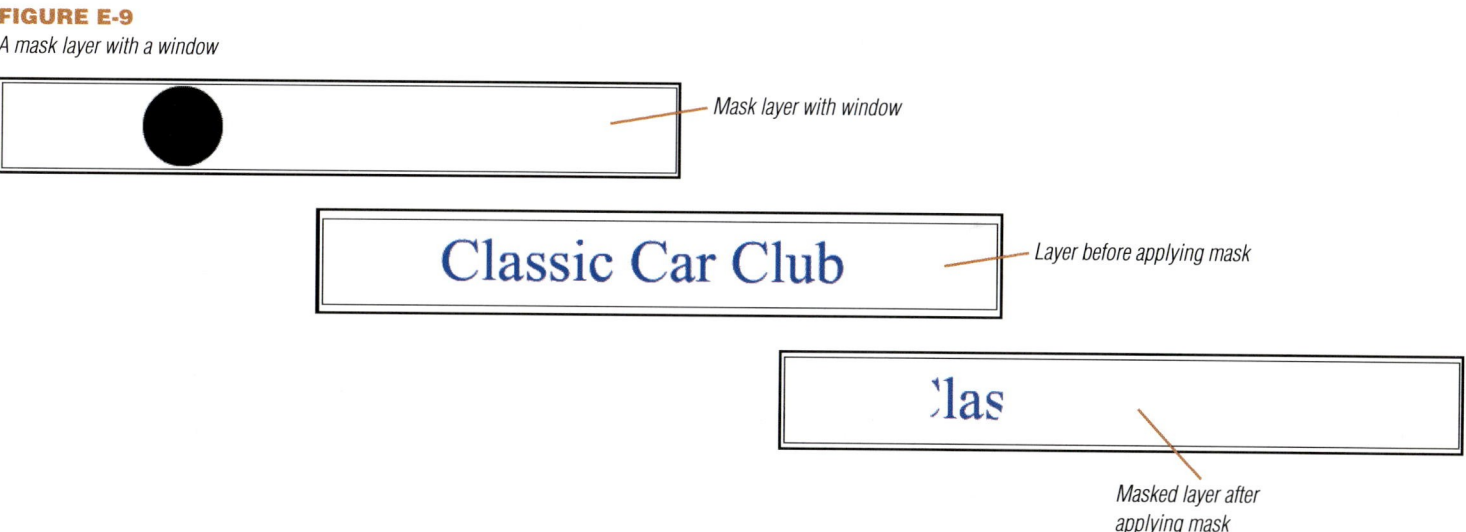

Mask layer with window

Classic Car Club

Layer before applying mask

las

Masked layer after applying mask

Create a mask layer

1. Open fle_4.fla, then save it as **classicCC.fla**.

2. Create a new layer on top of the heading layer, then rename it **mask**.

3. Click the Oval Tool on the toolbox, click the Stroke Color Tool, then click the No Stroke icon on the top row of the color palette.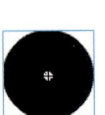

4. Click the Fill Color Tool on the toolbox, then click the black color swatch in the left column of the color palette.

5. Draw the circle shown in Figure E-10, click the Arrow Tool on the toolbox, draw a marquee around the circle to select it, click Insert on the menu bar, then click Create Motion Tween.

6. Insert a keyframe in Frame 40 on the mask layer, then drag the circle to the position shown in Figure E-11.

7. Click the mask layer on the timeline to select it, click Modify on the menu bar, then click Layer to open the Layer Properties dialog box.

8. Verify that the Show option is selected in the Name section, click the Lock option, click the Mask option in the Type section, then click OK.

   The mask layer has a shaded mask icon next to it on the timeline.

9. Play the movie and notice how the circle object covers the text in the heading layer as it moves across the stage.

10. Save your work.

You created a mask layer.

FIGURE E-12

The completed Layer Properties dialog box

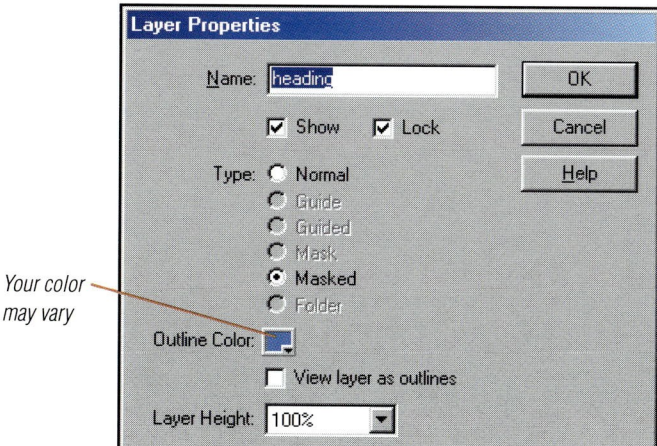

Your color
may vary

Create a masked layer

1. Click the heading layer to select it, click Modify on the menu bar, then click Layer to open the Layer Properties dialog box.

2. Verify that the Show option is selected in the Name section, click the Lock option, click the Masked option in the Type section, compare your dialog box to Figure E-12, then click OK.

   The heading layer appears indented and has a shaded masked icon next to it on the timeline.

3. Play the movie and notice how the circle object acts as a window to display the text on the heading layer.

4. Save your work, then close the movie.

You created a masked layer.

ADD SOUND

What You'll Do

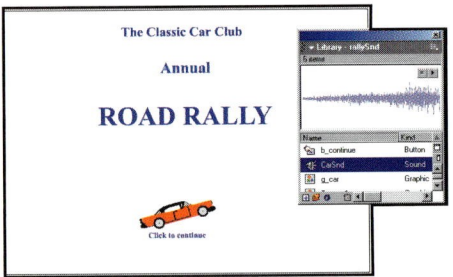

In this lesson, you will add sound to an animation.

Incorporating Animation and Sound

Sound can be extremely useful in a Macromedia Flash movie. Sounds are often the only effective way to convey an idea, elicit an emotion, dramatize a point, and provide feedback to a user's action, such as clicking a button. How would you describe in words or show in an animation the sound a whale makes? Think about how chilling it is to hear the footsteps on the stairway of the haunted house. Consider how useful it is to hear the pronunciation of "Buenos Dias" as you are studying Spanish. All types of sounds can be incorporated into a Macromedia Flash movie: for example, CD-quality music that might be used as background for a movie; narrations that help explain what the user is seeing; various sound effects, such as a car horn beeping; and recordings of special events such as a presidential speech or a rock concert.

Following is the process for adding a sound to a movie:

- Import a sound file into the movie; Macromedia Flash places the sound into the movie's Library.
- Create a new layer.
- Select the desired frame in the new layer and drag the sound symbol to the stage.

You can place more than one sound file on a layer, and you can place sounds on layers with other objects. However, it is recommended that you place each sound on a separate layer as though it were a sound channel, as shown in Figure E-13. In Figure E-13, the sound layer shows a wave pattern that extends from Frame 1 to Frame 40. The wave pattern gives some indication of the volume of the sound at any particular frame. The higher spikes in the pattern indicate a louder sound. The wave pattern also gives some indication of the pitch. The denser the wave pattern, the lower the pitch. You can alter the sound by

adding or removing frames. However, removing frames may create undesired effects. It is best to make changes to a sound file using a sound-editing program.

You can use options in the Property inspector (shown in Figure E-14) to synchronize a sound to an event—such as clicking a button—and to specify special effects—such as fade in and fade out. You can import the following sound file formats into Macromedia Flash:

- WAV (Windows only)
- AIFF (Macintosh only)
- MP3 (Windows or Macintosh)

If you have QuickTime 4 or later installed on your computer, you can import these additional sound file formats:

- AIFF (Windows or Macintosh)
- Sound Designer II (Macintosh only)
- Sound Only QuickTime Movies (Windows or Macintosh)
- Sun AU (Windows or Macintosh)
- System 7 Sounds (Macintosh only)
- WAV (Windows or Macintosh)

A sound symbol displayed on the timeline

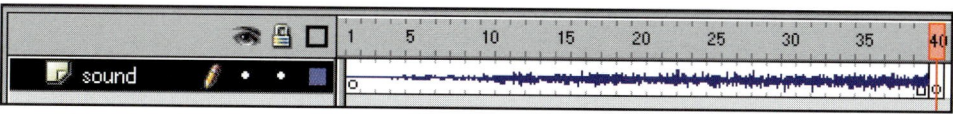

The sound options in the Property inspector

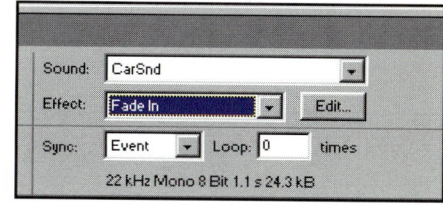

Add sound to a movie

1. Open fle_5.fla, then save it as **rallySnd.fla**.

2. Click the stopmovie layer, insert a new layer, then rename it **carSnd**.

3. Insert a keyframe in Frame 72 on the carSnd layer.

4. Click File on the menu bar, then click Import.

5. Use the Import dialog box to locate the CarSnd.wav file, then click Open.

6. Click Window on the menu bar, then click Library.

7. Drag the CarSnd sound symbol to the stage, as shown in Figure E-15.

8. Test the movie, then close the test movie window.

9. Save your work.

You imported a sound and added it to a movie.

FIGURE E-15
Dragging the CarSnd symbol to the stage

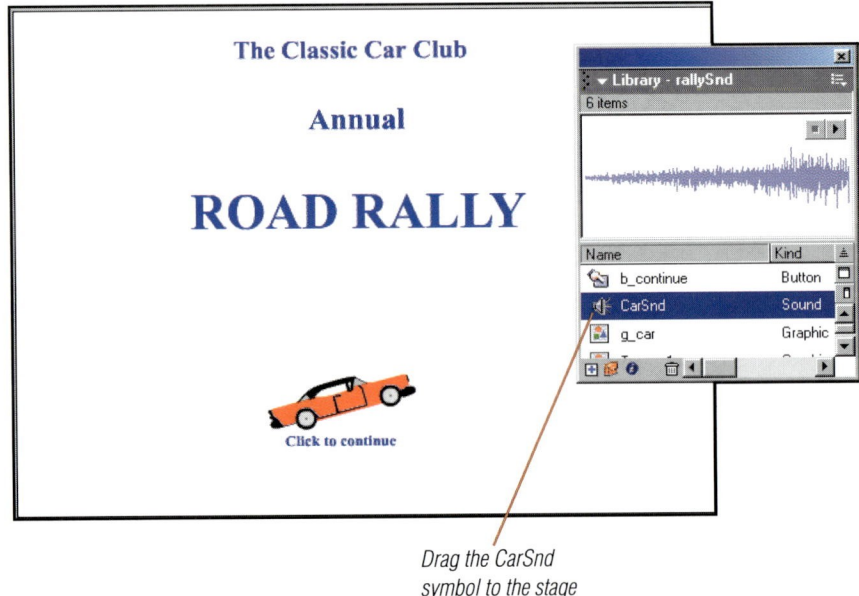

Drag the CarSnd symbol to the stage

FIGURE E-16

The button timeline with the sound layer

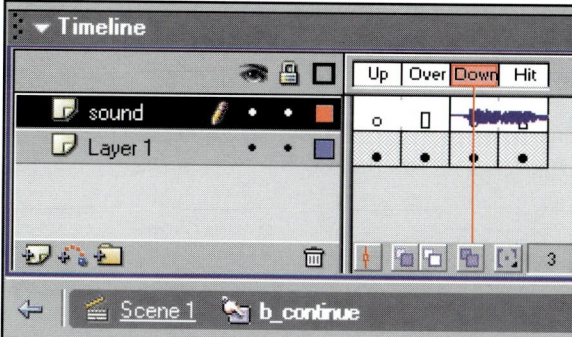

ADD SCENES

What You'll Do

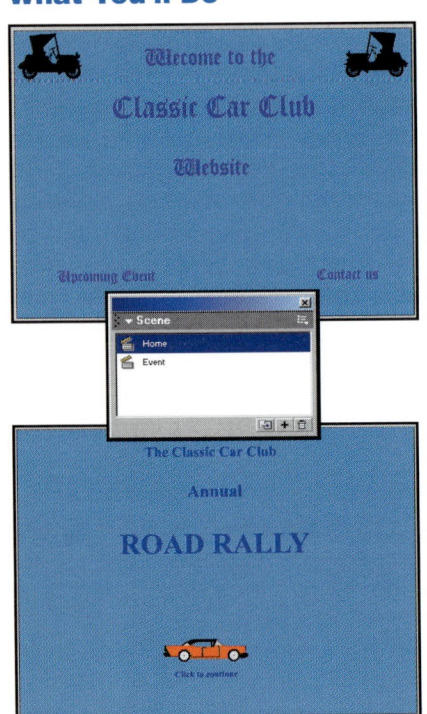

 In this lesson, you will add scenes to a movie and combine scenes from multiple movies into one movie.

Understanding Scenes

Until now you have been working with relatively short movies that have only a few layers and less than 100 frames. However, movies can be quite complex and extremely large. One way to help organize large movies is to use scenes. Just as with their celluloid equivalent, Macromedia Flash scenes are discrete parts of a movie. They have their own timeline and they can be played in any order you specify, or they can be linked through an interactive process that lets the user navigate to a desired scene.

QUICKTIP

There are no guidelines for the length or number of scenes appropriate for any size movie. The key is to determine how best to break down a large movie so that the individual parts are easier to develop, edit, and combine.

Working with Scenes

To add a scene to a movie, you choose Scene from the Insert menu or use the Scene command from the Modify menu. This displays the Scene panel and allows you to add a new scene. The Scene panel can be used to accomplish the following:

- Rename a scene by double-clicking the scene name, then typing in the new name.
- Duplicate a scene by selecting it, then clicking the Duplicate Scene icon.
- Add a scene by clicking the Add Scene icon.
- Delete a scene by selecting it, then clicking the Delete scene icon.
- Reorder the scenes by dragging them up or down the list of scenes.

When a movie is played, the scenes are played in the order they are listed in the Scene panel. You can use the interactive features of Flash, such as a stop action and buttons with `goto` actions to allow the user to jump to various scenes.

Following is the process for combining scenes from several movies into one movie:

- Open the movie that will be used as Scene 1.
- Insert a new scene into the movie.
- Open the movie that will be used as Scene 2.

- Copy the frames from the second movie into Scene 2 of the first movie.
- Continue the process until the scenes for all the movies have been copied into one movie.

The home page for the Classic Car Club Web site, shown in Figure E-17, will become the first scene of a multi-scene movie.

FIGURE E-17

The Classic Car Club home page

Add and name a scene

1. Open fle_6 movie, then save it as **cccHome.fla**.

2. Click Modify on the menu bar, then click Scene to open the Scene panel.

3. Double-click Scene 1 in the Scene panel, type **Home**, then press [Enter] (Win) or [return] (Mac).

4. Click the Add scene icon, double-click Scene 2, type **Event**, compare your Scene panel with Figure E-18, then press [Enter] (Win) or [return] (Mac). ⊞

   The stage is blank when the new scene, Event, is created.

5. Click Home in the Scene panel and notice that the timeline changes to the Home scene.

6. Click Event in the Scene panel and notice that the timeline changes to the Event scene, which is blank.

7. Test the movie and notice how the movie moves from Scene 1 to the blank Scene 2.

8. Close the test movie window, then save your work.

You added a scene and used the Scene panel to rename the scenes.

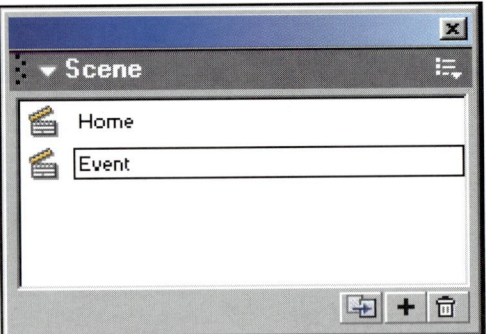

FIGURE E-19

Selecting all the frames

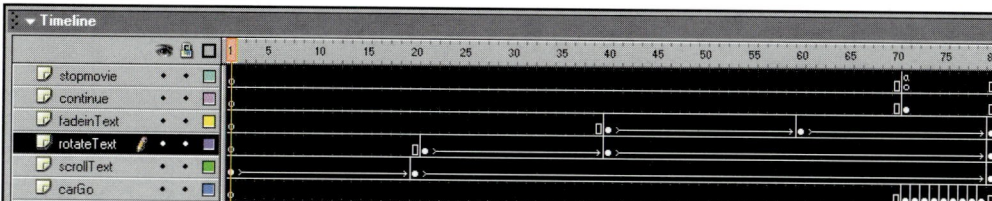

Copying frames to add to a scene

1. Open rallySnd.fla.

2. Click Edit on the menu bar, then click Select All Frames to select all the frames in all the layers, as shown in Figure E-19.

3. Click Edit on the menu bar, then click Copy Frames.

4. Close rallySnd.fla without saving the changes.

5. Click Window on the menu bar, then click cccHome.fla.

6. Make sure that the Event scene is selected.

7. Click Frame 1 on Layer 1 of the Event scene.

8. Click Edit on the menu bar, then click Paste Frames.

   The layers and frames from rallySnd.fla appear in the timeline.

9. Click Home in the Scene panel.

10. Test the movie and notice how the Home scene is played, followed by the Event scene.

11. Close the test movie window, then save your work.

You copied frames from one movie into a scene of another movie.

Add interactivity to scenes

1. Make sure that the Home scene is displayed.

2. If necessary, click the Arrow Tool on the toolbox, then click the Upcoming Event text button on the stage.

3. Click Window on the menu bar, then click Actions.

4. If necessary, click Actions, click Movie Control, then double-click goto in the Actions panel.

5. Click the Scene list arrow in the Actions panel, click Event, then compare your Actions panel to Figure E-20.

(continued)

MACROMEDIA FLASH E-22

FIGURE E-20

The completed Actions panel

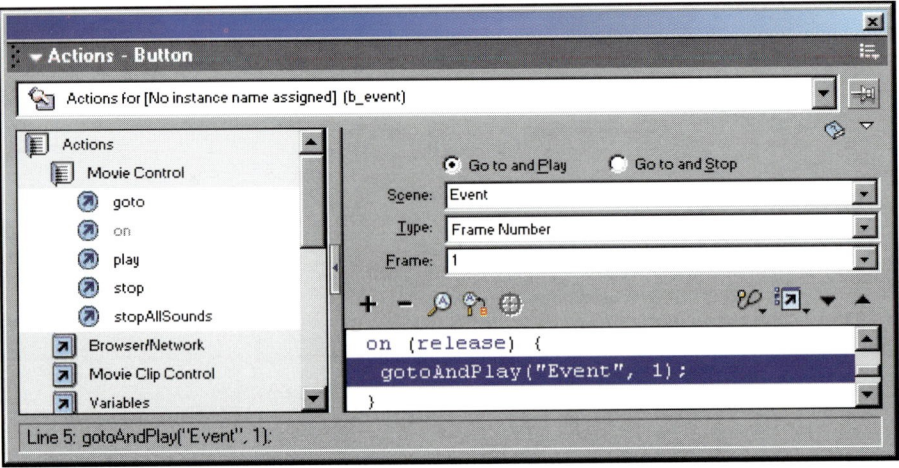

Creating Special Effects

6. Click Frame 1 on the stopmovie layer, double-click **stop** in the Actions panel, then compare your Actions panel to Figure E-21.

7. Test the movie, click the Upcoming Event button, then notice how the Home scene plays, followed by the Event scene.

8. Close the test movie window.

9. Save your work, then close the movie.

You added a scene, used the Scene panel to rename the scenes, and added interactivity to jump from one scene to another.

FIGURE E-21

Adding a **stop** *action*

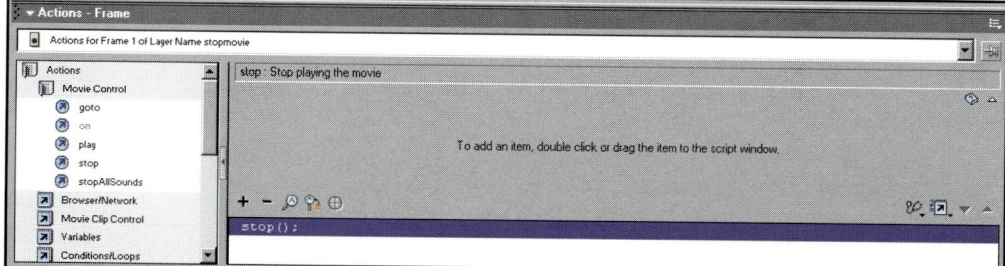

CREATE A SLIDE SHOW PRESENTATION

What You'll Do

 In this lesson, you will make changes to a slide show presentation by adding interactivity and transition effects.

Electronic Slide Shows

Electronic slide shows are useful when making presentations, such as a salesperson to potential buyers, a businessperson to interested investors, an executive to the Board of Directors, keynote speaker to an audience, or a professor to a group of students. The slide show can be stored on the hard drive or CD-ROM/DVD of a computer and projected on a large screen or simply delivered through the Internet to individual viewers. Slide shows—especially those that incorporate multimedia, including animation—can greatly enhance a presentation. The slides can include graphics that help illustrate specific content, bullets that summarize the main points, and sounds that add variety. Slide shows help in keeping the viewer interested in the content and in keeping them on track throughout the presentation.

There are various programs, such as Microsoft PowerPoint, that are specifically designed to create electronic slide shows. These programs have several advantages. They are relatively inexpensive, easy to

learn, and easy to use. They come with templates for the layout of the slides, color scheme, and overall design, as shown in Figure E-22. In addition, they can include sound, video, and animation developed with other programs. Despite this, there are some disadvantages to using these programs. The programs create presentations that are primarily linear, with limited ability to jump easily from one slide to any other except the previous or next slide. The slide shows are designed to be controlled by a presenter or to self-run, with no interaction by the viewer. If you use a design template, the slide show may resemble others in its look and feel. Finally, these programs allow you to assemble various elements, but are limited in their capabilities to create or edit these elements, especially animations.

You can use Macromedia Flash to create an electronic slide show that provides the viewer more flexibility. Each scene in a movie could be a slide. The show could be designed to be controlled by either a presenter or a viewer by providing navigation buttons that allow them to jump to any scene. Alternately, the show could be self-running and include only start and stop buttons. In addition, you can use special effects, such as dissolves or wipes, to transition from one scene to another. A dissolve transition effect could be created with a motion tween that includes a zoom out and an alpha setting that goes from 0 to 100. A wipe transition effect could be created by using a mask that reveals each scene by moving from off the stage to covering the stage from various angles.

Macromedia Flash provides a great deal of flexibility and sophistication when designing and developing electronic slide shows and can be used to create compelling and unique presentations.

FIGURE E-22

Templates provided by a slide show program

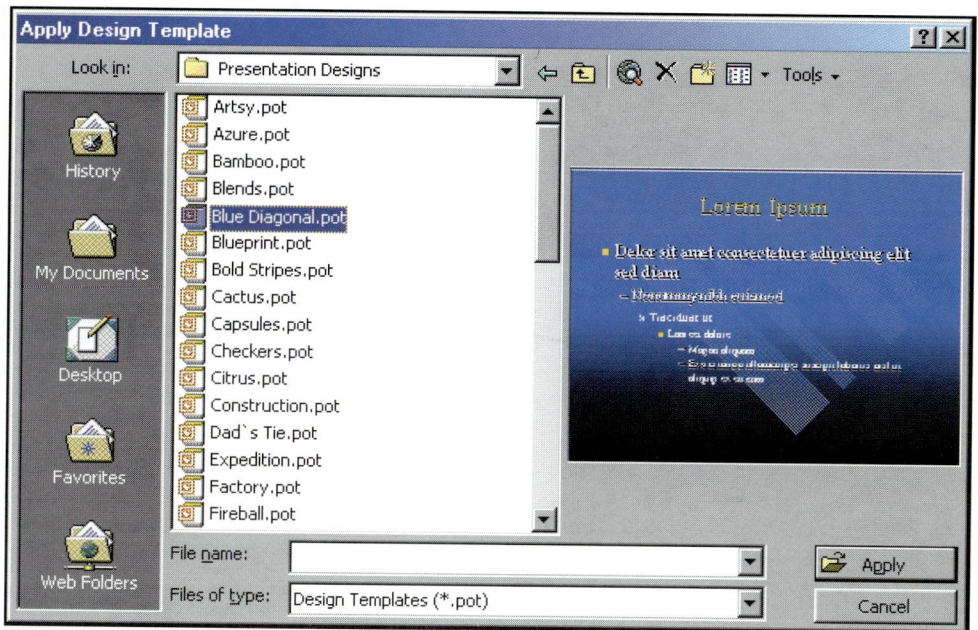

Test a slide show presentation

1. Open fle_7.fla, then save it as **coolCars.fla**.

2. Verify that the Scene panel is open, then click Car1 to display the Car1 scene.

3. Repeat Step 2 for the other scenes, then click Start to display the Start scene.

4. Click Control on the menu bar, then click Test Movie.

5. Click the go button on the road sign to display the next scene.

6. Click the navigation buttons to display each scene, as shown in Figure E-23.

7. Close the test movie window.

8. Click View on the menu bar, point to Magnification, then click 50%.

9. Save your work.

You tested a slide show presentation.

The navigation buttons

Navigation buttons

Creating Special Effects

FIGURE E-24

Positioning the rectangle

Add transition effects

1. Click Car1 in the Scene panel, then add a new layer named **mask** above the image layer.

2. Click the Fill Color Tool on the toolbox, then click the black color swatch in the top left column of the color palette.

3. Click the Rectangle Tool on the toolbox, draw a black rectangle over the stage, then drag it to the left of the stage, as shown in Figure E-24.

4. Create a motion tween using Frames 1 through 20 that scrolls the rectangle to the right until it covers the entire stage.

5. Click the mask layer on the timeline, click Modify on the menu bar, click Layer, click the Lock check box, click the Mask option, then click OK.

6. Click the image layer on the timeline, click Modify on the menu bar, click Layer, click Lock, click Masked, then click OK.

7. Repeat Step 5 for the backgrnd layer.

8. Test the movie and notice the transition effect (wipe from left to right) when the Car1 scene is displayed.

9. Close the test movie window.

10. Repeat Steps 1 through 6 for the Car2 and Car3 scenes, but have the mask (rectangle) scroll in from top to bottom for Car2, and diagonally from left to right for Scene 3.

11. Test the movie, close the test movie window, then save your work.

You created transition effects.

Create a shape-tweened animation.

1. Open fle_8.fla, then save it as **skillsdemoE.fla**.
2. Insert a keyframe in Frames 45 and 65 on the face2 layer.
3. Use the Arrow Tool to drag and reshape the mouth of face2 into a smile.
4. Display the Properties panel.
5. Click anywhere between Frames 45 and 65.
6. Use the Properties panel to specify a Shape Tween.
7. Play the movie.
8. Save your work.

Create a morphing effect.

1. Insert a keyframe in Frame 65 on the number1 layer.
2. Use the Arrow Tool to select 1, then break it apart.
3. Insert a blank keyframe in Frame 85 on the number1 layer.
4. Display the Library panel.
5. Click Edit Multiple Frames on the timeline to turn on this feature.
6. Drag the g_number2 symbol and place it directly over the 1.
7. Break apart the 2 symbol.
8. Turn off the Edit Multiple Frames feature.
9. Click anywhere between Frames 65 and 85 on the number1 layer.

10. Use the Properties panel to specify a Shape tween.
11. Play the movie, then save your work.

Use shape hints.

1. Click Frame 65 of the number1 layer.
2. With the 1 selected, add two shape hints, one at the top and one at the bottom of the 1.
3. Click Frame 85 of the number1 layer, then position the shape hints accordingly.
4. Play the movie, then save your work.

Create and apply a mask layer.

1. Insert a layer above the heading layer, then name it **mask**.
2. Click Frame 1 on the mask layer.
3. Drag the g_face graphic from the Library panel to the left side of the word "How".
4. Insert a Motion tween.
5. Insert a keyframe in Frame 45 on the mask layer.
6. Drag the face to the right side of the word "faces?".
7. Click the mask layer on the timeline, click Modify on the menu bar, then click Layer.
8. Use the Layer Properties dialog box to specify a Mask layer that is locked.
9. Click heading in the timeline, then use the Layer Properties dialog box to specify a Masked layer that is locked.
10. Play the movie, then save your work.

Add and name a scene.

1. Display the Scene panel.
2. Rename Scene 1 **faces**.
3. Add a new scene, then rename it **correct**.
4. Type a heading, **That's correct**, with red, Arial, 72 pt, and center it near the top of the stage.
5. Change the name of Layer1 to **heading**.
6. Insert a keyframe in Frame 30 on the heading layer.
7. Test the movie.
8. Save your work.

Add interactivity to a scene.

1. Display the faces scene, add a new layer above the face2 layer, and rename it **stopmovie**.
2. Insert a keyframe in Frame 85 on the stopmovie layer and add a `stop` action to it.
3. Use the Arrow Tool to select the Continue button on the stage.
4. Use the Actions panel to assign a `goto` action to the Continue button that jumps the movie to the message scene.
5. Test the movie.
6. Save your work.

Creating Special Effects

Add sound to a movie.

1. Use the Scene panel to display the correct scene.
2. Add a layer and name it **applause**.
3. Click Frame 1 on the applause layer.
4. Display the Library panel and drag the applause sound symbol to the stage.
5. Test the movie.
6. Save your work.

Add a transition effect.

1. Display the correct scene.
2. Add a layer, name it mask, then specify it as a mask layer.
3. Draw a rectangle, then create a motion tween that causes the rectangle to move from above the stage to covering the stage.
4. Specify the heading as a masked layer.
5. Test the movie.
6. Save your work, then compare your images to Figure E-25.

FIGURE E-25
Completed Skills Review

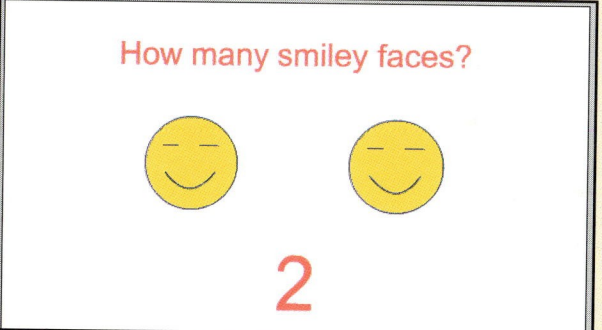

The Ultimate Tours travel company has asked you to design several sample animations for their Web site. Figure E-26 shows a sample Cruises screen with morphed and shape-tweened animations, as well as a mask effect. Using these or one of the sites you created in Unit D as a guide, complete the following for the Cruises screen of the Ultimate Tours Web site:

1. Open ultimatetoursD.fla (the file you created in Unit D Project Builder 1) and save it as **utlimatetoursE.fla**. (*Hint*: If you did not create ultimatetoursD.fla in Unit D, see your instructor.)
2. Create a morph animation.
3. Create a shape-tweened animation.
4. Create a button that goes to another scene.

For the new scene:

5. Create a scene and give it an appropriate name.
6. Rename Scene 1.
7. Create an animation using a mask effect in the new scene.
8. Add a sound to the scene.
9. Add an action to go to the Cruises screen when the animation is done.
10. Test the movie, then compare your image to Figure E-26.

FIGURE E-26
Completed Project Builder 1

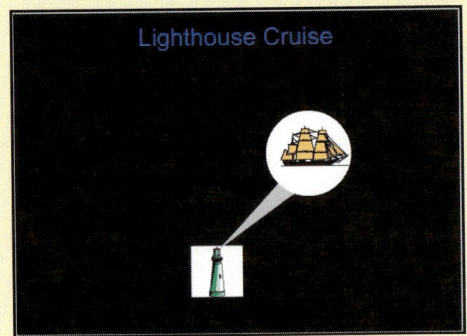

Creating Special Effects

This is a continuation of Project Builder 2 in Unit D, which is the development of a personal portfolio. If you have not completed the previous project, see your instructor. The homepage has several categories, including the following:

- Personal data
- Contact information
- Previous employment
- Education
- Samples of your work

In this project, you will create several buttons for the Sample Animations screen and link them to the animations.

1. Open portfolioD.fla (the file you created in Project Builder 2, Unit D) and save it as **portfolioE.fla**. (*Hint*: In this file, the Tahoma font is used. You can replace this font with Impact or any other appropriate font on your computer.)
2. Display the Sample Animations screen.
3. Add layers and create buttons for a shape-tweened animation, morph animation, and an animation using shape hints.
4. Add a new scene and create the morph animation in this scene.
5. Rename the new scene and Scene 1 using appropriate names.
6. Add a sound to the scene.

7. Create frame actions that cause the movie to return to the Sample Animations screen after each animation has been played.
8. Test the movie.

FIGURE E-27
Completed Project Builder 2

9. Save your work, then compare your image to Figure E-27.

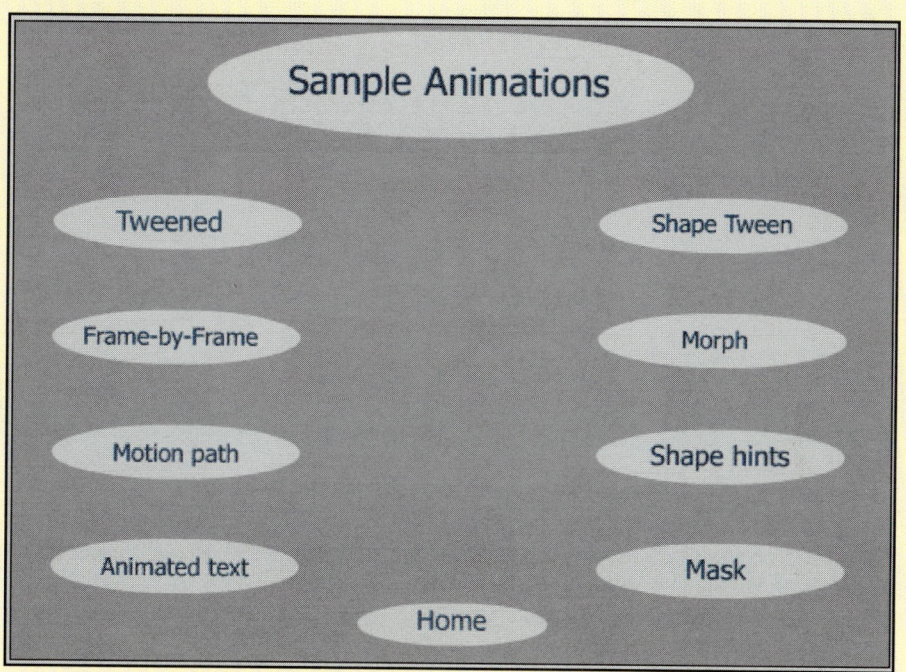

DESIGN PROJECT

Figure E-28 shows the homepage of a Web site. Study the figure and complete the following questions. For each question, indicate how you determined your answer.

1. Connect to the Internet and go to *www.course.com*. Navigate to the page for this book, click the Student Online Companion, then click the link for this unit.
2. Open a document in a word processor or open a new Macromedia Flash movie, save the file as **dpuUnitE**, then answer the following questions. (*Hint*: Use the Text Tool in Macromedia Flash.)
   - What seems to be the purpose of this site?
   - Who would be the target audience?
   - How might a shape-tweened animation be used in this site?
   - How might a morph animation be used?
   - How might a mask effect be used?
   - How might sound be used?
   - What suggestions would you make to improve the design and why?

FIGURE E-28
Design Project

GROUP PROJECT

Your group can assign elements of the project to individual members, or work collectively to create the finished product.

Your group has been asked to develop a Web site illustrating the signs of the zodiac. The introductory screen will have a heading with a mask effect and links to the 12 zodiac signs. Selecting a sign will display another screen with a different graphic to represent the sign and information about the sign, as well as special effects such as sound, shape animation, and morphing. Each information screen will be linked to the introductory screen.

1. Open a new movie, then save it as **zodiac.fla**. (*Hint*: In this file, the Stonehenge font is used. You can replace this font with any appropriate font on your computer.)
2. Create an introductory screen for the Web site with the following:
   - A heading
   - A mask layer that creates a spotlight effect
   - Several graphics
   - Two graphics that are buttons that jump to another scene when clicked
3. Create a second scene that has
   - A morph animation using two graphics
   - A sound
   - A Home button with a sound when clicked

4. Create a third scene that has
   - A shape animation using shape hints
   - A Home button with a sound when clicked

5. Rename all of the scenes.
6. Test the movie.
7. Save the movie, then compare your image to Figure E-29.

FIGURE E-29
Completed Group Project

UNIT A

GETTING STARTED WITH FIREWORKS MX

1. Create a new document and import files.

2. Learn about the Macromedia Fireworks window.

3. Work with bitmap and vector images.

4. Create and modify text.

GETTING STARTED WITH FIREWORKS MX

Fireworks MX is a graphics program for the Web. Fireworks is designed so that Web enthusiasts and professionals, such as developers and graphic artists, can create, edit, and apply functionality to optimized files. Many Fireworks MX tasks are compartmentalized—artists can enhance or create designs without disturbing the programming added by developers, and vice versa. In Fireworks, you can work with files created by other graphic design programs, and save and export files you create in Fireworks to other programs. Fireworks MX integrates seamlessly with other Macromedia applications, including Dreamweaver, Macromedia Flash, FreeHand, ColdFusion, and Director. It operates smoothly with key associated applications, such as Adobe Photoshop and Microsoft FrontPage.

Tools You'll Use

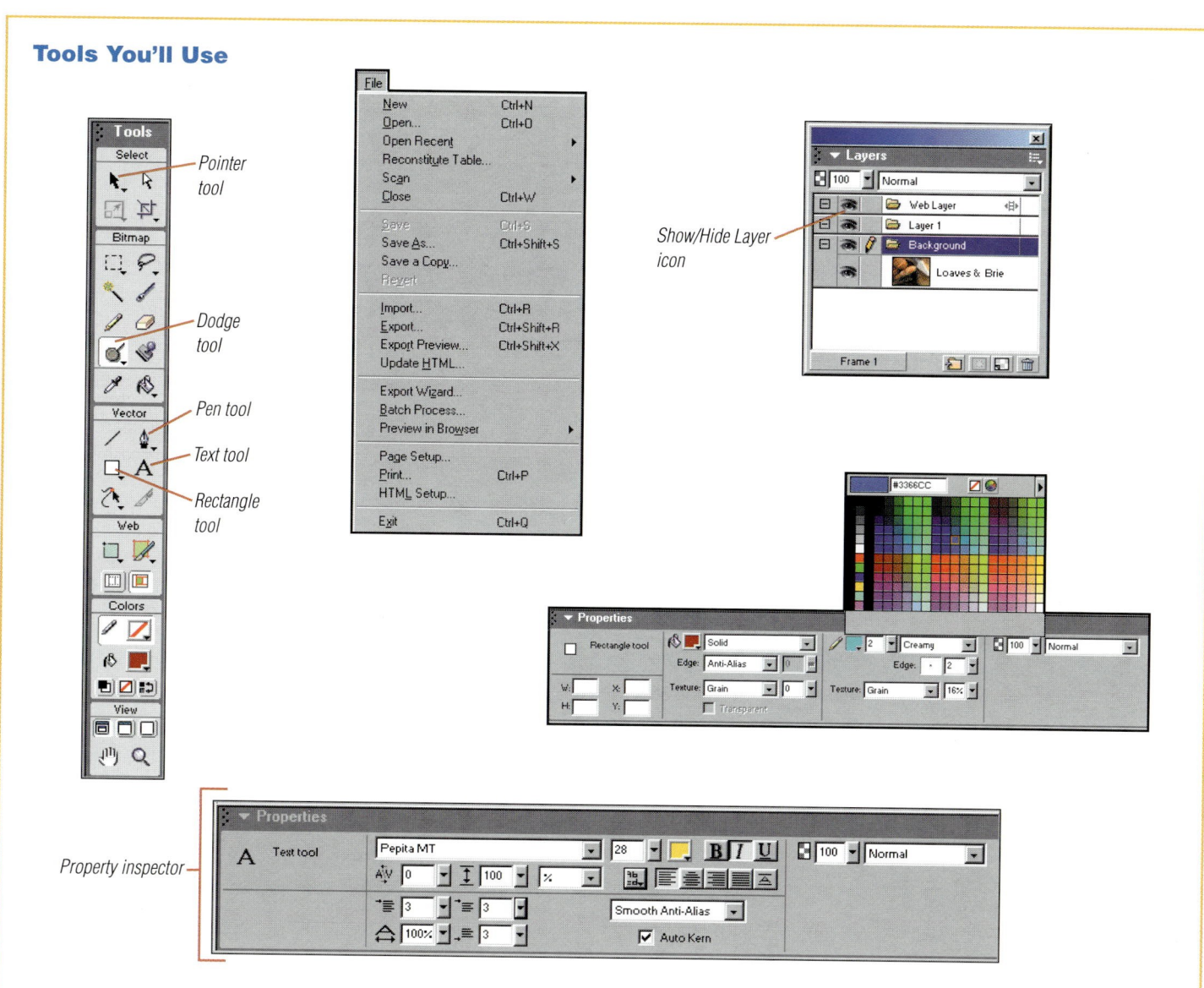

Pointer tool

Dodge tool

Pen tool

Text tool

Rectangle tool

Show/Hide Layer icon

Property inspector

CREATE A NEW DOCUMENT AND IMPORT FILES

What You'll Do

▶ In this lesson, you will start Fireworks, and then create a document and import files into it.

Understanding Fireworks

Fireworks MX is available on both Windows and Macintosh platforms. Its functions are geared toward creating dynamic graphics that will operate and interact efficiently on the Web. Many features maximize your ability to work with different file formats and different programs. For example, you can create, edit, and work with bitmap and vector images in the same document. You can easily add JavaScript-enabled interactive and animation to Fireworks images. The process Fireworks uses to optimize files is extremely effective in balancing the need for image quality with the requirement for reduced file size.

Working with Files

Fireworks files are known as **documents**. Although you can open or import a wide range of file formats, the files you create in Fireworks are **PNG** (Portable Network

Graphics) files and have a .PNG extension. Working with PNG files affords you substantial flexibility in how you export all or part of your image. You can slice an image into various parts and then individually optimize and export them in different formats. For example, you can save a photograph in your image as a JPEG and a line art portion of your image as a GIF. If you want to save a Fireworks PNG file as a PNG file for the Web, you must follow the standard optimization and export procedures that you would use for optimizing any file format. Table A-1 lists the file formats Fireworks supports for various functions.

You can create a new document, open an existing file, or import a file into a Fireworks document. You can also copy and paste or drag and drop images or text from other applications or from a scanner or digital camera into a Fireworks document.

To copy an image, select the image in the document window, press and hold [Alt] (Win) or [option] (Mac), then drag the object to a new location in the current document or to another document. You can also select the object on the Layers panel, click Edit on the menu bar, click Copy, make the target document active, click Edit on the menu bar, and then click Paste.

QUICKTIP

You can access Help in Fireworks by clicking Help on the menu bar and then by clicking Using Fireworks (Win), or Fireworks Help (Mac). You can also obtain updates and tips and search for information at the Fireworks MX Web site: *www.macromedia.com/software/fireworks* and by clicking links in the Answers panel.

TABLE A-1: Import and Export File Formats Supported in Fireworks MX

import & open		export
Adobe Illustrator	.ai, .art	CSS Layers
Animated GIF	.gif	Director
ASCII text	.txt	Dreamweaver Library
BMP	.bmp	Frames to Layers
CorelDRAW (uncompressed)	.cdr	HTML & Image
EPS	.eps	Illustrator 7
Fireworks MX PNG	.png	Images Only
FreeHand FH7 or higher	.fh	Layers to Frames
GIF	.gif	Lotus Domino Designer
HTML file	.htm, .html, .xhtm	Macromedia Flash SWF
JPEG	.jpg, .jpe, .jpeg	Photoshop PSD
Photoshop PSD	.psd	
PICT (Macintosh only)	.pict	
RTF	.rtf	
Targa	.tga	
TIFF	.tif, .tiff	
WBMP	.wbmp, .wbm	

Start Fireworks and create and save a new document

1. Click the Start button on the taskbar, point to All Programs, point to the Macromedia folder, then click the Macromedia Fireworks MX program icon (Win).

   TIP To start Fireworks on a Macintosh, double-click the hard drive icon, double-click the Applications folder, double-click the Fireworks MX folder, then double-click the Macromedia Fireworks program icon.

2. If necessary, close the Welcome dialog box.

3. Click File on the menu bar, then click New.

4. Type **375** in the Width text box, press [Tab], then type **375** in the Height text box.

5. Compare your dialog box to Figure A-1, accept the remaining default values, then click OK.

6. Click File on the menu bar, click Save As, type **sweetface** in the File name text box (Win) or Save As text box (Mac), click the Save in list arrow (Win) or Look in list arrow (Mac) to choose your destination drive, then click Save.

7. Compare your renamed document to Figure A-2.

You started Fireworks and then created and renamed a new document.

FIGURE A-1

New Document dialog box

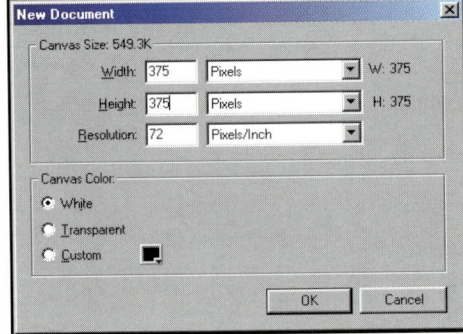

FIGURE A-2

Renamed document

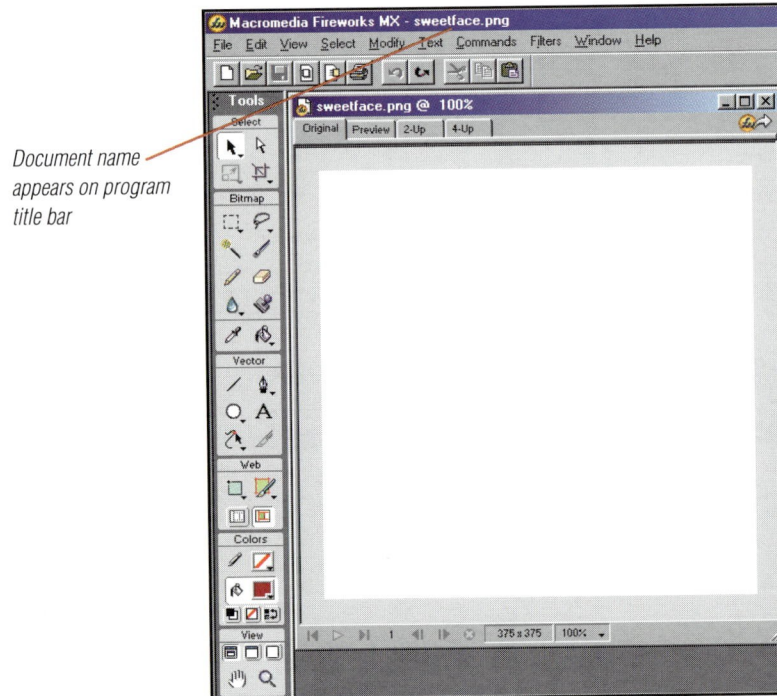

Document name appears on program title bar

Getting Started with Fireworks MX

FIGURE A-3

Importing a file into the full document window

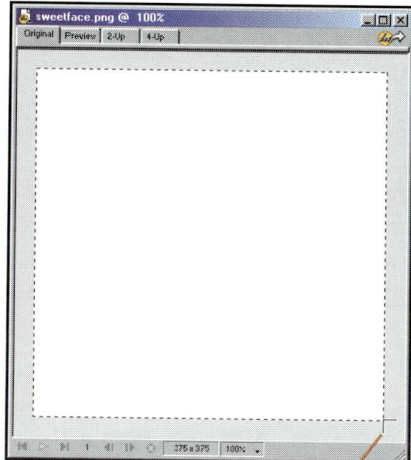

Import cursor at the end point of the import area

FIGURE A-4

Defining the import area

Begin dragging here

FIGURE A-5

Importing an eps file

FIGURE A-6

Completed document with imported files

Lesson 1 Create a New Document and Import Files

Import different file types

1. Click File on the menu bar, then click Import.

2. Navigate to the drive and folder where your data files are located, click m&m.jpg, then click Open.

   TIP If the drive containing your data files is not displayed, click the Save in list arrow (Win) or Look in list arrow (Mac).

3. Click and drag the pointer from the upper-left corner of the document window diagonally to the lower-right corner of the document window, as shown in Figure A-3.

   The m&m image fills the document window.

4. Click File on the menu bar, click Import, click smile.gif, then click Open.

5. Using Figure A-4 as a guide, click and drag the pointer across the lower width of the image.

6. Repeat Step 4, but import eyes.eps, accept the default values in the Vector File Options dialog box, then click OK.

7. Using Figure A-5 as a guide, click and drag the pointer across the top width of the image.

8. Click a blank area surrounding the document window, then compare your image to Figure A-6.

9. Click File on the menu bar, click Close, then click Yes (Win) or Save (Mac) to save your changes.

You imported different file types into a document.

LEARN ABOUT THE FIREWORKS WINDOW

What You'll Do

▶ *In this lesson, you will open and rename a document, learn about features in the Fireworks window, use the Show/Hide Layer icon to hide and show an object on a layer of the Layers panel, drag an object to a different layer, and then delete the object on the Layers panel.*

Viewing the Fireworks Window

The Fireworks window contains the workspace—the area where you work with documents, tools, and panels. You work with objects and images on the canvas. The overall Fireworks environment emulates the familiar interface in other Macromedia applications. Tools are housed in the **Tools panel**, other functions are contained in specific panels, such as the Optimize and Layers panels. The Tools panel is separated into sections: Select, Bitmap, Vector, Web, Colors, and View, so you can easily locate the tool you need. You can modify selected objects and set tool properties and other options using the **Property inspector**. Depending on the activity or action you are performing, information in the Property inspector constantly changes—properties specific to a selected tool or command appear on the Property inspector. You can move panels around the workspace based your preferences; by default, the Property

inspector is docked at the bottom of the workspace.

If you want to move or resize a panel, you must first undock it by dragging the gripper. An undocked panel has a blue bar (Win) or a gray dotted bar (Mac) above the title bar. Figure A-7 shows the main components in the Fireworks window, including docked and undocked panels. Note that displaying all of the panels at one time can easily obscure your view of your document window, and that panels differ slightly between Windows and Macintosh.

If you are using Windows, you can access additional features, such as toolbars and the status bar. You can open the Main and Modify toolbars from the Window menu. The Main toolbar includes icons for common tasks, while the Modify toolbar contains icons for modifying objects. You can open the status bar, which displays tips and other information about selected tools, from the View menu.

The document window contains four tabs: Original, Preview, 2-Up, and 4-Up. When you select the 2-Up tab or 4-Up tab, you can select different optimization settings and evaluate them side-by-side. For example, you can compare the original PNG settings against various TIFF or JPEG settings. The bottom of each document window also contains VCR buttons for playing animation.

Understanding the Layers Panel

Although a *layer* is a common term among graphic design applications, layers are used differently, depending on the program. For example, in Adobe Photoshop, you use layers to manipulate *pixels*. **Pixels** are small squares of color value used to display a digital image on a rectangular grid, such as a computer screen. However, in Fireworks and other programs, such as FreeHand or Adobe Illustrator, you use layers to manipulate *objects*. **Objects** are the individual elements in your document, such as text or images. The Layers panel arranges and structures objects as discrete pieces of your image. In Fireworks, a **layer** functions like a folder divided into sections that contain objects, just as folders on your computer house individual files. You can place as many objects as you wish on a layer, arrange them in any order, select one or more of them, and apply effects to them. For example, you can apply a mask or blending effect to all of the objects on one layer. While you can place nearly as many objects as you want on a layer, it is often easiest to use a layer to logically combine objects—for example, creating a layer that contains all the buttons in a Web page, or the design elements in a logo. You can modify one or more objects at a time and easily hide objects in the document. You can also collapse or expand the Layers panel to show just the layer or all of the objects on a layer. Figure A-8 shows the components of the Layers panel.

FIGURE A-7
Fireworks window

Menu commands
Tools panel
Document window tabs
Document title bar
VCR buttons
Property inspector

Docked panel has dots
Undocked panel has blue title bar

FIGURE A-8
Layers panel

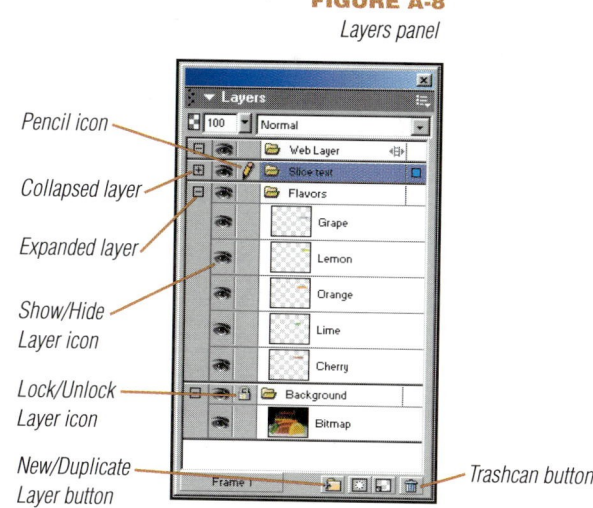

Pencil icon
Collapsed layer
Expanded layer
Show/Hide Layer icon
Lock/Unlock Layer icon
New/Duplicate Layer button

Trashcan button

Open a document and display the Layers panel

1. Click File on the menu bar, then click Open.

2. Navigate to the location where your data files are stored, click fwa_1.png, then click Open.

   TIP You can also double-click the file-name to open it.

3. Click File on the menu bar, click Save As, type **breads** in the File name text box (Win) or Save As text box (Mac), click the Save in list arrow (Win) or ▲ (Mac) to choose your destination drive, then click Save.

4. Click Window on the menu bar (if necessary), click Layers to display the Layers panel, then compare your screen to Figure A-9.

You opened and renamed a document and displayed the Layers panel.

Hide, move, and delete an object using the Layers panel

1. Click the Show/Hide Layer icon next to the Great Crusts object in Layer 1 of the Layers panel to hide the layer. 👁

   Notice that the Show/Hide Layer icon toggles between an eye icon and a blank box, depending on whether the layer is being hidden or shown.

   TIP To hide all the objects on a layer, click the Show/Hide Layer icon next to the layer name. If you do not see an object in a layer, click the Expand Layer icon. ⊞

   (continued)

Displaying the Layers panel

FIGURE A-10
Object hidden on the Layers panel

Show/Hide Layer icon (blank box) indicates layer is hidden

Click Show/Hide Layer icon to hide object or layer

Text is no longer visible

FIGURE A-11
Object moved between layers

Double line indicates location of layer when you release the mouse

Object being moved to Background layer

2. Compare your image to Figure A-10, then click the Show/Hide Layer icon next to the Great Crusts object in Layer 1. ☐

   The text reappears in the document.

3. Click the Great Crusts object in Layer 1 of the Layers panel, then drag it beneath the Background layer, until a double line appears beneath the Loaves & Brie layer, as shown in Figure A-11. ▸

   The Great Crusts object has become the bottom-most object in the Background layer, and it is no longer visible in the document.

   TIP Although it is difficult to discern, as you move an object in the Layers panel, a double line appears beneath the target layer, indicating where the object will be placed.

4. Verify that the Great Crusts object is still selected, click the Delete Selection icon on the Layers panel. 🗑

5. Save your work.

You hid and displayed an object in a layer on the Layers panel and moved and deleted an object.

Renaming layers and objects

To rename a layer, double-click the layer name on the Layers panel, type a new name in the Layer Name dialog box, then press [Enter] (Win) or [return] (Mac). To rename an object, double-click the object name on the Layers panel, type the new name, then press [Enter] (Win) or [return] (Mac).

WORK WITH BITMAP AND VECTOR IMAGES

What You'll Do

 In this lesson, you will adjust and retouch a bitmap, lock and create a layer, display rulers, and create and modify a vector object.

Understanding Bitmap Images and Vector Objects

Fireworks allows you to work with both bitmap and vector graphic images in your document. A **bitmap graphic** represents a picture image as a matrix of dots, or pixels, on a grid. Bitmaps allow the computer screen to realistically display the pixels, and is well-suited to displaying photographic images. In contrast, **vector graphics** are mathematically calculated objects composed of anchor points and straight or curved line segments. When you work in a document, bitmap graphics are referred to as images and vector graphics are referred to as objects.

Because a bitmap image is defined pixel by pixel, when you scale a bitmap graphic, you lose the sharpness of the original image. **Resolution** refers to the number of pixels in an image (print graphics require greater resolution). Onscreen resolution is usually 72 or 96 pixels per inch (ppi). Bitmap images are, therefore, resolution-dependent—resizing results in a loss of image quality. The most visible evidence is the all-too-familiar

jagged appearance in the edges of an image. Examples of bitmap file formats include BMP, GIF, JPEG, JPG, PNG, PICT (Macintosh), TIFF, and PSD (Adobe Photoshop).

Because they retain their appearance regardless of how you resize or skew them, vector graphics offer far more flexibility than bitmap images. They are resolution-independent—resizing retains a crisp edge. Because vector graphics can be asymmetrical, you can place them over another image and still see what lies beneath, unlike a rectangular bitmap. The disadvantage of a vector graphic is its inability to accurately depict the colors and detail in a photograph.

Using the Tools Panel

Although you can use many tools on both bitmap and vector graphics, graphic mode-specific tools are housed in separate sections of the Tools panel. Based on the object, layer, or tool, Fireworks automatically determines whether you are editing a bitmap or a vector graphic, and switches to activate or nullify the tool appropriately. Figure A-12 shows the Blur tool (a bitmap tool) actively blurring the floral bitmap image, but the tool is nullified from blurring the text because it is a vector object. You can create vector objects using the Pen, Text, Line, and Rectangle tools. You can use the Blur, Sharpen, Burn, Dodge, Smudge, and Rubber Stamp tools to modify the pixels in a bitmap image, which makes them useful for retouching photographic images. For example, to erase a small flaw or imperfection in an image, you can use the Rubber Stamp tool to replicate the pixels in one area and then stamp them over another area.

Some tools have multiple tools associated with them. A small arrow in the lower-right corner of the tool icon indicates that more tools are available. To select additional tools, press and hold the tool, then click the tool you want from the list, as shown in Figure A-13.

QUICKTIP

When you select a tool on the Tools panel, the options and settings available for that tool are displayed in the Property inspector. Not all tools have options associated with them.

Precisely Aligning and Positioning Objects

Fireworks provides rulers, guides, and a grid to help you align and position objects in your document. You can turn them on or off using the appropriate command on the View menu. Ruler measurements are always measured in pixels. You can snap objects directly to guides and the grid and modify the color and appearance of these lines and points at any time. To change guide and grid colors, point to the Guides command on the View menu, then click Edit Guides.

FIGURE A-12

Using a bitmap tool on different graphic types

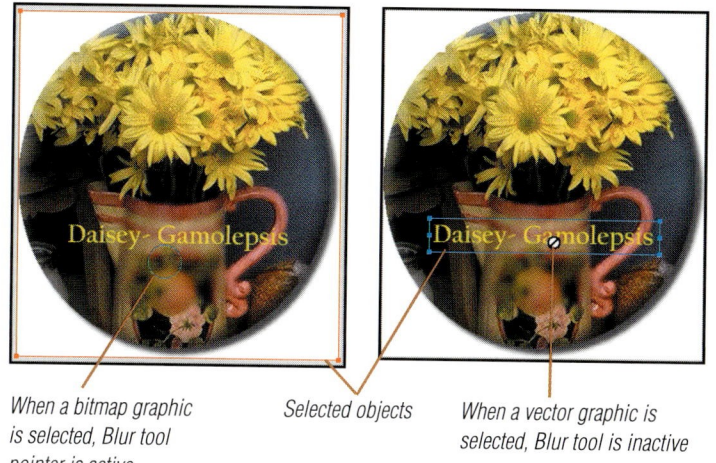

When a bitmap graphic is selected, Blur tool pointer is active

Selected objects

When a vector graphic is selected, Blur tool is inactive

FIGURE A-13

Selecting tools on the Tools panel

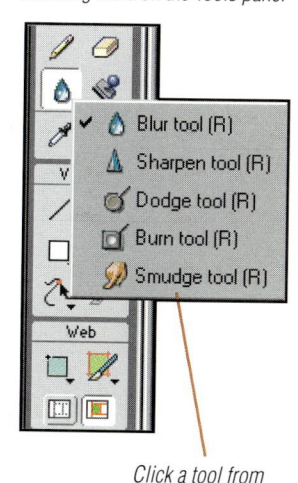

Small arrows indicate additional tools available

Click a tool from the list to select it

Edit a bitmap image and lock a layer

1. Make sure that the Layers panel is displayed.

   TIP You can undock and move panels to match your work preferences.

2. Click the Loaves & Brie object in the Background layer of the Layers panel to select it (if necessary).

3. Click Filters on the menu bar, point to Adjust Color, then click Brightness/Contrast.

4. Drag the Brightness slider to **-6**, then drag the Contrast slider to **20**.

   TIP To view changes as you make them in the document, make sure that the Preview check box is selected.

5. Compare your Brightness/Contrast dialog box to Figure A-14, then click OK.

   The colors in the image appear richer.

6. Make sure the Background layer is selected, then click the Pencil icon in the column next to the Background folder icon to lock the layer.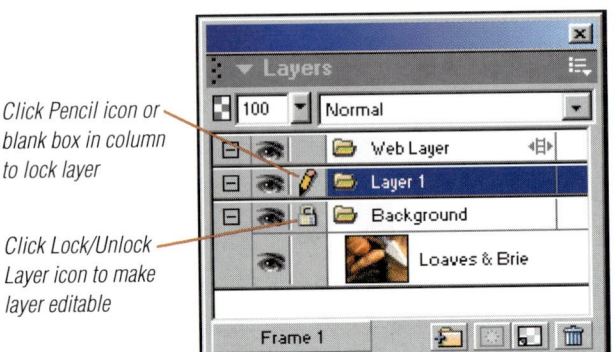

   TIP Locking a layer automatically locks all of the objects on the layer; once a layer is locked, you cannot edit, move, or delete the layer or any of its objects until you unlock the layer.

7. Compare your Layers panel to Figure A-15, then save your work.

You adjusted the brightness and contrast of the Loaves & Brie object and then locked the layer.

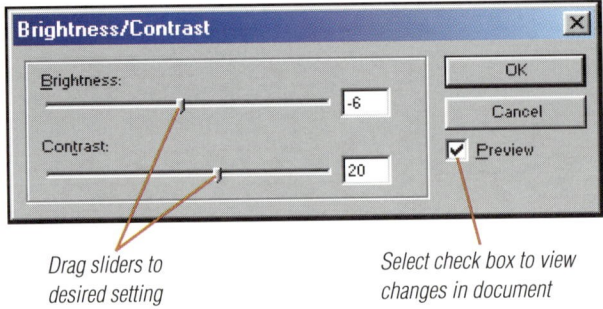

Drag sliders to desired setting

Select check box to view changes in document

FIGURE A-15
Layer locked on Layers panel

Click Pencil icon or blank box in column to lock layer

Click Lock/Unlock Layer icon to make layer editable

Properties for the Dodge tool

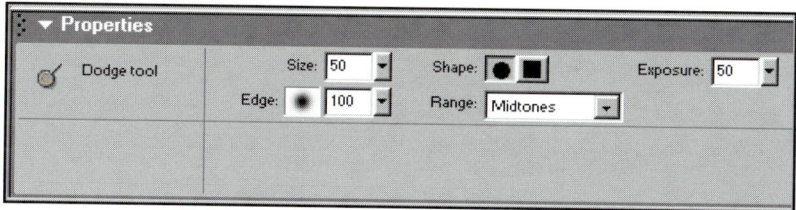

Using the Dodge tool to lighten pixels

Finish dragging
pointer across the
grains of wheat

Pixels in dodged
wheat shaft are
lighter

Begin dragging here

Retouch a bitmap

1. Click the Lock/Unlock Layer button in the column next to the Background folder icon on the Layers panel to unlock the layer.

2. Click the Loaves & Brie layer to select it.

3. Click Window on the menu bar if necessary), then click Properties to display the Property inspector.

4. Press and hold the Blur tool on the Tools panel, then click the Dodge tool from the list.

5. Click the Size list arrow in the Property inspector, drag the slider to **50**, press [Enter] (Win) or [return] (Mac), then compare your Property inspector to Figure A-16.

   TIP   If properties for a tool are not displayed in the Property inspector, click the small arrow in the lower-right corner of the panel to expand the panel.

6. Position the pointer in the lower-left corner of the image, then click and drag the pointer across the wheat, as shown in Figure A-17.

7. Save your work.

You used the Dodge tool to lighten the wheat image pixels.

Create a new layer and display rulers

1. Click Layer 1 to make it active (if necessary), then click the New/Duplicate Layer button on the Layers panel to create a new layer, Layer 2.

   TIP Fireworks automatically places a new layer above the active layer.

2. Double-click Layer 2, type **Ad Copy** in the Layer Name text box, then press [Enter] (Win) or [return] (Mac).

3. Click View on the menu bar, then click Rulers.

   Rulers display at the top and left sides of the window. The units of measurement adjust when you zoom in or out of the image.

4. Save your work, then compare your image to Figure A-18.

You created a new layer and displayed rulers.

Create a vector object

1. Click the Rectangle tool on the Tools panel.

2. Click the Fill category list arrow in the Property inspector, click Solid (if necessary), then click the Fill Color box to open the color palette.

3. Click the right-most swatch in the second row from the bottom, as shown in Figure A-19.

   TIP If you know a color's hexadecimal value, for example: #FFFFCC, you can type it in the text box on the Fill Color pop-up window.

(continued)

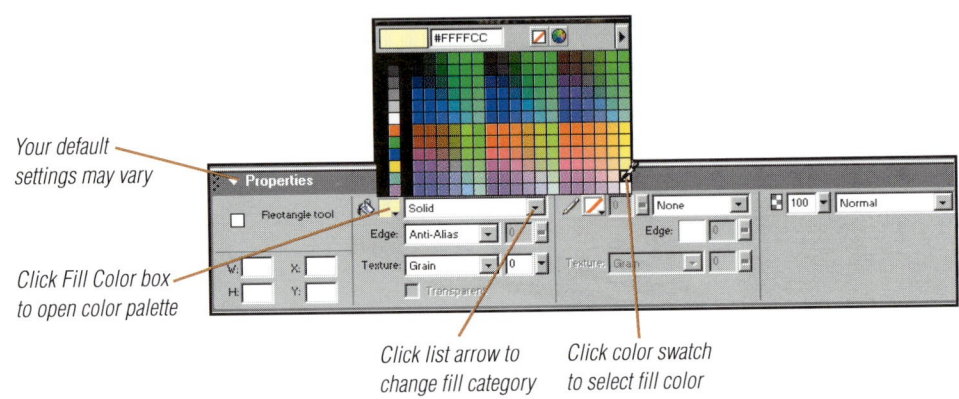

Your default settings may vary

Click Fill Color box to open color palette

Click list arrow to change fill category

Click color swatch to select fill color

Newly created rectangle

Your default border
may vary

FIGURE A-21
Stroke properties

Drag slider to select
edge softness

Click list arrow to
select texture intensity

Click list arrow to
select texture

Click list arrow
to select the
roundness of
the corners

FIGURE A-22
Border applied to rectangle

Completed rectangle

Click anywhere
in blank area to
deselect object

4. Click the Edge of fills list arrow, click Anti-Alias (if necessary), click the Texture name list arrow, click Grain, click the Amount of texture list arrow, drag the slider to **10**, then click the Transparent check box.

5. Click and drag the pointer to create the rectangle shown in Figure A-20. ┼

> TIP   Fireworks automatically applies the last selected stroke and fill to an object.

6. Save your work.

You set properties for the Rectangle tool in the Property inspector, and then created a rectangle.

Apply a stroke to an object

1. Click the Stroke Color button on the Property inspector, double-click the hexadecimal text box, then type **#FF9900**.

2. Click the Tip size list arrow, drag the slider to **6**, click the Stroke category list arrow, point to Charcoal, then click Creamy.

3. Enter the remaining stroke values shown in Figure A-21.

> TIP   Drag the Rectangle Roundness slider to 0 for square corners and to 100 to create an ellipse.

4. Click Select on the menu bar, click Deselect, then compare your image to Figure A-22.

> TIP   You can also deselect an object by clicking the border outside the document window.

5. Save your work.

You selected stroke properties and applied a stroke to the rectangle.

CREATE AND MODIFY TEXT

What You'll Do

 In this lesson, you will create text and a path, attach the text to the path, save your document, and then exit the program.

Using Text in a Document

The text features in Fireworks are typical of most desktop publishing programs—once you select the Text tool, you can preview the font family and modify properties, including size, color, style, kerning, leading, alignment, text flow, offset, and anti-alias properties. **Kerning** adjusts the spacing between adjacent letters or on a range of letters, while **leading** adjusts the amount of space between lines of text. **Anti-aliasing** blends the edges of type to the color behind them. You can choose four anti-alias settings: No, Crisp, Strong, or Smooth. Figure A-23 shows Text tool properties in the Property inspector—you can automatically preview the changes you make to Text tool properties in your document.

Once you create text, you can edit the text block as a whole, or edit just a range of text. To edit a text block, select the Pointer or the Sub-selection tool and then click the text block. To edit a range of text, double-click the text block using Pointer, Sub-selection, or Text tool, then highlight the text you want to modify. To apply your changes, click outside the text box, or click another tool or command. If you press [Enter] (Win) or [return] (Mac), you will insert a blank line of text in the text block. When you create text, you can create auto-sizing or fixed-width text blocks. Auto-sizing means that the text block expands to accommodate the type you enter. If you delete text, the text block contracts. You can create an auto-sizing text block by selecting the Text tool on the Tools panel, then begin typing in your document. In contrast, you can determine the width of a fixed-width text block by dragging the Text tool to create a text block before you begin typing. To spell check text, select the text block you want to check, click Text on the menu bar, then click Check Spelling.

QUICK TIP

You can use the Text Editor panel to view and modify text that may be difficult to see in your document. To open the Text Editor panel, select a text block or a range of text, click Text on the menu bar, then click Editor.

Attaching Text to a Path

You can manipulate text to follow an interesting direction in your image. You can create the path and then attach text to it. A **path** is an open or closed line consisting of a series of anchor points. **Anchor points** join path segments—they delineate changes in direction, whether a straight line, a corner, or a curve. To create a path, you use the Pen tool to define points in your document. To attach text to a path, select the text and the path, and then use the Attach to Path command on the Text menu. You can edit the text after you've attached it to a path.

Fireworks also allows you to edit text with most other functions after you've combined them). You can edit the path, but only if it is not attached to text. To detach text from a path, select the path/text object, click the Detach from Path command on the Text menu, then edit the path. Figure A-24 shows text attached to paths.

To edit a path, you can adjust the anchor points. To adjust the anchor points, select the path, select the Subselection tool on the Tools panel, and then drag points to new locations on the path as desired. You can also modify the appearance of text on a path by changing its alignment and orientation. To change alignment, select the path/text object, then select one of the options from the Align command on the Text menu. To change orientation, select an option under the Orientation command on the Text menu. Figure A-25 shows the options for the Align and Orientation commands.

Text properties in the Property inspector

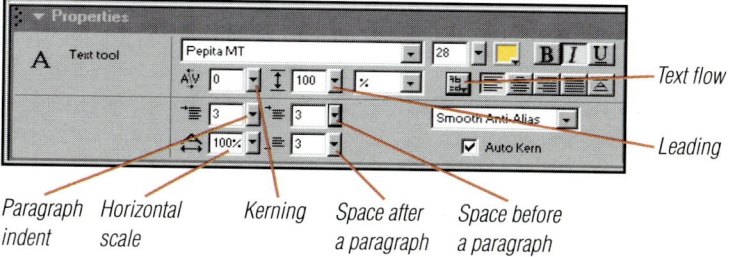

Paragraph indent   Horizontal scale   Kerning   Space after a paragraph   Space before a paragraph

Text flow

Leading

FIGURE A-24

Text on a path

FIGURE A-25

Align and Orientation command options

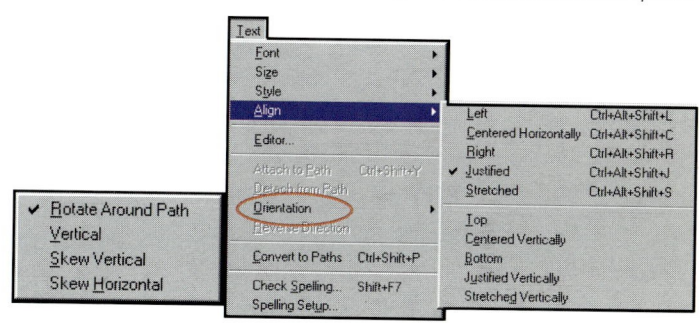

Create text using the Text tool

1. Verify that the Ad Copy layer is selected on the Layers panel, then click the Text tool on the Tools panel. **A**

2. Click the Font list arrow in the Property inspector, click Times New Roman, double-click the Size text box, then type **36**.

3. Click the Bold and Italic icons to select them. **B**

4. Click the Italic button to select it. **I**

5. Click the Color box, double-click the hexadecimal text box, type **#663300**, then press [Enter] (Win) or [return] (Mac).

6. Verify that the Center alignment icon and Smooth Anti-Alias option are selected, then compare your Property inspector to Figure A-26.

7. Click the document in the middle of the rectangle, type **Old World**, press [Enter] (Win) or [return] (Mac), then type **Taste**.

   TIP Center the text in the rectangle (if necessary).

8. Click the top of the cheese wedge, click the Font list arrow, click Century Gothic, double-click the Size text box, type **24**, then verify that the Bold and Italic buttons are selected.

9. Type **Fresh daily!**

   TIP You can nudge a selected object by using the arrow keys on your keyboard.

10. Click Select on the menu bar, click Deselect, then compare your image to Figure A-27, save your work.

You created text using the Text tool.

FIGURE A-26
Setting Text tool properties

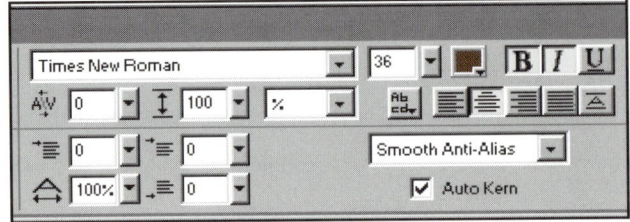

FIGURE A-27
Newly created text

Fresh daily!

Last path point
created is solid

FIGURE A-29
Text on path

Text follows
points on path

Create a path, attach text to it, then exit Fireworks

1. Click the Pen tool on the Tools panel. 🖋

2. Click the document in the locations shown in Figure A-28.

   A blue path appears on the canvas.

3. Click the Pointer tool on the Tools panel, press and hold [Shift], then click the Fresh daily! text to select both the path and the text. ▶

4. Click Text on the menu bar, then click Attach to Path.

5. Click Select on the menu bar, click Deselect, then compare your image to Figure A-29.

6. Save your work.

7. Click File on the menu bar, then click Exit (Win) or click Fireworks, then click Quit Fireworks (Mac).

You created a path using the Pen tool, attached the Fresh daily! text to it, then saved the document and exited the program.

Exporting text

When you export Fireworks text to Macromedia Flash, you can choose to convert the text to a path, even if you did not originally do so. This way, you can maintain the formatting and, thus the appearance you applied to the text in Fireworks.

Start Fireworks and open a document.

1. Start Fireworks for the platform you are using.
2. Create a new document and set the Width to **255** and the Height to **440**.
3. Save the document as **pasta_1**.png.

Import files.

1. Import ingredients.jpg so that it fills the full document window.
2. Import elbow.gif into the top of the document. (*Hint*: Drag the cursor from the upper-left corner until it reaches the right border, approximately 1 inch down.)
3. Import shell.tif into the document, directly beneath the elbow image.
4. Save your work, compare your document to Figure A-30, then close the document.

View the Fireworks window.

1. Open fwa_2.png.
2. Save the file as **pasta_2**.

3. Select the Varieties object on the Background layer of the Layers panel.
4. Hide and display the Varieties object on the Layers panel.
5. Move the Ingredients object from Layer 1 above the Varieties object so that it is now in the Background layer.
6. Delete the Ingredients object, then save your work.

Work with bitmap and vector graphics.

1. Select the Varieties layer.
2. Select the Dodge tool, set the Size to **50**, then click and drag the pointer over the pasta on top of the table.
3. Lock the Background layer.
4. Save your work.

Create a layer and display rulers.

1. Create a new layer above Layer 1.
2. Rename the newly created layer **Proper Names**.

3. Display rulers.
4. Select the Rectangle tool.
5. Enter the following properties in the Property inspector: Color: **#66CC00**, Category: Solid, Edge: Feather, Feather amount: **4**, Texture: Burlap, and Texture amount: **20%**.
6. Using Figure A-30 as a guide, draw a rectangle on the first pasta jar.
7. Apply a stroke with the following properties: Color: **#339900**, Tip size: **2**, Category: Air Brush Basic, and Texture amount: **0%**.
8. Save your work.

Create and modify text.

1. Select the Text tool.
2. Enter the following properties in the Property inspector: Font: Garamond, Size: **22** pt, Color: **#000000**, Bold, and Left alignment.

3. Click the pointer in the middle of the rectangle, then type **Rotelie**.

4. Center the text in the rectangle (if necessary). (*Hint*: Use the arrow keys on your keyboard.)

5. Enter the following properties: Font: Impact, Size: **65** pt, Color: **#990000**, Bold, Center alignment.

6. Click the pointer on top of the hinge on the spaghetti jar, then type **Pasta Shapes**.

7. Deselect the Pasta Shapes text.

8. Select the Pen tool, then create a path as shown in Figure A-30.

9. Attach the Pasta Shapes text to the path.

10. Save your work, then compare your document to Figure A-30.

FIGURE A-30
Completed Skills Review

You are in charge of new services at Crystal Clear Consulting. You're preparing to roll out a new crisis solutions division, designed to help companies that are in a management or financial difficulty. You plan to brief your coworkers on the services at an upcoming company lunch. Each department head—including you—is going to submit a sample introductory Web ad announcing the division. You'll use your Fireworks skills to design a simple ad.

1. Obtain images that symbolize the new consulting service. You will import this image to a layer in the document. You can obtain an image from your computer, from the Internet, or from scanned media.
2. Create a new document and save it as **crystal.png**.
3. Import the image you downloaded so that it serves as the background.
4. Rename Layer 1 with **Background**.
5. Create a new layer and rename it with an appropriate name.
6. Copy another image to the newly named layer and retouch it if necessary.
7. Retouch one of the images, and lock layers as needed. (*Hint*: The clouds background image in the sample has been retouched using the Blur tool.)
8. Create a new layer and name it **Text Objects**.
9. Create at least one vector object and apply a fill or stroke to it. (*Hint*: The rectangle in the sample has a Hatch border applied to it.)
10. Create at least two text objects. (*Hint*: The font in the sample is Matisse ITC and Eras Demi ITC. You can substitute these fonts with other fonts on your computer.)
11. Apply a stroke to at least one of the text objects.
12. Attach at least one text object to a path, then rename the object on the Layers panel.
13. Save your work, then compare your document to Figure A-31.

FIGURE A-31
Completed Project Builder 1

You've just completed your first class in Fireworks. Afterward, you met with your boss to summarize some of the neat features. She is intrigued by the various ways you can change the appearance of text on a path and has asked you to prepare a few samples for the next staff meeting, illustrating the way Fireworks can manipulate text.

1. Create a new Fireworks document and name it **meandering_paths.png**.

2. Create a text object that is at least 20 characters long (you can use the font of your choice and as many words as you like). Note the alignment of the text in the Property inspector.

3. Create an interesting path, then attach the text to it.

4. Rename the Text on a Path object on the Layers panel **Path 1**.

5. Note the orientation of the text on the path. (*Hint*: Use the Orientation command on the Text menu.)

6. Create a text object with the words **Alignment** and **Orientation:** on separate lines, as shown in the sample. This text will describe the settings you choose.

7. Type the alignment and orientation of the Path 1 object next to their descriptive labels.

8. Rename the newly created text object on the Layers panel **Description 1**, then drag the Description 1 object next to the Path 1 object in your document.

9. Copy the Path and Description objects, then drag them below the first pair in your document.

10. Rename the objects **Path 2** and **Description 2**, respectively.

11. Change the alignment and orientation of the text to the path, then update the Description text accordingly. (*Hint*: To quickly change the alignment, use the Align command on the Text menu.)

12. Repeat Steps 9–11, but name the objects **Path 3** and **Description 3**, respectively.

13. Save your work, then compare your image to Figure A-32.

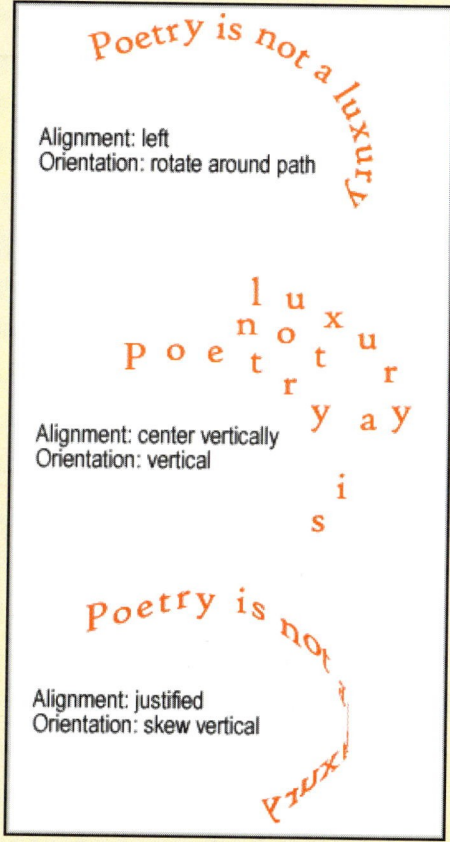

Alignment: left
Orientation: rotate around path

Alignment: center vertically
Orientation: vertical

Alignment: justified
Orientation: skew vertical

DESIGN PROJECT

You can develop your design and planning skills by analyzing Web sites. Figure A-33 shows a page from the Rock and Roll Hall of Fame Web site. Study the image and complete the following questions. For each question, indicate how you determined your answer. Because, by their very nature, dynamic Web sites are updated frequently to reflect current trends, this page may be different from Figure A-34 when you open it online.

1. Connect to the Internet and go to *www.course.com*. Navigate to the page for this book, click the Student Online Companion, then click the link for this unit.
2. Open a document in a word processor, or open a new Fireworks document, then save the file as **rocknroll**. (*Hint*: Use the Text tool in Fireworks.)
3. Explore the site and answer the following questions. For each question, indicate how you determined your answer.
   - What vector shapes does the page contain?
   - What fills or strokes have been added to vector shapes?
   - Do objects appear to have been manipulated in some manner? If so, how?
   - Have photographs been retouched? If so, how?

- Do objects or text overlap? If so, list the order in which the objects appear in the Layers panel.

- Has text been attached to a path?
- What is the overall effect of the text?

FIGURE A-33
Design Project

Your group can assign elements of this project to individual members, or work collectively to create the finished product.

Your team serves on the Education Committee for Cultural Consequence, a cultural anthropology group. The group is constructing a Web site that examines facial expressions and moods in people around the world. The committee is in charge of developing emoticons—a shorthand method of expressing moods—for the Web site. The images will be in the style of the smiley face. You can use the facial expression of your choice in developing the emoticon.

1. Choose an emotion and the emoticon that conveys that feeling.
2. Obtain and retouch at least two images for the expression you've chosen. You can obtain images from your computer, from the Internet, or from scanned media.
3. Create a new document, then save it as **emoticon.png**.
4. Create an object for the background and apply a fill to it. (*Hint*: The sample has a solid rectangle.)
5. Create a new layer named **Faces** and import the images you've obtained to the new layer.
6. Create a new layer and name it with the expression you selected in Step 1.

7. Create the emoticon on the layer created in Step 6, using tools on the Tools panel, and apply fills and strokes to them as desired. (*Hint*: The emoticon in the sample was created with the Ellipse tool and the Brush tool with a Basic Soft Rounded tip setting.)

8. Create a text object that identifies the expression. (*Hint*: The text in the sample is Pristina.)
9. Save your work, then compare your document to Figure A-34.

FIGURE A-34
Completed Group Project

UNIT B

WORKING WITH OBJECTS

1. Work with multiple objects.

2. Modify color in objects.

3. Apply effects to objects and text.

4. Apply a style to objects.

UNIT B
WORKING WITH OBJECTS

Transforming Objects

Fireworks provides a bevy of tools that can transform objects and shapes into interesting graphics. You can combine multiple objects to create entirely new shapes, or you can fill an object with color and texture and then adjust its appearance. In addition to menu commands, you can add and manage effects using the Effects section of the Property inspector. Once you select a tool on the Tools panel, you can adjust several options associated with it. The Stroke, Fill, and Effect sections maximize your ability to experiment—you can create multiple versions of a stroke, fill, or effect, and turn them on or off at will.

You can also create different effects by rearranging the order in which they appear in the list of applied effects on the Property inspector. The end result will vary depending on which effect appears first.

Tools You'll Use

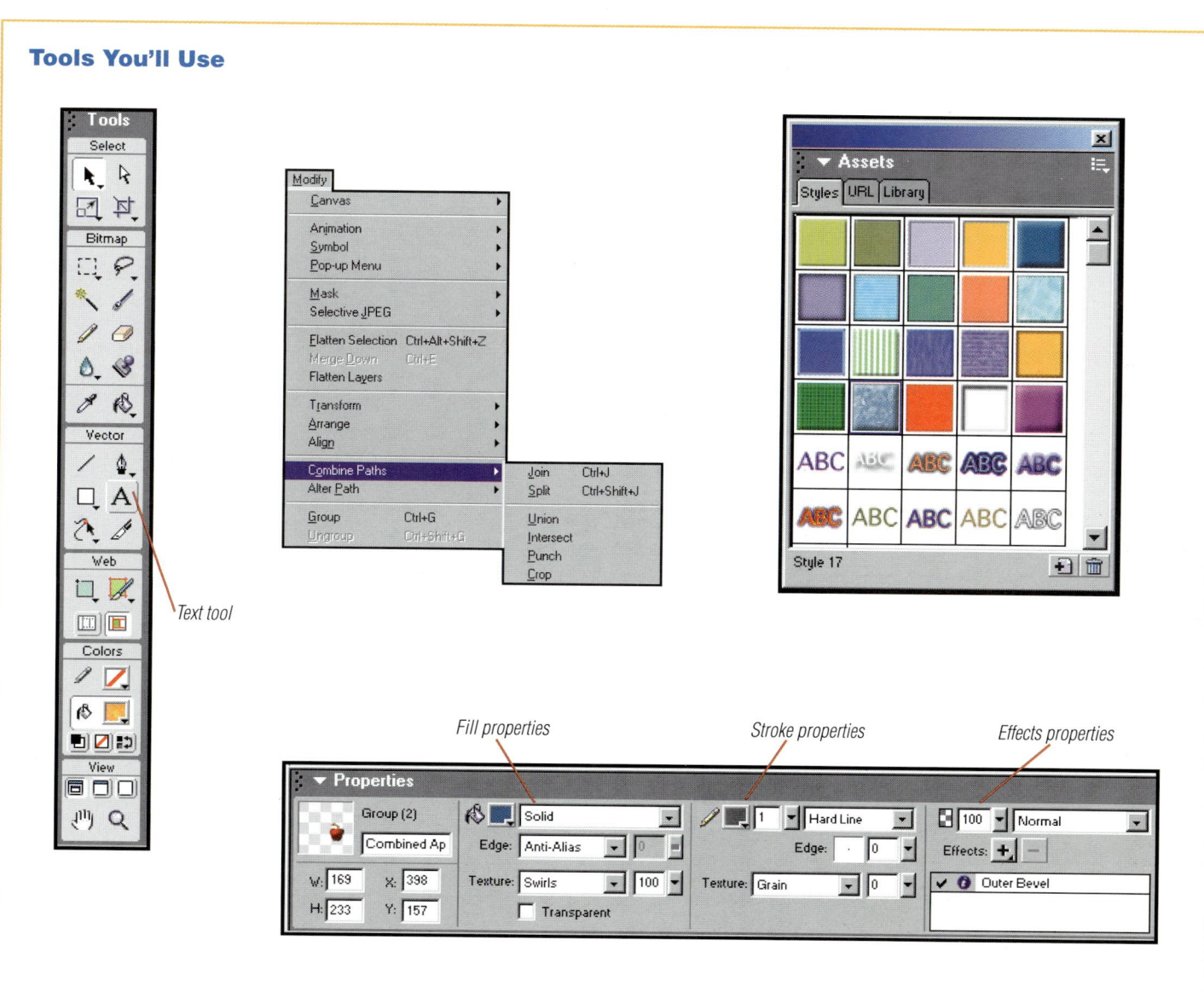

Text tool

Fill properties

Stroke properties

Effects properties

WORK WITH MULTIPLE OBJECTS

What You'll Do

 In this lesson, you will open and rename a file, select and move a vector object, then combine two vector objects and move them together, before placing them behind another vector object. Last, you will group the objects and reposition them.

Selecting and Combining Objects

Using vector shapes allows you to work with limitless individual objects. You can manipulate these shapes by joining them, using the Group and Combine Paths commands on the Modify menu. The **Group** command allows you to manipulate multiple objects as a single selection. You can group any objects in your document: vector images, bitmap images, text, and so on. Fireworks preserves each individual object's shape and its configuration to the other objects. Once you group objects, you can modify the group as a whole, such as by changing the color or applying a stroke. If you want to change any one of the objects, you can easily ungroup the objects, apply the change, and then regroup them. For example, if a group consists of title text and an image, you must first ungroup the objects before you can edit the text.

Fireworks offers six options for combining paths: Join, Split, Union, Intersect, Punch, and Crop. Each command produces a different effect. You must select two or more vector objects before you can apply a combination option to them. The Combine Paths commands are described below and some are illustrated in Figure B-1.

Join—The Join command allows you to combine the paths of two or more objects to create a single merged object that includes all the points of both paths. However, the area where the two paths overlap appears empty; the images and objects on layers beneath it will show through the overlapped area. You can also use the Join command to join selected end points of open paths.

Split—You can split the paths of two or more objects that had been combined using the Join command. The Split command creates two or more simple paths. Note that the Split command is not the same as performing Undo.

Union—The Union command creates a path that is the sum total of all selected areas. In Figure B-1, the union includes the portions of the yellow and blue objects that extend beyond the borders of the wood object.

Intersect—The area that is common to all selected paths of all three objects is included. In Figure B-1, this is a small wood area.

Punch—The outline of the top-most object carves its outline through all lower selected images. In Figure B-1, the yellow *shape* slices through the other objects.

Crop—The area of the topmost path is used to remove the areas of the paths beneath it. In Figure B-1, the curve is wood and blue.

Arranging and Aligning Objects

You can arrange and align objects at any time, using the Arrange and Align commands on the Modify menu. When you arrange an object, you can move its location on the Layers panel and its appearance in your document. Fireworks contains standard arrange options: Bring to Front, Bring Forward, Send Backward, and Send to Back. You can align objects in relation to each other by their sides or centers, or distribute them evenly in your document, either horizontally or vertically. For additional aligning and distributions options, you can open the Align panel by clicking the Align command on the Window menu. Options in the Align panel allow you to match and align the spacing of multiple objects along both horizontal and vertical axes, and align a vector object's anchor points.

Combine Paths command examples

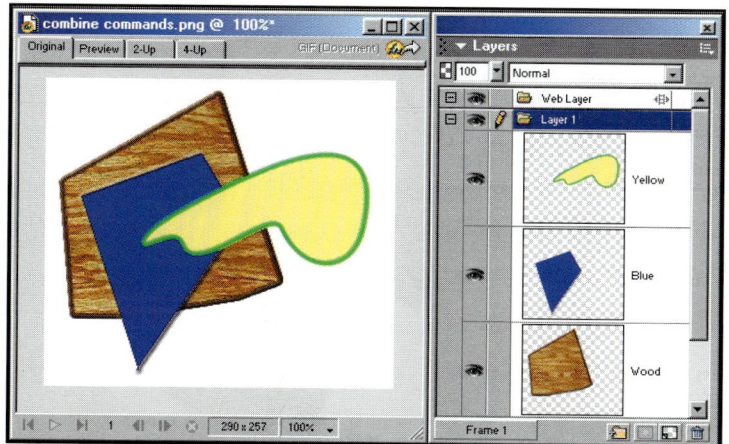

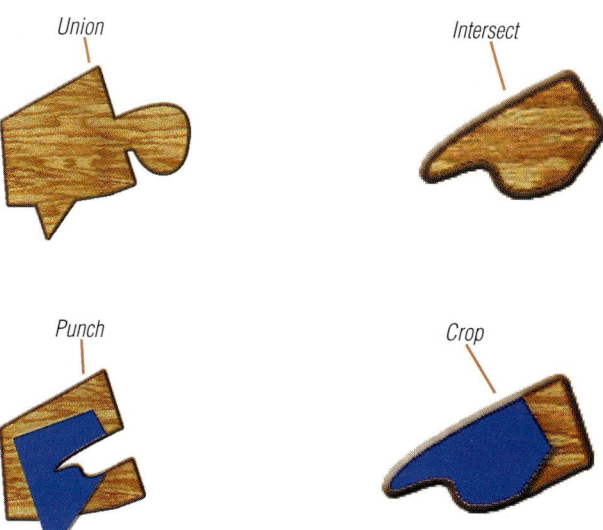

Move and select multiple objects

1. Open fwb-1.png, then save it as **a=apple**.

2. Display the rulers, then click the Pointer tool on the Tools panel (if necessary). 🔧

3. Click the Stem Bottom object, then drag it to the location shown in Figure B-2.

   > TIP You can use the Info panel on the Property Inspector to position objects precisely.

4. Press and hold [Shift], click the Stem Top object, then compare your image to Figure B-3.

   The two stem pieces are selected.

5. Save your work.

You opened and renamed a file, and then moved and selected objects.

Combine and arrange objects

1. Click Modify on the menu bar, point to Combine Paths, then click Union.

   The two stem pieces combine to create a single continuous path, which is renamed Path on the Layers panel.

2. Double-click the Path object on the Vector Apple layer of the Layers panel, type **Stem**, then press [Enter] (Win) or [return] (Mac).

   > TIP Fireworks automatically renames objects after you perform certain actions.

(continued)

Object being moved

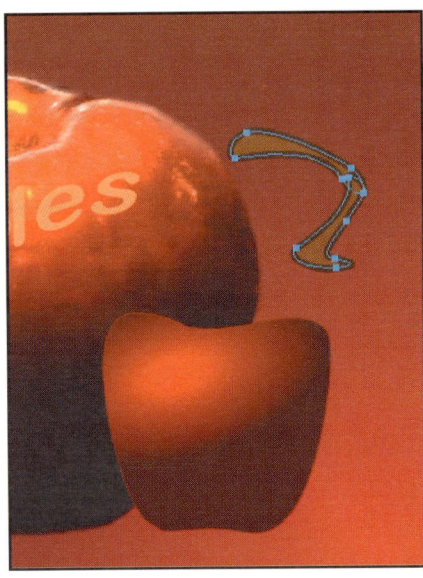

Working with Objects

Rearranged object

Stem appears
behind apple

FIGURE B-5
Grouped object

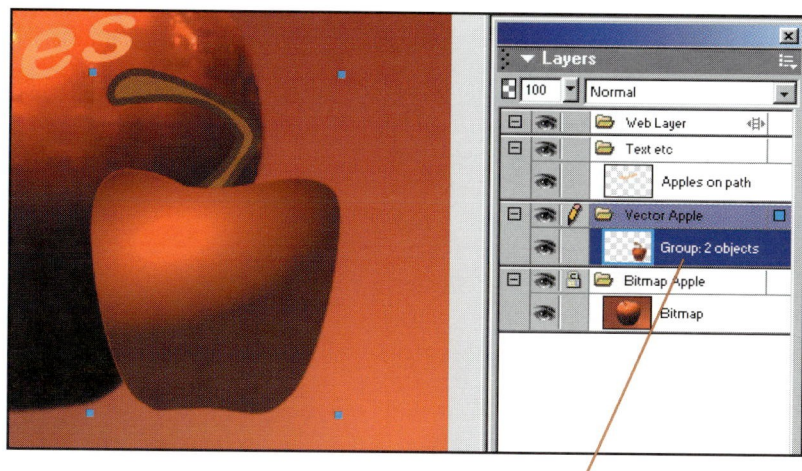

Grouped objects renamed in Layers panel

3. Verify that the Pointer tool on the Tools panel is selected, click the combined stem, then drag the combined stem to the middle of the apple.

4. Click Modify on the menu bar, point to Arrange, then click Send to Back.

   The stem appears behind the apple shape, although the full path is still visible.

5. Click Select on the menu bar, click Deselect, then compare your image to Figure B-4.

6. Save your work.

You combined, moved, and arranged the two stem objects.

Group objects

1. Press and hold [Shift], click the Stem object, then click the Apple Shape object.

2. Click Modify on the menu bar, then click Group.

   The apple and stem objects become one object in the document, and the original objects on the Layers panel combine into a new object named Group: 2 objects.

3. Compare your image to Figure B-5, then save your work.

You grouped the stem and apple.

MODIFYING COLOR IN OBJECTS

What You'll Do

In this lesson, you will add and modify a gradient fill to the Stem object.

Modifying Objects

When you select an object, the Property inspector contains specific areas that allow you to change nearly every attribute pertinent to that object. For example, you can modify an object's name and dimension; its fill and stroke color, pattern, edge and texture; and its opacity and blend mode. You also can apply effects.

Understanding Fills and Gradients

After you create a vector shape, you can modify its appearance by changing its interior, or fill. The Property inspector provides powerful tools for enhancing fills in objects. You can use a **fill** to apply a solid color, a pattern, or a gradient to an object. Fireworks offers dozens of preset patterns from which you can choose, or you can apply a pattern created in another program. A **gradient** consists of two or more colors that blend into each other in a fixed design. Fireworks offers several fill, pattern, and gradient categories, shown in Figure B-6. You can easily change a pattern

or gradient after you've applied it, and modify additional fill characteristics such as edge, texture, and transparency.

QUICKTIP

You can change an object's fill color by clicking the Fill Color box on the Tools panel on the Property inspector, or on the Color Mixer panel.

You can choose a gradient or fill pattern from the Fill category list arrow. The middle section of the Fill category menu includes 11 preset gradient options. If you a select a gradient as a fill, you can choose one of the preset gradient colors for the gradient by clicking the Fill Color box on the Property inspector, and then clicking the Select a color gradient preset list arrow. You can change gradient colors at any time without affecting the type or appearance of the gradient. To edit a gradient, open the Edit Gradient pop-up window by clicking the Fill Color box on the Property inspector or on the Tools panel. You can modify gradient colors by manipulating the color swatches beneath the color ramp in the Edit Gradient pop-up window. You can modify the transition from one color to the next by dragging a color swatch along the color ramp. To change color, click the color swatch, then select a new color swatch from the pop-up color window. You can add a color by clicking an area beneath the color ramp; to delete a color, drag it off the color ramp.

You can preview a pattern fill before you select it. To preview a fill, select an object, and verify that Pattern is selected from the Fill category list. Click the Fill Color box on the Property inspector, click the Pattern name list arrow, and then point to a pattern name, as shown in Figure B-7.

In Fireworks, you can easily transform the appearance of a pattern or gradient to suit your design needs. When you select an object with a pattern or a gradient fill, a set of round and square fill handles appears on the object. You can drag the fill handles to adjust the position, angle, and width of the gradient, as shown in Figure B-8.

Understanding Edges and Textures

You can alter the edge of a fill by selecting a hard or soft line, or feather the edge to make it appear to blend or fade into the background. Finally, you can add and modify the amount of texture to any fill. Fireworks offers dozens of textures from which to choose, or you can use your own bitmap format file or another Fireworks file for a customized texture. To add a custom texture, click Other in the Texture name list, select the file you want to use, and then click Open.

FIGURE B-6
Fill categories

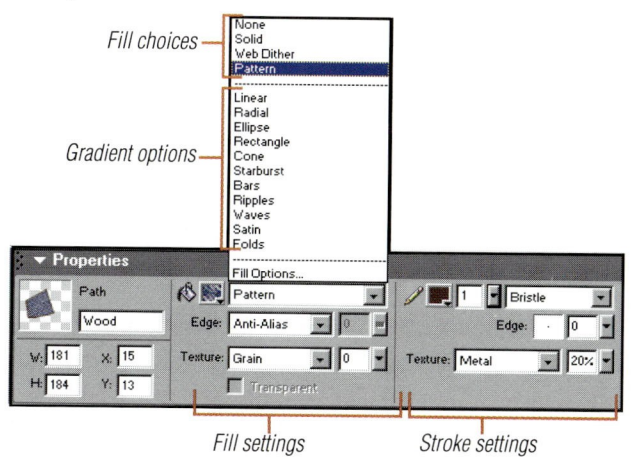

Fill choices
Gradient options

Fill settings   Stroke settings

FIGURE B-7
Pattern options

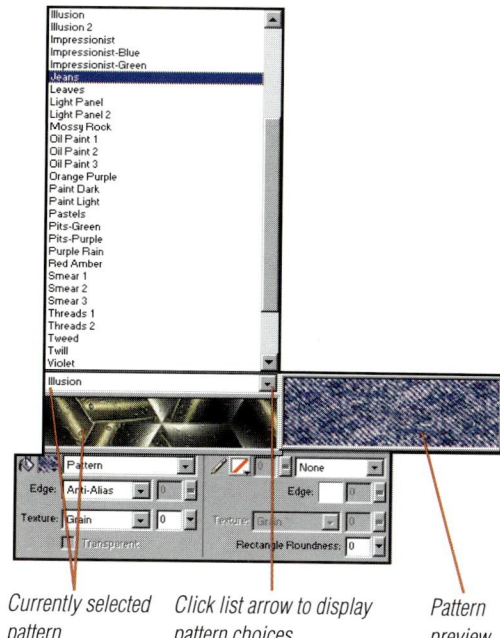

Currently selected pattern
Click list arrow to display pattern choices
Pattern preview

FIGURE B-8
Sample gradients

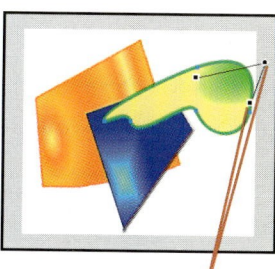

Move handles and adjust length to modify gradient

Add a gradient fill to an object

1. Verify that the Group: 2 objects object is selected, click Modify on the menu bar, then click Ungroup.

   The individual paths of the two objects reappear.

2. Click Select on the menu bar, then click Deselect.

3. Click the Stem object on the Vector Apple layer of the Layers panel.

4. Click the Fill category list arrow on the Property inspector, click Ripples, then click the Fill Color box on the Property inspector.

5. Click the left color swatch, double-click the hexadecimal text box, type **CCCC99**, then press [Enter] (Win) or [return] (Mac).

6. Click the right color swatch, double-click the hexadecimal text box, type **996600**, then press [Enter] (Win) or [return] (Mac).

7. Compare your Edit Gradient pop-up window to Figure B-9, then press [Enter] (Win) or [return] (Mac) to close the window.

8. Save your work, then compare your image to Figure B-10.

You added a gradient fill to the stem and changed the colors of the gradient to give the stem a more natural appearance.

unused
unused

FIGURE B-9
Gradient options on the Edit Gradient pop-up window

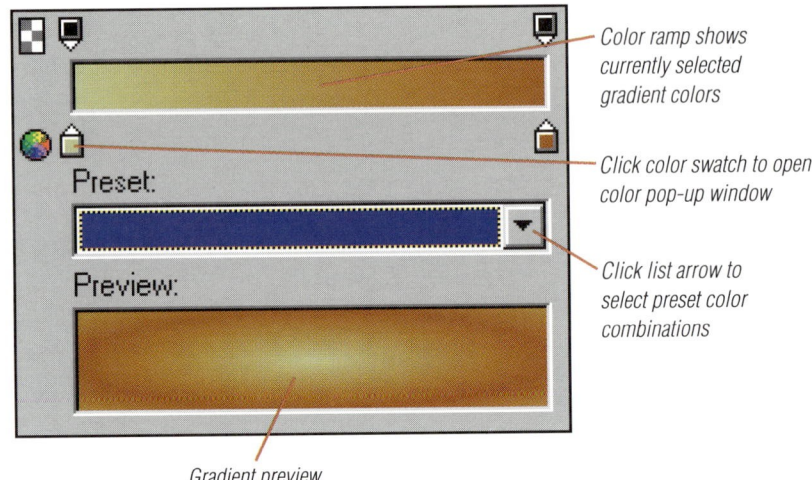

Color ramp shows currently selected gradient colors

Click color swatch to open color pop-up window

Click list arrow to select preset color combinations

Gradient preview

FIGURE B-10
Gradient applied to object

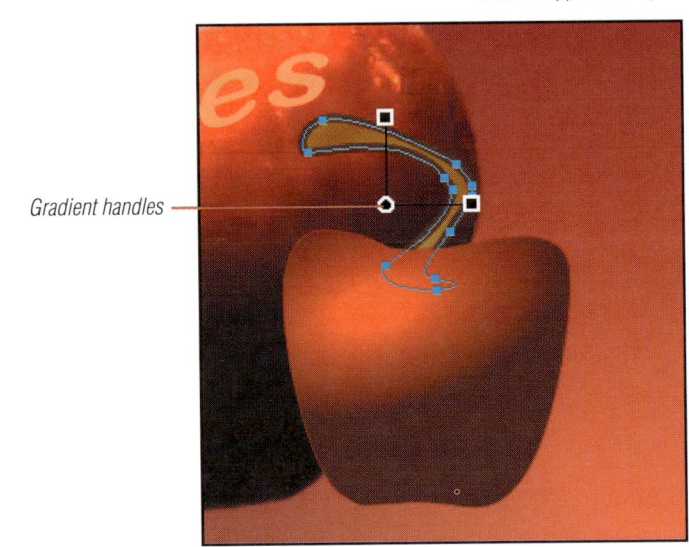

Gradient handles

FIGURE B-11

Fill and stroke settings

FIGURE B-12

Completed fill

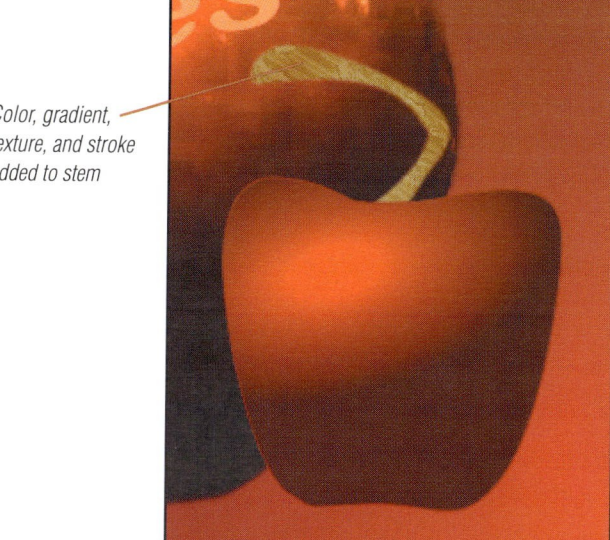

Color, gradient, texture, and stroke added to stem

1. Verify that the Stem object is still selected, then click the Edge of fills list arrow in the fill section of the Property inspector.

2. Click Feather, click the Amount of feather list arrow, drag the slider to **1**, then press [Enter] (Win) or [return] (Mac).

3. Click the Texture list arrow, click Onyx (if necessary), click the Amount of texture list arrow, drag the slider to **35%**, press [Enter] (Win) or [return] (Mac), then verify that the Transparent check box is not selected.

4. Click the Stroke category list arrow in the Stroke section of the Property inspector, click None (if necessary), then compare your Property inspector to Figure B-11.

5. Press and hold [Shift], click the Apple Shape object, click Modify on the menu bar, then click Group.

6. Click Select on the menu bar, click Deselect, then compare your image to Figure B-12.

7. Double-click the Group: 2 objects object on the Vector Apple layer of the Layers panel, type **Grouped Apple**, and then press [Enter] (Win) or [return] (Mac).

8. Save your work.

You modified a fill's edge, texture, and stroke, and renamed an object on the Layers panel.

APPLY EFFECTS TO OBJECTS AND TEXT

What You'll Do

▶ *In this lesson, you will add an Outer Bevel effect to the Vector Apple and an Inner Shadow effect to the Apples text, and then adjust the transparency of the Inner Shadow effect.*

Understanding Effects

Using the Stroke and Fill sections in the Property inspector, you can alter the appearance of vector objects in your document. In addition to those adjustments, you can use the Effects section to add the effects found on the Filters menu, as well as others such as the illusions of dimension and depth. The features in the effects section are similar to filters, labs, or renders used by other graphic programs, such as Adobe Photoshop or advanced 3-D landscaping programs, such as Corel Bryce. Fireworks refers to effects as Live Effects because you can always edit and preview changes to them. The Effects section affords you flexibility to experiment with multiple effects. You can add, edit, delete, or hide effects in the Effects section at your convenience. To edit most effects, select the object(s) to which the effect is applied, then click the Info icon or double-click the effect name in the Edit and arrange Effects list to open its pop-up window or dialog box.

Figure B-13 shows the commands available in the effects section.

Just as you can move objects on the Layers panel to affect their appearance in your document, you can modify the overall look of an object by changing the order of effects. Figure B-14 shows how changing the stacking order of effects in the Edit and arrange Effects list can produce very different results in a document. Each macaw has the same settings and effects applied to it, but in a different order. To move an effect, drag it to a new location in the Effects list.

Using the Filters Menu

You can apply many effects from the Filters menu. Although the Filters menu and the effects section share several features, be aware that the effects you add from the Filters menu do not appear in the Effects section of the Property inspector and you cannot alter their settings after you apply them. You can edit or remove filters only in the current work session—more precisely, you can *undo* a filter, not edit it. You can undo an action by clicking the Undo command on the Edit menu—once you save or close the document, the Undo actions are lost.

QUICK**TIP**

You can also undo a command by dragging the marker above a state on the History panel.

Relating Effects and File Size

Although effects generally contribute to increased file size, disabling an effect instead of deleting it does not significantly add to file size. Some effects, such as the Blur, Blur More, and Gaussian Blur effects, may actually decrease file size, because blurring an object decreases the total number of colors in the graphic. The fewer colors used in your document, the less storage space required—hence, smaller file size.

Understanding Transparency

You can adjust the transparency of images in your document by changing their opacity settings. The **opacity** setting determines if your image is completely opaque (100%), or completely transparent (0%). To adjust the opacity of an object in your document, select the object on the Layers panel, click the Opacity list arrow, then drag the slider to the desired opacity. You can also adjust the opacity of certain effects in the effects section. Fireworks applies the same concept to the opacity settings you use to adjust the amount of texture in strokes and fills, contrast in effects, and so on.

FIGURE B-13

Effects options

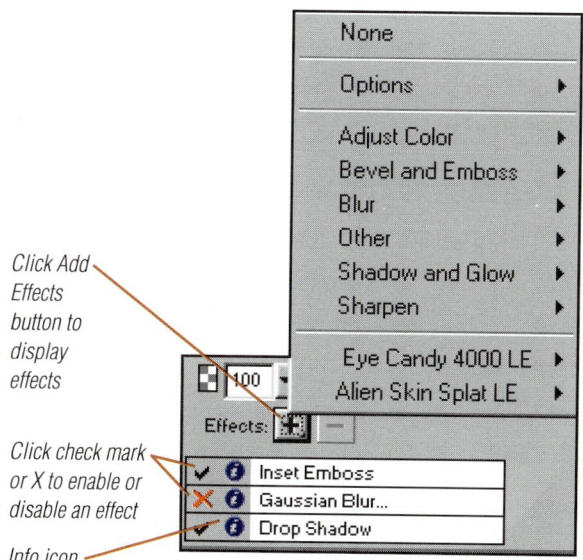

Click Add Effects button to display effects

Click check mark or X to enable or disable an effect

Info icon

FIGURE B-14

Effects rearranged in the Edit and arrange effects window

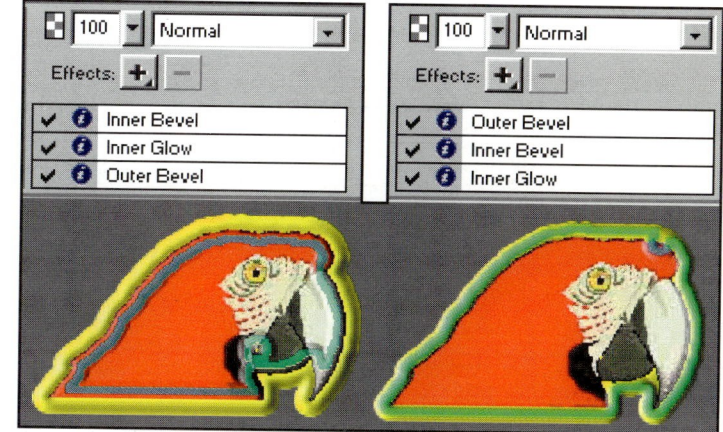

Apply an effect to a vector object

1. Click the Grouped Apple object to select it (if necessary), then click the Add Effects button in the Effects section of the Property inspector.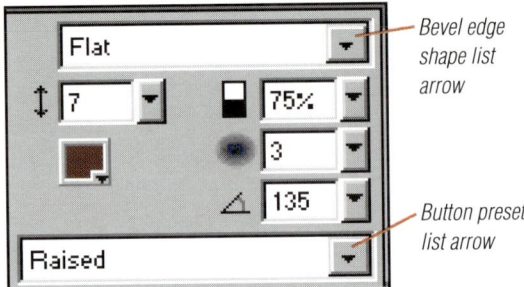

   TIP To delete an effect, select the effect in the Effects list, then click the Delete Effects button.

2. Point to Bevel and Emboss, click Outer Bevel, then verify that the Bevel edge shape is Flat.

3. Click the Width list arrow, then drag the slider to **7**.

4. Click the color swatch, double-click the hexadecimal text box, type **663300**, then press [Enter] (Win) or [return] (Mac).

5. Click the Button preset list arrow, then click Raised (if necessary).

6. Accept the remaining default settings, compare your Outer Bevel pop-up window to Figure B-15, then press [Enter] (Win) or [return] (Mac).

   The effect, Outer Bevel, appears in the Effects list.

   TIP To temporarily disable an effect, click the applicable check mark in the Effects list.

7. Click Select on the menu bar, click Deselect, then compare your image to Figure B-16.

8. Save your work.

You added an Outer Bevel effect to the Grouped Apple object.

FIGURE B-15

Outer Bevel effect settings

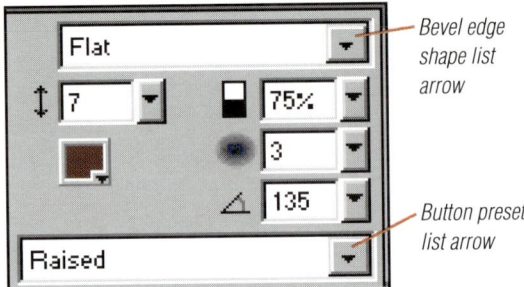

Bevel edge shape list arrow

Button preset list arrow

FIGURE B-16

Outer Bevel effect applied to object

Outer Bevel effect

Working with Objects

Apply an effect to a bitmap object

1. Click the Apples on path object on the Text etc layer of the Layers panel.

   TIP If an object or layer name is not completely visible on the Layers panel, double-click the name to see the full name.

2. Click the Add Effects button, point to Shadow and Glow, then click Inner Shadow. +

3. Click the Distance list arrow, drag the slider to **5**, click the color box, double-click the hexadecimal text box, type **990000**, then press [Enter] (Win) or [return] (Mac).

4. Compare your image to Figure B-17.

You applied an Inner Shadow effect to text.

FIGURE B-18
Setting opacity and softness

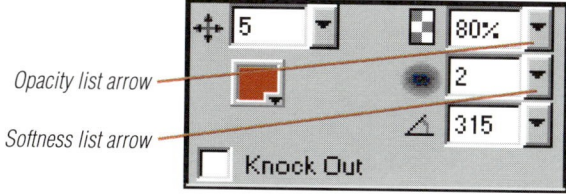

Opacity list arrow

Softness list arrow

FIGURE B-19
Completed Inner Shadow effect

Inner Shadow effect

Adjust the transparency of an effect

1. Click the Opacity list arrow, drag the slider to **80**, click the Softness list arrow, drag the slider to **2**, then compare your pop-up window to Figure B-18.

2. Accept the remaining default settings, then click a blank area of the work area.

3. Click Select on the menu bar, click Deselect, then compare your image to Figure B-19.

4. Save your work.

You set the opacity for the Inner Shadow effect.

Lesson 3   Apply Effects to Objects and Text

APPLY A STYLE TO OBJECTS

What You'll Do

In this lesson, you will use the Styles panel to apply a style to text.

Using Styles in Documents

Styles are preset attributes, such as size, color, and texture that you can apply to objects and text. Fireworks manages styles on the Styles panel, which you can open from the Window menu. You easily can apply a style to an object by selecting the object, then clicking the style in the Styles panel. When you hold the mouse over a style, its name appears in the lower-left corner of the Styles panel. Figure B-20 shows style samples applied to different objects. You can edit an existing style, or you can create your own style from scratch and then save it in the Styles panel. You can also import or export preset or custom styles. Custom styles appear at the bottom of the Styles panel. To save a custom style, apply the properties you want to an object, then click the New Style button on the Styles panel to open the New Style dialog box. Name the style, and then select the attributes you want to include. Figure B-21 shows a new style added to the Styles panel. Fireworks will always apply the precise attributes associated with the style, which may not always be convenient

or exactly what you want. For example, many text styles change the font style and font size when you apply them. You can edit the style so that applying the style will change only the fill, stroke, and effect, not the font style or size. To edit a style, select the style in the Styles panel, click the Styles panel list arrow, click Edit Style to open the Edit Style dialog box, then select the attributes you want the style to apply and deselect the ones you want the style to ignore. To maintain the font style and size, for example, you would deselect the Text Font and Text Size check boxes.

Using Plug-ins

A **plug-in** adds features or enhancements to an application. You can install plug-ins from other software applications into Fireworks. Some plug-ins augment existing features. For example, Fireworks includes a sampling of effects from two Alien Skin products: Eye Candy 4000 LE and Alien Skin Splat LE. Additional information about Alien Skin plug-ins is available at *www.alienskin.com*.

Fireworks requires that you install the correct plug-ins, software drivers, and modules before you can import files from scanned or digital cameras. Note that plug-ins are platform-specific: TWAIN module (Win) or Photoshop Acquire plug-in.32 (Mac).

Using Adobe Photoshop Plug-ins and Features

Adobe Photoshop plug-ins and other import features are of common interest to Fireworks users. You can readily locate external sources of Photoshop features in the Fireworks Preferences dialog box. Options on the Folders tab of the

Preferences dialog box allow you to access the folders containing Photoshop plug-ins, textures, and patterns. Options on the Import tab allow you to determine how Fireworks translates Photoshop layers and text, such as by sharing layers across frames or allowing you to edit text after you import it.

Plug-ins and text features from Photoshop 5.5 translate smoothly into Fireworks MX—features from Photoshop 6 and 7, however, do not. Photoshop 6 and 7 text editability is compatible, but plug-ins are incompatible with Fireworks MX. For

general information on using Photoshop plug-ins, search for the Importing Photoshop filters and plug-ins topic in the Search section of the Using Fireworks help system. For additional information on Photoshop and Fireworks compatibility issues, visit the Fireworks Support Center at *www.macromedia.com/ support/ Fireworks*, then search the site using the keyword Photoshop. You can also search Macromedia Online Forums at *http://webforums.macromedia.com/fireworks/*.

FIGURE B-20
Style samples

FIGURE B-21
New style added to Styles panel

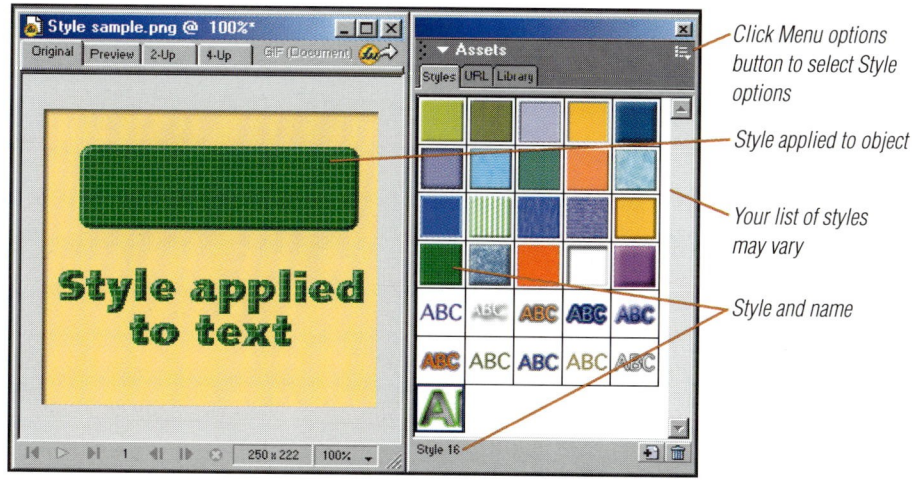

Click Menu options button to select Style options

Style applied to object

Your list of styles may vary

Style and name

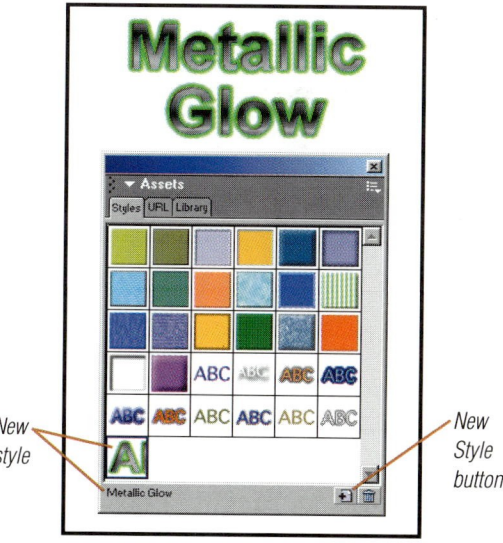

New style

New Style button

Apply a style to text

1. Click Window on the menu bar, then click Styles

   > **TIP** Drag the panel to the side of the work area so it does not obscure your view of the image.

2. Click the Text tool on the Tools panel, click the Font list arrow in the Property inspector, click Arial, double-click the Size text box, then type **175**.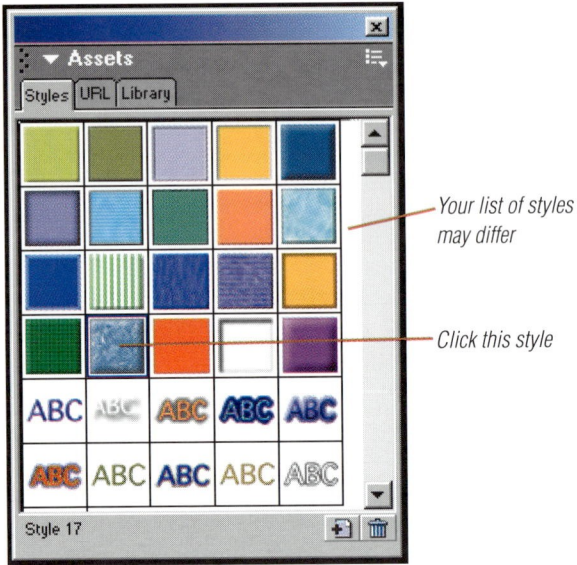

3. Click the Fill Color box, then click the first swatch in the top row of the color pop-up window.

4. Click the Bold button, then click the Center Alignment button.

5. Click the document next to the left side of the apple, then type **A**.

6. Click Style 17 in the Styles panel, as shown in Figure B-22.

   Fireworks applies the style to the text.

7. Click Select on the menu bar, then click Deselect.

8. Compare your image to Figure B-23, move the text to match the figure (if necessary), then save your work.

You created text and then applied a style to it.

FIGURE B-22
Styles panel

Your list of styles may differ

Click this style

FIGURE B-23
Style applied to text

Style 17 applied to text

Working with Objects

Drop Shadow effect settings

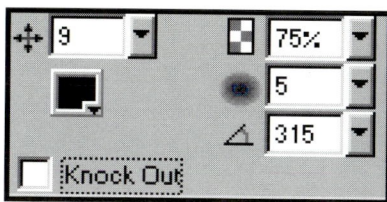

Drop Shadow effect applied to style

Drop shadow
effect added
to letter

Apply an effect to a style

1. Click the Pointer tool on the Tools panel, then click the letter A to select it.

2. Click the Add effects or choose a preset list arrow in the Effects section, point to Shadow and Glow, then click Drop Shadow.

3. Enter the values shown in Figure B-24.

4. Click Select on the menu bar, then click Deselect.

5. Save your work, then compare your image to Figure B-25.

You added an effect to the style.

Using automation features

In the course of Web design, you inevitably will need to make global changes to objects, text, files, and so on. Fireworks offers two features that will increase your efficiency. The Batch Process command on the File menu changes files you've already created. For example, you automatically can convert a collection of graphic files to another format or optimization setting. The Find and Replace command on the Edit menu works within your document to change colors, text, fonts, and so on.

Select, combine, and group objects.

1. Open fwb_2.png, save it as **confection**, then verify that the rulers are displayed.
2. Click the right green wing, then use the arrow keys to move it up and left to merge it with the left green wing.
3. Select both the left and right wings.
4. Combine the paths of the two objects, using the Union command.
5. Rename the combined object **Insignia**.
6. Select the purple circle, then move it behind the multicolored circle. (*Hint*: Use the Send to Back command under the Arrange command.)
7. Align the purple circle behind the multicolored circle so that it looks like the largest ring on the multicolored circle.
8. Group the purple circle and multicolored circles.

9. Rename the combined object **Lollipop**.
10. Move the lollipop object to the location shown in Figure B-26.
11. Select the right stick, and move it behind the lollipop.
12. Save your work.

Add a gradient fill to an object.

1. Select the pink ellipse.
2. Select the Folds fill from the Fill section on the Property inspector.
3. Click the Fill Color box, then change the left color to **FF99CC** and the right color to **FFFFFF**.
4. Change the Edge to Feather and the amount of feather to 8.
5. Change the Texture to Plaster and the amount of texture to 30%.

6. Group the pink circle and the left stick.
7. Rename the grouped objects **Cotton Candy**.
8. Save your work.

Apply effects.

1. Select the Insignia object.
2. Apply an Inner Bevel effect with the following settings: shape: Flat, width: 10, and button: Raised.
3. Add a stroke to the insignia with the following settings: category: Felt Tip, type: Dark Marker, size: 2.
4. Drag the insignia to the middle of the bottom green gumdrop.

5. Select the Text tool on the Tools panel, then choose the following settings: font: Times New Roman, size: 30 pt, color: white (#FFFFFF), style: Bold, Italic, and Center Alignment.

6. Click the document in the middle of the black blank area at the top, then type **Sugarless Tastes Great**.

7. Center the text on the page, if necessary.

8. Save your work.

Apply a style to text.

1. Display the Styles panel, then apply Style 1 to the text. (*Hint*: Substitute a different style if necessary.)

2. Select the gumdrops image, then adjust the opacity on the Layers panel to 80%.

3. Save your work, then compare your document to Figure B-26.

FIGURE B-26
Completed Skills Review

You're in charge of office security at your business. In the last four months, several employees, including the owner, have neglected to engage their screen savers when they've left their desks for lunch, meetings, and so on. Unfortunately, your office consists of cubicles that are open to many visitors passing through at any given time. So far, friendly reminders and rewards haven't done the trick, so you're going to e-mail the same obnoxious message and attachment to everyone. You'll use your Fireworks skills to develop a simple, but effective, message.

1. If desired, obtain images that will reinforce your message delivery and enhance the vector shapes you will create. You can obtain images from your computer, from the Internet, or from scanned media.

2. Create a new document and save it as **remember_me**.

3. Create a background image using any of the vector tools, rename it, and apply a fill, stroke, style, or effect to it, or adjust its transparency. (*Hint*: The background in the sample is a rectangle filled with a Twill pattern at 40% opacity.)

4. Create the primary vector object and apply a fill and at least one effect to it. (*Hint*: The ruler in the sample has a Linear gradient, Inner Bevel, Drop Shadow, and stroke applied to it.)

5. Create at least one other vector object and apply a fill, stroke, style, or effect to it, or adjust its transparency. (*Hint*: The polygon in the sample has an Outer Bevel effect and the Folds gradient applied to it.)

6. Create text objects as desired and apply a fill, stroke, style, or effect to them, or adjust their transparency. (*Hint*: The ruler text in the sample has an Inner Emboss effect applied to it; other text has a Drop Shadow effect applied to it.)

7. Group or combine objects as necessary, then rename the objects on the Layers panel.

8. Experiment with changing the order of effects in the Property inspector.

9. Save your work, then compare your document to Figure B-27.

FIGURE B-27
Completed Project Builder 1

Impact Potions, a new energy drink aimed at the teen market, is sponsoring a design contest. They want you to introduce the drink by using the design in a pop-up window on other teen Web sites. They haven't decided on the container yet, so you can create the bottle or can of your choice.

1. If desired, obtain images that will reinforce your message delivery and enhance the vector shapes you will create. You can obtain images from your computer, from the Internet, or from scanned media.
2. Create a new document and save it as **impact_potion**.
3. Create a beverage container using the vector tools of your choice, apply a fill, style, or stroke, and combine as necessary. (*Hint*: The can in the sample is an oval and a rectangle combined with the Union command.)
4. Create a label for the container, applying fills, styles, transparency, and effects as necessary.
5. Create text for the sign, applying fills, styles, transparency, and effects as necessary. (*Hint*: The Impact text in the sample has a style and the Drop Shadow effect applied to it; the text objects on the can were attached to paths.)

6. Rename objects or layers on the Layers panel as appropriate.
7. Experiment with changing the order of effects in the Property inspector.

FIGURE B-28
Completed Project Builder 2

8. Save your work, then compare your image to Figure B-28.

DESIGN PROJECT

One of the many advantages to using Fireworks for your images is the ability to combine vector and bitmap images into one document. For an artist, such as the country musician Dwight Yoakam, an official Web site can reinforce both artistic message and mood. Photographs and Fireworks-generated images combine to convey the feel of an old-time café and street scene. Each image also links the visitor to other pages within the site.

Because, by their very nature, dynamic Web sites are updated frequently to reflect current trends, this page may be different from Figure B-29 when you open it online.

1. Connect to the Internet and go to *www.course.com*. Navigate to the page for this book, click the Student Online Companion, then click the link for this unit.
2. Open a document in a word processor, or open a new Fireworks document, then save the file as **yoakam**. (*Hint*: Use the Text tool in Fireworks to answer the questions.)
3. Explore the site and answer the following questions:
   - When they were created in Fireworks, which objects could have been grouped?
   - Do objects appear to have been combined? If so, which Combine Paths commands could have been used and why?

- Identify gradients, textures, styles, or other effects applied to objects.
- Are there objects that appear to be a combination of a photograph and vector shape, or photographs that appear to have an effect applied to them?

FIGURE B-29
Design Project

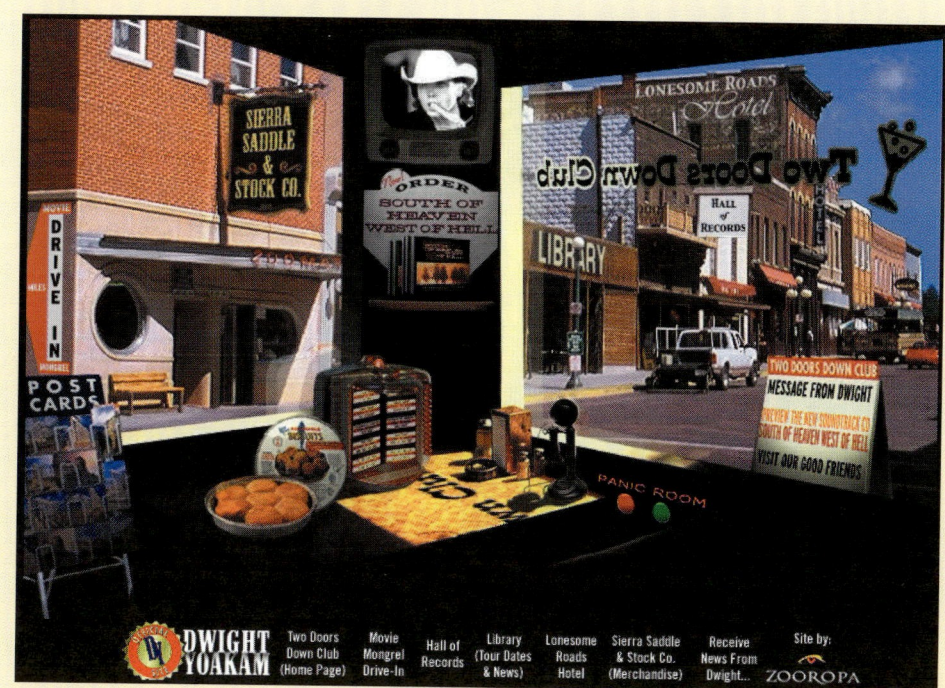

(*Hint*: Visit the site during the day and at night.)

4. Save your work, then compare your image to Figure B-29.

GROUP PROJECT

Your group can assign elements of the project to individual members, or work collectively to create the finished product.

You own a coffee shop and bakery, Existential Pastries, located near a convention center. You've just learned that two large conferences are being held the same week: the Intercontinental Philosophy Society and the Twilight Zone Crowd. With your strong-brewed coffee, international magazines, and rich desserts, these folks are your target audience. You want to buy time on the hotel's conference TV channel to promote the shop, but first, you need to create a design intended for all attendees.

1. If desired, obtain images for the ad that will support the vector objects you will create. You can obtain images from your computer, from the Internet, or from scanned media.
2. Create a new document and save it as **existential_pastries**.
3. Use the vector tools of your choice to create a baked item and authenticate its appearance. Apply fills, effects, styles, and strokes. (*Hint*: The donut ring in the sample has an Ellipse gradient with Parchment texture fill, Inner Bevel, and Drop Shadow effects applied to it. The texture has been rotated.)
4. Apply at least one Combine Paths command to the objects. (*Hint*: The donut hole in the sample was created using the Punch command.)
5. Create title text and other text that relates to the baked item, using fills, effects, styles, and strokes.
6. Create a background image.
7. Rename layers and objects on the Layers panel as appropriate.
8. Experiment with changing the order of effects in the Property inspector.
9. Save your work, then compare your document to Figure B-30.

FIGURE B-30
Completed Group Project

WORKING WITH INTERACTIVITY AND ANIMATION

1. Create slices and hotspots.

2. Create links in Web pages.

3. Create rollovers from slices.

4. Create basic animation.

5. Add tweening symbol instances to create animation.

UNIT C
WORKING WITH INTERACTIVITY AND ANIMATION

Understanding Web Functionality

Web pages contain various types of functionality that perform specific tasks or change appearance following input from the user, usually via the mouse. You can build in this functionality when you design and create your Web page. Fireworks provides you with easy-to-use tools, commands, and behaviors that allow you to add animation and interactivity to your Web graphics. You can create slices and hotspots that have links to other Web pages, rollovers, and animation. Best of all, you don't need to learn any programming language. In addition to being a graphic optimization and creation program, Fireworks comes with complete JavaScript behaviors ready to be inserted. You can easily add the functionality you want to an object or area of a Web page. From a functionality perspective, Fireworks makes it easy to add a lot of onscreen activity—it may be tempting to animate everything you can. However, from a design perspective, you must keep your viewers in mind. Your end users may very well leave a site that is over-the-top in animation and sound just as quickly as they would a static, dull site.

Tools You'll Use

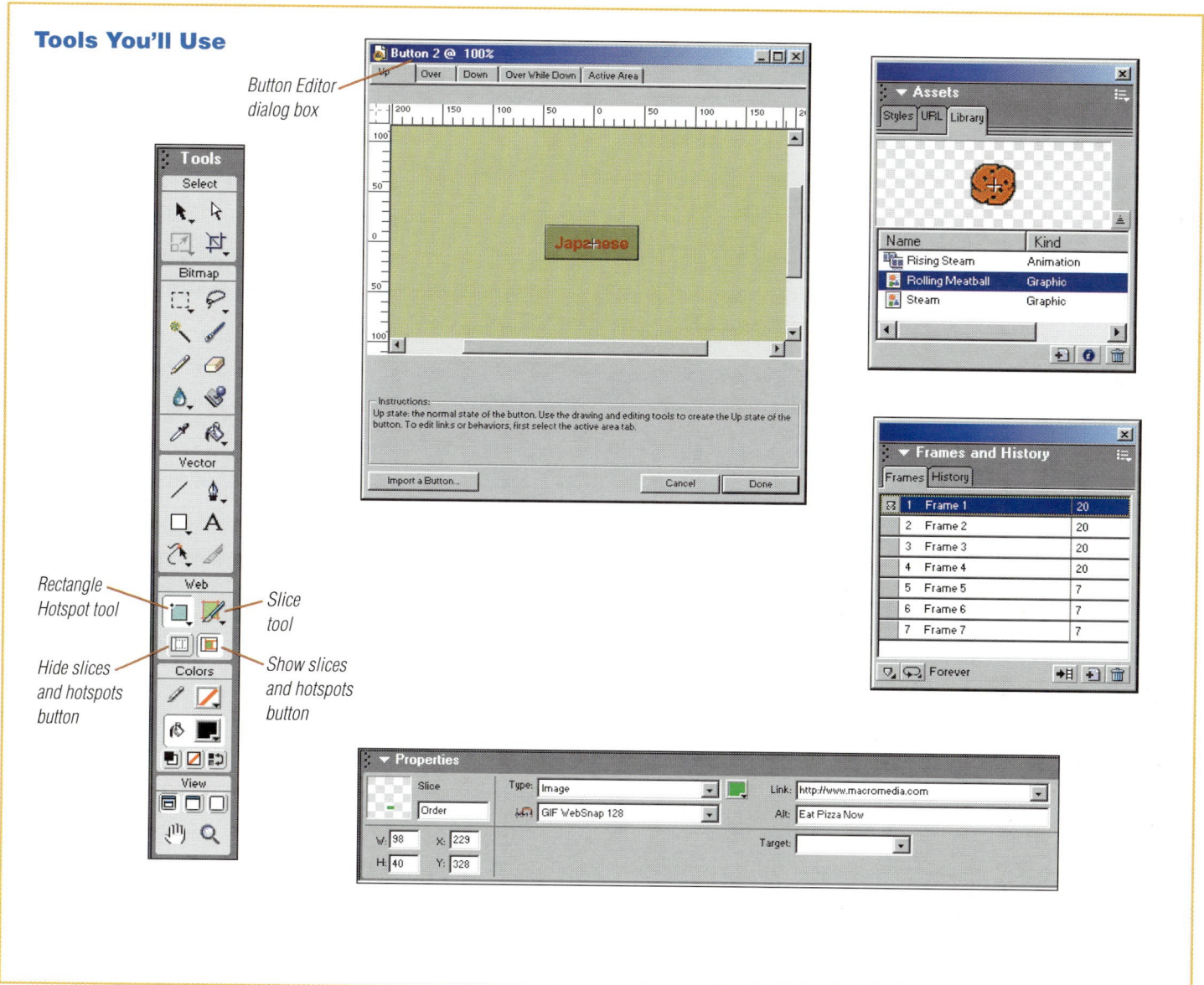

Button Editor dialog box

Rectangle Hotspot tool

Slice tool

Hide slices and hotspots button

Show slices and hotspots button

CREATE SLICES AND HOTSPOTS

What You'll Do

 In this lesson, you will open and rename a file, add slices and a hotspot to different objects, and rename objects on the Layers panel.

Understanding Slices and Hotspots in Fireworks

You use slices and hotspots to add interactivity to your Web document. **Interactivity** allows visitors to your Web site to affect its content by moving or clicking the mouse. You determine the areas for this mouse action by creating **slices**. Slicing a document into segments has distinct advantages—you can add individual functionality to each slice, and you can export it in the file format that best matches its use in your Web page. For example, you may want to export a photograph as JPEG, or line art as a GIF. To create a slice, you can use the Slice tool or Polygon Slice tool on the Tools panel and then draw the slice shape you want. You can automatically insert a slice on an object by selecting the object and then clicking the Slice command from the Insert command on the Edit menu. Slices appear as green translucent rectangles in your document.

Exporting slices

Fireworks exports slices, which define the table cells in the exported HTML file. Fireworks exports the area of the image that lies beneath the slice as a single image. You can export one, all, or selected slices in a document. You can choose the HTML editor of your choice, such as Dreamweaver, which will read the code and reassemble the slices into an HTML table. You can also copy the image map onto your Clipboard and then paste it directly into Dreamweaver or another HTML editor.

A **hotspot** is an area that you define in your document to which you can assign a URL (Web address) or other type of interactivity. Hotspots initiate specific actions, such as linking to a new Web page, after being triggered by a mouse action. You can create a hotspot of just about any shape, using the following hotspot tools on the Tools panel: Rectangle Hotspot tool, Circle Hotspot tool, or Polygon Hotspot tool. Hotspots are displayed as blue translucent objects in your document. You can also create a single hotspot from multiple images. You can select many of the same options, such as inserting a URL link, to slices and hotspots. The options on the Property inspector change slightly, depending on whether you

select a slice or a hotspot. An **image map** is a graphic containing several hotspots. You can assign a different URL to each hotspot.

Slices and hotspots write HMTL code when you export them that instructs your Web browser to execute certain commands, such as changing a button color, swapping an image, or linking to a URL. Once you create a slice or hotspot, you can add interactivity or functionality, which you'll learn about in a later lesson. Because slices and hotspots are Web objects and not graphic objects, Fireworks stores them on the Web Layer of the Layers panel. The Web Layer is always the topmost layer on the Layers panel. You can name, hide, show, create,

and delete objects on the Web Layer in the same way as you do with document objects. To create and edit slices and hotspots, you must click the Show slices and hotspots icon on the Tools panel. To completely view and assess the configuration of all your slices and hotspots, select the Slice Guides and Slice Overlay commands on the View menu. For optimal functioning, slices should be contiguous (adjacent to each other); if they do overlap, Fireworks will apply the attributes assigned to the topmost slice. The sample document shown in Figure C-1 depicts slices and hotspots turned on and off in a document, respectively.

FIGURE C-1

Slices and hotspots in document

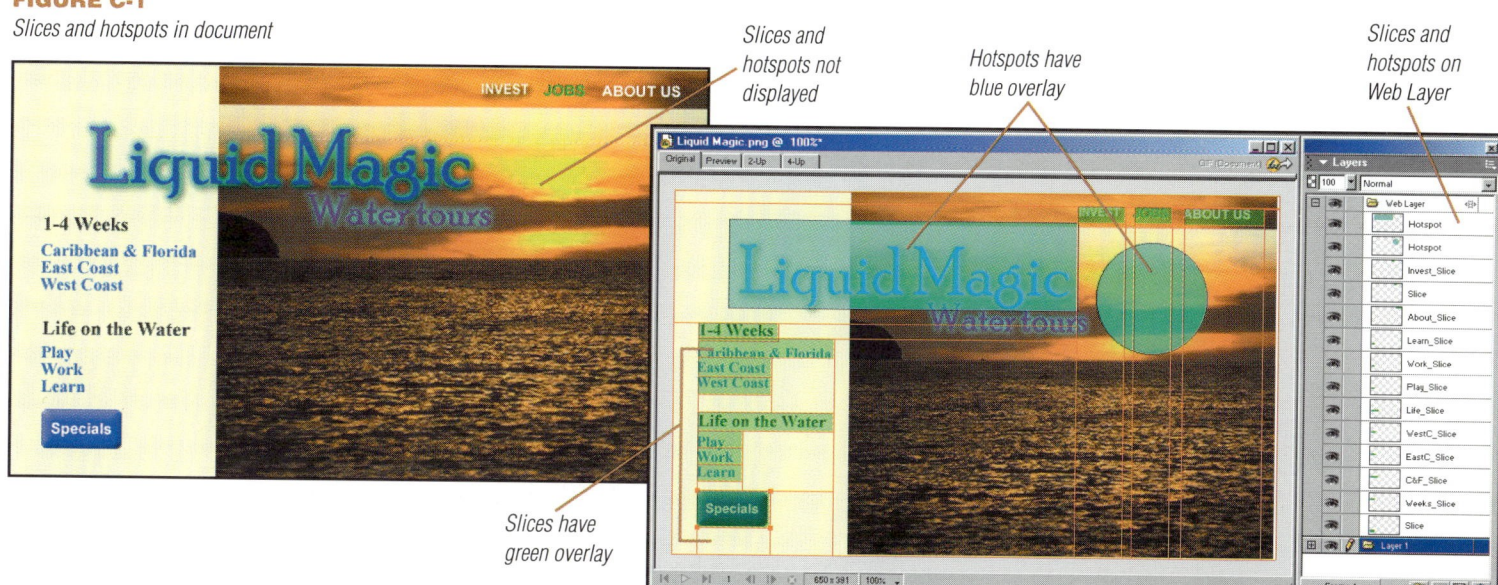

Slices and hotspots not displayed

Hotspots have blue overlay

Slices and hotspots on Web Layer

Slices have green overlay

Create a slice from an object

1. Open fwc_1.png, then save it as **pizzeria**.

2. Verify that the slice guides and slice overlay commands are selected on the View menu.

   > TIP To display slice guides and the slice overlay, click the respective command on the View menu.

3. Click the Order 'Za object in the document.

4. Click Edit on the menu bar, point to Insert, click Slice, then compare your image to Figure C-2.

5. Double-click the Slice object on the Web Layer on the Layers panel, type **Order**, then click a blank area of the screen.

   > TIP Separate words in a slice with an underscore or a hyphen.

6. Save your work.

You opened and renamed a file, inserted a slice on an object, and then renamed the slice object on the Layers panel.

Create a slice using the Slice tool

1. Click the Slice tool on the Tools panel.

2. Draw a slice that covers the Japanese pizza photo, then compare your image to Figure C-3.

   > TIP To change the color of a slice line or guide line, click View on the menu bar, point to Guides, click Edit Guides, click the color swatch you want, then click OK.

(continued)

FIGURE C-2
Slice added to object

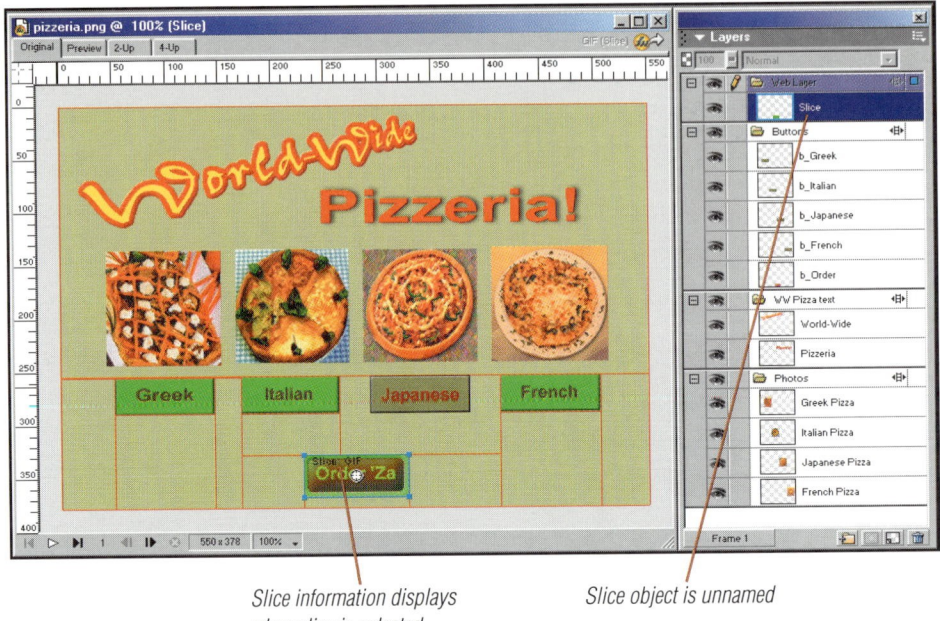

Slice information displays when slice is selected

Slice object is unnamed

FIGURE C-3
Slice added using Slice tool

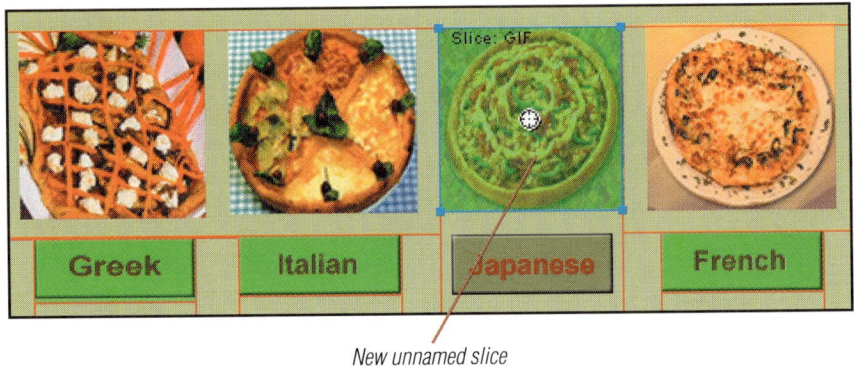

New unnamed slice

FIGURE C-4

Renamed slices on Web Layer

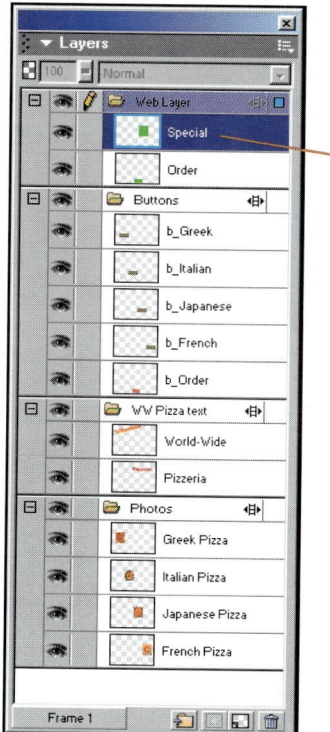

Slices added on
Web Layer

FIGURE C-5

Hotspot added to object

Hotspot overlay
is light blue

3. Double-click the Slice object on the Web Layer on the Layers panel, type **Special**, then click a blank area of the screen.

    TIP You can also rename a slice on the Property inspector.

4. Compare your Layers panel to Figure C-4.

5. Save your work.

You created a slice on an object using the Slice tool and then renamed the slice object on the Layers panel.

Create a hotspot using the Polygon Hotspot tool

1. Press and hold the Rectangle Hotspot tool on the Tools panel, then click the Polygon Hotspot tool.

2. Using Figure C-5 as a guide, click the mouse to create a hotspot that covers the World-Wide text.

    If the hotspot is not exactly how you want it, you can undo each mouse click until the hotspot is gone or delete the hotspot, and then start over.

3. Double-click the Hotspot object on the Web layer on the Layers panel, type **World-Wide**, then click a blank area of the screen.

4. Save your work.

You created a polygon hotspot on an object, then renamed the hotspot object on the Layers panel.

CREATE LINKS IN WEB PAGES

What You'll Do

 In this lesson, you will add a link to a slice and a hotspot, add text to the slice's URL information, and preview the links in Fireworks and in a Web browser.

Adding a URL to a Slice or a Hotspot

After you place a slice or hotspot on an object, you can assign a URL to the slice or hotspot. Once you select the slice or hotspot in the document, you can enter a URL and other options in the Property inspector. You can insert a URL in the Link: text box, and also select a URL from previously entered addresses. When your users click the link in a Web browser, the browser will navigate to that Web page. The text you enter in the Alt: text box appears when you position the mouse over a slice or hotspot. The text resembles a ToolTip in Fireworks, which appears when you hold the mouse over a tool on the Tools panel. Note, however, that alternate text behaves differently (or not at all) depending on your browser and computer platform. In some Web browsers, this text may appear as the linked URL is loading in the browser. You can

determine how the linked Web page will be displayed in the browser by selecting an option in the Target: text box. For example, the Web page can open in a separate window, or replace the current Web page.

Fireworks automatically assigns a unique name to a slice, based on its row and column number. By default, Fireworks does not name hotspots in the Property inspector. You can change the name to something more meaningful by changing the object name on the Web Layer in the Layers panel or in the Property inspector. Figure C-6 shows slice settings on the Property inspector.

QUICKTIP

You can edit hotspots using the Pointer, Subselection, and transform tools (Scale, Skew, and Distort).

Accessing URLs

You may want to add the same URL to several slices or hotspots in different documents, such as a Home or Contact Us button. Fireworks stores each URL you enter in the Current URL list on the Properties panel. You can add, delete, or edit URLs on the URL panel. Once you open a document that contains a URL list, you can access these addresses for every document you open during the *current* editing session. To add a URL to a library, open the URL panel from the Window menu, select the URL, then click the Add current URL to library icon. By default, Fireworks adds URLs to the URLs.htm library. You can add individual URLs to the URLs.htm library, create your own **libraries** (groups of URLs), and import URLs. If you use a URL repeatedly, you can permanently add it to a URL library. You can also create a new library to store related URLs. In addition, you can import URLs from a Netscape Navigator Bookmarks file or from an Internet Explorer Favorites file. You can reference a URL library where your operating system stores application data, under Macromedia/Fireworks MX/URL Libraries.

Understanding Preview Options

When you add interactivity, such as a URL link to a slice, you can preview the mouse change in the Preview tab of the Document window. The Preview tab displays the document as it would appear in a Web browser, using the current optimization settings. To actually link to the URL and view alternate type, you must preview your document in a Web browser. Fireworks allows you to preview your document in two different browsers. To set a browser, click the applicable primary or secondary browser option from the Preview in Browser command on the File menu as shown in Figure C-7, select the folder where your browser software is located, click the executable (.exe) filename (Win) or the application (Mac), then click Open. Depending on the computer and the browser, your Web document may appear and function differently—it's a good idea to preview your Web page using as diverse a mix of computers, software, and settings as possible.

FIGURE C-6

Slice settings on the Property inspector

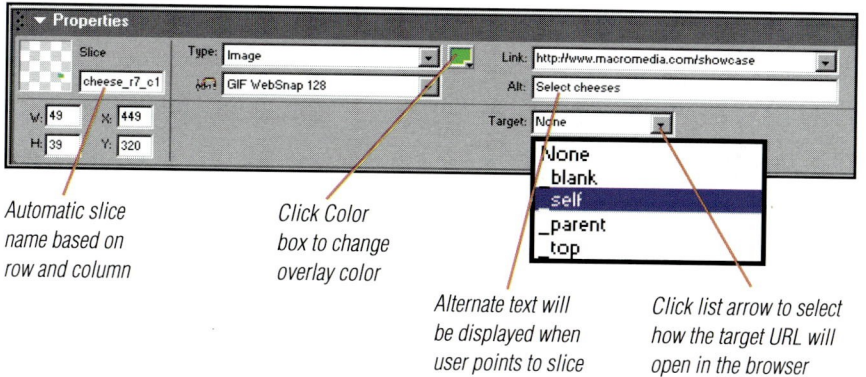

Automatic slice name based on row and column

Click Color box to change overlay color

Alternate text will be displayed when user points to slice

Click list arrow to select how the target URL will open in the browser

FIGURE C-7

Browser preview options

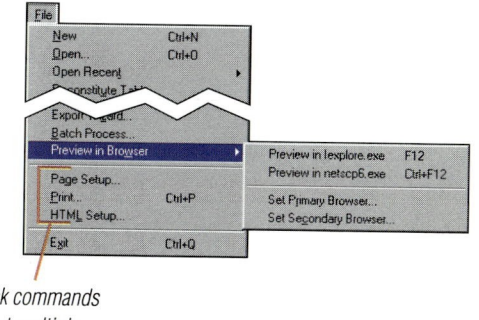

Click commands to set multiple preview browsers

Add a URL to a slice

1. Click the Pointer tool on the Tools panel, then click the Order slice. ▶

2. Click the Link: text box on the Property inspector, then type **http://www.macromedia.com**.

   TIP   You can select a previously entered URL by clicking the Link list arrow and then clicking an address.

4. Click the Alt: text box, type **Eat Pizza Now**, press [Enter] (Win) or [return] (Mac), then compare your Property inspector to Figure C-8.

5. Save your work.

You selected a slice, then added a URL link and alternate text to the slice using the Property inspector.

Insert a link in a hotspot and change the hotspot shape

1. Click the World-Wide hotspot.

2. Click the Link: text box, then type **http://www.macromedia.com/showcase**.

3. Click the Hotspot shape list arrow, click Rectangle, then compare your image to Figure C-9.

   The hotspot changes to a rectangle, which overlaps onto other objects.

(continued)

FIGURE C-8
URL entered for hotspot

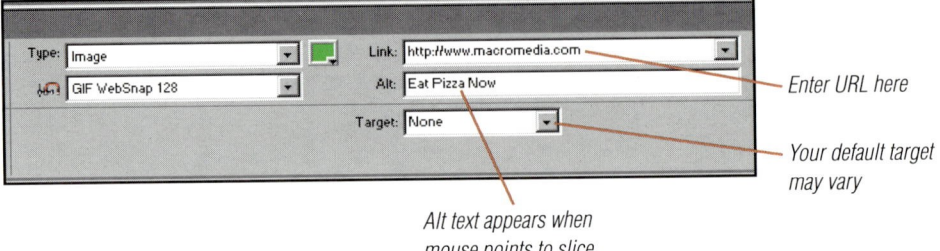

Enter URL here

Alt text appears when mouse points to slice

Your default target may vary

FIGURE C-9
Changing a hotspot shape

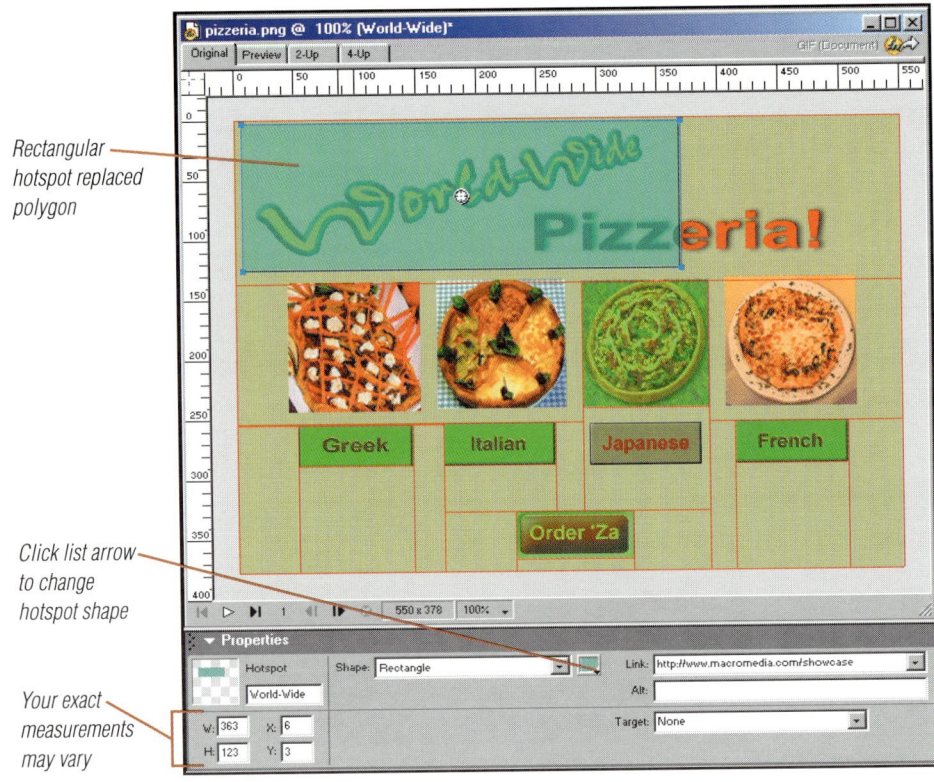

Rectangular hotspot replaced polygon

Click list arrow to change hotspot shape

Your exact measurements may vary

Working with Interactivity and Animation

FIGURE C-10

Preview in Fireworks

Pointer indicates
interactivity

FIGURE C-11

Preview in Web browser

Alternate text

4. Click Edit on the menu bar, then click Undo Edit Hotspot to restore the polygon.

> TIP You can also edit a hotspot by clicking the Subselection tool on the Tools panel and then dragging the hotspot's anchor points to new locations.

5. Save your work.

You added a link to a hotspot, changed the shape of a hotspot, then restored the original shape.

Preview in Fireworks and in a browser

1. Click the Hide slices and hotspots button on the Tools panel to hide the slices, then click the Preview tab.

2. Move the mouse over the World-Wide hotspot and the Order slice, then compare your image to Figure C-10.

3. Click File on the menu bar, point to Preview in Browser, then click the browser in which you want to preview the document.

4. Move the mouse over the World-Wide text and the Order 'Za button, then compare your image to Figure C-11.

> TIP Depending on your browser, alternate text may not be visible.

5. Click the Order 'Za button to test the link, then close your browser.

6. Save your work.

You previewed the document in Fireworks and in your default browser.

CREATE ROLLOVERS FROM SLICES

What You'll Do

In this lesson, you will create a rollover for the Japanese pizza image by first adding text to a new frame. You will then create and add a drag and drop behavior to a new button, create and modify button states, and then preview the rollovers.

Understanding Rollovers

In a basic Web page, graphics change appearance—they are often swapped for other graphics in response to mouse actions. Usually, the first indication of an action occurs when you move, or roll, the mouse over an object or area of the Web page. A **rollover** is a behavior on a graphic element in your Web page that your mouse triggers. The trigger can be a roll or a click. In order to create a rollover, you need to coordinate a few items: first, you need to create at least two images and at least one new frame, attach slices or hotspots to the images, and finally, add a behavior that sets the slices or hotspots in motion. You create a rollover effect by adding a behavior to a slice or hotspot. A **behavior** is a preset piece of JavaScript code. **JavaScript** is a Web-scripting code that interacts with HTML code to create interactive content, such as rollovers.

You can add a behavior by dragging and dropping a behavior from a slice or hotspot onto the same or different slice, by adding a behavior from the Behaviors

panel, or by writing your own JavaScript. The easiest and fastest way to add a behavior is to drag and drop one onto an object. To add a drag and drop behavior, select the object, then drag the Behavior handle to the target object. You can use the drag and drop behavior to attach a behavior to one or more slices, and to easily swap an image in a rollover. If you know JavaScript, you can write a custom behavior. Figure C-12 shows the drag and drop behaviors available for slices and hotspots, and the preset behaviors available on the Behaviors panel.

QUICKTIP

Because Fireworks and Dreamweaver behaviors are identical, you can edit your Fireworks HTML behaviors using the Dreamweaver Behaviors panel.

Usually, you create two images for a rollover: one for the trigger, or *before* version, and another copy of the object as the target, or *after* version. In Fireworks, you can create a simple rollover in different ways. In a sense, when you execute a rollover, the image changes over time (from *before* to *after*). The Frames panel contains frames that are used to play animations or it can contain various rollover and button state images. By default, each document contains one frame, Frame 1, where the images that appear when the Web page first loads are found. When you add a rollover, you create a new frame if needed. A rollover requires that you add at least one new frame to your document; you create a new frame for a new image. In a simple rollover, the original version appears in Frame 1, and the target of the rollover appears in Frame 2. After you create a rollover, you can modify or move the images in your document without affecting the behavior. You can edit the objects that lie beneath a slice or hotspot. You must first hide the slice or hotspot before you

can edit the object. To hide a slice or hotspot, click the Hide slices and hotspots button on the Tools panel, or click the Show/Hide Layer icon next to the object on the Layers panel.

Understanding Button States

You can create a button that contains a slice and different states that determine the button's appearance based on the mouse action. A button can have up to four **states** associated with it, although most contain two: Up and Over. Modifying a button in the Over state will cause the button's appearance to change when you roll the mouse over it. A button is a special type of graphic symbol that represents an object, text, or combination group. You can assign button states using the Button Editor. The button states are described below.

Up—Default state, not affected by mouse movement.

Over—State when mouse passes over button.

Down—State when user clicks mouse.

Over While Down—State when mouse passes over button after user clicks it (in Down state).

Active Area—The slice (or hotspot on top of a slice) to which a behavior is attached. The Active Area includes the four button states and the size of any swap image.

QUICKTIP

Keep in mind that the more button states you add, the more graphic files you generate when you export Fireworks files into HTML.

FIGURE C-12
Behavior options

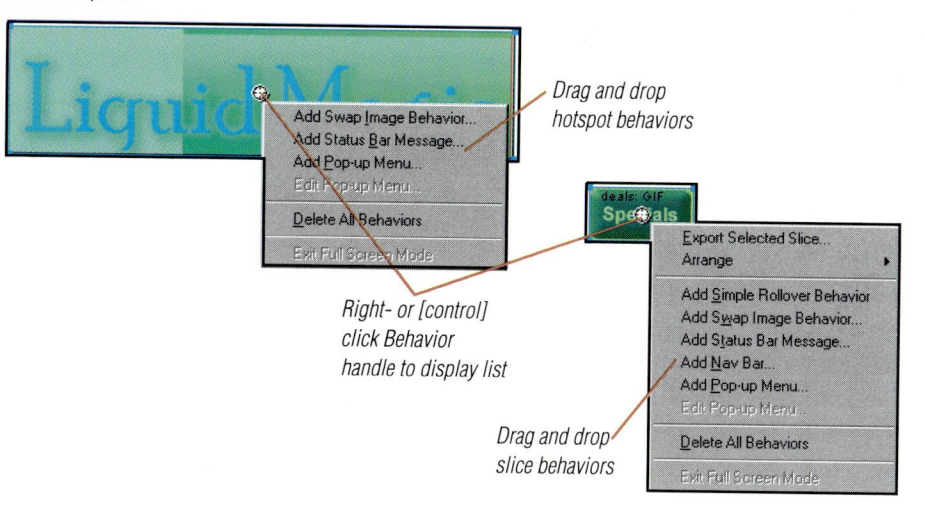
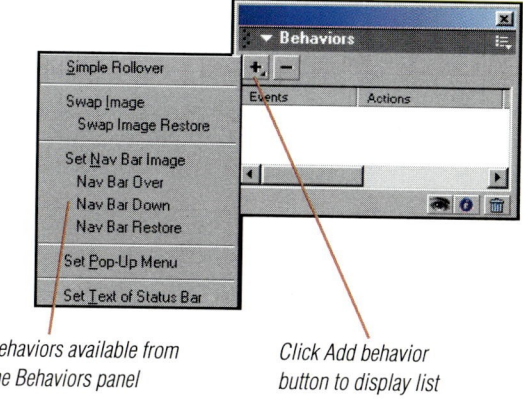

Drag and drop hotspot behaviors

Right- or [control] click Behavior handle to display list

Drag and drop slice behaviors

Behaviors available from the Behaviors panel

Click Add behavior button to display list

Create text in a new frame

1. Click the Original tab, then click the Japanese pizza slice in the document.

2. Click Window on the menu bar, click Frames, then click Frame 2 in the Frames panel.

   This document already has rollovers inserted, so you do not need to add a new frame.

   | TIP All the Over images are visible in Frame 2 (flags on the buttons).

3. Click the Text tool on the Tools panel, then click the document in the middle of the Japanese pizza image. A

4. Click the Font list arrow, click Arial, double-click the Size text box, type **22**, click the Color box, click the light blue swatch in the far left column of the color pop-up window, (#00FFFF), click the Bold button, then click the Center Alignment button.

5. On three separate lines, type **Shrimp Mayo Squid**.

6. Click the Pointer tool on the Tools panel, then center the text over the image (if necessary).

7. Click Select on the menu bar, click Deselect, then compare your document to Figure C-13.

8. Save your work.

You added rollover text to a slice in Frame 2.

FIGURE C-13
Adding rollover text

Existing rollovers visible in Frame 2

New rollover text

FIGURE C-14

Drag and drop behavior

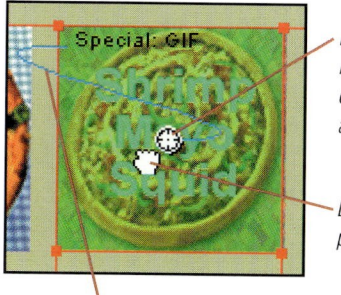

Special: GIF

Drag Behavior handle until blue connection line appears

Drag pointer

Blue line indicates rollover connected to slice

FIGURE C-16

Behavior added to Behaviors panel

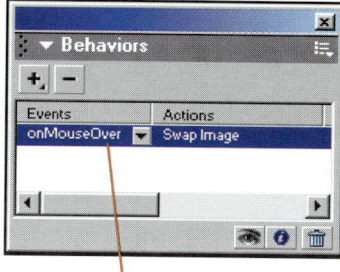

Swap image behavior added to slice by drag and drop behavior

FIGURE C-15

Swap Image dialog box

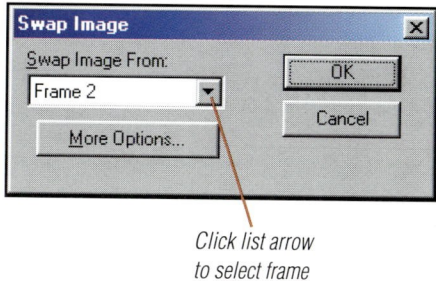

Click list arrow to select frame

FIGURE C-17

Text rollover preview

Text appears when mouse rolls over pizza

1. Click the Show slices and hotspots button on the Tools panel, then click the Japanese pizza slice.

2. Using Figure C-14 as a guide, click the behavior handle in the middle of the Japanese pizza slice, then drag it to the top left corner of the slice.

   A blue line attaches the behavior to the slice and the Swap Image dialog box opens.

3. Verify that Frame 2 appears in the Swap Image From text box, then compare your Swap Image dialog box to Figure C-15.

4. Click OK, click Window on the menu bar, click Behaviors, then compare your Behaviors panel to Figure C-16.

   The behavior appears on the Behaviors panel.

5. Click the Preview tab, then click the Hide slices and hotspots button on the Tools panel to hide the slices.

6. Roll the mouse over the Japanese pizza photo, then compare your image to Figure C-17.

You added text and a rollover behavior to the slice, then previewed the rollover.

Create a new button state

1. Click the Original tab, then click the Show slices and hotspots button on the Tools panel to display slices.

2. Click the Japanese text object in the document, click Edit on the menu bar, then click Copy.

   You will copy the object to use it as the Up state, or normal version, of the object.

3. Press [Delete] (Win) or [delete] (Mac) to delete the Japanese object and text in the document.

   You will add interactivity to the object copy in the Button Editor.

4. Click Edit on the menu bar, point to Insert, then click New Button.

   The Button Editor opens with the Up tab selected, where you can create and edit buttons for each rollover state.

5. Click Edit on the menu bar, then click Paste.

   The Japanese object from the document appears in the Up state.

6. Click the Over tab, click the Copy Up graphic button, then compare your Button Editor to Figure C-18.

   Fireworks pastes the copy of the button from the Up state.

You selected, copied, and deleted an object, then pasted it in the Up and Over states in the Button Editor.

FIGURE C-18
Object copied to Over state

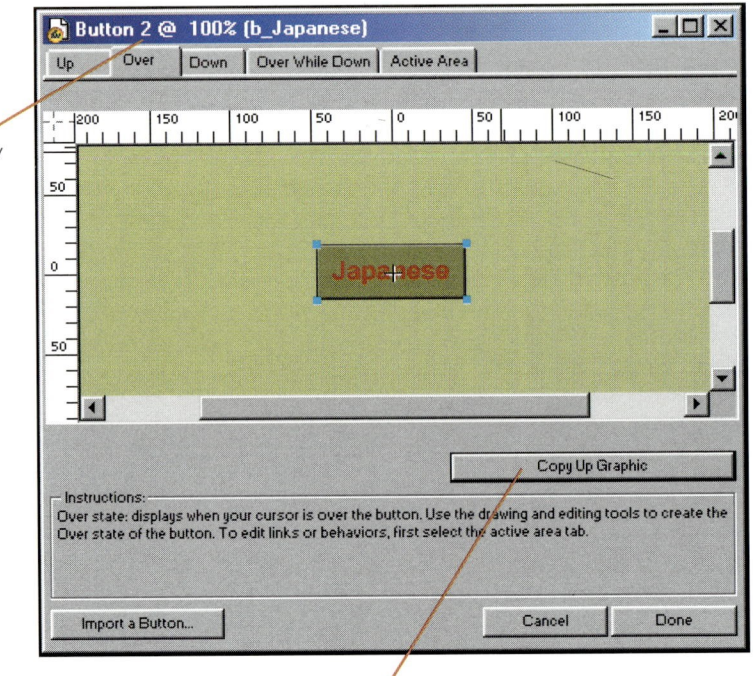

Your button number may differ

Click button to copy objects from Up state

FIGURE C-19

Modifying an object in the Over state

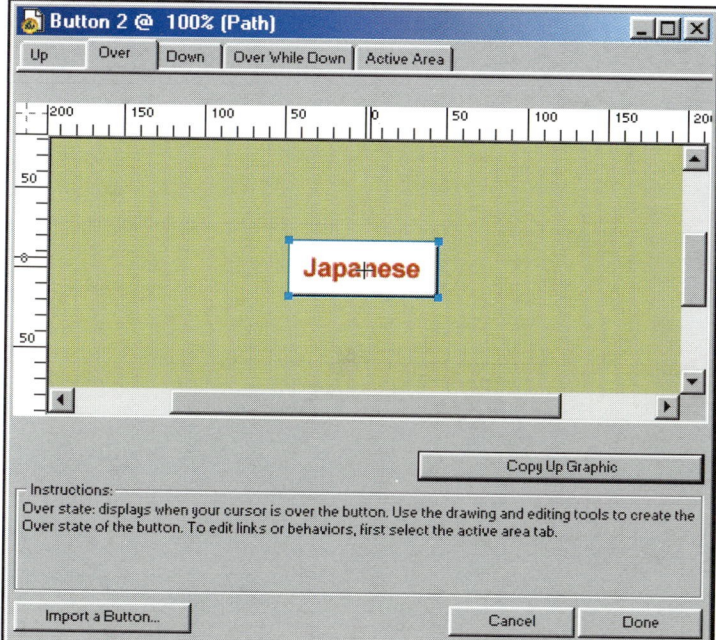

Lesson 3   Create Rollovers from Slices

Modify an object in the Over state

1. Click Modify on the menu bar, click Ungroup, click a blank area of the Button Editor, then select the green rectangle.

2. Click the Fill Color box on the Property inspector, click the white color swatch (#FFFFFF) in the left column of the color pop-up window, press (enter) (Mac), if necessary, then compare your image to Figure C-19.

3. Press and hold the Rectangle tool on the Tools panel, then click the Ellipse tool.

4. Click the Fill Color box on the Property inspector, then click the red color swatch (#FF0000) in the left column of the color pop-up window palette.

5. Press and hold [Alt][Shift] (Win) or [option][Shift] (Mac), place the pointer on the cross hair of the rectangle, then drag a circle from the middle of the button to the top and bottom borders of the rectangle.

   TIP   Press and hold [Alt] (Win) or [option] (Mac) to draw an object from the center outward.

6. Click the Pointer tool on the Tools panel, center the red circle (if necessary), click the Japanese text, click the Color box on the Property inspector, then click the black swatch (#000000) in the left column of the color pop-up window.

(continued)

7. Click Modify on the menu bar, point to Arrange, click Bring to Front, then compare your button to Figure C-20.

8. Click the Done button on the Button Editor.

   The new Japanese object appears in the middle of the document.

9. Drag the Japanese object beneath the Japanese pizza, then use the arrow keys to center it precisely, as shown in Figure C-21.

10. Double-click the Button Symbol object on the Buttons layer of the Layers panel, type **b_Japanese**, click a blank area of the screen, then save your work.

You modified the Over state of the Japanese object by changing the object and text color and adding a new design element to it. You positioned the object in the document, and renamed the object on the Layers panel.

FIGURE C-20
Modified button

FIGURE C-21
Button repositioned under pizza

Arrow icon indicates symbol

Working with Interactivity and Animation

FIGURE C-22
Rollover preview

Stop button   Current frame

1. Click the Hide slices and hotspots button on the Tools panel to hide slices, then click the Preview tab. 🔲

2. Roll the mouse over the Japanese object to display the flag.

   > **TIP** To edit a button, double-click the button in any frame, then click the tab of the button state you want to modify.

3. Roll the mouse over each of the other text buttons and the Japanese pizza photo.

4. Click the Play button, then click the Stop button at the bottom of the document window to alternate views between the Up and Over states, as shown in Figure C-22. ▷

5. Click File on the menu bar, point to Preview in Browser, then click the browser of your choice.

6. Roll the mouse over the buttons and the Japanese pizza photo.

7. Close your browser, then save and close pizzeria.png.

You previewed the rollovers in the Preview tab of the document, cycled through the frames, and previewed the document in a browser.

CREATE BASIC ANIMATION

What You'll Do

In this lesson, you will animate a selected object, and then animate another object by modifying frames on the Frames panel.

Understanding Animation In Fireworks

Animation is created playing a series of images in a sequence, which creates the illusion of movement, fading out, and so on. Fireworks makes it easy to add animation to your document. However, even with the best tools at your fingertips, the most important aspect of successful animation is you, the designer. Developing and following a plan when you create an animation ensures that your outcome will match your vision. Otherwise, you could spend a lot of time redoing pieces of your animation, or could discover that

it does not function properly in a browser or look at all the way you had intended.

Fireworks offers different techniques to animate objects. The easiest way is to select an object and then to animate it by clicking the Animate Selection command on the Modify menu. This process turns an object into a animation symbol, which is an element that you can reuse in any document. When you animate an object, Fireworks will prompt you when the number of animation frames exceeds the total number of frames in the document.

Understanding animated GIFs

When your animation is complete, you can export it for playback in a Web page as an animated GIF. To export a file or slice, select Animated GIF from the Export file format list in the Optimize panel, click the Export command from the File menu, navigate to the location where you want to save the file, then click Save.

You can animate several objects in a document. You can also copy an object into different frames and then modify the object in each frame, a process known as **frame-by-frame** animation. You can change physical attributes, such as color and effects, by modifying an object in the document. You can adjust the animation trail in your document by dragging the animation motion path. To extend the animation, drag the green or red animation handles. To move the animation (and the object), drag a blue animation handle. Figure C-23 shows animation handles on objects.

To edit an animation, select it, then modify settings on the Property inspector.

Using the Frames Panel

You use the Frames panel to manage the frames in your animation. You easily can rename frames (by default, they are numbered sequentially), and add, delete, move, copy, or hide frames as needed. You can also set the number of times your animation will play in the browser and its direction: forward or reverse. You can use **onion skinning** to view one or more frames while in the current frame. The term "onion skinning" refers to the super-thin sheets of transparent paper used in traditional animation as overlays to view an animation series. By seeing where and how the preceding and following frames interact with the image in the current

FIGURE C-23
Animation handles

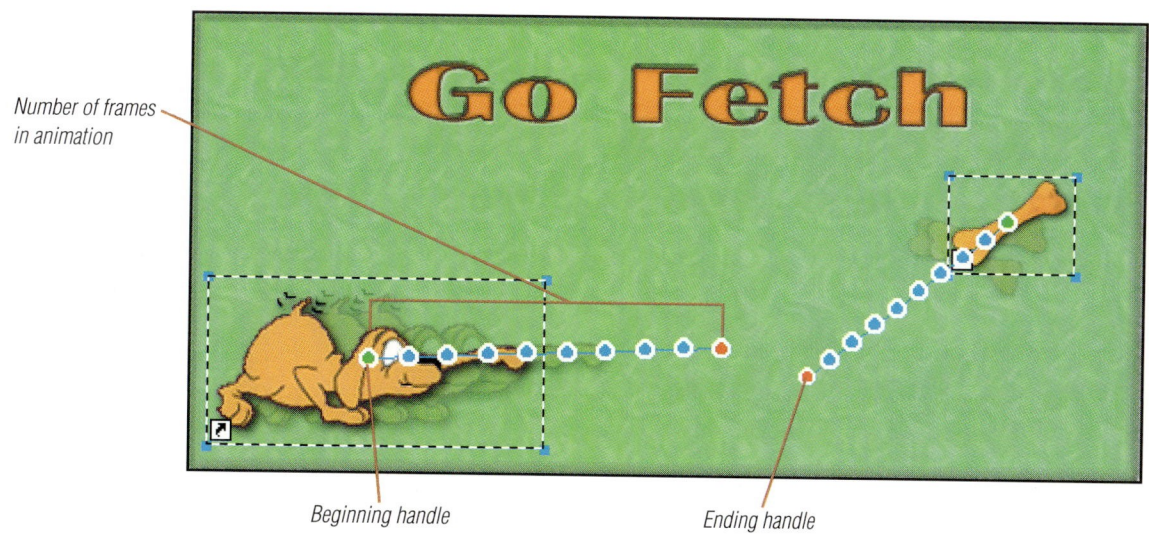

Number of frames in animation

Beginning handle

Ending handle

frame, you can precisely align your animation. Figure C-24 shows onion skinning in a document.

Sharing Layers Across Frames

If you want an image to display in every frame, set the layer to share across frames. Otherwise, when you play an animation, an image will be visible only in the first frame. You must select entire layers to share across frames; you cannot select individual objects on a layer. You can edit an object in a layer that is shared across all frames at any time; Fireworks automatically updates the changes in every frame. To share a selected layer across frames, select the Share This Layer command in the Layers panel options pop-up menu.

Choosing the Number of Times a Movie Will Play

Web designers often assume that viewers will want or need to watch an animation repeatedly. For example, an e-mail image, such as an animated envelope or mailbox, may continuously open and close, in a process known as **looping**. You can choose how many times your movie will play by clicking the GIF animation looping button in the Frames panel, then clicking an a number or option in the list. For example, None means the movie will play once and then stop, 5 means it will play five times and then stop; and Forever means it will never stop.

FIGURE C-24
View onion skinning

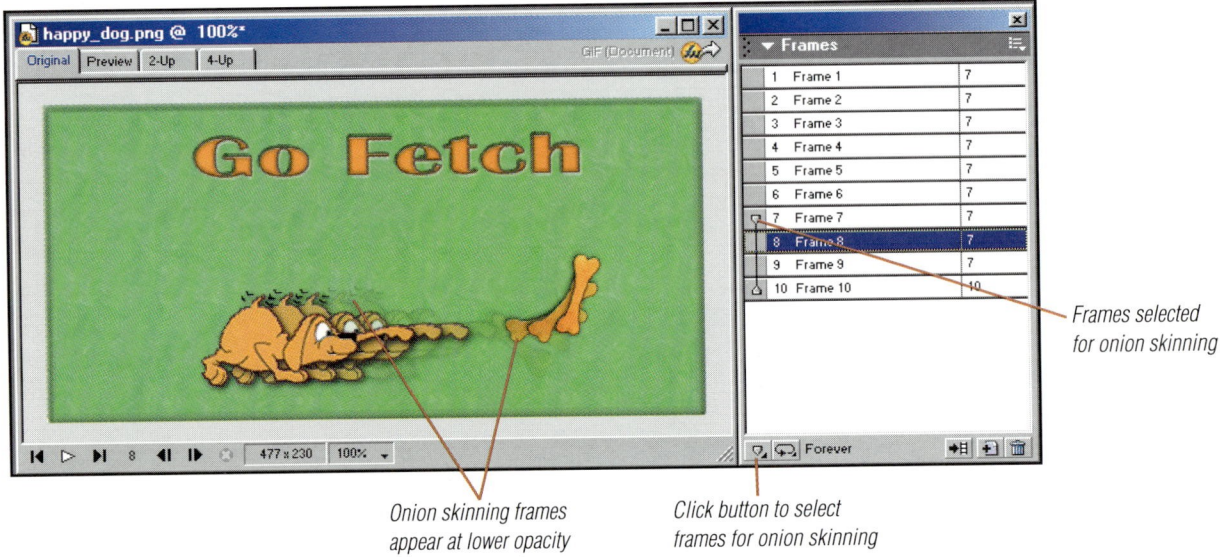

Onion skinning frames appear at lower opacity

Click button to select frames for onion skinning

Frames selected for onion skinning

FIGURE C-25
Animate dialog box

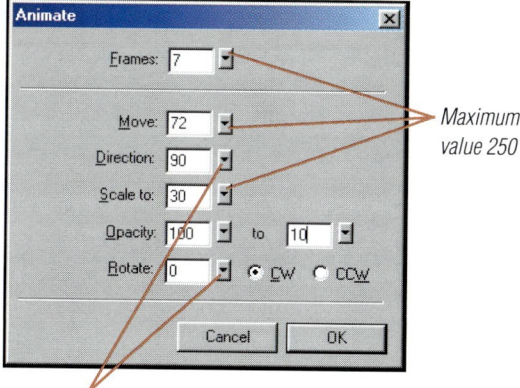

Maximum value 250

Maximum value 360

FIGURE C-26
Animated steam in Frame 5

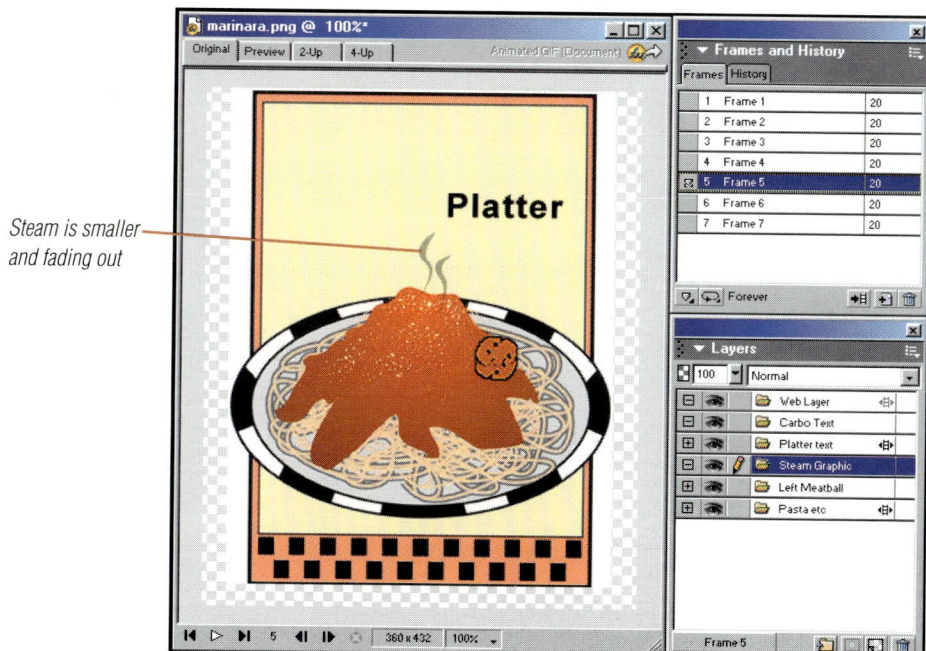

Steam is smaller and fading out

1. Open fwc_2.png, then save it as **marinara**.
2. Make sure that the Layers and Frames panels are displayed.
3. Click the Rising Steam object on the canvas.
4. Click Modify on the menu bar, point to Animation, then click Animate Selection.
5. Enter the settings shown in Figure C-25, click OK, then click OK again if a warning box appears asking if you want to add frames.

   TIP   The steam will rise, become smaller, and fade out.

6. Double-click the Animation Symbol object on the Layers panel, then type **Rising Steam**.

   TIP   Because Fireworks automatically names new objects on the Layers panel, you may frequently need to rename them.

7. Click the Play button on the document window to preview the animation, then click the Stop button to stop the animation. ■

   The animation plays in the document in the direction determined by the animation motion path.

8. Click Frame 5 on the Frames panel, then compare your image to Figure C-26.
9. Save your work.

You animated an object.

Modify an animation motion path

1. Click the Previous frame button on the document window until you reach Frame 1.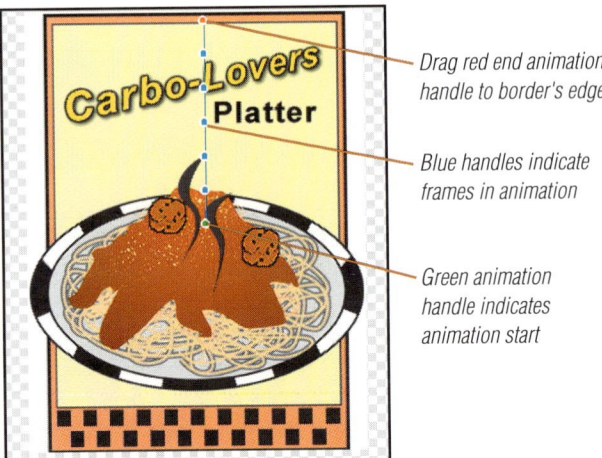

   TIP To edit an animation motion path, you must be in the first frame of the animation.

2. Click the Rising Steam object on the canvas.

3. Click the red animation handle, then drag it to the location shown in Figure C-27.

   TIP To constrain your selection to a straight line, press and hold [Shift] when you drag.

4. Click the Play button, then click the Stop button on the document window to preview and then stop the animation.

   Notice how the animation cycles through the Frames panel as the animation changes in the document.

5. Click Frame 3 on the Frames panel, then compare your animation to Figure C-28.

   The animation begins to fade out, and objects that are not shared across frames, such as the left meatball and Carbo-Lovers text, are no longer visible.

   You adjusted the animation motion path and then played the animation.

FIGURE C-27
Modified animation path

Drag red end animation handle to border's edge

Blue handles indicate frames in animation

Green animation handle indicates animation start

FIGURE C-28
Animation cycling through Frames panel

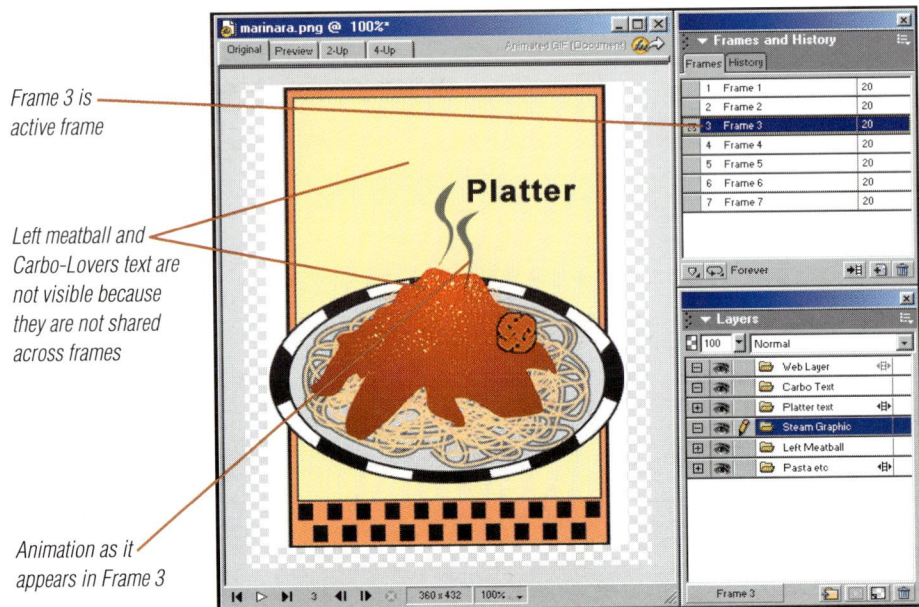

Frame 3 is active frame

Left meatball and Carbo-Lovers text are not visible because they are not shared across frames

Animation as it appears in Frame 3

Working with Interactivity and Animation

1. Click the Previous frame button on the document window until you reach Frame 1. ◀|

You can also click the First frame button on the document window if you are not in Frame 1.

> TIP You can determine which frame is active by looking at the Frames panel or looking at the number next to the Last frame icon at the bottom of the document window.

2. Click the Carbo-Lovers text on the canvas, click Edit on the menu bar, then click Copy.

3. Click Frame 3 on the Frames panel, click Edit on the menu bar, then click Paste.

4. Repeat the paste instruction in Step 3 for Frames 2, 5, and 7.

5. Click Frame 2, then click the Carbo-Lovers text to select it.

6. Click the Color box on the Property inspector, double-click the hexadecimal text box, type **FF9900**, press [Enter] (Win) or [return] (Mac), then compare your image to Figure C-29. ■

7. Click Edit on the menu bar, then click Copy.

8. Click Frame 4, click Edit on the menu bar, click Paste, then repeat for Frame 6.

9. Click the Play button, click the Stop button on the document window to preview and then stop the animation. ▷

10. Save your work.

You modified the fill color of an object in different frames to create the appearance that the object's color continuously changes as the animation plays.

FIGURE C-29
Modified object in Frame 2

New text color
in Frame 2

ADD TWEENING TO ANIMATION

What You'll Do

In this lesson, you will convert an object to a symbol, copy and modify an instance, add tweening frames, adjust the frame delay, trim the document, and then preview the animation.

Using Animation Symbols and Instances

You can create animation by converting an existing object to a symbol, or by creating a new symbol by clicking the New Symbol option from Insert command on the Edit menu. A **symbol** can be a graphic, animation, or button that represents an object, text, or combination group. When you animate a selection, Fireworks automatically converts the selected object to an animation symbol. By default, a new symbol has five frames. When you drag a symbol to the canvas, it is known as an **instance**. When you edit the original symbol, all instances of the symbol update as well.

You need at least two instances of the same symbol in order to tween an animation: one for the start of the animation, the other for the end. You can create animation that is more complex by adding more instances. You can import or create any image you want to animate and convert it to a symbol. Fireworks adds the new symbol to the Library panel and the original object used to create the symbol becomes an instance of that symbol on the canvas. Fireworks stores symbols in the Library panel, where you can edit and have the option to reuse them in other documents. Using symbols helps to reduce file size because Fireworks stores the symbol's

Importing animation files

You can easily open several files at once and set up a document for animation. Place the files you want to use in a folder, then, in Fireworks, click Open, select all of the files you want in the Open dialog box, then select the Open as Animation check box. Fireworks opens the files en masse, placing them on one layer on the Layers panel and each in its own frame on the Frames panel. Files that contain rollovers are placed over two frames.

properties in the Library panel, not in your document. If you have animations that appear in multiple frames, creating animation symbols has distinct advantages. Figure C-30 shows a sample Library panel that contains different symbol types. Note that before you can preview an animation in your browser, you must first open the Optimize panel, and then set the Export file format to Animated GIF.

QUICKTIP

You can create a Macromedia Flash SWF file from an animated Fireworks document.

Understanding Tweening

Animation mimics motion, but the movement may not always seem to flow evenly from one action to the next. The solution is to ease the transition between motion frames—the more frames in an animation, the more smoothly it plays. **Tweening** modifies, or blends, two or more instances and distributes them to frames so that the movement appears more fluid and less jerky. In Fireworks, you can add as many tweened instances of the symbol as you need to create just the animation you want.

Understanding Frame Delay

You can fine-tune your animation by adjusting the display time for each frame, known as **frame delay**. Frame delays are measured in hundredths of a second—even a small change can affect your animation dramatically. If the frame delay is too short, the image will appear indistinct; if it is too long, the image will appear jerky or erratic. The frame delay is displayed in the right column of the Frames panel; the default frame delay for a new symbol is .07, or seven-hundreths of a second. You can adjust the delay for one or more frames at any time. To simultaneously adjust the frame delay for multiple frames, press and hold [Shift] as you click the frames whose frame delay you want to change. In addition to setting the frame delay, you can select frames that will be included when you export the animation. When you deselect a frame, a large red X appears in place of the frame delay setting on the Frames panel, as shown in Figure C-31.

QUICKTIP

To exclude an animation frame from the exported file, double-click the frame delay column, then deselect the Include when Exporting check box.

FIGURE C-30
Sample Library panel

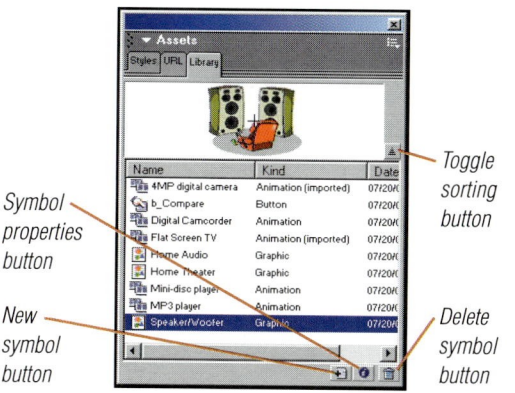

Symbol properties button

New symbol button

Toggle sorting button

Delete symbol button

FIGURE C-31
Excluding frames in the Frames panel

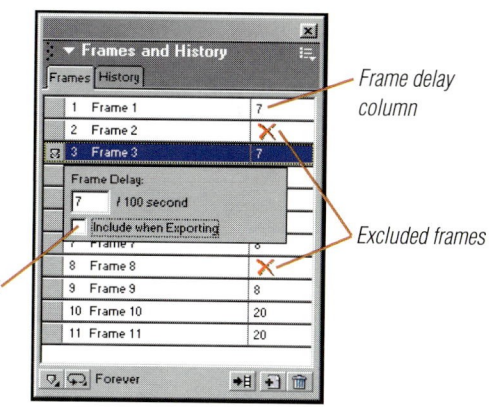

Frame delay column

Excluded frames

Deselect checkbox to hide a frame

Create a symbol and an instance

1. Click the First frame button on the document window (if necessary), click Window on the menu bar, click Library, then click the Symbol in the Library panel (if necessary).

2. Double-click the Symbol animation in the Library panel, type **Rising Steam** in the Name text box of the Symbol Properties dialog box, then click OK.

3. Right-click (Win) or [control] click (Mac) the left meatball in the document, then click Convert to Symbol.

4. Type **Rolling Meatball** in the Name text box of the Symbol Properties dialog box, verify that the Graphic option is selected, compare your dialog box to Figure C-32, then click OK.

   The left meatball object represents one instance of the new symbol.

   > TIP Symbols are listed alphabetically in the Library panel.

5. Click the Rolling Meatball symbol in the Library panel, then compare your image to Figure C-33.

(continued)

FIGURE C-32
Symbol Properties dialog box

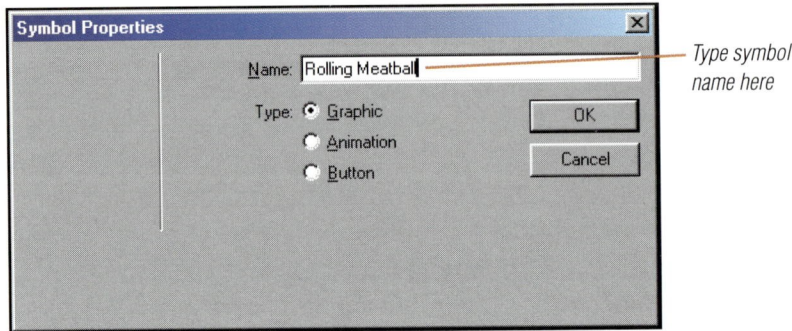

Type symbol name here

FIGURE C-33
Converted symbol

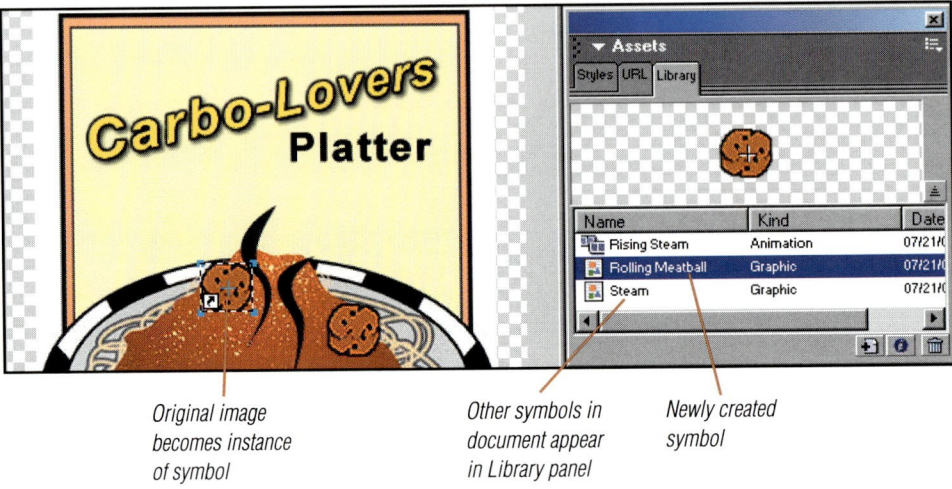

Original image becomes instance of symbol

Other symbols in document appear in Library panel

Newly created symbol

FIGURE C-34

Instance added to document

Drag instance of Rolling Meatball symbol to edge of plate

6. Drag an instance of the Rolling Meatball symbol in the Library panel to the location shown in Figure C-34.

The two instances of the Rolling Meatball symbol represent the animation's beginning point and endpoint.

> **TIP** Symbols are identified by an arrow icon in the lower-left corner.

7. Click Modify on the menu bar, point to Transform, then click Rotate 180°.

> **TIP** Deleting instances from your document window does not remove the corresponding symbols from the Library panel.

8. Save your work.

You converted an object into a symbol, and placed an instance of the symbol on the canvas as an endpoint for the animation.

Tween animation

1. Press and hold [Shift], then click the original meatball instance to select both objects.

2. Click Modify on the menu bar, point to Symbol, then click Tween Instances.

3. Type **5** in the Steps text box, click the Distribute to Frames check box (if necessary), then click OK.

Because Frame 1 is selected, you see only the beginning of the animated path of the meatball.

(continued)

4. Click the Play button, then click the Stop button on the document window to preview and stop the animation.

5. Click the Last frame button on the document window (if necessary), then compare your image to Figure C-35.

6. Save your work.

You added tweening frames to an animation.

Set frame delay

1. Click Frame 5 on the Frames panel, press and hold [Shift], then click Frame 7 on the Frames panel to select Frames 5, 6, and 7.

2. Double-click the highlighted area of the Frame delay column, type **7** in the Frame Delay dialog box, shown in Figure C-36, then click a blank area of the screen.

3. Click the Play button, then click the Stop button on the document window to preview and stop the animation.

   The meatball appears to speed up as it rolls toward the edge of the plate.

4. Save your work.

You adjusted the frame delay of three frames on the Frames panel.

FIGURE C-35
Result of tweening

Meatball rolls off plate

FIGURE C-36
Modified frame delay

Double-click column to open Frame Delay dialog box

Enter new time

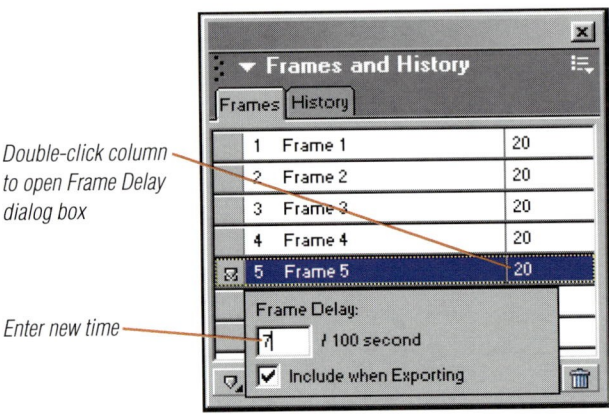

Working with Interactivity and Animation

FIGURE C-37
Trimmed image

FIGURE C-38
Optimize panel

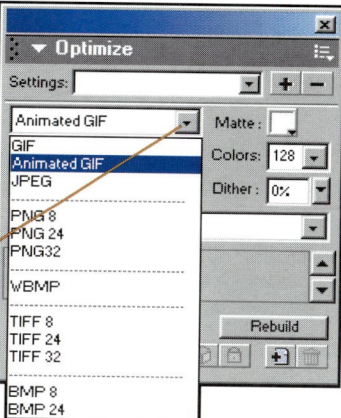

Click list arrow
to display file
format list

Trim the image and preview the animation

1. Click Modify on the menu bar, point to Canvas, click Trim Canvas, then compare your image to Figure C-37.

    The excess space around the graphic is trimmed.

2. Click Window on the menu bar, then click Optimize to open the Optimize panel.

3. Click the Export file format list arrow, then click Animated GIF (if necessary), as shown in Figure C-38.

4. Click File on the menu bar, point to Preview in Browser, then click the browser in which you want to preview the animation.

5. Close your browser, then save and close marinara.png.

You trimmed the canvas to the image area, set the export file format, and then previewed the animation in a browser.

History of tweening

In traditional film animation, a cadre of artists was needed to create just a few seconds of animated film. Senior artists would draw the animated objects' major action points as keyframes. Junior artists, known as *tweeners*, were responsible for completing the frames in between—from 8 to 24 frames were required for one second of film. In contrast, computer animation usually displays 10 to 20 frames per second.

Insert slices and hotspots.

1. Open fwc_3.png, then save it as **moon_fest**.
2. Select the learn more text, then insert a slice from the Insert command on the Edit menu.
3. Rename the slice **learnmore** on the Web Layer.
4. Select the Slice tool.
5. Draw a slice around the Chinese calligraphy and the white space directly below it.
6. Rename the slice **Translation** on the Web Layer.
7. Select the Circle Hotspot tool. (*Hint*: Press and hold the currently displayed hotspot tool, then click the Circle Hotspot tool.)
8. Draw a hotspot from the center outward that covers the full moon photo. (*Hint*: Press [Alt] (Win) or [option] (Mac) as you draw the hotspot.)
9. Rename the hotspot **LunarLinks** on the Web Layer.
10. Save your work.

Insert links.

1. Select the learnmore slice.
2. Type **http://www.macromedia.com** in the Link text box on the Properties panel. (*Hint*: Previously entered text may appear in the Alt text box.)
3. Add the following Alt text: **Chinese Calligraphy** using the Property inspector.
4. Select the LunarLinks hotspot.
5. Insert the following URL link: **http://www.spacelink.nasa.gov**.

6. Add the following Alt text: **Lunar Links**.
7. Save your work.

Change a hotspot shape.

1. Verify that the LunarLinks hotspot is selected.
2. Change the hotspot to a rectangle using the Property inspector.
3. Save your work.

Preview in Fireworks and in a browser.

1. Hide the slices, then click the Preview tab to preview the document.
2. Preview the document in a Web browser.
3. Test links, then close your browser.
4. Save your work.

Add a text rollover.

1. Click the Original tab.
2. Display slices, then select the calligraphy object on the Layers panel.
3. Click Frame 2 on the Frames panel.
4. Click the Text tool on the Tools panel, select font: Arial, size: 11, color: Red, alignment: Center.
5. Click the document in the white space above "A" in Autumn, then type **Have a joyful mid-autumn festival**.
6. Select the behavior handle for the Translation slice, drag it to the top left corner of the slice, then swap an image from Frame 2.
7. Hide slices, then preview the rollover.
8. Save your work.

Add a button rollover.

1. Click the Original tab, show slices, then click the Cakes object.
2. Copy the Cakes object, then delete the object in the document.
3. Create a new button from the Insert command on the Edit menu, then paste the Cakes object in the Button Editor.
4. Create a copy of the Up graphic in the Over state.

Modify a button state.

1. Ungroup the Cakes object in the Over state.
2. Change the color of the text to bright green (#**00FF00**), then close the Button Editor.
3. Center the Cakes object under the Tropical Luck mooncake.
4. Rename the Button Symbol on the Layers panel and in the Library panel **Cakes**.
5. Hide slices, then preview the document in Fireworks and in a browser.
6. Close your browser, compare your image in Frame 2 to Figure C-39, then close moon_fest.png.

Create basic animation.

1. Open fwc_4.png, then save it as **moon2moon**.
2. Select the moon photo object and animate the selection with the following changes to default settings in the Animate dialog box: Frames: 7, Opacity: 100% to 0%.
3. Play the animation.

4. Change the animation motion path so that the endpoint of the animation is vertical, approximately two-thirds up to the top of the canvas.
5. Play the animation.
6. Rename the Animation Symbol object on the Layers panel **moon_photo**.
7. Verify that the Library panel is open, then rename the animation symbol in the Library panel **rising_moon**.
8. Save your work.

Modify images in frames.

1. Click Frame 1, then select and group the Moon to Moon text.
2. Rename the Group: 3 objects **moon2moon** on the Layers panel.
3. Copy and paste the text in Frames 2, 3, 5, and 7.

4. Click Frame 2, then change the text color to **#66FFCC**.
5. Copy the text in Frame 2, then paste it in Frames 4 and 6.
6. Play the animation.
7. Save your work.

Create a symbol and an instance.

1. Select Frame 1, select the moon_character object, then convert it to a graphic symbol.
2. Rename the symbol **moon_character**.
3. Rename the Graphic Symbol object **Moon1** on the Layers panel.
4. Drag the moon_character symbol from the Library panel to the middle of the canvas.
5. Rotate the direction of the moon_character instance 180°, then change the opacity of the original Moon1 object to 20%. (*Hint*: Use the Opacity list arrow on the Layers panel.)

6. Select the two instances, then tween them, adding five frames that are distributed to frames.
7. Play the animation.
8. Save your work.

Set frame delay.

1. Set the frame delay of Frame 7 to 20.
2. Trim the canvas of the document.
3. Preview the animation in Fireworks in and your browser.
4. Save your work, then compare your image to Figure C-40.

FIGURE C-39
Completed Skills Review

FIGURE C-40
Completed Skills Review

Working with Interactivity and Animation

You manage the Web site for Train That Critter, an obedience clinic for pet owners. It's time to update the training section with a new animation that introduces the service. The only requirement is that you depict a pet caught in the act of misbehaving. You can use the pet of your choice.

1. Obtain images of a pet and the relevant situation. You can draw your own images in Fireworks, or obtain images from your computer, from the Internet, or from scanned media.

2. Create a new document and save it as **busted**.

3. Create a background layer, using an image or any of the vector tools, rename it, and apply a fill, stroke, style, or effect to it, or adjust its transparency.

4. Copy or import your images into the document, animate them, then apply tweening to at least one animation. (*Hint*: The fish in the sample have been tweened.)

5. Create **Busted** text, then animate it. (*Hint*: Each letter in the sample is a separate text object and has been copied

into different frames. The text used in the sample is Perpetua Titling MT. You can substitute another font on your computer.)

6. Rename symbols, objects, and layers as appropriate in the Library panel and on the Layers panel.

7. Save your work, then compare your document to Figure C-41.

FIGURE C-41
Completed Project Builder 1

Your class on Modern Mythology is examining how extraterrestrials would investigate urban culture. Your group will discuss the many uses of camouflage and disguise as they relate to cultural study. You've volunteered to create a humorous animation for the opening sequence of a presentation.

1. Obtain images that will convey the topic and your interpretation. You can create your own images, or obtain images from your computer, from the Internet, or from scanned media.
2. Create a new document and save it as **incognito**.
3. Copy or import your images into the document, then create one original and one disguised image. (*Hint*: The alien in the sample was created with vector tools; they have multiple effects and fills applied to them.)
4. Create at least one animation, using the animation technique of your choice.
5. Create text as desired and animate it.
6. Create at least one fade-out effect or dramatic size change.
7. Rename symbols, objects, and layers as appropriate in the Library panel and in the Layers panel.
8. Save your work, then compare your image to Figure C-42.

FIGURE C-42
Completed Project Builder 2

You and a few friends, all avid Fireworks users, have been discussing function versus form as it specifically relates to animation and rollovers. After reaching an impasse, you've decided to find a Web site that totally bolsters your opinion, whichever side you happen to take. You're going to find a site that illustrates your point exactly, and then analyze the technique.

1. Connect to the Internet, and go to *www.course.com*. Navigate to the page for this book, click the link for the Student Online Companion, then click the link for this unit. The Web page is shown in Figure C-43.

2. Scroll to the list in the middle under CoolHomepages Design Academy, then click a category such as Animation, Rollovers, or Fun.

3. Open several Web pages, then, when you find one that interests you, open a word processor or use the Text tool in Fireworks to record your answers, then save the file as **cool page**.

4. Discuss the following points. You may also refer to linked related pages in the site, referencing their URLs in your discussion.

   ■ What animation is immediately active in the page?

■ Can you distinguish the type of animation? Can you tell if it has been tweened?
■ How many times does the animation play in the page?
■ How well does the animation play in your browser?

■ If possible, view the page using another browser, then compare the results.
■ Describe the rollovers—is animation involved? If so, how?
■ Describe how hotspots are used.

FIGURE C-43
Design Project

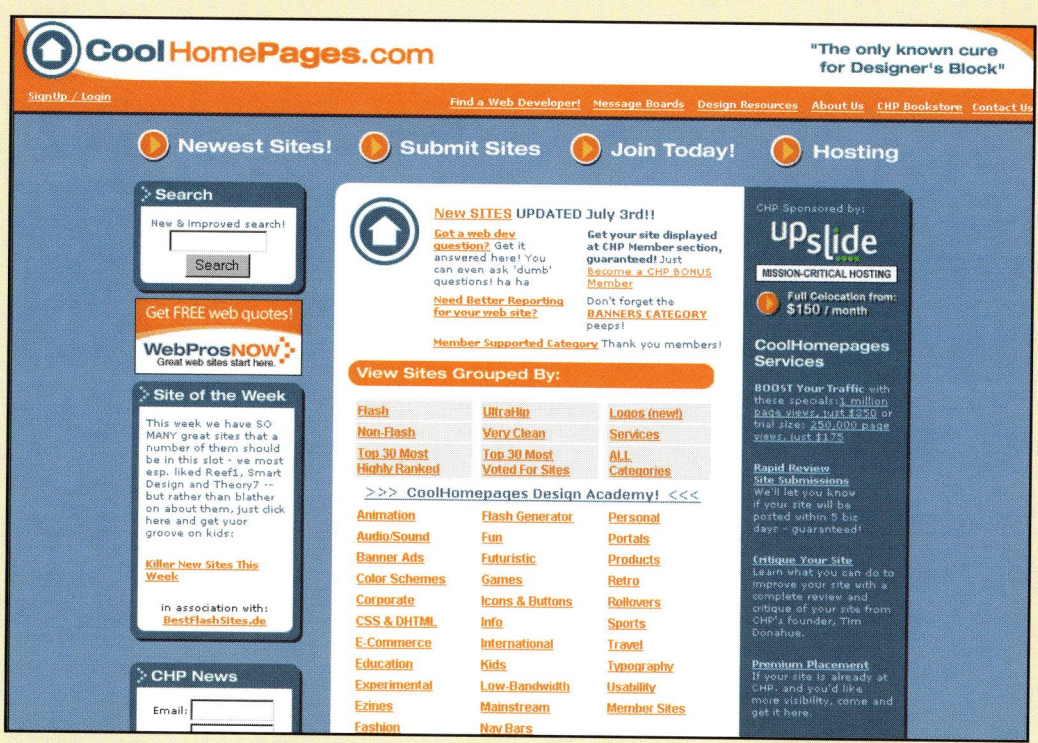

Your group can assign elements of the project to individual members, or work collectively to create the finished product.

Your apartment complex is one of several co-sponsoring a huge yard sale with a retro theme. A local Internet service provider has donated server space for Web pages listing the sale items. Before you and your friends venture into your respective clothes closets, you would like to help design and create one of the Web pages. You can use the category of your choice and fit it into the retro theme.

1. Obtain images for the Web page, including design elements. You can create your own images, or obtain images from your computer, from the Internet, or from scanned media.
2. Create a new document and save it as **retrofit**.
3. Create design elements for the theme, and animate them using the animation techniques of your choice.
4. Create title text as desired and animate it.
5. Create at least three button or text rollovers.

6. Add URLs to at least two slices or hotspots.
7. Create and add tweening to animation, or add a rollover to additional text as desired.

8. Rename symbols, objects, and layers as appropriate in the Library panel and in the Layers panel.

9. Preview the animation in Fireworks and in a browser.
10. Save your work, then compare your document to Figure C-44.

FIGURE C-44
Completed Group Project

UNIT A

INTEGRATING MACROMEDIA MX PRODUCTS

1. Set up the work environment.

2. Place Fireworks images into a Dreamweaver document.

3. Edit Fireworks images from a Dreamweaver document.

4. Insert and edit Macromedia Flash movies in Dreamweaver.

UNIT A

INTEGRATING MACROMEDIA MX PRODUCTS

Introduction

The Macromedia MX suite of integrated Web development products includes Dreamweaver, Macromedia Flash, and Fireworks. Used together, these tools allow you to create Web sites that include compelling graphics, animations, and interactivity. Recognizing that developing a Web site often involves team members with varying expertise (graphic designers, animators, programmers, and so on), Macromedia has designed these products so that they integrate easily.

This integration allows you to move from one tool to another as you bring together the elements of a Web site. For example, you can create a graphic image using Fireworks, import the image into Dreamweaver, and then edit the image starting from the Dreamweaver environment. While each of the products can stand alone, they have a similar look and feel, with common features and interface elements, such as the Property inspector, that allow you to transfer your skills from one product to another.

Tools You'll Use

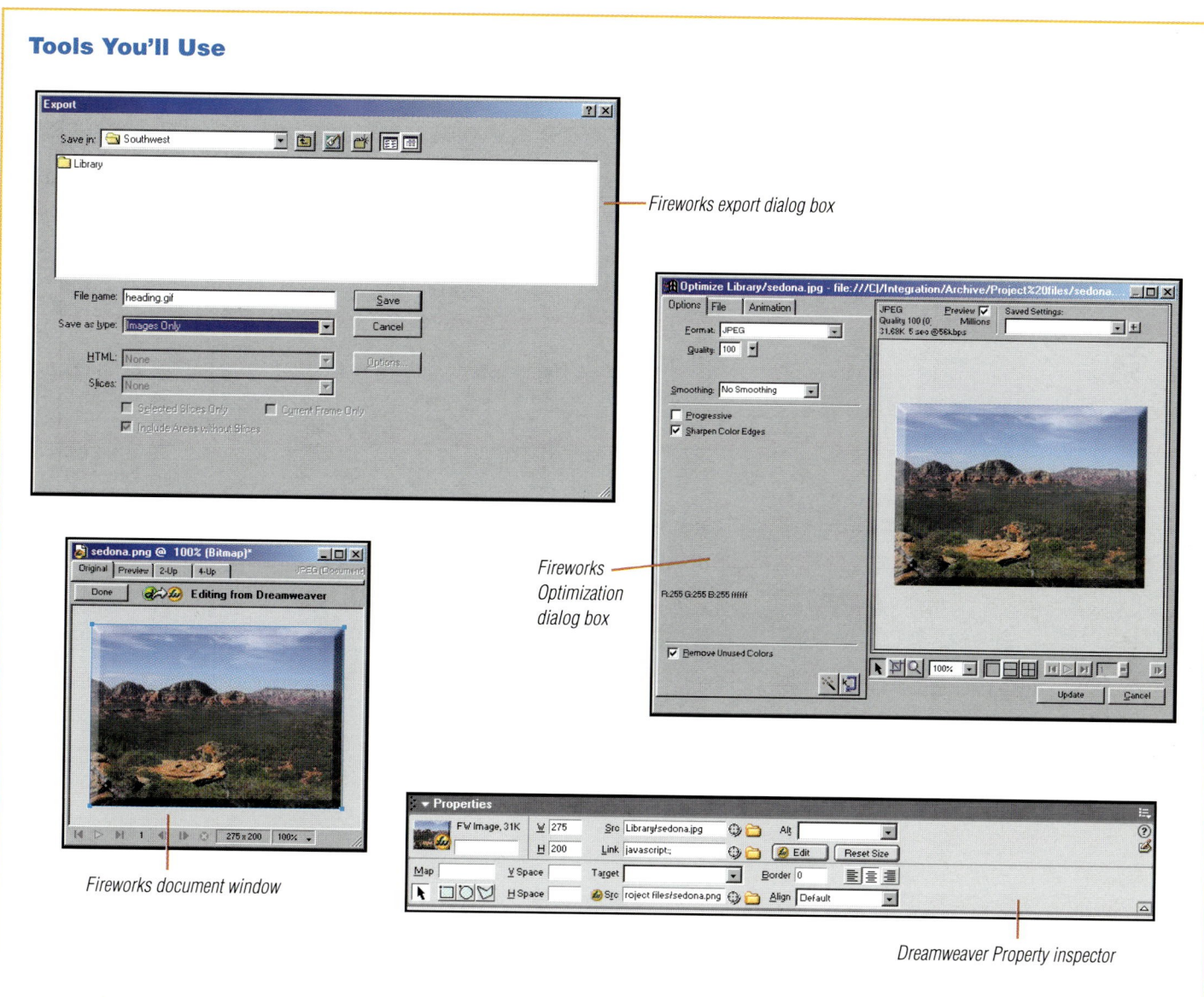

Fireworks export dialog box

Fireworks Optimization dialog box

Fireworks document window

Dreamweaver Property inspector

SET UP THE WORK ENVIRONMENT

What You'll Do

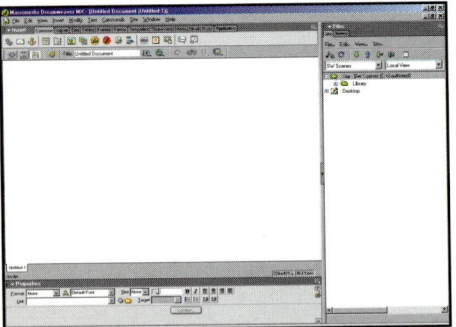

 In this lesson, you will set up the work environment to facilitate integrating Fireworks images into a Dreamweaver document.

Setting Fireworks as the Primary External Image Editor

You can import a Fireworks image into a Dreamweaver document. Later on, when desired, you can edit the graphic by launching the Fireworks program from within Dreamweaver. This requires that you set Fireworks as the primary external image editor for GIF, JPEG, and PNG files in Dreamweaver. You can set the external image editor using settings in the Preferences dialog box for Dreamweaver.

Using Design Notes

When you export a Fireworks document or Macromedia Flash file to Dreamweaver, information about the original source file (PNG or FLA) is saved in a Design Notes file (MNO). For example, if you open air-plane.png in Fireworks and export it as air-plane.jpg, Fireworks creates a Design Notes file named airplane.jpg.mno. The Design

Notes file contains references to the source PNG file that created the exported file, which allows you to access the original PNG file for editing. You should save your Fireworks source PNG file and exported files in a Dreamweaver site. Saving in this location ensures that any developer sharing the site will be able to access the source PNG file when launching Fireworks from Dreamweaver. Figure A-1 shows the contents of a Design Notes file. The code indicates that the Fireworks source file (airplane.png) is located on the C: drive in a folder named Images.

Specifying Launch-and-Edit Preferences

The Fireworks launch-and-edit settings allow you to specify how to deal with source PNG files when editing Fireworks images from another program, such as Dreamweaver. You use the Fireworks

Preferences dialog box to specify one of the following launch-and-edit settings:

- Always Use Source PNG, which automatically launches the Fireworks PNG file specified in the Design Notes. Updates are made to both the source PNG and the exported file.

- Never Use Source PNG, which automatically launches the exported Fireworks image. Updates are made to the exported image only.
- Ask When Launched allows you to specify whether or not to launch the source PNG file.

Setting up the Dreamweaver Site

Figure A-2 shows the structure for the Web site you will be developing in this Unit. Initially, the site will contain only a Library folder that you will use to export a Fireworks image. As you work through the Unit, you will integrate Fireworks images and a Macromedia Flash movie into the site.

FIGURE A-1

The contents of a Design Notes file

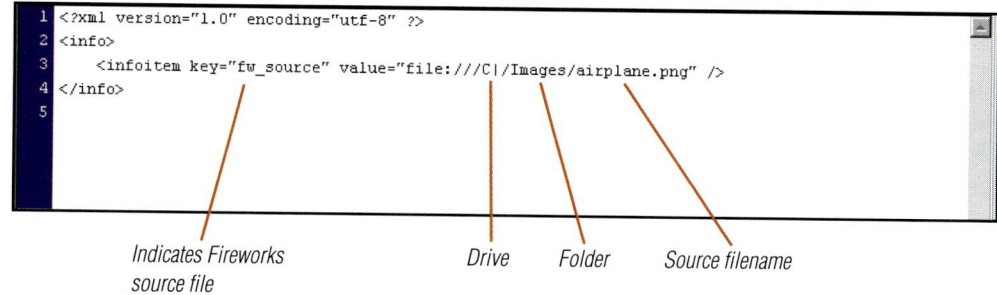

Indicates Fireworks source file   Drive   Folder   Source filename

FIGURE A-2

The structure of the Web site

Designate the primary external image editor

This Lesson requires that you have Dreamweaver and Fireworks MX installed on your computer.

1. Start Dreamweaver MX.

2. Click Edit on the Menu bar, then click Preferences.

3. Click File Types / Editors to display the options shown in Figure A-3.

4. Make sure that .png is highlighted in the Extensions column, then verify that Fireworks is displayed in the Editors column and that Fireworks is set as the primary editor.

5. Click .gif in the Extensions column, then make sure that Fireworks is displayed in the Editors column, then repeat for .jpg .jpe .jpeg.

6. Click OK.

You set Fireworks as the primary external editor for .png, .gif, and .jpg files.

FIGURE A-3

The Dreamweaver Preferences dialog box

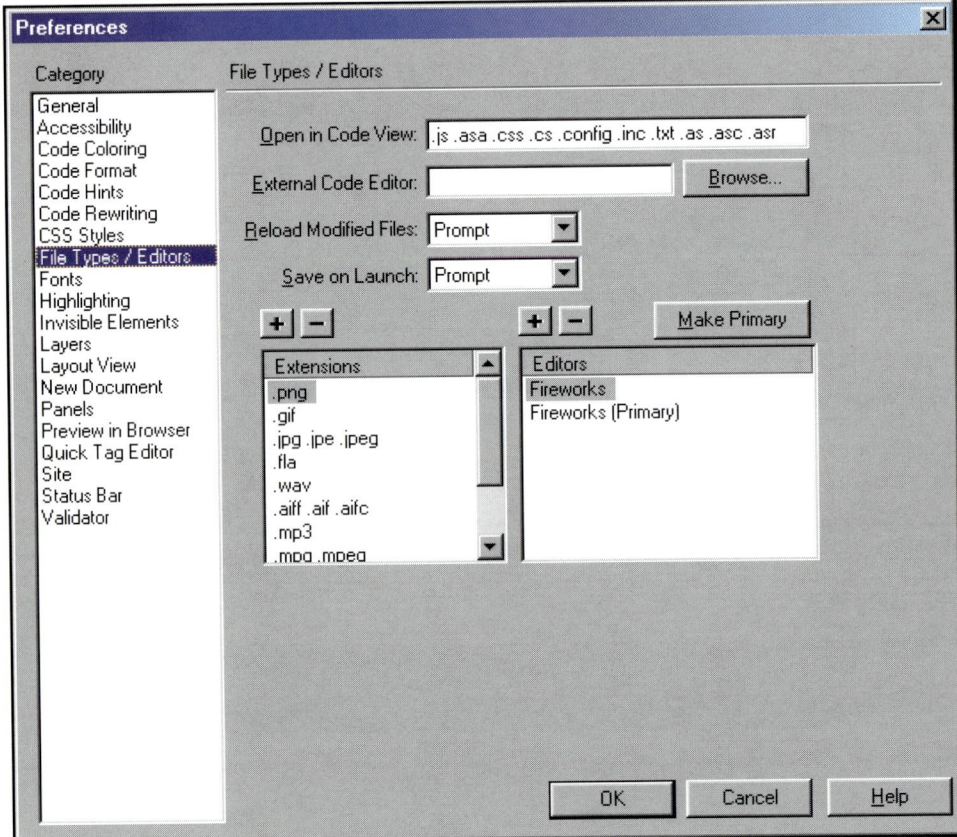

FIGURE A-4

The Fireworks Preferences dialog box

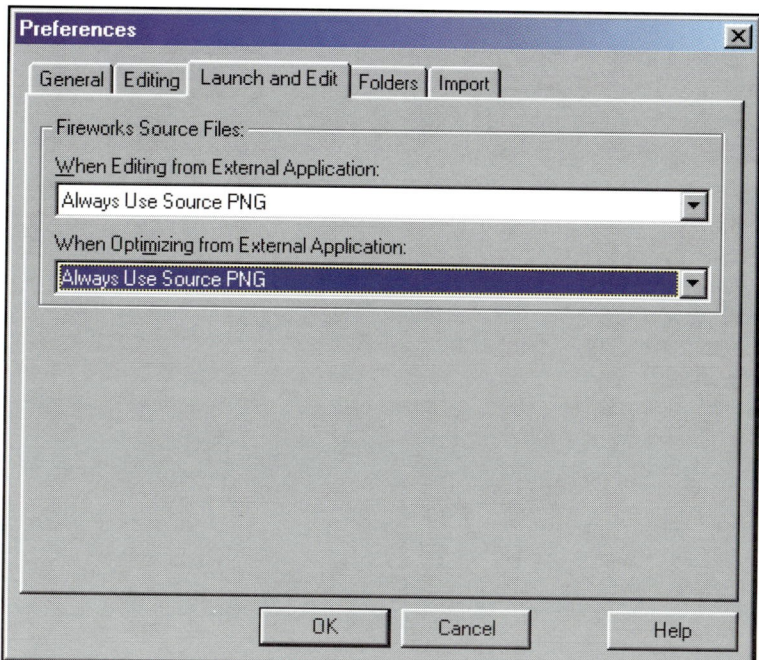

This Lesson requires that you have Fireworks MX installed on your computer.

1. Start Fireworks MX.

   TIP To maximize your computer's use of resources, close other programs not relevant to the lessons.

2. Click Edit on the menu bar, then click Preferences (Win), or click the Fireworks menu, then click Preferences (Mac).

3. Click the Launch and Edit tab to display the source file options (Win), or select the Choose category of preferences to edit list box, then choose Launch and Edit (Mac).

4. Click the When Editing from External Application list arrow, then click Always Use Source PNG.

5. Repeat Step 4 for the When Optimizing from External Application option, then compare your dialog box to Figure A-4.

6. Click OK.

You set the Fireworks launch and edit preferences.

Set up the Dreamweaver site

1. Open the file management tool that is on your operating system, create a folder on your hard drive, then name it **Southwest**.

2. Create a new folder named **Library** in the Southwest folder.

3. In Dreamweaver, click Site on the menu bar, then click New Site.

4. If necessary, click the Advanced tab, as shown in Figure A-5.

5. Type **SW Scenes** in the Site Name text box.

(continued)

FIGURE A-5

The Site Definition dialog box

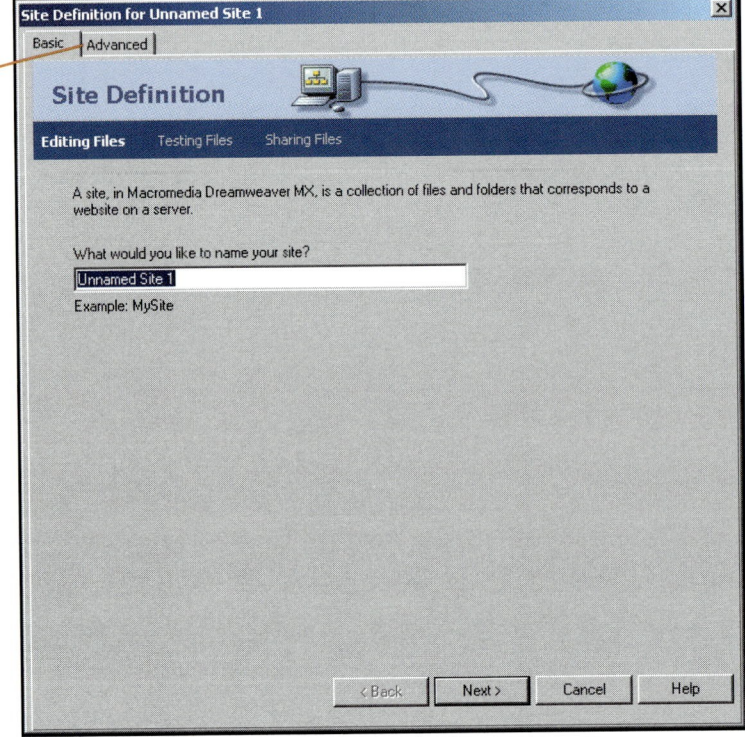

Advanced tab

FIGURE A-6

The completed Site Definition for SW Scenes dialog box

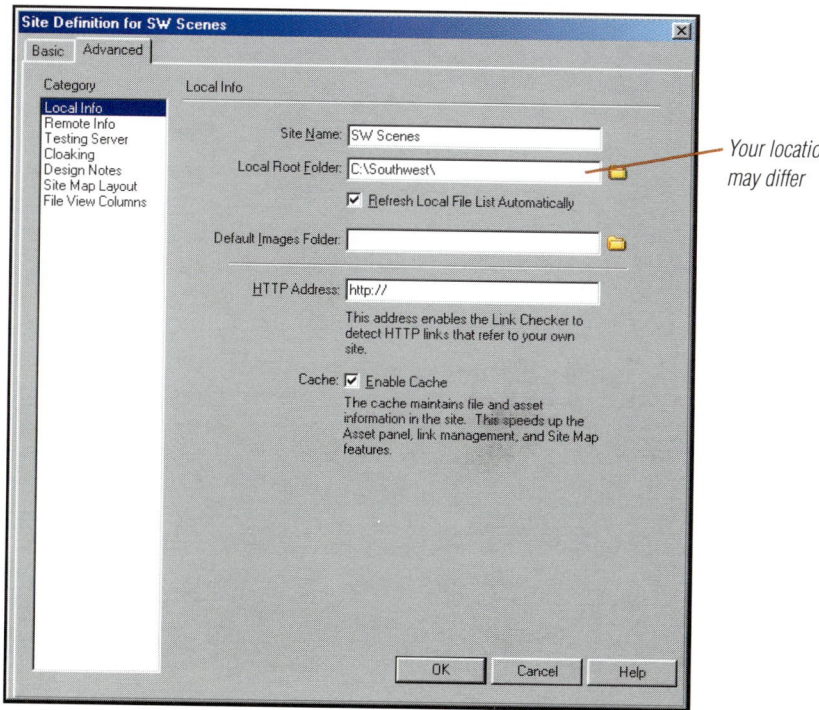

Your location may differ

6. Click the folder icon next to the Local Root Folder textbox, then navigate to the Southwest folder.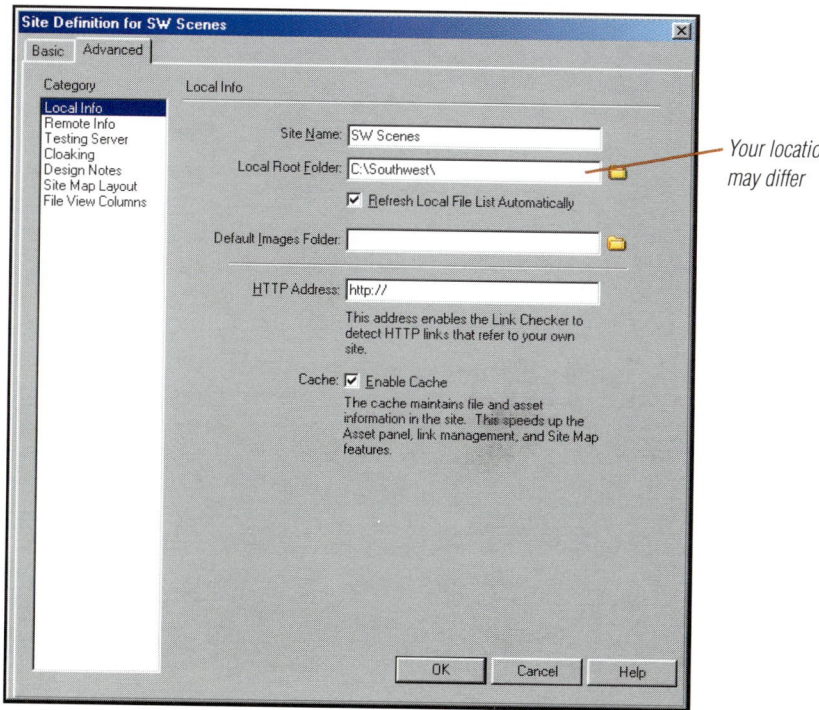

7. Double-click the Southwest folder in the Choose Local Root Folder for Site SW Scenes dialog box, then click Select (Win) or choose (Mac).

8. Verify that your Site Definition for SW Scenes dialog box resembles Figure A-6, then click OK.

You created a folder for the Dreamweaver site and then created the site.

PLACE FIREWORKS IMAGES INTO A DREAMWEAVER DOCUMENT

What You'll Do

In this lesson, you will place a Fireworks image into a Dreamweaver document and edit the image from within Dreamweaver.

Placing a Fireworks Image into Dreamweaver

You can place PNG, JPEG, and GIF images created in Fireworks directly into a Dreamweaver document. The process is to select the position in the document where you want the image to appear, then use the Image command on the Insert menu to specify the image file to insert. Alternately, you can export an image from Fireworks into a Dreamweaver site folder. Placing an image in the Library folder of the site allows you to insert the image in a document as a library item. Then you can change the image and have it update all occurrences of the image throughout the site. The process is to create a folder named Library in the Dreamweaver Web site, then use the Export command on the File menu in Fireworks to specify the type of file to save (Dreamweaver Library or Image Only). When you export an image file as an image

Using Libraries

Libraries allow you to store items such as graphic images and text that you want to reuse or update throughout your Web site. When you place an item from the Library into a document, Dreamweaver inserts a copy of the item and a comment containing a reference to the original item. This makes it possible to update all occurrences of the item by merely changing the original item in the Library. An example of the use of a Library item would be a "Thought for the day" that appears in several locations in a Web site. Each day, this Library item would be changed, and all the pages that display it would be updated to show the new item.

only, one file (.jpg or .gif) is created. When you export it to a Dreamweaver Library, two files are created, the image file and an .lbi file that contains information on the source filename and the dimensions of the image. Figure A-7 shows the Dreamweaver Site panel after exporting a .gif file to the root folder and a .jpg file to the Library folder.

FIGURE A-7

The Site panel after exporting images from Fireworks

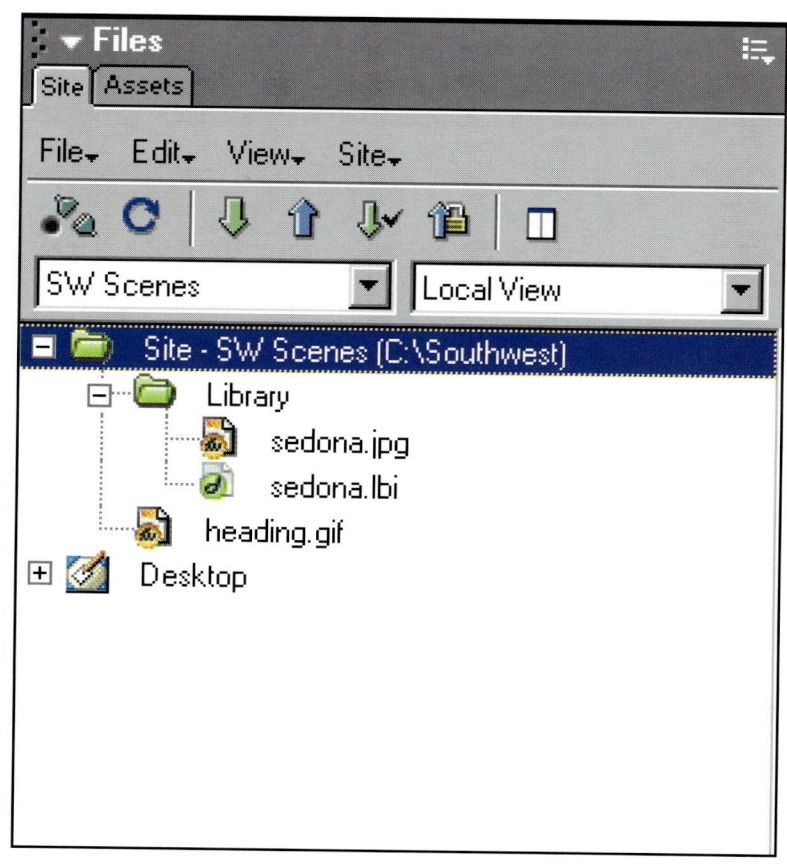

Export a Fireworks graphic as an image

1. Open heading.png in Fireworks.

2. Click Window on the menu bar, then click Optimize to open the Optimize panel (if necessary).

3. Verify that GIF is selected in the Export file format box in the Optimize panel.

4. Click File on the menu bar (Win), or the Save A: arrow (Mac), then click Export.

5. Click the Save as type: (Win) or Save As (Mac) list arrow, then click Images Only (if necessary).

6. Select Southwest as the Save in: (Win) or Where (Mac) folder (Win) or the Where folder (Mac), then compare your screen with Figure A-8.

7. Click Save.

8. Close heading.png without saving changes.

You exported a Fireworks graphic as a GIF image.

The Export dialog box specifying the save type as Images Only

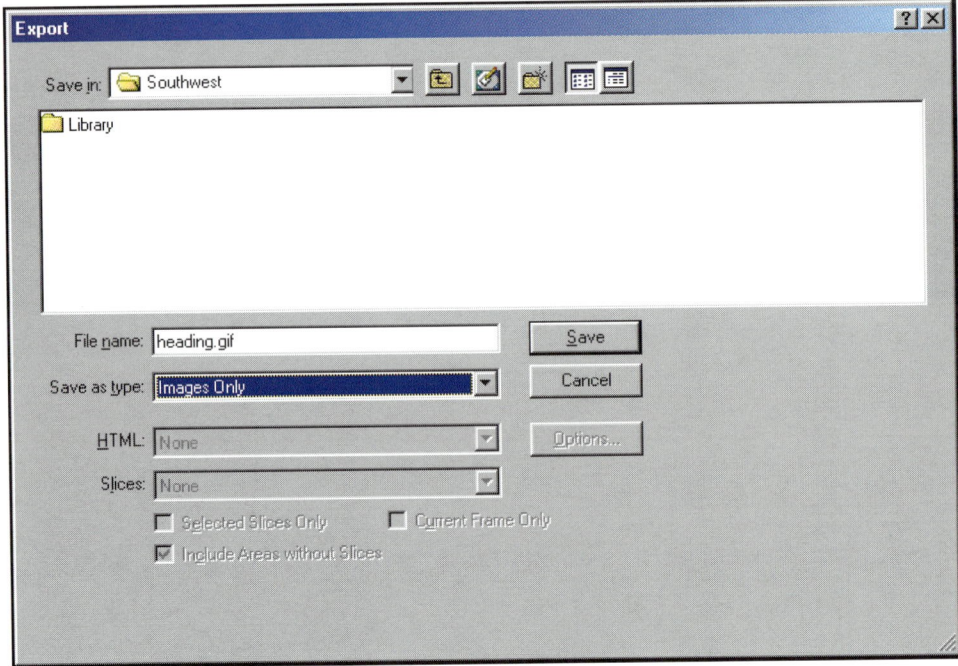

FIGURE A-9

The Export dialog box specifying the save type as Library

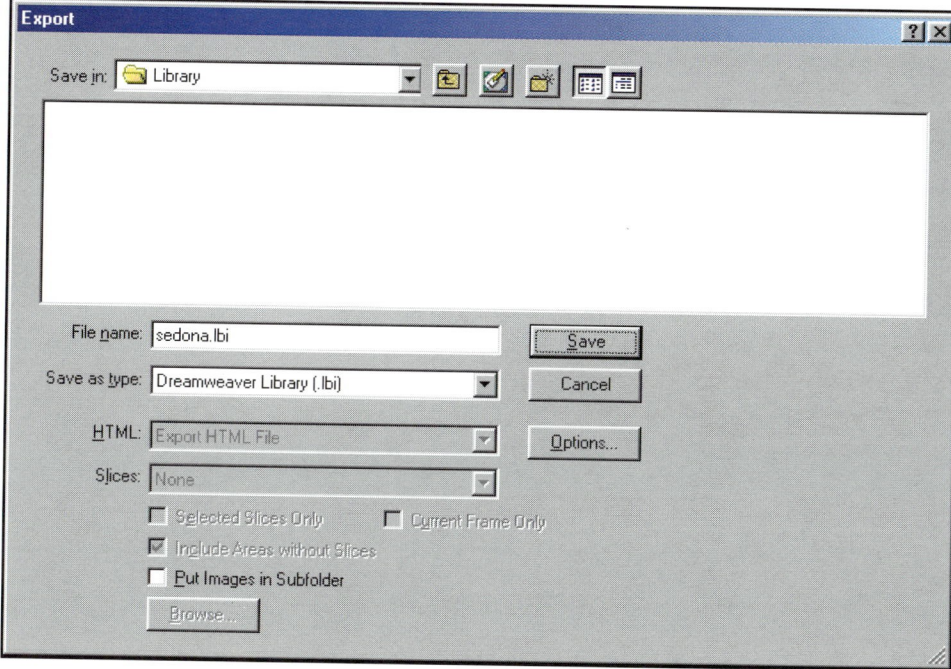

1. Open sedona.png in Fireworks.

2. Click File on the menu bar, then click Export.

3. Click the Save as type: list arrow (Win), or the Save As arrow (Mac), then click Dreamweaver Library (.lbi).

4. Click OK when the message appears asking you to locate a Library folder.

5. Double-click (Win) or click (Mac) Library in the Select Folder dialog box, click Open, then compare your dialog box with Figure A-9.

6. Click Save in the Export dialog box.

7. Close sedona.png without saving changes.

You exported a Fireworks graphic to a Dreamweaver Library folder.

Insert a Fireworks image into a Dreamweaver document

1. Verify that the SW Scenes site in the Site panel is open in Dreamweaver.

2. Open a new HTML document and save it as **home.htm**.

3. Click Insert on the menu bar, then click Image.

4. Click heading.gif to select the file, as shown in Figure A-10, then click OK (Win) or choose (Mac).

5. If a "This file is outside of the root folder..." message appears, click Yes, then click Save when the Copy File As dialog box appears.

   The image is placed in the Dreamweaver Southwest folder so that it can be associated with the other files in the site.

6. Make sure that the image is selected, then click the Align Center button in the Properties panel. ≣

7. Click File on the menu bar, then click Save.

You created a Dreamweaver document and inserted a Fireworks image into it.

FIGURE A-10

Specifying an image to insert

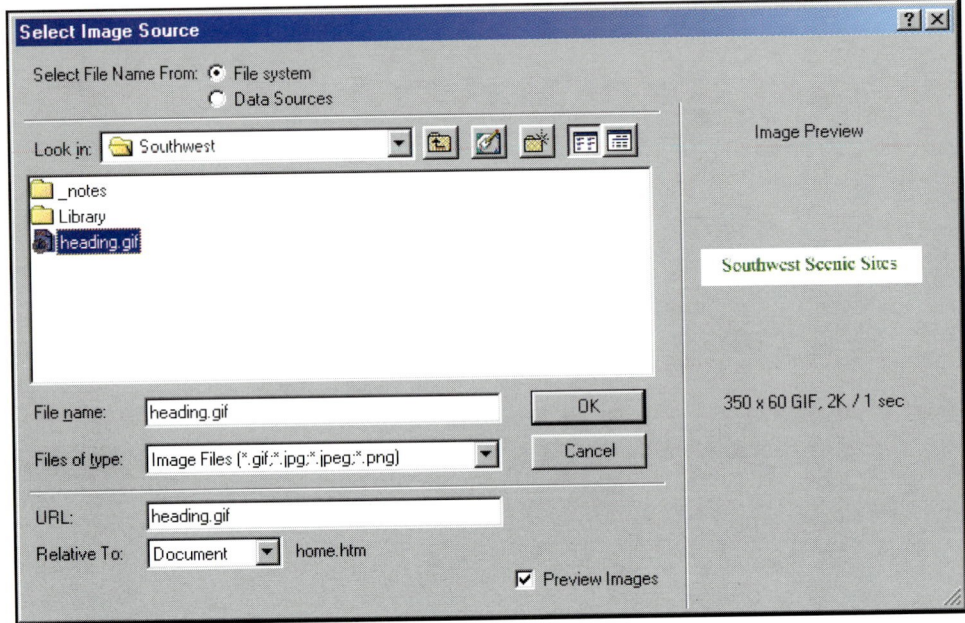

FIGURE A-11

Inserting the image to the document

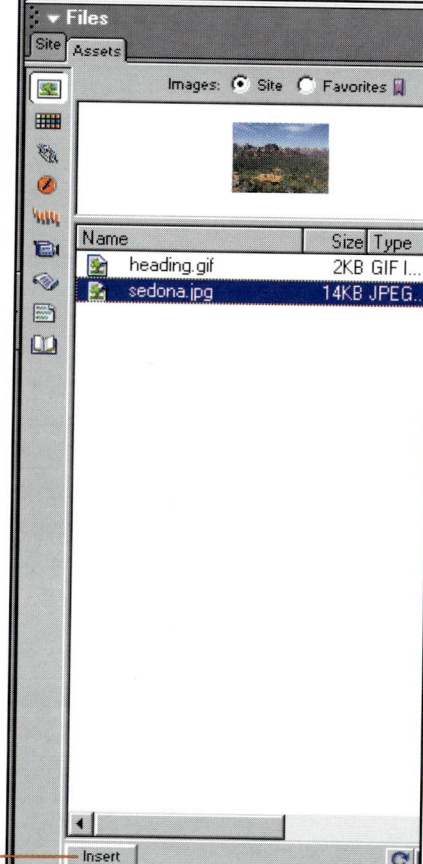

Insert button ——— Insert

1. Point to the right side of the heading text image, then click to set an insertion point.

2. Press [Enter] (Win) or [return] (Mac).

3. Click Window on the menu bar, then click Library.

4. Click the Assets tab.

5. Click sedona.jpg in the Assets panel, then click the Insert button as shown in Figure A-11.

6. Save your work.

You inserted a Fireworks image from the Assets panel into a Dreamweaver document.

EDIT FIREWORKS IMAGES FROM A DREAMWEAVER DOCUMENT

What You'll Do

 In this lesson, you will edit a Fireworks image from a Dreamweaver document.

Editing a Fireworks Image from Dreamweaver

When you edit a Fireworks image from a Dreamweaver document, the Fireworks program is launched and the selected image is displayed. You complete the desired changes and then return to Dreamweaver without having to resave or re-export the edited image. The programs automatically update the image files. The process is to select the image in the Dreamweaver document, then select the Edit button in the Property inspector, as shown in Figure A-12. The Fireworks program is launched, and the image appears in an edit window. After making your changes, click the Done button to return to the Dreamweaver document. If you need to make quick export changes, such as resizing the image or changing the file type, you can use the Optimize Image in Fireworks command to display the Optimize dialog box.

FIGURE A-12
The Edit button in the Property inspector

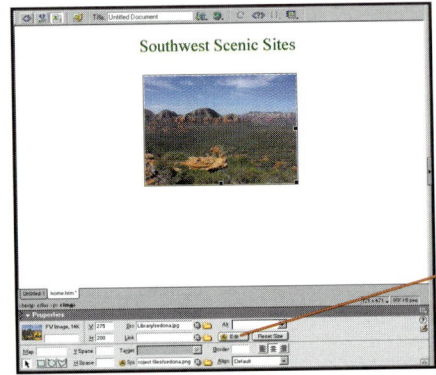

Click button to edit the image in Fireworks

FIGURE A-13
The Done button

FIGURE A-14
Changing the quality setting

Quality text box

Your optimization settings may vary

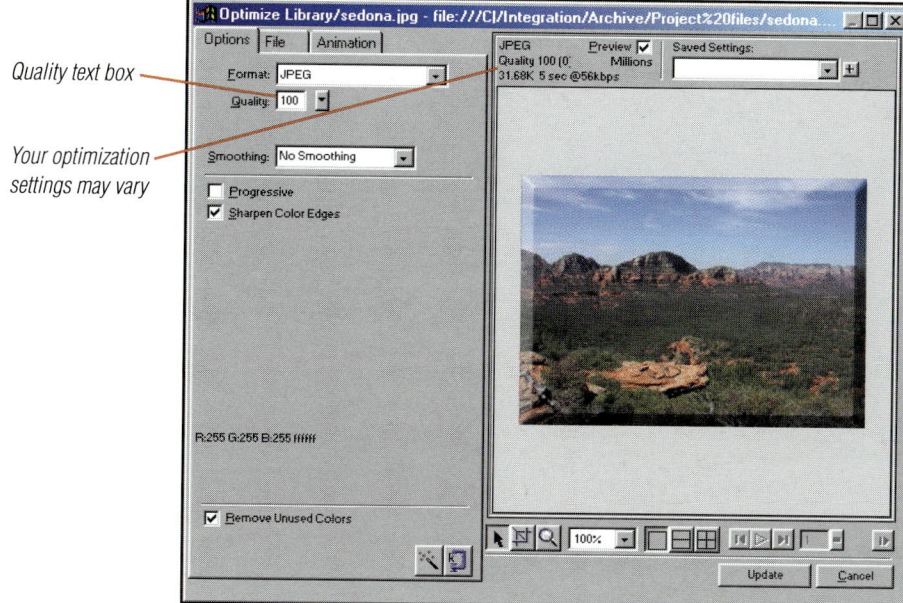

Lesson 3   Edit Fireworks Images from a Dreamweaver Document

Edit a Fireworks image from Dreamweaver

1. Click the sedona.jpg image to select it.
2. Click the Edit button in the Property inspector.

   The image opens in Fireworks.
3. If necessary, click the Pointer tool on the Tools panel, then click the sedona image to select it. ![pointer]
4. Click the Add Effects button in the Property inspector, point to Bevel and Emboss, then click Inner Bevel. ![plus]
5. Accept the default values, then click a blank area of the screen.
6. Click the Done button in the Editing from Dreamweaver window, as shown in Figure A-13, to return to the Dreamweaver document.

   The image in Dreamweaver displays the bevel effect.

You edited a Fireworks image from Dreamweaver.

Optimize a Fireworks image from Dreamweaver

1. Verify that the sedona.jpg image is selected in Dreamweaver.
2. Click Commands on the menu bar, then click Optimize Image in Fireworks.
3. Double-click the Quality text box, then type **100**, as shown in Figure A-14.
4. Click Update.

   The Optimization dialog box closes.

You edited a Fireworks image from Dreamweaver.

INSERT AND EDIT MACROMEDIA FLASH MOVIES IN DREAMWEAVER

What You'll Do

Southwest Scenic Sites

SEDONA, ARIZONA

In this lesson, you will insert a Macromedia Flash movie into a Dreamweaver document and edit the movie within Dreamweaver.

Inserting a Macromedia Flash Movie into a Dreamweaver Document

You can easily insert a Macromedia Flash movie (.swf) into a Dreamweaver document. The process is to set the insertion point where you want the movie to appear, and then use the Media command on the Insert menu to select Flash as the media to insert. If the file is not in the root folder for the Web site, you will be asked whether you would like to copy it into the root folder. It is recommended that you copy the file to the root folder, so that it will be accessible when you publish the site. When the insert process is completed, a placeholder appears at the insertion point in the document.

Viewing Information About the Movie

When you click the placeholder to select it, the Property inspector displays information about the movie, including the dimensions and the filename, as shown in Figure A-15.

Setting an Image to Control the Movie's Playback

The Control Shockwave or Flash action feature of Dreamweaver allows you to specify an object, such as an image, to control the actions (play, stop, rewind, or goto a frame) of a Macromedia Flash movie. For example, you could specify that the movie plays when the mouse rolls over an image. The process is to select the movie in the Dreamweaver document that is to be controlled and name it in the Property inspector, as shown in Figure A-16. You can select the object to control the movie and use the Behaviors panel to specify the type of action.

FIGURE A-15

The Property inspector with a movie selected

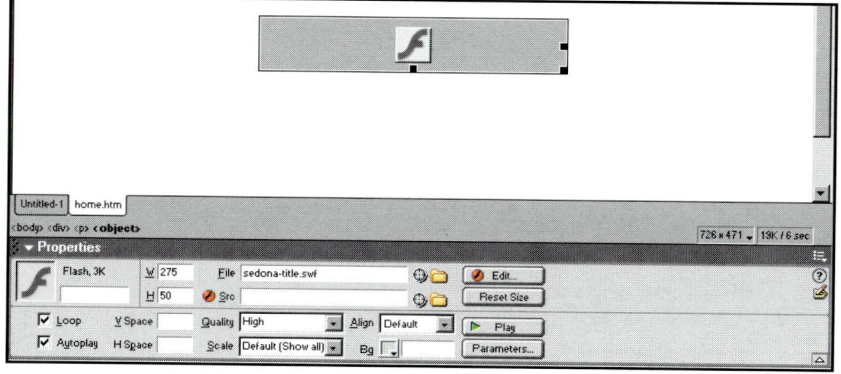

FIGURE A-16

Naming the movie in the Property inspector

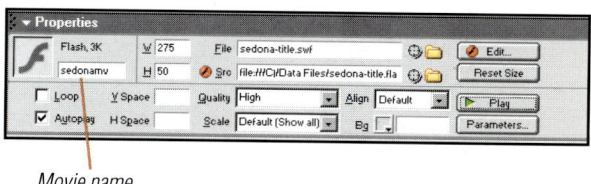

Movie name

Insert a Macromedia Flash movie into Dreamweaver

1. Click an insertion point to the right of the image.

2. Press [Enter] (Win) or [return] (Mac) to center the insertion point below the image, as shown in Figure A-17.

3. Click Insert on the menu bar, point to Media, then click Flash.

4. Navigate to the folder containing your data files, click sedona-title.swf, then click OK (Win), or click Choose (Mac).

5. If a "This file is outside of the root folder..." message appears, click Yes, then click Save when the Copy File As dialog box appears.

6. Save your work.

You inserted a Flash Macromedia movie into a Dreamweaver document.

Insertion point

FIGURE A-18

Changing the movie window height

Type new height here

1. Click the Flash movie placeholder to select it (if necessary).

2. Click the Play button in the Property inspector.

3. Click the Stop button in the Property inspector.

4. Click the Loop check box in the Property inspector to deselect it.

5. Double-click the height box (H), type **100**, as shown in Figure A-18, then press [Enter] (Win) or [return] (Mac).

6. Click the Reset Size button in the Property inspector to restore the previous setting.

7. Save your work.

You played a Macromedia Flash movie and changed its settings in Dreamweaver.

Edit a Macromedia Flash movie from Dreamweaver

1. Click the Flash placeholder to select it, then click the Edit button in the Property inspector.

2. Navigate to the folder containing your data files, click sedona-title.fla, then click Open.

3. If necessary, click the Arrow Tool on the toolbox to select it.

4. Click Frame 1 on the Heading layer.

5. Click Sedona on the stage.

6. Click the Color option (Win) or Color Styles (Mac), list arrow in the Property inspector, then click Alpha (if necessary).

7. Double-click the Alpha Amount text box, type **0**, as shown in Figure A-19, then press [Enter] (Win) or [return] (Mac).

8. Click the Done button in the Editing from Dreamweaver window.

9. Click Play on the Dreamweaver Property inspector.

10. Click File on the menu bar, point to Preview in Browser, then click iexplore (Win), or click InternetExplorer.app (Mac).

   | TIP   Your default browser may vary.

11. View the movie, then close the browser.

You edited a Macromedia Flash movie from Dreamweaver.

Changing the Alpha setting

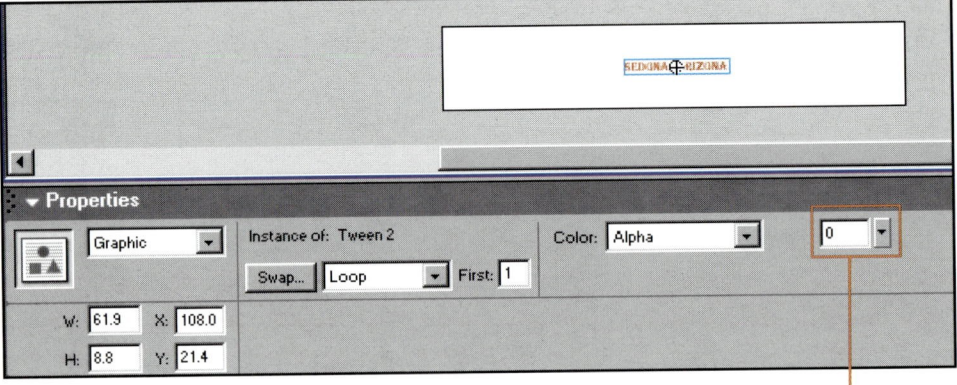

Type new Alpha setting here

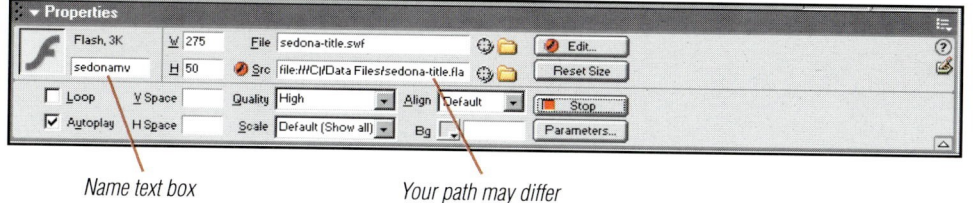

Name text box   Your path may differ

FIGURE A-21

The completed Control Shockwave or Flash dialog box

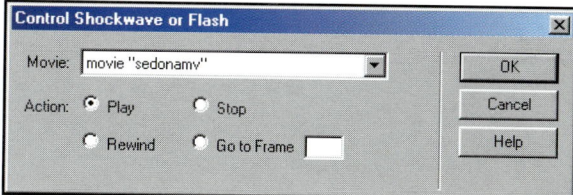

Control the movie

1. Click the Flash placeholder to select it, click the Name text box in the left side of the Property inspector, type **sedonamv**, then compare your Property inspector to Figure A-20.

2. Click Autoplay in the Property inspector to deselect it.

3. Click the sedona.jpg image to select it.

4. Click Window on the menu bar, then (if necessary) click Behaviors.

5. Click the Add Behaviors button in the Behaviors panel, then click Control Shockwave or Flash.

6. Make sure the Control Shockwave or Flash dialog box has the same settings as shown in Figure A-21, then click OK.

7. Verify that the Events setting in the Behaviors panel is on Mouse Over.

8. Click File on the menu bar, point to Preview in Browser, then click iexplore (Win), or click Internet Explorer.app (Mac).

   | TIP   Your default browser may vary.

9. Point to the image to play the movie.

10. Point away from the image, then point to the image to play the movie again.

11. Close the browser, then save your work.

You set a Fireworks image as the control for play-ing a Macromedia Flash movie.

Designate the primary external editor.

1. Start Dreamweaver MX.
2. Display the Preferences dialog box and display the File Types / Editors option.
3. Verify that Fireworks is set for .png, .gif, and .jpg files.

Specify the launch and edit settings.

1. Start Fireworks MX.
2. Display the Preferences dialog box.
3. Set the Launch and Edit options to never use the source PNG when editing from an external application.
4. Set the Launch and Edit options to always use the source PNG when optimizing from an external application.

Set up the Dreamweaver site.

1. Create a folder on your hard drive and name it **Foods**.
2. Add a folder within the Foods folder named **Library**.
3. Create a new Dreamweaver site named **Foods-for-Thought**, using the Foods folder as the root folder.

Export a Fireworks graphic as an image.

1. Open bread-heading.png in Fireworks.
2. Export the file as an image-only GIF file to the Foods folder.
3. Close the edit window without saving the changes.

Export a Macromedia graphic to a Dreamweaver site Library folder.

1. Open bread-photo.png in Fireworks.
2. Export the file as a JPEG file to the Library folder in the Foods folder.
3. Close the edit window without saving the changes.

Insert a Fireworks image into a Dreamweaver document.

1. Open the Foods-for-Thought site in Dreamweaver.
2. Start a new document and save it as **food-home.htm** in the root folder.
3. Insert the bread-heading.gif file into the document.
4. Center-align the heading across the document, then save your work.

Insert a Fireworks image from the Assets panel into a Dreamweaver document.

1. Place an insertion point below the heading.
2. Insert the bread-photo.jpg file from the Assets panel to the insertion point.
3. Save your work.

Edit a Fireworks image from Dreamweaver.

1. Select the bread-photo.jpg image and click the Edit button in the Property inspector.
2. Add an inner bevel effect to the image.
3. Click the Done button to return to the document.

Optimize a Fireworks image from Dreamweaver.

1. Select the bread-photo.jpg image (if necessary).
2. Display the Optimize Image dialog box.
3. Change the quality setting to **100** and click Update.

Insert a Macromedia Flash movie into a Dreamweaver document.

1. Set an insertion point below the image.
2. Insert the bread-An.swf file below the photo image, and accept copying the image if asked.
3. Save your work.

Play a Macromedia Flash movie and change the movie settings from within Dreamweaver.

1. Select the Macromedia Flash movie placeholder.
2. Click the Play button, then click the Stop button.
3. Deselect the Loop feature.
4. Change the movie window height to **250**, then reset the size.
5. Save your work.

Edit a Macromedia Flash movie from Dreamweaver.

1. Select the movie placeholder, then click the Edit button.
2. Select the bread-An.fla file.

3. Create a motion animation that causes the word Bread to scroll in from the left side of the stage.
4. Click Done to return to the document in Dreamweaver.
5. Display the Web page in a browser.

Control a movie from within Dreamweaver.

1. Select the movie placeholder and name the image **breadmv**.
2. Deselect the Autoplay feature.
3. Select the bread-photo.jpg image.
4. Set the Behavior to have the image control the playing of the breadmv movie.
5. Display the document in a browser and point to the image to play the movie.
6. Close the browser and save your work.
7. Compare your movie to Figure A-22.

FIGURE A-22
Completed Skills Review

Ultimate Tours travel has asked you to develop a Dreamweaver Web site for their company. The site will include the Macromedia Flash animations that were developed in Flash Unit E. (*Hint*: If you did not create ultimatetoursE.fla in Flash Unit E, see your instructor.)

1. Create a folder on your hard drive and name it **UTours**, then create a folder within the UTours folder named **Library**.
2. In Dreamweaver, create a new site named **UltimateTours**, using the UTours folder as the local root folder.
3. Open utours_home.htm and save it to the root folder for the UltimateTours site.
4. In Fireworks, export UTours-heading.png as an image-only file to the UTours folder.
5. Export the UTours-photo.png as a Library file to the Library folder.
6. In Dreamweaver, display the utours_home.htm document and insert the UTours-heading.gif image.
7. Insert UTours-photo.jpg to the right of the heading, and center the heading and photo across the page.
8. Insert ultimatetoursE.swf below the heading, and center it.
9. Turn off the Loop and Autoplay features, then name the movie **UTmv**.
10. Select the photo and choose to edit it in Fireworks by adding an inner bevel effect.
11. In Dreamweaver, select the photo and set it to play the Macromedia Flash movie.
12. Save your work, display the document in a browser, then compare your image to Figure A-23.

FIGURE A-23

Completed Project Builder 1

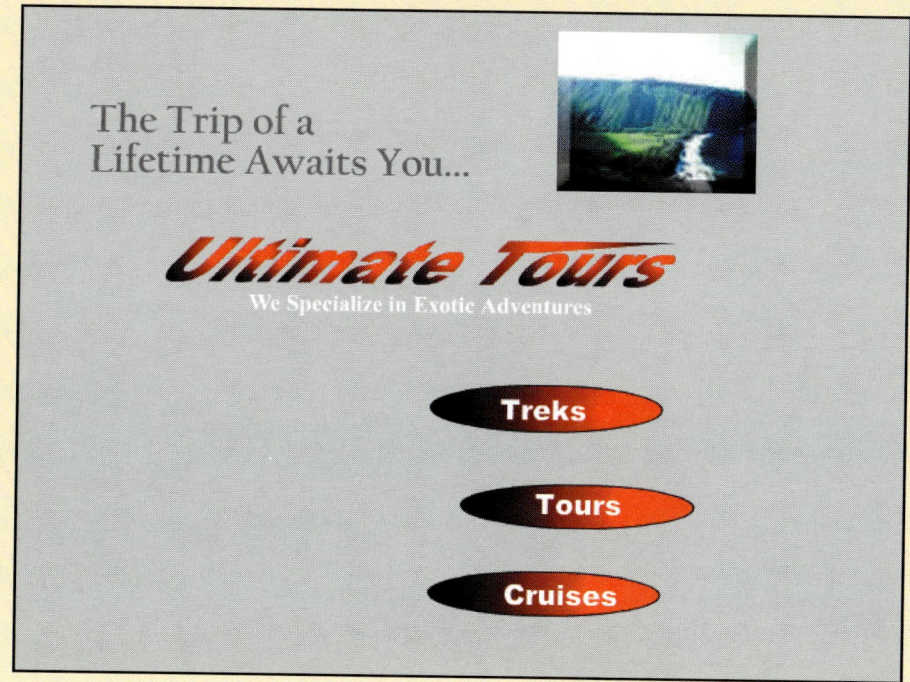

This is a continuation of Project Builder 2 in Macromedia Flash Unit D. If you have not completed the previous project, see your instructor. You will create a Web site in Dreamweaver and import portfolioE.swf into it. The home page of the Web site will include a heading and photo image (of your choice), as shown in Figure A-24.

1. Create a folder on your hard drive and name it **Mywebsite**, then create a folder within the Mywebsite folder named **Library**.

2. In Dreamweaver, create a new site named **MyWeb**, using the Mywebsite folder as the local root folder.

3. Open myhome.htm and save it to the Mywebsite site.

4. In Fireworks, export my-heading.png as an image-only file to the Mywebsite folder.

5. Export my-photo.png as a Library file to the Library folder.

6. In Dreamweaver, display the myhome.htm document and insert the my-heading.gif image.

7. Insert my-photo.jpg from the Library folder to the right of the heading and center the heading and photo across the page.

8. Insert portfolioE.swf below the heading and center it.

9. Turn off the Loop and Autoplay features, then name the movie **mymv**.

10. Select the heading and edit it in Fireworks to apply a drop shadow.

11. Select the photo and choose to edit it in Fireworks by adding an inner bevel effect.

12. In Macromedia Flash, edit the movie by adding a graphic that resembles a portfolio case to the initial screen.

13. In Dreamweaver, select the photo and set it to play the Macromedia Flash movie.

14. Save your work, display the document in a browser, then compare your image to Figure A-24.

FIGURE A-24
Completed Project Builder 2

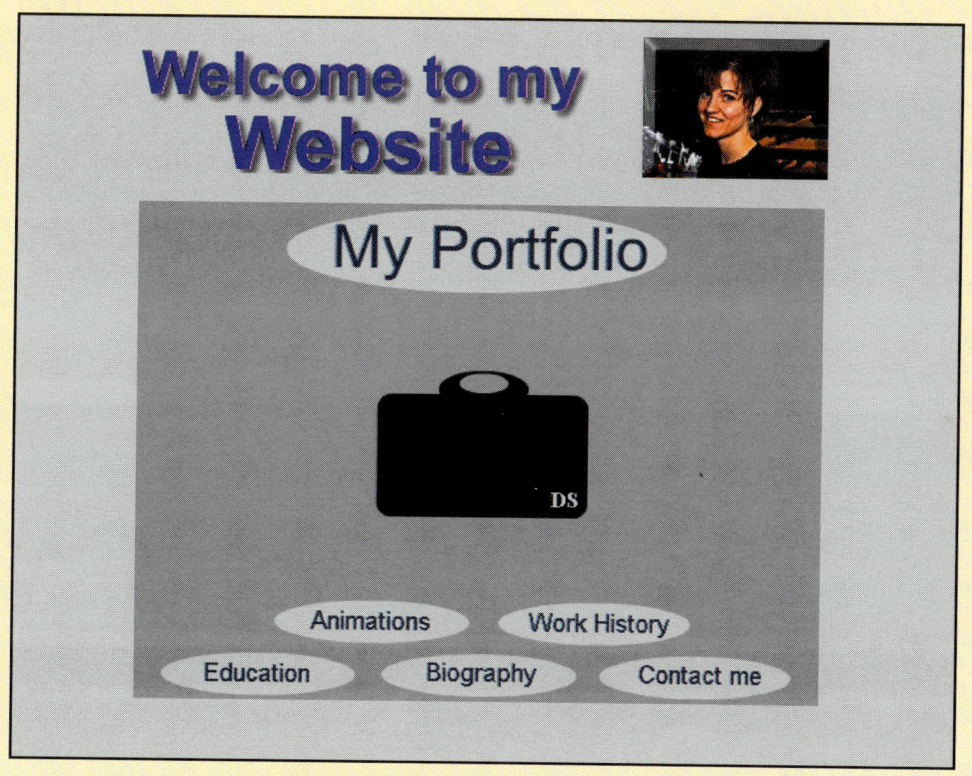

Figure A-25 shows the home page of a Web site that was developed using Macromedia Dreamweaver, Flash, and Fireworks. Study the figure and complete the following questions. For each question, indicate how you determined your answer.

1. Connect to the Internet, and go to *www.course.com*. Navigate to the page for this book, click the Student Online Companion, then click the link for this unit.

2. Open a document in a word processor or in Flash, save the file as **dpuIntegration**, then answer the following questions.
   - What seems to be the purpose of this site?
   - Who would be the target audience?
   - Identify three elements within the Web page that could have been created or enhanced using Fireworks.
   - Identify two elements on the page and indicate how you would use Fireworks to enhance them.

   - Identify an animation that could have been developed by Macromedia Flash.
   - Indicate how you would use Macromedia Flash to enhance the page.
   - What would be the value of using Macromedia Flash, Dreamweaver, and Fireworks to create the Web site?
   - What suggestions would you make to improve on the design, and why?

FIGURE A-25

Design Project

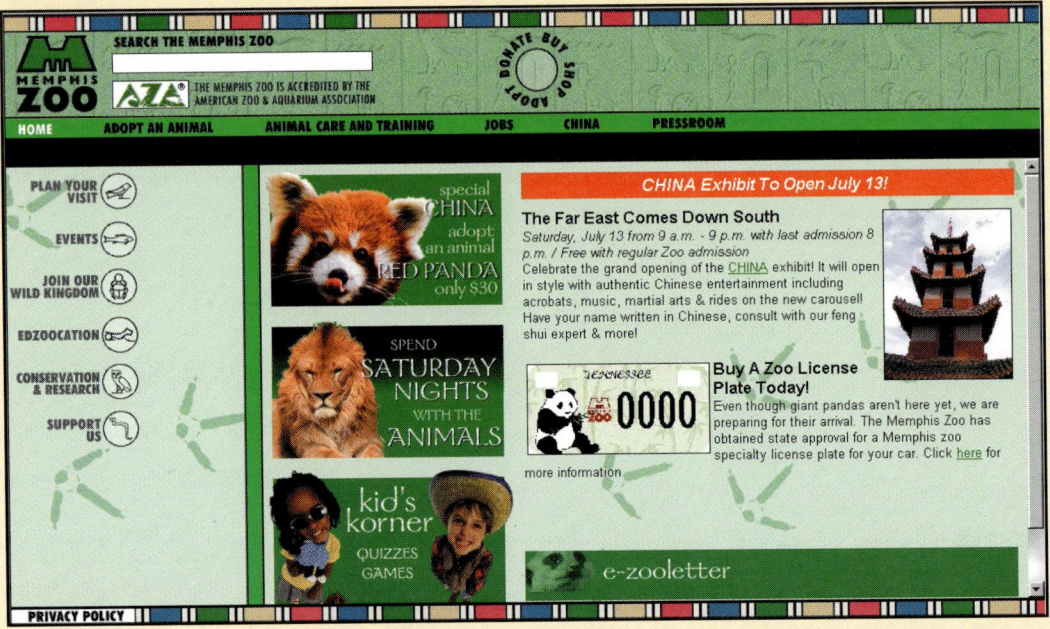

GROUP PROJECT

Your group can assign elements of this project to individual members, or you can work collectively to create the finished product. This project begins with the Rapids Transit Web site created in Dreamweaver Unit E. (*Hint*: If you did not create this site, see your instructor.)

Your group has been asked to enhance the Rapids Transit Web site by adding a Flash movie and changing a graphic image on the Our Guides page. Figure A-26 shows the completed page for this part of the Web site.

1. In Macromedia Flash, create an animation using the kayak.png image. Use a motion guide that causes the image to dip up and down as it moves across the screen from right to left. Save the movie as **kayak-an.fla** and publish it.

2. In Dreamweaver, display the Rapids Transit site files in the Site panel.

3. Display the guides.htm document and insert the kayak-an.swf movie above the body text, then center it.

4. Select the movie and turn off the Loop and Autoplay features, then name the movie **kayak animation**.

5. Select the photo and choose to edit it in Fireworks by adding an inner bevel effect.

6. In Dreamweaver, select the photo and set it to play the Macromedia Flash movie.

7. Save your work.

FIGURE A-26
Completed Group Project

We have four of the best river guides you will ever find — Buster, Tucker, Max, and Scarlett. Buster has been with us for thirteen years and was born and raised here. Tucker joined us two years ago from the big city, but we've managed to make a country boy out of him! Max and Scarlett are actually distant cousins and joined us after they graduated from college last year. They're never happier than when they're out on the water floating and fishing. Each of our guides will show you a great time on the river.

Our guides will pack your supplies, shuttle you to the put-in point, maneuver the raging rapids for you, and then make sure someone is waiting at the take-out point to shuttle you back to the store. They haven't lost a customer yet! Give us a call and we'll set up a date with any of these good people. Here's a photo of Buster showing off his stuff. The river is always faster and higher in the spring. If you want to take it a little slower, come visit us in the summer or fall. Leave your good camera at home, though, no matter what the time of the year. You may get wet! Life jackets are provided and we require that you wear them while on the water. Safety is always our prime concern.

Read the following information carefully!!

Find out from your instructor the location of the Data Files you need and the location where you will store your files.

- To complete many of the units in this book, you need to use Data Files. Your instructor will either provide you with a copy of the Data Files or ask you to make your own copy.

- If you need to make a copy of the Data Files, you will need to copy a set of files from a file server, standalone computer, or the Web to the drive and location where you will be storing your Data Files.

- Your instructor will tell you which computer, drive letter, and folders contain the files you need, and where you will store your files.

- You can also download the files by going to *www.course.com*. See the inside back cover of the book for instructions to download your files.

Copy and organize your Data Files.

- Use the Data Files List to organize your files to a zip drive, network folder, hard drive, or other storage device.

- Create a subfolder for each unit in the location where you are storing your files, and name it according to the unit title (e.g., Dreamweaver Unit A).

- For each unit you are assigned, copy the files listed in the **Data File Supplied** column into that unit's folder.

- Store the files you modify or create in each unit in the unit folder.

Find and keep track of your Data Files and completed files.

- Use the **Data File Supplied** column to make sure you have the files you need before starting the unit or exercise indicated in the **Unit** column.

- Use the **Student Saves File As** column to find out the filename you use when saving your changes to a provided Project File.

- Use the **Student Creates File** column to find out the filename you use when saving your new file for the exercise.

Files used in this book

Macromedia Dreamweaver MX

Unit	Data File Supplied	Student Saves File As	Student Creates File	Used in
A	dwa_1.htm contact.swf newsletter.swf services.swf tours.swf assets/tripsmart.jpg assets/trps_log.gif			Lesson 2
	dwa_2.htm assets/tripsmart.jpg	index.htm assets/tripsmart.jpg	accessories.htm catalog.htm clothing.htm newsletter.htm services.htm tours.htm	Lessons 4 and 5
	dwa_3.htm dwa_4.htm assets/bloom_log.gif assets/blooms.gif	index.htm assets/blooms.gif	plants.htm workshops.htm tips.htm	Skills Review
	dwa_5.htm assets/rapids.jpg	index.htm assets/rapids.jpg	guides.htm rentals.htm store.htm	Project Builder 1
	dwa_6.htm assets/jacobs.jpg	index.htm assets/jacobs.jpg	directions.htm menus.htm recipes.htm	Project Builder 2
	none			Design Project
	none			Group Project
B	dwb_1.htm packing_essentials.htm assets/tidbits.jpg assets/tripsmart.jpg	newsletter.htm assets/tidbits.jpg assets/tripsmart.jpg		Lesson 2
	dwb_2.htm gardening_tips.htm assets/blooms.gif assets/planting_tips.jpg	tips.htm assets/blooms.gif assets/planting_tips.jpg		Skills Review

Unit	Data File Supplied	Student Saves File As	Student Creates File	Used in
	none			Project Builder 1
	none			Project Builder 2
	none			Design Project
	none			Group Project
C	how_to_pack.htm			Lesson 1
			tripsmart.css	Lesson 2
	dwc_1.htm assets/tripsmart.jpg assets/giraffe.jpg assets/lion.jpg assets/zebra_mothers.jpg	tours.htm assets/tripsmart.jpg assets/giraffe.jpg assets/lion.jpg assets/zebra_mothers.jpg		Lesson 3
	assets/seamless_bak.gif assets/tile_bak.gif	assets/seamless_bak.gif assets/tile_bak.gif		Lesson 5
	dwc_2.htm dwc_3.htm gardening_tips.htm assets/blooms.gif assets/daisies.gif assets/iris.jpg assets/pansies.jpg assets/planting_tips.jpg assets/tulips.jpg	tips.htm plants.htm assets/blooms.gif assets/daisies.gif assets/iris.jpg assets/pansies.jpg assets/planting_tips.jpg assets/tulips.jpg	blooms.css	Skills Review
	dwc_4.htm assets/buster_tricks.jpg assets/rapids.jpg	guides.htm assets/buster_tricks.jpg assets/rapids.jpg	rapids.css	Project Builder 1
	dwc_5.htm rolls.htm assets/cheesecake.jpg assets/jacobs.jpg assets/oranges.jpg assets/poached_pear.jpg	after_theatre.htm recipes.htm assets/cheesecake.jpg assets/jacobs.jpg assets/oranges.jpg assets/poached_pear.jpg	jacobs.css	Project Builder 2
	none			Design Project
	none			Group Project

Unit	Data File Supplied	Student Saves File As	Student Creates File	Used in
D	dwd_1.htm assets/tripsmart.jpg	services.htm assets/tripsmart.jpg		Lesson 1
			top.swf	Lesson 3
	assets/nav_catalog_down.jpg assets/nav_catalog_up.jpg assets/nav_home_down.jpg assets/nav_home_up.jpg assets/nav_news_down.jpg assets/nav_news_up.jpg assets/nav_services_down.jpg assets/nav_services_up.jpg assets/nav_tours_down.jpg assets/nav_tours_up.jpg	assets/nav_catalog_down.jpg assets/nav_catalog_up.jpg assets/nav_home_down.jpg assets/nav_home_up.jpg assets/nav_news_down.jpg assets/nav_news_up.jpg assets/nav_services_down.jpg assets/nav_services_up.jpg assets/nav_tours_down.jpg assets/nav_tours_up.jpg		Lesson 4
	dwd_2.htm assets/blooms.gif assets/blooms_ask_down.jpg assets/blooms_ask_up.jpg assets/blooms_home_down.jpg assets/blooms_home_up.jpg assets/blooms_plants_down.jpg assets/blooms_plants_up.jpg assets/blooms_tips_down.jpg assets/blooms_tips_up.jpg assets/blooms_workshops_down.jpg assets/blooms_workshops_up.jpg	master_gardener.htm assets/blooms.gif assets/blooms_ask_down.jpg assets/blooms_ask_up.jpg assets/blooms_home_down.jpg assets/blooms_home_up.jpg assets/blooms_plants_down.jpg assets/blooms_plants_up.jpg assets/blooms_tips_down.jpg assets/blooms_tips_up.jpg assets/blooms_workshops_down.jpg assets/blooms_workshops_up.jpg	top.swf	Skills Review
	dwd_3.htm assets/buffalo_fall.gif assets/rapids.jpg	before.htm assets/buffalo_fall.gif assets/rapids.jpg		Project Builder 1
	dwd_4.htm assets/jacobs.jpg	menus.htm assets/jacobs.jpg		Project Builder 2
	none			Design Project
	none			Group Project
E	assets/headphones.jpg assets/packing_cube.jpg assets/passport_holder.jpg assets/tripsmart.jpg	assets/headphones.jpg assets/packing_cube.jpg assets/passport_holder.jpg assets/tripsmart.jpg		Lesson 3

Unit	Data File Supplied	Student Saves File As	Student Creates File	Used in
	headphones.htm packing_cube.htm passport_holder.htm			Lesson 4
	dwe_1.htm dwe_2.htm assets/hat.jpg assets/hats_on_the_amazon.jpg assets/nav_catalog_down.jpg assets/nav_catalog_up.jpg assets/nav_home_up.jpg assets/nav_home_down.jpg assets/nav_news_down.jpg assets/nav_news_up.jpg assets/nav_services_down.jpg assets/nav_services_up.jpg assets/nav_tours_down.jpg assets/nav_tours_up.jpg assets/pants.jpg assets/vest.jpg	clothing.htm catalog.htm assets/hat.jpg assets/hats_on_the_amazon.jpg assets/nav_catalog_down.jpg assets/nav_catalog_up.jpg assets/nav_home_up.jpg assets/nav_home_down.jpg assets/nav_news_down.jpg assets/nav_news_up.jpg assets/nav_services_down.jpg assets/nav_services_up.jpg assets/nav_tours_down.jpg assets/nav_tours_up.jpg assets/pants.jpg assets/vest.jpg		Lesson 5
	assets/tearoom.jpg assets/texas_rose.jpg assets/yellow_rose.jpg agenda.htm exhibition.htm nursery.htm tearoom.htm	assets/tearoom.jpg assets/texas_rose.jpg assets/yellow_rose.jpg		Skills Review
	rental_info.htm store.htm assets/fruit_basket.jpg assets/kayak.jpg	store.htm assets/fruit_basket.jpg assets/kayak.jpg		Project Builder 1
	directions_paragraph.htm assets/signature_dish.jpg	assets/signature_dish.jpg		Project Builder 2
	none			Design Project
	none			Group Project

Macromedia Flash MX

Unit	Data File Supplied	Student Saves File As	Student Creates File	Location
A	none		devenvironment.fla	Lesson 1
	fla_1.fla	demomovie.fla		Lesson 2
	none		tween.fla	Lesson 3
	none		layers.fla	Lesson 4
	none	none		Lesson 5
	fla_2.fla	skillsdemoA.fla		Skills Review
	none		demonstration.fla	Project Builder 1
	fla_3.fla	recycle.fla		Project Builder 2
	none		dpuUnitA	Design Project
	none	none		Group Project
B	none		tools.fla	Lesson 1
	none		tools.fla	Lesson 2
	none		tools.fla	Lesson 3
	none		tools.fla	Lesson 4
	flb_1.fla	layersB.fla		Lesson 5
	none		skillsdemoB.fla	Skills Review
	none		ultimatetoursB.fla	Project Builder 1
	none		portfolioB.fla	Project Builder 2
	none		dpuUnitB	Design Project
	none		jazzclub.fla	Group Project
C	flc_1.fla	coolcar.fla		Lesson 1
	flc_2.fla	CarRace.fla		Lesson 2
	none		CarRace.fla	Lesson 3
	none		CarRace.fla	Lesson 4
	flc_3.fla	skillsdemoC.fla		Skills Review
	none			Project Builder 1
	none			Project Builder 2
	none		dpuUnitC	Design Project
	none		isa.fla	Group Project

Unit	Data File Supplied	Student Saves File As	Student Creates File	Location
D	fld_1.fla	frameAn.fla		Lesson 1
	fld_2.fla	carAn.fla		Lesson 2
	fld_3.fla	carPath.fla		Lesson 3
	fld_4.fla	carRotate.fla		Lesson 4
		frameAn.fla		Lesson 5
	fld_5.fla	skillsdemoD.fla		Skills Review
	none			Project Builder 1
	none			Project Builder 2
	none		dpuUnitD	Design Project
	none		summerBB.fla	Group Project
E	fle_1.fla	antiqueCar.fla		Lesson 1
	fle_2.fla	morphCar.fla		Lesson 1
	fle_3.fla	shapeHints.fla		Lesson 1
	fle_4.fla	classicCC.fla		Lesson 2
	fle_5.fla beep.wav CarSnd.wav	rallySnd.fla		Lesson 3
	fle_6.fla	cccHome.fla		Lesson 4
	fle_7.fla	coolCars.fla		Lesson 5
	fle_8.fla	skillsdemoE.fla		Skills Review
	utlimatetoursD.fla applause.wav click.wav	ultimatetoursE.fla		Project Builder 1
	portfolioD.fla	portfolioE.fla		Project Builder 2
	none		dpuUnitE	Design Project
	none		zodiac.fla	Group Project

Macromedia Fireworks MX

Unit	Data File Supplied	Student Saves File As	Student Creates File	Used in
A	none		sweetface.png	Lesson 1
	fwa_1.png	breads.pg		Lessons 2–4
	ingredients.jpg elbow.gif shell.tif	pasta_1.png		Skills Review
	fwa_2.png	pasta_2.png		
	none		crystal.png	Project Builder 1
	none		meandering_paths.png	Project Builder 2
	none		rocknroll.doc	Design Project
	none		emoticon.png	Group Project
B	fwb_1.png	apple.png		Lessons 1–4
	fwb_2.png	confection.png		Skills Review
	none		remember_me.png	Project Builder 1
	none		impact_potion.png	Project Builder 2
	none		yoakam.doc	Design Project
	none		existential_pastries.png	Group Project
C	fwc_1.png	pizzeria.png		Lessons 1–3
	fwc_2.png	marinara.png		Lessons 4–5
	fwc_3.png fwc_4.png	moon_fest.png moon2moon.png		Skills Review
	none		busted.png	Project Builder 1
	none		incognito.png	Project Builder 2
	none		cool page.doc	Design Project
	none		retrofit.png	Group Project

Integration

Unit	Data File Supplied	Student Saves File As	Student Creates File	Location
A	none	none		Lesson 1
	heading.png	home.htm		Lesson 2
	sedona.png			
	none	heading.gif		Lesson 3
	sedona-title.fla	home.htm		Lesson 4
	sedona-title.swf	sedona.jpg		
		sedona-title.swf		
		sedona-title.fla		
	bread-An.fla	bread-An.fla		Skills Review
	bread-An.swf	bread-An.swf		
	bread-heading.png	bread-heading.gif		
	bread-photo.png	bread-photo.jpg		
		food-home.htm		
	none			Project Builder 1
	none			
	utours_home.htm	utours_home.htm		
	UTours-photo.png	UTours-photo.jpg		
	UTours-heading.png	UTours-heading.gif		
	myhome.htm	myhome.htm		Project Builder 2
	my-photo.png	my-photo.jpg		
	my-heading.png	my-heading.gif		
	none			
	none			
	none		dpuIntegration	Design Project
	before.htm	before.htm		Group Project
	buffalo_fall.gif	buffalo_fall.gif		
	buster_tricks.jpg	buster_tricks.jpg		
	fruit_basket.jpg	fruit_basket.jpg		
	guides.htm	guides.htm		

Unit	Data File Supplied	Student Saves File As	Student Creates File	Used in
	index.htm	index.htm		
	kayak.jpg	kayak.jpg		
	kayak.png	rapids.css		
	rapids.css	rapids.jpg		
	rapids.jpg	rentals.htm		
	rentals.htm	store.htm		
	store.htm	kayak-an.fla		
		kayak-an.swf		
		kayak-an.html		

A

Absolute path
A path containing an external link that references a link on a Web page outside of the current Web site, and includes the protocol "http" and the URL, or address, of the Web page.

ActionScript
A scripting language that allows those with programming expertise to create sophisticated actions.

Aligning an image
Positioning an image on a Web page in relation to other elements on the page.

Alternate text
Descriptive text that can be set to display in place of an image while the image is downloading or when users place a mouse pointer over an image.

Anchor points
Joins path segments to delineate changes in direction.

Animation
The perception of motion cause by the rapid display of images in a sequence.

Anti-aliasing
Smoothes the edges of curved or diagonal lines, such as type, so that the appearance does not appear jagged.

Assets folder
A subfolder in which you store most of the files that are not Web pages, such as images, audio files, and video clips.

Assets panel
A panel that contains nine categories of assets, such as images, used in a Web site. Clicking a category button will display a list of those assets.

B

Background color
A color that fills the entire Web page, a frame, a table, a cell, or document.

Background image
A graphic file used in place of a background color.

Balance
In screen design, balance refers to the distribution of optical weight in the layout. Optical weight is the ability of an object to attract the viewer's eye, as determined by the object's size, shape, color, and so on.

Bandwidth profiler
A feature used when testing a Flash movie that allows you to view a graphical representation of the size of each frame.

Banners
Graphics that appear across the top of the screen that can incorporate the company's logo, contact information, and navigation bars.

Behavior
A preset piece of JavaScript code.

BMP
Bitmapped file. A file format used for images that is based on pixels.

Body
The part of a Web page that is seen when the page is viewed in a browser window.

Border
An outline that surrounds, a cell, a table, or a frame.

Broken links
Links that cannot find the intended destination file for the link.

Browser
Software used to display Web pages, such as Microsoft Internet Explorer or Netscape Navigator.

C

Cascading Style Sheets
A file used to assign sets of common formatting characteristics to page elements such as text, objects, and tables.

Cell padding
The distance between the cell content and the cell walls.

Cell spacing
The distance between cells.

Cell walls
The edges surrounding a cell.

Cells
Small boxes, within a table, that are used to hold text or graphics. Cells are arranged horizontally in rows and vertically in columns.

Child page
A page at a lower level in a Web hierarchy that links to a parent page.

Code and Design Views
A Web page view that is a combination of Code View and Design View.

Code View
A Web page view that shows a full screen with the HTML code for the page. Use this view to read or directly edit the code.

Columns
Table cells arranged vertically.

Comments
Helpful text describing portions of the HTML code, such as a JavaScript function.

Contents
The Macromedia Help feature that lists topics by category.

Controller
A toolbar that contains the playback controls for a movie.

Debug
To find and correct coding errors.

Declaration
The property and value of a style in a Cascading Style Sheet.

Default base font
Size 3 (Dreamweaver).

Default font color
The color the browser uses to display text, links, and visited links if no other color is assigned.

Default link color
The color the browser uses to display links if no other color is assigned. The default link color is blue.

Defining a Web site
Specifying the site's local root folder location to help Dreamweaver keep track of the links among Web pages and supporting files.

Definition lists
Lists comprised of terms with indented descriptions or definitions.

Delimiter
A comma, tab, colon, semicolon, or similar character that separates tabular data.

Description
A short summary of Web site content that resides in the Head section.

Design notes
A file (.mno) that contains the original source file (.png or .fla) when a Fireworks document or Macromedia Flash file is exported to Dreamweaver.

Design View
The view that shows a full-screen layout and is primarily used when designing and creating a Web page.

Document toolbar
A toolbar that contains buttons for changing the current Web page view, previewing and debugging Web pages, and managing files.

Document-relative path
A path referenced in relation to the Web page that is currently displayed.

Documents
Fireworks and Dreamweaver files.

Domain name
An IP address expressed in letters instead of numbers, usually reflecting the name of the business represented by the Web site.

Down Image state
The state of a page element when the element has been clicked with the mouse pointer.

Download time
The time it takes to transfer a file to another computer.

DSL
Digital Subscriber Line. A type of high-speed Internet connection.

Enable Cache
A setting to direct the computer system to use space on the hard drive as temporary memory, or cache, while you are working in Dreamweaver.

Export data

To save data that was created in Dreamweaver in a special file format so that you can bring it into another software program.

External links

Links that connect to Web pages in other Web sites.

Favorites

The Dreamweaver Help feature that allows you to add topics to the Favorites window that you might want to view later without having to search again.

Fill

A solid color, a pattern, or a gradient applied to an object.

Flash Button Objects

Flash graphic and text objects that you can insert onto a Web page without having the Macromedia Flash program installed.

Flash text

A vector-based graphic file that contains text.

Floating workspace

A feature of Macromedia products that allows each document and panel to display in its own window.

Font combination

A set of three fonts that specifies which fonts a browser should use to display the text on a Web page.

Frame animation

An animation created by specifying the object that is to appear in each frame of a sequence of frames (also called a frame-by-frame animation).

Frame delay

The display time for each frame in an animation.

Frame-by-frame animation

Animation that creates a new image for each frame (also called Frame animation).

Frames

Individual cells that make up the timeline in Flash or that contain an animation's images and objects in Fireworks.

FTP

File Transfer Protocol. The process of uploading and downloading files to and from a remote site.

GIF file

Graphics Interchange Format file. A GIF is a type of file format used for images placed on Web pages that can support both transparency and animation.

Gradient

Two or more colors that blend into each other in a fixed design.

Group

A command that manipulates multiple objects as a single selection.

Head content

The part of a Web page that is not viewed in the browser window. It includes meta tags, which are HTML codes that include information about the page, such as keywords and descriptions.

Headings

Six different styles that can be applied to text: Heading 1 (the largest size) through Heading 6 (the smallest size).

Hexadecimal value

A value that represents the amount of red, green, and blue in a color and is based on the Base 16 number system.

History panel

A panel that lists the steps that have been performed in a Macromedia application while editing and formatting a document.

Home page

Usually, the first Web page that appears when users go to a Web site.

Horizontal and vertical space

Blank space above, below, and on the sides of an image that separates the image from the text or other elements on the page.

Hotspot

An area that you define in your document to which you can assign a URL (Web address) or other type of interactivity. A clickable area on a graphic that, when clicked, links to a different location on the page or to another Web page.

HTML

Hypertext Markup Language, the language Web developers use to create Web pages.

Hyperlinks

Graphic or text elements on a Web page that users click to display another location on the page, another Web page on the same Web site, or a Web page on a different Web site. Hyperlinks are also known as links.

I

Image map

A graphic that has one or more hotspots defined on it that, when clicked, serve as a link that will take the viewer to another location.

Import data

To bring data created in another software program into an application.

Index

The Macromedia Help feature that views topics in alphabetical order.

Insert bar

A toolbar that contains icons that allow you to insert objects, such as images, tables, and horizontal rules.

Instances

Representations of symbols after you drag them from the Library panel to the canvas.

Integrated workspace

The acronym for Multiple Document Interface layout where all of the windows and panels are integrated into one large window with the panels docked on the right side of the screen.

Interactivity

Allows visitors to your Web site to interplay with and affect its content by moving or clicking the mouse.

Internal links

Links to Web pages within the same Web site.

IP address

An assigned series of numbers, separated by periods, that designates an address on the Internet.

ISP

Internet Service Provider. A service to which you subscribe in order to be able to connect to the Internet with your computer.

J

JavaScript

A Web-scripting code that interacts with HTML code to create dynamic content, such as rollovers or interactive forms.

JPEG file

Joint Photographic Experts Group file. A JPEG is a type of file format used for images that appear on Web pages. Many photographs are saved with the JPEG file format.

K

Kerning

An adjustment to the spacing between adjacent letters or a range of letters.

Keyframe

A frame that signifies a change in an object being animated.

Keywords

Words that relate to the content of the Web site and reside in the Head section.

L

Layer (Fireworks)

An element that functions like a folder divided into sections that contain objects. A document can be made up of many layers.

Layers (Flash)

Rows on the timeline that are used to organize objects and that allow the stacking of objects on the stage.

Layout View

A Dreamweaver view that is used when you draw your own table.

Leading

An adjustment to the amount of vertical space between lines of text.

Library

A panel containing graphic symbols, button symbols, and animation symbols. You can use multiple Libraries in a document and share Libraries between documents.

Local root folder
A folder on your hard drive, zip disk, or floppy disk that will hold all the files and folders for the Web site.

Looping
The number of times an animation repeats.

Macromedia Flash Player
A program that needs to be installed on a computer to view a Flash movie.

Mailto: link
An e-mail address that is formatted as a link that will open the default mail program with a blank, addressed message.

Mask layer
Used to cover up the objects on another layer(s) and, at the same time, create a window through which you can view various objects on the other layer.

Menu bar
A bar across the top of the program window that is located under the program title bar and lists the names of the menus that contain commands.

Merge cells
To combine multiple cells into one cell.

Meta tags
HTML codes that include information about the page such as keywords and descriptions and reside in the head section.

Morphing
The process of changing one object into another, sometimes unrelated, object.

Motion guide layer
A path used to specify how an animated object moves around the Macromedia Flash stage.

Motion tweening
The process used in Macromedia Flash to automatically fill in the frames between keyframes in an animation that changes the properties of an object such as the position, size, or color.

Movement
Movement in screen design refers to the way the viewer's eye moves through the objects on the screen.

Named anchor
A specific locations on a Web page that is used to link to that portion of the Web page.

Navigation bar
A set of text or graphic links that viewers can use to navigate between pages of a Web site.

Nested table
A table within a table.

Non-breaking space
A space that will be left on the page by a browser.

Objects
The individual elements in a document, such as text or images.

Onion skinning
A setting that allows you to view one or more frames before and after in the current frame.

Ordered lists
Lists of items that need to be placed in a specific order and are preceded by numbers or letters.

Orphaned files
Files that are not linked to any pages in the Web site.

Over Image state
The state of a page element when the mouse pointer is over the element.

Over While Down Image state
The state of a page element when the mouse pointer is being held over the element.

Panel groups
Groups of panels such as Design, Code, Application, and Files, that are displayed through the Window menu. Sets of related panels are grouped together.

Panels
Components in Macromedia Flash used to view, organize, and modify objects and features in movie.

Panels
Individual windows in Dreamweaver that display information on a particular topic, such as Answers or History.

Parent page
A page at a higher level in a Web hierarchy that links to other pages on a lower level.

Path (vector object)
An open or closed line consisting of a series of anchor points.

Path (file location)
The location of an open file in relation to any folders in the Web site.

Pixels
Small squares of color value used to display a digital image on a rectangular grid, such as a computer screen.

Playhead
An indicator specifying which frame is playing in the timeline of a Macromedia Flash movie.

Plug-in
A module that adds features or enhancements to an application.

PNG file
Portable Network Graphics file. A PNG is a file format used for images placed on Web pages that is capable of showing millions of colors, but is small in file size. The native file format in Fireworks.

Point of contact
A place on a Web page that provides viewers a means of contacting a company.

PPI
Pixels per inch.

Property inspector
A panel where properties and options specific to a selected tool or command appear. In Dreamweaver, a panel that displays the properties of the selected Web page object. You can change an object's properties using the text boxes, drop-down menus, and buttons on the Property inspector. The contents of the Property inspector vary according to the object currently selected.

Publish
The process used to generate the files necessary for delivering Macromedia Flash movies on the Web.

Publish a Web site
To make a Web site available for viewing on the Internet or on an intranet.

Reference panel
A panel that is used to find answers to coding questions, covering topics such as HTML, JavaScript, and Accessibility.

Refresh Local File List Automatically option
A setting that directs Dreamweaver to automatically reflect changes made in your file listings.

Relative path
A path used with an internal link to reference a Web page or graphic file within the Web site.

Remote server
A Web server that hosts Web sites and is not directly connected to the computer housing the local site.

Resolution
The number of pixels in an image.

Rollover
An effect on a graphic element in a Web page that your mouse triggers.

Root-relative path
A path referenced from a Web site's root folder.

Rows
Table cells arranged horizontally.

Sans-serif fonts
Block-style characters used frequently for headings, subheadings, and Web pages.

Scene
A section of the Macromedia Flash timeline designated for a specific part of the movie. Scenes are a way to organize long movies.

Screen reader
A device used by the visually impaired to convert written text on a computer monitor to spoken words.

Seamless image
A tiled image that is blurred at the edges so that it appears to be all one image.

Search
The Macromedia Help feature that allows you to enter a keyword to begin a search for a topic.

Selector
The name assigned to a style in a Cascading Style Sheet.

Serif fonts
Ornate fonts with small extra strokes at the beginning and end of the characters used frequently for paragraph text in printed materials.

Shape hints
Indicators used to control the shape of an object as it changes appearance during an animation.

Shape tweening
The process of animating an object so that it changes into another object.

Site map
A graphical representation of how Web pages relate to each other within a Web site.

Site panel
A window very similar to Windows Explorer (Windows) or Finder (Macintosh), where Dreamweaver stores and manages files and folders. The Site panel contains a list of all the folders and files in a Web site.

Slices
A Web element that divides an image into different sections, which allows you to apply rollover behaviors, animation, and URLs to those areas.

Soft return
A shortcut key combination which forces text to a new line without creating a new paragraph, creating a <BR> tag.

Split cells
To divide cells into multiple rows or columns.

Stage
That area of the Macromedia Flash workspace that contains the objects that are part of the movie and that will be seen by the viewers.

Standard toolbar
A Windows toolbar that contains icons for some frequently used commands on the File and Edit menus.

Standard View
A Dreamweaver view that is used when you insert a table using the Insert Table icon.

State
Each state represents the button's appearance based on a mouse action.

Status bar
A bar that appears at the bottom of the Dreamweaver or Fireworks document window. The left end of the status bar displays the tag selector, which shows the HTML tags being used at the insertion point location. The right end displays the window size, and estimated download time for the page displayed.

Storyboard
A small sketch that represents each page in a Web site. Like a flowchart, a storyboard shows the relationship of each page to the other pages in the site.

Symbol
A graphic, animation, or button that represents an object, text, or combination group.

Tables
Grids of rows and columns that can either be used to hold tabular data on a Web page or can be used as a basic design tool for page layout.

Tabular data
Data that are arranged in columns and rows and separated by a delimiter.

Tag Selector
A location on the status bar that displays HTML tags for the various page elements, including tables and cells.

Target
The location on a Web page that the browser will display in full view when an internal link is clicked or the frame that will open when a link is clicked.

Templates
Web pages that contain the basic layout for similar pages in the site.

Tiled image
A small graphic that repeats across and down a Web page, appearing as individual squares or rectangles.

Timeline
The component of Flash used to organize and control the movie's contents over time, by specifying when each object appears on the stage.

Toolbox
The component of Flash that contains a set of tools used to draw, select and edit graphics and text. It is divided into four sections.

Tools panel
A panel in Dreamweaver and Fireworks separated into categories containing tools and their options.

Tweening
The process of adding tweened instances and distributing them to frames so that the movement appears more fluid.

Unity
In screen design, intra-screen unity has to do with how the various screen objects relate. Inter-screen unity refers to the design that viewers encounter as they navigate from one screen to another.

Unordered lists
Lists of items that do not need to be placed in a specific order and are usually preceded by bullets.

Unvisited links
Links that have not been clicked by the viewer.

Up Image state
The state of a page element when the mouse pointer is not on the element.

Upload
The process of transferring files from a local drive to a Web server.

URL
Uniform Resource Locator.

Vector graphics
Mathematically calculated objects composed of anchor points and straight or curved line segments.

Visited links
Links that have been previously clicked, or visited. The default color for visited links is purple.

Web design program
A program for creating interactive Web pages containing text, images, hyperlinks, animation, sounds, and video.

Web server
A computer dedicated to hosting Web sites that is connected to the Internet and configured with software to handle requests from browsers.

Web site
Related Web pages stored on a server that users can download using a Web browser.

Web-safe Colors
Colors that will display consistently in all browsers, and on Macintosh, Windows, and Unix platforms.

White space
An area on a Web page that is not filled with text or graphics.

Workspace
The area where you work with documents, movies, tools, and panels.